PENGUIN BOOKS

THE YELLOW CROSS

René Weis was born in 1953. He is Professor of English Literature at University College London and the author of numerous scholarly publications. He is also the author of *Criminal Justice: The True Story of Edith Thompson*, published in Penguin. He lives in London.

The Yellow Cross

The Story of the Last Cathars 1290–1329

RENÉ WEIS

PENGUIN BOOKS

PENGUIN BOOKS

Published by the Penguin Group
Penguin Books Ltd, 80 Strand, London WC2R 0RL, England
Penguin Putnam Inc., 375 Hudson Street, New York, New York 10014, USA
Penguin Books Australia Ltd, Ringwood, Victoria, Australia
Penguin Books Canada Ltd, 10 Alcorn Avenue, Toronto, Ontario, Canada M4V 3B2
Penguin Books India (P) Ltd, 11 Community Centre, Panchsheel Park, New Delhi – 110 017, India
Penguin Books (NZ) Ltd, Cnr Rosedale and Airborne Roads, Albany, Auckland, New Zealand
Penguin Books (South Africa) (Pty) Ltd, 24 Sturdee Avenue, Rosebank 2196 South Africa

Penguin Books Ltd, Registered Offices: 80 Strand, London WC2R 0RL, England

www.penguin.com

First published by Viking 2000
Published in Penguin Books 2001
6

Copyright © René Weis, 2000
All rights reserved

Photographs (unless otherwise acknowledged on pages ix–x)
copyright © René Weis, 2000

The moral right of the author has been asserted

Set in Monotype Bembo
Printed in Great Britain by Clays Ltd, St Ives plc

To the memory of
Cécile Hansen-Roger
and
my father, Guy Weis

Contents

List of Illustrations and Maps

Illustrations

1. Caussou and the Val de Caussou.

2. The square of Montaillou from the main track, looking west towards Prades.

3. The main medieval track passing the square of Montaillou.

4. *La fontcanal* and the track entering Montaillou from Ax.

5. Montaillou and the area known as *a-la-cot*.

6. *La laviera*, where the women of Montaillou did their washing in the Middle Ages.

7. Les Granges, the spur of the Gazel, and the *haute montagne* of Montaillou.

8. The church of Unac, where Béatrice met Raymonde de Luzenac in 1300.

9. Lordat in its setting as seen from the castle.

10. Larnat as seen from the meadows of *le fusan*.

11. The rocky shelf of the Martys' home in Junac.

12. Pierre Authié's rock of Bugarach.

13. Salted fish at a fourteenth-century fishmonger's (*pisces saliti*, *Codex Vindobonensis Series Nova 2644*, *Tacuinum*, f.82v, Courtesy of Österreichische Nationalbibliothek).

14. Ax-les-Thermes and the Rocher de la Vierge.

15. The Perfects' gully at Larnat.

16. Cubières and its medieval church.

17. Women carding, spinning, and weaving (from an illuminated fourteenth-century manuscript, BN FR 12420, f.71r, Courtesy of Bibliothèque Nationale de France).

Photographs, unless otherwise acknowledged, are the author's own.

Maps

Acknowledgements

In the last five years I have accumulated a number of debts which it is a pleasure to acknowledge.

In Languedoc I want to thank Alain Fayet, the mayor of Montaillou, for his advice and guidance, and Georges Clergue and Michel Descat for their hospitality. I am grateful to André Rieu and Philippe Barthe of Dalou for welcoming a stranger into their homes in the same square where Béatrice de Planisolles once lived. I must thank Louis Claeys in Pamiers and the staff at the Archives Départementales de l'Ariège in Foix. I am also grateful to Jean-Claude Dupuis of the Institut Géographique National for his expert advice on the toponymy of France. The mayors of Larnat and Junac cheerfully fielded my queries about their respective villages during the Middle Ages, and André Vacquié from Mérial showed me the hidden church of Gebets.

The three most important manuscripts for this book are evenly distributed across three great libraries: the Fournier Register at the Vatican Library in Rome, the d'Ablis Register at the Bibliothèque Nationale in the Richelieu in Paris, and Limborch and MS 4697 at the British Library in London within a few minutes' walk from my office at University College London. I must thank the staff and curators of these invaluable collections, as well as the staff of the UCL library, and particularly John Allen.

As a teenager in a *lycée classique* it was my good fortune to study Latin under Eugène Leytem, whose deep learning and dedicated teaching provided me with a passport to the medieval Inquisitorial registers which form the basis of this book. I also want to record here my gratitude to Lex Jacoby for sharing his experience as a writer with me, and for his encouraging words.

Closer to home I must thank Emmanuela Tandello from the UCL Italian Department, and Diego Zancani of Balliol College, Oxford, who were both generous to a fault with their time and offered invaluable assistance. Karl Miller has been a source of inspiration ever since I was his student, and I want to thank him further for his faith in this project. I also wish to express my gratitude to Dan Jacobson for his continuing support, wisdom, and friendship. I am indebted to David Henn of the Department of Spanish and Latin American Studies at UCL for discussing the Pallars valley in Catalonia with me. In my own department Sarah Wintle alerted me to a misreading of the topography of modern Montaillou, and Richard North advised me on Gothic names. Charles Mitchell of King's College London shared his legal expertise with me, and I enjoyed a brief spell as the tutee of my student Sarah Lee, one of the most talented young photographers in the country. It is thanks to her that the pictures in this book are no worse than they are. I am grateful to the Dean's fund at UCL for a generous financial contribution to my work in the Vatican, and to Sonja Weis and Patrick Thill for bringing to my attention an important source of Cathar studies.

My publishers chose the meticulous and astute Annie Lee to copy-edit my manuscript. I am grateful to her, as I am to Reginald and Marjorie Piggott for doing a superb job on the maps, and to Carol Janeway for her comments on the typescript. It is a pleasure to express my thanks to Bill Hamilton and Sara Fisher of A. M. Heath for their calm efficiency and staunch backing, and to Andrew Kidd at Viking for being the most genial of editors. Finally, in writing on the Cathars I am deeply indebted to the seminal work of Jean Duvernoy and Emmanuel Le Roy Ladurie.

I want to thank Michael Worton for his support, and Maryse Brochard-Hansen for her affectionate *amitié*. My greatest debt is again to Jean. Without her encouragement and forbearance this book would not have been written, and I want to thank her for all that she has done for me.

René Weis
University College London, 2000

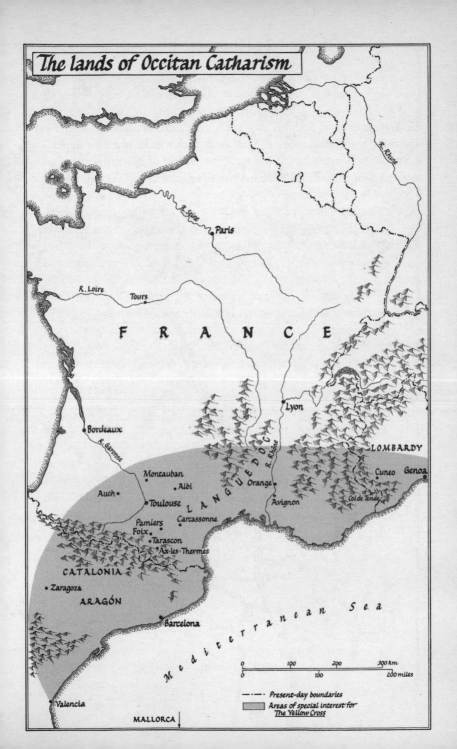

The lands of Occitan Catharism

Paris

R. Seine

R. Loire
Tours

F R A N C E

Lyon

R. Rhône

Bordeaux

R. Garonne

Montauban
Albi
Auch
Toulouse
Carcassonne
Pamiers
Foix
Tarascon
Ax-les-Thermes

L A N G U E D O C

Orange
Avignon

LOMBARDY
Cuneo
Genoa
Col de Tende

CATALONIA

Zaragoza

ARAGÓN

Barcelona

M e d i t e r r a n e a n   S e a

Valencia

MALLORCA

| 0 | 100 | 200 | 300 km |

| 0 | 100 | 200 miles |

- - - Present-day boundaries

Areas of special interest for
The Yellow Cross

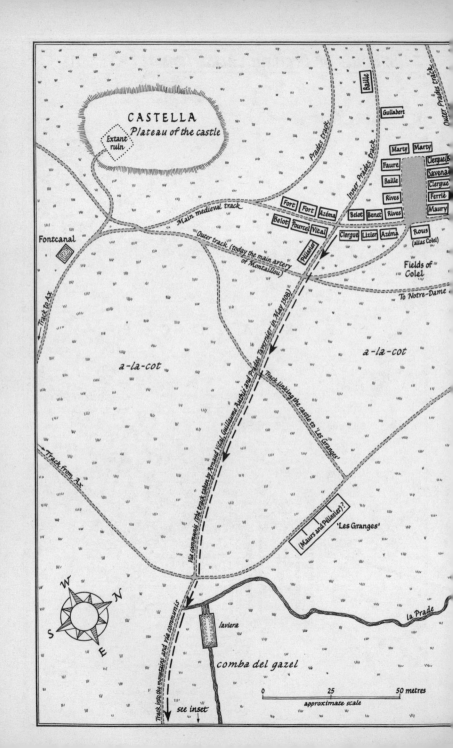

CASTELLA
Plateau of the castle

Extant ruin

Baille

Guilabert

Marty Marty

Faure Clergue (B

Baille Savenac

Rives Clergue

Fort Fort Azéma Belot Benet Rives Ferrié

Belot Fourcet Vital Maury

Pélissier Clergue Lizier Azéma Rous (alias Colet)

Prades track

Inner Prades track

Outer Prades track

Main medieval track

Outer track (today the main artery of Montaillou)

Fontcanal

Track to Ax

Fields of Colet

To Notre-Dame

a-la-cot

a-la-cot

Track linking the castle to 'Les Granges'

Via au revers: (the track whereby Bernard Vital, Guillaume Authié and Prades Tavernier in May 1308)

Track from Ax

(Maurs and Pélissier)? 'Les Granges'

Track into the mountains and via communis

see inset

laviera

comba del gazel

la Prade

0   25   50 metres
approximate scale

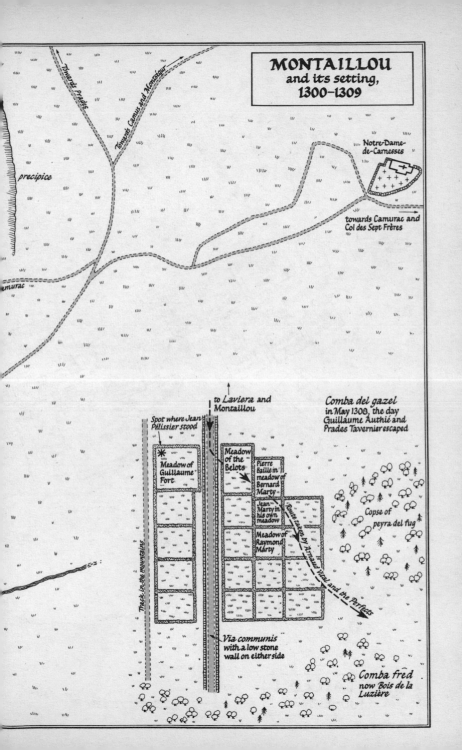

MONTAILLOU
and its setting,
1300–1309

precipice

Towards Prades

Towards Camus and Montaillou

Notre-Dame-
de-Carnesses

towards Camurac and
Col des Sept Frères

Camurac

to *Laviera* and
Montaillou

Comba del gazel
in May 1308, the day
Guillaume Authié and
Prades Tavernier escaped

Spot where Jean
Pélissier stood

Meadow of
Guillaume
Fort

Meadow
of the
Belots

Pierre
Baille in
meadow of
Bernard
Marty

Copse of
peyra del fug

Jean
Marty in
his own
meadow

Meadow
of
Raymond
Marty

Route taken by Arnaud Vital and the Perfecti

Track in the mountains

Via communis
with a low stone
wall on either side

Comba fred
now *Bois de la
Luzière*

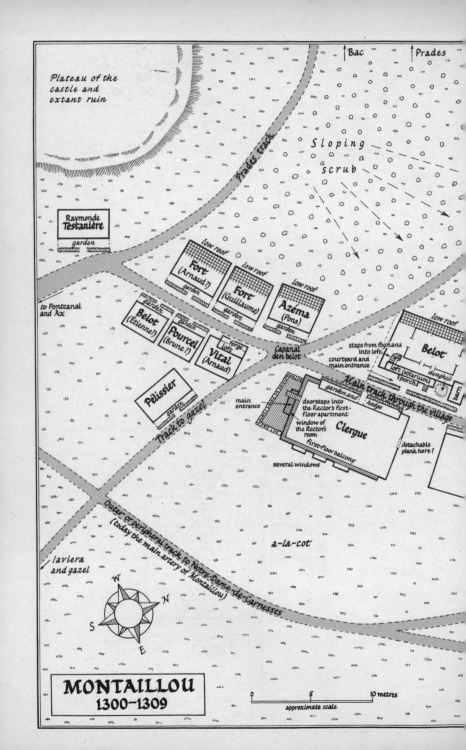

Plateau of the castle and extant ruin

Bac   Prades

Prades track

Sloping

scrub

Raymonde Testanière
garden

low roof

Fort
(Arnaud?)
garden

low roof

Fort
(Guillaume)
garden

low roof

Azéma
(Pons)
garden

low roof

to Fontcanal
and Ax

garden

Belot
(Étienne?)

garden

Pourcel
(Brune?)

forge
loft

Vital
(Arnaud)

Capanal
den belot

Belot

steps from foghana
into loft

courtyard and
main entrance

loft (solarium)
porch

dunghill

bath

Pélissier

garden

Track to gazel

main
entrance

doorsteps into
the Rector's first-
floor apartment

window of
the Rector's
room

garden and

hedge

Main track through the village

Clergue

detachable
plank here?

first-floor balcony

several windows

Outer or peripheral track to Notre-Dame-de-Carnesses
(today the main artery of Montaillou)

a-la-cot

laviera
and gazel

W

N

S

E

MONTAILLOU
1300-1309

0   5   10 metres
approximate scale

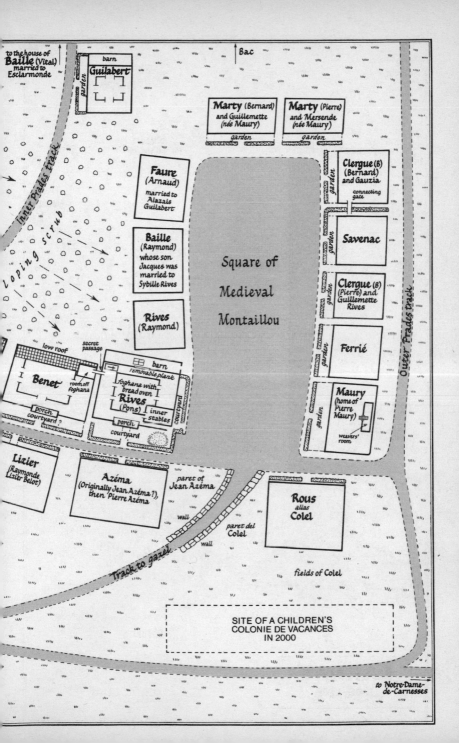

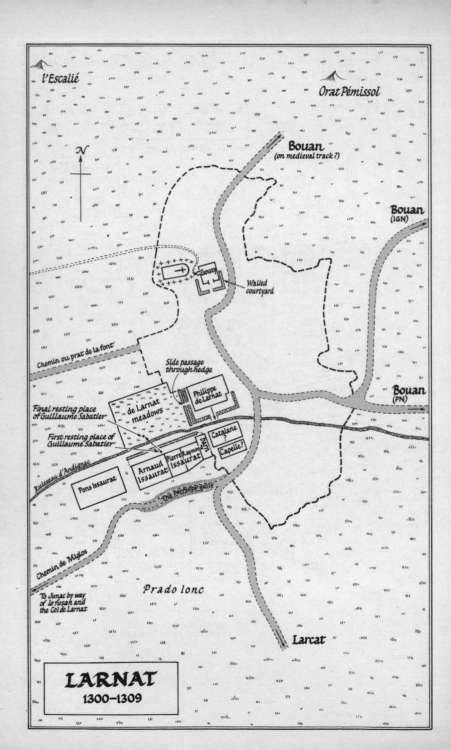

l'Escalié

Orat Pémissol

N

Bouan
(on medieval track?)

Bouan
(IGN)

Goury

Walled
courtyard

Bouan
(PN)

Chemin ou prat de la font

Side passage
through hedge

de Larnat
meadows

Philippe
de Larnat

Final resting place
of Guillaume Sabatier

Catalane

First resting place of
Guillaume Sabatier

Capelle?

Arnaud
Issaurat

Pierre Raymond
Issaurat

Ruisseau d'Andignac

Pons Issaurat

The Perfects' gully

Chemin de Miglos

Prado lonc

To Junac by way
of le fusah and
the Col de Larnat

Larcat

LARNAT
1300–1309

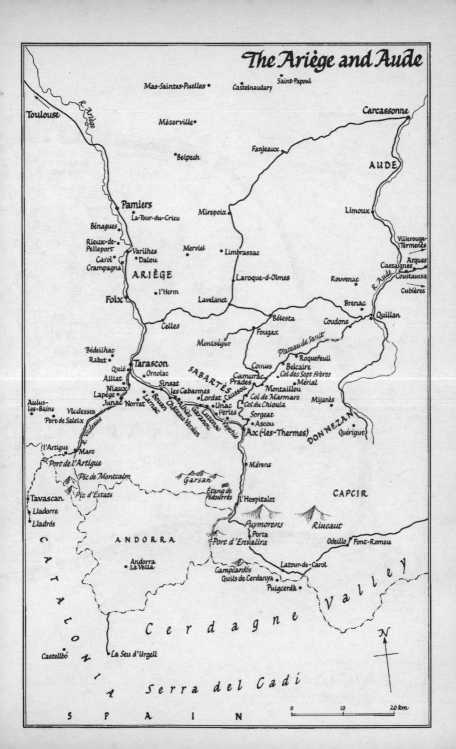

The Ariège and Aude

Toulouse

Carcassonne

AUDE

Mas-Saintes-Puelles • Castelnaudary • Saint-Papoul
R. Ariège
Mézerville•
•Belpech
Fanjeaux
Limoux
Villerouge-
Termenés
Mirepoix
Pamiers
La-Tour-du-Crieu
Bénagues•
Rieux-de-
Pelleport• Merviel Limbrassac Cassaignes• Arques
Varilhes • •Dalou • Coustaussa
Carol• R. Aude
Crampagna ARIÈGE Laroque-d'Olmes Rouvenac Cubières
l'Herm
Foix Brenac Quillan
Lavelanet Coudons
Celles Bélesta
Fougax
Bédeilhac Montségur Plateau de Sault
Rabat Roquefeuil
Quié• Tarascon Comus Belcaire Col des Sept Frères
Alliat• Ornolac SABARTÈS Camurac Mérial
Niaux• Sinsat Prades
Lapège• les Cabannes Caussou Montaillou
Junac• Norrat Lordat Col de Marmare Mijanès
Aulus- Vicdessos Bouan Uriac Col du Chioula
les-Bains Lercat Perles
Port de Saleix Sorgeat DONNEZAN
Ascou
Ax (-les-Thermes) Quérigut
l'Artigue Maro
Port de l'Artigue
Pic de Montcalm Mérens
Garsan CAPCIR
Tavascan Pic d'Estats Étang de
Pédourrés l'Hospitalet
Lladorre Riucaut
Lladrós Puymorens
Porta Odeillo Font-Romeu
ANDORRA Port d'Envalira
Andorra Latour-de-Carol
La Vella Campcardós
Guils de Cerdanya
Puigcerdà
CATALONIA
Cerdagne Valley
N
Castellbó La Seu d'Urgell
Serra del Cadi
0 10 20 km
SPAIN

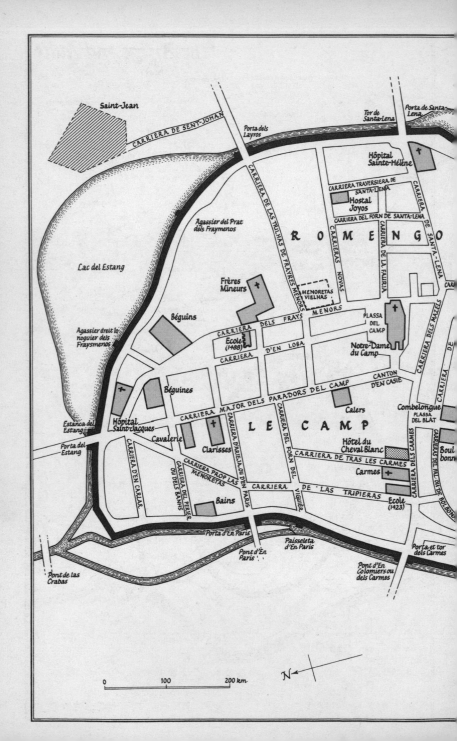

Saint-Jean

CARRIERA DE SENT-JOHAN

Porta dels
Layros

Tor de
Santa-Lena

Porta de Santa-
Lena

Hôpital
Sainte-Hélène

CARRIERA TRAVERSIERA DE
SANTA-LENA

Hostal
Joyos

CARRIERA DEL FORN DE SANTA-LENA

R O M E N G O

Agassier del Prat
dels Fraymenos

CARRIERA DE LAS TRILHAS DE FRAYRES MENORS

CARRIERAS NOVAS

CARRIERA DE LA FAURIA

CARRIERA DE SANTA-LENA

Lac del Estang

Frères
Mineurs

MENORETAS
VIELHAS

CARRIERA DELS FRAYS MENORS

PLASSA
DEL
CAMP

Béguins

Agassier dreit lo
noguier dels
Fraysmenos

Ecole
(1488)

CARRIERA

D'EN LOBA

Notre-Dame
du Camp

CARRIERA DELS MAZELS

CARRIERA DE

Béguines

CARRIERA MAJOR DELS PARADORS DEL CAMP

CANTON
D'EN CASIE

Combelongue

PLASSA
DEL BLAT

Calers

L E C A M P

CARRIERA D'ARELA OU DEN PARIS

Estanca del
Estang

Hôpital
Saint-Jacques

CARRIERA DEL FORN DEL

CARRIERA DELS CARMES

CARRIERA DEL OU DEL POI

Porta del
Estang

Cavalerie

Hôtel du
Cheval Blanc

Boul
bonn

Clarisses

CARRIERA DE TRAS LES CARMES

Carmes

CARRIERA D'EN CARLAR

CARRIERA PROP LAS
MENORETAS

CARRIERA DEL PEAER
OU DELS BANHS

CARRIERA DE LAS TRIPIERAS

Ecole
(1423)

VIGUIER

Bains

Porta d'En Paris

Paisseleta
d'En Paris

Pont d'En
Paris

Porta et tor
dels Carmes

Pont de las
Crabas

Pont d'En
Colomiers ou
dels Carmes

0   100   200 km

N

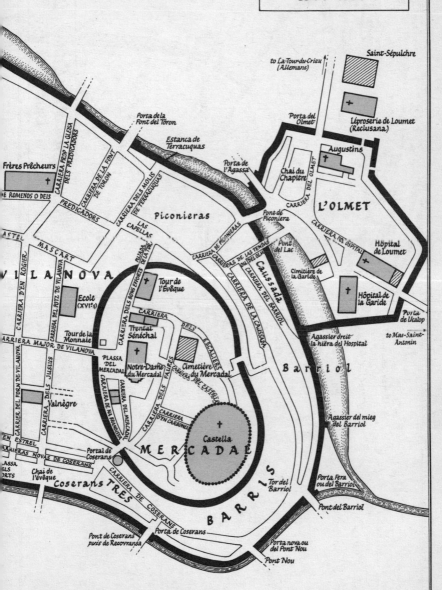

PAMIERS
1300–1550

to La-Tour-du-Crieu
(Allemans)

Saint-Sépulchre

Porta del
Olmet

Léproserie de Loumet
(Reclusana)

Porta de la
Font del Toron

Augustins

Estanca de
Terracuquas

Porta de
l'Agassa

Chai du
Chapitre

Frères Prêcheurs

L'OLMET

DE ROMENOS O DEIS

PREDICADORS

Piconieras

Pont de
Piconiera

Hôpital
de Loumet

LAS
CAPELLAS

Pont
del Lac

CASTEL

MASCART

Tour de
l'Evêque

Cimitière de
la Garide

Hôpital de
la Garide

VILANOVA

Ecole
(XVIe)

CARRIERA

Porta
de Ucalop

CARRIERA MAJOR DE VILANOVA

Tour de la
Monnaie

Trental
Sénéchal

Agassier dreit
la hiera del Hospital

to Mas-Saint-
Antonin

Barriol

PLASSA
DEL
MERCADAL

Notre-Dame
du Mercadal

Cimetière
du Mercadal

Valnègre

Agassier del mieg
del Barriol

EN ESTREL

Portal de
Coserans

MERCADAL

Castella

Chai de
l'Evêque

Coserans TRES

Porta Fera
ou del Barriol

Tor del
Barriol

Pont del Barriol

BARRIS

Pont de Coserans
puis de Recovransa

Porta de Coserans

Porta nova ou
del Pont Nou

Pont Nou

(After François Baby, 1980, by kind permission
of the Office de Tourisme du Pays Pamiers.)

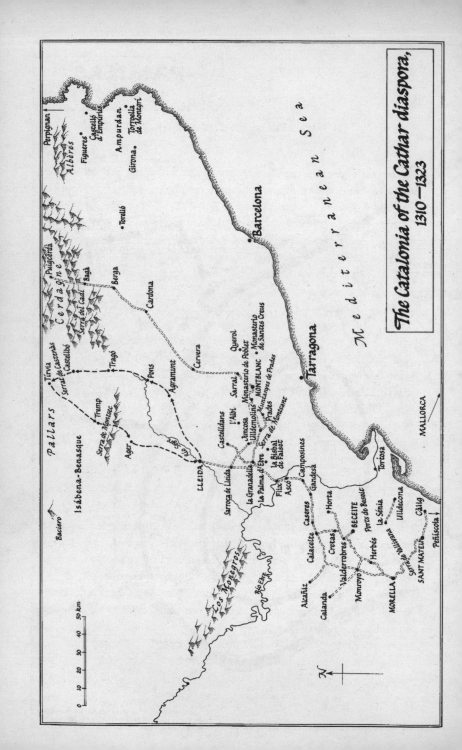

The Catalonia of the Cathar diaspora, 1310–1323

Perpignan

Albères
Figueres
Castelló d'Empúries
Ampurdan.
Girona.
Torroella de Montgrí.

Torelló

Barcelona

Mediterranean Sea

Puigcerdà
Cerdagne
Serra de Casserras
Bagà
Berga
Cardona

Serra del Cadí

Pallars

Tírvia
Serra de Castelló
Trago
Pons
Agramunt
Cervera

Querol
Monasterio de Poblet
Monasterio de Santes Creus

Tarragona

Baciero
Isábena-Benasque
Tremp
Serra de Montsec
Ager

Sarral
MONTBLANC
Muntanyes de Prades
Prades
Serra de Montsant
L'Albí
Juncosa
Ulldemolins
Castelldans

LLEIDA
Sarroca de Lleida
la Granadella
la Palma d'Ebre
Flix
Asco
la Bisbal de Falset

Camposines
Gandesa

Tortosa

MALLORCA

Río Ebro

Los Mongeros

Alcañiz
Calanda

Valderrobres
Cretas
Calaceite
Caseres
Horta
Monroyo
Herbés
BECEITE
Ports de Beceit
la Sénia
Ulldecona
Càlig
Peñíscola
MORELLA
Serra de Vallivana
SANT MATEU

N

0 10 20 30 40 50 km

Introduction:
In the Tracks of the Last Cathars

In the early years of the fourteenth century the Inquisition of Carcassonne unleashed a major offensive against a small community of
heretics in a remote corner of the Pyrenees. These were known as
Cathars, and they believed that the devil was co-eternal with God and
that the material world and the flesh were his evil creation. The pedigree
of this dualist, Manichean heresy reaches back at least to the eleventh
century. The word 'Cathar' itself probably derives from the Greek
katharós, which means 'pure' or 'purified' (*pace* Duvernoy 1976, 303),
and their theology may have been influenced by Eastern metaphysics.

Among medieval heresies Catharism stands out as the most striking
and anachronistic. Here was a dissident faith with, at its doctrinal core,
gentleness and the promise of universal redemption. It was inspired by
the New Testament, and it was Christ and his Disciples whom the
spiritual leaders of the Cathar church, the so-called 'Perfects' or 'Good
Men', emulated. The Cathars' opposition to all forms of killing
extended to human and animal life alike, and like Christ they intended
to forgive those who persecuted them. To encounter such a philosophy
in the long-distant past is in itself surprising; to learn that in thirteenth-
century Languedoc it inspired tens of thousands of ordinary men and
women to risk their lives is astonishing. The popular perception of the
Middle Ages is of a cruel and benighted period in which the Church
held absolute sway and the sun was thought to revolve around the
earth. Catharism, on the other hand, has become a beacon of light in
that darkness through providing a moral and spiritual model whose
idealism has rarely been matched in the history of Europe.

The Cathars themselves viewed their doctrine and that of the established Catholic church in just such contrasting images of light and
darkness. These they probably borrowed from St John's Gospel, which
more than any other biblical text inspired them.

In the third verse of John they read that 'in the beginning' the creator
God

was life; and the life was the light of men. And the light shineth in darkness; and the darkness comprehended it not. (1:4–5)

According to the same Gospel, Christ's incarnation ensued from a mysterious act of divine will, and he became 'the true Light, which lighteth every man that cometh into the world' (1:9). In him the Word was made flesh, and through Christ, God's 'only begotten Son',

light is come into the world, and men loved darkness rather than light, because their deeds were evil. For every one that doeth evil hateth the light, neither cometh to the light, lest his deeds should be reproved. But he that doeth truth cometh to the light, that his deeds may be made manifest, that they are wrought in God. (3:19–21).

It was the intense mysticism of St John's Gospel which chimed remarkably with the Cathar faith, and indeed profoundly influenced it. No part of the Scriptures with the exception of the Lord's Prayer played such an important role in the ritual which governed the transmission of the most important Cathar sacrament, the *consolamentum*. This term was applied equally to the ordination of the Cathar spiritual leaders and to the Cathar consolation of the dying. Both involved the consoling Perfect in a laying-on of hands and of the Gospels, the palm-sized 'book' which is repeatedly mentioned by the various witnesses to such events.

St John's Gospel provided the Cathars with scriptural authority for their profoundly metaphorical and symbolic interpretations of the mysteries of the Bible. Their hostility to the human body and its physical needs and rituals was anticipated in John's vision of the Word becoming flesh without the agency of the Virgin Mary who, though immaculate, was nevertheless physically a woman. The Cathar Perfects preached that Christ could self-evidently not have issued from the womb of a real woman, and that the virgin birth was to be understood symbolically: Christ was not born of Mary, but *shadowed* in her. Similarly, the transubstantiation of bread and wine into the body and blood of Christ could be demonstrated to be an absurdity, because there would never be enough of Christ's body to be thus consumed; not to mention the fact that his transubstantiated body would linger in the bowels of priests after mass.

The Cathar antipathy towards the human body was deeply rooted in their metaphysics, according to which the original fall of the souls from heaven was followed by the devil's cladding them with 'tunics' or bodies. In every human being, therefore, the eternal soul belongs to God, the mutable and decaying matter to the devil. The same logic stipulated that the resurrection of the consoled would not be in the body, as Catholic theology maintained, but would be a spiritual phenomenon, with the soul journeying to heaven to meet its Maker. If a man or woman died without the benefit of a Cathar consolation, their soul was destined to migrate into another living creature, animal or human, until it found the body of a 'good Christian'. For the Cathar believers the physical world was full of erring souls in search of the right incarnation that would take them to salvation.

Once a dying patient had received the consolation from the hands of a Perfect or Good Man, they were forbidden any sustenance other than water. This state of being consecrated to death and salvation by fasting was called the *endura*, which was intended to safeguard the integrity of the consolation. From now on the dying person was in a state of grace, and could no longer be touched by women. Some were lucky to be consoled shortly before death, whereas others embarked on an awesome hunger-strike to the bitter end.

As the emphasis on the abstinence of food after consolation indicates, diet played a defining role in Catharism. Whereas the ordinary Cathar believer, known as *credens* (or *credentes* in the plural), was at liberty to eat anything, including meat, the Perfects avoided every source of food associated with animal fat, including eggs. Their staple fare consisted of bread and fish, which they consumed in moderation; and they ate fish only because the engendering of fish in water was deemed to be free from the corruption that attached to mammalian intercourse.* It was this same revulsion for meat, because it was created by coition, that caused the Perfects to avoid pregnant women. According to strict

---

* Although the fish is an ancient symbol for Christ and the Eucharist, the Perfects' diet of fish does not obviously seem to be connected to this. If the roots of this diet are biblical at all, they are more likely to derive from the feeding of the five thousand with five loaves of bread and two fishes (Mark 6:38–44); and, perhaps, from Jesus's eating broiled fish after the resurrection (Luke 24:42), or handing out bread and fish to his Disciples during his third visit after rising from the dead (John 21:13–14).

Catharism the foetus was a creation of the devil which awaited its redeeming soul. Moreover, some Cathar versions of the Fall averred that the devil seduced the souls away from their heavenly home by introducing into it a beautiful woman whom all the souls desired to possess. Women were thus cast from the beginning as one of the instruments of the Fall and the devil's creatures. Notwithstanding such misogyny, there had been Cathar *Perfectae* (women Perfects) in the period leading up to the fall of Montségur in 1244, and women played a crucial role in the story of the last Cathars.

The Cathar followers were inspired by the Perfects. As we shall see in the course of this narrative, the Good Men's sacrifices were many and legendary. Whereas they seemed to be following in the true steps of Christ, their enemies, the Catholic priests, all too frequently trod the libertines' primrose path of dalliance. In the words of the Perfect Pierre Authié whose apostolate is recalled to this day in Languedoc, the people had to choose between the Cathar church

which flees and forgives, and the other which fetters and flays: the former holds to the straight path of the apostles, and does not lie and deceive; the latter is the Church of Rome. (FR, f.249v)

At a time when human life was precarious and salvation in the next world was seen to compensate for the sorrows and sufferings in this one, it is not entirely surprising that so many people preferred to make common cause with the Cathar church; the more so since it enjoyed considerable support from the local political power.

Such was the spread of Catharism by the middle of the twelfth century that at the Third Lateran Council of 1179 Pope Alexander III publicly denounced the Cathars, noting that they were thick on the ground in Gascony, the Albigeois, the Toulousain and elsewhere, and that they were poisoning the minds of ordinary people. Between 1209 and 1255 the Cathars were savagely persecuted in Languedoc, which at that time was not part of France. Their challenge to the established Church was strongest in this region, probably because here they enjoyed the protection of powerful sympathizers and fiercely independent warlords such as the Counts of Foix and Toulouse and the Trencevals of Carcassonne.

In response to the murder in 1208 of his legate Pierre de Castelnau, Pope Innocent III proclaimed a crusade against the 'Albigensians', as the French invaders, who spearheaded the crusade, called the heretics (after the Tarn town of Albi). A cycle of death and destruction ensued. The massacres at Béziers (1209), Minerve (1210), and Lavaur (1211) were chronicled in the contemporary epic about Simon de Montfort's crusades, the vernacular *Chanson de la Croisade Albigeoise*, and the havoc wreaked in the region by de Montfort and his crusaders lives on in the local folklore to this day. The bloodletting ended only with the fall of the Cathar fortresses of Montségur (1244) and Quéribus (1255).

Catharism had been contained, but not eradicated, by the French crusades, and the continuing suppression of heresy was entrusted in 1233 by Pope Gregory IX to the Dominicans. One of their number was the Inquisitor Geoffroy d'Ablis. It was he who almost exactly 100 years after the first crusade of 1209 oversaw the crushing of the last Cathars. By 1310 most of the leaders of the Cathar *risorgimento* had perished on pyres in Carcassonne and Toulouse. A decade later the Bishop of Pamiers, a Cistercian called Jacques Fournier, tied up the remaining loose ends, and by 1325 Catharism was a spent force. It would never rise again.

This book tells the story of the Cathar twilight between 1290 and 1329. The focus of the Inquisition had by now contracted to a number of small mountain villages in an area of Languedoc known as the Sabartès, with the spa town of Ax-les-Thermes at its centre. It was from this important border city at the gates of what are today the autonomous principality of Andorra and the region of Catalonia, in Spain, that in the 1290s a new Cathar leadership emerged in the guise of a talented and wealthy bourgeois family called Authié. They and other Perfects eventually expired in the flames of the Inquisition. But of their faithful followers, who included most of the ordinary people of the Ariège, a single person only, one Guillaume Fort from Montaillou, is recorded as ending his life at the stake during this wave of repression.

In the broader context of the bloodstained annals of medieval Languedoc this final conflict between the Church and its opponents rates as little more than a footnote. But the small-scale historical significance of these events is belied by the fascination that they have exerted ever since the relevant source records became available towards the end of the nineteenth century. It was then that the vast Fournier Register became more widely known for the first time after centuries of semi-oblivion in the vaults of the Vatican in Rome. As Emmanuel Le Roy Ladurie puts it in his masterly book on the village of Montaillou, Occitan Catharism resembles a dead star which after an eclipse of five centuries again gives off 'a cold and fascinating light'.*

The clue to the appeal of this story lies in the nature of the evidence preserved in the Registers of Geoffroy d'Ablis (MS 4269) and especially that of Jacques Fournier (MS 4030). In them the glimpses of life in medieval Languedoc are so vivid and visual that turning the pages of the two manuscripts becomes like sitting through televised documentary footage from seven centuries ago. The reader, not unlike Alice in Wonderland, may feel that he or she has crossed over into a country where nothing is quite as expected; and the biggest surprise of all is that these medieval texts sharply mirror our own experiences of everyday life on the threshold of the third millennium. There are, of course, minor barriers such as, for example, some of the women's first names. While we still use names like Raymonde and Béatrice, which are also in the Registers, others like Alamande, Alazais, Brune, Esclarmonde, Gauzia, Guillemette, Mengarde, Montane, Rixende and Serafina have long since gone out of fashion; but after a relatively short immersion in the documents even they acquire a kind of well-thumbed familiarity.

From these fourteenth-century manuscripts the homes and villages of the medieval Sabartès rise to the surface in a manner that is probably unique in the recorded history of Europe. We are taken inside thir-teenth-century houses in Ax-les-Thermes, Junac, Larnat, Luzenac, Montaillou and further afield in Catalonia. There we are made to eavesdrop on people watching other people who are Cathar militants and who gather at night in lofts, cellars, barns and dovecotes where the hinges of doors have been cunningly silenced to avoid detection. Moreover the villages, the tracks in and out of them, and of course the

---

* 'Le catharisme n'est plus aujourd'hui qu'un astre mort, dont nous recevons à nouveau la lumière fascinante et froide, après un demi-millénaire d'occultation' (Le Roy Ladurie 1982, 625).

surrounding landscapes are still largely intact and are mostly identified by the same names today as they were then.

The intrinsic merit of the extant Inquisitorial Registers has long been recognized, but the pieces of the puzzle have heretofore not been gathered into a whole, perhaps because single depositions, such as the long testimony of Pierre Maury, stand alone and in themselves provide fascinating and self-contained objects of analysis. If the published literature on these materials occasionally errs in this respect, it is because of its eclecticism.

The intention of this book is to discover what really happened on the ground during the d'Ablis and Fournier Inquisitions, and to that extent researching the story turned into a kind of detective work. It did not seem to be enough, for example, to state that the whole of the village of Montaillou was arrested on a given day in the late summer or early autumn of 1308. I wanted to find out why it had happened at that particular time, whether there was a significant connection between this and an earlier raid on the village in May that year, and how the Inquisitorial posse managed to take the village unawares. As always, wherever Montaillou is concerned, it was crucial to understand the role that the most powerful family in the village played in this series of events. They sat, spiderlike, at the centre of the resistance network against the Church during the years from 1290 to 1320, and they were fabulously wealthy. That they played a decisive part in the recrudescence of Catharism has long been known, but quite how their power operated through its links with the Inquisition has never been fully appreciated. Nor has it been adequately explained how they eventually fell from grace, when they had so successfully weathered the initial storms of the Inquisition which destroyed the Cathar ringleaders.

The name of this family was Clergue, and seven centuries later they remain pre-eminent in the present-day skeletal village of Montaillou. The insignia of status in the 1990s, such as a silver-streaked, top-of-the-range BMW and the latest Peugeot 406, both of them owned by Clergue cousins, bear witness to the Clergue families' continuing hegemony here. From the window of the apartment that I rented from Georges Clergue, I sometimes spotted his cousin's BMW silently crawling up the track which connects 'Les Granges', an area down by the creek of Montaillou, to the heart of the village, before heading for Ax-les-Thermes or Belcaire; even the descendants of medieval godfathers have to go shopping. The owner of the BMW is nowadays actively promoting the village's Cathar heritage, which is so intimately enmeshed with the Clergues' family history.

But this battle to revive the standing of Montaillou may already be lost. To date there is no café here to welcome visitors, and the indigenous population is shrinking at an alarming rate. Indeed, the entire Ariège is being depleted of its people, notwithstanding the regional powers' efforts to staunch the haemorrhage from the villages. There are no teenagers in Montaillou, and the only children are those who spend time here during the summer in the *colonie de vacances* which occupies the corner where once the outer medieval track intersected with the track running from the square of thirteenth-century Montaillou.

The piecing together of the multiple bits of evidence in this book could never be a straightforward collage of fragments, because of the manner in which the evidence was obtained in the first place. The fact is that many of the testimonies convey only a partial truth at best. Sometimes the accused are afraid to tell all in case they implicate themselves too deeply or offend the local power, which would be there long after the Inquisitors had moved on; at other times they are desperately trying to save somebody else and as a result they offer half-truths.

The deposition of the genial Montaillou shepherd Pierre Maury before Jacques Fournier, for example, is legendary in Cathar studies, but it has all too often been taken at face value. The assumption was presumably that Maury was too upright to tell an untruth. But the fact that this courageous and likeable figure might be lying to shield his brother ought not necessarily to diminish him in our eyes. After all, he did not accept the spiritual authority of the Church of Rome to judge him. It is only when we realize how artfully disinformative parts of his testimony are that the deeper ramifications of his story become apparent.

The Cathar movement in the late-thirteenth-century Sabartès was an underground organization, and the Inquisition of Geoffroy d'Ablis never penetrated to its core in spite of the fact that it executed most of their leaders. It has been asserted confidently by a seminal writer on this material that the chief figurehead of the movement, Pierre Authié from Ax-les-Thermes, revealed more to the Inquisitors than others did while he was in custody in Toulouse (Duvernoy 1970, 46). His faith forbade him to lie, and we cannot rule out the possibility that he may have been tortured. But while he did tell them a great deal, he did *not* reveal to Geoffroy d'Ablis and Bernard Gui, his fellow Dominican Inquisitor rendered infamous in Umberto Eco's *The Name of the Rose*, that the Clergues of Montaillou were Cathar collaborators. Clearly he answered questions, but he never volunteered the single most significant piece of information about the Cathar contamination of the Sabartès. As long as the Clergues were pulling the strings at Montaillou the Cathar flame was not extinct there.

The magnetism of this story stems in large part from the way it draws us into the minutiae of its world. The obvious next step, to get closer still, was to follow literally in the characters' footprints, particularly since locations played such a large role in these records. Thus I wondered whether the Cathar track which ran from Larnat to the top of the mountain and from there down to Junac could be found, and if so what, if anything, could be learnt from this. Would it be possible 700 years on to locate the ravine on the Miglos side of the same mountain where a traitor was murdered in the spring of 1300 (see below, page 116)? Could I retrace the route that the châtelaine of Montaillou took whenever she returned to her father's home to visit him and her sister?

I hoped that the experience of immersing myself in the landscape of the Sabartès might in some unforeseen ways illuminate the story. This did not seem impossible. These events had happened mostly in a rural and mountainous world that had topographically probably not changed much, if at all, in seven centuries. The visual impact of the passage of time was bound to be of a different order here from that of my own habitat in London, which has of course been transformed since the Middle Ages. If the fourteenth-century poet Geoffrey Chaucer were to return to London, he would find that his native metropolis had become an unrecognizable place; but the people from this Occitan story might simply walk back into their own landscape.

Because the writing of this book involved a fair amount of fieldwork, I heavily depended on local IGN maps, the justly famed French equivalents of British Ordnance Survey maps. They not only helped to guide me safely through my walks, but crucially they also recorded place names that in many cases have been forgotten even by the local people. The IGN maps needed, however, to be supplemented by the *Plans Napoléoniens* (PN), on which the whole of France was mapped during the first half of the nineteenth century. Every *mairie* in France has a copy of the PN for the area under its jurisdiction, and the collected Ariège ones are under legal deposit in the departmental archives in the city of Foix. Even the briefest research in the place names from the d'Ablis and Fournier Registers reveals that the PNs are still not being drawn on as extensively as they should be by writers on the last Cathars. This is a loss, not least because some of the PNs are delicately executed drawings of the kind rarely produced nowadays. Most important of all, they show a countryside which was still largely rural and pre-industrial, so that paths which were in use and remained visible for many centuries are now solely preserved on the PNs. For orientation in a medieval landscape, and for much else, they proved invaluable, and will continue to do so.

I set off in the Cathars' tracks to discover nuggets of information, anything in fact that might shed light on my story. The location that I wanted to find above all others was *comba del gazel* near Montaillou.★ In 1308 a young shepherd called Jean Pélissier had witnessed two Perfects' flights through it, and in his dramatic account of it he had included specific details of the landscape (see below, pages 210–11).

On an oppressively hot July day I arrived in Montaillou in search of the *comba*. It was not marked on IGN 2148 ET, the map for the Ax-les-Thermes sector of the region, although the spur of the *gazel* was. The documents indicated that in *comba del gazel* there was a *comba fred*, and such a location was indeed listed as being in the *haute montagne* above Montaillou. The problem was that this particular *comba fred*, which turned out to be the wrong one, sat in a depression beyond the peaks of Pénédis and Roc de Quercourt, so that the village itself was not visible from there.

I nevertheless trekked up to the crest of the mountains, and this

---

★ The Occitan phrase *comba del gazel* literally means 'the comb of the Gazel', a comb (or coomb) being a hollow or valley.

took about two hours. From up here Montaillou seemed small and insignificant. I wondered how Pélissier could possibly have observed two men coming from the village at such a distance. He could hardly have seen more than I could from this vantage point, since I happen to have perfect vision. I knew then that I had strayed too far afield.

In the blue distance south of me snow-tipped peaks stretched far away into the Cerdagne and Catalonia, and I thought of Pierre Maury of Montaillou. He had ceaselessly trekked through this same majestic landscape, and he had known the Pyrenees better perhaps than anyone ever will again. Generous to a fault, he had rescued his abused sister with the same determination that made him guide Perfects safely through the darkest nights. Nearly 700 years on, the idea of this free spirit ending his life in the dank cells of a prison near Pamiers was almost unbearable.

I was woken from my reverie by the racks of cloud that were starting to stack low over the Puymorens and the Capcir mountains. Almost immediately afterwards the skies darkened dramatically in the Ax-les-Thermes region down in the valley. Only then did I realize that the flies had been aggressive on the ascent because of an impending storm. Such inexperience can be fatal in the mountains, and I scrambled back towards Montaillou.

Raindrops were spitting when I stumbled across a narrow trench which widened downwards. The track that I was on cut right across its uppermost point. It seemed to be an obvious short-cut to Montaillou, and I took it notwithstanding a sea of nettles and snapped, jagged tree trunks everywhere, the handiwork of past gales and lightning. The storm broke when I was half-way down the furrow. Visibility shrank to a few yards in seconds, and immediately lightning was everywhere around me. I stretched out flat on the squelching woodland floor, and covered myself with my raincoat, never having experienced such a vehement rainstorm at close quarters. The lightning was terrifyingly low, and I remembered hearing from the local people that cows and sheep are struck down here every year. The word '*paratonnerre*' comes readily to the lips of Montalionians (that is, people from Montaillou) when discussing anything, from the ruin of the castle to the unsightly electricity pylons which run along the lower slopes of the mountain in full view of Montaillou.

The eye of the storm settled above the grove of saplings where I sheltered for what seemed aeons, but was probably little more than ten minutes. Eventually I could rise safely and limp down into Montaillou; my bare legs, another beginner's folly, were sore for three days from the wet nettles. I gazed back towards 'my' niche in the copse, to take with me the memory of a place where for the briefest moment I had endured a fraction of the outdoor trials that were a routine experience to the people of the thirteenth century. My spot among the new spruces was slightly recessed east from the hollow of the trench, and from Montaillou I could no longer see it. Later, when I came to know the area more intimately, when the topographical details of the medieval documents and the late-twentieth-century landscape seamlessly blended into each other, I realized that by sheer serendipity I had taken cover where *comba del gazel* and the medieval *comba fred* merge into each other: the very same spot where two Cathar Perfects hid from the Inquisition one day in the summer of 1308.

In a recent guidebook on the Pyrenees (1998), Marc Dubin writes of 'the magnificent Pays de Sault', which at the convergence of the two *départements* of the Aude and Ariège includes the four villages of Camurac, Comus, Prades and Montaillou. Locally the people proudly declare, '*Le pays est beau, il est ouvert.*'⋆ A striking illustration of this was afforded me by one of my walks from Montaillou to Caussou by way of Prades and the Col de Marmare. It was winter, and it was warm. This combination can be lethal in the higher Pyrenees because it may induce avalanches, but at 4,000 feet it spelled ideal walking conditions: good visibility, since the trees were bare, no flies, and snow wherever there was shade. It is quite common here for the lee side of a path to be frozen solid while the more exposed part, a few inches across, is soaking in warm sunshine.

I did not quite know what to expect as I made my way down for the first time from the crest of the Marmare towards Caussou, the home village of the most famous character in the Fournier Register, Béatrice de Planisolles. But two miles or so above the village the valley gradually widened and before me there opened a harmonious, almost pastoral, prospect of meadows and river. My track was undoubtedly the medieval

⋆ 'The countryside here is beautiful and spacious.'

one, and this was therefore almost exactly what the young châtelaine saw during the last leg of her journey home from Montaillou or Prades to see her family.

It was over 20° Celsius when I strolled into Caussou. The solitary café in the village looked as if it had ceased trading some time ago, and it certainly would not open in the lunch hour. The shutters were down everywhere, and the only noises to be heard were the growling sound of the torrent cutting through the village, and the clinking of knives and forks on plates.

At the entrance to Caussou I had picked up a canine companion who insisted on chaperoning me through this *terra incognita*. I knew some of the names of the village's inhabitants in 1300, and from the Ariège telephone directory I guessed that descendants of the families from that period still lived here in the 1990s. My new friend joined me in staring at a house in the village on which, in large letters, the word 'Planisolles' had been inscribed; at least somebody here would have understood why I desired to visit Caussou.

I sat on the wall of the cemetery down from the church, and my friend joined me. He clearly did not greatly care for the mountain cheese in my sandwich, but he graciously accepted what I gave him and stayed anyway. In my mind I called him Argos, because he was so true, and because I so enjoyed his company as we both sat '*au soleil*'. I tried to figure out where the seigneurial de Planisolles had lived, and concluded that it had probably been in the prime spot of this mountain ledge, an area directly east of the stream where the natural heart of the village still is today; quite close in fact to the twentieth-century 'Planisolles' villa.

If so, Béatrice's uncle Pons de Planisolles's house may also have stood near here. It was in his garden that in 1322 Pons's son Raymond and an accomplice called Bourret buried a shepherd whom they had murdered. While the aristocrat from Caussou went unpunished, the peasant Bourret was hanged at Foix, but not before vengefully implicating another de Planisolles, a brother of Béatrice's, in heresy. Bourret had wanted to destroy him through evoking the great class leveller of fourteenth-century Languedoc; heresy brought peasant and aristocrat alike under the jurisdiction of the Church. As we shall see, in the years preceding 1322 charges of 'heresy' had ruthlessly been exploited by the

Church in just such a way to consolidate its economic power base in this corner of Languedoc.

The single most memorable convergence of the documents and the modern landscape was, for me, the discovery of the Perfects' fording point in the Agly river at Tournefort. I was driving from Rasiguères towards a dot on IGN 2448 OT called Tournefort, when I saw a sign for this location not far ahead of me. The river bed was to my left some thirty feet below. The road bulged out convexly towards it, and I pulled up into this natural parking space to continue my search on foot. If a ford did indeed exist, then the documents placed it near enough to here. As I stepped away from the car and looked down at the Agly, I found that I stood right above it. There could be little doubt: not only was this where the river had been crossed for centuries, but the bulge in the road may also have been formed to meet the passage across the river.

If fording the Agly ultimately left little to the imagination, the opposite was the case with the church at Gebets near Montaillou. Medieval Gebets had been an important sister village of Montaillou, and it had been more intimately linked through family ties to it than either Prades or Camurac, both of which are considerably closer. Gebets is now officially a vanished location, but its existence is recalled in the place name 'Crête de Gebets' on IGN 2148 ET (11B). This marks a hilltop crest some three miles east of Montaillou and on the way to a village called Mérial, which once housed the biggest iron forges in the region. In the 1990s Mérial hides bleakly at the bottom of a cramped valley, the Défilé d'Adouxes. The sun only ever visits here grudgingly for a few hours each day, and Mérial is on the verge of extinction.

Some 200 yards up the mountain, right above Mérial and now completely gone, sat Gebets. Unlike its neighbour Mérial, this south-east-facing village would have enjoyed a degree of sunshine comparable to the villages of the Pays d'Aillou, as Prades and Montaillou are also known. A kindly local woman gave me instructions on how to get there from beyond the church of Mérial. Although I did indeed find signs of habitations off a semi-metalled woodland track, I could not be sure; and I could not find the ruins of the church of Gebets, which I knew had been visible only thirty years earlier.

I returned to Mérial at just the point when the grocer's van appeared and *le tout Mérial* converged on this vital lifeline. It was my good fortune that the first person I asked for assistance happened to be a local farmer called André Vacquié. He explained how hard it was to find the church, that there was a small trail that I absolutely needed to take to get there. But it happened to be completely '*envahi*' (overgrown) during summer, and there was therefore no way that I could find it. '*Et voilà!*'

André considered the logic of this, and then insisted that we take his truck. We stopped off close to where I had been earlier, and then penetrated downhill into a veritable jungle. After a mere five minutes we emerged into a half-clearing and, indeed, into the apse of the ruins of the tiny church of Gebets. Bits of wall still rise knee-high, and apse and front entrance could be distinguished. Pierre Maury's uncle, who ended up in Sant Mateu in Catalonia, must once have stood inside this very same building, and so must young Raymonde Cléments of Gebets, whom her aunt Alazais Faure would save from the rampant Pierre Clergue of Montaillou.

My gallant host waited in silence 'outside' the church while I repeatedly photographed this green, dappled scene. So thick was the canopy of the young silver birches that neither of us noticed when it started to rain. Only a generation ago this same area had not only been clear of growth, but had been surrounded by arable land. It seems that the local farmers assiduously ploughed the soil around the church of old Gebets, and not infrequently turned up human bones, since their fields sat on top of the medieval churchyard.

I found it hard to tear myself away from the serenity of this spot. Where once people had worshipped there was now a strangely harmonious *mélange* of masonry and nature. I thought of San Damiano in Assisi. When the crucifix spoke to St Francis in that church and invited him to rebuild it, the chapel at Gebets would have risen proudly at the heart of this Pyrenean village. Now it was poised to disappear for ever.

Its neighbour across the mountain, however, the pilgrimage church of Notre-Dame-de-Carnesses in Montaillou, is a medieval manmade place which survives almost intact. There is no question about the authenticity of this building, notwithstanding various changes to it over the centuries, including a raising of the height of its walls. The chapel is the most noteworthy ancient building in the immediate area. Its apse, where the priest Pierre Clergue propositioned the châtelaine Béatrice de Planisolles, is perfectly preserved, and under its floor rests Pierre Clergue's mother. The fact that Notre-Dame is still used as a church only serves to enhance its importance as a living fossil. Its counterpart in Prades, Saint-Pierre, another church with echoes of Pierre Clergue and Béatrice de Planisolles, also still stands, although its architectural history is rather more chequered.

The outstanding importance of Notre-Dame-de-Carnesses does not, however, mean that there are no other remains of interest on the site itself. The latest archaeological view appears to be that most of the medieval village has been gradually washed down the hill; and it is likely that when 400 years ago the villagers abandoned the old site and moved further down the hill, they cannibalized their former abode. Even so there *are* extant foundations in several different areas of the medieval site, notably north of the square and at *paret del colel* (the wall of Colel), where a still visible track from *a-la-cot* emerged opposite the old square; in other words where I have placed the house of Raymond Rous alias Colel.

Other manmade places survive in this area from the Middle Ages. The buildings of Pamiers from where Jacques Fournier launched his Inquisition may have largely disappeared, but the city's street-grid is medieval and its names reflect its history; and one crucial street directly down from Fournier's former palace has survived almost inviolate from the passage of centuries.

Once the cemetery of Saint-Jean, or (today) Saint-Jean-Martyre, lay outside the city walls of Pamiers. It no longer does so now that the walls are down. From the railway line to Toulouse, which passes close to it, it looks as ornate, crowded and slightly sinister as many other French cemeteries. Its shape and dimensions are not very different from what they used to be, so that this is to all intents and purposes the same place. Because of its elevation on a hill the cemetery commands an impressive prospect of Pamiers and its many churches. This very spot was the most infamous plot of land in Languedoc during the Fournier persecutions. It was here that Béatrice de Planisolles was sentenced along with others, and it was in this same place that Guillaume Fort of

Montaillou was burnt at the stake in front of an audience which included his sister and his niece.

The grim prison of Allemans in the village of La Tour-du-Crieu has disappeared in its entirety. The houses which now ring-fence a space that doubles as parking area and children's playground probably sit on the old ramparts, and the church of Saint-Paul is the only (partial) survivor of the massive set of buildings that once rose here. An entire subterranean world of dungeons and oubliettes once sprawled directly beneath the surface of the village square at La Tour-du-Crieu, and that same space where there is now only air once housed a number of the most important characters from this story. They were all brought together here, and the brothers Pierre and Jean Maury may have died right here too, as there is no mention of their release in 1329 when some of the other inmates were set free.

It is the oddest thing to be walking in the peaceful and relatively inaccessible countryside of the highlands of the Sabartès, and to recall the intensity of the Cathar faith which once prevailed in these same locations and this identical landscape. Did that faith make these immutable vistas appear differently to them than to us? One of the enduring mysteries surrounding this story is why it should have been right here that the Cathar or Albigensian faith flared up again one last time in the years from 1290 to 1320.

Almost anywhere in the Sabartès is off the beaten track after five minutes, and my abiding memory of trekking from Montaillou to Caussou, or through the Gorges de la Frau to Montségur, or in the snows of Jasse de Balaguès, or in the mountains above Larnat, or of resting on the crest of the Port de l'Artigue looking down into Catalonia, is of silence and solitude; no sounds from traffic or flight-paths intrude here, only the trickle of a creek, a sudden flutter in the bushes, and the beat of my walking-stick on the track. The Perfects and their *passeurs* similarly carried sticks to haul themselves up these severe escarpments and, perhaps, to fend off the occasional viper. When one considers that they trekked mostly at night, their achievements seem the more remarkable.

Although I spent time at night on the site of the former medieval village of Montaillou, and in Unac and Caussou, my one serious attempt at a night-time walk predictably ended in failure. What light there was did not suffice, and within minutes I needed to resort to a torch. It is easy to forget how impenetrably black night can be in the countryside under cloud, and yet this path led through a relatively open part of the landscape, not a gully full of boulders deposited by mountain torrents during spring, or a secret track perilously winding its way up a moun-tainside. I had previously wondered why local Perfects, who after all knew the region fairly well, needed pathfinders. Now I understood that the human equivalent of a feline sixth sense was required to advance any distance at all here at night; and even when thus accompanied, the Perfects still needed to be physically fit enough to cope with these strenuous journeys.

While I trekked extensively in the Sabartès, there were distances that required a more practical twentieth-century mode of transport, the car. To the extent that I drove some 15,000 miles in search of the last Cathars, researching this book at times assumed the character of a road movie.

When I was preparing the groundwork for this story, I repeatedly encountered the misleading assertion that the town of Ax-les-Thermes in the Ariège and the village of Arques in the Aude circumscribed its geographical boundaries; anything that happened beyond this grid was deemed to show exceptional initiative on the part of the people of the Registers. But Occitan shepherds travelled well beyond the confines of Languedoc, let alone Arques or Ax. The culture of the internal combustion engine takes it for granted that large distances can be covered in quick time only because of the horsepower under the bonnet. But this is not the case. One of the more striking aspects of the Registers was the evidence of people's mobility and the huge distances that they travelled in relatively short spaces of time.

The arch of transhumance, as the seasonal moving of livestock to regions of a different climate is known, stretched from Montaillou into Catalonia. Indeed, at the approach of winter the shepherds of the Pyrenees took their flocks all the way to the coast near Valencia. They did so across the Puymorens or Capcir mountains such as the Riucaut, and then headed south through the Cerdagne and across the Cadí range. Around Easter they would do the same trek in reverse and head back towards the summer pastures in the mountains. I could not walk in their footsteps, partly because the medieval tracks across the passes can no longer be easily picked up, and partly because such treks are beyond the scope of all but the hardiest and toughest walkers.

When I drove from Montaillou to the coastal town of Peñíscola above Valencia I had a choice of several possible itineraries. I decided to go by way of the Puymorens from Ax-les-Thermes, because we know for certain that this was one of the tracks that medieval shepherds used to take. They do not seem to have used the direct route to La Seu d'Urgell, which cuts through Andorra and across the Port d'Envalira, perhaps because of the tensions that existed between them and the Andorrans (see below, pages 309–10).

I scheduled my drive to coincide roughly with the beginning of the medieval September transhumance, which started around St Michael's (29 September). It was a wet, dark and fog-bound morning when I set out from Montaillou around 6 a.m. As I turned the ignition, the temperature gauge indicated 4° Celsius. Even the reassuring purr of the engine did little to relieve the oppressiveness of the drive to Ax-les-Thermes.

About three miles south-west from Montaillou I turned into the short ascent to the top of the Col du Chioula. It was here, on this very spot where the road curves left to begin the climb, that in May 1308 two boys from Montaillou had, in the middle of the night, met a leading local Cathar. At that precise moment shortly after 6 a.m., in a place which was once known as the *superius del angle*, the temporal gap between 1308 and the late 1990s seemed suddenly acutely real. It was one thing to walk in the Cathars' tracks on sun-drenched days of spring; it was quite another to struggle up a stony gully in the pitch dark in a rainstorm or a blizzard. I then realized, as Jack London and George Orwell had done when trying to join the lives of the poor and dispossessed in London, that one can never truly be there as long as the chance of getting out remains entirely a matter of choice. Just as it was only ever possible to be a tramp-in-disguise rather than the real thing during a few weeks of well-intentioned research, so it was impossible now to experience the harshness of life in the medieval Cathar Languedoc. And not only did the Cathars struggle with the elements in a way that I never did or could, but this entire drama was played out against the

background of a savagely repressive regime that thought burning people
was not necessarily wrong. Jacques Fournier reputedly wept grievously
(*multum plangebat*) for having to burn the Valdensian Raymond de la
Côte whom he knew to be a good man (FR, f.27r); but burn him he
did.

On that particular September morning of my drive to Spain the Ax-les-
Thermes slope of the Puymorens was shrouded in mists, and I therefore
chose to go through the Puymorens tunnel rather than across the
mountain. When I emerged on the Latour-de-Carol side day was
dawning; the skies were clear, and the stars were fading as the sun rose
beyond the south-eastern mountains of the Cerdagne valley.

I crossed into Spain at Bourg-Madame and then made my way to La
Seu d'Urgell from where I drove to Lleida past places called Tragó and
Pons; they both featured in a famous episode towards the very end of
the Cathar diaspora in Catalonia. The climactic change was dramatic,
and when I passed Lleida around 11.30 a.m. the temperature had risen
to 30° Celsius. The roads were straight, empty and somnolent, and I
relied on the air-conditioning to keep me alert. What a contrast from
the freezing start to my day. I could not have wished for a more apposite
illustration of why the Occitan shepherds descended with their flocks
to Catalonia year after year to spend the winter months there.

From Lleida I drove into Los Monegros, before turning south at
Fraga. I crossed the Ebre river at Mequinenza, and pushed on to Alcañiz
and towards Morella. Some stretches on this road were so desolate that
they might have been in New Mexico or Arizona. I thought of young
Arnaud Sicre, the 'iceman' of this story. Like me he had headed south
towards those same far-off blue hills beyond the vanishing point of this
heat-shimmering strip of road; further still lay the olive groves and lush
pastures of Càlig and Sant Mateu, and the sea. But Arnaud had *walked*
all the way, and later he would recall the depth of his weariness as he
arrived in Sant Mateu. He could hardly have dared to hope that it
would deliver so much more than he had ever imagined.

By the time I embarked on the last leg of my journey to Morella,
through the solitary hills of the Sierra de la Molinera and Els Ports, I
had driven for eight hours. It was around 3 p.m. when I coasted through
the narrow cobbled streets of Morella and made for the municipal

car-park high up on the hill. That afternoon, under a hot and cloudless sky, the city was being lashed by parching winds that were sweeping down from the distant Pyrenees through the open plains of Catalonia.

Among the many new (to me) villages and cities that I visited during the writing of this book, Morella was the most spellbinding. Its elevated, almost haughty, position confers on it a sense of grandeur. I did not stay there long enough to get to know its people, to learn how the Morellans view themselves, but I somehow suspected that there would be a certain chic defining them. For me Morella held the additional excitement, on my first night there, of hearing the news in my hotel bedroom in both Castilian and in Catalan; for Catalan is the closest anyone can come now to the *langue d'oc* that was spoken by all the characters in this story. The two are virtually identical.

Approaching Morella by night from the south and Sant Mateu, as I did on another occasion, is both a memorable and an intimidating experience. Rather than climbing gently towards the walled city and its sea of lights, the road dips from Port de Querol all the way down to the bottom of the mount so that during the short, brusque ascent which follows Morella gradually fills the car's windscreen until finally it dwarfs driver and vehicle alike. From this perspective Morella at night is a medieval New York. It was partly here, and partly in Sant Mateu down towards the coast, that the Cathar church survived in exile, loosely grouped around Guillaume Bélibaste who made Morella his home.

All the main players who wrote the last chapter in the Catalonian exile after 1310 passed through this place. By the time I reached Morella I was familiar with the sites where they had trodden. But visiting this particular city was different, and what made it so was the knowledge that in my memory were stored images from the Sabartès that they would have shared as a memory before me; images of *comba del gazel* and the *haute montagne* of Montaillou, of the Val de Caussou and, most poignantly of all perhaps, of Cubières and Junac, the Languedoc home villages of Bélibaste and his lover Raymonde respectively. I had stood on that same rocky shelf in Junac that once housed Raymonde Marty's home and that of her sister Blanche, and on two different occasions I had walked through Guillaume Bélibaste's home village of Cubières, and now I was in Morella, where in the 1310s they spoke of home to visitors. Today Bélibaste's Cubières is a place that time forgot, but its

exquisite location and the *esprit de corps* of its villagers ensure that it is a
modern *village fleuri*. When I last stayed in Cubières, an azure-painted
wheelbarrow, delicately decked in geraniums, occupied pride of place
on the del Saouzé creek. It probably stood within a few yards of
where the Bélibastes' homestead once rose, because we know that the
Bélibastes' paddock rolled down towards the river.

Bélibaste never saw Cubières again, but I returned in 1999. If there
is a commemorative plaque or any other kind of memorial to him in
his native village, I missed it. But the place of his death, Villerouge-
Termenès, has become a shrine to this last Cathar Perfect; and the very
fortress where he lingered in chains as a prisoner is now largely dedicated
to paying homage to him, thus proving that some version at least of the
dictum *sanguis martyrorum semens christianorum** even came true for him.
There would have been, one imagines, many a worthier man than the
former shepherd-turned-Perfect in the Corbières in the course of these
long centuries, but it is Guillaume Bélibaste who is remembered; and
not only here, but also in Catalonia. Both Morella, which is in the
Comunidad Valenciana, and Sant Mateu in Catalonia refer to him in
their tourist publicity.

In the intervening centuries since the arrest of the Maury brothers
in Catalonia in 1323, only a handful of people will have travelled
through these parts with an internalized knowledge of this particular
history and its settings in the Sabartès. I suddenly found that sharing
another community's tribal memory became a weighty and even guilty
knowledge, because unlike them I was free and unbounded. I had the
choice to drive back into France, as I did, simply because I had by good
fortune been born in a free country in the second half of the twentieth
century.

Whenever I have stayed in Montaillou, I have been acutely conscious
of the fact that nearly seven centuries earlier, within yards of my
rented apartment in *a-la-cot*, the people of Montaillou had sat fearfully
anticipating every next move by the Inquisition. Although they enjoyed
considerable freedoms as far as the secular powers were concerned, the
Church demanded that they surrender their souls and spirits to it, and
for punishment their bodies. And there was nothing they could do

---

* 'The blood of martyrs becomes the seed of Christians.'

other than nurture their true faith secretly in the innermost recesses of their hearts.

The abiding impression from this story is one of the value of the enchanting small change of everyday life in medieval Languedoc. The Registers of Geoffroy d'Ablis and Jacques Fournier introduce a gathering of intelligent, sensuous, food-loving, witty and warm people. In spite of all the pains and sorrows unjustly inflicted on them, the people interrogated in the d'Ablis and Fournier Registers held the Inquisition in check for two decades. Although they lost the uneven contest in the end, this account intends to show that the Church never succeeded in quashing their spirit. They were simply ordinary people following their instincts to protect their loved ones, and it was their misfortune that their tiny part of the country fell under the scrutiny of a vindictive established Church.

Sources and Procedures

The primary written sources of this book are two fourteenth-century Inquisitorial Registers: MS 4269 (Bibliothèque Nationale, Paris), which concerns Geoffroy d'Ablis's Inquisition at Carcassonne, and MS 4030 (Vatican Library), which contains the testimonies given before Jacques Fournier at Pamiers. These are complemented by the *Sentences* of the Pamiers Inquisition, which survives in the British Library as BM MS 4697, and as the *Liber Sententiarum Inquisitionis Tholosanae 1307–1323* inside Philip Limborch's printed *Historia Inquisitionis* (1692). In addition a number of volumes in the Doat collection (Bibliothèque Nationale, Paris) contain relevant materials which have been used in this book.

Both the d'Ablis and Fournier Registers have been authoritatively edited. The vast MS 4030 appeared in 1965 in a magisterial, three-volume edition with notes by Jean Duvernoy, who followed it in 1978 with an annotated French translation. The much less substantial, but equally interesting, d'Ablis volume was published in a parallel Latin–French text in 1984, with notes and a full *apparatus criticus* by Annette Pales-Gobilliard. MS 4697 remains unedited, probably because of Limborch's printed version, which is almost universally used in writing on this fourteenth-century history. In this respect I have followed suit, while also consulting MS 4697.

In quoting from the Registers I have in each case gone to the original manuscripts, which I have checked against the standard editions in the case of d'Ablis and Fournier. I have always followed manuscript unless otherwise indicated. I have not marked upper case in my Latin quotations, because the manuscripts do not, but I have followed precedent in spelling out every word rather than attempting to reproduce the extensive abbreviations used by the medieval clerks.

In a number of significant instances my readings of the Fournier Register differ from the ones supported by its editor. On MS 4030, f.44r, for example, the word *eruca*, meaning rocket, occurs. Although the proposed correction to *bursa* ('leather bag, purse': Duvernoy 1965, 1.248) makes good sense of an admittedly awkward passage, *bursa* is too far off manuscript's *eruca* to be attributed to a scribal mistake. With some reservations I have therefore retained *eruca* in my translation.

A further example is provided by MS 4030, f.265r, where Duvernoy suspects three scribal errors, one of which, *eadem*, is silently and rightly emended to *eodem* (Duvernoy 1965, 3.198). But the other two corrections are substantive: for the first name *Ramunda* the word *hereticus* is substituted, and manuscript's verb *venisset* (*venio*: to come) becomes *vidisset* (*video*: to see). Both these changes distort the reading of manuscript, which is colourful and kinetic in its own right.

Where I have departed from manuscript, or adopted a previously proposed editorial reading, this is indicated. Thus at MS 4030, f.43r, where manuscript offers a seemingly meaningless *muicture*, the phrase '*iuncture*' has been proposed as an emendation (Duvernoy 1965, 1.244). In MS 4030 only the string '-*cture*' seems safe, and in this instance I have adopted the editorial emendation, which makes good sense and allows for minim confusion and transposition of letters, both of which are familiar characteristics of manuscripts.

All translations are my own, and there are inevitably differences of emphasis and meaning from my predecessors. Where, for example, Duvernoy glosses '*habebimus inter vestrum de vobis*' as 'mais nous aurons votre mort', I follow Niermeyer (1984) in translating *inter* as a preposition (rather than a noun) meaning 'for this as well as that'; accordingly my text reads 'for these reasons we will strip you of all your belongings' (FR, f.96v; Duvernoy 1978, 463).

Another source of confusion originates from the closeness of the two cognate languages of fourteenth-century Languedoc: Medieval Latin, which was the written language, and Occitan, which was universally spoken in the Sabartès. It is not always clear whether a particular phrase is one or the other, as the case of *druda* illustrates; it *sounds* like Occitan, but in the particular instance in the text it is, probably, Latin.

For *druda* the two languages afford related glosses, but that is not the case with the use of *posticium* at MS 4030, f.76r. I take the phrase *posticium* to be Latin rather than Occitan and concur with the generic meaning of 'small door' (Lewis and Short 1969; Niermeyer 1984; DuCange 1840); I consequently read *intra* ('inside') where others have read *infra* ('under'), logically so since they follow Levy (1892–1924) in taking *posticium* to be Occitan and meaning 'plank'. While the Occitanians therefore hide the present for the Perfects under a plank or palette, the Latinists put it inside the oven door (see below, page 16).

Throughout I have used Lewis and Short and Gaffiot (1934) for Classical and post-Augustan Latin, Niermeyer and DuCange for Medieval Latin, Levy and Mistral (1968) for Occitan, and Pompeu Fabra's *Diccionari general de la llengua catalana*.

Where there are transcription errors or omissions in the edited texts of the manuscripts, I have ignored them in accordance with the principle of working from manuscript as my copy-text. Rather than carrying a set of detailed notes and collations, I have, for reasons of conciseness, cross-referenced particularly important and substantial references to their sources through parentheses. I have used 'FR, f.ooo' for the foliation references to the Fournier Register (MS 4030), 'd'AR, f.ooo' for the d'Ablis Register (MS 4269) and 'L, ooo' for parenthetical page references to Limborch. (See page 406 for a full list of abbreviations used in the text.) In the same spirit I have used the Harvard system of bibliographical referencing, which means that I give the name of the cited author and page references in parentheses in my text, corresponding to the Bibliography on page 407.

In my longer quotations I have, as a rule, turned all indirect speech in the Registers into direct speech. There are only two authentic first-person testimonies in the documents, those by Pierre de Luzenac and Pierre de Gaillac in the d'Ablis Register. Whereas the ones taken down by the scribes of the court are congested with punctilious, legalistic formulae and sound highly artificial, the two first-person depositions are free from all that.

I have, however, not gone so far as to remove legal literalism from my quotations of others' testimonies. I have chosen to be conservative in this respect, partly to preserve the flavour of the original court documents, and partly not to stray too far from my copy-text. The rhetorical register of each deposition, while being legally generic, is also affected by the situation in which the accused appeared, so that to turn their speech into overly free and idiomatic discourse might seriously misrepresent what was actually spoken on any given occasion.

All my dates are New Style, in which the year is taken to start with 1 January, whereas all the documents use Old Style, that is the Julian calendar, which was current in Europe until Pope Gregory XIII's reform of 1582, and in England until 1752.

Although establishing a chronology for the events of this story is an art rather than a science, the dates of the major events are not really in doubt. These include the return of the Authiés to Languedoc in 1300, Pierre Maury's departure from Arques in December 1305, the marriage of Bernard Clergue of Montaillou in September 1307, the two raids on Montaillou, and the arrests of the various Perfects in 1305, 1307 and 1309. Local difficulties with constructing the sequence of events, as in the case of the death of *Na* Roche in Montaillou, or the meetings in Toulouse between the returning Perfects and Pierre de Luzenac, are acknowledged and set out in my text.

It is events in the Catalonian diaspora which pose the most awkward dating problems, simply because the Church only caught up with the Catalonian Cathars fairly late, so that there are no extant judicial minutes relating to this until October 1319. Our information about this ten-year period comes primarily from the brothers Pierre and Jean Maury, Guillaume Maurs, Guillaume Baille and Arnaud Sicre, and this mosaic needs to be scrupulously collated. The dating of the arrival of Arnaud Sicre in Sant Mateu provides a good example (see below, pages 314–15). Not the least of the difficulties with some dates in the diaspora stems from the fact that the two Maury brothers sometimes offer different versions at different times of the same events to the Aragonian Inquisition and to Jacques Fournier. The brothers' sense of time and sequence is mostly sound, but for good reasons they deliberately muddied the waters with regard to certain aspects of their lives in Catalonia.

Money was a key lubricant in the peasants' and shepherds' transactions. This was to be expected during a period when banking dynasties first started to emerge in Europe. The Cathar high command itself dealt with bankers to fund their movement. The documents abound with references to pennies, shillings, pounds, florins, gold angels and Barcelona money. By the time this story gets under way, royal French coins such as the popular *gros tournois*, which was a large silver coin also known as *tournois d'argent* (issued in 1266), were circulating widely in

Languedoc. They gradually superseded the older currency of the region, particularly the *sous toulzas* and *deniers toulzas*, or Toulouse shillings and pennies. These continued to be set at a higher value than the French coins, as two of the characters in this story would discover, literally to their cost (see below, page 123).

The accounting system of the late-thirteenth-century Sabartès was the Carolingian one. In money of account the *gros tournois* was the equivalent of a shilling (*solidus*) and was worth twelve pence (*denarius*). Twenty shillings in turn equalled one pound (*libra*), while the *petit tournois*, on the other hand, had the same value as a penny. Both shilling and pound were monies of account rather than minted coins, unlike the silver *tournois*, the penny, or the prestigious florin, which became the medieval equivalent of the dollar. The florin eventually emerged as the common unit of account where larger sums were involved; when it was first issued in 1252, its value was set at 240 pence, or one pound of money of account.

More important than knowing the monetary system, however, is appreciating the purchasing power of money at the time. Wherever it was possible to do so, I have tried to convey a sense of the real material value of any given sum of money. This also usefully illuminates the structure of the economy of medieval Languedoc and Catalonia. Thus, it reveals that labour was relatively cheap, but far from uniformly priced: head shepherds such as Pierre Maury clearly made a very good living, whereas card-makers like Guillaume Bélibaste struggled and needed to freelance to supplement their earnings. Similarly, razors were dear, and so was fish, both freshwater and marine. Meat, on the other hand, was relatively inexpensive. Why this should be so is unclear, but it chimes intriguingly with the modern traveller's experience of Catalonia and Languedoc.

Unless otherwise indicated, my distances are necessarily given as the crow flies. There is no foolproof way of equivalencing fifty miles on a map with the true distance on the ground in mountainous terrain. The one certainty is that a road and track distance will be several times longer, particularly in the Pyrenees and the *serras* of Catalonia.

All Catalonian locations are given in Catalan, not least because Catalan and medieval Occitan are almost the same language. Pierre

Maury therefore visited Catalan Sant Mateu rather than Castilian San Mateo, and a mountain range is now as then called *serra* rather than *sierra*. I have consistently given the characters' names in modern French rather than attempting to anglicize them or trying to preserve Occitan or Midi forms; when in doubt I have checked the spellings of names against the current telephone directories of the Ariège and Aude. The people of the Register address us with an immediacy that transcends the centuries, and to that extent it seemed right to prefer, for example, 'Pierre Clergue', which is the usage current in Montaillou today, to both 'Peter Clergue' and the now obsolete form 'Peyre (or Peire) Clerc'.

My quotations from the Bible are taken from the Authorized Version. I have resisted the temptation to engage in lengthy expositions of the doctrines of Catharism *per se*. In the Registers we are offered different perspectives on the 'true' faith through the proselytizings of Perfects and of good and bad Cathars. By choosing to let the documents speak for themselves as often as possible, I hoped to be true to the spirit of this book, which tries to preserve the uniqueness and integrity of this story and of its highly individuated characters. This strategy furthermore allowed me to spread the more overtly doctrinal parts of the book across wide areas of the text.

Given the nature of my evidence I have resorted to the indefinite wherever it was appropriate to do so. I have used 'may', 'might', 'perhaps', 'probably', 'almost certainly' and the conditional with as much nuancing as was consonant with common sense. I have resisted the temptation to allow hypotheses to harden into fact, and to that end I have approached the various testimonies with a measure of scepticism, bearing in mind that these were obtained under duress, notwithstanding the refraining from torture by these particular Inquisitors.

The raw materials which I set out to investigate have been touched on many times, and the editors of the Registers and their predecessors such as Döllinger and Vidal have helped to unlock this past which unique historical circumstances have preserved for us. In *Montaillou*, Le Roy Ladurie provided trenchant analyses of the socio-economic politics of the Pays d'Aillou at the time of the d'Ablis and Appamanian Inquisitions. But his work on family, home, marriage and sex inevitably involved a degree of conceptual abstraction which submerged the individual in the tribe, when it is precisely the irreducibility of the men and women of the Registers which makes them address us with such freshness from those ancient pages. In what follows I have attempted to tease out the *story* of these events on the ground, to tell it as a narrative simultaneously from within and, to the extent that I write with hindsight, from without.

Finally, unlike my predecessors, I have undertaken a full-scale reconstruction of the topography of the last Cathars' story, drawing on a combination of *PN*, IGN, local lore, and my own extensive trekking in the region. That so many tracks, valleys, nooks and corners from this medieval tale could be retraced in the landscape of the Sabartès is a tribute to the thoroughness of the Inquisitorial Registers, which have left us a wealth of geographical detail. But if mountain ranges are by nature timeless, the same does not hold true for towns and villages, not even in the relatively inaccessible upper Ariège. Here my reconstructions became necessarily more a matter of hypotheses and deductions. This was the case, to varying degrees, with places such as Ax-les-Thermes, Tarascon, Junac, Larnat and Montaillou and, in Catalonia, Beceite, Sant Mateu and Morella.

It was Montaillou, however, which posed the greatest challenge. The Clergues' dominance there had made it the focal point of the Authiés' movement, and Fournier had rightly concentrated his attention on it, hence the number of testimonies from the village. That no one has so far drawn an in-depth map of the medieval village is mildly surprising, because there is no shortage of data. The Fournier Register supplies a mass of information about various key locations and about the structural relationships between a number of houses. Thus, for example, we know for a fact that the Clergues lived opposite the Belots, that the Belot and Benet houses were secretly connected to each other, and that the Ferriés and the Maurys were direct neighbours on the same side of the square of Montaillou. But it was only after a close study of the *PN* of Montaillou that I could imaginatively superimpose the template of the written record on the present-day site and understand the shape of thirteenth-century Montaillou. The *PN* unmistakably retains the medieval village's main track pattern. Although the existence of these paths was attested by the Fournier Register, it was important and exciting to see the topography of the medieval manuscript confirmed in a hand-drawn map from the early nineteenth century. My reason for offering as much detail about Montaillou and its people as I legitimately could was to consolidate its immediacy and presence in the mind of the reader. More is known about this site and its inhabitants than about any other comparable medieval place in Europe, certainly as far as the 'ordinary' people of the Middle Ages are concerned. For that reason alone I deemed it desirable to recreate their microcosmic world as minutely as possible. It did not seem enough to state, for example, that after her marriage young Guillemette Rives frequently watched people coming and going from her father's wealthy Cathar house. While this information is factually correct, it fails to explain why and how she did this; she was, after all, a very minor cog in the Cathar machine, if that. A profounder understanding of Guillemette's watching is garnered from an appreciation of the topographical fact that her married home sat only a few yards away across the square from her parents', and that it was her numerous pregnancies and children that kept her pinned down in her husband's house. She became an observer *malgré elle*, because she dared not leave her children alone. Thus, sitting in her garden or standing in the square, Guillemette, the niece of a Perfect, innocently witnessed the Cathar story of Montaillou unfold, literally, in front of her house.

Prologue:
The Châtelaine of Montaillou

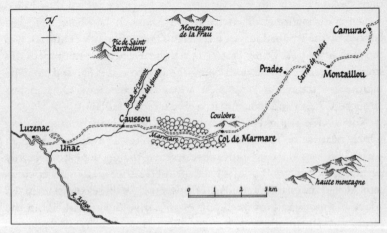

The châtelaine's way

On Saturday 26 July 1320 an aristocratic woman in her mid-forties appeared at an Inquisitorial hearing in the Episcopal Palace of the ancient city of Pamiers in Languedoc.

She was twice-widowed, and her married name in 1320 was Béatrice de Lagleize. Thirty years earlier she had become Béatrice de Roquefort, when she married her first husband and became the châtelaine of a Pyrenean hilltop village called Montaillou. Before then she had been Béatrice de Planisolles. It is by her euphonious maiden name that the châtelaine of Montaillou is affectionately remembered to this day in Languedoc, and I shall consequently refer to her as Béatrice de Planisolles throughout.

She had been summoned by the Bishop of the see of *Pamias*, as the city was called in the language of the region, to answer charges of blasphemy, witchcraft, and above all heresy. Her adversary on this summer weekend in the fourteenth century was a Cistercian by the name of Jacques Fournier. He was born in nearby Saverdun, and in

1320 he was in his mid-thirties. Fourteen years from now he would become Pope at Avignon, the third pope of the 'Babylonian captivity', as Petrarch, Fournier's younger contemporary, called the period when the papacy was exiled from Rome to Provence (1309–77).

Since the aristocrat and the Bishop were both natives of the Ariège, they spoke to each other in Occitan, the language which they called *roman* to distinguish it from Latin and *frances*. It had been rendered famous by the troubadours of the twelfth and thirteenth centuries, and the Florentine poet Dante (1265–1321), the exact contemporary of this story, is usually credited with being the first to call it *lingua d'oco*. The Latin name for it was *vulgare*. As a language, medieval Occitan was closer to Catalan and Italian than to French or Castilian.*

Not much transpired in the course of this preliminary hearing, during which Béatrice de Planisolles was invited to testify without taking an oath. This was standard procedure to save the accused from hastily perjuring themselves. The evidence against Béatrice was largely circum-stantial, and the charges varied in seriousness. The three counts included a lack of enthusiasm for attending mass, a frivolous remark about the Host, and accommodating a single night-time visit by a 'sorceress'. They probably did not worry the Bishop too much. What did concern him was Béatrice's descent from a house with a pedigree of Cathar loyalties, and the fact that twenty-five years earlier she had resided in the notorious Cathar-revivalist village of Montaillou. She had moreover known the most famous heretical family of the region, the Authiés of Ax, three of whom had been Perfects, the title bestowed by the Cathars on their spiritual leaders.† Even if Fournier had not entertained deeper

* Indeed, contemporary Catalan and the language spoken by the characters in this story are intimately related, and they were so in the Middle Ages, when the shepherds from Occitania poured into Catalonia without encountering a language barrier. Of course they were recognized in Catalonia by their accents for being Cerdagnians, but that was no different from the Cerdagnians themselves being astutely aware of regional variations between their own accents. The accent of the Pays d'Aillou, the two villages of Montaillou and Prades, for example, differed from that of Ax, now Ax-les-Thermes, just down the mountain. It was one such chance recognition of a particular intonation in a far-away place that proved to have terrible consequences in this story.
† Unlike the Montségur Inquisitors of the 1240s, Fournier did not allow anyone to use that title in evidence; instead Perfects had to be called '*heretici*', and in Fournier-speak the Cathar ritual of 'consoling' the dead was always referred to as 'hereticating'.

reasons for calling her in, he would have suspected that the woman before him had been implicated in the last Albigensian renaissance of the early fourteenth century. With reference to her Cathar father, he quoted Matthew 7:17 at her, that 'every good tree bringeth forth good fruit; but a corrupt tree bringeth forth evil fruit'.

The châtelaine must have wondered why she in particular was so important to Fournier, and why he was raking up the past all around her. The resurgence of Catharism a quarter of a century earlier in the highlands of the Sabartès, the Pyrenean mountain range in which most of this story is set, had after all been crushed by the Dominican Geoffroy d'Ablis, who in 1303 had acceded to the office of Inquisitor in Carcassonne, where he was joined in 1307 by his fellow Dominican, the redoubtable and scholastic Bernard Gui.

Some of Béatrice's fellow accused suspected the new Bishop of Pamiers of using the Inquisition to subdue a populace that stubbornly resisted his taxation demands. This was partly correct. Jacques Fournier was bent on turning himself into God's banker, and during the three years before his first interviews with Béatrice de Planisolles he had inflicted a savage regime of new taxes on the people of the Ariège. But the Bishop's most pressing spiritual reason for relaunching the Inquisition was the irritating presence of a rump of Cathar die-hards and recidivists across the Pyrenees in Catalonia. Fournier showed his grasp of the suasive power of money by setting bounties on their heads. He could hardly have guessed that in response to this a young man by the name of Arnaud Sicre would appear before him one day in October 1319 and offer to bring in the chief Perfect of the diaspora Cathars. Moreover, it seems as if at the far-flung Cathar hearths and campfires of Catalonia this daring freelancer had gathered some astonishing intelligence about the heretical years in the village of Montaillou where, coincidentally, the new Bishop had a distant relative.

We have no conclusive proof that it was the bounty-hunter who first alerted Jacques Fournier to the role played by a family called Clergue twenty years earlier in the Cathar recrudescence, but the signs are that he was the initial source of this information. Nobody living locally in the Ariège, the Aude and the Toulousain would have dared incriminate one of the wealthiest and most ruthless families on the ground in Languedoc, but Catalonia was a different matter, and the Clergues' sway did not hold there.

Even Fournier could not take on this family without the strongest proof of presumed guilt. But take them on he would. Here was his opportunity to eradicate the hidden core of the Cathar cancer that had eluded his predecessors. And the chief culprit had been close, it turned out, to the former châtelaine of Montaillou, who now lived in the village of Varilhes near Pamiers. She, Fournier reckoned, could turn out to be the chink in the armour of the Clergues.

The chronology and focus of the interviews with different Montalionians in Pamiers during the summer and autumn of 1320 establish beyond doubt that the foremost reason for summoning Béatrice de Planisolles was her connection with the Clergues of Montaillou, although this was never made apparent to her. Instead, Fournier consistently tried to convey the impression that his onslaught on the Clergues was as a result of Béatrice's revelations and corroborative evidence from other witnesses.

The widow's stalling during their first encounter did not fool the Bishop. After a short session he appointed the following Tuesday, 29 July, as the date of Béatrice's next court appearance; she would then be expected to give a sworn testimony. She agreed to this, and then, that same weekend, she fled. A few days later, on Wednesday 30 or Thursday 31 July, Béatrice was arrested at Mas-Saintes-Puelles in the diocese of Saint-Papoul, some twenty miles north-east of Pamiers. With her was a young priest who was her lover.

On Friday 1 August she appeared again before Fournier. This time she was invited to identify as her property a number of items found in her purse and leather bag. These consisted of two male umbilical cords, bits of cambric stained with menstrual blood, a seed of rocket, grains of slightly burnt frankincense, a mirror and a small knife or *canivet*, which was wrapped in a piece of linen, and a grain of an unidentified plant which was wrapped in silk. Her bag also contained dried pieces of a bread called *tinhol*, short lists, and many pieces of linen. Because of all this, the clerk of the tribunal faithfully notes, there was a strong presumption that Béatrice was a sorceress and used divinations.

In her deposition the contents of her purse and bag were itemized twice: at her appearance under arrest on 1 August, when she formally acknowledged them as hers, and three weeks later, on Monday 25 August, when the list of them was read out to her and she was invited to speak.

By Monday 25 August 1320 Béatrice was into her ninth, and last, session with Fournier and his fellow Inquisitors. She was exhausted, and she was reported to be very sick. Here is what she said regarding the contents of her bag, with no attempt, it seems, at evasion except regarding the bread, because it was nearly conclusive proof of Cathar contamination. Her candour is a hallmark of her entire deposition whenever it concerns the human body; and the body looms large in this story.

I had the boys' umbilical cords from the sons of my daughters, and I kept them because I was advised to do so by a woman who had been Jewish before being baptized. She told me that if I had such male umbilical cords, and carried them with me, I should not lose a lawsuit against anyone if I were to become involved in litigation. That is the reason why I had and kept my grandsons' umbilical cords. But since then I've not been involved in any lawsuit to test their efficacy. The bloodstained pieces of linen were soaked in the menstrual blood of my daughter Philippa, because the same baptized Jewish woman told me to collect some of the first period that flowed from my daughter, and to give it to drink to her husband or any other man and thereby ensure that the man in question would not be interested in any woman other than the one whose first period he drank.

Therefore when, quite some time ago, my daughter Philippa first started to menstruate, I observed from looking in her face that she seemed uncomfortable. I asked her what was wrong, and she replied that she was losing blood through her vulva. Remembering then the converted Jewish woman's words, I cut a piece off Philippa's bloodstained shift. But there did not seem to be enough of her period on that piece. I therefore gave my daughter Philippa a different piece of linen which was fine blue cloth and told her to impregnate it and entirely soak it with her period.* This Philippa did, and I afterwards

---

* The Latin text has '*alium pannum lineum blosetum et subtile*'. The use of '*blosetum*' is unclear, but the word may correspond to '*bluetum*', which means 'blue cloth' and of which '*blouetum*' is an alternate spelling (N).

dried the pieces of linen intending, when Philippa married, to give them to her husband to drink after wringing out her period from the re-soaked pieces of cloth. And when this year Philippa became engaged, I twice contemplated giving her period to drink to her fiancé. In the end, however, I thought it was better for this to happen after Philippa and her husband had had sex, and that it ought to be Philippa herself who should feed her period to her husband. And since I was arrested before the marriage could be consummated between Philippa and her husband, and indeed before they were married, I therefore did not give him any of her period.

The pieces of linen were not put on the rocket with the grains of frankincense for any nefarious purpose, but by accident. It was not to perpetrate evil deeds that I kept the incense, but because this year my daughter suffered from bad headaches, and I had been told that incense mixed with other things would cure her sickness. The grains of incense that were found on my person in my bag or elsewhere remain from that, and I never intended to do anything else with them. [Similarly] neither the mirror nor the wrapped-up knife, nor the pieces of cambric, were carried for the purpose of divination, or the making of mischief. As for the seeds wrapped in the silk fabric, it is a seed of a plant which is commonly known as 'herb ive'. It was given to me by a pilgrim who told me that it had medicinal properties to cure the falling sickness; and since this year my grandson by my daughter Condors suffered from the falling sickness, I wanted to use the seed. But my daughter informed me that she had taken her son to the church of Saint-Paul, where he was cured of the illness. She did not wish me to do anything about her son's sickness, and so I did not use the seed. (FR, f.44)

Although most of Béatrice's possessions could be construed as mildly incriminating, the Bishop would have recognized that they were innocuous charms and love philtres, which were not different ultimately from other local superstitions regarding, for example, clippings of nails and hair from corpses to safeguard the houses of the dead. An uncharacteristic *pudeur* made her gloss over the rocket (*eruca*), which was thought to enhance the quantity of sperm and the vigour of sexual intercourse (cf. Poirion 1995, f.30v). The carrying of an aphrodisiac proves that even in full flight Béatrice had her lover's sexual welfare at heart.

But the pieces of dried bread signalled Cathar associations. Fournier

would have guessed at once that it was bread which had been consecrated by Cathar Perfects. The talismanic carrying of the bread so many
years after her last alleged contact with heretics proved that the former
châtelaine harboured deep-rooted Cathar sympathies. It would not
have escaped the Inquisitor's notice that she omitted the bread from
her itemizing of her possessions.

If Fournier did not press her on it, he had his reasons. Before starting
her detailed refutation of the charge of heretical contamination implied
by the contents of her bag, the former châtelaine tried to retract the
cornerstone from her confession of the preceding days. Why she chose
to do so now remains a mystery, although later I shall argue that this
may have been due to her being bearded by the chief villain of this
story. In the days leading up to 25 August Béatrice de Planisolles had
indeed made certain statements that sent shock-waves through the
ecclesiastical establishment of the Ariège. If proven true, they would
render her own past meddling in heresy almost an irrelevance by
comparison. She gave Fournier more than he ever expected to hear,
and almost more than even he could handle.

By 25 August it was too late for a retraction. Since she had first made
certain allegations on Thursday 7 August about Pierre Clergue, the
rector of Montaillou, Fournier had received independent proof of
them. The most treacherous Cathar of the Authié era, it turned out,
was none other than a seemingly loyal, highly esteemed and immensely
rich local priest. This double-dealing prelate had not only weathered
the various inspections and purges, but had actively participated in
them. At the time of Fournier's interview with Béatrice de Planisolles
he had never been challenged, let alone arrested. Béatrice knew him
well. Indeed, like many other women she had been his lover, and the
priest seems to have held her in considerable affection. But no one
other than she would have dared give his name to the Church, because
locally he *was* the Church; and even in provincial capitals such as
Carcassonne and, probably, Foix and Pamiers, he wielded huge power.
He seems to have enjoyed immunity from suspicion, let alone prosecution.

The combing of the Sabartès two decades earlier in the search for
heretics had nevertheless been thorough, and virtually all the leaders of
the Cathar revivalist movement had perished at the stake by 1310. It

was therefore particularly shocking that it was only now that the full scale of the Authié family's challenge to the Church should be exposed; and that one of the main culprits, a multiple saboteur of the Church who was the priest of Montaillou, was happily at large.

Fournier found himself marching into battle against the ghosts of the Authiés and their adherents, dead and living, in the Pays d'Aillou. In the months and years which followed Béatrice's testimony, many who were resting in the cemeteries of Ax, Montaillou and Prades, and other parts of the Ariège in both the highlands and the lowlands, were exhumed and their corpses burnt on pyres. They were the consoled ones, men, women and children, who had been administered the last Cathar rites by various Perfects. After fifteen years of persecutions, from 1295 to 1310, the battered people of the Ariège were about to suffer yet another onslaught in 1320, probably the fiercest to be inflicted on them since the dark days of Simon de Montfort and his crusaders over 100 years earlier.

It was Béatrice de Planisolles's evidence that unleashed this final offensive against a community that had once been her own. Although, as we shall see, she had carefully distanced herself from any direct Cathar activities at the height of this heretical *risorgimento*, the Good Men repeatedly sought out the châtelaine of Montaillou as the ultimate prize. In the end, however, it was sex and not a religious conversion to Catharism, or rather sex under the guise of doctrine, that landed her quite literally in bed with heresy.

Her role in this medieval drama is pivotal. By virtue of her rank in the society of the time she knew all the main players. Hers is moreover one of the most recognizable voices in a series of depositions which are overwhelmingly characterized by their simple humanity and directness. Fournier's persecutions caused intense misery to the sorely tried people of early-fourteenth-century Occitania. But his hounding of them produced a set of records in which they address us with such dignity in the face of impossible odds that it turns their defeat into a moral victory. In their story the châtelaine is *prima inter pares*, and just as Fournier deemed her to be the key that would unlock the secrets of Montaillou, so I propose to follow her closely as this story unfolds, and for much the same reason.

★

Béatrice de Planisolles was born into minor nobility in the Ariège in, probably, about 1274. Her birth would coincide therefore approximately with that of Robert the Bruce, and it was in this same year that in Florence the nine-year-old Dante Alighieri fell in love with the eight-year-old Beatrice Portinari, whose first name he immortalized in the *Divina Commedia*.

The place of Béatrice's birth was almost certainly the mountain village of Caussou, the headquarters of the de Planisolles family. Now as then the village perches on the side of a mountain 2,970 feet above sea-level, and it lends its name to the Val de Caussou, a six-mile trench which connects the Ariège valley to the Col de Marmare (Pl. 1). Caussou has changed little in seven centuries, and overlooks the confluence of two streams, the Ruisseau de la Coume d'Amont and the Marmare. The Coume d'Amont, which was known in the thirteenth century as the 'brook of Caussou', bisects the village in a deep cut on a north–south axis, while the Marmare issues three miles up to the east from near the top of the Col de Marmare (4,465 feet).

Beyond the thickly wooded range of the Marmare lie the villages of Prades and Montaillou. In the thirteenth century the track across the *col* became a lifeline for the Cathars. The taxing seven-mile trek from Caussou to Prades and Montaillou at first leads up a gentle gradient past the Marmare in the meadows to the right, before steeply rising for two miles to the *col*, under a canopy of trees and with the booming sound of the Marmare in the ravine down below.

After moving to Montaillou at the age of seventeen, Béatrice walked this way whenever she visited her family, and particularly her sister Ava, who was married in Caussou. An important landmark in late-thirteenth-century Caussou, probably as it was entered from Unac and Bestiac, was 'the door of Raymond Tinhol', where various characters were in the habit of chewing the fat. Other places that would have been instantly recognized by the young châtelaine in her home village were *els esshars*, which was a location on the path up to Prades close to where today the metalled road turns into a track, and *comba del ginesta* or 'comb of the broom', which was the cut that runs up above the village.

Caussou was the de Planisolles' family-fee, and the clan was deeply entrenched here. It was headed by two brothers, Philippe and Pons de

Planisolles. Pons had at least two children, Raymond and Raymonde, and Philippe fathered three daughters who bore the ruling-class names of Béatrice, Ava and Gentille, and two sons, Guillaume and Bernard. This latter was also known by the nickname *de na mengo* or *den amengo*, which may mean 'the scowler' (*mengano* = grimace: *LT*). Béatrice's brothers were not to be trifled with, and many years later she was convinced that they would hurt her if she disgraced them through her unbecoming sexual conduct. Like the rest of the Sabartès, Caussou had been profoundly affected by the upheavals of the six decades which preceded Béatrice's birth, and particularly by the ripples from the Holy Inquisition, which Pope Gregory IX had set up in 1233 to complete the task of purging Occitan lands of heresy, and which was administered by the Order of Preachers, the Dominicans. In the ensuing years they zealously littered the country with yellow crosses, the symbol of shame which those regarded as heretics were forced to wear on their tunics and coats.

By the 1290s the de Planisolles had been steeped in heresy for two, if not three, generations.* Béatrice would probably not have seen her father displaying the yellow crosses he had been sentenced to wear when she was a little girl, because around Caussou, and indeed almost

---

* At about the time of Béatrice's birth or during her infancy, there took place a famous exodus from Caussou to Lombardy in northern Italy, which, as we shall see, had become a sanctuary for Occitan Cathars. The exodus was recalled fifty years later by old Guillemette Bec, whose maiden name, Rauzy, survives in Caussou today. A woman called Alazais Record, who was the cousin of Guillemette Bec's mother, departed for Lombardy with another woman called Gauzia and two children, a brother and a sister called Simon and Mathende. Of the foursome who left, Simon returned home in the mid-1290s. He was accompanied by a Lombard wife and stayed in the house of Pierre Rauzy, Guillemette's father.

The 'Lombardian' was friendly with the squire Pons de Planisolles, Béatrice's uncle, and it does not come as a surprise to learn that Béatrice's father, Philippe, had been sentenced to wear the yellow crosses. Indeed, *his* father, and therefore Béatrice's grandfather, may have been the Cathar Arnaud de Planisolles, whose wife was called Béatrice (D 24, f.275v). It is likely that Arnaud was the brother of the Guillaume de Planisolles who in April of 1241 visited the legendary Perfect Bertrand Marty at Montségur (D 22, f.127r). Their father, Béatrice's great-grandfather, was probably the Raymond de Planisolles who hid Perfects in Garanou (see below, page 12). All of them lived in Caussou.

anywhere else in the region, it is unlikely that nobility like the de Planisolles would have heeded the injunction of the Church to exhibit the crosses at all times.

The yellow crosses were popularly called *las debanadoras*, which literally translates as reels or winding-machines. The idiom is obscure, but the general meaning may be that the Cathars imagined that the crosses tied them to the end of a line that could be pulled in or wound up; an analogous phrase would perhaps be the proverbial expression 'carrying a millstone round one's neck'. The sentence stated that the penitents

shall carry from now on and forever two yellow crosses on all their clothes except their shirts, and one arm shall be two palms long [8 inches], while the other transversal arm shall be a palm and a half long [6 inches], and each shall be three digits wide [2.25 inches], with one to be worn in front on the chest, and the other between the shoulders. (L, 214)*

Moreover they were instructed not to 'move about either inside or outside' their houses without openly displaying the crosses, and they were obliged to 'redo or renew the crosses if they are torn or are destroyed by age' (L, 191).

Many of the Cathars released under licence by the Inquisition and sentenced to the crosses did not comply. Nor for that matter were they particularly penitent. The moment that Cathar Perfects were back in the Sabartès at the turn of the century, Béatrice's father enthusiastically aided and abetted their cause, not least by offering them a safe house in

* The crosses were yellow (*de filtro crocei coloris*), and their actual size depends on whether one interprets Latin *palmus* as the length of a hand (LS), that is 7–9 inches, or its breadth (G, N), in which case it measured 3–4 inches. This latter was probably the 'palm' the Inquisitors had in mind, since otherwise the crosses, and particularly the double crosses (*duplices*), would have become too huge to wear. The crosses imposed by Geoffroy d'Ablis on Guillaume Fort of Montaillou were, however, longer, with one of the transversals being 'two palms and a half long' and the other 'two palms' (FR, f.93v). This may suggest that he was sentenced to the more serious penalty of the double crosses, which were in fact two and half palms long (L, 286). Like the single (*simplices*) crosses, the double yellow crosses were worn simultaneously at the front and on the back.

Garanou, which had already been used fifty years earlier by his grand-father for the identical purpose. He also accommodated them in his house in Caussou (d'AR, f.3v).

At some point Béatrice and, presumably, other members of her family moved to the village of Celles, which is situated half-way between Tarascon and Foix. At the end of the twentieth century Celles is a comely, honey-toned village which would not be out of place in the Cotswolds or the Dordogne. Béatrice lived here in the mid-1280s. It was at Celles that she once heard a stonemason make a flippant comparison of the body of Christ to a prominent local landmark. This was, as we shall see, a classic Cathar idiom for dismissing transubstanti-ation, and years later she foolishly echoed it in front of witnesses.

In about 1291, at the age (probably) of seventeen, Béatrice de Planisolles married Bérenger de Roquefort, the châtelain of Montaillou. Whereas she is specific about the date of her second marriage, she is oddly unforthcoming about when her first one took place. But by August 1294 she had two sons and was expecting another baby. It is therefore probably safe to conclude that the correct date for her wedding is close to 1291–2, even though a period not long before 1296 is misleadingly suggested by her referring in 1320 to her wedding as happening 'at least twenty-four years ago or thereabouts', while simultaneously claiming to have been married, with children, by 1294 (FR, f.37r).

Béatrice may have been considerably younger than her husband Bérenger, who was frequently absent from Montaillou and predeceased his wife by many years. Nothing is known about him. Was he a 'politician' at Foix or Pamiers, where there were de Roqueforts, or was he a steward for the Count of Foix? Although Philippe de Planisolles would probably not have married off his daughter to an enemy of the dissident faith, Béatrice's conversations with her servant Raymond Roussel might suggest that her husband was not a Cathar.

Where her wedding ceremony was conducted we cannot now determine, although the illustrious pilgrimage church of Montaillou, Notre-Dame-de-Carnesses, cannot be ruled out. The de Planisolles–de Roquefort wedding would have been a major event in the social calendar of the region. We may be sure that nobility was bidden to the feast, but so were members of the local bourgeoisie and intelligentsia, because the guests included Guillaume Authié from Ax. The Authiés were among the most powerful professional families in the Ariège. They were those *ric borzes* (wealthy bourgeois) of Languedoc who, according to Guillaume de Tudèle, the thirteenth-century chronicler-poet of the crusades, stood to lose everything through the spread of heresy.* Guillaume Authié was a younger brother of Pierre Authié and, like him, a public notary. Notaries drafted legal documents such as contracts and wills, and formed the backbone of everyday legal culture in Languedoc. They were by definition literate, and their offices and homes tended to be sited conspicuously in public squares.

It was probably Guillaume Authié who drafted the marriage contract and the prenuptial deeds concerning Béatrice's dowry, for her and Bérenger's papers were processed by the Authiés' firm. As was customary in Languedoc, the return of Béatrice's dowry was guaranteed by her future husband's estates should she become widowed. This reversion clause was known as *donatio propter nuptias*.

Guillaume Authié was a fun-loving, fastidious, and charismatic figure with a beautiful wife and two young children. He had famously danced at the de Roquefort–de Planisolles wedding, and his social skills were legendary in the region. His wife Gaillarde, from Ax, was the niece of Guillaume Benet, the head of a notable Montaillou family, so that Guillaume Authié had domestic reasons for visiting Montaillou.†

Guillaume Authié's elder brother Pierre, the head of the Authié family, was also known to Béatrice and her husband. At some point between 1291 and September 1296 he drafted a sales bill for Bérenger de Roquefort, which Béatrice needed to ratify by oath and in person, because her dowry and her husband's property were intermeshed. It is likely that for this transaction they visited the Authiés' offices in Ax.

* In the language spoken by the characters in this story, '*serian enpaubrezit/ De lor grans manentias, don eran eriquit*', which translates as 'they will forfeit their great possessions of which they were enriched' (*Chanson*, 1931–61).

† On at least one occasion after his ordination as a Perfect, Guillaume Authié teamed up with another Perfect, Prades Tavernier, to help his in-laws with the harvest, and Guillemette Garsen later recalled that she took them wine and prunes for sustenance. During these timeless seasonal rituals, even revered Perfects such as Guillaume Authié in true peasant style temporarily reverted to the status of farm hands.

In the legalistic culture of late-thirteenth-century Occitania, the Authiés were thriving as the leading law firm in the region, and they were an obvious choice to transact the nobility's paperwork. But there may be another reason why they were preferred by the de Planisolles in particular: Béatrice's father was implicated in the Cathar recrudescence that was building up momentum then, and so were the Authiés, even though it would be another five years before they left to become ordained, and nearly ten years before they returned as Perfects to the Sabartès.

From 1291 to 1301 Béatrice de Planisolles, the new châtelaine, was to spend eleven eventful years in the Pays d'Aillou, nearly ten of them in Montaillou. During this period the village experienced the most tumultuous upheaval in its recorded history, as a result of which this tiny community has become the most intimately documented medieval site in the world.

Before the narrative is taken further, therefore, it will be essential to pay a visit to the Montaillou of the 1290s, to understand its landscape and its network of tracks, to meet its inhabitants, its heroes and its villains, and to confront its Cathar heritage. For although the châtelaine lived in her castle and overlooked the village from its height, hers was no ivory tower. She freely mingled, and in more ways than one, with the people of Montaillou, and it was this which ultimately caused her to bring the village to its knees without ever intending to harm it.

In the 1290s Montaillou sat on the south-eastern slopes of a hill which was wide enough to accommodate, above the village and on an elevated plateau, a keep with a castle square on its south-eastern side. This highest point of the hill stands 4,468 feet above sea-level. Hillside fortifications guarded the Pays de Sault, as the highlands of the Sabartès are known, during the Wisigoth occupation from the fifth century until 719 AD, when the Saracens overran the area. The name of Montaillou itself, which in the Registers is Latinized to *Mons Alionis*, derives from the Germanic proper name Agilo (Dauzat and Rostaing 1963), so that 'Mont-aillou' means the 'hill of Agilo', Agilo having presumably been a Gothic warlord. The linguistic formation has an analogue in the Anglo-Saxon etymon of Aylesbury in England, which means 'Aegeles-burh', or 'Aegel's fort'. Aylesbury and Montaillou are therefore respectively the fort and hill of Aegel-Agilo.*

Little remains of the thirteenth-century fortress of Montaillou, and today's desultory ruin may be only tenuously connected to the time when Béatrice de Planisolles resided here as châtelaine from 1291 to 1298. But the outline of the castle square and its perimeter can be clearly traced by the naked eye on the plateau. As for the village, modern Montaillou is a shadowy reflection of its buoyant medieval self. Since the end of the sixteenth or early seventeenth century the village has occupied its present site some fifty yards down the slopes of the hill from its medieval emplacement. It now straddles an area which in the Middle Ages verged on cultivated fields. In the 1990s some fourteen people live here during the winter months, and although the figure swells to more than ten times that during the summer, it nevertheless hardly compares to the permanent population here in the 1290s of well in excess of 230.

In the late thirteenth century the Sabartès was thriving. The trauma of the crusades' atrocities was receding, and as two Ariégeois generations grew up in peace, prosperity rewarded the hard work of these unsubjugated communities who were free from feudal bondage. The people of the Pays d'Aillou were dedicated to intensive agriculture, stock-raising and transhumance, and carding and weaving. Although they were not rich, they always seemed to have enough mutually to support themselves and one another, including their various illegitimate children. These were largely assimilated into the legitimate families, as if the thirteenth-century people of the Sabartès were following the communal child-rearing model proposed 1,700 years earlier by Plato in the *Republic*. No one starved in Montaillou, and there were no beggars as such. And just as after Christmas the women of Montaillou crushed or 'braked' the hemp, which they grew for its valuable fibre, so in late June they made cheese. The production of food played an important part in the village's economy. Bread and brassicas, particularly turnips and cabbage, formed its staple diet, and the villagers grew their own herbs such as parsley for flavouring various bouillons of chicken and pork.

* A different etymology, one deeply rooted in local history, is proposed by Alain Fayet in his fascinating study *À la recherche de Montaillou*, 2000.

Not everybody had a suitable oven for baking bread, and they therefore borrowed the facilities of those who did. Thus Brune Pourcel, the illegitimate daughter of the Perfect Prades Tavernier and named 'Brune' after one of his sisters, called at the Rives house one day with kneaded loaves for baking. Alazaïs Rives, née Tavernier, was her aunt, and the Rives were rich. Brune spread the loaves on a pallet, but she needed help with heaving them into the oven. At that point her father came up and, since no one else was there, he nervously assisted her; by then he had already gone under cover.*

The importance of bread and flour meant that the men and women of the Pays d'Aillou undertook regular trips to the flour-mills down in Ax, from where they returned dragging mules carrying sacks of freshly ground flour. The diet in the area was, however, far from vegetarian. A number of the villagers farmed chickens, and mutton and pork were consumed, the latter in the salted form of ham and sausages which were smoked over woodfires. Fish, particularly trout, were readily available in the plentiful mountain streams of the Sabartès, but were associated above all with the Perfects' diet; and in spite of their abundance, the people of the Registers repeatedly *bought* their fish in local markets. The markets, a flourishing ready-cash culture, and the local fairs, fed the economic cycle in the Ariège in this period.

---

* An inadvertently comic incident involving both heresy and the baking of bread occurred when another young woman from Montaillou, Guillemette Clergue (B), Alazaïs Rives's married daughter and the niece of Prades Tavernier, and of course Brune's half-cousin, used the same Rives oven. She had prepared the bread in a kneading-trough and had taken it to her father's house. There she lit a fire in a brazier to put in the oven to heat it. At that moment Arnaud Belot, a neighbour, entered, carrying under his coat something wrapped in a shirt. When he spotted Guillemette, he surreptitiously hid this bag, on her mother's instructions, inside the small door of the oven and left.

Was Guillemette distracted by his furtive behaviour? The fact is that she failed to look inside the oven before inserting the brazier into it, so that the bag with small fish, spoons, and some other items caught fire. When she noticed that there was something burning inside the oven she tried to pull it out, but the heat was too intense. Shortly afterwards her mother inquired whether she had checked the oven before putting the fire in it. When Guillemette owned up to her oversight, her mother furiously cursed her. Eight days later, presumably the time it took for them to be reconciled, Guillemette learnt from her mother that the bag contained fish which Prades Tavernier had given her a few days before when he stayed there.

Since the fairs were held annually in honour of the patron saints of the various towns, they also provided key points of reference in the year, which were often used by the people of the Fournier and d'Ablis Registers for the purpose of orientating themselves in the past. Thus the fiesta was held at Laroque d'Olmes every year on 16 June (Sts Ciricus and Julitta), at Pamiers on 2 September (St Antonin), at Ax on 14 September (the Exaltation of the Holy Cross), at Tarascon on 29 September (St Michael), and at Foix on 13 October (St Géraud), to mention only some of the festive saints' days which feature most prominently in this story, and which were haunted by villains and saints alike. Further landmarks in the year's calendar were provided by the great seasonal rituals of this agrarian society such as the interdiction and the cutting of the grass, the picking of crops, transhumance, and the all-important wine harvests in October.

In addition to honouring saints' days through fairs, Béatrice and her contemporaries lived their daily lives by the wider Christian festivals and the feasts of universally celebrated saints such as John the Baptist, Peter and Paul, and particularly the Virgin Mary, whose Assumption and Birth were second in importance only to Easter and, perhaps, Christmas.

In the third millennium the Christian calendar remains largely intact, but increasingly fewer among us are familiar with it. For this reason I offer a sample here of the medieval calendar, choosing as representative example the leap year 1300, which was the year of the Authiés' return to Ax and therefore marks the start of the Cathar renaissance in the Sabartès. I include here only the main festivals which everybody at the time associated with specific times of the year.

1300

Circumcision	Friday 1 January
Epiphany	Wednesday 6 January
St Vincent	Friday 22 January
Candlemas	Tuesday 2 February
Septuagesima	Sunday 7 February, the third Sunday before Lent and therefore the ninth before Easter
Quinquagesima	Sunday 21 February, the Sunday before Ash Wednesday

Shrove Tuesday	Tuesday 23 February
Ash Wednesday	Wednesday 24 February
Lent	24 February to Easter, a period of six and a half weeks of fasting
Quadragesima	Sunday 28 February, the first Sunday in Lent
Annunciation	Friday 25 March
Passion	Sunday 27 March (the start of Passiontide and the fifth Sunday in Lent)
Palm Sunday	Sunday 3 April
Good Friday	Friday 8 April
Easter Day	Sunday 10 April
Quasimodo	Sunday 17 April
Mark Apostle Evangelist	Monday 25 April
Rogation Sunday	Sunday 15 May
Ascension	Thursday 19 May
Whitsun	Sunday 29 May
Nativity of John the Baptist	Friday 24 June
Sts Peter and Paul	Wednesday 29 June
Assumption	Monday 15 August
Martyrdom of John the Baptist	Monday 29 August
Nativity of Mary	Thursday 8 September
Matthew Apostle Evangelist	Wednesday 21 September
St Michael	Thursday 29 September
All Saints	Tuesday 1 November
All Souls	Wednesday 2 November
St Andrew Apostle	Wednesday 30 November
Christmas	Sunday 25 December

The perception of time among these mostly illiterate thirteenth-century inhabitants of Languedoc may at first strike the twenty-first-century reader as vague at best. They did not always know exactly how old they were, and their sense of history was strictly local. They remembered events, of course, and some are more accurate than others in doing so. Some of the mothers of the story like Guillemette Benet (but not Alamande Guilabert), for example, can be relied upon to recall the span of time since the death of a child, while being otherwise vague about chronology. This renders precise dating difficult, but not impossible, since a careful collation of the various depositions soon pinpoints those whose memory can be trusted and those who are unreliable. Accuracy is rarely a matter of class here, since the lowly Alazais Azéma, for example, is generally as unerring in her dates as the châtelaine, whose head for times and approximate dates was good.

Life in late-thirteenth-century Montaillou was, unusually, not centred around the oval-shaped village square, which was located on the north-eastern edge of the plateau; the reason being probably that the church was not in the square (Map 2). The square, which measures approximately eighty-four feet by forty-two, was then as now skirted by the main track running down to the church of Montaillou, Notre-Dame-de-Carnesses (Pls. 2 and 3). This romanesque chapel counted among the foremost in the land, because the Virgin Mary had, it seems, appeared to a shepherdess on a spot nearby. It was also known as Sainte-Marie-de-Carnesses, or simply Sainte-Marie, and was located some 300 yards north-east of the village. Whereas throughout Languedoc men congregated after mass on benches under large elms near their village churches, this was not the case in Montaillou. Here it was indoors and at night that the real business of the village came to be conducted.

The village's essential commodity was water. In this respect it was typical of the mountain communities of Languedoc, which endure parching heat during the summer and deep frosts and heavy snows during the winter. The main source of water in Montaillou was known by the names of *la fontcanal* or *lacanal*. It was situated just beyond the top of the village and down from the castle, from where it would have been reached by a short path. The main track into Montaillou coming from Ax passed *fontcanal* before turning right and descending to the village (Pl. 4).

Fontcanal played a crucial role in the life of Montaillou. Although then as now there were other sources of water such as the non-identified *cortal sec* and *del buc*, *fontcanal* was clearly the main source of fresh water

supply for the village. Because many of the women and the female
servants of the various families gathered here daily to collect their water,
the track into Montaillou was constantly busy with women carrying
heavy loads of water on *cabessals*, that is head-cushions. During these
water treks the women gossiped, and their topics were mostly children
and, of course, love affairs. Rumours about the young châtelaine's sex
life started after she was widowed, and then, as the thirteenth century
drew to a close and the new one started, the villagers' talking point
became increasingly their role in the Cathar resurgence.

The panoramic view from *fontcanal* of Montaillou and its setting,
with Camurac in the middle distance, is today in all essentials the same
as it was nearly 700 years ago, and particularly on a sunny, snow-free
winter day when the trees are bare and the sight-lines are clear. It is a
stirring experience to stand here in the late 1990s and look towards the
spur to which modern Montaillou clings just as its precedessor did,
albeit fractionally higher up the hill (Pl. 5). To this day an ancient and
substantial house sits defiantly on the spot where in the thirteenth
century stood the home of the most powerful family in Montaillou,
the Clergues.

A mile and a half north-east of the village lies Camurac with the Col
des Sept Frères, a mountain which is distinct in the 1990s for its bald
pate. In the thirteenth century it denoted a boundary landmark for the
people of Montaillou.★ Some 300 yards south-east from *fontcanal*, at the
bottom of the valley of the *Prade* creek, lies a grove which encloses a
rectangular hole. Directly beyond it, and between two mountain spurs,
a dell rises towards the *haute montagne* of Montaillou from where tracks
lead into the Cerdagne and Andorra. This is *comba del gazel*, which takes
its name from the Bois del Gazel on whose north-eastern flank it sits.
In the Middle Ages *comba del gazel* was extensively cultivated, with
every meadow and field carefully demarcated from its neighbour by
low dry-stone walling. The spruces and saplings did not then encroach

★ When Pons Clergue tried to shield the shepherd Pierre Maury from his son Pierre
Clergue, the village priest, he instructed Pierre Maury's father to urge young Pierre
not to trust a treacherous priest: 'Tell Pierre Maury that, if he is on the Col des Sept
Frères to flee to the Col de Marmare, and from the Col de Marmare to the Puymorens
where the jurisdiction of the bishopric of Pamiers ceases; and even then he ought not
to stop but flee further' (FR, f.155r).

nearly so far as they do now down into the *comba* itself. Nor were there trees in the *a-la-cot* area, the rolling south-eastern slopes of the village; the summer and winter prospects across the fields to *comba del gazel* were therefore virtually identical.

A shepherd by the name of Jean Pélissier stood at *fontcanal* early one morning in May 1308, a year that was to prove fateful for Montaillou. He was taking his sheep to the pastures when he caught sight of Arnaud Vital down in *comba del gazel* and wondered why the village shoemaker was out and about so early. At least that was what he told the Inquisition; in reality, he knew full well, because the day before he had himself been in *comba del gazel* and, as we shall see, witnessed at first hand how Arnaud Vital orchestrated an escape from the Inquisition.

Closer inspection of the hole in the grove in front of *comba del gazel* reveals it to be a gently inclined broad trench some ten feet wide and twenty feet deep, which narrows to a funnel before decanting its mountain water into the *Prade*. The sides of this trench are firmed by boulders. This is the place that was known in thirteenth-century Montaillou as *la laviera*, and it was here that the women of the village did their washing (FR, f.246r) (Pl. 6). It sits in a direct sight-line of the castle. It was in this very spot that in around 1300–1301 Alazais Faure noticed that Mengarde Clergue, the young and illegitimate daughter of Bernard Clergue, was rinsing cambric shirts and handkerchiefs. She realized then that there must be Cathar Perfects in the village, since no one in Montaillou used such fine linen; and the use of cambric suggests that the Perfect was an Authié, and probably Guillaume Authié, who was making Montaillou his base.

The north-facing prospect from *la laviera* at the bottom of *comba del gazel* afforded a full view across the sloping fields of *a-la-cot*, the profile of the village itself and the fortress. Clearly a direct track was needed to connect *la laviera* to the village, although it could be reached circuitously by way of *fontcanal*, which is indeed the route the shepherds took. They did so presumably in order not to have their flock trample across the cultivated fields. The cross-fields track, which linked Montaillou, *la laviera* and *comba del gazel*, was what Jean Pélissier called the *via communis*.

It is time to enter the medieval village of Montaillou, and I propose to do so on the main track from the Col de Marmare and Ax, which passes *fontcanal* before descending into the village from the south-west. Some fifty yards down from *fontcanal* the track splits into two at a junction which still exists today. From here the thirteenth-century village's main street, the through-road, arches to the left and upwards towards the village proper, while the down-track curves convexly around its outside and runs more or less straight down to Notre-Dame-de-Carnesses. This peripheral path is today the principal road of Montaillou, logically so since the village has moved further down the hill. Together the through-road and the outer track form an ellipsis around part of the old village.

The main artery of old Montaillou has not been used for centuries, but its outline remains clearly visible. After rising at first, it then gently slopes down towards the erstwhile village square, which it passes on its eastern side. A short distance beyond the square it again bifurcates, just as it did almost seven centuries ago.

One of the tracks turns left and, passing the ruins of at least three substantial properties which once gave on to the square, heads to Prades. In doing so it traces a semi-circular swathe around the northern brow of the hill, thus skirting the steep drop on the fringe of the spur. This path was the 'outer' Prades track, as opposed to the 'inner' one with which it merged on the uninhabited north-western side of the hill.*

The other path turned right from the fork beyond the square and reconnected with the direct down-route from which it parted 300 yards further up. Today this short connecting segment curves gently around the outer edge of the converted former presbytery, which now houses a children's holiday camp.

Medieval Montaillou had several sub-arteries. Thus, on its downward loop towards the square, the village's through-road intersected with two north-west-running tracks, which cut right across the hill. The more northerly (and therefore lower) of these was the inner track to Prades, which overlooked the houses in the square as it passed closely behind them. At least two houses from the story are known to have stood on the inner Prades track, and one of them was the Guilaberts'. It

---

* It is the 'outer' Prades track that Pons Rives and Prades Tavernier took to go to the castle from the Rives house: 'they ascended towards the castle of Montaillou on the track which goes to Prades' (FR, f.66v). This also proves that the castle had a western entrance as well as a south-eastern one leading to *fontcanal*, *la laviera* and, in an emergency, the mountains.

apparently rose near its north-western extremity where a short-cut ran from the inner Prades track to the castle. The particular significance of its location at that point from where it commanded a view across the *bac*, that is the north-western aspect of the spur, will become evident later.

The inner Prades track started at the intersection with the through-road, and it is this crossroads which was known, almost certainly, by the name of 'the crossroads of *capanal den belot*', because the powerful house of the Belot family stood here.* It is likely that the inner Prades track did not stop at *capanal den belot*, but carried on down south-east through the cultivated terrain of *a-la-cot* or, today, 'à la côte'. The reason was the need for a route of access to *la laviera*. This track would have been the one that was referred to by Jean Pélissier as running down towards *comba del gazel* from Montaillou (FR, f.241v).

A further track, which is still distinguishable, started down south-west through *a-la-cot* from directly opposite the village square. On the 1826 *PN* it is shown intersecting with the outer artery, and from this fork it probably carried on down towards the fields, 'Les Granges' and *la laviera*. This track seems to have been dry-walled near the village, and it is this spot which, I believe, was known by the name of *paret del colel*, or, alternatively, the '*parede* of Jean [*sic*] Azéma'. The reason why both names were used interchangeably may be because this track seems to have emerged in the village between the houses of Pierre Azéma, whose father may have been 'Jean', and Raymond Rous, who was commonly called '*rous alias colel*'. If this is correct, then the Colel house would have overlooked the square of Montaillou, while down from his house were 'the fields of Colel'.†

---

* Both *capanal* and *caparal* are used in the Register, and an 'n/r' minim confusion in the manuscript is probable (FR, ff.162v, 95v). I suggest that *capanal* is the right phrase, by analogy with *fontcanal-lacanal*, and that *capanal* denotes a water point, though not, of course, the main fresh water one. Perhaps water from *fontcanal* was channelled here for sewage. The fact that Arnaud Vital's forge stood nearby further suggests that water flowed through *capanal*, since water was an essential commodity for that business.

† Little is known about Raymond Rous-Colel, but he had an affair with Gauzia Clergue (B), and the consolation of one Raymond Banqui took place in his house in 1307-8. Banqui was consoled by Prades Tavernier, who was smuggled into Montaillou in broad daylight disguised as a pedlar. At that time Pierre Clergue, the rector, had acted as look-out in *la parede* of Jean Azéma. Rous himself died consoled, and his bones were later dug up and burnt.

The track pattern of Montaillou therefore ran from south-west to north-east to connect *fontcanal* to Notre-Dame-de-Carnesses, and from north-west to south-east, thereby linking the northern edge of the spur through *capanal den belot* with *la laviera, comba del gazel,* and the *haute montagne.*

1. The People of Montaillou

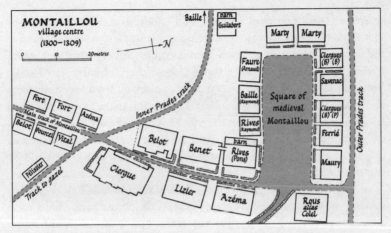

The heart of medieval Montaillou

When Béatrice de Planisolles arrived in Montaillou to be married, the village counted some thirty-five separate family names and nearly fifty families, if the different branches of the same family are counted separately. The family names of Montaillou in the last decade of the thirteenth century were Argelier, Arzelier, Authié (*not* related to the Axian Perfects and *passim* Authié (B)), Azéma, Baille, Bar, Belot, Benet, Bonclergue, Capelle, Caravessas, Castanier, Clergue, Clergue (B), Faure, Ferrié, Fort, Fournier, Guilabert, Julia, Lizier, Mamol (?), Martre, Marty, Maurs, Maury, Moyshen, Pélissier, Pourcel, Rives, Rous (alias 'Colel'), Savenac, Tavernier (?), Teisseyre, Trilhe (or Trialh?), and Vital.★

For the purpose of counting the people of Montaillou over a period of eighteen years, the years from *c.* 1291, the arrival of

★ Many of these names designate more than one family, and for two of them, Bonclergue and Castanier, the only source is D 27, ff.147v–148r.

Béatrice, to 1308, the year the village was raided, seem an appropriate time-span since they coincide with the main Cathar episode. In this period the majority of the villagers whom we will encounter in these pages were born, or grew from their teens and twenties into early middle age. My focus therefore will be mostly the 1280s to mid-1290s generation.

Some 160 of the men, women, and children of Montaillou can be identified by name, and there were probably some 250 people living in the village, if the average household is conservatively estimated at five bodies, to include two parents and at least three children per family. Various illegitimate children as well as grandparents and servants were also looked after in nuclear families. In addition there may have been a handful of families residing in the village whose presence is not specifically recorded in the Registers. And the figure of 250 does not include the occupants of the castle, the châtelaine, her husband, their children and their staff.

In this deeply rural culture men and women needed to be able to depend mutually on one another for survival, hence family links were a bastion of strength. It was the blood ties between clans and families that ultimately provided the Authiés, and other local Perfects such as Prades Tavernier, Pons Sicre and Arnaud Marty, with a century-old safety net that could never quite be shredded by the Inquisition. Even the Bishop of Pamiers would be aided in his task by family connections. For that reason it is essential to map out the major families of Montaillou before proceeding any further; families from other villages and towns, notably Prades, Ax, Luzenac, Larnat, Tarascon and Junac, and from the Toulousain also played a leading role in the dissemination of Catharism, and they will be met in due course.

Although it is not possible to locate with certainty the whereabouts in the village of *all* the participants, the homes of the most important among them can be identified on the grid with some confidence (Map 3). My conclusions are generated from a mosaic of mutually corroborative, and mostly incidental, remarks by various witnesses. These are crucially complemented by a striking passage in Pierre Maury's testimony, which appears to offer a semi-structured survey of the village's households (FR, f.257v; see below, page 36). It is a major source for confirming and, in some cases, determining the location in Montaillou of several among the lesser houses in the village.

In the 1290s and in the early years of the fourteenth century Montaillou was dominated by four powerful and variously affluent clans whose houses clustered in the vicinity of the square of Montaillou. They were called Belot, Benet, Rives and Clergue.

The Cathar trio and the Clergues

The houses of the Belots, Benets and Rives were built into the slope of the hill on the north-western side of the main artery so that their fronts faced south or south-east. These properties occupied the space between the junction of *capanal den belot* and the village square itself, and they were easily overlooked from the plateau. In clement weather their back-roofs provided a favourite place for the social and physical ritual of mutual delousing. All three were substantial dwellings with barns, vegetable gardens and dry-walled courtyards with gates or portals which verged on the village's track. Even the poorer houses of Montaillou usually had vegetable and herb gardens at the front, as did some of the houses in the square. Some properties, like the Pélissiers', were separated from the road by hedges.

THE BELOTS: This large house was low-roofed (*bassum*) at the back, because of the slope and the convex arching of the 'inner' path to Prades which ran down past it into *capanal den belot* (FR, f.60v). In front of its substantial porch extended the Belots' south-east-facing courtyard, which overlooked the Clergues. It was an obvious place for gossiping matriarchs to take the sun. Slightly apart from the porch was a spot called '*las penas*', which may have been reserved for servants, and from here the servants would eavesdrop on their mistress's conversations. The Belots were the second-wealthiest clan in the village. They were rich enough to recruit and employ servants, and the boundaries between servant and master were repeatedly transgressed in this household, which was a hive of sexual activity.

There were two parents, four sons and two (or perhaps three) daughters.* The sons were called Raymond, Bernard, Guillaume and

---

* Three, if Arnaude den Terras was a Belot (see below, page 195).

Arnaud, and the daughters were Raymonde and Alazais, and perhaps Arnaude. The Belot patriarch's name is not known, but he may have been dead by the end of the 1290s because by then the Belots' house was commonly called 'Raymond Belot's house', which probably indicates that Raymond was the eldest son and the new head of the family; unless, of course, the father was also called Raymond, in which case the name of the house simply continued. That the Belot brothers Raymond and Bernard shared the house as owners was noted by the new châtelaine when she lived in the village during this period. The younger Belot brothers were ruffians, and while Bernard Belot sexually assaulted the wife of another Montalionian, his brother Arnaud fathered an illegitimate child called Étienne when he was still, it seems, in his teens. The Belot mother was called Guillemette, and she would have been in her forties or early fifties in the 1290s. She was on intimate terms with her neighbour and contemporary Mengarde Clergue, the matriarch of the richest and most powerful family in Montaillou. In their devotion to the Cathar cause the Belots did not lag far behind the illustriously connected Benets.

THE BENETS: The Benets' house stood a few yards north-east and down the hill from the Belots'. It was their home which provided the initial channel for the Cathar reawakening in Montaillou, because Guillaume Benet of Montaillou was the uncle of the Perfect Guillaume Authié's wife.

Guillaume and Guillemette Benet had three sons and four daughters. When Montane Benet was born *c.*1301–2 her sisters Esclarmonde and Guillemette were 'little girls', and her brother Bernard was still only a child in 1308. The relative youth of the Benet children suggests that Guillemette, the mother of the household, was younger than either of the neighbouring matriarchs Guillemette Belot and Mengarde Clergue, who were direct contemporaries. Guillemette Benet may not have been much older than Béatrice de Planisolles. She repeatedly expressed her horror of the pain inflicted by fire, and later had to endure the agony of seeing her brother-in-law being burnt at the stake.

Whereas all the major houses owned livestock and farmed, there was also a need for skilled craftsmen. Just as there were weavers in the village, so the Benets may have been builders, that is masons or roofers, because they owned tools.* It is significant that the rich Belots' extension was built *for* them rather than *by* them, which suggests that a labour market operated in Montaillou. The wood for roofing, barns and enclosures came from the plentiful thick forests to the south-east of the village. As the wheel does not seem to have existed in the Pays d'Aillou in the thirteenth century, tree trunks needed either to be dragged into the village by oxen, or transported on the back of mules.

THE RIVES: The house of Bernard and Alazais Rives was the next one down from the Benets', and was in fact partly terraced with it. Theirs was a large and wealthy corner-house at the intersection of the main artery of Montaillou and the south-eastern side of the village square, and it could be entered either from the square or from the road. Its front boasted a porch where picked vegetables and fruit were kept. It had interior stables for beasts whose waste was carried outside through the main entrance of the house and deposited on a dunghill in the courtyard on the side of the square. The Rives also owned a barn which was an extension of the house while having a separate outside entrance. In this place, which had a skylight, grass and bales of hay and straw were stored.

We have already noted that the house contained a much-used bread-oven, which was in a roomy space serving as both hearth and dining-room. The Occitan term for this nerve centre of a thirteenth-century Sabartesian house was *foghana*. To translate it as 'kitchen', as Pales-Gobilliard does, fails to convey its importance as the preferred area for eating and sitting as well as for cooking, drying meat and baking, and for laying out the dead. It was in the *foghana* that life was played out during the winter, when the gossips gathered around the fire, and the bedrooms as well as the stables were usually off it. For these reasons I propose to retain the Occitan phrase to

---

* When Gauzia de Savenac and her husband Pierre did roofing work, they needed an auger to bore holes in the wood for the pegs to support the shingles (for 'auger' FR f.294r has *tarabellum*, which is not in N, LS, G; but *taratrum* = auger is listed in N). Gauzia borrowed her auger from the Benets, who at that very moment, in November, were themselves doing roofing work. It seems that they kept a spare auger in a chest of oats. The houses of Montaillou had shingle roofs, which means that they were tiled with thin, layered pieces of beech wood. These had one end thicker than the other and were stepped on the rising roof.

denote this inclusive core area where so many key events took place.

The Rives owed their economic importance to their local landhold-ing. They were prosperous farmers, who also kept animals for food and work; and they were active weavers. Next to the main Rives property, in the square of Montaillou itself, stood a junior Rives house which probably belonged to Bernard's brother Raymond Rives. The two Rives houses may have been almost merged into one. If so, they formed an impressive block which took in the south-eastern corner of the square and a section of its southern side.

By 1291 the senior Rives were linked, through the marriage of Bernard Rives of Montaillou and Alazais Tavernier of Prades, to a family of thriving weavers from neighbouring Prades. The couple had a son, Pons, and three daughters, of whom the youngest, Guillemette, was about eleven years old in 1291; she would later provide some of the most fascinating details about daily life in Montaillou. By marrying Alazais Tavernier, Bernard Rives had joined a committed Cathar family, because Alazais's brother was the weaver and future Perfect Prades Tavernier. Consequently the Rives house would become as much of a focus for heresy as its direct neighbour, the Benets'. Indeed, it was at the Rives' that the Perfects set up a small Cathar chapel, and the Rives and Benet houses were eventually connected by a secret passage which, through a movable partition, led from the Rives' house into a room off the Benets' *foghana*.

THE CLERGUES: In the late thirteenth century there were at least five families by the name of Clergue in the village, two of which are called Clergue (B) in this book to distinguish them from the main Clergue family.

The two branches of the pre-eminent family were those of Pons Clergue and his wife Mengarde, who was a Martre from the neighbour-ing village of Camurac, and the truncated family of Pons's (unmarried?) brother Guillaume and his two illegitimate children Fabrisse and Ray-mond, who was also known as 'Pathau'. This may be the name of his mother's family (there were Pathaus in Ax), or '*pathau*' may correspond to modern French '*pataud*' (*LT*), which means lumpish or oafish. It was Raymond Pathau who would assault the new châtelaine. The third Clergue family in Montaillou, which was headed by one Arnaud Clergue, was only tenuously related to the others. None of these families seems to have had family ties with the Clergue (B) family into which Guillemette Rives, one of our key witnesses, married.

THE MAIN CLERGUE FAMILY: Pons Clergue and Mengarde Martre had four sons and two daughters, and they lived opposite the Belots in a large two-floor house which probably sat on top of a cellar and stables. Both the Clergue parents were uncompromisingly Cathar, and Mengarde was close to a notorious Cathar matriarch from Montaillou called *Na* (i.e. '*domina*') Roche.

Among the Clergues' four male offspring the eldest was Pierre Clergue, who became the village priest. He remains to this day the most infamous son of Montaillou. The next was Bernard who, before the Carcassonne Inquisition, cast himself as an inveterate romantic. This canard, which Bernard Clergue peddled successfully to the Inquisition, seems also to have fooled twentieth-century students of the documents. He was ruthless, adored his elder brother Pierre, and was the *bajulus* or *bayle* of Montaillou. As such, he was invested locally with the authority of the Count of Foix, and his brief included administrative duties and judicial powers of arrest. He was the village's chief constable. He was also the father of an illegitimate daughter whom, as a dutiful son, he named Mengarde after his mother; and young Mengarde worked as a servant in the large Clergue household.

The two senior Clergue brothers were probably in their late teens when the new châtelaine arrived in Montaillou in 1291. They would prove to be, in the words of one of their contemporaries, a '*mala cadelada*', that is a 'bad brood' or a 'bad bitch's litter'. While Pierre Clergue seems to have been absent from Montaillou during the first half of the last decade of the thirteenth century, his younger brothers Bernard, Guillaume and Raymond as well as his sisters Guillemette and Esclarmonde probably lived in the village. The two sisters, however, married before the end of the century and left the village during the 1290s.*

---

* There is no mention anywhere in the depositions of them residing in Montaillou during the troubles, because they clearly married out of the Pays d'Aillou. Bernard Clergue refers to one of his brothers-in-law as a close associate of the temporal lord of Mirepoix (FR, f.176r). This may have been the father of his nephew Pons Gary, who came to the assistance of his uncles in Montaillou in 1321. The marriages of the Clergue daughters were the only ones in the village to be contracted outside of its immediate field of vision.

While their neighbours were doing well, the Clergues were truly rich. Over the years they lined the pockets of some of the highest officials of the Inquisition in Pamiers, Carcassonne and even Toulouse with princely bribes. The source of their wealth remains a mystery, but it is a fair guess that it originated from three generations of two-timing the Inquisition.

A fatal flaw in the Inquisition's operational network was its dependency on the local clergy for the issuing of summonses and for monitoring the observance of its decrees. This allowed families like the Clergues to play both sides and operate lucrative protection rackets.★ In spite of their wealth, however, the Clergues, like the semi-literate Sicilian godfathers of a later age, remained stubbornly rooted in their fee.

The Clergues and their allies were thus gathered in the same corner of Montaillou. They formed a caucus of families whose interests were intimately linked. But several other families, not all of them Cathar, were destined to play an important part in this story, and at different times three of them would be drawn into bitter feuds with the Clergues. The remaining families successfully eked out a living as the clouds gathered, and they even weathered the first Inquisitorial storms of 1308.

Two Catholic loyalists in Montaillou: Lizier and Azéma

Next to the Clergues, on the way down towards the square and opposite the Benets, stood the house of Lizier. The family was headed by Arnaud Lizier, a staunch Catholic. His wife was called Raymonde (née Argelier), and they had a son named Pierre and a daughter. Arnaud Lizier proved to be a thorn in the side of the Cathars, and eventually they moved against him.

From the extant testimonies it might appear at first that the Catholic family headed by Pierre Azéma and his powerful and feared mother, Raymonde Azéma (known locally as 'Na Carminagua'), was a less zealous opponent of the Cathars than Lizier. Pierre Azéma certainly

---

★ Thus Guillaume Mondon of Ax paid Pierre Clergue the huge ransom of five pounds, the equivalent of ten sheep, to be allowed to shed the yellow crosses (FR, f.51v). This would not only remove those visible emblems of shame, but in more practical terms it would render Mondon employable again, and others would be less likely to avoid him for fear of being drawn into the maelstrom of the Inquisition.

kept his head down until near the very end of the cycle of intrigue and persecution that ensued after the mid-1290s. The reason for this may have been partly that his brother Pons's wife Alazais and their son, another Raymond, were ardent Cathars;* also, like others in Montaillou who were either Catholic or agnostic, Azéma realized that to oppose the Cathars was to swim against the tide, particularly once Pierre Clergue's complicity with the heretical cause became evident.

The Azémas were farmers and owned pigs, and Pierre Azéma and his waspish wife Guillemette had two children.† They seem to have lived in the next house down from the Liziers and opposite the Rives, with a full view of the village square. If this is correct, then the two confirmed Catholic households of Montaillou, those of Arnaud Lizier and Pierre Azéma, stood shoulder to shoulder. If the house of the priest next door had indeed been a loyal Catholic household, the Clergue–Lizier–Azéma block would have formed a powerful geographical, as well as orthodox, spiritual alliance. It also suggests that the house of Pierre Azéma, like the Clergues' and the Liziers', may have been wealthy, because it occupied one of the prime sites in the village.

The houses of Maury and Maurs

Backing into the square of Montaillou from its northernmost point today are the remains of at least three houses, two of which are marked on the *PN*. Their south-west-facing frontages would have given on to the square, while in the 'basement' their stables overlooked the outer Prades track.

One of these ruins may have been the home of Pierre Maury, since

* The evidence from Pierre Maury's list and Raymonde Testanière's testimony tentatively suggests that Pons Azéma's house stood on the junction of *capanal den belot*, and therefore would have faced the Clergues' and Belots', as well as the house which was to become Arnaud Vital's forge. The Belots' 'big' door, as Bernard Clergue called it, seems to have been visible from the Azémas', and so was the Clergues' (FR, f.95v). Moreover, Alazais Azéma was in and out of the Belot house in a manner which indicates not just kindred interests but proximity.

† 'Azéma' is the Midi form of 'Adhémar' which means 'famous father' (Dauzat 1951). The family enjoyed the friendship in Montaillou of the Pélissiers, the Fourniers, and the family of Raymonde Martre, or '*Na* Longa' as she was known.

the Maury house stood on the north-eastern side of the square of Montaillou, next door to the Cathar house of Pierre Ferrié and opposite the large Rives house (FR, ff.240r, 257v). Pierre Maury's father Raymond was a weaver and was assisted in his trade by his son Guillaume who made shuttles in the '*sotulum*', that is the ground floor of his house or, in this case, the basement since weavers required humidity to protect their threads. Hence perhaps the Maurys' round, wood-panelled room which Guillemette Arzelier described as being located very deeply inside the house, where Perfects would eventually hide (FR, f.243v). Given its position on the north side of the square and therefore not leaning into the hill, the Maurys' house, like the Clergues', would have been on at least two different levels, lower at the front and higher at the back, with the drop down to the outer Prades track.

Raymond Maury enjoyed the reputation of being an honest work-man who could be trusted not to cheat his clients by purloining parts of their material. His wife Alazais was a Faure by birth, and her brother Arnaud, Pierre Maury's uncle, also lived close by in the village square.*

There were eight Maury children, and in the case of four of them we have, exceptionally, approximate birth dates provided by the characters themselves.

The oldest seems to have been Pierre. According to himself, he was born in about 1282, which makes him a youth of eighteen at the launch in the Sabartès of the Cathar *risorgimento*. Next-born after Pierre may have been Guillaume, to whom Pierre was particularly devoted. Guil-laume was followed, probably, by his two sisters. Raymonde was born *c.* 1287 and, true to the family tradition, married a Marty of Montaillou with whom she had at least one son, Guillaume. It appears that Ray-monde's husband was not a Cathar *credens*, and this may have created

---

* Raymond Maury had at least two sisters and two brothers. His sister Ermessende or Mersende was married to a Pierre Marty in the village, and they had two children, a daughter called Jeanne and a son by the name of Raymond. Their house had a garden, and they lived in the square of Montaillou. Raymond Maury's other sister, Guillemette, also married a Marty called Bernard, although her children Jean and Arnaud, and indeed she herself, were always known by the name of Maury. Raymond Maury had two brothers, Bernard and Pierre, another Pierre Maury who lived in Gebets. This Pierre Maury from Gebets followed his sisters Mersende and Guillemette into exile in Catalonia.

some tension in the family. Raymonde's marriage to Guillaume Marty meant that two of Pierre Maury's aunts and now his sister Raymonde had married Marty men.★

The Maurys' next daughter, Guillemette, followed in 1288, a year after her sister. While still in her teens she married a brutal cooper from Laroque d'Olmes; as we shall see, her suffering at his hands would lead her to the most renowned Occitan Perfect before her twentieth birthday. She was followed by Bernard and Raymond (the order is uncertain), and then came (perhaps) Jean (b. *c.* 1296) and Arnaud, who was the baby of the family.

The Maurys and their triple in-laws, the Martys, formed an influential clique, and they commanded a certain respect; even the châtelaine would socialize with them. The Maurys became related through the Martys to a minor family in the village, the Guilaberts. Circumstances would eventually thrust the relatively insignificant Guilaberts into the eye of the Inquisitorial storm. A similar fate befell a family called Maurs, who were also connected by ties of kinship to the Maurys.

The Maurs family lived on the way down to *la laviera*, probably near what is now Les Granges (Pl. 7). It is possible that they resided at Les Granges itself, since this clump of buildings was inhabited in the Middle Ages; and it is marked 'la Grange' on Cassini's eighteenth-century map of the Sabartès.

Pierre Maurs who in the 1280s married Mengarde Bar, from another Montaillou family, descended from a line of zealous Cathars that reached back to beyond the fall of Montségur. Pierre and Mengarde produced four sons and two daughters, and it was one of the sons, the young shepherd Guillaume Maurs, who launched into an almost twenty-year vendetta against Pierre Clergue.

In the 1290s the six Maurs children were probably in their early teens. Their first cousins were the offspring of Bernard and Guillemette Maurs, who also happened to be their neighbours near *la laviera*. Such

---

★ In view of such blood ties, it is worth noting the absence of cretinism in the village. The genetic material of Montaillou was as robust as it could be in a thirteenth-century village that was feeding itself adequately, and there is furthermore no evidence of real inbreeding. If anything, it would appear that the villagers were aware of its dangers, and real incest did not occur, notwithstanding the sophistic arguments used by the likes of the priest Pierre Clergue to justify it.

clusterings of families in the same area were a characteristic pattern of Montaillou.

At various times two members of the Pélissier family, the shepherd Jean and his brother Bernard, also lived with Bernard and Guillemette Maurs. The two Pélissier boys were family, because Jean Pélissier's mother, the wife of Bernard Pélissier, was Alazais Maurs, a sister of the Guillaume Maurs of the feud. Jean Pélissier's claim to have been born in about 1287 is roughly accurate, because it makes him a contemporary of the Maurs children, who are his cousins.*

When Pierre Maurs married Mengarde Bar, her Faure connections allied them to the Maurys, because Mengarde Bar's brother-in-law was Pierre Faure whose younger sister was Pierre Maury's mother. It follows that two of the major shepherd players in this drama, Pierre Maury and Guillaume Maurs from Montaillou, were related, albeit distantly. This must have contributed to the cementing of their friendship later when they found themselves in Catalonia.

The people of the square of Montaillou

Once it is understood that Pierre Maury's survey of Cathar houses mirrors a true-to-life grid of the village, five further important houses and families on the square can be identified.† They are Pierre Maury's maternal uncle Arnaud Faure and his wife Alazais Guilabert; his paternal aunt Mersende and her husband Pierre Marty; Raymond Rives of the Rives family; Raymond Baille and his wife; and Pierre Clergue (B) and his wife Guillemette (née Rives).

* All four of Jean's brothers, Raymond, Guillaume, Bernard and Pierre, were presumably born either late in the 1280s or in the early 1290s.

There was another Pélissier family, that of Julien Pélissier to whose house Jean refers. This may be Jean Pélissier's father's brother, but we cannot be certain. What does seem to be the case is that his father died some time before his mother, who was alive in 1306.

† That Pierre Maury's recollection is structured rather than random can be demonstrated from his references to the Rives, his own family, their neighbour in the square Pierre Ferrié, and the groupings of Belot–Vital and Lizier–Benet–Rous. The material from '*et domus bernardi riba . . .*' to '*. . . erat bona credens hereticorum*' (FR, f.257v) appears to recall the people of the square, before Pierre Maury, in his mind, journeys up south-west towards *capanal den belot* and the Azémas and Belots.

Pierre Maury's list consolidates the conclusion, urged by other evidence, that Guillemette Clergue (B) lived in the square, on the same side as the Maurys and almost opposite her parents, the Rives. The position of Guillemette's home afforded her a good view of the routes of access to the Rives house from both square and street (FR, f.67v), and knowing this allows us to make sense of the topographical patterning of a fleeting moment in the life of Montaillou in the 1290s. One day Mersende Marty was in her garden and called out to Guillemette, asking whether she could take some freshly picked cabbages to her mother (for the Perfect Prades Tavernier). Guillemette replied that she dared not leave her house, because she had little children near the fire. Mersende therefore took them herself to the Rives 'in my full view', a phrase Guillemette also applies to other people entering her mother's house. What this cameo episode further reveals is that the Martys lived west of Guillemette Clergue (B)'s house in the square, and were consequently further away from the Rives than the Clergues (B).*

Guillemette repeatedly reports 'seeing' people frequent her parents' house, because she spent whole days sitting opposite it in her garden or at a window, as she was continuously either pregnant or looking after babies. Her residing in the square also explains why, on returning from the water or *la laviera*, she had to pass the house of Raymonde Belot-Lizier which stood further up the hill. Living on the northern side of the square made Guillemette Clergue (B) a neighbour, to the west, of the Ferriés and of Pierre Maury's family. Further west of her may have stood the house of her father-in-law Bernard Clergue (B) and his wife Gauzia, since in Montaillou families commonly gathered in the same corner. If this was so, then the house of Pierre de Savenac also intervened between Guillemette and her in-laws, because Bernard Clergue (B) and de Savenac were direct neighbours, with a gate connecting the Clergue (B) house and de Savenac's garden.

This leaves two households which also appear to have inhabited the square: Arnaud Faure and his wife Alazais (née Guilabert), and Raymond Baille and his wife Guillemette, whose son Jacques was married

---

* The fact that the Martys and Clergues (B) were neighbours in the square may explain why Gauzia Clergue (B) reported that on All Souls' Day (2 November) 1301 she took Pierre Marty a large piece of bread as alms, 'as was the custom in Montaillou' (FR, f.293v).

to Sybille Rives, Guillemette Clergue (B)'s sister.* The square of Montaillou was a stronghold therefore of, in descending order of importance, Rives, Maurys, Martys, Clergues (B), Faures and Bailles.

At the margins of Montaillou

That a second Baille house stood near the junction where the climb up to the west entrance of the castle and the inner track to Prades part company is suggested by the consolidated evidence of Guillemette Clergue (B) and her cousin Fabrisse's daughter, Grazide Lizier (née Rives). This may have been the family of Vital Baille, his wife Esclarmonde, and their son Jacques. Since in Montaillou the best houses clustered near the square and enjoyed prime south-facing aspects, any habitation towards the *bac* or north-western side of the hill may have signalled a lower social or economic class. It may therefore be the case that the Baille house, which appears to have been standing further towards the *bac* on the same track as the Guilaberts', was even poorer than the Guilaberts'.

If the Guilaberts and the Bailles inhabited the north-western fringes of the village, Raymonde Testanière's house was the last one in Montaillou, or the first one as one entered Montaillou from above after passing *fontcanal*. She was the sister of Prades Marty, and she was known in the village by the name of 'Vuissane'. In the Montaillou of the late thirteenth century, to walk 'beyond the Testanière house' commonly meant to put oneself out of range of eavesdropping, although this seems odd since this track must have been busy with women bringing water into the village from *fontcanal*.†

---

* Raymond Baille from the square of Montaillou headed the main Baille family with his wife, Guillemette. They were both strongly Cathar, and had four boys, the youngest of whom, Guillaume, was born in the first few years of the fourteenth century. He was only a child when his father was arrested. Perhaps also living with them was 'old Arnaud Baille'. He proved a faithful friend to Pierre Maury on his return to Montaillou in 1305, and he found him work with his daughter's husband in Ax. Years later Pierre Maury in turn looked after the Bailles when they were refugees in Catalonia.

† The phrase 'beyond' here means 'above', hence we can deduce that the house stood high up the track and therefore south-west of the main square.

Doubtful locations

There remain a number of houses which cannot be located with any certainty. One of the most enigmatic ones is the 'Mamol' house, which had a courtyard and seems to have stood in the vicinity of the Clergues' and Benets' houses, but no 'Mamols' as individuals are ever mentioned in the documents (FR, f.80r).

Since Pierre Maury collocates the Belots, Arnaud Vital and Guillaume Fort, I would conjecture that the house of Guillaume Fort stood south-west of *capanal den belot,* perhaps up from Pons and Alazais Azéma and Arnaud Vital's forge.* Pierre Maury similarly lists Guillaume Pourcel and his wife Brune (née Tavernier) alongside Guillaume Fort, and we may tentatively assume that these two families were also neighbours. If so, Brune Pourcel would have lived on the way to Vuissane's. The Pourcels were poor, and their house had only an open space next to it, unlike the richer houses with their courtyards.

Not far, it seems, from the Pourcels lived Étienne Belot, the illegitimate son of Arnaud Belot. He was born some time in the early to mid-1290s, and would consequently seem to have been too young to own a house in the late spring of 1308, the purported date of Pierre Maury's survey. Giving a house to Étienne Belot may be a further slip in Pierre Maury's Cathar-listing conversation of 1324, all of which was almost certainly a fiction, and which fails moreover clearly to distinguish between 1308 and sixteen years later.

The other unidentified homes include the ones of Raymond and Guillemette Argelier, and of Arzelier, a different household.† Then

---

* There seems to have been a second Fort house, that of 'Arnaud' Fort, whose house in Montaillou was burnt by the Inquisition at the same time that two Perfects fled down *a-la-cot* from the Belots' house. While it is not impossible that 'Arnaud' is a mistake for 'Guillaume', Guillaume Fort was convicted of heresy only in 1316, by which time all the Perfects who frequented Montaillou were long dead. It follows, therefore, that the coinciding of the burning of a Fort house with escaping Perfects points probably to another Fort house, perhaps belonging to one of Guillaume's brothers.

† Guillemette, the daughter of Pierre Caravessas, owner of another unidentified house, married one Guillaume Arzelier whom she described as '*malum vel austerum*', which means 'nasty and strict' (FR, ff.243v,244r).

there was the house of Raymond and Guillaume Capelle, who may have been father and son. Theirs was a notable Cathar family during the period leading up to Montségur, when Perfects visited their house in Montaillou (D 24, f.73r). There was another Cathar family called Julia, who may have been related to the Julias and Benets from Ax. As for the militant Cathar *Na* Roche, she and her family may have lived not far from Brune Pourcel (see below, page 172). A family called Fournier lived in the village at the time, but they play no part in the extant records, and they were not related to the Bishop of Pamiers.

Little is known about one Raymond Vital and his wife Brune, other than that he predeceased her. Was he related to the cobbler and *passeur* Arnaud Vital, or to another Vital called Bernard who was said to be of Arnaud Vital's family? What about the Cathar house of Guillaume Authié (B), whose wife Bernard Belot tried to violate? And where did Arnaud Teisseyre and his daughter Sybille live? She worked as Béatrice's servant in the late 1290s during the châtelaine's affair with Pierre Clergue, and she accompanied her mistress when she left the Pays d'Aillou for good. Eventually Sybille Teisseyre became the lover of the man who raped the châtelaine.

When Béatrice de Planisolles took up residence at Montaillou, a number of the main players in the coming Cathar adventure were still only children or teenagers. For them the immense upheaval of the Cathar resurgence coincided with puberty. Their parents had grown up in relatively quiet times since the fall of Montségur forty-five years earlier, but they had remained resolutely Cathar at heart. When it looked as if the true faith was going to be rekindled, they rose ready to welcome it. It was their children who paid the penalty for their zeal. But few could have anticipated such an outcome, since in the early 1290s there were only a handful of Catholic families left in the village. The fact that *all* the ruling clans, and particularly the omnipotent Clergues, were Cathar must have reassured any doubters in Montaillou. Moreover, the new châtelaine was a de Planisolles, and could be trusted to be sympathetic to her family's long-standing loyalties to the *entendensa del be*, the Cathar 'discernment and understanding of the Divine Good'. Her forbearance towards Catharism was soon tested by none other than her household steward, Raymond Roussel.

2. The Steward, the Châtelaine and the Demon Priest: 1291–1301

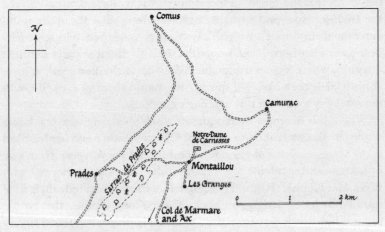

The Pays d'Aillou

It was during the month of August in 1294, Béatrice de Roquefort, as she now was, was barely twenty, the mother of two little boys, and newly pregnant for the third time, when the superintendent and steward of the castle, Raymond Roussel from Prades, started to press her to run away with him and join the good Christians who were sheltering abroad.

Raymond Roussel had long harboured Cathar leanings, and even before the 1280s he had been convicted of heresy and sentenced to the wearing of the yellow crosses. He desired the charismatic young châtelaine, whose father's heretical past was well-known; and his continued involvement in heresy was probably suspected locally as well. Although Béatrice did ask the obvious question, 'How can I leave my husband and my sons?' and pointed out that she was moreover pregnant and wondered about the fate of the baby if she left with Raymond Roussel to join the good Christians, she did not otherwise balk at his proposition. Indeed, it was mostly the unborn baby that preoccupied her.

Raymond Roussel explained to her that the souls of men and women transmigrated through up to nine bodies in search of a good Christian in order to achieve salvation. In response Béatrice pertinently asked, 'How can the spirit of a dead man or woman enter through the mouth of a pregnant woman, and through her mouth arrive at the mouth of the foetus that she carries in her stomach?' Raymond Roussel offered the lame, obvious and perhaps suggestive reply that the spirit could enter the foetus inside a woman's stomach through penetrating whichever part of her body he chose to. He similarly failed to parry her next question, whose logic is irrefutable: 'Why don't children speak at once at birth since they have old spirits?' Raymond Roussel evoked God's inscrutability to answer this ingénue's question.

Where was Bérenger de Roquefort while his young wife was being wooed by this Malvolio of a steward? Clearly Béatrice and her husband at this stage enjoyed a physical relationship, and she was enough in awe of him to fear for her life at his hands if she were caught eloping with Raymond Roussel. Roussel suggested that they should bide their time until Bérenger de Roquefort took off for a long journey that would remove him a little way from the Sabartès. He probably guessed rightly that the châtelaine was as complaisant as she was because of her Cathar upbringing. He decided therefore to assuage her fears of scandal and play simultaneously on her maternal anxieties by telling her a story of female Cathar martyrology, a story which she may well have known already.

Two local women of noble descent from Château-Verdun, the small Ariège town inhabited in the 1290s by the devoutly Cathar Stéphanie de Château-Verdun, chose to go to the stake at Toulouse rather than recant their Cathar beliefs. One of them was Serena de Mirepoix, who died in 1247, three years after the fall of Montségur, which her brother Pierre-Roger de Mirepoix had defended (D24, ff.261v–263v). It was (probably) Serena, a mother like Béatrice, who could not bear to be separated from her baby in a cradle before departing to meet her fate in Toulouse. In the end she had to order the wet-nurse to remove the baby so that she could leave.

'Raymond told me this story to inspire me to do likewise,' Béatrice commented later. As Raymond Roussel's next move showed, this was indeed his intention. Béatrice held out and expressed a wish to have as travelling companions two or three ladies of her rank to obviate the charge of sexual elopement, which would otherwise be levelled at her since she was still young. To allay her scruples, Raymond Roussel suggested to Alazais Gonelle, the mistress of Guillaume Clergue and a frequent caller at Béatrice's, that she should offer to accompany the châtelaine and himself; moreover, Alazais noted, Algée de Martre from Camurac, who was the sister of Mengarde Clergue and the mother of Guillaume Clergue, would also join them. Their 'elopement' would thus be morally safeguarded by two women closely connected to the Clergues, one of them being a middle-aged matron.

How much of these projects were wild diversions provided for the bored châtelaine by the middle-aged Cathar faithful is hard to gauge. Raymond's true designs, however, were about to become translucent. One evening, after what appears to have been a tête-à-tête dinner with the châtelaine, he secretly entered her bedroom and hid under her bed. What followed is best rendered in her own words about that late summer's night in the castle of Montaillou in the 1290s:

I tied up my household affairs and went to bed. Everyone in the house ['*de domo*': she is thinking of her living quarters] was quiet and sleeping. I was asleep myself when Raymond emerged from under my bed, lay next to me in his nightshirt, and started to act in a manner which suggested that he desired to have sex with me. When I exclaimed, 'What does this mean?' he urged me to keep quiet. To this I replied, 'How now, you peasant, shall I keep quiet then!' and started to scream and call my maidservants who slept next to me in my bedroom [presumably in an *adjacent* bedroom], telling them that there was a man in bed with me. On hearing this Raymond left my bed and chamber. The following morning he apologized for doing me the wrong of hiding next to me. I said to him, 'Now I see clearly that the intention behind your feigned words about us going to join the good Christians was only to possess me and to have sex with me. If it were not that my husband might assume that I acted dishonourably with you, I would at once have you thrown into the deepest dungeon.' (FR, f.38r)

Béatrice and Raymond Roussel had no further heretical conversations, and shortly afterwards Raymond Roussel left the castle and returned to Prades, to rejoin, it appears, his wife Alazais, a Cathar sympathizer and a cousin of Pierre Clergue (B), the husband of the young Guillemette Rives. With his wife in tow Raymond Roussel seems to have moved to Laroque d'Olmes beyond Montségur, perhaps to be safely out of the ken of the châtelaine, should she change her mind about his attempted assault on her.

Béatrice's picaresque escapade with Roussel suggests that her marriage to Bérenger de Roquefort may have been less than completely fulfilling. She seems to have been in the habit of sleeping alone, thought nothing of dining with her steward, and was intimate with him to the point where he and she freely spoke of eloping.

In the spring or early summer of 1295 Béatrice gave birth to (probably) 'Béatrice', the first of her five daughters. This girl was alive in 1308 when Pierre Clergue visited her mother in Varilhes, but she had died by 1320, unlike the four sisters who followed her.

One day in July 1295 when Béatrice was recovering from the birth, Alazais Rives, who was then probably in her early forties, knocked at the door of the castle. Béatrice knew, of course, that Alazais was one of the two younger sisters of Prades Tavernier, that Prades was rumoured at this time to be seeing a great deal of Stéphanie, the widow of Guillaume-Arnaud of Château-Verdun, and that they were thought to be planning to leave for Lombardy to seek out other Cathar Perfects.★ Béatrice would have been cautious about frequenting a 'contaminated' family; she would also have known that Alazais's fifteen-year-old daughter Guillemette was heavily pregnant and due any moment, and that this was being used as the pretext for Alazais's calling.

When Béatrice sent a servant to inquire what Alazais wanted, the

---

★ The reason why parts of northern Italy and particularly Lombardy provided Cathars with relatively safe havens was because these regions had been fought over since the twelfth century by the Guelphs (the papacy) and the Ghibellines (the imperial party). Wherever the Ghibellines ruled the Cathars were tolerated. It was not until the mass burning of Cathars in the arena of Verona on 12 February 1278 that the Cathars' hold on the Italian peninsula began to weaken. Even so, it is clear from the Fournier Register that in places like Cuneo, where Pierre and Guillaume Authié headed in 1296, the Cathars continued to be well entrenched long afterwards. It is worth noting that in the thirteenth century 'Lombardy' was sometimes used in an inclusive sense to mean Italy (as in e.g. *Chanson* 1931–61).

reply came back that she needed vinegar. Béatrice ordered it to be given to her, understanding perhaps that the vinegar was needed for the imminent childbirth at the Rives house. But Alazaïs's explanation came back that she did not in fact require any vinegar. Instead, she hoped for an interview with the châtelaine. Béatrice declined to grant this, and Alazaïs departed. The subterfuge to get access to the châtelaine had failed, but contact had been established.

Later the same day Alazaïs returned to the castle, and again knocked at the door. This time she claimed that her daughter was in great pain from contractions: could Béatrice therefore descend to her house, because Guillemette desired to see her very much? Again Béatrice refused to comply, pointing out that she herself was recovering from childbirth. Before long Alazaïs was back for the third time, now pleading passionately with Béatrice to come and see her daughter. Again the answer was negative.

From Alazaïs's insistence it is fairly obvious that she was being urged by someone in the village to entice the châtelaine into the Rives house. To have secured the unqualified support of the châtelaine of Montaillou for the Cathar cause would have been an important link in the dissident chain that was being fashioned throughout the area at the time; and the more deeply the local nobility was implicated, the harder it would be for the Church and the secular powers to persecute the good Christians. It says something about the local perception of the châtelaine that Alazaïs and her Cathar allies, like her steward Raymond Roussel, thought that 'baby-business' constituted a fail-safe way of swaying Béatrice. In particular, the tender-hearted châtelaine's compassion for another woman's labour pangs might overcome her reluctance about meeting Cathars at the Rives'; the more so since the suffering girl was the sweet-natured teenager Guillemette, who was married to the brutal Pierre Clergue (B) who reputedly beat her and loathed the Cathars.*

* Shortly after her mother's failed attempts to involve the châtelaine in heresy, Guillemette gave birth to a baby daughter, and so in the autumn of the year 1295 both she and Béatrice were rearing little girls. The solidarity of women in a thirteenth-century village like Montaillou was undoubtedly strong, and women depended on other women to assist them with childbirth above all. From generation to generation mothers, aunts and other women in the village acted as midwives to their daughters and nieces. The fact that there are no recorded deaths in childbirth in Montaillou

Béatrice's curiosity may have been irresistibly aroused by Alazais's persistent visits, because later that same day she decided to go to Notre-Dame-de-Carnesses, a journey that would inevitably take her either directly through, or closely past, the village. She had made a baptismal candle ([acc.] *retinctam*: LS, N) and wanted to take it to the church, presumably to celebrate her new baby; or the candle may have been part of the ritual of purification.

Béatrice arranged for a woman who was staying at the home of Pierre d'Espère, the then rector of Montaillou, to accompany her. This woman, who was from Limbrassac (between Laroque d'Olmes and Mirepoix), was either an acquaintance or a servant, and she was probably seeing the priest on an errand for the castle household. Why Béatrice should need to call on someone staying at the village rector's is puzzling, since her household included several other servants. To summon somebody from the heart of the village expressly to join her on the walk to the chapel was bound to advertise her intentions. Perhaps she half-wanted to be met on the way to the church. It would be easier to plead in mitigation of a church-bound 'chance' encounter with heretics than to answer a charge of an intentional full-blown conference with frontline dissidents.

The two women set out on the half-mile trek towards the pilgrim chapel outside the village. On the way down Alazais Rives, leading

---

confirms one's sense of its people as well-fed and generally of sound constitutions.

Childbirth was literally a communal labour, but not every young woman was therefore inured to its physical aspects. To its shame the Pamiers Inquisition made its very first victim (15 July 1318) of one such woman, the twenty-five-year-old epileptic Aude from Merviel. She had heard in church how the night before a woman had given birth to a little girl in the public street before she could reach her home. In the course of the service, Aude recalled, 'I started to ponder about the foulness women expel during childbirth, and when I saw the elevation of the Host on the altar I thought that It was contaminated by such foulness. For this reason I fell into the error of faith, that the body of our Lord Jesus Christ was not on the altar' (FR, f.136r).

The gulf between the high spirituality of Christianity and the physiological realities of incarnation in a feeding and evacuating human body was seen by the Cathars as self-evident proof of the purely symbolic nature of transubstantiation and of the consuming of the Host. Aude's response to childbirth was probably never intended as a Cathar pronouncement, but that is how the Church and her neighbours chose to interpret it.

two geese, ran into them. She reiterated her plea for Béatrice to come and call on her daughter. When she met with the same rebuff, Alazais came clean. She told Béatrice that her brother Prades Tavernier was staying in her house and wanted to speak to her, because Stéphanie de Château-Verdun had charged Prades with a message for Béatrice. But Béatrice resolutely held out in her refusal, because she knew the dangers and penalties ensuing from witnessed contacts with Perfects, or aspiring Perfects as Prades was at this stage.

In 1295–6 Montaillou and Prades were in a state of spiritual ferment, and by late autumn of 1296 it was bruited throughout the Sabartès, and particularly in the Pays d'Aillou, that the rich and powerful Authiés from Ax had converted to Catharism and had left for Lombardy to be ordained Perfects there. The Authiés were related by marriage to the Benets of Montaillou and the Savignans of Prades; they were intimate with the feared Clergues, and they knew the châtelaine and her husband. It was through their contacts in Ax and Montaillou that on their return from exile in 1300 the Authiés relaunched the Albigensian heresy in the Languedoc.

But the Authiés were rather grand and aloof figures in the Pays d'Aillou. From the perspective of the 'ordinary' people of the region, their first-hand experience of a heretical conversion-in-the-making was that of their brother, father and uncle Prades Tavernier, and his links with Stéphanie de Château-Verdun.

There were few whose outlook on these matters was more innocent than Prades's niece Guillemette Clergue (B)'s. One of her last encounters with her uncle Prades before he disappeared into Catalonia may have been about a year later, on 29 June 1296. That Friday morning, which was a holiday to mark the feast of St Peter and St Paul, Raymond Roussel's wife, who was Pierre Clergue (B)'s cousin, appeared at Guillemette Clergue (B)'s house in the square of Montaillou and invited Guillemette to join her for mass at Saint-Pierre in Prades. When Guillemette replied, 'I dare not go without my husband's permission,' Alazais intervened and secured her friend's temporary manumission.

And so the two young women took off for Prades to go to church. But, of course, they went there above all to enjoy the fiesta and, in Alazais Roussel's case, to meet Prades Tavernier. On the way across the hill between Montaillou and Prades, Alazais took off a blouse that she was wearing and gave it to Guillemette to put on. This was probably a gift to give the impoverished girl some festive confidence.

After mass at Saint-Pierre, the very church where the châtelaine would four years later have sex with the village priest of Montaillou, the two women lunched at the house of Guillemette's uncle, Bernard Tavernier. How the rest of the day passed off is best related by Guillemette herself:

When we sat at table, Alazais asked Bernard, 'And where is Prades Tavernier? The house looks almost deserted to me because I don't see him here,' to which Bernard replied that he did not know where Prades was and that it was already four days since he had last seen him. He thought it was odd that Prades had not come to the fiesta.

After lunch I played and danced with other boys and girls from Prades, and in the evening Alazais and I had dinner in the house of Bernard Tavernier. As we were dining and dusk fell, Prades Tavernier arrived. He hastily entered the house in which we were dining and from the upper fold of his tunic he drew dead squirrels and threw them there. Then he sat down at table with us and had dinner. While we were eating, Prades told Alazais that she had done well to visit them (the Taverniers) and to bring me along. Alazais replied that she had come to the Taverniers' for love of him and trusting in him. Prades then said to both of us, 'And why did Alazais – my mother – not accompany you? It seems that she does not care.' We replied that we had not informed my mother of our coming to Prades.

After we had finished dinner Albie, Bernard Tavernier's wife, and I ascended to Prades Tavernier's loft, while Alazais and Prades spoke apart for a moment. I don't know what they said to each other, but before they spoke, as we rose from the table, Alazais had told Prades, 'It does surprise me that you wander thus at large and are giving up weaving since you were doing so well from weaving.' Prades replied that he was tired of weaving, and that in future he no longer wanted to weave.

After Alazais had spoken to Prades apart, he invited us to stay there that night. But this we declined, and the two of us departed and arrived at my house in Montaillou. Bernard accompanied us until we were outside Prades. As we thus strode along, Alazais asked Bernard, 'And why does Prades no longer weave his canvases as he used to, since he made a good enough living from that craft?' Bernard replied that Prades no longer wanted to weave because he was tired of it and was therefore selling off the tools of his craft; and if he worked one day, he went out three or four days, and he visited Château-Verdun a great deal. (FR, f.66r)

Was Guillemette Clergue (B) conscious of the fact that the Pays d'Aillou was about to turn itself inside out? She probably did not think that those matters were hers to ponder. Intelligence about events in Montaillou came her way mostly through minute domestic details. One day, for example, her son Arnaud, who was then very little, returned from his grandmother Alazais Rives from across the square with 'three or four apples or medlars'. He explained to his mother that Mersende Marty had taken the fruit to the Rives in a blanket, and that she had given these to him; 'I did not know whether Mersende gave them to my mother to give them to the Perfects or for another reason,' Guillemette remarked (FR, ff.67v–68r).

In late August or early September 1296, one morning between 6 and 9 a.m., Guillemette and her mother were harvesting wheat in one of her father's fields in *a-la-cot*, the south-eastern slope down from the village which levels out at the bottom of the valley in front of *la laviera* and *comba del gazel*. Here they met Guillemette's brother Pons, who was on his way back from accompanying his uncle Prades to the Col de Marmare. Prades was bound for Château-Verdun where Stéphanie de Château-Verdun was in the process of selling her goods in readiness to leave for Barcelona, to be received there by the Good Men. Pons's accompanying of Prades must have been for social and, perhaps, spiritual reasons, because Prades hardly needed a guide for this easy first leg of the journey down the mountains. Eventually Pons, like Raymond Azéma, Pierre Maury, Arnaud Vital and others, became a *passeur*-guide for the various Perfects, ready at the slightest request to drop everything to ensure safe, mostly nocturnal, passage across the rugged terrain of the Sabartès.

A few days later, on a public holiday, Guillemette stood in the square of Montaillou cradling her baby in her arm when her uncle Bernard Tavernier came up to her. He wanted to know whether she had recently seen his brother Prades. She replied that she had not, and then asked Bernard why he was looking for Prades, and Bernard explained that he had found someone who was interested in buying the household tools that Prades was in the process of selling off separately. Guillemette then asked why her uncle was seeing so much of Stéphanie de Château-Verdun, and Bernard explained that Stéphanie and Prades were seeking out the Good Men who put the souls of men and women in Paradise. When she replied, 'How can they be Good Men since the priests say so many bad things about them, and if they could catch them they would burn them?' Bernard stayed silent and left.

Guillemette's memory may be somewhat disingenuously edited here, because she claimed in evidence to have asked this same question of her brother and mother, and of her uncle and aunt Guillemette Tavernier-Dejean in the space of a few days. Each time the question-and-answer ritual shows an artless teenager, who reports that her mother even called her *pega* (fem. for *pec*), that is, 'silly', for her ignorance. The truth is probably rather different, namely that the generally guileless Guillemette was a willing Cathar sympathizer, not least because her vile husband hated the heretics. If her elders did not want to implicate her too deeply, and therefore, like her brother, at times tried to prevent her from seeing a Perfect, this may well have been on account of both her husband and her youth. Even so, Guillemette saw Prades Tavernier repeatedly in her father's house, and she overheard him mentioning Stéphanie de Château-Verdun in conversation with the Cathar die-hard Raymond Roche. She also met him at her aunt's in Prades during the phoney-war period of 1295–6, and nine years hence, in the barn of her father's house, Guillemette would innocently stumble across the fugitive Prades at prayer sitting in a ray of sunlight (see below, page 167). The reason why Guillemette visited her parents' house so frequently was primarily to borrow wheat, hay and straw, as well as bread, flour, combs for carding hemp, and occasionally a mule or an ox to work in the field. In the mid-1290s she thus inevitably witnessed her uncle Prades Tavernier's transition from a popular weaver to an aspiring Perfect trying to raise cash for his travel expenses to Barcelona by selling the tools of his trade.

Prades Tavernier left the Sabartès in the company of the aristocratic Stéphanie de Château-Verdun and her daughter, the Lady Catalane. This latter was already of marrying age, and her skill as a seamstress stood them in good stead financially, since silk Barcelona blouses were coveted luxury items at the time. It is tempting to date their departure to October 1296 and synchronize it with that of the Authiés, who left for Lombardy then.

The weaver and the aristocrat were away for a long time, and at some point Stéphanie and her daughter were arrested, though not, it seems, Prades. Stéphanie lost almost everything, but she may have been granted her freedom under house-arrest, in deference perhaps to her rank. She was certainly back in her home in Château-Verdun during the first decade of the fourteenth century, under the watchful eye of her son. She seems to have been so indigent that Prades lent her the sum of 100 shillings (the cost of about ten lambs), which he later tried in vain to recover from her.

It is likely that Prades was ordained in Catalonia, notwithstanding Vidal's assertion that he became a Perfect only after the Authiés' return in 1300 (Vidal 1906b, 78). While there is no explicit record of a Tavernier consolation in Montaillou between 1295 and 1300, he may well have had a hand in the consolation of Guillemette Faure-Bar, which happened in the winter of 1299 while the Authiés were in the process of returning. Within a short time Prades Tavernier had become an underground figure who needed to tread a lonely and clandestine path through the Sabartès at night. On assuming the mantle of a Perfect he took the first name of André, one of Christ's Disciples. During his apostolate André Tavernier was known for his tall stature and white hair, both characteristics which he shared with his master Pierre Authié.

The departure of Prades Tavernier seems to have been neatly synchronized with that of the village priest of Montaillou, Pierre d'Espère. He was succeeded by Pierre Clergue, a scion of the richest and most powerful family in Montaillou. He was the kind of priest whom the thirteenth-century troubadour Pierre Cardenal had targeted in a scabrous popular poem:

> Clergue se fan pastors
> et son aucizedor
> e par de gran sanctor
> qui los vei revestir

which translates as: 'Priests pretend to be shepherds, when really they are murderers, and they seem of great holiness when you see them in their habit'; in other words, they are wolves in sheep's clothing.

Where Pierre Clergue studied before arriving back in Montaillou cannot be ascertained, but we may be fairly certain that the timing of his arrival was not fortuitous. Did his predecessor die, or was he removed because he was too steeped in orthodox Catholicism? The fact that the Cathar renaissance in the Pays d'Aillou coincided with the incipient tenure of a Cathar-tainted priest from a ruthless family of Cathar sympathizers suggests that the highest echelons of Occitan power and gentry were colluding with the new movement and its controllers in exile, the Authiés.

The Clergues' grip on the village tightened even further when the priest's appointment was matched by that of his younger brother Bernard to the office of *bayle*. Such was their political astuteness and the depth of their pockets that they held these two positions unchallenged for the next twenty-four years, thus achieving a virtual stranglehold on the village. Between them they embodied the Stendhalian 'Rouge et Noir' in the miniature fiefdom of Montaillou.

Was it this which emboldened their half-cousin Pathau to take his chances with the châtelaine? We will never know, but in January or February 1297 Pathau Clergue took Béatrice de Planisolles by force in her own home. Bérenger de Roquefort was still alive. Pathau walked away scot-free from this serious offence; a crime which, as the case of Bernard Belot and the wife of Guillaume Authié (B) proved, was not taken lightly at the time. Was Bérenger too sick by then to be told of the violation of his wife and home, or was Béatrice so ashamed and humiliated by what had happened that she could not speak of it? Did she feel partly to blame? Is this why the châtelaine felt somehow less offended by this sexual assault than one might have expected from her? For when Bérenger died in February 1298, a year after the incident, she became Pathau Clergue's kept mistress. Rumours about this in the village were rife.

In the course of 1298 Béatrice moved out of the castle and into a house adjacent (*iuxta*) to it (FR, f.39r). Is it entirely fanciful to imagine that this could be the substantial ruin which today sits near the castle in the hillside, up at the top of the village's main road, just down from *fontcanal*? She did not inherit the manor, since under medieval Occitan law, when the mother of the house was widowed her dowry reverted to her, and the first-born son inherited the estate. This custom is alluded to by Alazais Azéma as well as by Béatrice (FR, ff.40r, 58v; Duvernoy 1965, 1.308–9n.143).

Nothing can be established about the new châtelain. If one took up residence, it might have been as 'regent' for one of Béatrice's two sons, who were both children under ten when their father died. Béatrice's reference to granting acquittance from her dowry to her 'husband's heirs' rather than 'my children with him' may suggest that there were de Roquefort brothers and family unconnected to her who inherited the manor of Montaillou; or there may have been sons from a previous marriage of her husband. It is a surprising feature of this story that as the village lurched towards its most turbulent recorded period and, in 1308, plunged into the eye of the storm, the châtelain of Montaillou seems to play no part in it, any more than the one of Prades.

Through Pathau, Béatrice de Planisolles strayed into the orbit of the Clergue family. At the very least her experience of the thuggish Pathau must have meant that she could have harboured few illusions about the Clergues. Did Pathau make her pregnant? It seems not.

During her approximately seven-year-long marriage to Bérenger, Béatrice seems to have produced two sons and three daughters, including little Béatrice who was born in May or June 1295. The two who followed between 1295 and early 1298 were two further girls, Condors and Esclarmonde. Béatrice's brother Bernard from Caussou agreed to become the girls' guardian, presumably because of Bérenger's death. From her later conversations with Pierre Clergue, and particularly the reference to her father's sense of decorum where her sexual honour was concerned, it appears that she conceived no illegitimate children during her time between marriages.

It was a year later, in March 1299 and during Lent, the period of forty weekdays from Ash Wednesday (4 March) to Easter Eve (18 April). During this time of abstinence, which honours Christ's forty days of fasting in the wilderness, canon law did not just regulate the

intake of food, but it also prohibited sex (Paterson 1993, 272).* Béatrice
went to confess herself to Pierre Clergue, the rector of Montaillou,
who heard confession behind the altar of Notre-Dame-de-Carnesses.
The moment she knelt in front of him he kissed her and declared,
'There is no woman in the world I like as much as you.' The fact
that he used *diligere* (like) rather than *amare* (love) or *adamare* (love
passionately) is interesting in itself. Although he knew that she was
being kept by Pathau, this did not stop him from propositioning her.
It may even have roused him to do so. She was so stunned that she left
abruptly without confessing herself.

That Easter of 1299 Pierre Clergue repeatedly visited Béatrice to try
to seduce her. She asked him, 'How can you invite me to be your
mistress, when you know full well that your cousin Raymond has had
me? He will reveal everything.' Clergue replied, 'I know all about it,
but I can be more useful to you and give you more presents than that
illegitimate.' He then suggested that he and his cousin might share her
favours, but this she declined, saying that the two of them would quarrel
because of her, and as a result they would both despise her. While she
implied that her being a widow made his pass even more serious, it
may have had the opposite effect on the priest. He was partial to
widows, as the case of Mengarde Buscailh from Prades demonstrates
(see below, pages 247–8), the more so since they tended to live alone,
and there was no need to worry about a husband at night.

Béatrice retorted that she would rather have sex with four strange
men than one single priest, because she had heard it said that no woman
who had copulated with a priest could see the face of God.

'You are deeply foolish,' Pierre Clergue replied, and then proceeded
to spin her a casuistic line of sub-Cathar cant, noting that

It is just as great a sin if a married woman is carnally known by her own
husband as it would be if she were known by anybody else, the same sin
whoever the man, whether he be her husband or a priest. It is [indeed] a

* But Lent in Languedoc also included spring, and it inspired Guillaume de Tudèle,
the poet of the first part of the *Chanson*, to a flight of Occitan lyricism that Béatrice
would have recognized: '*A l'intrat de caresma, cant baicha la freidor/ E comensa a venir lo
dous temps de Pascor . . .*' (At the beginning of Lent, when the cold is abating/ And
there approaches the mild weather of Easter . . .) (*Chanson* 1931–61, 1.62).

greater sin to have intercourse with a husband, because the wife is not conscious of sinning during sex with her husband, but she certainly believes herself to be sinning if she has sex with other men. Therefore married sex is a more serious sin than sex with another man. (FR, ff.38v–39r)

In Occitan, he might have sounded just like his contemporary Arnaud de Savinhac, who claimed to echo a common Sabartesian sentiment when he said, '*tostemps es e tostemps sira qu l'home ab autru moilher jaira*,' which translates as 'such a time is and will be when man sleeps with somebody else's wife' (FR, f.25v).

Béatrice responded to Clergue's sophistry by asking how as a priest he could say such a thing, since in church matrimony was said to be instituted by God, and the first *ordo*, that is divine decree, was marriage, which God instituted between Adam and Eve so that married sex should be no sin. To this Clergue replied, 'If God created the institution of marriage between Adam and Eve, if He did in fact create them, why didn't He ensure that they didn't sin?' On hearing this, Béatrice professed later, she understood that the priest denied that God had created Adam and Eve and instituted marriage between them. Pierre Clergue concluded by noting that many of the Church's doctrines were false and that the priests maintained them because otherwise they would be neither honoured nor feared: 'Except the Gospels and the Pater Noster, all the other Scriptures are *affitilhas*,' he remarked, using a popular phrase from the local patois which signified the fantastical embroidering by people of others' tales.

Pierre Clergue was not done. He seems to have warmed to the challenge of simultaneously seducing the widowed châtelaine and proselytizing on behalf of his Cathar friends. Indeed, in his mind sexual conquests and Cathar doctrine were conveniently never separated. It was to the injunction against incest that he now turned, little knowing that this particular canard would come to haunt him many years later in the shape of Grazide Lizier, his niece's daughter, who was born in this same year that he was propositioning the châtelaine.

In the predatory world order according to Pierre Clergue it was the deplorable oppression of sexual desire which lay at the root of the orthodox Christian interdiction against a brother marrying his sister. At the beginning, he explained, brothers and sisters freely enjoyed one another. But then it would sometimes happen that a large number of brothers had only one or two beautiful sisters whom they all desired to possess, and this led to many murders among the brothers, hence the Church's injunctions against incest. Sexual intercourse, Pierre Clergue noted, was the same sin in the eyes of God whatever shape or form the partnering ultimately assumed; and the worst offence was married sex, because it took place without obloquy attaching to it.

In any case, he concluded, the Church's marriage rites were just a bit of secular pomp. His punchline and the carefully angled goal of his counsel was that men and women were at liberty to commit whatever sin they fancied in this world and act entirely according to their inclination so long as they were received in the faith of the Good Men at the end, because that alone ensured their salvation.

It seems that Béatrice was not as yet quite swayed by Clergue's unorthodox and skewed views, although from her experience of Raymond Roussel she must have guessed what this was tending towards. Pierre Clergue next moved from theory to an applied illustration of his creed:

Look, we Clergues are four brothers. I am a priest and don't want to have a wife. If my brothers Guillaume and Bernard [Béatrice may be misremembering here, because Bernard was not yet married then] had married my sisters Esclarmonde and Guillemette, our house wouldn't have been destroyed by the fortune that my sisters had as dowries. Rather our estate would have stayed whole. And with only one [new] woman brought into our house by our brother Raymond, we would have had plenty of women and our house would be the richer for it. This is why it would have been better for a brother to marry his sister and for the sister to take her brother for a husband, rather than for her to be sent forth from the paternal home with a large dowry to marry a stranger by which action the paternal home is ruined. (FR, f.39r)

The priapic priest's wilful twisting of Cathar teaching on incest nevertheless reflected widely held views among ordinary Albigensians. But we have already noted in connection with the Maury–Marty intermarriages that the old taboos held firm, and the proof of it lay in the absence of malformation in Montaillou, as if some atavistic gene had embargoed consanguineous sex whatever its dubious Cathar sanctions.

Thus Raymond Delaire, who stood accused before Fournier a year after the châtelaine, also confessed to having viewed incest as free from sin during his time as a Cathar. Although he claimed to have found the idea of incest shameful, he, like Pierre Clergue, had sex with his sister-in-law. 'However,' he remarked, 'for a man to have sex with a second cousin or other women is neither sinful nor shameful, because I go along with the common saying in the Sabartès, namely "*a cosina secunda tot leli afonia*",' which literally translates as 'to a second cousin shove her it all in' (FR, f.144r).

Raymond was not given to fine-tuning his expressions, as his naturalistic views on Christ's conception further indicate. Christ, he jauntily remarked, was produced by '*foten e coardan*', which translates unedifyingly as 'fucking and giving tail' (FR, f.144v). A pleonastic variant of this was Raymond's assertion that God was the result of '*masan e foten ayshi co nos*', which means 'plain fucking like the rest of us', and this he cheerfully illustrated by striking the palms of his hands together (FR, f.143v). It is not surprising that neither of these locutions was translated into Latin by the clerks of the Inquisitorial court. What matters here above all is the evoking of Ariégeois folk-wisdom which, since time immemorial it appears, circumscribed the boundaries of licit sex (which stopped with intercourse between second cousins) in such a way as to minimize genetic mistakes.

Béatrice held out for over three months. Then, one night during the first week in July, which in 1299 lasted from Monday 29 June to Sunday 5 July, she surrendered to Pierre Clergue in her house close to the castle. After this initial encounter they often had sex, and she allowed herself to be 'kept' by him for the next year-and-a-half (FR, f.39r). He regularly spent two or three nights a week in her house, and she visited his on two other nights, which suggests that they spent most nights of the week together, with the exception perhaps of Sunday. The Clergue house is described in the documents as 'the house of the rector and his brothers', and three generations of Clergues (counting in Bernard Clergue's illegitimate daughter) lived together in the same large house at some time or other (FR, f.99r). Pierre Clergue occupied a first-floor room above the main entrance, and it was in all probability in this room that he slept with the châtelaine. That they were involved was commonly rumoured in Montaillou. It appears moreover that the priest did not need to take heed of his parents or anybody else when entertaining women upstairs. The fact that his room, which was off a large hall, seems to have had independent external access must have helped. It was probably on these premises that Mengarde Clergue one day told Béatrice that it was a good deed to tend to the needs of *Na* Roche and her son Raymond Roche, the two formerly imprisoned Cathars. If their property was confiscated, they would certainly have been indigent; and they seem to be the only Cathars from Montaillou who were actively persecuted during the 1290s and spent some time in gaol. But they were free by 1298–9, and *Na* Roche, a friend of Mengarde Clergue and Guillemette Benet, was consoled and died in Montaillou in 1305. Her son also was in circulation again, because in about 1300 he was testing the political waters down in Sorgeat talking to Guillaume Escaunier about the Authiés' return (FR, f.119).

During the period of Béatrice's involvement with Pierre Clergue, which lasted for eighteen months until January 1301, Pathau occasionally made a play for her again, but she denied him each time. A 'hidden hate' thus arose between the two Clergue cousins, she noted.

When Béatrice and Pierre Clergue first started having sex together, she asked him, 'And what will I do if I become pregnant by you? I should be utterly lost.' Clergue replied that he had a certain herb which had contraceptive properties. In fact, what he proposed to use seems to have been an improvised combination of condom, pessary and spermicide. Here is how Béatrice described her 'safe-sex' encounters with Pierre Clergue, in words which are consciously refined, since her audience consisted of the Inquisitorial court; they also reflect in their stilted repetitiveness the characteristics of legal evidence.

I replied to him, 'And what kind of herb is that? Is it the one that cowherds put over the pot of milk in which they have put the rennet, the herb which does not allow the milk to curdle as long as it stays on the pot of milk?' He replied that I should not trouble myself over what kind of herb it was, but the herb was such that it had that particular quality and that he had the herb. And from then on, when he wanted to know me carnally, he wore something that was wrapped and tied [around his penis] by a piece of linen cloth, the thickness and length of an inch, or the joint [*sic* Duvernoy 1965, 1.244] of the small finger on my left hand.

He had a certain kind of long piece of string that he put around my neck when we had sexual congress. This thing which he called a herb was suspended from the string. It descended between my breasts and stayed over my vagina [literally 'the orifice of my stomach']. He always put it there when he wanted to know me carnally. It stayed around my neck until the priest wanted to rise; and during his wanting to rise the priest took it from my neck. And sometimes when he wanted to know me carnally twice, or more often, during the same night, the priest asked me, before he joined himself to me, where the herb was. I took it, finding it by the cord around my neck, and put it in his hand. The priest took the herb and put it over the orifice of my stomach, the cord running between my breasts. And so he joined himself physically to me, and in no other way.

Sometimes I asked the priest that he should surrender the herb to me, to which he replied that he would not do so because I could then join myself to another man without being impregnated by him, if I wore the herb. And because of this, to prevent me from having intercourse with another man out of fear of getting pregnant by him, he did not want to surrender the herb to me.

The priest did this above all because Raymond Clergue who is also called 'Pathau' and who kept me first before the priest, a cousin-german of Raymond Clergue, had me. Because of this the two were jealous of each other over me.

The priest also told me that he did not want me to be impregnated by him as long as Philippe de Planisolles, my father, was alive, because my father would be deeply ashamed of it; but after his death, he would be very happy for me to become pregnant by him. (FR, f.43)

Pierre Clergue and Béatrice discussed heresies at her place when she was delousing him near a window in her house overlooking the road, or in front of the fire, or in bed, always careful not to be overheard by anyone (FR, f.39v). Béatrice's servant at this stage was Sybille Teisseyre from Montaillou. One day in December 1299, at a time when the Authiés' return to the Sabartès was well and truly under way, Béatrice was warming herself with Alazais Maury in front of the fire in the Maurys' house in the square of Montaillou. Gauzia, the wife of Bernard Clergue (B), and therefore probably the mother-in-law of Guillemette Clergue (B)-Rives, entered and asked Alazais whether Guillemette Faure was dead. This Guillemette (née Bar) was the widow of Pierre

Faure from Montaillou, the sister of Mengarde Maurs, and Alazais Maury's (née Faure) sister-in-law.

Alazais Maury replied that Guillemette was dead and already buried:

GAUZIA: And did you do well?
ALAZAIS: Yes, by my faith, well.
GAUZIA: And you have done well, well? You were not short of
           anything?
ALAZAIS: We did well, and there was no hindrance.
GAUZIA: Thanks be to God.

Béatrice knew of course that this was Cathar code, but when she quizzed Alazais Maury about it a few days later the latter refused at first to enlighten her. After some reassuring cajoling, she eventually told Béatrice that Guillemette was consoled by the Good Men and went through the *endura*, the Cathars' purifying death-fast. She took only cold water for fifteen days before dying, an act of courage and a calvary that impressed Béatrice enough for her to share the memory of it many years later in a moment of tenderness with her then lover (FR, f.45v). Alazais Maury persuaded Béatrice to send the Perfects some food in the form of a peck, that is two gallons, of flour. It seems to be at this stage that Béatrice became implicated in Catharism, after resisting its earlier overtures in July 1295. Since this happened in December 1299 the Perfect in question was probably Guillaume Authié accompanied by, perhaps, Pierre-Raymond de Saint-Papoul.

Notwithstanding a half-hearted attempt later at disowning her heretical loyalties, Gauzia Clergue (B) was a committed Cathar. She was related to the dominant Clergue family through marriage as well as by birth. In the village she was sometimes referred to as Gauzia Longa, after her mother, *Na* Longa, whose husband was a Martre from Camurac and a brother of Mengarde Clergue.* One Saturday morning in Febru-

---

* Gauzia's father was therefore the uncle of Bernard and Pierre Clergue, and she was their cousin. Before marrying her husband Bernard Clergue (B) she had been the mistress of Raymond Rous of Montaillou and Ax, whose bones were later exhumed and burnt (FR, f.273v; d'AR, f.11v). Gauzia was moreover friendly with the sisters Guillemette Benet and Sybille Fort, the wife of Guillaume Fort, both of whom were devout Cathars.

ary or March 1303 Gauzia also assisted in the consolation by Prades Tavernier of her dying daughter Esclarmonde, the godchild of Guillaume Benet. On falling ill Esclarmonde had come home to her father's house from Comus, where she was married, to recover or die in Montaillou. She lingered on for three years. Raymond Belot had fetched Prades all the way from Junac or Larnat (FR, f.295r). Several years later, at the entrance to the gaol of Carcassonne, Raymonde Belot-Lizier, who was visiting her incarcerated husband Arnaud, was told by her brother-in-law Raymond Belot that she should tell Gauzia Clergue (B) that she as well as her dead daughter, who would therefore be dug up and burnt posthumously, had been betrayed.

Towards nightfall one day in the winter of 1299–1300 Béatrice was visiting at Alazais Azéma's, and there she saw Alazais's son Raymond with a bag of victuals. He was off to feed the Good Men. The châtelaine's presence in one of the village's humblest homes can confidently be attributed to its active role in furthering the cause of Catharism in the region. At first Alazais stalled when Béatrice asked where her son might be going at such a time. She even accused her inquisitive aristocratic guest of being *cilharda*, which means having large eyebrows, that is being nosy. Then, extracting from her a promise of secrecy, she revealed that Raymond was a *passeur*.

It was probably during that Christmas Eve of 1299 rather than the following one of 1300 that Pierre Clergue pressed the châtelaine for sex (FR, f.39r). When she said, 'How can you want to commit such a great sin in such a holy night?' Clergue retorted that the sin of sex was the same on this night as on any other. She surrendered and they consummated their passion.

The following morning Clergue unabashedly said Christmas high mass in Montaillou without first confessing himself. He often, Béatrice remarked, did so after a night of sex with her. His excuse was that the power of absolution lay with an omniscient God alone. He particularly enjoined her not to confess her relationship with him to any other priest. Not even the Pope and his bishops, he noted, have the power to absolve man's sins, but only the Good Men who suffered persecutions at the hands of the Church. Béatrice then asked why in that case he himself heard confession, granted absolution and imposed penances.

'Even though it's useless,' he replied, 'I and other priests have to do so, because if we didn't we would lose our revenues; no one would give us anything if we didn't do as the Church instructs us to' (FR, f.39v).

In the new year 1300 Béatrice moved to Prades, and there she started to live in a small house close to the church of Saint-Pierre. It was wedged between the substantial residence of one Pierre Guillaume from Prades and the house of the Prades rector Jean Clergue. This latter was not related, or at least not closely, to the Clergues of Montaillou. Gauzia Clergue (B) later claimed, unconvincingly, to have confided in him about the heretical activities of Mersende Maury-Marty, the aunt of Pierre Maury.

The fact that Béatrice emphasizes that her new dwelling was small, even perhaps pint-sized (a *domuncula*), may suggest that she was experiencing financial difficulties at this stage (FR, f.43r). Did she take her children with her to Prades? Where were they when she was having sex with Clergue in her house in Montaillou? Were they being looked after by a nanny or a wet-nurse? At this stage the two boys and their three younger sisters, Béatrice, Condors and Esclarmonde, were still all under ten, and the girls' ages ranged from three, the youngest, to five or six for Béatrice Junior.

Because her house in Prades abutted on to Jean Clergue's and the sound-proofing was poor, she and Pierre Clergue could not have sex there without being heard in the house next door (FR, f.43r). One day therefore, Pierre Clergue told Béatrice that he would send his 'student' Jean to fetch her the following night to have sex in the church of Saint-Pierre. Clergue did indeed at this time have a disciple to run errands for him. This boy was called a '*scolaris*' by Béatrice and by another witness, who remembered the student being mentioned in 1301 by Guillaume Authié (FR, ff.43r, 51v). He was now deployed as a pander by his master.

That night, 'at around the time of the first sleep', Béatrice waited for the hapless student, and then duly followed him through 'a very black night' into the church. Here they found Pierre Clergue waiting (FR, f.43r). He had arranged for a bed to be made up for them. What his ecclesiastical jurisdiction in Saint-Pierre's in Prades was is not at all clear. Nor is it likely that he shared the former châtelaine's *pudeur* about her priestly neighbour, who was hardly likely to turn on one of the powerful Clergues of Montaillou.

According to Béatrice, she exclaimed, 'Really! How can we do such a thing in the church of Saint-Pierre?' to which Pierre Clergue scoffingly replied, '*O que gran dampnagge y aura sent peire!*' ('O what grievous harm this will do St Peter!') After these words they lay down in the bed, and that night and in that church Pierre Clergue had sex with her. Then, before dawn, Clergue walked Béatrice back to the door of her house.

The church at Prades it still called Saint-Pierre, and it already stood here in the early twelfth century (Moulis 1970, 130–31). It was badly damaged in a fire in 1648, which almost obliterated the village. That Béatrice de Planisolles had sex '*dans l'église de Prades*' is known to this day in Montaillou; and while the villagers laugh about it, they are also mildly disapproving. Did Béatrice move to Prades partly to escape the attentions of the priest? After all, he was not somebody that she could marry and, unlike him, she was worried about her reputation, as well as being frightened of her brothers. She was still only in her late twenties at this time. But her affair with the libidinous Clergue continued until the end of the year 1300.

In the course of that same year, while living in Prades, Béatrice visited her sister Ava in the de Planisolles' home village of Caussou, where she was married to one Vérèze. Ava, who may have been younger than Béatrice, had just had a baby and was recovering from the birth. The journey there would have taken not much more than two hours of solid walking.

The Sunday after arriving in Caussou, Béatrice attended mass at the priory church of Unac, a village nearly two miles down the Val de Caussou towards the Ariège. The priory has long since disappeared, but the magnificent church of Unac survives (Pl. 8). This twelfth-century romanesque building with its eleventh-century clocktower was the parish church of Caussou and, it seems, of Luzenac, since the squires of Luzenac attended high mass here. The priory of Unac rose around the present church and probably encompassed most of the space east of the church where today cars park. It was here in this priory that Jacques Fournier held several summer sessions. Outside the church Béatrice encountered Raymonde de Luzenac, the widow of Guillaume-Bernard de Luzenac. The de Luzenacs were minor nobility, a family of squires like the de Planisolles. Raymonde was considerably older than Béatrice, and whereas the young de Roquefort widow from Montaillou had five small children, the youngest of whom, Esclarmonde, may have been barely weaned, Raymonde's three boys were grown up, the youngest being nineteen in 1301.

Since the de Planisolles and de Luzenacs both resided in the Val de Caussou, it is not surprising that they were related. Moreover, there was a castle at Luzenac, and Raymonde was probably its châtelaine. As Béatrice remarked, Raymonde embraced and kissed her 'because she was of my family'.

Then, near the entrance to the church, Raymonde asked Béatrice, 'And you, cousin, who are from the good country [the Pays d'Aillou], have you not so far seen these Good Men? If I were there, I should be eager to see them.' When Béatrice replied that she had not seen any of them, and furthermore professed to lack the courage to do so, Raymonde assured her that 'If once you have seen and heard them, you will never want to hear anything else again; and after hearing them once, you will always be in a state of grace wherever you go.'

After this Cathar exchange the two women entered the church to hear mass. When twenty years later, and before the Inquisitor, a seemingly guileless Béatrice casually pointed out that Raymonde and she were related, she may well have been trying to lay any familiarity between them at the door of blood relations. Although she was highly susceptible to Cathar approaches, her instincts for self-preservation and good common sense made her shun any overt involvement with the cause. But she had no power over her father's and family's actions, and she may not even have been aware of the full extent of their share in the Authiés' adventure. What she must, however, have known was that the de Planisolles' and de Luzenacs' homes were staging-posts for the likes of Prades Tavernier as he shuttled between the Ariège valley and the Sabartès.

The fact is that by 1300 an extensive network of safe houses and *filières* had been organized to receive the Authiés back in the Sabartès. It criss-crossed the region, and way beyond it, from east to west and from north to south. In the Val de Caussou, which provided a strategic short-cut between the Ariège river and the highlands of the Pays de

Sault, the de Luzenacs' role was pivotal. Raymonde was a dyed-in-the-wool Cathar among whose assignments seems to have been the task of ensuring safe passage to the Luzenac and Garanou regions of the valley, liaising with the de Planisolles, who from Caussou monitored the northern sector of the same deep trench connecting the Marmare to the lower valley.

Mobility and speed were of the essence if the Cathar resurgence was to succeed. In achieving her mission Raymonde was assisted by her niece Lorda and her three boys, Guillaume-Bernard, the eldest son, who became squire after his father's death, his brother Arnaud and the youngest, Pierre.* It was through her niece Lorda's marriage to Guillaume Bayard, however, that Raymonde de Luzenac wielded real influence. Bayard was a lawyer and judge by profession as well as being the châtelain and governor of Tarascon. After the Count of Foix he was probably the single most powerful person in the Sabartès, and Pierre Authié spoke of him and Roger-Bernard III in the same breath. His crucial place in the Authié network will shortly become clear.

In addition Raymonde could count on a faithful servant, Rixende Palharèse. Although Rixende was Raymonde's servant as well as, coincidentally, her eldest son's mistress, she enjoyed a considerable degree of autonomy. She owned a small house in Luzenac on the Ariège, and she was favoured with free access to Raymonde as well as various Perfects and aristocrats in the region, including the châtelain of Junac and Stéphanie de Château-Verdun. She was once observed conferring in secret with this latter to the intense frustration of Stéphanie's son, who was anxious not to invite further retaliation on his house. One of the social impacts of Catharism was to level the differences between the rich and poor, upper and lower classes, as they struggled towards a common goal. Thus Rixende was made welcome by the rich Belots of Montaillou when she went there to help with the harvest, particularly since two Perfects, Guillaume Authié and Prades Tavernier, were due to spend a night there at the same time as her. And it was Alazais Azéma, one of the poorest inhabitants of Montaillou,

---

* Twenty-three years on from their mother's meeting with Béatrice de Planisolles in Unac, Arnaud and Guillaume-Bernard de Luzenac could be found dutifully attending mass in exactly the same church, rehabilitated and precariously re-established in their possessions.

who vouched for Rixende and whose word was accepted by the Belots.

If Alazais enjoyed some status in Montaillou during the renascent Cathar adventure, it was as the mother of Raymond Azéma, who became a leading scout and pathfinder for the Perfects. Alazais was in turn welcomed by the widow of the squire in Luzenac, because of her son's prowess at chaperoning Perfects over the mountains at night. But her own need to earn a living through trade meant that she was frequently on the move, and could therefore double as a messenger and gatherer of intelligence. Her chosen trade was of that of cheesemonger, buying and selling cheeses.

When she was at Luzenac, Rixende saw her and asked whether she wanted to buy cheeses.

I said yes, and then Rixende said that she knew of six cheeses for sale. I instructed her to take them to her house so that on my way back to her house from Guillaume de 'Serras' where I was collecting my cheeses, I would find her six. When I returned to Rixende's house, she told me that she had gone for the cheeses to the house of Raymonde de Luzenac, the mistress of the place, who desired to know who wanted to purchase the cheeses. Rixende explained that it was the mother of Raymond Azéma of Montaillou. I then bought her cheeses, and when I had bought them Raymonde de Luzenac came to Rixende's house and immediately embraced and kissed me. She told me that she liked me very much, because of my son Raymond who accompanied the Good Men. (FR, f.59v)

This incident occurred some time after 15 August 1301, within a year or so of Béatrice's exchange with Raymonde de Luzenac. By then the Perfects were back in the Sabartès, and known to be so. But when Béatrice spoke to Raymonde at Unac she may well not have known, even though Guillaume Authié had already touched base at the Benets' in Montaillou.

Raymonde de Luzenac's question may have been more probing than its innocuous-seeming enthusiasm for the Cathar cause implies. If the châtelaine was unaware of the Perfects' resurfacing, then that might suggest that the undercover operation was working well at grass-roots level. Moreover, it appears that Pierre Clergue, who certainly knew about the Authiés' homecoming, had decided to keep his châtelaine in the dark. That Clergue acted in this manner in order to protect her may be doubted. Perhaps he felt that she could not quite be trusted in these fragile early stages of the Authiés' return, in spite of the fact that his proselytizing was beginning to bear fruit. Indeed, she later professed to have felt so passionately about the Cathar faith between Easter and August of 1301 that she was prepared to pay any penalty for it. By then Clergue was no longer her lover, and she was looking elsewhere. Perhaps she had already met her second husband by the time she saw Raymonde at Unac, and Raymonde's question may artfully reflect unease about Béatrice's new suitor's lack of the *entendensa del be*, which was in any case not nearly as entrenched in the lowlands, where Béatrice was heading, as it was in the Sabartès. That Béatrice gives August 1301 as the termination of her Cathar spell further points in that direction.

At some point in 1300–1301 Béatrice met the squire Guillaume-Othon de Lagleize, and became betrothed to him (FR, f.45v). If she ended her relationship with Clergue when she met her second husband, then we may surmise that Othon and she met during the winter of 1300–1301, because it was around January 1301 that the affair between the priest and the châtelaine ceased.

The parting from Clergue seems to have been amicable; and it was not permanent, as it turned out. But when she announced her intention to marry de Lagleize from Dalou and follow him to the lowlands, the vile Bernard Belot of Montaillou called on her. Pierre Clergue, he said, wept much for her, because in the lowlands the 'good Christians' would not be there to save her soul. It was therefore important that she should see the Good Men now, since the Perfects dared not readily venture into the lowlands, and no one could be received by them if they had not seen or heard them before. Béatrice steadfastly refused. Others from Prades pressed her similarly, and warned her that in the lowlands she would be joining the company of 'dogs and wolves' (FR, f.45v). But Béatrice was not swayed, and on (probably) 15 August 1301 she left Prades for good.*

---

* She described this leave-taking as 'descending' from the Pays d'Aillou. She also, confusingly, gave Assumption Day, Tuesday 15 August, as being both the day of her leaving Prades to marry *and* the date of her second marriage (FR, ff.40v, 42r). If she did indeed depart from Prades on the same day as marrying Othon in Crampagna,

Othon was a prosperous aristocrat, with residences in Crampagna, Dalou and Varilhes, and this may have played a part in his union to the former châtelaine and her five children, the more so since her financial circumstances seem to have been rather straitened by 1301. Béatrice and Othon started their married life in the village of Crampagna in a house or estate called *carol*, after the neighbouring hamlet and the river Carol, which flows north-west of Crampagna before decanting into the Ariège.

Béatrice soon moved from Crampagna to nearby Dalou. Here she and her husband took up residence in the château of Dalou, which rose on the south-western end of the village's main square, with its back towards the Pech of Dalou and the hill of Margail.* A church stood in the vicinity, and this may well have been an earlier version, on the same site, of the one which today overlooks the horseshoe square from the rue des Nobles.

Around St Michael's (29 September, which fell on a Friday) of that year, barely six weeks after her marriage, Bernard Belot called on her in Crampagna with yet another message from Pierre Clergue. His pretext for thus approaching her was to forward her marriage contract and papers relating to her dowry. Although she had indeed lodged these with Pierre Clergue, perhaps after her solicitors' departure into exile, she no longer required them, because she had already acquitted the heirs of her first husband from her dowry. She guessed, of course, at the true purpose of this visit, and therefore took Belot aside to confer with him in secret. She explained that she no longer wanted to know about the Cathars and forbade him to seek her out again in case her husband should become suspicious. Then she gave him five shillings to give to Guillaume Authié (FR, ff.40v, 59r). Bernard Belot left crest-fallen, saying that 'they', that is Bernard, the rector, and their Cathar

---

she would have needed to make the considerable journey on horseback and descend through the Val de Caussou, where members of her family would have joined her. It is not an impossible scenario, but it is implausible. It is more likely that she left Prades for Caussou on 15 August 1301, and that from here she proceeded a few days later to Crampagna to be married there on Saturday 19 August 1301.

* The Midi word *pech* denotes a high place or hill with a rounded top; it translates Latin *podium* and corresponds to northern French *puy*.

friends, had not thought that their good words would have been so quickly forgotten.

But Pierre Clergue was not so easily dissuaded. Two or three weeks later, in October 1301, at the time of the wine harvest, he appeared himself (FR, f.42r). By now Béatrice and her husband had moved to Dalou. The day before meeting Béatrice in person he sent her a luxury gift through Sybille Teisseyre, Béatrice's servant from Montaillou days. It consisted of a blouse in the Barcelona style, with silk lacework of carmine and saffron (FR, f.42r). He also instructed Sybille to tell her mistress Béatrice that he and she could have undetected sex provided Sybille stood in the middle of the door of the cellar. He evidently did not need to mince his words with the servant from Montaillou.

The following day he entered de Lagleize's mansion. He introduced himself as a Limosian, and pretended to salute Béatrice from her sister Gentille. Playing along with the charade, perhaps for the sake of some of her new husband's servants, she bid him enter. Then they proceeded into the cellar, and here they had sex while Sybille guarded the open door. After this Béatrice accompanied Clergue out of the house, and inquired after the destination of the money she had given to Bernard Belot.

This was the last Béatrice saw of Pierre Clergue for a while. In about 1303 (or 1302?) Ava, who was named after her aunt, was born. Since Béatrice was always having sex, it is probable that she was doing so with her new husband and that Ava was the offspring of this union. Her sister Philippa followed in 1305, since the two girls were said to be between six and seven and four and five in 1310 (FR, f.36v). The consolidated evidence suggests that Philippa was the younger of the two and therefore the youngest of Béatrice's children. Both Ava and Philippa appear to have been Othon's children, although there is an outside chance that Pierre Clergue was the father of Ava. It is not likely that he would have had the luxury time-wise to use contraception in the cellar in Dalou. Nor was there the same need for it, since any pregnancy could now be attributed to the hapless husband.

Did Béatrice consent to more sex with Clergue simply to reward him for a choice present? We will never know, but there can be little doubt that he cared about her and that she enjoyed sex with him. But while Clergue was drawn increasingly into the political storm that was brewing in Montaillou, Béatrice was concentrating on bringing two more daughters into the world and rearing them. Her recorded life now reassumed a familiar domesticity.

Thus in 1305 we find her visiting her sister Gentille, who was married in Limoux to one Paga den Post, in the very year when two Perfects were arrested in that same city in September. Although they escaped, Limoux would have been buzzing with the news, as well as the worrisome realization that the Authiés' luck and support was not fail-safe.

Modern Limoux is a buoyant small city, with cafés, bookshops, traiteurs and pâtissiers to rival Carcassonne. At the eastern edge of the main square sits the old town church of Saint-Martin, with its crescent-shaped romanesque apse backing on to the Aude. On the fringe of Limoux, under a mile from the town centre and on a plateau, rises the imposing and august pilgrimage church of Notre-Dame-de-Marceille. The romanesque choir chapel of the north transept is a place of pilgrimage to this day, and here there stands a famous madonna-with-baby carved from eleventh- or twelfth-century wood, an object of worship since the Middle Ages. It was here when Béatrice came to confession, although we know that she did *not* confess to heretical activities. By paying a conspicuous visit to Notre-Dame-de-Marceille with her sister, and probably with plenty of witnesses to hand, her 'confession' was most likely a gesture intended to deflect suspicion at a time of crisis.

If this was indeed her intention, she rather defeated its long-term purpose by unguarded swipes at the Host two or three years later in Dalou. At the time, in about 1307–8, she was not called to account, perhaps because her husband Othon was locally too powerful for his wife to be challenged.

Her offences were, however, reported to Guillaume de Montaut, the rector of Dalou, by two different witnesses, one of whom was Othon's niece Mabille Vacquié. She had berated Béatrice for not attending church and for saying, 'Do you really believe that what the priests hold up at the altar is the body of Christ? Believe me, even if the Lord's body were as huge as the mountain over there, it would already have been eaten by the priests.' She pointed at the hill of Margail not far behind her mansion in Dalou to emphasize her point about the manifest absurdity of the Catholic belief in transubstantiation. She repeated this archetypal Cathar offence in front of another witness, thus laying herself open twelve years later to a corroborated hostile testimony against her.

In the meantime she continued her life in her grand house with her daughters. When we next encounter her, the spiritual aspirations of the Sabartès lay in tatters, and its former châtelaine was very ill.

3. Exodus to Lombardy: 1296

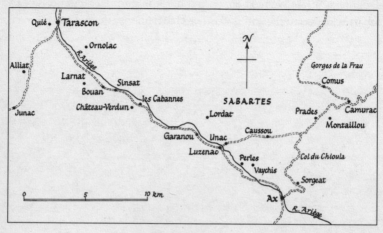

The Authiés' way

In the early 1290s, the Authiés of Ax were at the apogee of their reputation. Twenty years earlier Pierre and Guillaume Authié, and their brother-in-law Guillaume de Rodes, had come to the rescue of Roger-Bernard III, Count of Foix, in the course of the territorial disputes which turned him into a vassal of France.* Since then the firm had done the state further service by virtue of their high standing in the Ariégeois legal community. Why then would this highly respectable and rich family take the plunge into heresy, since they can have entertained no illusions about the consequences of such an action?

The farmers, shepherds, and the poor of the Sabartesian countryside may not always have appreciated fully that the long arm of the Inqui-

---

* It was the Authiés who in 1272 conducted the protracted negotiations over the conflicting claims of France and Aragón regarding the castles of the Sabartès, trying to assert the rights over them of Jacques I of Aragón, to whom Roger-Bernard had pre-emptively made over his properties, in case his defiance of France should fail, as it did (Pailhès 1996, 47, 73).

sition was able to smoke out heresy even from the deepest recesses of the mountains. The Authiés, on the other hand, knew that they were about to defy the most powerful institution of their time, and one that was not confined by national boundaries. Nor was its grip exclusively, or even primarily, political. Rather, the Church was seen above all as oppressing the human spirit in the interest of its own mercenary end, and its benign posturing fooled no one. By rising up against the Church, the rich and successful Authiés of Ax exhibited a degree of *contemptus mundi* that inspired an intense loyalty among their followers from all classes. They may also have been true to a family tradition, since in the 1230s there was already a father-and-son team of Perfects in Ax called Pierre and Raymond Authié respectively (D 24, ff.268–9).*

By the time of his capture Pierre Authié is repeatedly described as an old man (*senex*) in Limborch; he seems to have been in his mid- to late sixties then. He had another brother apart from Guillaume, and this sibling, Raymond, who was probably the second eldest, seemingly showed no taste for becoming a Perfect. Like his brothers he seems to have been a notary, because he refers to pleading a case at the royal court in Carcassonne (d'AR, f.11r). There was also a sister who was called Raymonde, and she lived in Tarascon where she was married to a minor noble, Guillaume de Rodes the elder of Tarascon. They had several children, and it was Raymonde who at Tarascon raised Guillemette, Pierre Authié's second illegitimate child from his mistress; eventually Guillemette married the tailor Guillaume Carramat of Tarascon, and thus further consolidated her father's foothold in that city. Raymonde de Rodes, her children and her brother Raymond from Ax all played important roles in the events that were about to be triggered by their two brothers Pierre and Guillaume.

* It is unlikely that this earlier Raymond Authié was the father of the Authiés who left in the 1290s. He would have had to give up his calling in order to marry and to have children, which is improbable in the years leading up to Montségur, when 'heretical' attitudes were hardening. It is more likely that the Authié family of the 1290s were collateral relatives of Raymond Authié, that is, our Authiés were probably the children of a brother of the Perfect Raymond Authié, so that the father of Pierre, Guillaume and their siblings was himself born during the second decade of the thirteenth century. This Authié Senior from Ax would have been a direct contemporary of the holocaust of Montségur and the fall of Quéribus, and may have instilled

Pierre Authié was married to a woman called Alazais, and he had at least seven children with her.* One of them, Guillemette Authié, married a wealthy doctor and notary by the name of Arnaud Teisseyre from Lordat, some twelve miles west of Ax (Pl. 9). Their alliance was to produce a significant link in the chain of communications that would eventually be forged throughout the region. It did not, however, bring happiness to Guillemette herself.

Equally important is the fact that one of Pierre's sons, Jacques, who was born around 1281–2, would follow his father's calling and become a Perfect, probably the youngest as well as the most eloquent preacher in the Cathar Languedoc; and perhaps the boldest, because on one occasion Jacques was to preach at night in the lion's den, in the church of Sainte-Croix in Toulouse (L, 159).

But in addition to his wife Pierre Authié had a mistress, a widow called Monète Rouzy, who was the sister of a fellow solicitor in Ax.† With her he had two more children, a son who was affectionately and invariably called 'le Bon Guilhem', and another daughter by the name of Guillemette (FR, f.161r).

Pierre Authié embarked on his Cathar odyssey at an advanced age, and his health did not always stand up to the rigours of the life of a Perfect in the Pyrenees. When in true Cathar tradition he became '*l'Ancien*' (that is, a kind of high priest) among the Perfects, his years as well as his status were thereby acknowledged (L, 37, 81). His domestic sacrifices were of a lesser order than they would have been for a younger man. With nine children, all of them grown-up, Pierre was arguably free to leave and find salvation.

This was not the case with his brother Guillaume. In the extant documents, it is in 1284 that Guillaume first appears as a witness, and therefore perhaps as junior partner, in the Authié firm, and the signs

---

that history into his children, whose names Pierre and Raymond may have been traditional names in their family.

* Their names were Jean, Arnaud, Montane, Jacques, Mathende, Gaillarde and Guillemette.

† She is described in the documents as his *druda*, which, if it is Latin, translates as 'intimate counsellor' (N) or 'mistress' (DuCange 1840); the Occitan phrase '*drudarié*' is glossed in *LT* as '*cajolerie, caresses d'amour*'.

are that he was considerably younger than Pierre. He may have been born as late as 1260.

We have already noted that he danced at the wedding of the beguiling châtelaine. Guillaume Authié was famed for his refined manners, and for his sense of fun; his laughter was infectious, and almost anything could set it off. There was a story he told about how some time before he became ordained he was at the fair in Pamiers with a fellow believer. This *credens* spoke apart to Bertrand de Taix, a well-known local Cathar. When de Taix noticed Guillaume standing close by, he asked, referring to Guillaume, 'Isn't that one the devil?' When Guillaume told this story he joked about it and laughed. The fact that it involved Bertrand de Taix probably contributed to his mirth, for, as we shall see, de Taix's real-life experience of the opposite sex could have been penned by Plautus or Molière.

Within a year of the Authiés' return to Ax as Cathar Perfects, Alazaïs Azéma asked Raymonde de Luzenac, Béatrice's sparring partner from Unac, how it came

... that Guillaume has now thus left his wife and children, and all his goods, when he had a beautiful wife and children with her, and given that he was rich and greatly loved to have fun? and now he is hiding and does not dare move about openly. (FR, f.59v)

Raymonde Testanière similarly reported hearing Guillaume commended by the Belots of Montaillou for being an expert dancer who knew how to enjoy himself (FR, f.94r). Guillaume Authié's contemporaries were impressed, and even baffled, by the scale of the contrast between his present and his past existences. Such questions were rarely, it seems, asked about his elder brother.

At Sybille Baille's in Ax one day the question was put to Guillaume himself. When he was asked why he was now solitary when previously he had been in the habit of being full of fun, Guillaume simply replied that 'those were different times, and these are different again', '*aliud tempus erat illud et aliud istud*'(FR, f.117r).

What these new times of Guillaume Authié's apostolate were like was succinctly summed up by Raymonde de Luzenac when she remarked that Guillaume had left the world and was keeping to the road of God:

... he no longer eats meat, animal fat, eggs, cheese, milk, and in a year he
keeps three Lents. In each week he fasts for three days on bread and water,
and lives a life of integrity, because he does not touch women and he does
not lie; nor does he kill anything that lives, and he suffers many persecutions
because of God. He has the power to save souls with God, just like the
apostles, by saying the words that Christ spoke to his Disciples. It would be a
great sin for anyone to do bad to Guillaume Authié. (FR, f.59v)

The path to heaven was ever steep and thorny, and not just for the
individual who chose to tread it. What Raymonde failed to mention
were the penalties exacted from the families of Perfects. The Inquisition
knew that for any underground movement to function effectively in
this kind of society, its leaders would, sooner rather than later, and
inevitably, have to fall back on their extended families. At the precise
moment that contact was made between Perfects and their relatives,
their freedoms were forfeit, since all such contact was censurable. It is
not surprising that the entire Authié clan, with their wives and children,
not excluding Pierre Authié's ageing wife Alazaïs, were incarcerated
by the Inquisitors, although not, it seems, for life. In reality, however,
even shortish terms could spell death, since the gaols of thirteenth-
century Languedoc were harsh and insalubrious places. Crossing the
line to ordination inevitably imperilled one's entire family.

As we have seen, the Authiés' connection with Montaillou ran
through Guillaume Authié's wife, Gaillarde, whose mother was a
Savignan from Prades, and thus assured the Authiés of a foothold there
as well. Gaillarde later played a prominent part in the consolation of
her grandfather Arnaud Savignan.

Guillaume may have been in his early thirties at the start of the 1290s,
and Gaillarde was young enough to bear him two male children then.
These boys, who were named Pierre and Arnaud after their uncle and
cousin, may have been the latest arrivals rather than the only ones,
although no mention is ever made of other, older children by the couple.

Throughout the nine years of his mission Guillaume kept closely in
touch with his wife. Although they could no longer be lovers and were
in fact divorced in the eyes of the Cathar church, the bond between
them remained deep. He could never altogether wrench himself free
from either his children or his wife, and on one particular occasion,

sitting opposite each other on two benches in a loft-bedroom in Ax, he and Gaillarde were seen discussing their young sons (FR, f.188).

Their children would eventually be spirited to the relative safety of Catalonia after the crackdown of 1308–9, but Gaillarde herself appeared before the Carcassonne Inquisition, and she was probably gaoled there. No one in the region could have foreseen that Fournier would try to tear its heart out again after so much suffering.

Guillaume Authié was the most glamorous Perfect of the Authié renaissance, and the one who was deemed to have paid the highest price for his precariously privileged position. He seems to have become the 'best' people's Perfect, with some extraordinary consolations to his credit. Guillaume's elegance of mind is distilled in the Montaignian stylishness of his succinct response about time present and time past, and his courage, humanity and resilience will become increasingly evident as this narrative unfolds.

The story of the Authiés' conversion was widely known in the region. The details of it resonate with Augustinian and Pauline echoes and may render it generic, and therefore bogus, as far as the literal facts are concerned. Nevertheless, the importance of a book, or *the* book in it, may contain more than just a grain of authenticity, since books are of paramount importance in this narrative.

According to Sybille Peyre's deposition, which is as distinguished as Pierre Maury's by its minute recall of Authié sermons and of details of incidental conversations from the early years of the fourteenth century, Pierre Authié was one day reading a book in his brother Guillaume's presence. He told him what he had found in the book. Guillaume then in turn briefly studied the text, and when Pierre asked him what he thought, Guillaume replied, 'It seems to me that we have lost our souls.' Then Pierre said, 'Let us go therefore, brother, and look for the salvation of our souls.' And, so the story went, they abandoned everything and left for Lombardy, where they became 'good Christians'. The book would almost certainly have been St John's Gospel.

The intensity of the Authiés' spiritual passion cannot be in doubt, although their integrity was questioned shamefully, in a moment of dejection, by a fellow Perfect who envied them their class and learning (see below, page 147). The Church's ham-fisted attempts to blacken

the moral character of the Perfects by implying, among others, that
their travelling in pairs, each with a *socius* (i.e. companion) suggested
sexual deviancy, fell on deaf ears among the people (Oldenbourg 1998,
62). They knew that the Perfects walked thus in honour of Christ's
Disciples, who had done likewise.

It is precisely the Authiés' unquestioned idealism which may shed
new light on something that has long cast an awkward shadow over
Pierre Authié's decision to flee in 1296, the business of his debt to a
nobleman from Ax called Simon Barre. Rather than turning his flight
to Lombardy into a rejection of the material world, the undischarged
debt to Barre made it look like an escape from a powerful creditor.

Simon Barre was the hereditary châtelain of Ax and Mérens who,
however, lived in an ordinary house in Ax and slept in a bedroom close
to the front door.* This might mistakenly suggest a rather domestic
and small-scale character, but Barre was no more so than the Clergues
of Montaillou. His real power was probably wielded through money-
lending, since at least two of the characters in this story may have been
insolvent debtors of his. There can be little doubt that Simon Barre was
feared, and when his *bayle*, Arnaud de Sobrenia from Tignac, drowned it
was widely rumoured that Simon Barre had had him silenced so that
he could not betray his master's heretical secrets (FR, f.52r). Like the
Clergues of Montaillou, the Barres of Ax were two-timing the Inquisition with impunity. When the Inquisitor from Carcassonne came to
take depositions in Ax, it was at the house of another Barre, Arnaud, that
they stayed, unaware of the fact that the Barres were themselves Cathar.†

* Through the marriage of another Axian Barre, Raymond, to Raymonde de Junac, a
Cathar aristocrat from the Larnat–Junac–Tarascon triangle, the Barres came into contact
with the powerful Bayards, who were also friends of the de Junacs.
† It may not be a coincidence that a notorious murder in Ax of 1319–20 involved
yet a further Barre, Valentine Barre, this time as a victim (FR, ff.23r, 24r). It happened
in the cemetery of the 'old town', where today the road starts its climb of the Chioula
towards Prades and Montaillou.
   In the longer term the Barre family returned to the fold in time to deflect the
Inquisition's onslaught, although Simon did not escape gaol. Within a generation of
the d'Ablis visit, the Barres had hugely enhanced their local grip on power by a
well-timed contribution to the Fuxian (i.e. of Foix) treasury in the war against England
(Moulis 1970, 127).

Barre was prepared to threaten, and probably exact, the death penalty from his debt defaulters, as in the case of Pierre de Gaillac Senior, a fellow nobleman and the father of an unscrupulous young lawyer of the same name. But as the younger de Gaillac knew, Barre was vulnerable to charges of heresy, and if the clerical climate hardened in an orthodox direction, then Barre, and many others like him, could be hurt by those far less powerful than themselves.

The Barres may have shared with the Authiés the distinction of being the first family of thirteenth-century Ax. In the 1230s the two families' ancestors had been involved together in the Cathar movement, and Bertrand Marty, Pierre and Raymond Authié, and Guillaume Barre, the *bayle* then of Ax, had all met at the Authiés' house (D 24, f.268r). As a fellow Axian, Pierre Authié would have been well aware of this common past history, and it is moreover likely that the Authiés were more than once contracted by the Barres on legal business.

The official version of Pierre Authié's debt, and perhaps the true one, was given by Pons Cog of Tarascon, who seems to have been a hired thug and enforcer for Simon Barre; the fact that he could read and write does not necessarily argue against his being a menial. Cog had been instructed to render to Pierre Authié his promissory notes on settlement of his debt. This would simultaneously release Arnaud Carot from his obligation, because Carot, a Cathar faithful from Ax, had stood security for sixty 'shillings'.

This sum can only have been a fraction of what Pierre Authié owed to Barre, since his debt was commonly thought to have been substantial, not least by Arnaud Teisseyre. Although sixty shillings is not negligible, it was the sale price in the Tarascon area of five lambs. A herd of twenty sheep and five lambs, for example, fetched sixteen pounds, or 320 shillings in the money of account of the period, over five times Pierre Authié's debt. Even allowing for the fact that the sale of a flock of twenty-five sheep included no less than ten pounds for wool, as in Arnaud Marty's contemporary sale of just such a herd, the fact remains that the rich solicitor from Ax must have owed vastly more than the security tendered by Arnaud Carot (FR, f.281r). His intention to part with his entire herd of cows may indicate that his debt was in excess of twenty pounds.

The anticipated date for this transaction was Saturday 29 September

1296, the three-day-long fair of St Michael at Tarascon. Pierre Authié
had assembled his entire herd of cows in the market at Tarascon and
intended to sell them all, at an auction presumably, on the third and
(probably) last day of the fair, on Monday 1 October. The deal was that
from the proceeds he would settle with Barre the day after the sale, but
on the Tuesday Cog was stalled by Pierre, who told him that he would
pay up the following day.

   That same Tuesday night Pons Cog was out on two different patrol
errands. The first one took him and three other vigilantes south of
Tarascon to Axiat. On returning into Tarascon at midnight they nar-
rowly escaped being arrested by the town's *bayle* near the Ariège bridge,
perhaps for breaking the curfew. Cog's second call that night was to
take him into the upper part of the city to a place called *al pech*, to
inspect a barn with hay in it which belonged to another Cog, Bernard.
To dodge a second meeting with the *bayle*, the four men walked up a
track called 'the street of the gardens of St Michael'.

   When they were half-way there they saw, in the full moon, two
men leaning against a garden fence, looking towards Tarascon. Seeing
that they were not armed, Cog asked them to identify themselves.
Pierre Authié and his son-in-law Arnaud Teisseyre of Lordat turned
round towards him and told him who they were. Cog recognized them
in the moonlight. It was now gone midnight and early in the morning.
To Cog's question about what they were doing out at this hour,
Pierre replied that they had dined late and did not want to suffer
any after-effects from dinner; hence this fresh-air constitutional. Cog
invited them to sleep at Bernard Cog's that night; perhaps he was
concerned about Simon Barre's money, and deemed it to be safer to
have Pierre Authié to hand. But the two men declined, explaining that
they had beds waiting for them elsewhere.

   What did Pierre Authié and Arnaud Teisseyre talk of as they stood
in the early hours of, probably, Wednesday 3 October 1296, looking
towards Tarascon, a blacked-out medieval city on a river, illuminated
only by the eerie sheen of the full moon, and surrounded by an
immutable and majestic panorama of high mountains, which still bear
the traces of prehistoric habitation?

   This was a momentous occasion. Pierre had sold his entire herd two
days earlier, and the money would fund his and his brother's time

abroad. The approximate cost of the journey to Lombardy from the Toulousain was in the area of fifteen shillings.* By comparison the cost of a round-trip from Montaillou to Carcassonne was one shilling. For Pierre Authié the die was cast, and after the morrow there would be no going back; if on the Wednesday morning Pierre Authié disappeared from view, his life would change for ever. Even his brave heart must have felt some trepidation as he stood in the street-of-the-gardens on his last night before starting the 'midnight run'. And at the end of his journey death by fire was almost certainly awaiting him. Although some of their followers pretended to believe that God took away the Perfects' pain during those terrible final moments, because they suffocated before the flames reached them, Pierre Authié preached the contrary. Unlike their adversaries' founding father, Dominic de Guzman, the Cathar Perfects were rarely heard yearning for martyrdom.

Were Pierre and Arnaud discussing the practicalities of setting up a resistance network in the region when they were encountered by Pons Cog? Did they have a hand, for example, in securing the post of rector of Montaillou for a member of the Clergue family? Was the young Pierre Clergue a friend of Guillaume Authié's already then, or did that come later? How friendly were the Authiés with the Clergues, and had they cultivated the rural clergy as part of a long-term strategy? Was the fact that Pierre Authié's nephew was himself a Dominican at Pamiers, up-river from Tarascon, significant? Why was it that a mere four years from this night the Authiés were welcomed back to the Sabartès by hundreds, if not thousands, of people ready to risk everything for them?

We shall never know whether or not Pierre Authié's debt with Simon Barre was real, or whether Carot somehow managed to pay it on Pierre Authié's behalf with the help of other Axian members of the rich Authié family. While Pierre Authié immediately settled with Arnaud Carot on his return in 1300, through the intermediary of his brother in Raymond Authié's cellar in Ax, there is no record of him dealing in this manner with Barre. Is that because the Authiés' house was ceded to him? On the Authiés' return Barre and the new Perfects traded gifts, and Barre uncapped himself in the presence of the Authié

---

* At least that was the sum that Martin Francès was paid for taking Amiel de Perles back to Lombardy to be sanctified afresh by *l'Ancien* Bernard Audoyn (L, 68).

Perfects. His own wife Sicarde became so passionate about Catharism
that she nearly eloped to Lombardy with a fellow believer.

As much as the charisma of the Good Men, it may have been Barre's
philandering that caused this particular Ariégeoise to want to elope.
Simon Barre found in Catharism a sexual haven, not to say heaven.
Like Pierre Clergue, he had discovered erotic bliss in the conquest of
two sisters, Saurmonde and Grazide Tourte from Ax; and indeed, the
Jacqueline den Tourte from Ax with whom Clergue had sex in the
hospital there may have been a third sister. This form of incest, as
understood by the Bible, became a particular Cathar obsession, as we
have already seen in the case of the châtelaine and Clergue.

Barre was one day boastfully regaling two of his cronies with this
when they were staying at Grazide Tourte's, noting that sleeping
with women other than one's spouse was not a sin. One of his two
interlocutors was the violent Raymond Vaissière, a Cathar recidivist
who became a supergrass for the Inquisition to save his skin. The other
one was Pathau Clergue from Montaillou, who is not recorded as
contributing anything to this men's talk. He did not need to; he was a
rapist, and any woman, including a châtelaine, was fair game for him.
He did not require the dubious sophistications of Cathar doctrine as an
excuse.

It might be wise to keep an open mind about the true nature and
purpose of Pierre Authié's debt. That it was real cannot easily be
doubted. At the same time it could have been part of an elaborate
charade to dupe the ever-vigilant Inquisition, whose ears were everywhere. It may have been a perfectly natural thing for Pierre Authié to
be selling up to become solvent again; it was quite another for him to
sell everything for no obvious reason. The 'debt' to Barre may have
ensured that the search for the Authiés did not develop immediately
into an international, or at least boundary-crossing, ecclesiastical affair.
By the time the Inquisitors at Carcassonne or the Dominicans at Pamiers
realized that the Authiés had turned out to be heretics, they were
probably beyond their reach, at least temporarily.

A month before he left the Sabartès, some time in late August or
September 1296, Pierre Authié was in Lordat tending his son-in-law

Arnaud Teisseyre. Like the wealthier houses of the period, Arnaud Teisseyre's boasted a hall (*aula*) with rooms off it, as well as a study (*scriptorium*), which had a window giving on to the street. Behind Arnaud's house there was an orchard, and it was here that Michel Cerdan of Lordat one summer night, just before dawn and during full moon, at the height of the Authiés' activities, spotted two men who were holding up a map as if they were trying to read it by the light of the moon (FR, f.158r).

Relations between Arnaud and his father-in-law were said to be strained at times, because Arnaud mistreated his wife Guillemette. Arnaud himself alludes to this in his testimony, as does Pierre de Gaillac, who became his clerk. But now, in 1296, Arnaud was very sick, and for three days his life hung by a thread. Pierre Authié and the *bayle* of Lordat and Château-Verdun, Pierre-Arnaud of Capoulet, a retainer of the Lady Stéphanie, drew a *cordon sanitaire* around Arnaud; if he were to die, they wanted to be at hand to find him a Perfect so that he could be received into the Cathar faith.

It was (probably) shortly afterwards that Pierre Bela, the rector of the Pech of Lordat, paid a visit to Arnaud. In a scene that might centuries later have come straight out of *Oliver Twist*, he peered through a casement window into Arnaud's study, and there he spotted Pierre Authié who sat away from the window, behind Arnaud. By then Arnaud seemed to have recovered his faculties enough to be startled by Bela's sudden appearance and to demand to know whether there was anything Bela wanted. Bela subsequently claimed that he was so taken aback by the sight of Pierre Authié that he replied 'No', and left. Later Bela remembered confusedly that this took place 'three days' after Pierre Authié was commonly thought to have fled Ax due to debts, or leprosy, or heresy (FR, f.158r).

Arnaud Teisseyre recovered, and it was probably on or around Thursday 4 October 1296, the day after the encounter with Cog in Tarascon, that the Authiés left the Sabartès for Lombardy, accompanied by one Pierre de na Sclana and Bon Guilhem. Before leaving, Pierre entrusted his son-in-law with a book for safe-keeping. It was bound with linen cloth, measured about 'the length of the palm of a hand', or approximately eight inches, and was three to four inches thick. To judge by its thickness this was a substantial tome, and was therefore probably the Gospels bound together with the Epistles of St Peter and St Paul. After their return the Authiés would treat the lending of Cathar Gospels as a tribal gesture of friendship and esteem.

When it was publicly announced in Ax by Simon Barre that a defaulting Pierre Authié had absconded, his house became a debtor's forfeited property and was seized by the Count of Foix. For the time being, it seems, the Authiés' departure remained a strictly secular and local affair, involving Roger-Bernard III and his faithful counsellor of old, Pierre Authié. As we shall see, the Count, as well as his deputy, kept faith with the old Perfect, and the favour was almost certainly repaid in full. The public confiscation of the Authié home may have been in settlement of the debt owed by Pierre to Barre; or else Barre was keeping the house in trust for the wider Cathar church. It is worth noting that the Authié house is never again mentioned after this. Instead, a set of safe houses with some ingenious hideaways would become the new homes of the Authiés.

At the time that Pierre Authié departed for Lombardy, his son Jacques lived in the castle of Castellbó in the diocese of Urgell, as the guest of its châtelain, Arnaud del Pech. After his father's departure, Jacques Authié returned to Ax. He stayed there for about two months, but rumour locally had it that he would follow his father to Lombardy, and indeed he vanished and went underground to start the life of a fugitive shortly after.*

Pierre Authié's daughter Mathende and her husband Pierre-Eugène both joined the aspiring Perfect on their way to Lombardy (L, 221). Also, the intensely active Guillaume Falquet of Verdun (Ariège) assured a constant traffic of letters and messages between the Ariège and Lom-

---

* It is likely that during the four years of his father's and uncle's absence Jacques stayed at Arnaud Teisseyre's from time to time. If he did become a 'sleeper' in the Cold War sense of the word, his task would have been to help coordinate an infrastructure in the Ariège ready for the Authiés' eventual return. Although he himself was young, older and more experienced heads, some undoubtedly from his own family, lent a helping hand. We may be fairly certain that Stéphanie de Château-Verdun was kept posted of the new Perfects' progress through her *bayle*, and that Prades Tavernier, and indeed the local aristocracy, worked hard at preparing the ground for their coming back.

bardy both during the Authiés' absence and after their return. On his fourth trip to Lombardy, Falquet pushed on all the way from Lombardy to Sicily, taking two Perfects there, one of whom was Pons Baille, the son of Sybille Baille (L, 13).*

The Authiés had a choice of two routes to cross into Lombardy (Nelli 1969, 264–5). They could either go via Nice and then journey up across the Col de Tende, which is thirty miles north of Menton and Ventimiglia, or they could approach it by crossing the Col de Larche in the Alpes-de-Haute-Provence. Both were regularly used, and on these *cols* Perfects and faithful alike hoped to escape the agents of the Inquisition as they blended in with the many pedlars, merchants, shepherds, pilgrims and others who regularly flowed across these mountains. From the mountains they proceeded to Cuneo, which lay at the gates of Lombardy and had been the regional capital of emigrant Occitan Catharism since 1250 (Duvernoy 1965, 1.269n.107). Here they sojourned for two months, while Pons-Arnaud of Château-Verdun stayed in a nearby city. It was at Cuneo that Pierre and Guillaume were ordained Cathar Perfects (d'AR, f.10r).

A year later, it seems, Bon Guilhem returned on a reconnaissance mission to the Sabartès. He visited his brother-in-law Pierre Argen of Ax, and then, together with him, Raymond Authié. He arrived at Arnaud Teisseyre's in Lordat on or around St Martin's day, which fell on Monday 11 November 1297. He stayed with Arnaud, and here he probably made contact with his half-brother Jacques. The exciting news was that Pierre and Guillaume Authié had become ordained abroad, and that they were keen to come back, if they could be safe.

* Like Lombardy, Sicily harboured its share of exiled Cathars, at least since 1282, when the Angevines and the French barons, who were allies of the papacy, were expelled during the Sicilian Vespers, and Pedro III of Aragón took over the reins of the troubled island.

4. The Last Perfects' Return: 1299–1300

The Tarascon triangle

The return of the Authiés to the Sabartès was gradual and involved two separate, but simultaneous, operations with different personnel. The first one was headed by Pierre Authié himself and led to Toulouse, from where the Authiés proceeded to Ax (FR, f.55r); the second one, under Guillaume Authié, was intended to secure Tarascon and its region.

The Authiés must have hoped that the biggest city in Occitania, with some 35,000 inhabitants, would guarantee them a degree of anonymity; and it was close enough to the Sabartès for them to run messengers backwards and forwards through the Ariège valley, and particularly to Tarascon and Ax. Moreover, Pierre Authié's daughter Gaillarde lived in Toulouse, where she was married to Raymond Sartre from Sorèze, and this provided an extra incentive (L, 68; d'AR, f.62v). It seems that the Authiés usually stayed in the house of one Gentille in the suburb of Saint-Cyprien, across the Garonne from the main city (L, 69).

An additional reason for Pierre and Guillaume Authié to stop over in Toulouse was to open a credit line at the counters of a well-known firm of Toulousain money-changers, the Ysalguiers, probably Raymond Ysalguier, who is recorded in 1295 as being both money-changer or banker and consul (L, 183).* The Authiés were practically minded businessmen, and may even have had dealings in the past with the Ysalguiers. The spiritual insurgency needed funds, and these had to be readily accessible in different places. While the Authiés were securing credit in Toulouse, their treasurer Martin Francès from Limoux in the Aude joined them there. Both he and his wife Montolive were ardent Cathars. The fact that Francès was staying with Pierre Authié in Toulouse at the start of the return suggests that the Cathar spearhead was methodically establishing and consolidating its financial base. According to Jean Maury, reporting the words of the two diaspora Perfects Raymond de Toulouse and Guillaume Bélibaste, the Authiés' war-chest was worth well over 100,000 pounds (!) and was strategically spread over Toulouse, Mirande and Castelsarrasin; and all of it was later left in trust, it was alleged, to the surviving Authiés of Ax (FR, f.217r).

Nobody could have foreseen that, shortly after arriving in Toulouse, Pierre Authié's cover would be blown almost immediately by a chance encounter. During a stroll in Matabiau, near Saint-Sernin and the site of today's railway station of Matabiau, Pierre Authié was passed and recognized by Raymonde de Luzenac's youngest son, Pierre, who was studying the *Decretales* at the city's university.† Pierre Authié knew the young de Luzenac through frequenting his mother, and in 1296, the year of his leaving the Sabartès, he had attempted to convert the then fourteen-year-old boy to the Cathar faith. For a while de Luzenac, like his mother and brothers, was in thrall to Pierre Authié, who in turn

---

* In 1306 this same Ysalguier turned enthusiastic carpetbagger during the expulsion of the Jews by Philippe le Bel. He was charged with the liquidation of their property in Toulouse, and thereby grossed a profit of 75,265 *livres tournois*, a truly enormous sum (Chalande 1919, 420; Ramet 1935, 184).

† The *Decretales* gave a juridical framework to the study of canon law as formulated by Gratian in his standard text-book *Decretum Gratiani* (*c.*1140). Pierre de Luzenac and Pierre de Gaillac were decretalists at Toulouse around the same time. Later these two Ariégeois law students came to know each other well and would play a major role in the unfolding Cathar drama in the Sabartès.

seems to have been fond of this intelligent teenager; he was a promising member of the Ariégeois intelligentsia and a future lawyer who liked books and could be trusted to choose them for the Perfects (see below, page 121).

The day after Matabiau, Pierre Authié's lieutenant Pierre Sans (*Sancius*) searched out Pierre de Luzenac at his lodgings hoping to secure his silence and cooperation through bribes. In de Luzenac's words, 'Throughout that entire winter and spring [of 1299–1300] Pierre Sans frequently came to see me and brought me many food-dainties in the form of capons and lamb' (d'AR, f.62r).* And in the course of the following summer, Pierre de Luzenac recalled later, he ate 'good salmon and trout' at a dinner party during which Pierre Authié asked a lot of probing questions about the situation in their native land. Present at the same dinner were Guillaume Peyre of Limoux, two otherwise unknown Toulousains, Pierre Sans, and Raymond Sartre and his wife Gaillarde, the old Perfect's daughter. Sartre was there because Pierre de Luzenac was sub-letting his lodgings to him that summer of 1300 to raise additional cash, and it was on a return to his living quarters one day that he encountered Pierre Authié in the courtyard, visiting, one imagines, his son-in-law (d'AR, f.62v).

It seems as if the Perfects understood that the best way to retain de Luzenac's loyalty was through buying it. Although in general loyalty, and indeed money, were freely given to the Perfects, sometimes with staggering generosity, in this case the tables were turned. They were dealing with a feckless young man who was perennially in debt while studying in Toulouse, perhaps because he gambled. He owed over ten pounds by the time he met the Authiés, and they appear to have bailed him out. But his debts were mounting, and from now on Pierre de Luzenac constantly borrowed from the Authiés. He continued to do so even when they were safely entrenched in their fiefdom of the upper Ariège. When his family could no longer afford to keep both him and his brother as students at the same time, Pierre abandoned his studies

* Although Pierre de Luzenac's deposition of 28 November 1308 is muddled about the dates of his first encounter with Pierre Authié, his recall of the seasons and his placing of the Michaelmas school-term in the narrative sequence strongly argue in favour of 1299 as the date of this encounter. So does the fact that Pierre Authié had not yet been back in the Sabartès when he met de Luzenac.

and proceeded to practise at the bar of the Count of Foix as well as at the court of the King.

By exploiting de Luzenac's insolvency the Perfects also controlled him; on the other hand, they would have been alert to the fact that he might secure better terms in the form of blood money by stepping into the Dominicans' monastery not very far from Matabiau and offering them the new Perfects. Why the Authiés kept in with him we cannot now determine, and hindsight rarely provides a fair perspective. Perhaps they ought to have known better than to trust a profligate youth, but they clearly thought that he could be a useful ally, particularly when it came to pleading cases in law, as when they asked him to help out with Pierre de Mérens, who stood accused of a crime at the court of the Count of Foix (d'AR, f.66r). We shall never know whether his was above all a hired affection, and whether he did in the end sell his friends for a price. He himself later asserted that he dared not break with them because of the monies he owed them. The fact remains, however, that by the time the Inquisitor Bernard Gui proclaimed the capture of Pierre Authié as the foremost goal of the Catholic church in Languedoc in August 1309 (see below, pages 237–41), the price on *l'Ancien*'s head must have tempted the weaker and more venal among his followers. By betraying his friends, Pierre de Luzenac stood to gain money as well as some remission for his mingling with the heretics.

While Pierre Authié was organizing the movement's finances in Tou-louse, Guillaume Authié and Pierre-Raymond de Saint-Papoul were busy preparing the ground at Junac and Larnat near Tarascon. From All Saints 1299 until the spring of 1300 they stayed at the Martys of Junac, their operational base, as well as at Quié, Larnat and, probably, other places. The Martys were the family of the local blacksmith, and they would provide a Perfect in the person of Arnaud, and a *passeur* in the always awkward Bernard.

Their home village of Junac lies five miles south-west of Tarascon, and some six miles west of Larnat across the Col de Larnat. Junac and Larnat, and beyond Larnat the hamlet of Bouan, form the base of a topographical triangle, with Tarascon as its apex. The west-to-east base-line connects the Vicdessos and Ariège valleys (in the thirteenth century they were both Ariège valleys), which provided escape routes from the County of Foix into Catalonia and the kingdom of Aragón. The rugged terrain around Larnat particularly offered a safe haven from persecution, as it could only be reached up the precipitous *côte* from Bouan, or from the top of the Col de Larnat itself. Not long after Guillaume Authié and Pierre-Raymond de Saint-Papoul had settled into the dovecote of the Martys' that winter, Arnaud Marty's younger brother Bernard returned home. He had fallen ill with a fever while working as a shepherd for Guillaume-Arnaud de Castel, the châtelain of Rabat, which is about five miles north of Junac. He had joined de Castel's service because of alleged disagreements with his father and brothers.*

When his sickness worsened, Bernard Marty was set up on a bed in the *foghana*. He was not expected to live, and his brother urged him to be received into the Cathar faith. It was Guillaume Authié who conferred the *consolamentum* on Bernard. The latter later claimed that he knew Guillaume Authié and de Saint-Papoul to be Good Men, but that until that moment he did not know their names, even though he had watched them coming and going at his father's.

The *endura* started, and for three days Bernard survived on nothing but water. But then he rallied and became very hungry. He demanded to eat, which would inevitably render the consolation void. Eventually his brother Arnaud yielded to Bernard's entreaties in disgust and instructed his sister to feed him meat. The fast of the *endura* probably saved Bernard's life by starving the fever.† Arnaud, the future Perfect, was mortified by the weakness of his brother's flesh, and when he had recovered asked him whether he wanted his soul to be saved or not. Bernard elected to be saved, and was then taken into his father's dovecote for the *convenenza*, that is the formal 'contracting' of his soul to the Cathar cause.

---

* In his sly deposition Bernard portrays himself as an insignificant and reluctant cog in the Cathar machine. But this same Candide had successfully tricked the d'Ablis Inquisition into leaving him alone while they summoned every other member of his surviving family, including his two sisters. Years later he mustered the resourcefulness of a Telemachus while wandering through Languedoc in search of his sisters, both of whom eluded d'Ablis *and* Fournier.

† When shortly afterwards Bernard returned to the castle of Rabat, he learnt that his employers' three sons were dying. This seems to have been a severe case of winter flu

Here sat Guillaume Authié and Pierre-Raymond de Saint-Papoul.*
Bernard knelt before the Perfects, but he forgot to remove his cap. His
brother snatched it away and flung it to the ground, from where
Guillaume Authié picked it up and threw it so that it landed on a *palum*,
a stay for coats. The two Perfects laughed heartily at this, which puzzled
Bernard. But almost anything could trigger Guillaume Authié's famous
bursts of laughter, and he may have enjoyed hurling things since he
once challenged a companion to a stone-throwing contest on the
Ariège (FR, f.139r). In the dovecote at Junac his aim had clearly been
felicitous, and it was probably this which provoked his mirth.

The Marty estate where the Perfects were hiding sat up the slope on
the south-western edge of Junac, not far from the castle towards which
the main door of the estate opened. The church stood at some distance
in the valley towards Alliat and Tarascon. Bernard Marty describes
how one night his brother Arnaud, the Perfects Pierre-Raymond de
Saint-Papoul and Guillaume Authié, and Pierre Grat, the *bayle* of Junac,
passed under the wall of the castle until they arrived at a basement
window in one of its towers which looked towards the church of Junac.
Today the sole remains of the de Junacs' castle are the overgrown ruins
of a tower in which a roofless chamber has weathered the passage of
the years.

The courtyard with the dovecote of the Martys' house sat on the
massive rocky shelf which overhangs a shallow ravine and remains
plainly visible close to the castle ruins (Pl. 11). The main house was
recessed further back into the hill so that the estate sloped downwards.
This allowed the ever-watchful Bernard to observe everything that was
happening in or near the dovecote; and one night, he records, he
witnessed Guillaume Authié's bowel movement over the edge of the
bauz, an Occitan word which means 'a steep rock with a flat shelf at
the top' (FR, f.276v; gloss in *LT*).

---

rather than a full-blown epidemic. The Black Death had not yet reached Languedoc,
although it was at its doors, but influenza was not unknown.
* Pierre-Raymond de Saint-Papoul is described as *pulcrum* (acc.) in the documents,
which in this case may mean 'noble, illustrious, honourable' (LS); though when the
epithet was applied to young Sanche Mercadier, it is more likely that his good looks
were being described (L, 185; see below, page 237).

The Martys' house commanded a panoramic view of the pastures of *les plas e rosana* near Laburat, a vanished locality that may correspond to the area which is today called Labaure, and of the *valh*, or valley, of the Ariège. Between the house and next to the castle lay an area (it is still there) which was called the *planel* (plateau), and one night Pierre de Luzenac slept here in the open air until almost lunchtime the following day (FR, f.279r).

The Martys' estate sat up from the stone bridge across the Ariège in a fairly straight line, and it consisted of living quarters and a cellar, with a main door facing the castle and a subsidiary one overlooking the courtyard. Under the living quarters was a ground floor, which doubled as a basement where provisions such as nuts and apples were kept.

In the low-walled courtyard rose a number of other buildings, notably a set of stables which was terraced with the dovecote and connected to it by an internal door. There was also a barn for hay and straw, a sheepfold and, at the far end of the courtyard and nearest the precipice, a newly constructed building to accommodate animals. The garden of the Martys faced down south-east towards the *valh*, and verged on the property of their Cathar-friendly neighbour and fellow pathfinder, the *bayle* Pierre Grat.

The forge might have been expected to be the hub of the estate, but it is never referred to, although the charcoal used to power its mills is. We know that the forge stood at some distance from the house, and the obvious place for it was down on the Ariège itself, where it could draw on a plentiful supply of water; on the exact spot, in fact, where several centuries later Cassini marked a 'Forge' on his map.

Pierre Marty's family included his wife Fabrisse, three sons, Arnaud, Guillaume and Bernard, and three daughters, Bonnefemme, Blanche and Raymonde. Both Fabrisse and her daughter Bonnefemme were consoled by Guillaume Authié when they died in quick succession in the winter of 1304, perhaps of the same illness. Although old Marty seems to have been a keen fellow traveller of the Cathars, he oddly disapproved of the depth of his son's involvement in the new faith. Arnaud was heading for ordination, and started a regime of abstinences. He consequently stopped consuming meat, ate apart from the others, and confined his diet to cheese and fish. Above all, he used his father's property as a Perfects' haven. Although he muffled the hinges of the door leading into the dovecote, there was no hiding these nocturnal peregrinations.

Early one morning Bernard had come home from seeing an enthusiastic Cathar called Guillaume Delaire at Quié, and when his father challenged him about his movements, he stalled, undoubtedly in deference to his brother's injunctions. His father was furious, and remonstrated with him: 'You're going bad ways, you and your brother Arnaud, by this circulating at night.'

That evening over dinner, at a time when Arnaud still sat with the family, he and his father clashed spectacularly. Perhaps the old man resented being kept in the dark, but his sons may have done so because he was notoriously indiscreet, or perhaps they did not want to implicate him. So long as he was innocent of direct, and witnessed, dealings with the Cathars, the family's estate, which would all have been in his name, was safe.

Whatever the deeper reasons may have been, the following exchange happened at some point during that evening meal in early 1300:

FATHER: Arnaud, I don't like what you're doing, your comings and
           goings at night.
ARNAUD: Shut up, father, unless you want something bad to happen
           to you one day.
FATHER: You're telling me that?
ARNAUD: If you don't shut up, you will one day find your head
           between your feet. (FR, f.276v)

Old Marty grabbed a salt pestle and hurled it at his son, who lunged for it intending to throw it back at his father. He was restrained by their dinner guest Pierre Talha, who urged him not to assault his own father. Arnaud then threatened his father with retaliation by day or night. In response his father picked up the bench he had been sitting on and threw it at Arnaud swearing, calling him a bastard (i.e. illegitimate), and promising to bring him to perdition. Arnaud was hustled out of the house by his friend Talha, and for a long time afterwards father and son hated each other. Arnaud Marty may have been inspired by Guillaume Authié to follow in his footsteps, even though his temper was probably not best suited to the sacred calling of a Cathar Perfect;

but then, as we shall see, the last Occitan Perfect, who would become the lover of Arnaud's sister, was hardly well equipped for saintliness.

During the months of November and December 1299 Guillaume Authié repeatedly went up to Larnat. On at least two of these recorded hikes across the Col de Larnat he was chaperoned by, among others, Bernard Marty. On each occasion they left in the dark after the cock had crowed three times already, and made it to Larnat before the winter dawn.

During their first walk together down to the Ariège, and after crossing a bridge called Peyrapont, a stone bridge in the same place probably as the present one (if not partly the same stone bridge), they struck out beyond Capoulet towards Miglos where they collected Pierre de Miglos, the husband perhaps already then of the daughter of Guillaume Bayard (see below, page 125). His 'big dog' did not bark after them on this particular occasion, as they moved between Norgeat and Norrat across the *col* and then down to Larnat.

Some 150 yards above Larnat there was a meadow which the Register seems to call *fusan*, and which is marked on the *PN* for Larnat as *Suzan* or *Luzan* (Pl. 10); here the Perfects and their guides tended to stop to decide on which way best to approach the village on any given occasion.

There were at least five solid Cathar families in the village, the Capelles, Catalanes, de Larnats, Issaurats and Gouzys.* The last three, who were linked by marriage ties, would play a pre-eminent role in the Cathar relaunch in the Sabartès.

Approaching the Gouzys' main entrance from the *col* meant crossing the entire village, because their property was located in the lower part of the village towards its entry as it is approached from Bouan (FR,

---

* The Gouzys are probably the same family as the Regouzys, and although Bernard Marty in his 1324 deposition seems to differentiate between them, the Issaurats of Larnat do not in theirs of 1308. There was certainly more than one Gouzy family living here during these events, and I shall proceed on the assumption that Bernard Marty's Pierre Regouzy corresponds to the Pierre Gouzy of the d'Ablis deposition. His two sons were Bernard and Amiel, and his brother was probably the clog-maker Guillaume Gouzy, husband of Mathène and father of Raymond. The several young Gouzy women here at the time included Monète Gouzy and Cerdagne, the wife of Raymond Issaurat.

f.275v). The Gouzys' house stood at right angles to the church, and faced south-east into the heart of the village (Map 4). A door gave on to the church's eastern edge near the altar, and it was this side entrance that was sometimes used by nocturnal visitors, because it was more discreet. The location of the Gouzys' house is so precisely sketched in the documents that its site can easily be identified to this day, since the church still sits in the same spot in the lower part of Larnat. From the position of the church it is clear that the Gouzys' side entrance, unlike the main one, could easily be reached from across fields above the church and cemetery.

The Gouzys' house, like the Martys', boasted a walled courtyard with the house recessed inside it so that anyone visiting here was bound to pass through two doors. This must to some extent have been a status symbol. By the time Guillaume Authié paid his visits here, which were partly exploratory, partly consolidating, one of the daughters of the house, Sybille, had already left to marry Raymond Peyre from Sinsat, a village on the Ariège down the mountain from Larnat. She and her husband moved to Arques, where their prospering estate later provided a haven for Perfects and their sympathizers. Sybille probably left home with a substantial dowry, since the Gouzys were wealthy enough for the Cathar de Larnats to sanction the marriage of Philippe de Larnat's sister Guillemette to a Gouzy.

Almost seven centuries later the Gouzys are still here. Of the eighteen names listed in the 1997 Ariège telephone directory for Larnat, four were Gouzys, and another five Gouzys were to be found in Junac, under 'Capoulet-Junac'; and in the Commune de Miglos, which includes the former Cathar hamlets of Norgeat and Norrat, there are more Gouzys. Indeed, the mayor of Larnat is M. Sylvain Gouzy. When I told him where in the village the Gouzys lived in the thirteenth century, he chuckled and, with '*Et voilà la mienne!*', he pointed out his own south-facing house, which sits in the same location at the eastern end of the church.

The Issaurats of Larnat had been tied by marriage to the de Larnats even before the fall of Montségur in 1244 (D 24, f.270r). The head of the family in the 1290s was Arnaud Issaurat. The Issaurats were a militant and ruthless clan, as a local traitor discovered to his cost. Two Issaurat sons, Pierre and Raymond, gave evidence to Geoffroy d'Ablis, and later joined Pierre Maury in Catalonia in the years after the clampdown; Raymond's occupation may have been that of a grave-digger (FR, f.266r). The Issaurat sons' heads were to attract the same bounty as Pierre Maury's.

It was at the Issaurats of Larnat, and particularly in the house of Arnaud Issaurat, that Pierre Authié pitched his headquarters, movable though they were. Here the old Perfect was nursed by the Issaurats in his sickness throughout October 1300, after Guillaume de Luzenac had delivered him on a mule half-way up the climb of Larnat. A son of Pierre Amiel of Mérens later collected a still weak but convalescing Pierre Authié and took him to Mérens. Arnaud's was the main and very active branch of the family, and they lived in at least three houses owned by Arnaud and his sons.* These dwellings probably all clustered around the paternal one in the same corner above Larnat (d'AR, f.42).

The other Issaurat *padrone* at Larnat was Pons, who was the father of several daughters. One of his girls became a nun, even though the family were stoutly Cathar; but another one, Blanche, connected him to the Authiés of Ax, and that, in the deeply Cathar Sabartès of 1300, was tantamount to securing a place in heaven.

Arnaud Issaurat's garden, which lay outside and above Larnat, was separated by a brook from Philippe de Larnat's meadows. This creek was the Ruisseau d'Andignac, and it still runs past the medieval gully south-west of the village before decanting there into a trough. The Issaurats and de Larnats were therefore neighbours in the southern sector of the village. The squire's property would have reached back towards the centre of town while the Issaurats were south-western-most and both closer to the old track and further towards the *col*, with the Catalane family probably not far away. Down from the de Larnats' meadows was a garden hedge from where, through another side door, the de Larnats' house could be entered unseen by visitors descending from the *col* at night (FR, f.279v).

It was not far from this stream, and in a de Larnat meadow, that the Issaurats one summer night in 1303 or 1304 secretly reburied a certain

---

* Arnaud's family consisted of his wife Mengarde or Ermengarde (née Mir), the sons Raymond, Guillaume and Pierre, and four daughters, Guillemette, Margante, Sybille and Marguerite (assuming she is not the same as Margante), who seems to have been known also as 'Rose' and who worked in Pamiers as a servant of Bertrand de Taix's wife (see below, page 100) before marrying and moving to live in Ax (d'AR, ff.4r, 43v).

Guillaume Sabatier from Limoux. He had been hidden in a barn of theirs which was down from the house towards the village, where they kept wine, corn and hay, and where the Authiés and other Perfects lodged from time to time. He had been consoled by Pierre Authié and then underwent an epic *endura*, which was tantamount to a suicide through fasting (d'AR, ff.40r, 44v, 46v).*

Sabatier, who may have been related to the husband of Sybille Gouzy and whose brother was called Peyre-Sabatier, died in about Lent 1302. The Issaurats at first buried him in a trench in their garden, but then, within a year or eighteen months, they moved him across the creek. Did they fear an infection from a corpse rotting under their vegetables, or were they making assurance doubly sure by dumping the body on the unsuspecting de Larnats, in case the Inquisition saw fit to dig up their garden?

The posthumous fate of Guillaume Sabatier recalls that of one Cassagnas from Coustaussa who, after a long *endura* at the Rives' in Montaillou, was similarly buried secretly in a field belonging to the Rives or Belots.† In each case the clandestine funeral arrangements were dictated by the fact that they were outsiders and could therefore not be buried openly, as to do so would have drawn attention to the presence of a stranger.

*

* So was the death of Montolive Francès, whose *endura* turned into a six-week-long fast; she had been consoled by Pierre Authié (L, 28, 204).

† The longest *endura* in the Registers was that of a woman, again from Coustaussa, a small, hilltop village in the Aude and the home of the Perfects Raymond Faure and the popular Philippe d'Aylarac (d'AR, f.30r). She had fled from her husband and put herself through the *endura* at Sybille Baille's. She lasted *twelve* weeks, and her death can only be described as the result of a hunger-strike.

Suicide and *endura* similarly keep each other company in the case of Guillemette Marty, who was terrified of being caught by the Inquisition before she could die through the process of the *endura*. This happened shortly after the arrest in 1305 of Jacques Authié, which upset Guillemette terribly. Her friend therefore procured her 'a deadly brew of forest [wild?] cucumber juice and broken glass' and bought her a long sewing-needle with which to pierce her heart should the henchmen of the Inquisition come for her. In the end she apparently died of poisoning, which was a mercy, since the two women disagreed on which side of the body the heart was located (L, 71, 76).

Beyond the last house of the modern village and near the site of the former Issaurat property, an ancient gully turns right and up towards the *col*. This is the same medieval path which the Authiés, Issaurats, Martys and many other characters from this story walked many times on the half-hour journey to and from the Col de Larnat, or *lernayssol* as it was almost certainly known at the time (d'AR, f.43v; the Latin for Larnat is *Lernatum*). Shortly after leaving Larnat, the sunken path, which runs like a trench between boulders (Pl. 15), cuts across a wide terrace of meadows which in the fourteenth century were known as *prado lonc*, which translates as 'long or wide meadow'. The area is still so known in Larnat, and *Prat Loung* is marked on the early-nineteenth-century *PN* for the village. It was somewhere on *prado lonc*, under a rock (in a rocky cave?) that a woman called Esperte d'en Baby from Miglos reportedly met Pierre Authié to imbibe his teaching (FR, f.206r).

There may well have been a particular rock at *prado lonc* where the Perfects were regularly met as well as dropped off. The *filière* across the *col* usually operated simultaneous sending and receiving teams of *passeurs*. We know that on the western side of the mountain, if Perfects went from Larnat to Junac, the meeting-point was usually directly above Norrat, where the Issaurats would deliver a Perfect to the waiting Martys (d'AR, f.39v). I suspect that the rock above *prado lonc* was a similar place. Moreover, this meeting-place may be the same place as the one to which old Issaurat referred when he spoke of 'a [hidden] enclosure on the way out of the village' (d'AR, f.47v). This *could* be the rock or cave mentioned by Sybille Peyre (née Gouzy).*

There was another branch of the Issaurats in the nearby village of Larcat, which shares the same mountain with Larnat less than three miles to the south-east. These Issaurats were Catholic loyalists. Astonishingly,

---

* No such place has been found, but two huge rocks do rise near Larnat, and over the centuries they must have attracted their own mythologies. One is l'Escalié, which is north-west and above the village and therefore in the opposite direction from *prado lonc*; the other, to the north-east, is the sugar-loaf mountain of Orat Pémissol. Is there a fossilized echo in its name of sermons (*orationes*) that were held here in the distant past? If so, they would not have been Cathar ones, because we know from eyewitness accounts that Cathar clinics in Larnat convened in cellars and attendance was by invitation only.

the two branches of the family were confused with each other when, in 1301, an elderly wine-merchant from Pamiers mistakenly chose as his wife a Catholic Issaurat from Larcat instead of a Cathar one from Larnat. Bertrand de Taix was rich, aristocratic and devoutly Cathar. His first wife had been a 'Flors' Mir, which means that he may have been the brother-in-law of old Arnaud Issaurat. He was almost certainly in his fifties at the time of his remarriage, as he had been summoned by the Inquisition to be interviewed in the chapel of the castle at Varilhes as long ago as 1272. In the past he had been a great reciter of Pierre Cardenal's anti-clerical poem 'Clergues se fan pastors', and he once waggishly gave an inspiring rendition of it in the choir-stalls of the church of Saint-Antonin of Pamiers while mass was being said by the maverick Bishop of Pamiers, Bernard Saisset.

Bertrand de Taix had been a friend of Pierre Authié's long before the Authiés left for Lombardy, even though he professed not to know Guillaume Authié when he saw him. He was also distantly related to them through Pierre Authié's illegitimate daughter. While the marriage of this bumbling *senex amans* to the fierce Huguette Issaurat from Larcat has all the ingredients of a Plautine farce, his semi-castellated estate may have provided the Authiés with a welcome foothold in Pamiers, which was generally a dangerous place for the Cathars, as it was crawling with Dominicans and ecclesiastical staff. To have a rich ally there, in addition to a mole in the Dominicans, could certainly do no harm, although by 1300 Bertrand de Taix was probably too foolish to be a useful ally to the Authiés.

Even after his marriage of mistaken identity Bertrand de Taix inconsolably yearned for a daughter of Pons Issaurat's. Standing with him at the door of his orchard in Pamiers, Blanche de Rodes, one of Pons Issaurat's daughters, listened sympathetically to his plight, but could do little more than remind him of the fact that all her sisters, except the nun, were now married. Old Bertrand explained that his desire for an Issaurat wife from Larnat was partly because a Larnatian Issaurat would bring Perfects into his life again.

When he heard of the Authiés' return from Lombardy, he sent them provisions of good wine. But he did not dare cross his Catholic wife Huguette by using his own stock, and so he bought wine from another merchant and then dispatched it to the Perfects in Tarascon. As for seeing the Authiés, he at some point hit on the idea of using a visit to the thermal waters at Ax as a pretext for a journey into the Sabartès. Huguette, however, was aware of his intentions and blocked his project. All visitors to the house were henceforth primed not to broach the subject of the thermal baths at Ax, let alone praise them, to avoid emboldening him further.

When Bertrand met Pierre Authié's illegitimate daughter Guillemette in his kitchen one day, he was delighted. Patting her head, he told her that he loved her very much because of her father. He offered her and her husband a free house in Pamiers so that they could be close to him. He attributed this generosity to the fact that in the past he had short-changed his brother Jean de Taix, whom he called Guillemette's father-in-law or stepfather; why this should have been so is not clear from the documents, unless one assumes that Guillemette's husband Carramat was an illegitimate son of the same Jean de Taix.

As Huguette de Taix contemplated a lonesome existence at the side of a senescent husband, who thought he had married somebody else, she invited Rose Issaurat of Larnat to stay on to keep her company. This Rose did. The solidarity of the two young women, who may have been cousins, proved stronger than the sectarianism that was splitting their families.

The Issaurats of Larnat gave Pierre Authié the kind of base that was provided for his brother Guillaume in Montaillou. As in Montaillou, it was family connections as much as faith that bonded the local inhabitants to the Authiés, although here they were more convoluted. When Pons Issaurat's daughter Blanche Lombard was widowed she married Guillaume de Rodes, the son of Raymonde Rodes-Authié, Pierre Authié's sister, and the old Perfect's nephew. The three Rodes brothers from Tarascon were fiercely loyal to their uncles and their cause, and the Issaurats, their in-laws through Guillaume's marriage, stood shoulder-to-shoulder with them.

The link between the Authiés and the Issaurats was cemented further when Pierre de Gaillac, the chess-playing son of Gaillarde, the younger sister of Raymond Authié's wife Esclarmonde, married Raymonde Lombard-Issaurat, a daughter from Blanche's first marriage (d'AR, 47). By 1300, therefore, Pierre de Gaillac of Tarascon, the Authiés of Ax, and the Issaurats of Larnat were woven into a close web of family relations.

The village of Larnat was undoubtedly more densely populated in the early fourteenth century than it is now, but it was probably small enough even then to make it impossible for anyone to break ranks. Larnat was as secure as Montaillou, and more unassailable; and whereas family connections anchored Guillaume Authié in Montaillou, his brother Pierre was more commonly seen at Larnat, perhaps because his most influential *credens*, Guillaume Bayard, lived near here.

The communities of Larnat, Junac, Tarascon and Rabat were tightly linked through shared allegiances, which frequently cut across class divisions. At the height of the *risorgimento* the Cathar faith temporarily levelled social and other class differences, both in theory and in practice. Thus the châtelain of Junac and his entire family were eager members of the true Church, and regularly welcomed Arnaud Marty and his Perfect friends in the castle. Since they could not do so openly, they did it through a small window located at the bottom of a tower, which may be the one mentioned above. Through this 'secret' passage, the Perfects reached the bedrooms of the de Junac family.

As at Montaillou, the cross-caste mingling was not exclusively social. A young woman called Mersende, for example, who was a 'great friend' of Blanche Marty and the mistress of her brother Arnaud, the future Perfect, was subsequently sexually involved with Jacques de Junac from whom she had two children, a boy and a little girl called Guillemette; and the godmother of this girl of mixed pedigree was none other than Blanche Marty.

Both Guillaume Bayard (and his wife Lorda) frequented Junac during Guillaume Authié's stay there. He would usually arrive at the castle of Junac first and then, after dark, enter the Martys' dovecote opposite to meet and confer with the Perfect, passing through the *solarium* into the merged buildings of stables and dovecote just like everybody else. Once he was spotted riding up to the castle on a black mule rather than the kind of steed that befitted his rank. Even the second-most powerful man in the Ariège needed to tread guardedly when visiting the Authiés, who repaid the courtesy by in turn staying with Bayard and de Larnat.

We know this from the consignments of fish that were sent to them by the Martys. On one occasion Bayard received twenty-two salted trout from Arnaud Marty, and eight days later the same Arnaud sent another twelve, fresh ones this time, up to Philippe de Larnat, with an apology that he could not be more generous. In each case the fish was almost certainly intended for Perfects sojourning with them. Others also sent the Perfects fish, and on one particular occasion both Pierre and Guillaume-Bernard de Luzenac turned up independently of each other at the Issaurats of Larnat bearing trout for the Authiés.

In spite of its abundance in the rivers of fourteenth-century Langue-doc, fish was expensive, and the Martys' supply of it to the Perfects would have been mostly their own catches. That Arnaud and his brothers fished with rods and gosling feathers rather than nets is clear from the way they orchestrated daylight meetings with Perfects whom they wanted to shelter (d'AR, f.18r). Their strategy invariably was to meet them out of sight of the village on one of the Ariège bridges and pass them fishing-rods. Then the Perfects would join the Martys in fishing their way up the river into the village, and thus become invisible by blending into what was one of the most common activities of Junac (d'AR, f.39v). It may have been while fishing that the Martys met Arnaud Piquier, a fisherman from Tarascon, who would marry their sister Raymonde Marty in 1305 after his first wife Mathende had died after All Saints in 1304 (d'AR, ff.18r, 19r, 32r).

In some form or other the river and fish played a significant part in Junac. Were the fishing-grounds in Junac particularly well-stocked, and was that the reason why Junac had a fishmonger's where ordinary people as well as the 'best' people shopped? The fish that Arnaud Marty sent to the Bayards was salted, and this makes one wonder whether he might not have bought some of it, since it was easy enough to provide vast quantities of salted fish which kept. It was at the fishmonger's at Junac that Arnaud Sicre was to call in twenty years later in the course of one of his periodic returns from Catalonia, ostensibly to buy salted trout (Pl. 13). He had been sent to Junac on a fool's errand, it turned out, by Raymonde Marty (see below, pages 321–3).

As well as serving as bases for the spiritual colonizing of the Sabartès, the Cathar communities of Larnat and Junac were well placed for forays to Toulouse and, perhaps, Foix and Pamiers, although there is no record of Pierre Authié appearing in either of these two places.

*

The year 1300 was the first ever Jubilee year or Holy Year, that is a year in which special indulgences were granted to faithful Catholics who visited Rome. Jubilees or Holy Years happen every fifty years, and this first one was inaugurated by the supremacist Pope Boniface VIII with a papal bull which set out the conditions for obtaining indulgences. It was hugely successful. Up to 30,000 people may have attended the basilicas of St Peter and St Paul on the major holidays (Levillain 1994, 102–4). In the *Divina Commedia* Dante, who was in his mid-thirties during the Jubilee, recalled that the crush of people was such that the civic authorities in Rome had to institute a two-way flow across the Tiber bridge, with one lane facing towards the Castel Sant'Angelo and the Basilica Constantina, and the other towards Monte Giordano (Canto XVIII, 28–33).

By now the entire intelligentsia of the County of Foix knew that the Authiés had gone to Lombardy, and many would have been aware of the more important fact that they had already returned. In 1300 the renewed call for a spiritual renaissance fell on responsive ears in the Ariège valley, from the slopes of Puymorens and Envalira in the south to Toulouse in the north, by way of the canyon cities of Ax and Tarascon (Map 5).

Few of the main locations in this story lie much further than twenty miles away from Montségur, which had come to symbolize the Occitan Cathar church. Now the *entendensa del be* was about to be resuscitated with a fervour that matched anything that had gone before, and the Authiés and another dozen Perfects anointed by them became the catalysts of this Cathar twilight. The nine years of the Authiés' apostolate created the biggest recorded upheaval in the history of the region. Its consequences are felt to this day, even in the assimilation of Cathar history by the tourist industry, as in the network of '*Sentiers Cathares*' or '*Chemins des Bonshommes*'; and the thirteenth-century phrase '*bonshommes*' is still the phrase current in the Ariège for the Cathar Perfects.

Lent of 1300, which was a leap year, started on Ash Wednesday 24 February and finished the day before Easter, on Saturday 9 April. It was during the latter end of this period that one night there was a knock at the door of Raymond Authié. It was his brothers' messenger, confirming that the two Perfects were on their way, and asking whether he was ready to receive them. At this point they may have been in or near Château-Verdun, because Philippe de Larnat met them there briefly at the Ariège bridge on their way through, guided by Pons-Arnaud of Château-Verdun. De Larnat asked after Pierre-Arnaud de Capoulet, and learnt that he had stayed behind in Lombardy.

The following evening, towards midnight, Pierre and Guillaume Authié, accompanied by Bon Guilhem, arrived back in Ax for the first time since October 1296. They were welcomed 'with hugs and kisses' by Raymond and Esclarmonde Authié, and then they retired to bed (d'AR, f.10r). The next day the reunited Authié family spent their time talking about Lombardy, the brothers' ordinations, and also the plans for the impending campaign. The two Perfects impressed on their relatives the paramount importance of keeping their movements secret as well as their need for organized hiding-places. Much of the required underground infrastructure was already in place. It was a matter of consolidating it now, of making new converts, and above all of inspiring the rank-and-file faithful and the doubters by setting an example.

The two returned brothers were now probably wearing the clothes favoured by Perfects towards the end of the thirteenth century. These garments generally consisted of a dark blue hooded coat and a dark green tunic, and were assumed on ordination (d'AR, f.4r). Thus Guillemette Clergue (B) of Montaillou noted that she had seen two men in green cloth in the Belot house, and that this surprised her because no one in that house wore those colours. Raymonde den Arsen similarly described seeing Guillaume Authié in January 1308, 'a man dressed in dark blue or dark green' (FR, f.74v). And Pierre Authié had a cloak with a hood (*supertunicale & capucium*) made for himself from two ells of a green or bluish-green cloth (L, 50). For reasons of personal safety the Perfects no longer wore the black robes of the earlier thirteenth century and they now also shaved, but theirs was still a distinctive outfit, as the Inquisition's insistent questions about the dress code of suspected Perfects prove.*

★ Why dark blue or dark green should be more effective at protecting the identities of Cathar Perfects than black is mystifying, since ordinary people in Montaillou as well as the Inquisitors were clearly well aware of the new colour-coding. It is not inconceivable (though perhaps far-fetched) that the dark green and blue colours served the dual purpose of camouflage in the Pyrenean woodlands while still retaining the emphasis on sombre (and sober) clothing signalled by the traditional black of the earlier Perfects.

During the eight days (d'Ablis) or fortnight (Fournier) at Raymond's, Pierre and Guillaume followed their new dietary regime of fasting three days a week on water and bread, in addition to observing the customary abstinences of Lent. They explained to their family the Perfects' dietary requirements, a Cathar version of kosher, which entailed whenever possible using their own bowls and utensils. They were almost vegans in that they abstained from any kind of meat, cheese or eggs. They did, however, eat fish, although it had to be cooked in a pot which had never contained fat or lard.

A striking illustration of the fastidiousness of the Perfects' cuisine is provided by Guillaume Peyre's visit to the Rives in Montaillou. Although no date is given for this visit, it took place certainly before 8 September 1305, and probably in or before 1304, because Fabrisse Rives still seemed to be a member of that household. Peyre was not himself a Perfect, but he was Pierre Authié's personal assistant, and he was therefore a privileged figure.

When Fabrisse Rives spotted Guillaume Peyre in the *foghana* of the house, she noticed him leaning on a cushion, and was struck by the lordly treatment afforded him by Alazais Rives. Alazais was decanting a 'broth' made from nuts in a bowl, while in a separate pot she was cooking cabbage and meat, presumably for her family and herself. Alazais also brought him a wooden basin, water, and a pristine napkin, and he washed his hands while she poured water over them. Then, putting clean napkins in front of him, she waited on him with great care. This is clearly how Guillaume Peyre's master was used to being served, and Peyre perhaps saw himself already as a novitiate Perfect; but not long afterwards he was to betray his friends (see below, pages 152–3).

The deeper reasons for the Perfects' diet will become clear when we hear Pierre and Jacques Authié preach. During these first few days back in Ax, Pierre and Guillaume set about initiating their own kith and kin into the *melioramentum* or *melhorier*, the ritual observance due to the Perfects by the faithful. This consisted of the faithful kneeling in front of the Perfect and asking his blessing (or hers, since there had been several famous *Perfectae* earlier in the century) three times, and each time he would reply, 'May God bless you.' The exact words that were spoken on all these occasions, in Occitan of course, were the supplicant saying, '*Bon crestia la benediction de dieu e de vos*', to which the Perfect replied, '*De dieu las aiatz e de nos*', which literally translates as 'Have it from God and from us.' At the same time Raymond and Esclarmonde pledged that they desired to be consoled or received at the moment of death. The *convenenza* was intended to guarantee consolation in cases where the dying person had lost their rational faculties and could no longer choose at that moment to join the Cathar church.

From now on, and for the next nine years, the Authiés tirelessly moved from place to place throughout the Sabartès, and well beyond its borders. It is as if this difficult and harsh terrain posed no particular obstacles to these middle-aged men. It is only on getting to know the mountain passes and distances intimately that one appreciates the scale of the achievement of the last Occitan Perfects and their guides.

5. Betrayal and Consolidation: 1300

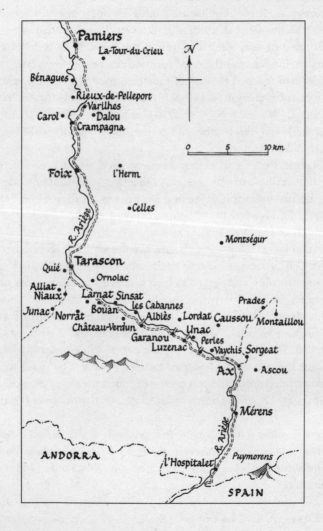

The Ariège of the Cathar revival

While staying at Raymond's, Pierre and Guillaume were visited by a select number of members of the inner Authié circle, including Guillaume and Géraud de Rodes from Tarascon and Pierre Amiel from Mérens. Geographically, Tarascon and Mérens are effectively the extreme poles of the upper Ariège valley.

Although Gaillarde, Guillaume Authié's wife, is not mentioned, we can safely assume that she visited him, even though both parents may have decided to keep their children in the dark. They were probably too small to understand the need for total discretion; conversely, if by then they had reached the age of fourteen, they would be counted as adults by the Inquisition and would be held responsible for any 'heretical' contact. We may be sure that Guillaume Authié saw his wife because he loved her, but his visit to her uncle's family in Montaillou was part of his mission.

Guillaume Benet had clearly been notified about a month or so before the Authiés arrived back in Ax that this would happen. He tried to prepare his wife for it, by telling her how good they were, how no one could be saved without being consoled by them, and that they should make them welcome.

One night after Guillemette Benet had already gone to bed, her husband let Guillaume Authié into their house. Guillemette saw him the following morning and agreed to hear him preach. He was not on this occasion fed by the Benets, because he carried his own provisions. He stayed in Montaillou all day, until Guillaume Benet returned from his work in the fields or woods. It would be interesting to know whether or not he also called in on the Clergues. That evening the Benets' neighbour Guillaume Belot came and collected the new Perfect. The fact that one of the Belots turned up in this open fashion to collect the new Perfect suggests that the organization was nearly ready to take on the might of Rome.

At Montaillou the Clergues were indispensable to the Authiés. Around Christmas in 1301, in a conversation at the house of Sybille Baille in Ax, Guillaume Authié said that the reason why he stayed in Montaillou so much was

because there we have a lot of good familiars and if we had so many good friends in all the towns of the world, you others could be the lords of all the entire clergy, and there would be no pope, no bishop, no priest that you couldn't lift out of his chair. Indeed, there are only two people there whom we have to guard against, namely a brother of Pierre Azéma [he means Pierre Azéma himself] and [Arnaud Lizier]. (FR, f.51)

The speaker, Raymond Vaissière, could not remember the name of the other person mentioned by Guillaume Authié, but it was Arnaud Lizier, and this was confirmed by Esclarmonde Authié. Indeed, she elaborated on this by reporting that Guillaume Authié had said that if it were not for Arnaud Lizier he could move about openly in the square of Montaillou.

When he was asked whether he was not worried about the priest of Montaillou and the people from the Clergue house, Guillaume Authié replied:

We don't need to worry about the priest of Montaillou or his student, or about anyone from the house of Clergue in Montaillou. Rather, if only all the rectors in the world were like the rector of Montaillou, then we wouldn't need to be afraid of any rector at all. (FR, f.51v)

Because of this as well as the profound family links, Montaillou became Guillaume Authié's most important away-base, whereas Prades Tavernier increasingly used Montaillou as his primary haven; for both, however, if not for most Perfects, the house of Sybille Baille in Ax remained their headquarters.

As with Gaillarde Authié, there is no record of Sybille Baille visiting the Authiés at this point, but she will certainly have done so. In the 1270s and 1280s Sybille Baille and her notary husband Arnaud Sicre were of the same generation as Guillaume and Gaillarde Authié, and like them they had young children in the late 1280s or early 1290s. Sybille's youngest, a daughter, was born in about 1298. This little girl was Raymonde, whom her brother Arnaud twenty years later used as bait. The presence of the little girl suggests that Sybille and her husband were still on good terms in the 1290s, when they also had Pierre and Arnaud, who as a child was affectionately called 'Naudy'. Many years later, and in another country, Pierre Maury claimed to remember

seeing Arnaud at his mother's breast, which suggests that either the
Sicre-Bailles visited Montaillou in the mid-1290s, perhaps to help out
with the harvests, or the Maurys saw them in Ax. At the time Pierre
Maury himself would have been a young teenager, since Arnaud
Sicre was probably born between 1294 and 1296. Esperte Servel, the
mother-in-law of Pierre Maury's brother Jean, recalled seeing young
Arnaud Sicre in Tarascon as a thirteen-year-old in about 1308–9.

The Sicre-Bailles probably belonged to the smart set of thirteenth-
century Ax. This included minor nobility such as the Barres, but it
consisted above all of an affluent and professional bourgeoisie that
enjoyed the business opportunities of a rich spa town, which happened
to straddle a major trading route between Spain and France. If the
Authiés seem to have been the first bourgeois family of Ax, with links
by marriage throughout the region, the Sicre-Bailles were probably
their *confrères* and will have been friends. Moreover, like the Authiés'
firm, Arnaud Sicre Senior may have done some work for the Count of
Foix.* The Sicres, like the Authiés, were clearly one of the main law
firms of the Sabartès during the second half of the thirteenth century,
but their base seems to have been Tarascon.

Sybille Baille, herself the daughter of a Cathar, became the most
ardent *credens* in Ax, and she eventually suffered the same fate as her
Perfect friends on a pyre in Carcassonne. It was her house which
became the crucible of Catharism in Ax. The house was visible from
one of the weavers' workshops in Ax, and these weavers probably lived
in the 'rue des Tisserands'. This ran roughly parallel to the Auze, and
cut through the heart of fourteenth-century Ax. It corresponds to
today's rue Mansart and rue de la Brancade, which contain some of the
oldest extant buildings in the city. We know that Pierre and Guillaume
Authié frequented the house of Bernard Arquetayre in the 'Tisserands',
and that it was a stone's throw from here to the Bassin des Ladres. I

---

* An Arnaud Sicre was contracted by Roger-Bernard of Foix in 1266, six years before
the Authiés were first recorded working for the same Count, and in a case in which
Béatrice's father Philippe de Planisolles bore witness. But this Sicre may have been
the grandfather of the Arnaud who went into Catalonia to track down the Cathars.
The Sicre of 1266 is described as '*Arnaldus Cicreda Notarius Publicus Savartesii*' in the
context of the granting of '*consuetudines, usus & libertates*' (i.e. customs and freedoms)
to Tarascon (Devic *et al.* 1872–1905, 9, c.692, 8 April 1266).

would surmise that Sybille Baille's house stood in or near the 'Tisserands'. At least one of its windows faced what was then called 'the Rock', the mighty excrescence at the heart of Ax which is now known as the Rocher de la Vierge (Pl. 14).

For the next eight years, the Perfects and their followers would weave in and out of the house in which a small secret bedroom, on the first or second floor and facing the Rock, was permanently kept as a hideout. Sybille Baille was incessantly baking, cooking and preparing fish for the Perfects and meat for their scouts, and it was to her that the faithful made their way when they were searching for a Perfect to come and console a loved one who was dying.

The depth of Sybille Baille's passion for the Cathar faith verged on the fanatical, and she allowed it to destroy her family. A year or so after the Authiés left, she drove her husband out of the marital home and returned to her maiden name; perhaps she wanted to be known as 'Baille' to signal an unbroken continuity between her faith and her father's. This action turned her husband into a sworn enemy of the Cathars. Sybille Baille subsequently sent her young son Pierre to her sister Alazais, a Cathar like herself living with her husband in La Seu d'Urgell in Catalonia; one of Alazais's best friends, Gaillarde Escaunier from Sorgeat (near Ax), was to become an important link in the chain connecting Ax and Sybille Baille to the Cathar families of Arques in the Aude.

Both the younger Baille boys were starting to talk, and it was too dangerous to have them around. In about 1300, or shortly afterwards, Sybille Baille sent the five-year-old Arnaud to his father in Tarascon, because his increasing articulacy rendered him a potentially dangerous witness to the activities in her home. Ironically, eighteen years later it was his acute ear for language that, in a square in Catalonia, gave him the break that he had almost despaired of ever achieving. Sybille's two elder boys, Pons and Bernard, stayed put. They shared their mother's faith, but the two younger sons would wreak a terrible revenge on the Cathars.

Sybille's husband, Arnaud Sicre, had probably moved back to Tarascon after the separation. His notary's offices, which may have been those of the family firm, stood on the main square. So did one of Blanche de Rodes's two houses in the city, where she would sometimes

accommodate her uncles Pierre and Guillaume Authié for a fortnight
or so over the summer of 1300. The presence on the square of Tarascon
of one of the Cathars' avowed enemies poses awkward questions in this
narrative, since various Perfects and other Cathars do not seem to have
been unduly worried by it. Arnaud Sicre Senior and the Authiés
certainly knew one another, but Sicre was probably neutralized as long
as Bayard ruled in Tarascon.

In the meantime Sybille Baille's devotion to the Cathar cause was
about to reach its apotheosis. Within months, if not weeks, of the
Authiés' return her son Pons was ordained simultaneously with Jacques
Authié, who may well have been a childhood friend, since the two of
them were probably of the same age, around eighteen or nineteen.

For the Authiés it was time to start consoling, and to do so Pierre
Authié needed to retrieve his 'book' from his son-in-law Arnaud
Teisseyre. He had left it behind because the book was too compromising
to carry. Raymond duly made his way to Lordat to collect his brother's
precious volume. When he appeared at Arnaud's, and greeted him with
the news of the Perfects' return, the latter anxiously walked him into a
room off the hall and wanted to know how they were and whether
they had been ordained. He then passed the book to Raymond.

Raymond fastened it by its binding to his belt and wrapped a fold of
his tunic around it, thus carrying it at the front as Guillaume Authié
also did when he came to console Bernard Marty, 'drawing out a book
from under his clothes'. With his precious cargo Raymond set out on
the three-hour walk back to Ax, where his brothers were by now
installed in his vaulted cellar, whose arches could provide emergency
cover (d'AR, f.4r).

On Saturday 9 April, the day before Easter, Pierre, Guillaume and
Jacques Authié stayed in Larnat with the Issaurat family. They were
visited here by the Issaurats' neighbour, the squire Philippe de Larnat.
He later recalled seeing Arnaud Issaurat as well as one of his sons,
Guillaume. De Larnat remembered that one of the Perfects was reading
from a book, but he pretended not to recall whether he was also
preaching or not. All he admitted to remembering was that there was
talk of some kind of vision.

Clearly he was stalling his interrogators. What almost certainly happened was that one of the Authiés read and the other one gave a running commentary. The most strikingly orchestrated example of this in the extant records was at Sybille Peyre's in Arques (see below, pages 135–9). It is noteworthy that de Larnat also reports meeting the two senior Authié Perfects in l'Herm, near Foix, one night during the second week in May. Guillaume Issaurat was their guide and was taking them to Garanou. De Larnat joined them, and thus witnessed their deferential reception at the entry into the village, probably at its ancient bridge, by the squire Pons de Lordat and his son. These two then led them into a house owned by the de Planisolles. This must have been the same house in which over fifty years earlier Raymond de Planisolles had provided shelter to an earlier generation of Cathars (D 24, f.274v). Béatrice's father was as deeply implicated in the earliest stages of the return of the Perfects as it was possible to be.

Their next foray was to Mérens, eight miles south of Ax, where Pierre Amiel welcomed them. From there they probably intended to push further south beyond l'Hospitalet and the Col de Puymorens to the village of Carol (today Latour-de-Carol), another place with strong Cathar connections and only three miles to the north of the important border city of Puigcerdà, which overlooks the Cerdagne (French) or Cerdanya (Catalan), the widest and most fertile valley in the Pyrenees, which is watered by the Segre river.

It was probably shortly after Easter that Raymond Authié himself passed through Mérens on his way to Puigcerdà to sell sheep, and stopped off to see his brothers. When he offered to bring them something from Puigcerdà, they asked for spices, particularly pepper and saffron. Although the Perfects lived austerely and chastely, some among them were also connoisseurs who before their ordination had been accustomed to luxuries. The Authiés used spices, consumed fish terrines, were keen experts on the cheeses of the different areas in the region, and drank 'good wine'. Thus it was with some regret that Géraud de Rodes, one of Pierre Authié's nephews, reported that, at Raymonde de Luzenac's, Guillaume Authié had been served wine 'which was not good; indeed, it was acidy' (d'AR, f.3v). Limborch repeatedly refers to Pierre Authié's penchant for good wine, and one Géraud d'Artigues is reported to have gone out specially 'in search of a better and more renowned wine than the one kept in his own residence' to serve it to Pierre and Jacques Authié (L,59). The old Perfect also enjoyed honey from Bouan. The beehives are still there off the narrow road as it winds its way out and up from Bouan to Larnat. The farmers and leading shepherds like Pierre Maury were of course knowledgeable about Ariégeois cuisine. But the Authiés' interest in condiments that were the equivalent of today's 'designer foods' betokens a sophistication which demonstrates that class differences in the Languedoc were never obliterated. Far from being hair-shirted, the elegant Authiés continued to wear cambric after their conversion.

The fact that they asked their brother for spices indicates that the meeting in Mérens happened after the end of Lent. Easter 1300 fell on Sunday 10 April. This Easter weekend of 1300 has become the most famous Easter in the imaginative history of Europe, because it is on Good Friday 8 April 1300 that Dante, who was himself thirty-five years old then, and therefore, according to the psalmist (Psalms 90:10), in the middle of his life, imagined the *Divina Commedia* as starting. In that year 1300 the patrician Dante still held high office in his beloved, albeit factionally riven, 'Fiorenza', but like the Authiés he would soon become an exile. Similar tensions to the ones which precipitated Dante's fall in Florence had earlier allowed the Authiés to thrive in their Lombardian enclave. They would, of course, not have known anything about Dante, or his hostility towards Pope Boniface VIII, who was ultimately their enemy as well. But his voice adds itself to theirs from this long-gone past with a searing intensity. That the author of the greatest poem of the Middle Ages should be a direct contemporary of this last Cathar renaissance, and indeed be imaginatively indebted to the love poetry which emerged from the Occitania of the Authiés, is in itself a fortuitous fact, a mere temporal coincidence of history. But to us who look back in time the two narratives, the story of the Authiés and Dante's imaginative masterpiece, complement each other as odysseys of the human spirit in the same historical moment.

In Mérens in the late spring of 1300 the new Perfects were not only visited by Raymond Authié. Somebody else called on them, a kind of Franciscan or *beguinus* by the name of Guillaume Dejean. He must have been a Cathar of note to be allowed to meet the Authiés so early into their return mission, and he seems to have spoken to the two Authiés for a while before taking his leave. He then made his way to Pamiers, and here he went straight to see a Dominican called Guillaume Pons.

Shortly afterwards, on what seems to have been Wednesday 25 May 1300 (literally 'a Wednesday shortly before Whitsun', which fell on 29 May), Brother Raymond de Rodes O.P., the son of Raymonde de Rodes-Authié, wrote a letter. It was addressed to his notary brother Guillaume in Tarascon, warning him that their uncles Pierre and Guillaume Authié were in danger: could he urgently come to Pamiers for a meeting? The following day Guillaume met his brother, perhaps inside the Dominicans' convent on the carriera de Romengos o dels Predicadors (Map 6).

Raymond took his brother aside and then told him of the plot to deliver their uncles into the hands of the Inquisition. His fellow Dominican Guillaume Pons had told him that he had been approached by a stool-pigeon called Guillaume Dejean, and Dejean had told Pons that he had seen Pierre and Guillaume Authié and was offering to bring them in. It was Guillaume Dejean's bad fortune that the tentacles of Catharism reached right into the nerve-centre of the Inquisition, and that both Guillaume Pons O.P. and Raymond de Rodes O.P. put friendship and family before calling; or perhaps their true calling was the Albigensian church all along. When Guillaume de Rodes was asked why he had supported the Authiés, he replied that it was 'because of his natural love towards them, because he was of their clan and family' (FR, f.17r).

With his dangerous knowledge Guillaume de Rodes returned to Tarascon and from there he at once headed for Ax. He needed to confer with Raymond Authié, the stand-in head of the Authié family now that Pierre inhabited the twilight world of barns, dovecotes, lofts, cellars, secret chambers, corn-pits, silos, wardrobes and large chests.

Although Guillaume de Rodes does not spell this out in his deposition to Geoffroy d'Ablis, he and Raymond Authié decided to lay a trap for the traitor. Speed was essential, and Guillaume Delaire from Quié, a zealous disciple of the Authiés, would act as the lure. Delaire was informed of what was afoot, and arranged to meet Dejean, as if by chance, in the main square in Ax. That at least is how it appears, and Delaire somehow managed to convince Dejean that he could help him capture the Perfects in a hiding-place in the mountain eyrie of Larnat.

The fact that the Authiés were indeed bound for the Tarascon area towards the end of the month may have rendered his ploy particularly plausible.

Dejean and Delaire seem to have headed for Larnat from Quié because it was on the bridge across the Ariège (now the river Vicdessos) at Alliat, before Junac, that Philippe de Larnat, Pierre Delaire, Guillaume's brother and Guillaume Issaurat of Larnat lay in wait (d'AR, f.39r). The two Delaires, Issaurat and de Larnat beat Dejean so severely that he could no longer cry out, and then dragged him up into the mountains of Miglos. Here they questioned the wretched informer about his intentions, and when he confessed to wanting to capture the Authiés they threw him over a high cliff into a pit or precipice in such a way that afterwards his body could not be seen. The place of this murder in June 1300 *may* have been the Ravin du Correc.

The entire episode, from the letter of 25 May to the death of the informer, took about a fortnight. Retaliation had been swift and efficient, something which Guillaume de Rodes had been loath at first to admit. The speed and ruthlessness with which Dejean's treachery had been squashed did not show the Cathars in too good a light.

The Albigensian creed was predicated on the spirituality and metaphors of St John's Gospel, and it specifically outlawed any violence. It singled out the shedding of blood and the killing of anything living, even the slaughtering of a chicken or the ensnaring of a squirrel (see above, page 48), as a mortal sin. The Catholic church repeatedly forced its Cathar prisoners to admit that they considered even judicial executions to be sinful, notwithstanding the Bible's authority to the contrary. But the Church's Bible was that of retribution, whereas the Cathars', in theory, was that of Christ's meekness and forgiveness. The practice was rather different, as the case of Dejean and the massacre fifty-eight years earlier of the Inquisitors at Avignonet by a posse from Montségur demonstrate. There is a tragic irony in the fact that the Authiés' return needed to be safeguarded almost immediately by the taking of a human life; and four years on the Cathars would stamp their seal on Montaillou with a second murder.

At around the time that Guillaume Dejean was set up, the Authié Perfects were visiting Guillaume de Rodes and his wife Blanche, the mother-in-law of Pierre de Gaillac. One early morning around Whitsun

(29 May) they were approaching Tarascon in the company of Raymond, when the light of dawn caught them out. They had reached a barn in a meadow belonging to a Tarasconian Cathar called Raymond Lombard, perhaps Arnaud Issaurat's son-in-law. Here they paused while Raymond Authié went into Tarascon to see Guillaume de Rodes. Together de Rodes and Raymond collected the key to the barn, and let the Perfects into it. Then, locking it, they returned into town.*

At about 6 p.m. Raymond Authié and Guillaume de Rodes took the Perfects bread, wine and water-boiled trout, but they could not stay with them because there were women nearby cutting the grass, and their suspicion might otherwise have been aroused. The Perfects stayed in the barn until nightfall, and then went into Tarascon, where they hid at Guillaume de Rodes's. They appear to have stayed for a fortnight, although they may have spent some of that time at the loyal Delaires' in neighbouring Quié. Here they hid in a grain-silo, which could be entered from the pantry through a huge upright chest. Inside the silo was a trapdoor, which was hidden under the grain and gave access to a hiding-place (FR, f.306r; d'AR, ff.16v–17r). For much of the time the last Perfects of Languedoc existed literally underground.

Pierre de Luzenac and his brother Guillaume-Bernard met them there to do them homage, and on parting Pierre Authié presented the younger de Luzenac with a Parma knife that he drew out of a basket. This basket he probably carried to authenticate his cover of pedlar, a disguise commonly adopted by Perfects, particularly when travelling during daylight hours.

Later in June the Authiés were once again in Tarascon, because on Thursday 23 June Pierre de Gaillac met them at Arnaud Piquier's. He was then on his summer holidays from Toulouse university. Shortly after 24 June, the feast of John the Baptist, the Authiés were reportedly back in the cellar next to the stables at their brother Raymond's in Ax,

---

* In the Middle Ages the main road from Ax to Tarascon, which is called '*ancien chemin dit d'Espagne*' on the *PN*, ran on the *right*-hand side of the Ariège through Ornolac and Ussat. Just before Tarascon the road skirts the wide meadows of 'le Pré Lombard'. Since these are the only meadows anywhere south of Tarascon, they have to be the same meadows belonging to Raymond Lombard where the Authiés sought refuge. There are Prés Lombards all over France, but in this case the onomastic arch linking the fourteenth and twentieth centuries may be more than a coincidence.

and asked to see Pierre de Luzenac. When he saw them, they were being waited on by Jacques Authié, who was not yet ordained.

Having done the trek between Ax and Tarascon repeatedly now, they discovered that the distance between the two towns, which is in excess of twenty miles, could not be covered safely during short summer nights, the more so since they could not always stick with the main road. They already had the run of the de Planisolles' house in the Lordadais, but they needed another safe house there. Since this was the de Luzenacs' backyard, Pierre promised to arrange it, but he was slow to deliver. He needed to be reminded of his undertaking in August that year when outside Ax, near the dovecote of yet another Barre, he met three men coming towards him in the 'pallor of the night'. When they were a stone's throw away from him, he whistled. They stopped, and one of them, Guillaume Authié, came up to him and demanded that he should assist their friend Pierre of Mérens in a criminal case brought against him in the courts of the Count of Foix. Then Guillaume inquired after the safe house, and de Luzenac promised to set it up, 'if it was necessary'.

In early July 1300 the Authiés were back in the Larnat–Tarascon area, and it was during July or August 1300 that Jacques Authié and Pons Sicre-Baille, or Pons d'Ax as he was also known, were ordained Perfects by Pierre and Guillaume Authié.

From the testimony of Pierre Bela we know that Jacques Authié stayed at Teisseyre's in Lordat for a fortnight before the initiation ceremony, because he saw him there by chance, when Jacques furtively put his head out of Teisseyre's first-floor *foghana*'s window in response to Bela's knocking at the door. Jacques's prolonged stay at his brother-in-law's may have been because of his leg-ulcer which Teisseyre tended and cured, even though the Register suggests that by the time this happened Jacques was already a Perfect; Jacques's ulcers may have been a chronic condition, and probably required regular nursing care (L, 69; FR, ff.157v, 159r).

That the ordination of Jacques Authié happened after 24 June and before September 1300 is suggested by Pierre de Luzenac, who stated that Jacques was not yet ordained when he saw him on 24 June 1300, but when he met him again in September that year he recalled that he thought that Jacques had recently become a Perfect (d'AR, f.66v). Pierre de Gaillac seems to confirm this in his deposition of 23 October 1308. He met Pierre and Jacques Authié, who was then already a Perfect, 'some eight years ago, before the feast of the nativity of the beatific John the Baptist which was recently celebrated'. Because de Gaillac uses 'recently', he must mean the *martyrdom* of John the Baptist, which falls on 29 August, rather than the nativity.

The ceremony of the ordination or the *consolamentum*, which differs from the act of consoling the dying, took place in the house of Arnaud Issaurat in Larnat, where the Authiés had a 'chapel' just as they did in Montaillou at the Rives', in Arques at the Peyres', and in Limoux at the Francès'. The *consolamentum* itself signified above all the conferring of the Holy Spirit on the novice. To be ordained the two kneeling young men, with their hands folded, were required to ask for permission to be received into the true Church, listen to the Ancient's (in this case Pierre Authié's) exegesis of the Lord's Prayer, repeat it after him, pledge themselves to a life of moral purity, never to lie or swear an oath, and to observe the dietary rituals that we have encountered already. After they had asked for, and been granted, remission of their sins, the Gospels were put on the postulants' heads, and *l'Ancien* put his hands on them. Then the Holy Spirit was transfused to them with the following words:

Bless and forgive us, Amen. May it be done unto us, O Lord, according to Your word. May the Father and the Son and the Holy Ghost pardon and forgive you your sins. Let us pray the Father and the Son and the Holy Ghost. Let us pray the Father and the Son and the Holy Ghost! Holy Father, receive Your servant into Your justice and infuse him with Your Grace and Your Holy Spirit. (Nelli 1969, 44)

This was followed by repeated recitations of the Lord's Prayer, and a brief reading of the Prologue to St John's Gospel in which Christ is presented as the eternal *Logos* or Word: 'And the Word was made flesh, and dwelt among us, (and we beheld His glory, the glory as of the only begotten of the Father), full of grace and truth' (1:14). The New Testament foundation of the Cathar church is then dialectically defined with the words: 'For the law was given by Moses, but grace and truth came by Jesus Christ' (1:17). It is this that Arnaud Issaurat remembered when he recalled vaguely that 'many words were spoken in the presence of the heretics of the apostles and the Gospels' not wanting to admit that he was perfectly familiar with the *consolamenta* in his house (FR, f.46v). The ordination ceremony finished with a further recitation of the Lord's Prayer, and then the Ancient kissed the two new Perfects on the mouth (FR, f.158r; Duvernoy 1978, 744 n.1; d'AR, ff.46v, 66v).

The fact that these two were young men barely out of their teens, who had sworn never to deviate from the true path, must have heartened the two older Perfects, even if Pierre Authié cannot have been insensible to the dangers now confronting his own son.★ Jacques Authié already carried a Disciple's name before ordination, but Pons did not. Neither did Guillaume Authié. Since Prades Tavernier became André Tavernier, why did neither Pons nor Arnaud Marty, the Perfect from Junac, change their name? Most of them did. Thus, within two years of ordaining his own son, Pierre Authié, assisted by Guillaume Authié, ordained two more Perfects in Larnat. Both men were in their thirties, and they were given the names Pierre and Paul respectively. This particular ceremony in 1302 was attended by no fewer than five Occitan Perfects, including the three Authiés, Prades (André) Tavernier, and Pierre-Raymond de Saint-Papoul. A year later, c.1303, Pons d'Avignonet was ordained by the Authiés, again at the Issaurats' in Larnat.

While there can have been little scope for luxury in the Authiés' lives on the run, they were attached to books and owned a library; and Pierre Authié had a special leather case made for his consolation-book (L, 50). As we saw, every Perfect always carried the Gospels on his person, usually in his tunic. But there were other books, which could only be purchased in major cities, and here Pierre de Luzenac's literacy came in useful.

It was in the cellar of the Issaurats' at Larnat one night in the autumn of 1300 that Pierre and Jacques Authié showed Pierre de Luzenac an

★ It is worth noting that we do not hear of consolations carried out by Jacques Authié, although we do hear him preach. This may mean that a newly ordained Perfect had to serve a period of apprenticeship as *socius* to senior Perfects, as for example Jacques Authié to Prades Tavernier, and Pons Sicre-Baille and Arnaud Marty to Guillaume Authié.

illuminated manuscript. It was 'a very beautiful book, with exquisite Bologna characters, which were splendidly illuminated with blue and vermilion and in the book there were the Gospels in Occitan and the Epistles of Saint Paul' (d'AR, f.64r).

The fact that the book was in Occitan clearly struck Pierre de Luzenac as noteworthy because some, or maybe even most, such gospels had parallel Latin–Occitan texts.* Jacques Authié read to the assembled congregation from this book for a while, and then invited Pierre to buy him a complete Bible next time he was in Toulouse: 'You may go up as high as twenty pounds or thereabouts.' This sum was equivalent to half a house in nearby Tarascon. The Authiés' readiness to spend that much on a book is an indication of their financial resources. Pierre agreed, and then asked for the money. The Authiés referred him to their Toulouse banker Ysalguier, and noted that Pierre Sans would arrange for it to be transferred to him. But de Luzenac had been arrested for debts at Toulouse and may have jumped bail, because he no longer dared return there. Instead, he proposed to continue his studies at Montpellier or at Lleida in Catalonia; if the Authiés advanced him the money, he would buy their Bible in Montpellier, where plenty could surely be found. Then he asked for a further advance of at least another ten pounds to redeem his own books from a loan shark in Toulouse, where he had pawned them. On this the Authiés stalled him, but at some point de Luzenac did bring them a book or pamphlet in Occitan containing the writings of St Peter and St Paul (d'AR, f.2r).

Possession of a book in this period was almost invariably construed as a sign of Cathar contamination, so that when Pierre Clergue of Montaillou was seen with a book, the villagers guessed that it came from Guillaume Authié. We have already seen how eager Pierre Authié was to retrieve his book from Arnaud Teisseyre of Lordat. Six years later, not long after Pierre Maury's return to Montaillou, the same Arnaud was employing Pierre de Gaillac, who was related to him through the Authiés. De Gaillac worked at Arnaud Teisseyre's as his

---

* Thus, at about the same time, Raymond Vaissière was sitting in the sun outside of his house in Ax when he spotted an acquaintance of his, Guillaume l'Andorran, reading to his mother from a book. Raymond asked to see the book. In it he read '*in principio erat verbum*', the opening of St John's Gospel, and he also noticed the fact that the entire volume consisted of a mixture of Latin and Occitan (FR, ff.52v–53r).

secretary after finishing his studies at Toulouse. He would have been something like an articled clerk, and this may have been a form of statutory pupillage. He was then probably in his mid-twenties, with a brother called Bertrand and two younger sisters, Raymonde and Alissende, who were then children, the latter being named after her grandmother.

He had been there for some six months when one day, searching through the ledgers of his employer, de Gaillac found among them a book. It was written, on paper, in Occitan, and it was bound with old parchment (FR, f.157r). It contained arguments for and against Manicheism, a dualistic heresy in which God and Satan are coeval, and the Catholic religion. The book was probably a Cathar treatise and may also have contained St John's Gospel.

Arnaud Teisseyre surprised his secretary in the act of reading this book and angrily snatched it from him. He then hid it. That night, according to Arnaud's wife, who was Pierre Authié's daughter, he beat her as well as his illegitimate son Guillaume (his son by Pierre Authié's daughter was called Raymond, after his uncle) for leaving it somewhere where de Gaillac could find it. Pierre de Gaillac claimed to have felt so deeply embarrassed and humiliated that he left Arnaud's house and returned to Tarascon. Three days later Arnaud visited him there and prevailed on him to return to Lordat. After that, whenever during their walks near Lordat Pierre alluded to Manicheism, Arnaud would just laugh and say nothing.

The body as well as the spirit needed tending, and on Friday 2 September, the first day of the fair of St Antonin at Pamiers, Raymond Authié and Arnaud Teisseyre went to buy a razor for Pierre and Guillaume Authié. To safeguard their anonymity the two Perfects needed to shave regularly, but they could not trust barbers, and therefore needed to shave each other or be shaven by adherents. Although Raymond had been given a shilling towards the cost of the razor, it was Arnaud who chose it. His knowledge as a doctor, and occasional surgeon who used razors for bleeding people, meant that he could be trusted to choose the best.

They went into a shop in the *Vilanova* or 'New Town' part of Pamiers, which corresponds to the area which today lies between the

Place de la République and the Mercadal. The shop stood next to the house of 'Compans Gras', a name casually mentioned by Raymond Authié as if he expected his interlocutor, the Bishop of Pamiers, to be familiar with it; as well he might, because a Pierre Compans Gras is named as one of the two consuls of Pamiers in a letter by the Count of Foix of 9 December 1303 (D 93, f.66r).

Raymond and Arnaud discovered that the instrument of their choice cost more than the Authiés' estimate of a shilling, even though a shilling of the period could hire a manservant for a day, or pay for overnight accommodation and food for a man and a woman at a hostelry. In other words, razors were expensive, and for this one Raymond had to pay out an additional three old-style pennies ([*deniers*] *toulzas*) to make up the difference between his French silver *tournois* and the total cost of ten *toulzas*. But Arnaud assured him that he had purchased the best. 'I chose,' he said, 'as if it were for myself' (FR, f.159v).

Nearly a month later, towards a cold end of September, Pierre de Luzenac was given notice by Raymond Authié that he should expect his brothers at the Perles bridge that night and put them up. And so, the same day the Perfects were due, de Luzenac commandeered Rixende Palharèse, whose house in Luzenac provided a suitable location. At first Rixende was unwilling to oblige. She professed to be frightened of having two strange men sleeping in her house when she was alone. What if they 'took me by force', she wanted to know. 'Don't worry, they won't talk to you about that, and they won't touch you,' he replied. When she insisted further he cut her off with, 'Shut up. And I expect there to be a fire when we arrive!'

That night he took himself off to the Ariège bridge to collect Pierre Authié and his son Jacques. They were chaperoned by their brother Raymond, who then returned to Ax while the two Perfects and de Luzenac hurried to Rixende's. They briefly warmed themselves at the fire, and then made up their bed and retired while Pierre returned to his home, perhaps the castle.

Early the following morning he joined them for a breakfast of fresh trout that they had brought with them from Ax, while Rixende ate apart in the pantry (d'AR, f.66v). Before breakfast Pierre Authié took napkins out of his bag and, giving one each to Jacques and de Luzenac,

put his around his neck like a stole and started to consecrate the bread.
In Pierre de Luzenac's own words: .

At the beginning of the meal and standing, Pierre Authié took half the bread,
held it in his hands with the napkin that he had put around his neck, and
started to say the Lord's Prayer over it. Then, softly between his teeth, he
spoke for a moment. Then he cut the bread with his knife, and put some on
the table in front of himself and then in front of each one of us, telling me
that this was what they called sanctified bread. When Jacques, who then
served us and put the food on the table, put out the dishes in front of us or
himself, he always said 'Bless us', and similarly when he cleared the dishes and
when he started to eat and drink. Both they and I had our stoles on the table
during the meal. (FR, f.66v)

After breakfast, de Luzenac claims, the Authiés wanted him to do the
melhorier, but he declined and offered to do it on another occasion.
Then Jacques gave him a four-page pamphlet which contained a Latin
exegesis of the Lord's Prayer.

After this they parted, with the Perfects returning to bed to be fit for
that night's trek. In the evening de Luzenac met up with them again,
and after dinner he escorted them as far as the bridge of Albiès, when
it started to rain. They took refuge in a disused mill, and there de
Luzenac did the *melhorier*. Shortly afterwards they heard whistling
outside the mill, which signalled that the relay-team had arrived. The
Perfects joined them, and Pierre headed home to Luzenac.

It would be another two months, near All Saints, before he needed
to incommode Rixende again. Not that she was generally unwilling.
Perhaps she just resented the callous selfishness of the young Pierre. His
mother, on the other hand, seems to have had no difficulty in motivating
Rixende. One day, for example, when the Authié father-and-son team
were at Raymonde's in Luzenac and were scheduled to push on to
Quié that night, Raymonde panicked at the thought that the two
Perfects might have to make do without blanket, sheets, and pillow-case
(FR, f.56v). She therefore sent Rixende ahead with what was needed,
and further instructed her to call on her niece Lorda Bayard for pro-
visions, since otherwise the Perfects might have to go without food in
Quié. At Quié Lorda equally willingly gave her bread, fish, and wine

for the Good Men. It was also Rixende Palharèse who eight years later rescued Arnaud Marty when he was on the run (see below, page 215).

By the time the year 1300 was drawing to its end, the Authiés were truly launched. They had survived at least one attempt at betraying them, and they had established solid foundations from which to wage their guerrilla warfare against the Catholic church.

In the Tarascon triangle, they enjoyed the support above all of Guillaume Bayard, his wife Lorda, niece of Raymonde de Luzenac, and his daughters Ricarde and Mathende. It was probably through the intermediary of Bayard that the Count of Foix, Roger-Bernard III, came to be consoled by Pierre Authié on his death-bed in March 1302 in the hall of the Tarascon castle, even though he was buried by the Bishop of Carcassonne and in the presence of several abbots (FR, f.206r; Devic *et al.* 1872–1905, 9, 232). Moreover, after the death of Roger-Bernard III Bayard's star was more than ever in the ascendant when he became regent (FR, f.51v).

What inspired Bayard to become a Cathar is impossible to determine, but like Simon Barre, he certainly revelled in the sexual licence of his new faith. In spite of a close relationship with his wife, who seems to have dominated him in some ways, he boasted of sleeping with not just two sisters, but with two sets of sisters.* That as a lawyer and judge Bayard was on the take was widely known, and his contempt for the judicial system is further evident from his strong-armed overturning of the lawful marriage of one of his daughters to Raymond-Arnaud of Château-Verdun, in favour of a second union with the squire Pierre de Miglos, the owner of the very large dog which was legendary in the region. On another occasion, Bayard colluded with Raymond Authié in hiding a rapist from the wrath of the governor of Mirepoix, because the rapist was a relative of a Cathar ally from Ax.

But in 1305 something happened that must have given Bayard pause

* They were Gauda and Blanche Faure, and the married Ermessende Magre and her married sister Arnaude. As already noted, this form of biblical incest had become fashionable and exciting in the fourteenth-century Ariège. Bayard dismissed objections to it with the commonly used word *faytilhas*, that is 'superstitions' (cf. Pierre Clergue's *affitilhas*, page 55), which the Cathars applied to everything Roman that they did not accept, such as transubstantiation.

for thought. At his wife's urging he intervened when the house of one Alamande de Sos was being raided by the men of the Count of Foix, while Guillaume Authié (d'AR, f.16r) or his nephew Jacques (FR, f.235r) was inside it. The men claimed to be recovering property in settlement of debts, and the raid happened to coincide with the presence in that house of a famous Perfect. Bayard stalled the guard long enough for the Authié Perfect to escape by the skin of his teeth through a door giving on to the Pech of Tarascon.

Arnaud of Bédeilhac, a clerk who was Bayard's messenger to the sergeant of the guard, did not believe that the raid was unconnected to the presence of an Authié in the house. He was surely right. The raid signalled that by 1305 the Inquisition was fighting back, and that its intelligence was so good that they knew that Bayard could not be trusted to supervise the seizure of Alamande's home. As we shall see, 1305 saw the first significant setbacks in the Ariégeois Cathar revival. The deliberate bypassing of the powerful Bayard may also have been intended as a shot across the bows. It may not be fanciful to conjecture that the local loyalist Arnaud Sicre Senior had a hand in this strike.

The Authiés cannot have been ignorant of the moral shortcomings of Bayard, just as they must have known that the priest of Montaillou was a leper in the face of God, whether theirs or that of the Roman Catholic church. Their preparedness to condone such depravity, with an eye to the greater good, casts a long shadow over their mission.

By the end of 1300 the Authiés' grip on the lower Ariège valley was assured by a formidable array of powerful alliances. An overarching Cathar junction had been effected between Tarascon and Ax (d'AR, ff.17r, 56r). In Ax itself the Perfects enjoyed the unconditional support of the Barre family, and of militant followers such as Sybille Baille and a number of others. From Ax their colonizing reached south beyond the Puymorens to Latour-de-Carol and Puigcerdà, and east to Mijanès and Quérigut in the Donnezan, and from there beyond the Fenouill-èdes. They fanned out north into the Pays de Sault, from where they radiated as far as Verdun-sur-Garonne north of Toulouse. The Aude down at Quillan could be reached in a long night's walk from Montaill-ou, and from Quillan it was twenty miles to Carcassonne and to Arques, a Cathar stronghold with close ties to the Sarbartès.

★

The energy, resourcefulness, and commitment of the Perfects is best illustrated from their consolations of the dying, which constituted their most dangerous duty. They were at their most vulnerable then to entrapment, but their ordination bound them to set out to console wherever they were needed. The group of fit young men who put themselves at the disposal of the Perfects as guides and messengers during these consolation journeys are among the unsung heroes of this story. Their knowledge of the area was matchless, and so were their speed and stamina. They were the eyes, if not the ears, of the Authiés by day and, crucially, *at night*. The pathfinders included Pierre Maury, Arnaud Vital, Raymond Azéma and Pons Rives from Montaillou, a Guillaume Dejean from Prades, the two Issaurat brothers from Larnat, Bernard Marty of Junac, and perhaps Guillaume Escaunier of Sorgeat. Sometimes a child would accompany a Perfect, as happened with Pierre-Raymond of Saint-Papoul when, in broad daylight, he called at Raymond Authié's in Ax. He wanted to look like a merchant, and this seems to have been one of his preferred, albeit risky, disguises (d'AR, ff.111, 39r). It was distinctly rare for a Perfect to be seen in daylight, and then only in an emergency, as happened at Montaillou one day when Pierre Clergue was roped in as look-out (see above, page 23).

Among the boldest and most spectacular consolations were the ones of Gentille in the hospital in Ax in September 1301 and of Pierre de Gaillac's mother in Tarascon three years later.

In 1301 the hospital at Ax was forty-one years old. Along with the Bassin des Ladres it had been commissioned by Louis IX, the son of Blanche of Castile, and the founder of the Sainte-Chapelle in Paris (c.1245–8). In 1297 Louis IX was canonized by Boniface VIII, and today the hospital Saint-Louis at Ax-les-Thermes bears his name. The purpose of the hospital and the pool, which sits in the same spot today as it did 700 years ago, was to nurse soldiers who had contracted skin diseases during the crusades in Palestine.

It was towards the end of September in 1301, and the time of 'the first sleep'. Raymond Vaissière of Ax was in his nightshirt and breeches, barefoot, and about to go to bed, when Guillaume Authié knocked gently on his door. Guillaume explained that he had come from his brother Raymond's house to ask Vaissière to accompany him to the hospital of Ax, where he intended to console a woman called Gentille d'Ascou.

Gentille may have belonged to minor nobility, as her name, which she shares with Béatrice de Planisolles's sister, indicates. She was staying at the hospital, he explained, to take the waters, but her main reason for being there was her desire to be consoled before dying. This was indeed the case, as Vaissière knew, since she had paid a substantial deposit of twenty-five shillings to the Authiés through his intermediary.

Putting on a fur coat, Vaissière joined Guillaume Authié and together they made their way to the hospital. When they reached its steps or stone staircase, they saw Marie, the wife of Pierre Amiel of Mérens, in the hospital's porch, and went up to her. Marie, who looked after the sick Gentille, then went inside the hospital to get Gentille, while Guillaume Authié and Raymond Vaissière entered a field at the back of the hospital.

Here they waited until Marie brought Gentille, who was so ill that she could neither walk nor stay upright unsupported. Gentille sat down, and Guillaume Authié consoled her. When he had finished, he suggested to Vaissière that he should either go home or go to the baths, because the company of Marie was enough. While Raymond Vaissière made his way to the baths, Guillaume Authié probably conferred with both Gentille and Marie about the *endura*. In Gentille's case, this lasted for another five or six days, before she found release.

Gentille had been a devout and even proselytizing Cathar, and her generous gift towards her consolation demonstrates as much. For Guillaume Authié to undertake a consolation in an open field verging on the hospital in Ax was to run the gauntlet of the Inquisition. Although these were early days, the plot of the year before against the Authiés proves that the Inquisition was rallying with the complicity of local collaborators.

Moreover, the hospital in Ax was not only frequented by the sick. The Montaillou priest's reign of sexual terror extended into this very place. Pierre Clergue regularly stayed over at the hospital after taking the thermal waters at Ax, and was himself visited here at night by various mistresses. They were rumoured to arrive wrapped in cloaks, presumably to hide their identities. Even so some names were common knowledge in Ax, among them those of *Na* Maragda, Jacqueline den

Tourte, and Alissende Pradon. What was also known, however, was that the women who serviced the demonic rector from Montaillou were intimidated by the power he wielded. In the words of a contemporary, 'there was no woman in Ax, or only a few, whom the rector could not possess when he was there, because of the fear of the Carcassonne Inquisition' (FR, f.51v).

It is possible that Pierre Clergue only started using the hospital as a place for assignations later, since at the time of Gentille's consolation he may have been mourning for the châtelaine, who had remarried six weeks earlier. On the other hand, his heart and his nether regions were not necessarily connected in a fashion that inspired this kind of abstinence. If Pierre Clergue used the hospital as a brothel, so perhaps did others such as Barre, Bayard, and the de Polignacs. When they came for the waters, as we know they did, the Clergues may have plied them with women, since prostitutes were known to frequent the area of the pool. However well consolidated the Cathar position was in Ax, Perfects still needed to take the utmost precautions, if only because they could not afford to compromise their friends. The extent to which theirs was a hugger-mugger, cloak-and-dagger existence is well illustrated by the consolation of Pierre de Gaillac's mother. The Perfect was again Guillaume Authié.

Gaillarde de Gaillac was dying in the August of (probably) 1304, and Guillaume Authié was smuggled into one of her husband's houses in Tarascon. The house stood close to another dwelling that also seems to have belonged to them; and nearby was the house of Guillaume de Rodes, a nephew of Pierre and Guillaume Authié, and husband of Blanche, de Gaillac's mother-in-law. Guillaume Authié waited for Gaillarde to reach the critical moment when she was close enough to death to start the *endura*. Later his nephew Guillaume de Rodes reported that this period lasted at least eight days.

Then, one very warm evening around six o'clock, Gaillarde was taken (literally 'dragged herself') to a secret place to die. In the room where she lay dying, de Gaillac, his maternal grandmother Alissende, his aunt Esclarmonde, and another fifty or so people from Tarascon had gathered to pay their respects. Esclarmonde urged him to get rid of them, because they needed total privacy for the consolation.

Turning to the assembled company, de Gaillac said, 'Gentlemen, let's go outside because the heat is oppressive and we are making my mother suffer.' Only Alissende and Esclarmonde were left in the room, which they locked from inside. After telling Pierre to sweep up, Esclarmonde climbed over beams and door-posts into the house next door to join Guillaume Authié. There she took off her cape and cloak and gave them to him to wear. It was disguised as Esclarmonde that the Perfect arrived in the room and consoled the dying woman. At dusk he left the house and entered that of his nephew Guillaume de Rodes, where he stayed that night and the following day. Then he was collected from the house by Bertrand Tournier of Tarascon who escorted him to Guillaume Bayard's.

By all accounts Guillaume Authié was scrupulously conscientious in carrying out his duties as Perfect. Whereas Prades Tavernier was repeatedly prevailed upon to console patients at the point where they had lost the faculty of reason, speech, and free choice, Guillaume Authié insisted on his patients having their mental faculties intact before consoling them.

In 1302 Guillaume's former sister-in-law was dying (FR, ff.54v, 55v). She had been born Sybille Benet and had married one Pierre Authié from Ax who was commonly known by the name of Pierre 'Pauc', that is 'little' Pierre. This was just as well, because the names of Sybille Benet's husband and brother-in-law duplicated those of the famous two Axian Perfects, so that this particular consolation became one of doubles; not only that, but *both* her brothers-in-law were called Guillaume Authié.

The night she died Sybille lay in her bed next to the fire. Tending her were her sister Gaillarde, her mother, and her brother-in-law Guillaume Authié. Sybille had yielded to Gaillarde's entreaties to be consoled, but she was frightened of her husband's reaction, since neither he nor his brother were Cathars. But the night she died her husband was asleep in his bed, perhaps lulled into a false idea about the true state of her health, since Gaillarde later claimed to have arranged for her sister's consolation to take place while he was asleep.

On Sybille's last night Raymond Authié's wife Esclarmonde visited the house. At some point Sybille Authié took a turn for the worse and it became clear that death was not far off. Gaillarde urgently needed to get the Catholic Guillaume Authié out of the house before she could smuggle into it her husband Guillaume. Esclarmonde Authié therefore turned to Guillaume Authié and asked him to grab a handful of straw to light up the way and see her home urgently. The unlit streets of medieval Ax may have been dangerous enough for a lone woman to require a night-time escort; on the other hand it is more likely that Esclarmonde's anxiety about her personal safety was a ruse to get him away.

While they were gone, Gaillarde rushed to Sybille Baille's and returned with the Perfect Guillaume Authié. By now Sybille was delirious and Guillaume Authié refused to console her: 'If she recovers her faculties, I'll come and receive her then,' he said.

Sybille Authié-Benet died that night without the benefit of a Cathar consolation. Although consolation did not guarantee a passport to heaven, it was intended to facilitate the way there, and it would ensure that the person would not migrate through a further reincarnation in this world. The people of medieval Languedoc seem to have considered that a greater blessing than we might now.

At the burial of Sybille Authié in the cemetery of Ax the following day, Gaillarde told a disappointed Esclarmonde that Sybille had died unconsoled. She blamed the Catholic Guillaume Authié for staying too long (which may have been his intention), and deplored the fact that Sybille had not earlier entered into a full *convenenza* with the Cathar Perfects (see above, page 90).

6. Pierre Maury and the Cathars of Arques

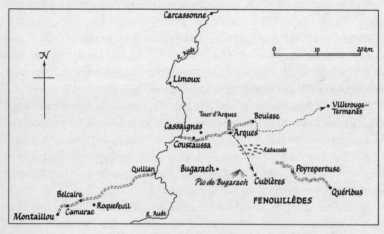

Arques in the Aude

Two years later, on a very wet and black night in April 1304, four men gathered in the same cemetery at Ax, not far down from today's railway viaduct. They were Prades Tavernier, Guillaume Escaunier and his brother Raymond, both from Ax, and their guide, the red-haired Pierre Montanié of Coustaussa. They intended to trek from Ax to the village of Arques, where Prades Tavernier was required for the consolation of Gaillarde Escaunier. In the dark they 'all climbed the mountain' by way of Sorgeat and got as far as the woods above Montaillou and Gebets.* Conditions in the gully in torrential rain must have been atrocious. The following day they pushed on until they reached Coustaussa in the Aude. Here they rested for a few hours at the Montaniés', and then, after midnight, they continued to Arques where they arrived before dawn.

Arques nestles in a wide valley which Pierre Maury, in Occitan,

* On this lost location, see pages xxxviii–xxxix.

called *la vayl d'archas*. It was linked to the Sabartès and the Pays de Sault through transhumance as well as marriage. In the winter shepherds drove their flocks down into the excellent pastures of the Aude valley, and in the summer they led them back up again. Although it seems that some pastures near Arques were also used during the summer, which is why Pierre Maury stayed there during that season, two of the most loyal Cathar families of Arques, the Peyres and the Maulens, used the summer pastures of the Pays d'Aillou.

The Maulens are called 'cousins' by Pierre Maury of Montaillou, which was why he went to stay with Raymond Maulen of Arques after leaving his father's house in the year 1299–1300. But the word 'cousin' is not strictly correct. Raymond Marty, who was indeed Pierre Maury's first cousin, seems to have been married to a sister of Raymond Maulen, so that when Pierre Maury calls Raymond Marty Maulen's 'brother' he means brother-in-law (FR, f.254r). It was this same Raymond Marty's sister Jeanne who became the Cathars' albatross in their Catalonian exile.

If herding duties and, perhaps, a row with his family in Montaillou brought Pierre Maury to Arques in the first instance (unless he left because he was threatened by Pierre Clergue), it was love that kept him there. Above all, a link was forged in Arques between Pierre Maury and the Perfects, and the seeds were sown here of the relationship between him and the luminary of the Catalonian diaspora, the shepherd-turned-Perfect, Guillaume Bélibaste.

Another Sabartesian who regularly visited in Arques was Guillaume Escaunier from Ax, who stayed with his sister Marquèse, the wife of Guillaume Botolh of Arques who employed his brother-in-law Escaunier as shepherd. At Arques Marquèse Botolh-Escaunier had become close friends with Sybille Peyre of the wealthy family of Raymond Peyre-Sabatier (*passim* Peyre), and Sybille seems to have named one of her daughters after Marquèse.

The fact that both women were Ariégeoises may have played a part in their friendship; Sybille Peyre was, as we have seen, a Gouzy from Larnat.* Marquèse Botolh-Escaunier may have stood as godmother

---

* Moreover, her brother had married Guillemette de Larnat, a sister of the squire Philippe. This Guillemette and her sister Sybille, who was married to a Miglos from the other side of the mountain, died almost simultaneously in the squire's house in

over her namesake, since a godparent system operated in the Sabartès. When therefore, in about 1302–3, little Marquèse died, Gaillarde Escaunier came all the way from Sorgeat to comfort Sybille and Raymond. But there may have been more to this visit than a mere mercy-errand. Gaillarde Escaunier was Cathar, like her close friend Sybille Baille from Ax. Her way of solacing Sybille Peyre and her husband was to offer them the spiritual services of the Authiés. To that extent Gaillarde may have been going forth to spread the Word, even if to do so meant exploiting another family's sorrow and their need for comforting.

Such was Gaillarde's persuasiveness that Raymond Peyre decided to visit the Authiés in Ax, and here he was converted. From now on he would be, in his wife's words, a good *pecol*, or 'foot' (meaning foot-soldier) of the Cathar church. The Peyres' grazing their sheep in the highlands of the Sabartès henceforth provided a watertight excuse for searching out the Good Men 'up there', and that was exactly what Raymond Peyre did. While visiting at later stages in the Pays d'Aillou Raymond may also have acted as a money courier.

Before long the Authiés visited their rich new recruit in Arques, and thus Sybille Peyre came to be present at the most extended Authié clinic on record. She later maintained that Pierre Maury had attended these occasions, but this was not the case, although he had been living and working for Raymond Maulen in Arques since the turn of the century. His reluctance at this stage was probably due to the fact that for two years, from 1302 to 1304, he was in love with a Catholic loyalist girl from Arques called Bernarde d'Esquinat, and it was for this reason that no one directly broached dissident ideas with him.

Altogether we have the texts of four major 'Arques-sermons'. Two of them were delivered on consecutive nights in the Peyre house, while the third one was given by Jacques Authié as he travelled with Pierre Maury. A fourth homily was delivered by Prades Tavernier in the cellar of the Maulens' house during the winter of 1304. Jointly they provide

Larnat in about 1302, and were consoled by the Authiés. There can be little doubt that the Authiés were eager to exploit the de Larnat–Gouzy (Larnat) and Peyre–Gouzy (Arques) bridgehead, which meshed furthermore with the Bayards, because of the eventual union of Pierre de Miglos and Ricarde Bayard.

a unique spotlight on the teachings of the Cathar doctrine of this period, and the fact that three of them are by the Authiés themselves, albeit mediated through two exceptional witnesses, Sybille Peyre and Pierre Maury, renders them compelling documents. While we know that the clinic at the Peyres' happened before the spring of 1304, we can only tentatively deduce a more precise date.

Young Marquèse Peyre had died some time before the Perfects Pierre and Jacques Authié first came to Arques. The night they entered the Peyres' house, Sybille and her daughter Bernarde, who was about five years old, were sleeping in the same bed. Since Bernarde turned six years old at Easter 1304, it would appear that the Perfects arrived in Arques some time in late 1303, which would date the conversion of the rich Peyres to the same period.

Like their counterparts elsewhere in Languedoc, the Peyres had prepared living quarters in their loft for the Perfects, and this loft had a balcony. For several years their friend Raymond Maulen had been a Cathar, and rumours about this were rife as far afield as Montaillou, where Pierre Maury first heard it. Now the Peyres and Maulens became rival zealots in the Cathar cause. As well as being friends of the Peyres in Arques, the Maulens may have been equally affluent. Raymond Maulen's wife was called Églantine, and her mother was Bérengère. Both of these were comparatively rare names, at least as far as the peasant culture of Occitania was concerned, and may indicate that Raymond Maulen was a wealthy farmer who, socially, had married above his station.

After resting the first night, Pierre and Jacques Authié seem to have spent their first day in Arques chatting to the Peyres and telling them about their recent lives. That evening they had a dinner of fish, apples, nuts, bread and wine, as well as cabbage, which they cooked themselves.

The following night, their third one in the house, they both preached. Although Sybille oddly could not well remember the contents of those sermons, she was struck by Jacques Authié's eloquence: he spoke, she claimed later, as if it were an angel talking.

The night after, the two Authiés enacted a well-rehearsed two-hander familiar to us from Larnat, with Jacques Authié reading aloud from a book in Latin while his father expounded its doctrine in Occitan. The Latin text would have been St John's Gospel. The reason why it was read in Latin was probably because Latin impressed the audience, and showed the learning of the Perfects, who were every bit as erudite as the corrupt priests of the Church of Rome. From the expository tone of the Authiés' sermon and the length of their stay at the Peyres', it is clear that this was an important foundation meeting.

The substance of this first reported Authié sermon, from their fourth night at the Peyres', consisted of a classic exposition of Cathar cosmography.

According to Pierre Authié, the devil sneaked into paradise after waiting 1,000 years at its door. Once he was inside, he inveigled the heavenly souls by telling them that they were subjects of the Heavenly Father: 'If you follow me into my world, I shall give you property in the form of fields and vineyards, gold and silver, wives, and other goods of that visible world.' Many spirits were seduced by this, and they fell from a hole in paradise for nine days and nine nights, like dense rain.

When the Father saw how depleted heaven had become, He rose from his throne, and put His foot on the hole. To the fallen souls He said 'Go for now,' thus leaving open the door of redemption. Everyone would be saved, even the bishops and high-priests, although they would be last, because their souls were the evil counsellors of Satan, and their journey back to the Father would be the hardest.

When the souls now on earth started to be saddened by their loss, the devil offered them as comfort such overcoats that would make them forget the bliss of heaven.

And so the devil created the human body, but the bodies could not move unless the Heavenly Father breathed life into them. The devil asked the Father to do so, which He did, on condition that what He put into the body was His, while the body was the devil's. Hence arose the dichotomy of body and soul, and the souls in their bodies forget what they hold in heaven.

No one can be saved or return to heaven unless they pass through the hands of the 'good Christians'. If one has not, one's soul at death is forced to re-enter another body, human or animal, and this metempsychosis continues until such time as the body's sins on earth have been expiated (FR, f.202).

Although Pierre Authié did not say so, or perhaps Sybille Peyre forgot to record it, there was a ceiling of nine on these transmigrations.

1. Caussou and the Val de Caussou.

2. The square of Montaillou from the main track, looking west towards Prades. The Rives house occupied the left-hand corner where track and square intersect.

3. The main medieval track passing the square of Montaillou.

4. *La fontcanal* and the track entering Montaillou from Ax.

5. Montaillou and the area known as *a-la-cot*.

6. *La laviera*, where the women of Montaillou did their washing in the Middle Ages.

7. Les Granges, the spur of the Gazel, and the *haute montagne* of Montaillou.

8. The church of Unac, where Béatrice met Raymonde de Luzenac in 1300.

9. Lordat in its setting as seen from the castle.

10. The rocky shelf of the Martys' home in Junac.

11. Larnat as seen from the meadows of *le fusan*.

12. The Perfects' gully at Larnat.

13. Salted fish at a
fourteenth-century
fishmonger's (*pisces
saliti*, from the
Tacuinum Sanitatis).

14. Ax-les Thermes
and the Rocher de
la Vierge.

15. Pierre Authié's rock of Bugarach.

16. Cubières and its medieval church.

Finally, these wandering souls arrive in a body in which they are consoled, and from there they return to heaven. Death with a Perfect in attendance, Pierre Authié implied, marked the end of the soul's odyssey.

Pierre Authié then proceeded to offer a parable, which I give here verbatim in Sybille Peyre's version of it:

The soul of a certain man left his body and entered that of a horse, and for a while he was the horse of a lord. When one night the squire rode this horse in pursuit of his enemies over rocks and stones, the horse put its hoof between two stones and could only extract itself with the greatest difficulty, leaving its horseshoe behind. When the horse died, its spirit entered a human body, that of a good Christian [i.e. a Perfect]. One day he was walking with another good Christian through that place where as a horse he had lost his shoe, and he told his companion about how as a horse he had there lost his shoe once. The two Perfects searched for the horseshoe between the two stones and found it. (FR, f.202v)

When Pierre Authié finished this story, Sybille Peyre recalls, 'we all laughed heartily'. The parable as well as the myth of the Fall echo, in different guises and variations, throughout the Cathar lore of this period; and of course the Manichean dualism which pits the soul, God's creation, against the body, the devil's counter-creation, lies at the heart of the Cathar heresy.

After the sermon was finished, they all did the *melhorier*, and then left the Perfects.

The following day they held court in their room, and before he preached again that night Pierre Authié was shaved by one of the faithful, one Raymond Gayraud from Arques.

His sermon, the third in three days, targeted specific issues, all of them commonplaces of the Cathar church. The 'Mother of God', he pointed out, was not a notion to be taken literally, since it was unimaginable for the body of Christ to have passed through a woman. Rather, it was a metaphor, as explained by the Evangelist, when he wrote that 'He who does the will of my Father who is in heaven, he is my brother, my sister, and my mother,' which paraphrases 'My mother

and my brethren are these which hear the word of God, and do it'
(Luke 8:21). In other words, those who want to do the will of God are
his 'mother'. This denial of Christ's literal incarnation was a key tenet
of Cathar doctrine, as was Pierre Authié's next point, that Christ neither
died nor suffered physical pain on the cross. Moreover Pierre Authié
insisted that one must not do reverence to the cross or representations
of it or of saints, because those are idols. Instead, 'just as a man should
with an axe break the gallows on which his father was hanged, so you
ought to try and break crucifixes, because Christ was suspended from
it, albeit only in seeming' (FR, f.202v).

The Father, Pierre Authié explained further, withheld the privilege
of divine amnesia to pain from his Disciples, because the servant must
not be greater than the master. If the faithful liked to believe, against
the evidence of their eyes surely, that the Perfects did not suffer at the
stake, Pierre Authié disabused them. But, he continued, pointedly
echoing the words of Christ's granting Peter the keys of heaven
(Matthew 16:19), the Son of God did grant them that what the Perfects
bound on earth would be bound in heaven.

Baptism was his next target. As well as implying that the baby's
weeping signalled a malaise with the entire process, he lampooned the
christening ritual as a meretricious charade in which adults answered,
and indeed lied, on behalf of an insentient child. The Cathar 'baptism',
on the other hand, did not consist of 'water' so much as of a visitation
by the Holy Ghost on adults.

Next on his list was transubstantiation, the turning of bread and wine
into the body and blood of Christ. With striking literalism, particularly
in a religion predicated on symbols and the mysticism of St John's
Gospel, Pierre Authié reiterated the Albigensian commonplace that
the body of Christ was not nearly big enough to satisfy the hordes of
greedy clergy out there. Even if it were the size of the nearby rock of
Bugarach (Pl. 12), the gluttonous priests would have devoured it long
ago.

Developing his offensive against the human body further, Pierre
Authié asserted that the only sacramental marriage was the union of the
soul to God. The marriage of the flesh, the union of man and wife, was
merely a union for intercourse, which was more sinful than extra-
marital sex, since sex within marriage happens more frequently and

usually without a sense of shame. All sex, in other words, was sinful, no matter how it was sanctioned.

On the subject of sin Pierre Authié had some good news, however. There was no sin, he claimed, in ignoring holy days; in fact it was always better to work than to be idle and gossip. Again, there was no point in observing meat-free days such as Good Friday, since eating meat was always a sin, on whichever day.

Finally he reverted to his theme of the preceding night. All those, he said, who were consoled by the good Christians would no longer be incarnated but would go straight to the Father. And so he finished.

The Authiés had worked hard in Arques. They had stayed five days (not four, as Sybille Peyre claimed) and five nights at the Peyres'. On each of these nights Jacques Authié ventured out into the main square of Arques, wearing a green coat borrowed from his host, Raymond Peyre. He thus mingled with the men of Arques for extended periods of time, safe in the knowledge presumably that he would not be recognized here, and could therefore gather easy intelligence about the mood in the village and the area generally.

From Arques the Authiés took off for Rieux-en-Val, to the north-east of Arques. While Raymond Maulen and Raymond Peyre were busy cooking the salted mullet that Peyre had got them as provisions for the journey, they decided that they would all go disguised as sheep traders, and if they were challenged they would explain that they were heading for pastures of theirs called *A Ser*.

There is no mention yet of Pierre Maury, as there undoubtedly would have been if he had been available as a guide; and indeed he was to walk Jacques Authié along this very route in late May 1304. Is it fanciful to believe that the Authiés encouraged Maulen and Peyre to woo Pierre Maury? They knew the Maurys through their family links with Montaillou, and they had probably been alerted to Pierre Maury's talents and single-mindedness. Here was perhaps a natural leader of men, a guide, and a commander whose energy and acumen would be an asset to the cause. The Authiés were by all accounts effective, far-sighted, and devious strategists. They had not hesitated, in the service of the greater good, to make common cause with the likes of Pierre Clergue; and for nearly eight years they successfully ran the wastrel Pierre de Luzenac as well as the unpredictable and dangerous Pierre de Gaillac. We may be reasonably certain that they also had a hand in recruiting Pierre Maury.

Did the Authiés' acolytes decide to act now because Pierre was poised to marry Bernarde? By the time Pierre Maury was approached he had bought a property in Arques. He was thriving and he was in love, and if he married his Bernarde he might be lost for ever to the good Christians. At some point towards the end of Lent 1304, or around Easter, which fell on 29 March, he was hired by Raymond Peyre. This was a first step. On a Sunday some eight days later, perhaps Quasimodo Sunday, 5 April, Pierre was bearded by Raymond Peyre and Bernard Bélibaste in the Peyres' sheepfold next to their house. Peyre came straight to the point, and urged Pierre not to marry a woman who was not of the *entendensa*, reminding him of his past affection for the good Christians before his love affair with Bernarde. If he married a Catholic he would never in the future be able to welcome or discuss the Good Men in his home. Why not find himself another bride? It could be arranged.

Raymond then stepped aside and Bernard Bélibaste, a scout and the brother of a future Perfect from the village of Cubières, made an offer that Pierre could not refuse. Instead of marrying Bernarde d'Esquinat, why not consider marrying Bernarde Peyre? She was admittedly only six years old, but she would come with a large dowry from her very rich father, who was prepared moreover to adopt Pierre Maury in the meantime. 'With her dowry and with what you already have in Arques, you will be rich enough no longer to need to work with your hands,' he was told.

The son of the weaver from Montaillou accepted the deal that was thus offered to him and, one must assume, broke off his affair with Bernarde d'Esquinat. As soon as Pierre had declared his readiness to be received, the Cathars wasted no time in making the necessary arrangements. Once the ritual of initiation had been undergone, it was that much harder to undo heretical affiliations, since seeing a Perfect, let alone honouring him, was a serious lapse in the eyes of the Church, and attracted commensurate penalties. Peyre and Belibaste had hoped to have Pierre received almost at once, but it was to take a little bit longer before a Perfect, *the* Perfect, was ready.

★

It was one evening some four or five days later, perhaps on Friday 10 April 1304, that Pierre Maury entered the *foghana* of the Peyres after returning the sheep to their pen. Preparations for a big dinner were under way. It must have been like a surprise birthday party, for this dinner was to celebrate Pierre Maury's reception into the Cathar faith. During the day, it seems, Pierre Authié had arrived with his bodyguard Guillaume Peyre and Martin Francès. The partakers of the main feast included Sybille Peyre, her husband and her mother from Larnat, Raymond Maulen, Pierre Maury, Bernard Vital from Montaillou (who resided in Arques and was a cousin of Arnaud Vital), Guillaume Escaunier, and his sister Marquèse. Pierre Authié and Martin Francès ate their dinner of fish apart in a side-room, while the others dined in the *foghana* or main hall. They were waited on by Guillaume Peyre, who frequently shuttled in and out between the room and the *foghana*; and once he brought out fish for Raymond Peyre from Pierre Authié.

After dinner Pierre Authié entered the *foghana* and saluted everyone by bestowing God's blessing on them. Then Raymond Peyre took Pierre Maury and led him into the room to Pierre Authié. The Perfect sat there with Guillaume Peyre, and both rose to meet Pierre. Authié took hold of young Maury's hand and made him sit next to him, while Raymond Peyre sat opposite them, probably as a witness, although he and Guillaume Peyre seem to have left Authié and Maury for the tête-à-tête of the *melhorier*.

The partnership between the Cathars and the twenty-six-year-old shepherd from Montaillou was about to be launched by *l'Ancien*, the most renowned living Perfect of Languedoc; and two or three years hence, the old Perfect's link with Pierre Maury would be poignantly consolidated when the latter's sister joined Pierre Authié and, probably, stayed with him until the end (see below, pages 238–9).

The Perfect's welcome to Pierre Maury was warm and intimate. He started by using the familiar '*tu*' instead of the second person plural '*vos*' throughout:

Pierre, it gives me such great pleasure! I've been told that you will be a good believer, if God so wills it, and I shall put you on the road to the salvation of God, if you want to believe me, just as Christ put His apostles there who never lied or deceived. And it is we who hold that road, and I shall tell you why we are called heretics: for this reason because the world hates us, which is not surprising, since it also hated our Lord whom it persecuted as it did His apostles. And we are hated and persecuted because of His law, which we observe with constancy, and those who are upright and want to maintain a steadfast faith allow themselves to be crucified and stoned when they fall into the hands of their enemies, as did the apostles, and they will not flinch from a single word of their stalwart faith. Because there are two churches, one which flees and forgives, and the other which fetters and flays. (FR, f.249v)

After this opening, with its classically Cathar statement about the two churches and a surprising enthusiasm for martyrdom, always a real, and often imminent, possibility for the Perfects of the period, Pierre Authié elaborated further on the contrast between the two churches. He elicited questions from Pierre Maury, and proceeded to the well-worn attack on Christian baptism. He noted that the Cathar version of baptism was predicated on a person's developed sense of moral discrimination, and that such a person should be at least twelve, and preferably eighteen, years old.

Eager to impress Pierre Maury with his trustworthiness, Pierre Authié then explained his own conversion:

Pierre, I have told you many things which are deeply true. I know everything that happens in the Church of Rome, and I was a public notary. I recognized then that I lived in great sin, because I did not live justly and truthfully, and I therefore relinquished sin and went in search of the truth. And after I found it and was received in the constant faith, I returned to these regions to make our friends understand its good teaching, and thus our faith has spread. And it goes from one to the other in such a way that in a short time there will be many good believers in these lands.

Then, switching to the second person plural, Pierre Authié exhorted him:

Be of good cheer and rejoice, because this is a happy day for us. If you knew the blessing promised to us, which we are not allowed to reveal to a man unless he becomes a good Christian, we would hardly stay on this earth. Pierre, I've given you to understand everything that must be given to understand by any good believer. Here it is. There are some who do not want to do what I'm going to ask of you now, but the majority of believers nevertheless comply. (FR, f.250r)

Pierre Maury replied that if God so wished, then he would do the good.

At that point Pierre Authié rose and closed the door of the room. The two of them were alone now, and the Perfect took a pillow, put it on the floor, and told Pierre to act as instructed, to which Pierre agreed. Kneeling in front of the Perfect, Pierre Maury asked for his blessing and then underwent the ritual *melhorier*.

Now Pierre Maury was a fully confirmed Cathar, and together he and the old Perfect issued forth into the *foghana*, where the others awaited them. Then they had a drink near the fire.

After that, and probably for the first time, Pierre Maury joined a group consisting of Guillaume Escaunier, Raymond Maulen, Guillaume Peyre and Bernard Vital to take the Perfect on the twelve-mile trek to Cassaignes, on the way to Limoux. If this was his first such night-time assignment, it came within a hair's breadth of disaster minutes after their leaving the Peyre house.

As they made their way past the 'mill of Arques' opposite the 'Tour d'Arques', which still rises on the Cassaignes road west of the village, they came face to face with the owner of the Tour, the squire Gilet de Voisins, and a posse of his men. The spot of this encounter in 1305 is today marked by the 'Auberge du Moulin'. De Voisins represented the secular arm of the Church in Arques, but the Cathars held their nerve, and the two groups exchanged greetings as they passed each other. The Authié party had undoubtedly taken the precaution of disguising itself as traders, pedlars or shepherds, but even so Gilet's suspicions ought to have been aroused by a group of men on the move late at night. Perhaps the brazenness of the Cathar group, walking, contrary to their usual practice, on the main road to the Aude, really did fool him, or perhaps it was the unlikely presence among the Cathars of his own *bayle*, Raymond Gayraud, which deceived him.

The long night of Pierre Maury's conversion was not over yet. Outside Cassaignes two young men rendezvoused with the Authié group and took them to the house of Guillaume de Cassaignes. Twenty years later Pierre Maury recalled this Guillaume's blue coat, which may suggest that he was an aspiring Perfect; if so, he may not have entirely enjoyed the blessing of Pierre Authié, because Maury also remembered that the old Perfect did not reciprocate his enthusiastic reception of them.

Pierre Maury was invited to stay for a drink and accepted. Before he left, the old Perfect impressed on him the need for discretion during future encounters with other Perfects. He advised him not to embarrass them with awkward questions, since if they were put on the spot and erred in their answer, they would then have to fast for three days. 'It is a sin to distress a good Christian,' he concluded.

With this admonition ringing in his ears, Pierre Maury made his way back to Arques where he arrived at dawn. He never again set eyes on Pierre Authié.

A few days later, one morning towards the middle of April, Pierre Maury returned from herding duties to the Peyres'. It seems that from the outside he spotted Prades Tavernier sitting on a bench and eating inside the very room where he had been received. He entered the house, and in the *foghana* he found Sybille Peyre's mother, who was frying eggs and bacon for herself. When he tried to enter the room to see Prades and found it locked, Sybille's mother told him that he would find something unexpected in there. Then she threw him the key, and he joined Prades. The Perfect blessed some of the bread he was eating and gave it to Pierre who took it with him on his way to his sheep.

Some eight days later Pierre Maury was back at the Peyres' to pick up more bread. In their cellar he encountered Guillaume Bélibaste Senior, who invited him over to the Maulens'. The Maulens' substantial house gave on to two streets at different levels, with their cellar and sheepfold being adjacent on the same level, while their *foghana* ran above the cellar.

Here, in the Maulens' cellar, poking his head around a barrel behind which he was hiding, stood Prades Tavernier. His stay in Arques was clearly a prolonged one, and old Guillaume Bélibaste did the *melhorier* but, Pierre Maury noticed, without kneeling because of his crippled (arthritic?) condition. Pierre Maury interestingly did not see fit to elaborate on why Prades hovered about at the Maulens' and Peyres'.

Was he trying to protect some of those involved who were still alive? Pierre Maury knew full well that Prades was lingering on at Arques because of two separate consolations. But in both cases Prades Tavernier and the Cathar church suffered a rare defeat at the hands of Raymond Peyre's wife Sybille.

She had been left inconsolable, as we saw, by the earlier death of her daughter Marquèse: 'I could not stop being sad and hurting,' she remarked, and Gaillarde Escaunier had tried to comfort her. But in the spring of 1304, Gaillarde herself was taken sick while staying at her daughter Marquèse Botolh's house, and it looked as if she might die. It was decided to console her, and her son therefore went to Ax and, as we saw, returned with his brother and Prades Tavernier. His other sister, called Gaillarde after her mother, was already at the Botolhs'.

By the time Prades met Gaillarde in mid-April 1304, she was hallucinating and moaning. Prades hesitated, because her mind was wandering. In the end he relented, and Gaillarde was received and put in the *endura*. Prades stayed on at Raymond Maulen's in Arques, waiting for the woman to die. While he did so the local adherents and aspirants had a chance to converse with him. Frequently Perfects would use the opportunity of a consolation for converting others of the same family or in the same village. These sessions were the equivalent of modern-day constituency clinics.

After five or six days on a diet of fresh water, Gaillarde rallied and asked for food. Her son Guillaume and her daughter Marquèse were reluctant to oblige, because eating would subvert the consolation. But as Gaillarde's luck would have it, Sybille Peyre visited her after hearing of her illness. When Gaillarde begged her for food, Sybille and Gaillarde's daughter, young Gaillarde, fed her wine and bread, and then cabbage cooked in oil. It was Sybille Peyre who apparently swayed Gaillarde's scruples about eating, although she and the younger Gaillarde hid their Samaritan deed from their families for as long as possible.

Perhaps the reason for Sybille Peyre's surge of compassion was that at the time of Gaillarde's *endura* she herself was nursing a small baby, Jacqueline, who was also very sick. She stood to lose another daughter, which would have left her with only young Bernarde. Sybille agreed with her husband that the baby should be consoled, and Prades once more, after pointing out its lack of sentience, yielded to their pleas.

The baby, her mother remembered later, was in 'agony' during the consolation. When the ceremony was over Raymond Peyre was delighted in spite of his deep sorrow; for like his wife, he loved his children and had long mourned for little Marquèse. At least, he said, Jacqueline would be an angel in heaven now. But when he briefly left the house with Prades and Bernard Vital, Sybille suckled the baby to still its distress. 'I could not bear,' she declared, 'to see her die like that.' Little Jacqueline lived for another year. When she did die in May or June 1305 she was not consoled afresh; perhaps her mother would not permit her child and herself to be put through such agony again.

When Raymond Peyre learnt of his wife's action, he was shaken and furious; and, as Sybille notes, he stopped loving his child and her for a long time. Others among the men, such as Pierre Maury, readily condemned her behaviour, and Jacques Authié, who seems to have arrived in Arques shortly after these events, probably did too; he had already accused Gaillarde Escaunier of being 'a bad old woman' for breaking her fast.

But if the headstrong Sybille temporarily lost her husband's esteem, her action won her the convalescent Gaillarde Escaunier's deepest friendship. Not only was Gaillarde, who had proselytized for the Cathars and then failed the *endura*, recovering, but she now allowed Sybille, in another defiant gesture, to feed her meat. Sybille's incensed husband told her to do as she liked where she herself was concerned, 'but do not push others into evil, because you know they say that "he who has bad neighbours has bad mornings" '(FR, f.204r).

But not long afterwards Raymond Peyre himself took ill, and thought that he was doomed. Prades was summoned, but delayed the consolation, since Raymond did not seem that sick. Perhaps the prospect of a third defeat at the hands of the determined Sybille had rendered him cautious. Raymond duly recovered, and Prades's good offices were, again, not needed.

When the local Cathars on this occasion collected the impressive sum of ten pounds for Prades Tavernier, Raymond noted approvingly that Prades needed the money more than the Authiés. They were learned, he remarked, and many people gave them many things, because it was deemed to be a privilege to give to them (FR, f.204r). Prades, on the other hand, was not nearly so highly regarded; he did not know Latin, and he was poor. Raymond Peyre should know, because it was his task locally to collect the many legacies left to the Authiés, and then deposit them in trust with the Francès family in Limoux where the Authiés' war-chest was kept (FR, f.204v).*

Rumours of the Authiés' wealth were rife at the time. As noted, they had been rich, literate, and cultivated before their ordination, and in spite of their Perfects' austerity they retained a certain remoteness that in the agrarian culture of thirteenth-century Occitania was associated with the ruling classes. That this caused some jealousy among the less fortunate is not surprising. Raymond and his wife Sybille heard Prades in a moment of frustration accuse the Authiés of greed. In an almost Molièrian vignette, Prades claimed that Guillaume and Gaillarde Authié loved handling their treasure:

> But I [Sybille Peyre] heard him [Prades] say at that time that if he had known from the beginning how Pierre and Guillaume Authié lived, he would not have put himself in their state, because they did not live how they ought to, because they were very greedy and envious and amassed money so that sometimes Guillaume Authié, after collecting money, came to his wife Gaillarde and the two of them frequently put their heads in a chest to pore over the money that he had gathered. (FR, f.204r)

Prades begrudged the Authiés their eminence in the movement, and to Pierre Maury he pettily recalled an incident when the Authiés helped themselves to the best part of a piece of woollen cloth, which had been given to all the Perfects to share. Could this be the piece of wool that Sybille Peyre took to Limoux for purple-dying, along with a cake, or a cheese, as a present for her hosts, the Francès family? On the same trip Guillaume Escaunier carried freshwater fish, which proves that

---

* It may have been for reasons of prudent housekeeping that the Authiés kept their money deliberately where it could not be accessed easily. When Pierre de Luzenac borrowed the sum of nine or ten pounds from Pierre Authié in Tarascon, he was told to collect the money in Limoux; but before he could do so, Pierre Authié warned him, he needed to discuss the loan first with other members of his kitchen cabinet. Getting de Luzenac to trek from the Ariège valley to Limoux made it that much more difficult for him to get his hands on anything other than petty cash.

they set out to meet Pierre Authié. From Sybille's description of the Francès home, it is clear that the treasurer of the Authiés was himself wealthy; rather astonishingly, he also owned 'an old serf' (*mancipius*: N; d'AR, f.11r).

Towards the end of May 1304 Pierre Maury was out on his sheep-pastures late one evening when he was summoned back to Arques, where at the Peyres' he found Jacques Authié, who had arrived with Pierre Montanié and required a guide to Rieux-en-Val.

Long before dawn the following morning Pierre Maury, Jacques Authié and Pierre Montanié set off on their twenty-mile-long journey. While the two guides walked, the young Perfect rode a mule provided for his comfort by Raymond Peyre. They went by way of a place called *la calm de linas*, and they lunched near Bouisse. Their destination was the house of one Guillaume de Rieux, a twenty-five-year-old clerk, who was tall and prematurely grey, and seems himself to have acted sometimes as a guide for the Perfects.

This was Pierre Maury's first encounter with the younger Authié, who, aware of Pierre's recent conversion, started to preach while they were on the road, as Perfects frequently did. The twenty-two-year-old Jacques Authié's reputation for being silver-tongued is illustrated by the narrative coloration and embroidery of his account of the Fall. Whereas his father's version was abstract and almost perfunctory, Jacques's was lively, visual, and anecdotal. It is interesting to note that, like his father, he used the familiar '*tu*' rather than '*vos*' to Pierre, who was several years his senior. He covered some of the same ground as his father, particularly with regard to transubstantiation and other rituals of the Roman church, except the bits of the Gospels it uses and the Lord's Prayer. What, he wondered rhetorically, was meant to become of the body of Christ once the Host has been eaten by human beings? To Cathar thinking the thought of Christ's body turning to human waste was as self-evidently impossible as was the idea that He Himself would issue into the world through a woman's vagina.

In the summer of 1304 Pierre Maury was up on the Rabassole pastures two hours to the south-east of Arques and some 950 feet above the village. From the Rabassole Pierre enjoyed a grand view westwards across the Val d'Arques. The area was less densely wooded then, because it was ceaselessly combed by herds of hungry sheep. His fellow shepherds during this period included his cousin Raymond Marty from Montaillou and a brother of Raymond Peyre.

It is worth pausing over this individual for a moment. Raymond Peyre seems to have had two brothers, Bernard and Pierre, who for some reason was called Pierre Sabatier rather than Peyre or Peyre-Sabatier. If the brother up on the pastures whom Pierre Maury described as a believer was Pierre Sabatier, as seems likely from Sybille Peyre's reference to his herding duties, then that casts an intriguing side-light on a significant part of her deposition.

She claimed that at some point her brother-in-law went up to their loft when Pierre Authié was in residence. When he discovered that he could not have access to one of the rooms there because of a Perfect, he apparently lost his temper. According to his sister-in-law, he cursed the Cathars and threatened them with physical violence. He only calmed down when his brother explained that the visitors were servants of the squire Guillaume-Arnaud de Château-Verdun and of his mother Stéphanie, and that they were stopping off on their way to the monastery of Lagrasse. Although this may be a true account, I rather suspect that it was an elaborate charade dreamt up between the Peyres to safeguard their property from the danger of confiscation. If the house, or at least part of the substantial Peyre estate, was made over to Pierre Sabatier, that would guarantee its continuance in the family so long as Pierre Sabatier was not himself implicated. It seems that the Inquisition's economic penalties could, in theory at least, be eluded by limited liability, where a person could in good time 'sell' or make over his/her belongings to a trusted third party and thus put them beyond the reach of the secular powers.

Pierre Maury spent most of the summer of 1304 on the Rabassole as 'head shepherd', looking after his sheep and making cheeses and bread. Towards the end of August, one day between noon and three o'clock, he was visited here by the Perfect Amiel de Perles and Raymond Bélibaste, who were on their way to the Bélibaste stronghold of Cubières, and the track there led them past the Rabassole. This was Pierre Maury's first meeting with the famous Amiel de Perles, a Perfect with a Cathar pedigree almost as impeccable as the Authiés'.

One Sunday that winter, after returning from church, which the Cathars attended to safeguard their cover, Pierre Maury met Prades

Tavernier once again in the Maulens' cellar, hiding behind the same barrel as before. Raymond Peyre and Pierre Maury laid a table in the cellar, and then joined Prades for dinner. While he ate lentils in oil, bread, wine and nuts, they had meat. At some point Peyre went upstairs to the *foghana* to retrieve some more from the pot and bring it down. Prades reacted by saying to Pierre, 'Get rid of that *feresa*,' using the disparaging term favoured by Perfects for gravy and meat.

It was the *feresa* which prompted Prades to preach. He explained that the Perfects only ate fish because fish propagate in water, and that their Lenten diet was intended to punish the flesh. His underpinning theme was that the ways of God are straight and narrow, whereas those of Satan indulge the flesh.

Later that winter, perhaps in January or February of 1305, Pierre Maury was visited at Arques by his brother Guillaume from Montaillou. Guillaume was about fourteen at this point. He had guided Prades Tavernier, who by now had pitched his tent more or less permanently at the Rives' in Montaillou, to Coustaussa where he had left him at the Montaniés'. Guillaume passed on greetings from Prades, and Pierre Maury gave his brother a shilling and a silver obole (worth half a penny), and four pence to give the Perfect so that he could buy himself new shoes.

At Easter of 1305 Pierre Maury was sent by Raymond Peyre on a debt-collecting mission to the Bélibastes of Cubières (Pl. 16). When early in the evening he arrived at their house near the river, he found several of the Bélibastes at home. They were Guillaume Bélibaste Senior and his wife, Raymond and his wife Estelle, and Bernard.

But Guillaume Bélibaste Junior, the future Perfect and companion of Pierre Maury in Catalonia, was conspicuous by his absence. Perhaps he was out on herding duties, or maybe he was already in hiding, because he had killed another shepherd and his own life was therefore forfeit (this seems to have happened some time before 1305: FR, f.256r). It is not known who ordained Guillaume Bélibaste, but it may well have been Pierre Authié. The connection between them could have been Pierre Maury's sister, who at some stage appears to have moved on from Guillaume Bélibaste to *l'Ancien* himself.

The Bélibastes were entertaining when Pierre Maury visited them in Cubières, and the guest of honour arrived shortly after him. He was Maître Pierre Girard, the public prosecutor of the Archbishop of Narbonne; two years from now Pierre Maury would stand before Girard accused of heresy.

After a dinner of meat, cheese, and milk, the prosecutor retired to bed. Raymond and Bernard Bélibaste now took Pierre outside and led him to the straw-barn, which sat away from the house towards the river-bank. Like the barn at Tarascon it required a key for access. Here Amiel de Perles and a recently ordained Raymond Faure from Coustaussa were sheltering. Pierre did the *melhorier* to Amiel and greeted him from his employer. Shortly afterwards, Estelle Bélibaste knocked on the door of the barn and asked Bernard and Pierre to leave. As they left, Pierre Maury noticed that two men were going to see the Perfects. He later professed not to have known them, in which case he must have understood that these were guides who would take them into the Fenouillèdes.

Perhaps; is it not also possible that one of these furtive visitors may have been the public prosecutor? Why was he dining in a sworn Cathar home? Was he another high-ranking official whom too much clerical corruption had turned against the Church of Rome? It seems an unlikely coincidence that two Perfects should have been staying at the Bélibastes' at the same time as one of the Bishop's chief executive officers. If Pierre Maury recognized Girard, he clearly later decided to pretend otherwise.

It was the end of August of 1305, and Pierre Maury was at 'Peyresols' directly north-west of Arques, which is the place that I take the *pars sors* of the Fournier Register to refer to.* Late one night Raymond Bélibaste arrived at Peyresols from Limoux with the Perfect Philippe d'Aylarac in tow. Pierre Maury fed them, while the Perfect drank only wine out of a tumbler that he carried on him. Then Bélibaste asked Pierre to take them to Cubières forthwith, without stopping in Arques, which later upset the Peyres. They set out south-east, past the Tour d'Arques, across the river, and towards Rabassole, which they skirted.

---

* It is not impossible that these pastures belonged to the powerful Peyres, and that the name 'Peyre-sols' ('the fields of the Peyres'?) reflects the fact that these lands had been part of their family's territory since time immemorial. Pierre Maury's companions here included Jean Maulen and Guillaume Marty from Montaillou.

The night was dark and the party could hardly see as they made their way through the woods and up steep escarpments. Their trek was so arduous that the Perfect fell repeatedly, and hurt his feet, exclaiming 'Holy Spirit, help me!' The effort of the journey sapped his energy to preach. Near Cubières they entered a sheepfold, or *cortal* in Occitan (*corral* in Spanish), belonging to the Bélibastes, and here they were welcomed by Bernard Bélibaste and his brother Guillaume, the future Perfect, together with a little boy who was their nephew. It was still dark, and the guides had a bite of bread and drank milk, while the Perfect settled down on his garments to sleep. The Bélibastes asked Pierre to stay over in their home, but he declined. Instead, alone, he returned to Arques. These long-distance treks must have tested even him to his physical limits, although they seem almost like hikes compared to his last fully documented trek fifteen years hence.

A few days later, in early September of 1305, Pierre Maury again met Amiel de Perles at the Peyres'. That brief encounter was to be his last with Perfects in the Val d'Arques, because shortly afterwards disaster struck.

Around 8 September 1305, the Nativity of the Virgin Mary, Jacques Authié and Prades Tavernier walked into a trap in Limoux. Although details of their capture and subsequent escape remain a mystery, we know that they had been lured there under the pretext of a consolation by none other than Guillaume Peyre, Pierre Authié's trusted aide-de-camp. Limoux was Peyre's home town, and he had been close to the Authiés from the start of their return to Languedoc in 1299–1300. Indeed both he and the other traitor, Pierre de Luzenac, had partaken five years earlier of a salmon and trout dinner in Toulouse in the summer of 1300.

He had operated the double-cross now because he felt let down by the Authiés and other Cathars who had refused him funds to acquit himself of a debt of forty shillings incurred during a spell in the Inquisitors' prison. He settled with his creditors by trading two of his friends for blood money. It is unlikely that anyone other than a member of the inner circle of the Authiés' organization could have duped Jacques Authié and Prades Tavernier, since generally the Cathars' security arrangements held fast. And none more so than those surrounding the Authiés themselves: they were after all the élite corps of this Cathar adventure.

Not only did Guillaume Peyre set up the two Perfects, he also provided valuable information to the Inquisition about the wider heretical contamination of the region. But the Cathar faithful did not always turn the other cheek, as we have already seen, and from now on Guillaume Peyre needed to tread warily. His brother was murdered in Carcassonne in retaliation, and as late as April 1321 this fourteenth-century Occitan supergrass was still in protective custody.

The impact of the arrests was devastating. There could be no question of either of the two men standing up to interrogation. They were pledged never to tell an untruth, and if the Inquisition resorted to torture, they would certainly talk. What none of the faithful could have anticipated was that the two captured Perfects gave the Inquisition the slip almost at once, before they were even taken from Limoux to Carcassonne. We can pick up their trail shortly afterwards in the village of Le Born, some twenty miles north-east of Toulouse, which proves that from Limoux Jacques Authié and Prades Tavernier fled north-west rather than doubling back instinctively to the Sabartès (L, 28). They hid here for eight days in the house of one Guillaume-Arnaud Faure (his family was known as '*Espanhol*'). This suggests that it was their treasurer Francès who organized the two Perfects' getaway, because four years later Francès's wife would die in the house of Guillaume-Arnaud's brother Bernard Faure in the same village. The Francès and Faure families were obviously closely linked.

When news of the capture of Jacques and Prades broke at Arques, Raymond Peyre was distraught, and when he briefed Pierre Maury about it he repeatedly struck his cheeks in a gesture of despair. Pierre was deeply upset, but he did not flee.

A fortnight later he returned to the Peyres' house. The night after, a council of war convened there. It consisted of Raymond Maulen, his brother-in-law Raymond Marty, Guillaume Escaunier and his sister Marquèse, Raymond and Sybille Peyre and her mother, Bernard Vital, Raymond Gayraud, the Cathar *bayle* of Gilet de Voisins, and Pierre Maury. The decision was taken to seek out the new Pope to confess their heretical activities, before they were summoned. Thus they would appear properly penitent, and that would count in mitigation.

By then it was widely known that the two Perfects had escaped, probably before they could be interrogated. But the traitor Guillaume Peyre had penetrated their homes with Pierre Authié, and they felt irrevocably compromised. They may have had intelligence to that effect, which would account for the savage reprisals they exacted from Peyre's family. Pierre Maury refused to agree to their plans to confess to the Pope, and the discussion which ensued degenerated into talk about money, with Pierre Maury complaining that he stood to lose the sixty shillings that he was owed if they did as planned, since they would not be able to repay him if the Inquisition confiscated their goods. But the die had been cast, and early the following morning the Peyres, Maulens, and the others left to sue for a papal pardon.

The new holder of St Peter's Chair was the Gascon Bertrand de Got, now His Holiness Pope Clément V (1305–14). He had been elected Pope at Perugia in Umbria on Saturday 5 June 1305, and was crowned in Lyon on Sunday 14 November 1305. Unlike his predecessor he would prove a pliable subject of the French Crown, and Philippe le Bel attended his instauration. It was Clément V who in 1306 famously excommunicated Robert the Bruce for killing 'Red Comyn', Lord of Badenoch, in the church of the Greyfriars in Dumfries. In the *Inferno* Dante cast Clément V as an even more degenerate character than the pharisaic Boniface VIII, who had after all caused the poet's exile from Florence. According to Dante, after Boniface 'shall come a lawless shepherd from the west of yet fouler deeds' than either Boniface VIII or Nicholas III (*Inferno*, Canto XIX). On the subject of the popes Dante and the Cathar Perfects were as one. In 1305 the papacy was still in Rome, but Clément V moved it to Avignon, where in 1316 he was succeeded by Jean XXII.* He is remembered today chiefly for his craven support for the meretricious oppression of the Templars by Philippe IV.

The morning the party from Arques left, Raymond Peyre and Raymond Maulen asked Pierre Maury to guard their sheep until their return, to which he agreed. Later that same morning Gilet de Voisins impounded the property and livestock of all the supplicants, while also

---

* Clément V settled in Avignon on 9 March 1309, and for the next sixty-nine years the Apostolic seat stayed in Provence rather than Rome.

instructing Pierre Maury and Jean Maulen to take good care of the Peyre and Maulen sheep. This solicitous remark may further suggest that Gilet de Voisins, like his *bayle*, was sympathetic to the Cathar cause. But now that the guilty parties were poised to own up to both the Pope and the Inquisitor he needed to be seen to be moving against them.

The Cathars from Arques were gone for more than ten weeks. They confessed to Bérenger, Bishop of Béziers and Grand Penitentiary of the Pope. Letters of absolution were issued to Guillaume Escaunier and his wife on Sunday 5 December 1305 and this indulgence was complemented by a second letter issued by the notary Barthélemy Adalbert on behalf of the Crown's public prosecutor at Carcassonne on Friday 24 December, which unconditionally restored all their property to the Escauniers.

It appears that the Peyres and Maulens were dealt with ahead of the Escauniers, since these two families were back in Arques about a fortnight before Christmas. They remonstrated with Pierre Maury for not joining them, and then made it clear that he could no longer lodge with them. For them the mere fact of not arresting him on sight now constituted an offence. During the falling-out which followed, Raymond Peyre refused to settle his debt with Pierre Maury, who visited his 'cousin' Maulen that night to confer. Maulen also urged him to go and see, if not the Pope, then the Inquisitor at Carcassonne; he even offered to accompany him. Pierre temporized and rejoined his flock.

A week or so later, leaving his sheep on winter pastures which seem to have been near Lavelanet, he was heading back to Arques to collect a measure of woollen cloth that he had arranged to have woven by a tailor there. He had reached Fougax just beyond Montségur, when he ran into his brother Guillaume, who had already heard that Pierre Maury had left the Peyres' employment. Together they journeyed on to Arques, and on the way met up with their brother-in-law Guillaume Marty.

The two Guillaumes waited at the Moulin d'Arques down from the Tour of the de Voisins, while Pierre retrieved the item of clothing that he had ordered. With this he hastily doubled back to the hamlet of Pontilhs, which survives today as a dot on the road-map between

Arques and Serres. Here he waited for the two Guillaumes, who may have wound up other outstanding business in Arques. Then the threesome returned to Coustaussa where they stopped at the house of Bernard Montanié who, it seems, like Pierre Maury, had decided to weather the storm rather than rush to confess.

This was Pierre Maury's last recorded visit to Arques. As he stealthily left the place, he was owed money by the Peyres, and he forfeited the property he bought, both the house and the fields. Later he claimed that this was the first time that he was ruined, the second being when he forfeited his share in his inheritance after 1308 for fear of being arrested; and the third time was in Catalonia.

Notwithstanding the precipitate confessions by the Cathars from Arques, the momentum of the movement in the area may have been only stalled, since there is some evidence to suggest that the Perfects returned to Arques after 1305, and that Pierre Authié imparted information to Sybille Peyre about Bernard Clergue that could have reached Arques only after the middle of September 1307, nearly two years *after* the Lyon and Carcassonne confessions.

From Coustaussa the two Maurys pushed on to Quillan, and the following day they went from here to Roquefeuil. 'After this we arrived in Montaillou, and this was some two or three days before Christmas, and it was nineteen years ago last Christmas,' Pierre Maury noted later (FR, f.254v).* Why should Pierre Maury feel safe in Montaillou, since the hateful Guillaume Peyre had earlier visited the Rives, and therefore must have told his new masters that the village was Cathar? Pierre himself had in fact left Arques for his home village noting airily that, if he was to be arrested, it might as well be in the Sabartès as elsewhere. Did someone tip Pierre Maury the wink that Montaillou was safe whatever happened?

This was Pierre's first Christmas at Montaillou since 1299–1300. His stock can rarely have been higher with the Perfects now that, at considerable cost to himself, he had refused to join the penitents of Arques. They would not be slow in using him again. When Pierre

---

* The fact is that he either meant '*eighteen* years ago' or '*this* Christmas', because his Pamiers testimony was given in the summer of 1324, and we know that he reached Montaillou at Christmas 1305.

Maury had left back then, the village was riding on the crest of hope, proud to be in the vanguard of the Cathar revival. Five turbulent years on it had absorbed a number of blows and setbacks, but now, in the autumn of 1305, the faithful of Montaillou, unlike their brethren at Arques, did not react to the arrests of Jacques Authié and Prades Tavernier.

This cannot have been simply because news of this setback took longer to reach the Sabartès than the closer Aude village, since such was the speed of the fourteenth-century bush telegraph and its fleet-footed operators that the time differential would have been slight.* Moreover, the Clergues' penetration of the Carcassonne Inquisition was so deep that they would probably have been apprised of the Perfects' arrests even before it was common knowledge.

The sequence of arrest and escape at Limoux seems to have been too swift for the Clergues to have had a hand in jumping the two Sabartesian Perfects from custody. But they were intimate with the gaoler of Carcassonne, Jacques de Polignac, who was also rector of the church of Caunettes-en-Val (Aude) in the diocese of Carcassonne. He would be present at a number of the extant despositions that form the d'Ablis Register. Both he and his nephew Hugues de Polignac, to whom Jacques seems to have delegated the day-to-day feeding and provisions of the prison, were true carpetbaggers in the flotsam of the Inquisition. Hugues was accused of top-slicing the Crown's subvention for the food of the Carcassonne prisoners for himself, and of pocketing monies from the families of convicted heretics for periods of up to two years after their deaths, of which he failed to notify them. In addition to this he misappropriated some of the Crown's timber and tiles to build a house for himself. His uncle stood similarly indicted of helping himself greedily to the confiscated goods of convicted heretics (Beugnot 1839–48, 3, 147–8; Devic *et al.* 1872–1905, 10, cc.650–52; *CR 1285–1314*: 8718).

Neither uncle nor nephew was convicted in the end, but the fact that their probity was called into question quite so strongly is proof of

---

* Indeed, the young *passeur* Raymond Azéma, carrying clothes for Perfects in Ax, covered the thirty-mile distance from Limoux to his mother's home in Montaillou in a single night; though he was so exhausted from the trek later that morning that he could not rise from his bed, and had to ask his mother to convey his freight to Sybille Baille in Ax.

the depth of their greed. How they knew the Clergues we may never discover, but they did and seem to have been beholden to them. Their game-plan was certainly similar to the Clergues', in that the Inquisition afforded immense opportunities for the unscrupulous to enrich themselves. But the Clergues were past masters at this scam and, unlike the de Polignacs, were not caught at it until much later. The fact remains that whatever the size of their operations, the Clergues had amassed the kind of wealth that allowed them comfortably to bribe, if not downright own, the de Polignacs.

7. Montaillou 1300–1305

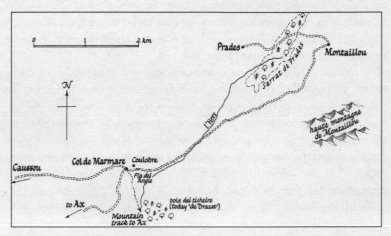

From the Marmare to the Pays d'Aillou

When Pierre Maury departed from Montaillou in 1299–1300, the village was poised to receive the Authiés. By the time he returned five years later, Guillaume Authié had established a semi-permanent base here alongside Prades Tavernier, through the offices of the Benets, Belots, Rives, and Clergues. If the village now gave the appearance of a homogeneous Cathar cell, this had come about at a price. Fear had played no small part in generating the Cathar consensus at Montaillou, and not everyone was happy with this state of affairs.

Once the village's ruling families had decided to provide the Perfects with a base in Montaillou, the need for secure accommodation became paramount. To this end the people of Montaillou started building full, and sometimes mezzanine, loft-extensions where beds with refined pillow-cases were kept for the exclusive use of visiting Perfects. The Clergue house already boasted a loft which dated from at least the return of Pierre Clergue in the mid-1290s, and probably from before that. When Guillaume Authié started to stay at the Clergues' cannot be ascertained for certain, but by the time he did he apparently could let himself in unannounced by displacing a board on the outside of the house, in a manner known only to him and the rector's family.

To have a loft became a status symbol, and the richest house in the village was keen to advertise its power. Given their village's position on a hill with solid rock underneath their houses, most of the villagers needed to extend upwards, if they desired to create additional space.* Only houses like the Clergues' and the Maurys' had basements, because of their dual-level position on the hill.

If Ariégeois houses in the mountains did not generally have basements, many of them had cellars; the differences between these two are sometimes blurred. Basements or *sotula* were common in the Ariège and Aude valleys and were generally integral parts of houses to which they were sometimes connected by trapdoors, whereas the cellars were occasionally separate and flush with the main house and barns, as for example at the Benets' in Montaillou and the Maulens' in Arques. Their function was the same, of course.

In Montaillou the Belots' *solarium* or loft became the most famous in the village. Whereas the Rives put up their relative Prades in a barn, the Belots housed the best-loved Occitan Perfect, Guillaume Authié, in some style. Their loft rose at mezzanine level next to the *foghana*, and could be accessed both from inside the house and from the exterior courtyard in front of it (FR, f.94v). The Belots' loft-extension, which they had built for them, probably dated from around 1300–1301.

One morning Vuissane, who was then a servant in the house, saw in it a richly decked bed, and on its pillow there sat a cushion of silk. She knew at once that Perfects had slept there the night before. It had in fact been Guillaume Authié, and the Belots would have made a special effort to make him more than just comfortable.

When Vuissane saw the bed, the loft-extension was so recent that it had not yet been 'covered with earth' (*interratum*, FR, f.94v), which may mean that it had not so far been daubed or insulated with wattle and loam, that is a paste of clay, sand, straw, and twigs commonly used

---

* In any other mountain village such a distinctive architectural feature might well have instantly signalled heretical contamination to an alert Inquisitor, but Montaillou was run by the Clergues, whose credit and credibility with the Carcassonne Inquisition were unlimited. They decided what was suspicious and what was not.

for this purpose in medieval houses. Next to their house and loft, and inside their courtyard, the Belots kept a huge and high dung-heap which, towards evening that day, provided a prying Vuissane Testanière with a platform from which to peer into the loft through a cranny when she heard a murmur of voices coming from it. She thus caught sight of Guillaume Belot and Bernard Clergue kneeling next to Guillaume Authié, with their hands linked in prayer.

Not only did the wealthier households such as the Rives and Belots now contain lofts for the Perfects, but former dependants in the village were thriving to the point not only of building or buying their own houses, but investing in extensions as well.

One of these, and a die-hard Cathar, was the Montaillou cobbler, blacksmith, and *passeur* Arnaud Vital, who was in fact a first cousin of the Belots. In the late 1290s Arnaud was running his business from a room at his cousins'. He also became the 'hayward' of Montaillou, which meant that he was the village's field-watchman and was responsible for keeping sheep from breaking into enclosed fields once they had been sown.

During this period the Belots employed three women servants, and they were all called Raymonde. The first one was Arnaud Vital's sister Raymonde, who later married Prades den Arsen. The Belots' staff therefore included two of their first cousins. Raymonde Vital may have left the Belots as early as 1300, perhaps to get married, even though Alazais Azéma's testimony has Raymonde still there in about 1302. In any case she would be recalled by the Belots when the plot thickened.

Next was Raymonde (Vuissane) Marty. As well as already having an illegitimate daughter by the name of Guillemette, between the late 1290s and the early 1300s Vuissane conceived two more illegitimate children by Bernard Belot who was, probably, the second Belot son. One of his illegitimate offspring by Vuissane was called Bernard after him. The reason why Vuissane was so complaisant to Bernard was because she hoped that he might marry her. Being the object of his desires and the mother of his children would surely persuade him to make her an honest *Na* Belot. But Bernard Belot was a sexual thug with a conviction, either past or to come, for attempted rape on the wife of a fellow Mountaillou resident; indeed, his is the most expensive fine recorded in the Register. Moreover, as Arnaud Vital told Vuissane,

Bernard would never marry her, because she was not a Cathar. So at least she claimed in front of Fournier. His true reason for not marrying her was spelled out to Vuissane in 1321.

While proselytizing for Catharism Arnaud Vital in turn offered his sexual services to Vuissane, who at the time still hoped to marry Bernard. At some point Arnaud sexually assaulted her, but he did not succeed in raping her. Vuissane remonstrated with Arnaud for pressing her for sex, saying that because she had two children from his cousin their intercourse would become incestuous.

The third Raymonde of the Belot household became Arnaud's wife in about 1300.* It is a fair guess that she was seduced by Arnaud while working at the Belots', since Arnaud propositioned most of the women he encountered, and generally successfully so.

As man and wife Arnaud and Raymonde lived at the Belots' from 24 June to All Saints of 1300, after which they moved into a home of their own, across the road from the Belots and up from the Clergues. It must have been good for business to be situated at the village's main junction of *capanal den belot*. Did the dowry from Raymonde allow them to move into their new house? Arnaud seems to have done well for himself, since their house, with its new loft, stood in the nobs' corner of Montaillou.

After his marriage Arnaud frequently left his young wife alone at night, only returning much later without, it seems, offering explanations. Because she knew him to be a village Lothario from her time at the Belots', she was naturally jealous, and his continued attentions to Vuissane must have fuelled her fears. She suspected that he was seeing Raymonde Rives, the niece of the Perfect Prades Tavernier and sister of the abused Guillemette, as well as one Alazais Gavelle about whom nothing is known.†

* After his death some ten years later she married one Bernard Guilhou from Vernaux, a village between Lordat and Unac, and became Raymonde Gilhou, which is the name under which she testified before Fournier.
† But there was an Alazais Gonelle from Gebets, who was the mistress of Guillaume Clergue, with whom she had a son. Could Gavelle and Gonelle be confused here? It has been suggested that Alazais Gavelle might be Alazais Faure, with whom Arnaud indeed became sexually involved (Duvernoy 1978, 488n.2); but that relationship, whose consequences spelt disaster for Alazais Faure and her loved ones, came several years later.

In truth Arnaud's night-time activities in Montaillou had less to do with sex and more to do with faith, for they coincided almost exactly with the burgeoning of Authié-inspired activity in the area. As a leading pathfinder, he put himself entirely at the disposition of Perfects, hence his many nocturnal absences. If Arnaud had loved his wife better, he might have discovered that she was someone who could be trusted to keep a secret. It was she who later openly challenged the Inquisition to do its worst. His contemptuous treatment of her may be why she sought solace in the arms of Pierre Clergue and, according to Vuissane's innuendo, Bernard Clergue.

Alazais Azéma, the mother of another *passeur* from Montaillou, Raymond Azéma, also found comfort in the arms of Pierre Clergue; and some twenty years later she would prove more loyal to him than most. She and her son were among the most active Cathars in the village during the 1300–1308 period of high heretical activity. By 1302 Alazais Azéma was so intimate with the Perfects that she was allowed to witness Guillaume Authié and Pons Sicre leaving the *foghana* of the Benets through a partition to get to the Rives'. The sticks they were carrying suggest either that they were about to be off on a long trek, or else had just returned from one.

Like others of the poorer women of Montaillou such as Brune Pourcel, Guillemette Clergue (B), and eventually Fabrisse Rives, Alazais Azéma was always in and out of the richer houses, in her case that of her neighbours opposite, the Belots'. As well as food, she borrowed cooking utensils such as a *payrola* (cauldron), although on one occasion, during the wedding of Bernard Belot and Guillemette Benet, she lent *them* a pot. In spite of her poverty Alazais Azéma, like everyone, gave the Perfects presents, which in her case consisted of bushels of wheat, because she could not afford much.

Montaillou was full of women observers because, unlike the men, they of necessity stayed put more because of their children. Much of our information about the comings and goings in the village therefore comes from women with small children.

One of these was Brune Pourcel, the illegitimate daughter of Prades Tavernier. At the time of the Authiés' return, Brune worked as a servant in the Clergue household, alongside Bernard Clergue's illegitimate daughter. During this period the two matriarchs Mengarde Clergue and Guillemette Belot were being more familiar with each other than usual, and they were repeatedly spotted in deep conference sitting in the track which ran between their two houses. The fact that the die-hard Cathar *Na* Roche was also a frequent visitor to the Clergues' house during this period leaves no doubt about the purpose of the meetings of the two middle-aged women.

One day Mengarde Clergue, the rector's mother, instructed Brune to take two loaves baked in hearth-ashes and wrapped in a tablecloth and a flask of wine to Guillemette Belot opposite. Brune professed to be astonished by this gift, because the Belot house was 'very rich'. When she asked what she should tell Guillemette about the bread and wine, Mengarde replied that she ought not to worry about it: 'Just give it to Guillemette, because I have spoken to her.'* Brune took the food and wine across to the Belots', and because she found their door closed she knocked. At once Guillemette Belot opened the door, but only by a fraction, and she stood in it to prevent Brune from seeing inside. She took the gifts and without further ado re-entered her house.

The reason for the secrecy was the presence inside of the Authiés, who avoided Pierre Clergue's house in these early stages for fear of compromising him. This meant that Mengarde was continually shuttling across the road, pretending that she was going to her neigh-bour's to sew or to do needlework, or getting her servants to do so. Like Brune, Bernard Clergue's daughter was employed on similar errands to deliver victuals to the Belots for the Perfects.

Mengarde Clergue provided the Perfects with flour, bread, honey, oil, and good wine from Pierre and Bernard Clergue. On the rector's instructions she also took them work to do. Thus during his stays at the Belots' Guillaume Authié sewed fur-linings on to some of Pierre Clergue's tunics, and patched up sleeves on his garments. He also repaired shoes, and he received money from Pierre Clergue for these services. When in 1308 Gaillarde Authié voiced concern about her husband to Guillaume Belot, he assured her that Guillaume Authié was

---

* Brune may have been disingenuous in her deposition before Fournier on this, or else she was genuinely puzzled because the Belots, like the Rives, Clergues, and others such as the Benets and Maurys, must have had their own bread-ovens.

well looked after in Montaillou, because Mengarde Clergue sent the Perfects all sorts of provisions. Moreover, Pierre Clergue was rumoured to be paying his Cathar friends a substantial annuity of wheat.

Guillaume Authié reciprocated Pierre Clergue's kindness by sending him a present of gloves, which formed a material part of the present-trading culture of Languedoc. The Perfects imported gloves from Lombardy, and were in turn given gloves themselves. Gloves, for which two different Latin words are used ([acc.] *cirothecas vel gans*, FR, f.75v), seem to have been both a luxury item, like the Lombardian knives or *canivets*, or Barcelona silk, as well as protective clothing against the Pyrenean cold.* But the most important present, symbolically speaking, that Guillaume ever sent to Clergue was a *calendarium*, a calendar bound together with the Gospels such as was used in consolations.

More than anyone else in the village, Brune lived off her relatives, and she did not hesitate to turn herself into a thieving magpie on occasions. Such excursions repeatedly brought her into contact with her father at the Rives, who seem to have been generous towards all their kith and kin.

When he lodged at the Rives', which he did with increasing frequency, he usually stayed in the hay-barn. One day Brune quietly entered the barn and was helping herself to a sheaf of hay when her father, Prades Tavernier, whom she had not seen because he sat on top of the straw, asked her what she was doing. She replied that she was taking hay because she did not have any, and then she fled.

Similarly, during the turnip harvest, Pons Rives had arranged for his turnip crop to be stored in a shed in or near the porch of his house. In the course of the same day Brune went there four times with a basket, and surreptitiously filled it with turnips. On each occasion she saw her father Prades, who was locked inside the house. When she approached, he opened the door a crack and, seeing her, asked her why she was

* The exchange of presents between Perfects and their followers was standard practice. In addition to money, the Perfects received from their followers any amount of comestibles as well as intricately patterned table-napkins, ells of cloth, towels and, on one recorded occasion, a long coat of black sheepskin. In return the Perfects dispensed linen hats, silken bonnets, gloves, blouses and jackets, jewels, Parma knives, and calendars.

stealing the turnips: 'To cook them for my children and to feed them,' she replied. He reprimanded her for taking them without the knowledge of the people of the house. When later Pons Rives appeared, she told him that she had taken the turnips, and he replied that she was welcome to them.

Another time Brune borrowed a flour-sieve from the Rives, who also shared their flour and bread with her, as well as various bowls, firewood, and their bread-oven. She was Prades's daughter, and the Cathars must have loved her partly for that reason, as we know they did Pierre Authié's daughter. Moreover, she was poor with a number of children, and once she had to decline to see her father, because she had left her children unattended. Where mothers with many children were concerned, the people of Montaillou rallied round them with heart-warming solidarity.

But there was a price to pay for being dependent on others. It was around Easter 1302. Brune had a six-month-old baby son, Raymond, whom she was breast-feeding. Her aunt Alazais Rives came to see her and asked whether she could bring her baby to her house to be suckled by a woman from Razès whose milk was causing her pain. At first Brune was loath to comply, explaining that the other woman's milk might be bad for her baby. Then she relented; she was too poor to refuse anything to her rich relatives.

When she arrived at the Rives house, the lactating woman sat next to the fire. At a door into one of the rooms off the *foghana* stood Brune's father, Prades Tavernier. Brune was instructed by Alazais to honour him with the *melhorier*, which she did after being initiated into it by her aunt. Alazais Rives and the woman from Razès did likewise. As Brune left the house to return home with her baby, her aunt gave her two pieces of bread: a large one for her son, and a small, blessed one, *tinhol*, for her.

During one of her visits to the Rives' *foghana* Brune witnessed the 'adoration' of Prades Tavernier by Mersende Marty in the presence of Arnaud Vital and Alazais Rives. Mersende on that occasion presented Prades with bread and oil wrapped in a blue item of clothing. Hers was a deep faith from which she never wavered. Another time, in about 1303–4, Mersende was seen entertaining the Perfects Guillaume Authié and Pons Sicre in her house in the square across from the Rives. Many years later and in another country, Mersende mournfully reminisced about the 'gallant' son of Sybille Baille.

Prades's sojourns in his sister's barn were witnessed by another opposite neighbour and great borrower from the Rives, their daughter Guillemette Clergue (B). She dates her encounter with Prades to 1304, and like her cousin Brune she also remembered it as being turnip-picking time. She asked her mother whether she could have a little bit of hay, and was told to get a small bundle from the barn and then depart at once in case her brother took it from her. By now (1304) Pons Rives headed the family. Although Pons was kind to Guillemette, he was irritated by his sister's frequent visits to the house, not least because she might expose the amount of Cathar activity there. In Guillemette's own words:

I entered the barn where the straw and hay were kept, and at the top of the chaff loft I saw Prades Tavernier who sat close in a ray of sunlight. He was reading in a black book the length of my hand. When he spotted me he rose, transfixed, as if he wanted to hide, and said to me, 'Is that you, Guillemette?', to which I replied, 'Yes, sir.' I then asked him how he came to be there, and he replied 'Come here [*veta pur* [?]]; I'm sitting here in a ray of sunlight.' When I wanted to take some hay, Prades asked me, 'Do you want to take hay?' I said, 'Yes, my mother has given me permission for it.' Then I took the hay and Prades entered my father's main house through a postern in this barn from which a plank had been removed. He held his head through the hole where the plank had been moved and, when I had taken all the hay that I wanted and desired to leave with it, Prades said, 'Won't you sit for a short while with me?' I replied that I could not, because I was afraid that my brother might turn up and take the hay from me. (FR, f.66v)

The reason why Prades needed to step into the main house was presumably to allow Guillemette to take the hay from the heap he had been sitting on.

The following day Guillemette and her odious husband were heading to Ax (FR, ff.66v, 67r). He was walking ahead of her driving a mule laden with corn to be ground, while Guillemette herself carried five chickens and some eggs to sell in Ax.

They had reached a place which was then called *pla del angle*, which literally translates as 'the level plain of the angle or corner of a deep valley' (FR, f.67r). It denotes the point where the valley of the Hers river coming from Prades and Montaillou narrows to a bottleneck under the Col de Marmare.

At *pla del angle* three tracks merged. One of them ran straight on west towards Caussou and connected the Sabartès to the Ariège valley at Luzenac, while the other two bore south towards Ax. Of these two one corresponded roughly to the present *départementale* and was commonly used by the Sabartesian highlanders when they carried goods to the market at Ax, or when they were driving a mule, as the Clergues (B) were doing on this occasion. The other one was steep and direct. It was known at the time as 'the mountain track' and was the Cathars' preferred route to Ax. It climbed from *pla del angle* to the crest of a wood known then as *del tisheire* (probably the modern Bois de Drazet), before descending towards Sorgeat by way of a steep escarpment known as 'l'Assaladou' (see below, pages 181–2).★

As Guillemette and her husband proceeded in the direction of the easier track she looked back towards *del tisheire*, and there she saw her brother Pons with a bundle on his shoulders, followed closely by Prades Tavernier with three or four sheepskins on his shoulders, in the disguise again, it seems, of a pedlar. To be safer Prades was keeping off the track itself by, as she put it, 'the length of a crossbow's arrow'. She waited for her brother to catch up with her, but he called to her to carry on and follow her husband. Pons did not wish for the Cathar-loathing Clergue to see Prades.

Guillemette did as she was told, and subsequently watched as her brother rejoined Prades and took the mountain track.

Very shortly afterwards, and maybe just a few days later, Guillemette Clergue (B) returned to Ax with her mother. They were taking hemp to a weaver's to work it into a piece of linen or hemp-linen. They wove there until Alazais Rives ran out of hemp and decided to go and

★ The two tracks down to Ax seem to have emerged there in two different places, with one descending into the street of the baths, presumably the heart of Ax near the Bassin des Ladres, and the other one coming down past the *Vieille Ville* and cemetery, roughly pre-tracing the present *départementale* from the Chioula.

buy some more (Pl. 17). Guillemette urged her to be quick about it, because night was falling and they needed to get back to Montaillou.

From her seat at the loom Guillemette watched her mother enter the house of Sybille Baille. When she did not return, Guillemette went to fetch her, probably because she was anxious about getting home late and having to face an angry, violent husband.

She entered the Baille house, and stopped at the foot of the staircase. Looking up towards the main hall, she saw her mother talking to Sybille Baille and two men, her uncle Prades Tavernier and (probably) Guillaume Authié, who were both leaning against a chest. From the bottom of the stairs Guillemette called out, '*e donna!*' ('hello, madam') to her mother. When Sybille Baille discovered that the caller was Guillemette Clergue (B), she furiously turned on Alazais Rives: 'How can you bring that young woman here, when she lives with bad people and has a bad man for a husband. In future we will not allow you to enter here again' (FR, f.67r). Her mother's lame defence, that she had left Guillemette at the weaver's, was of little avail against Sybille's ire and the reproaches of the two Perfects. She was ordered to make sure that her daughter would not breathe a word to her husband about seeing them. When on the way back up to Montaillou Guillemette tactlessly asked her mother who the second man was, she was told to shut up, that it was none of her business.

Guillemette's dealings with the Perfects were on the whole conducted innocently from the sidelines, although she was not quite as much of an ingénue as she pretended to be. But her husband gave cause for concern to the Cathars in Montaillou, although his animosity towards them seems to have expressed itself no further than striking his Cathar wife. The fact that she had so many children may suggest that he also possessed her sexually whenever he felt like it; or perhaps Guillemette put up with her husband's behaviour because she enjoyed sex with him. She was certainly not incapable of rallying to his defence when he was treated with hostility by others in the village.

It was around this time that she felt emboldened to ask for credit from the shoemaker and blacksmith after seeing Arnaud frequent her parental home because of the Perfects there. She took him some of her husband's shoes to repair, and asked him to defer payment until Whitsun, when she hoped to sell some chickens. Guillaume Belot was present during this interview. He had probably just walked across to talk to his old friend, the more so since Arnaud's forge and workshop were open-plan. Indeed Pierre Clergue was frequently deloused on one of the workshop tables by Vital's wife Raymonde while simultaneously flirting with the female passers-by; that he also eventually conducted an affair with his delouser was a matter of course.

Arnaud Vital refused Guillemette credit, saying that her husband was a nasty creature. She bristled at this and seems to have defended her husband with some vigour. She knew, of course, that 'nasty creature' was used because her husband was not Cathar. Guillaume Belot asked, 'Are you one of us?' and did she sometimes confide in her husband about their heretical activities? She replied that she dared not speak to him about it, because he had threatened to kill her or to throw her out, if she frequented the homes of Cathars.

But the small faction which opposed the Cathars in the village in turn had good reason to feel intimidated because of two events which both happened in the period from 1301 to 1304, the mutilation of Mengarde Maurs and the murder of Arnaud Lizier.

All we know about *l'affaire Maurs* is that Mengarde's tongue was cut out at the instigation of Pierre Clergue, and that the whole episode was somehow connected to heresy. This much we can deduce from our sole evidence about this business, a surreptitious conversation between Arnaud Vital and his neighbour Bernard Belot. In the course of it one of the men indignantly called Clergue a 'traitor' and accused him of cynical double-dealing: after all, he remarked, Clergue had been of the same faith as Mengarde and had moreover swapped presents with Guillaume Authié (FR, f.162v)!

The specific nature of the mutilation suggests that Mengarde Maurs may have been accused of speaking libellously of the Clergues. By so doing she would have fallen foul of an unwritten, but absolute, law of Montaillou: all the Cathars in the village knew that the rector and his family were 'heretics', but no one was allowed to say so under any circumstances. If they did, the Clergues would exact revenge through their friends in Carcassonne. Had Mengarde recklessly (or just fool-ishly?) incriminated the Clergues, and had they in turn dragged her before the secular arm for speaking against them?

The severity of the punishment was clearly intended to set an example, and the Clergues do not seem to have worried unduly about alienating others in the village (Pl. 18). Their sway in Montaillou had long been predicated on the wielding of naked power and the inspiring of fear. The fact that the ordeal of Mengarde Maurs antagonized the Maurs, Bar, Maury and Pélissier families, all of whom were related to her, as well as friends and neighbours such as Vital and the Belots, did not trouble them. But one of the Maurs' sons, Guillaume, who was away from Montaillou during these events, vowed to avenge his mother and family. As we shall see, he never wavered from the path of his vendetta.

What the Cathar Perfects made of the priest's action is not recorded, but the uncomfortable question of the friendship of Guillaume Authié and Pierre Clergue rears its head again.

If the Clergues punished Mengarde Maurs through the law, which was hardly 'law' since they owned it, the murder in Montaillou of Arnaud Lizier in 1304 may have been their most brazen demonstration yet of raw and unaccountable power. It was never specifically laid at their door, but nothing happened in the village without their connivance. That Lizier was an awkward customer is clear from Guillaume Authié's troubled reference to him. He was prosperous, and he lived next door to the Clergues so that he saw everything that happened in the square and at *capanal den belot*. Neither made him popular with the Montaillou Cathars, whom he seems to have openly defied.

It was Pierre Authié who told Sybille Peyre of Arques that 'Arnaud Lizier of Montaillou did not like the heretics, and they therefore arranged for him to be harshly dealt with, and he was found assassinated in front of the castle's entrance' (FR, f.206r). The fact that his body was discovered *in plano castri de monte alionis* (FR, f.59r), the castle plateau which was prominent above the village, suggests that his violent death was intended as an added deterrent to the likes of Pierre Azéma and perhaps Pierre Clergue (B).

We do not know how Arnaud Lizier died or where. He may have been stabbed or clubbed to death in an ambush in the nearby woods. It is unlikely that he was killed under the walls of the fortress. Even if there was no garrison there at the time, the caretaker incumbent of the castle would at the very least have commanded a watch, and they would have been alerted by the commotion of men fighting outside. The odds are that Lizier was murdered at night somewhere near the village, and then dumped close to the castle's main entrance. Had he perhaps sought an interview with the châtelain (if there was one) to alert him and the Count of Foix to the presence of Cathar Perfects in Montaillou? As the Clergues' neighbour he must have been aware of the fact that the priest and the *bayle* of Montaillou were actively aiding and abetting the Cathars. But he would also have known that Pierre Clergue frequented the castle long after the departure of Béatrice de Planisolles. If he nevertheless tried to secure the assistance of the Count of Foix, he would thereby almost certainly have signed his death-warrant, and the location of his body would become more sharply symbolic: not even the castle, it would seem to say, could offer a refuge from the vengeful arm of the Cathars.

As to who did the deed, there can be no doubt that several local Cathars were implicated, just as Cathars from Larnat and Quié had been involved in the murder of Guillaume Dejean in the mountains of Miglos. There are no obvious grounds for believing that Raymonde Lizier-Argelier was complicit with her first husband's killers, although the suspicion has arisen because three years later she married into a major Cathar family.

Arnaud Lizier's neighbour and fellow Catholic Pierre Azéma must have been enough of a realist to appreciate that he could do nothing but bide his time. But when it seemed to have come in 1308 the Clergues simply changed sides and thus remained untouchable for another twelve years.

Because of a kind of *omertà* (the Mafia's code of silence) reigning in Montaillou after 1304, Cathar activities in the village remained shrouded in secrecy. Thus, in January 1305, after being consoled by Guillaume Authié in her son's barn, *Na* Roche was at dusk carried in a blanket by Guillaume Belot, Raymond Benet, and Rixende Julia to Brune Pourcel's house to be put through the *endura* there. That night, according to Brune, she, Rixende, and Alazais Pélissier sat up with the old Cathar, who died on the third night. When she related these events Brune, eager to impress the Inquisitor favourably, insisted that two night-owls settled on her roof at *Na* Roche's death, and that she interpreted this as the devils having come to carry off the old woman's soul.

Early in the morning after *Na* Roche's death, Alazais Azéma arrived at Brune's house and helped her prepare the corpse. They wrapped it in a blanket belonging to Alazais Azéma, and then she was buried in the cemetery of Notre-Dame-de-Carnesses, with Pierre Clergue (probably) officiating at the burial ceremony. *Na* Roche was undoubtedly dug up later and burnt, like her son who died three or four years later. The Cathars who had buried the consoled Raymond Roche in, their garden were afterwards ordered to exhume him with their own hands (*propriis manibus extumulaverunt*, L, 79).

Within eight days of consoling *Na* Roche, Guillaume Authié was needed again, because his wife's cousin Alazais Benet from Montaillou was dying. She had been ill since late November or early December 1304, and was nursed by, among others, Fabrisse Rives. There could be no question but that this daughter of a leading Cathar house, and one so intimately allied to the Authiés, would be consoled by them.

When she started to sink, two of the Belot boys, Guillaume, who was a godson of Alazais Benet's father, and Raymond, went to fetch Guillaume Authié, probably in Ax. To reach his cousin's bedside that night Guillaume Authié and his guides braved a mountain blizzard on the snowbound ascent from Ax. Even by the trekking standards of the time this feat was a major achievement and proof of the dedication of Cathar Perfects. While Alazais was dying, her poor mother was suffering from earache, and years later Alazais's death and her earache were etched together on Guillemette's mind.

The party with Guillaume Authié arrived in Montaillou around dawn, and while the Belots checked the house first, the Perfect and, perhaps, another man, hid in the Benets' cellar, an outbuilding that stood next to the main house and was flush with it. Her parents and the two Belots assisted at the consolation, and Alazais died in the arms of her father and Raymond Belot.

The 'strangers' had been seen by Fabrisse, who promptly, and obtusely, reported this to her cousin Pierre Clergue (although he tended to repudiate their consanguinity on the grounds that Fabrisse was illegitimate).

The skies had obviously cleared, because Pierre Clergue was soaking up the winter sun at the door of Notre-Dame-de-Carnesses, when Fabrisse bearded him with news of the consolation. His reply was: 'Shut up, shut up, you don't know what you're saying, because there are no heretics in these parts; if there were, they would easily be smoked out' (FR, f.62v).

He may well have decided there and then that she lacked discretion, and that it was dangerous to have her so close to one of the main Cathar hearths. Already Pons Rives and his mother were adamant that Fabrisse made it impossible for Perfects to convene in her house. It would have been shortly after this that Pons Rives showed her the door.* Fabrisse's own testimony makes no mention of her forced expulsion, even though it would have shown her in a good light to be able to tell Fournier that she was ousted from her home because of her Catholic loyalties. Instead, she referred to the reception accorded Guillaume Peyre by Alazais Rives (see above, page 105), and the fact that afterwards she and her sister-in-law no longer openly fought with each other, 'in case either reproached the other with what had happened during the visit of Guillaume Peyre' (FR, f.62v). It would appear that Fabrisse and Alazais Rives were in the habit of quarrelling, and the Rives may have worried that her lack of discretion and her antagonistic temperament might combine to turn her into a traitor. It is equally evident from the brief reference to Peyre that Fabrisse, very foolishly, viewed this dangerous knowledge as a stick with which to threaten the Rives.

From being the wife of one of the richest Montalionians, Fabrisse now became as poor as Alazais Azéma and set herself up as an itinerant publican, mostly selling wine. Her expulsion from her home must have been sanctioned, if not prompted, by the rector of Montaillou; and her family connection to the Clergues may have saved her from the worse fates of Mengarde Maurs and Arnaud Lizier. It was an additional mercy that, unlike her sister-in-law Guillemette, Fabrisse had only one child, Grazide, who was now about five. The little girl presumably accompanied her mother into her internal exile, but whereabouts in Montaillou this was is not recorded. Somewhere near Les Granges cannot be

---

* Oddly both Pierre Maury and Doat wrongly record that Fabrisse Clergue was married to Raymond Rives, when in fact she was the wife of Pons Rives (FR, f.257v; D 27, f.147v).

ruled out, because there she would have been out of harm's way, while still being part of the community that she was servicing.

It is not known how Fabrisse operated her mobile tavern business. She would have needed to buy her wine (from the vast vineyards of Pamiers) in either Ax or Tarascon, and to this end she would have required a mule for transport. One imagines that the Rives, and particularly Pons Rives, the father of her daughter, helped her out as much as they could, albeit at arm's length. Even the Clergues may have assisted the mother and daughter who were their own flesh and blood, whatever the rector's equivocations to the contrary later (see below, page 247). Eventually Fabrisse was readmitted into the Cathar circles, and she and Grazide later lived, alone, in the large Rives house on the corner of the square.

Within five months of his sister Alazais's death, around Whitsun of 1305 (6 June), Raymond Benet died in his father's house. He had been a handsome and talented young man. His parents were present when Guillaume Authié consoled him, and so were Guillaume and Arnaud Belot and Arnaud Vital, who had escorted the Perfect to the Benet house at dusk. His father mourned his passing bitterly and, weeping, told Alazais Azéma, 'I have lost all I had through the death of my son. In the future I will have no one to work for me' (FR, f.61r). Since the eldest son, Pierre, had left home, the Benets were left with two teenage daughters and two children, Bernard and his five- or six-year-old sister Montane. When eventually Pierre Benet returned to Montaillou, he would have to endure the indignity of Pierre Clergue seducing both his wife and his sister-in-law.

Three or four months later the recently escaped Prades Tavernier seems to have taken up residence on a semi-permanent footing at the Rives'. Here, at the heart of the Clergues' fiefdom, he was as safe as it was possible for a Perfect to be.

8. The Cathars and Guillemette Maury: 1305–7

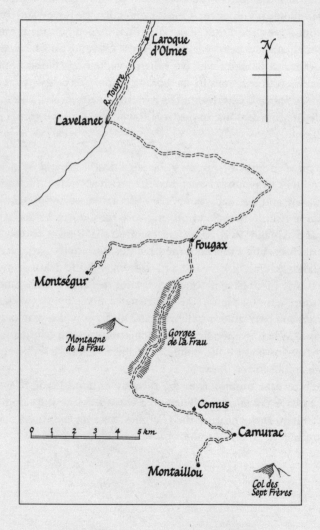

The itinerary of Pierre Maury's rescue mission

Pierre Maury spent the festive season of Christmas 1305 in Montaillou with his mother and father, and four of his brothers.* After Christmas Pierre started working as a shepherd for his mother's bachelor brother, Arnaud Faure of Montaillou. By now Pierre Maury was about twenty-three or twenty-four years old. When he asked Arnaud about Perfects in Montaillou, Arnaud replied that he was too young to concern himself with such matters: 'If you want to do good to them, do it without worrying about seeing them.' Arnaud was wary of his nephew, who was known to have flouted the Inquisition at Arques. There would have been a strong suspicion that the Cathars of Arques had given Pierre Maury's name to the Inquisition, making him a liability, especially since, as yet, no one in Montaillou had been summoned.

Although Montaillou was now steeped in Catharism, Pierre Maury's flaunting defiance of the Inquisition could not be tolerated, not least because it threatened to compromise the Clergues' façade of Catholic loyalty. It was quickly decided that he must go. Rather than facing Pierre Maury with the bad news, Arnaud Faure chose to dismiss him through Guillaume Belot and forbade him his house; and when Belot's message was endorsed by Pierre's own, younger, brother Bernard, who told him that their own household would suffer if he did not leave, Pierre knew that he had no choice. He professed to be surprised that Cathars were telling a believer like him to leave, and he never forgave Arnaud Faure. But unlike the villagers of Montaillou, he had not experienced at first hand the pressures that within the preceding eighteen months had produced both a case of torture and a murder in order to protect the village from having its heresies exposed.

It was old Arnaud Baille of Montaillou who came to the rescue of Pierre Maury by finding him employment with his son-in-law, a rich livestock-raiser in Ax by the name of Barthélemy Bourrel. Although Bourrel's family were not Cathar, his wife and his ambitiously named daughter, Bérengère, were. As soon as Pierre and Barthélemy had

---

* They were Guillaume, Bernard, Jean and Arnaud, who was still little. His brother Raymond may have been away from Montaillou at that moment, unless Pierre simply forgot to recall his presence two decades later. As for his two sisters, one of them, Guillemette, was married in Laroque d'Olmes, while the other one, Raymonde, who was married to Guillaume Marty of Montaillou, spent Christmas with her own family, although she may have visited the parental home at some point during that day.

agreed terms, Pierre was dispatched to the pastures of Tortosa in the
Ebre delta in Catalonia. The distance from Ax to Tortosa measures at
least 160 miles as the crow flies, and double that on the road. Although
a hardened shepherd like Pierre Maury could walk that stretch (which
is considerably further across the mountains) in four or five days, driving
a flock of sheep from Tortosa to the Sabartès would take three or four
times longer. The Maury–Bourrel partnership must have seemed like
a good deal all round: Bourrel had hired the best shepherd in Languedoc,
and Pierre Maury was out of harm's way in deepest Catalonia, where
the long arm of the Inquisition did not always reach. They might even
forget about him. One is bound to wonder whether Arnaud Faure and
Pierre Maury's father had not acted in concert to spirit him out of
Montaillou and Ax, for all their sakes, his own included.

In Lent that same year of 1306 the leading scout Raymond Issaurat
from Larnat was dispatched to Montaillou to find a Perfect to console
Alazais Gouzy, who lay dying. She was of the same Gouzy family which
was allied to the de Larnats and the Peyres of Arques. Issaurat was joined
on the mission by a local Cathar called Guillemette d'Arnaude.

They arrived at the Belots' early in the evening after trekking for
over twenty miles. Raymond explained their reason for coming, and
Raymond Belot took him to the Maurys' where the Perfect Philippe
d'Aylarac was staying. Pierre Maury's mother was there when Issaurat
arrived, and so was the Perfect. But d'Aylarac was already committed
elsewhere, and so advised Issaurat to go on to Ax, where he was bound
to find what he was looking for. Raymond Belot agreed to accompany
him.

It was about midnight when they reached Ax, and here Belot left
Issaurat and Guillemette d'Arnaude while he went in search of a
Perfect, probably from the house of Sybille Baille. He returned shortly
afterwards with Raymond Faure of Coustaussa. Raymond Belot then
went into Ax, presumably to spent the night there before his journey
back to Montaillou, while the new threesome made their way to
Larnat.

From Ax to Larnat was an eight-hour hike, or the length of a
midsummer night, as we know from Pierre Issaurat's description of the
same journey. When they were at the height of Unac, some eight miles

away from Ax, it was daylight. This suggests that they had rested somewhere, perhaps in Montaillou, and that they had arrived at Ax quite a bit later than midnight. Raymond Issaurat himelf, on a different occasion, refers to lying down one night on a bed at Sybille Baille's in Ax in order to recover from the weariness of a journey.

They pushed on past Unac to Château-Verdun, where they lunched on bread blessed by the Perfect and wine that they purchased at a local tavern. After lunch they made it to Sinsat and here, rather curiously, the Perfect asked them to proceed ahead without him; he would follow shortly, perhaps after seeing a friend.

So Raymond and Guillemette went on to Larnat, only to find on their arrival, after a round trip of over sixty miles, that Alazais had died. When Raymond Faure met up with them in the afternoon, he was no longer needed. But he stayed for several days, and during this period he was extensively visited by people from the area.

A few months later, towards the end of June, Raymond Issaurat's brother Guillaume, one of the murderers of the unfortunate Dejean, lay dying, and his brother Pierre went to Arnaud Authié in Ax in search of a Perfect. There he found the Issaurats' good friend Amiel de Perles, who was free to come, and Pierre was so overjoyed that the two men embraced. They trekked from Ax to Larnat through the night, and they arrived just before dawn and found Guillaume alive.

At some point the dying man requested water. But when his father put a spoonful of it to his mouth Guillaume indicated with slurred speech and through gestures that the water would not go down. This was the signal to Amiel de Perles to proceed with the consolation, which he duly did.

By the time this happened Pierre Maury was back in the Sabartès. He had returned around Whitsun (22 May 1306), since May was the time when the shepherds traditionally retreated from their lowland pastures before the onset of the summer heat. He spent the summer months of 1306 in the (unidentified) passes of Roserabat in the company of other shepherds from Ax. During this period his family in Montaillou, and particularly his brother Guillaume, were putting up Raymond Faure of Coustaussa, who before long was joined there by Philippe d'Aylarac.

It was in the winter of 1306–7 that the Cathars caught up again with

Pierre Maury through Sybille Baille. Pierre had met her several years earlier, and his flock now included *one* of her sheep. One wonders how many such lonely sheep Sybille Baille farmed out thus to different shepherds and livestock-raisers in the area, because they provided a wholly legitimate pretext for mingling with all sorts of different people, any one of whom might suddenly become a useful contact.

One winter night, after locking the sheep in their pens, Pierre Maury was chopping logs for fuel when Sybille Baille's son Bernard came to get him. Together they proceeded to his mother's house, and while Pierre Maury went in, Bernard sat outside on a stone bench that protruded outwards from the wall of the house as was customary in the medieval Ariège.

Pierre climbed the stairs into the living quarters of the house, and there, in the *foghana*, he met the Perfect Philippe d'Aylarac and also Bernard Bélibaste, whom he knew from his days in Arques. Sybille Baille was cooking. Her eight-year-old daughter Raymonde was also present. Pierre did the *melhorier* to d'Aylarac, and then explained that he could not linger because his employer Bourrel had guests staying that night who needed looking after. Sybille urged him to come back later when they had retired to bed, because the Perfect needed a guide to go up to Montaillou.

After helping out at Bourrel's, Pierre Maury and another servant of the Bourrel household, 'Mondine' (diminutive for Raymonde), went out to a tavern to buy wine. On the way there they passed the Baille house, and Mondine stopped. She explained that she needed to pass on a message from her mistress, either Esclarmonde or Bérengère, to Sybille Baille. On the way up the stairs Mondine was singing as she followed Pierre. At the top of the landing she and Sybille spoke in whispers. Then Pierre told Sybille that he definitely could not make it back that night to escort d'Aylarac, since the guests at Bourrel's were too many. She insisted that the two men absolutely needed to be taken to Montaillou that night, which they could only do with a guide since they were not familiar with the tracks. Could Pierre prevail on Bourrel to let him go, if he promised to be back by noon? This hushed conversation was not heard by Mondine, and the Perfect and Bernard Bélibaste had already retired further up the stairs to the hidden room that was reserved for Perfects staying the night.

Barthélemy Bourrel proved surprisingly complaisant. 'Why don't you rise quite early and aim to be at Montaillou before dawn,' he suggested, 'since that way you will be back here by 3 p.m.? I shall tend the flock until then.' When everyone at the Bourrels' had gone to bed, Pierre Maury made his way to Sybille Baille's and spent what was left of the night there on a bed next to her son.

At dawn, while Sybille waited on the Perfect in a separate room, Pierre Maury and Bernard Bélibaste enjoyed a hearty breakfast of cold meat left over from the night before. This was an unusual treat for Pierre Maury, and he told Sybille how much he enjoyed it. Finally the three men, with a generous bag of provisions provided by Sybille Baille, left for Sorgeat on the first leg of their haul up to Montaillou. From Sorgeat they climbed an escarpment called *lasitardor*, which almost certainly corresponds to today's 'l'Assaladou', the massive hump which rises north of Sorgeat (Duvernoy 1978, 1026n.58).*

The harshness of the wintry climb was accentuated by adverse weather conditions, and Pierre Maury referred to the *asperitatem itineris et temporis*. That the weather was bad was confirmed by Pierre's sister Raymonde, who recalled the rain and the cold on that day; and his younger brother Jean remembered that a thick cover of snow lay at Montaillou then, and from this he concluded that these events must have taken place in the month of January.

During the ascent d'Aylarac suffered from severe indigestion which may have been triggered by the fact that he undertook the climb on a full stomach. While 'l'Assaladou' is not exactly a hiker's Everest, its gradient is severe. Parts of the ancient track can be picked up above the campsite at Sorgeat, which is already some way up the *Coste*. The old gully runs through a trench on the eastern flank of 'l'Assaladou', alongside the Afouys mountain stream. In the summer it is largely

---

* It is probable that *lasitardor* is a phonetic spelling by Fournier's clerk of 'l'Asilador', which is close enough to 'l'Assaladou', the more so since 'l'Assaladou' above Sorgeat is still called *la Coste*, which is the phrase that Pierre Maury applied to *lasitardor* in 1324 (FR, f.256v). The difference between the two stages of the journey is reflected in the rhetorical nuancing of Pierre Maury's deposition; he states that they (my emphases) '**iverunt** *versus soriatum et deinde* **ascendentes** *per costam vocatam lasitardor*', which translates as 'They *went* towards Sorgeat, and then they *climbed* the escarpment called Lasitardor.'

overgrown, but in early spring it can be negotiated. The track here is steep and rocky, and a strenuous hour is needed to hit the *haute montagne* plateau above Montaillou, from where another hour's walk connects with *pla del angle*. Today, therefore, the hike from Sorgeat to Montaillou averages out at about three hours altogether. In the Middle Ages, when the paths were much better maintained by permanent usage, the entire trek, from Ax to Montaillou by way of Sorgeat, would have taken about four hours.

It may have been the Perfect's struggle with the colic as much as the sheerness of the *Coste* which delayed the party from Ax, for by the time they reached the wooded top of 'l'Assaladou' it was time for lunch. They made a small fire, and then consumed a fish pie, meat, cheese, bread, and wine that they had brought away from the house of Sybille Baille. Rather than proceeding straight after lunch into Montaillou, the Perfect advised them to wait until dark, which probably fell in late afternoon.

It was early evening when Pierre Maury and his two charges entered Montaillou and the house of his father. Pierre's sister Raymonde had just called at her parents' home to borrow a loaf of bread from her mother. She, her parents and her younger brothers Guillaume, Bernard, and Raymond were present when the men from Ax appeared. As for young Arnaud, he was probably in bed already, and the ten-year-old Jean was out guarding his father's sheep. He apparently came in later.

Pierre Maury's parents and the first-mentioned three brothers did the *melhorier* to the Perfect. After his sister had left for home with the bread, the Maurys, Philippe d'Aylarac, and Bernard Bélibaste all dined together. While the others ate turnips and meat, the Perfect ate cooked turnip, followed by fish, and then fruit.

The following morning Pierre Maury kissed d'Aylarac goodbye in his bed, and then set out for Ax. By the time he arrived back there he was nearly twenty-four hours later than promised. He found Mondine tending Bourrel's sheep, and she informed him that Barthélemy had been furious with him over his absence. This time Pierre Maury got off with a warning.

In his account of this mission Pierre Maury only ever refers to the same Perfect and to Bernard Bélibaste. But both his sister and his brother, who otherwise corroborate his story, make mention of

Philippe d'Aylarac *and* of Raymond Faure, who must therefore have overlapped with d'Aylarac at the Maurys' during this period.

During his second summer with Bourrel Pierre Maury visited his sister in Laroque d'Olmes. It was on the feast of Ciricus and Julitta, which fell on Friday 16 June 1307 and coincided with the town fair. Pierre Maury came to the fair to purchase rams at the market, and planned to stay that night with his sister and his brother-in-law, the cooper Bertrand Piquier.

The eighteen-year-old Guillemette seems to have married Piquier not long before Pierre Maury's return to Montaillou in December 1305. Piquier was by all accounts a coarse character, and Guillemette had already fled home from him once. At her father's in Montaillou then she had met the Perfect Philippe d'Aylarac and Bernard Bélibaste. Guillemette had pleaded with the *passeur* Bernard Bélibaste to take her to the Good Men because, dead or alive, she could never again stay with her husband: 'I'd prefer wandering aimlessly through the world,' she exclaimed, meaning, as the men understood full well, that she would rather be a prostitute than the wife of Piquier. Guillemette was barely eighteen when she said this, and her desire to be taken to the Perfects may well be connected to the fact that they never touched women. Guillemette's flight may have happened in the winter of 1306, when both d'Aylarac and Bélibaste were staying at the Maurys'. On the other hand it may well date from late spring or early summer 1307, in which case it probably prompted her brother Pierre's trip to Laroque d'Olmes; and the d'Aylarac–Bélibaste team was still operating in the Sabartès that summer.

Rather than sleeping at his uncle Bernard Maury's family home in Laroque d'Olmes, Pierre chose his sister's place. He was grudgingly received, and if he had hoped that his sleeping at the Piquiers' would provide Guillemette with a respite, he was mistaken, because that night the brutal cooper again beat his wife. Neither Pierre's presence nor, it seems, that of Piquier's mother and younger brother inhibited Guillemette's husband. The following morning Pierre Maury met Philippe d'Aylarac and Bernard Bélibaste, probably by appointment, near the pen where the animals for sale were corralled.

Over a late breakfast in a tavern they discussed his sister's predicament.

When Pierre suggested that they all three go and see her husband, d'Aylarac cautioned against it, since Piquier was bound to react badly to them turning up there together.

The three men decided to go for a constitutional along the river and head south out of town, alternately walking and sitting. In the end they found a private and secluded place and spoke again about Guillemette. Then they spotted Guillemette herself on her way to a field to make hay. They rose to follow her. As they were doing so, they encountered Pierre Maury's uncle Bernard from Montaillou, who invited all three of them for lunch. The Perfect and Bélibaste declined, and instead followed Guillemette. Pierre accepted, and together he and his uncle went into Laroque d'Olmes where, in a tavern in the town square, they had a meal which included meat.

Then Pierre Maury retraced his sister's steps and found her and his two friends in a field close to the river Touyre and the road. They had already spoken to one another, and Guillemette went up to Pierre Maury and said, 'Brother, please do what the *senher* tells you to.' But she could not expand on this, because the road was too busy with people passing. In order not to compromise their safety, Pierre and his two companions returned to the spot where they had sat earlier. Here d'Aylarac explained to Pierre that he was to take his sister to Rabastens, some twenty miles north-east of Toulouse, and should aim to be there a couple of days before St John's day (24 June) or on that day at the latest; he should leave his sister in a house there and proceed to mass at the main church, Notre-Dame-du-Bourg, where he would find either the Perfect, or one of the two Bélibastes, Bernard or Guillaume; if none of those could be there he would ensure that another trustworthy friend could be found to take care of Pierre's sister. 'Wait either in the church or next to it from morning until noon,' d'Aylarac advised Pierre. Pierre Maury was uncharacteristically anxious about embarking on this trek, since he did not know the way to Rabastens, but he complied anyway.

After this the threesome returned to the fair and checked into an inn. Bernard Bélibaste and Pierre bought conger or hake at the market and an earthenware pot in which to cook the fish. Pierre Maury's own account of that night's dinner, his third meal of the day, and the Perfect's 'kosher' requirements offers a fascinating snapshot of the night of Saturday 17 June 1307 in a hostelry in Laroque d'Olmes.

And since at the inn conger was already being cooked in another pot, when we wanted to cook ours separately in the newly purchased one, the hostess of the inn told us not to run up such an expense, but rather cook all the conger together in one. Bernard replied that she should not worry about the expense, because she would be well paid for the fire. From the same landlady we had a lid for our pot which Bernard rubbed very hard with ashes to remove all grease stains from it. Because there were many pots with meat on the hearth, Bernard and I were anxious to ensure that no *feresa*, that is meat or gravy from the meat, should enter our pot; even though our pot was covered, we therefore still stayed close to it until the fish were cooked.

During this time the Perfect slept. Bernard and I were about to sit down at the table when the Perfect advised us to buy eggs for two pennies and put them in front of us on the table, to ensure that our diet would not betray us as a heretical party. We bought the eggs. Then, after Bernard had prepared a dish of fish and fish broth for the Perfect, he lifted the [remaining] fish out of the pot, and he and I broke the eggs into it. Then Bernard and I ate the eggs as well as the fish, but the Perfect did not eat eggs, but only fish and broth. At the start of our dinner he blessed the bread in the same manner as he had done over breakfast, and gave of this blessed bread to both me and Bernard. In a low voice we said, 'Bless us, "*senher*",' and he replied in a similarly low voice, 'May God bless you.' Our bill was paid by myself and Bernard Bélibaste, and between us we spent that day about four shillings. (FR, f.255v)

This sum covered the fish, eggs, earthenware pot, rented stove-fire, and overnight accommodation for three people. At tuppence the basket of eggs cost the same as it would have done when bought directly from a farm. The total cost of forty-eight pence or four shillings was certainly high, which may be one of the reasons why Pierre Maury recalled it so clearly. By comparison, in 1320 Béatrice de Planisolles and her then lover paid only one shilling between them for an overnight stay and food in an inn. It may well have been the pot and the fire as well as the fish which increased the size of their bill since, as previously noted, fish could be very expensive, notwithstanding its abundance in the rivers of the Ariège. Guillaume Authié's sister-in-law Esclarmonde, for example, spent seven pence on buying fish for the Perfect, and Pierre de Gaillac reports buying a trout for twelve pence for the Authiés with money from Alissende Marty of Tarascon, the aunt (probably) of Blanche and

Raymonde Marty of Junac. A shilling was an impressive sum of money for a trout, which must have been intended as a special gift. On this occasion the Perfects themselves 'cooked the trout excellently after preparing it with good spices' (d'AR, f.54r).

After dinner that night the men retired to bed, with Bernard Bélibaste and Philippe d'Aylarac sharing one bed and Pierre Maury and a stranger another.

The following day, on Sunday 18 June, Pierre bought six rams at the market, and entrusted them to some people from Montaillou to take back. Pierre returned to the inn, but could not find his companions, who may have taken off with another party. He therefore called in on his sister for a late breakfast and to say his goodbyes. He ate with her, her mother-in-law, and a child who was a younger brother of Piquier's. Before departing he whispered to her, 'I'll come for you in three days. In the meantime get everything ready if you want to leave as instructed by the Perfect.' She replied that she was ready, and that he must not miss his appointment with her.

Then Pierre Maury set off on the thirty-mile trek to Montaillou which would take him past Montségur, through the Thermopylae of the Gorges de la Frau, and past Comus, where Pierre de Luzenac may already have lived. His travel companions were Guillaume Clergue, a brother of Pierre Clergue's of Montaillou, Clergue's cousin Gauzia Longa, and one Vital Teshendier.

When he returned to Laroque d'Olmes on, probably, Wednesday 21 June, he met up with his sister in the same field as before, and gave her money to buy bread, wine, and cheese for him. He could not afford to be spotted in the town by Piquier, whose suspicions would have been aroused by seeing his brother-in-law there.

Brother and sister ate together in Piquier's field, and then Guillemette went home. They agreed that Pierre would wait for her until late that night at the northern boundary of Laroque d'Olmes, next to a cross which stood near the cemetery which was overlooked by the high-lying old town. Nearly seven centuries later this cemetery and its ancient church still sit in the same place not far from the road to Mirepoix and next to the river Touyre.

It was 'at the time of the first sleep' that Pierre's sister joined him. She was carrying her wedding dress and her sheets, which were probably everything that she took into her marriage to Piquier. Then they set out on the 100-mile journey to Rabastens.

During the night from Wednesday to Thursday they reached Mirepoix. From here they pushed on to Beauville, and then to Caraman, which lies some twenty miles south-east of Toulouse. They arrived at Rabastens on Friday 23 June, and took up lodgings in a house near the church. The journey had taken from late Wednesday night until Friday. In the morning Pierre went to the west-facing portal of the church, and there he found Bernard Bélibaste, who took Pierre down to a house not far from the church. Bernard shared these quarters with his brother Guillaume, the future Perfect. Pierre had a drink with the two Bélibastes, and then he collected his sister. While he and Bernard attended high mass, Guillaume stayed behind with Guillemette, and the two of them prepared lunch. After lunch the Bélibastes promised to take as good care of Guillemette as of themselves, while she undertook to do everything to deserve their love and esteem.

It was time for Pierre Maury to return to Ax to his employer Barthélemy Bourrel. As he prepared to leave, Guillemette asked him to come and see her from time to time. Pierre replied that he could not, because he would be serving various masters, and so they parted. He never saw his sister again because, according to him, she was arrested with Pierre Authié in 1309 and taken to prison in Toulouse and, subsequently, in Carcassonne. But Pierre Maury heard about her from Guillaume Bélibaste, who over the next decade would become his good friend. Guillemette proved to be a good housekeeper, even though she was, apparently, quarrelsome and sometimes talked back with a sharp tongue. She does not seem to have been returned to Piquier after her arrest, although we cannot be sure. The fact is that she was dead by 18 February 1324, and possibly long before then; so were, by then, her mother and her father, and her brothers Guillaume, Bernard, Jean, and young Arnaud.

When Pierre Maury returned to Ax shortly after 25 or 26 June in 1307, he was informed by Barthélemy Bourrel that his services were no longer required. Pierre was cashiered because of his repeated absences, but it was to this sanction ultimately that Pierre Maury owed another fifteen years of freedom, as we shall see.

9. Wedding-bells in Montaillou: 1307–8

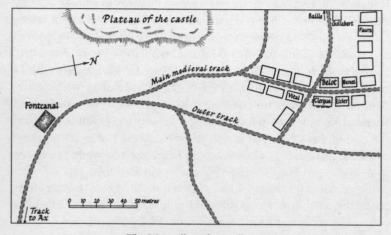

The *Montaillou* of new alliances

It was around Easter 1307 that Raymond Belot went to see his impoverished cousin Raymonde Vital in Pamiers. He told her that he and his
brothers were planning to marry their sister to Bernard Clergue, and
that she should come and join them again. By now, some seven years
after leaving Montaillou, she had a daughter, and her husband Prades
den Arsen may already have been dead. Raymonde accepted somewhat
grudgingly, but pointed out that she was indentured in Pamiers until
the end of August.

As soon as she was free that summer she took her daughter to be
reared by her husband's family, and then set off for the harvest in the
Val d'Arques. From there she proceeded to Montaillou, and when
she arrived there in the early autumn of 1307 Bernard Clergue and
Raymonde Belot were already married (FR, f.74r).

The approach to Raymonde den Arsen around Easter 1307 demonstrates that negotiations for a Clergue–Belot marriage were well under
way by then. This long-range, premeditated time-scheme further

underpins the suspicion that Bernard Clergue's romantic smoke-screen about his marriage was a concoction, and that the Clergue–Belot union owed more to their faith than to their hearts.

While the Clergues were plotting to broaden their power-base during the spring of 1307, the Issaurats of Larnat were hosting a conference of Perfects. It was Holy Week 1307 (from Palm Sunday to Easter Sunday, 26 March), and Guillaume Authié, Philippe d'Aylarac, and Amiel de Perles attended. Was this a council of war to discuss strategies to respond to Bernard Gui's appointment as Inquisitor at Toulouse on Monday 16 January 1307 (Baudrillart *et al.* 1909–, 8, 1935, cc. 677–81)? Or was it a gathering to ordain a new Perfect? Could the Larnat conference be related instead to the business of Raymond Belot's visit to Pamiers, the fashioning of a new order in Montaillou?

It was a year and a half since the arrests of Jacques Authié and Prades Tavernier, and the Cathars had regrouped. Peyre's evidence, which originated from the very core of the movement, did not, it seems, inflict irreparable damage to the Authiés' cause. And yet Peyre probably knew the names of just about every major player in the *risorgimento*. The containment of his testimony was probably due to some form of sabotage from within the Church's ranks, which had been deeply penetrated by the Cathars. Because of this the recent arrival on the scene of the formidable Dominican Bernard Gui must have exercised the Authiés and their allies. Bernard Gui would indeed turn out to become their most implacable foe.

That the Authiés' revival continued to inspire the people of the region is evident from a cameo scene in the fields of *a-la-cot* in Montaillou. It was early one morning in June 1307, and Guillemette Clergue (B) was on her way to make hay in *a-la-cot* when she met Guillaume Maury, Pierre Maury's favourite brother, leading a mule laden with flour. Guillaume was returning from Ax, and he was singing. Guillemette suggested teasingly that he must have been drinking his fill to be so merry. He replied that he had experienced happiness during the middle of the previous night while having his corn ground in Ax. 'How come,' Guillemette asked, 'you were in Ax in the middle of the night? Whenever my husband goes there to have our corn ground, he returns

home bone-tired from the wait and all the dust from the flour.'
Guillaume explained that he had spent only a short time at the mill,
but had stayed overnight in the house of Sybille Baille, where he
conversed with Guillaume and Jacques Authié.

When he was in Montaillou Guillaume Authié now resided permanently at the Belots'. He also visited the Clergues across the road,
although only *one* eyewitness account ever placed him there (see below,
page 199). It was only inside the Clergues' house that Guillaume Authié
openly conversed with the rector. But Bernard Clergue was not so
bound, and he frequently visited Guillaume Authié at their neighbours'.
On one such occasion in September 1307 he was at the Belots with
Guillaume Authié when, from his south-east-facing window which
overlooked the Clergues' house, Guillaume noticed that pigs were
disporting themselves in the Clergues' front-garden. 'How now! [*aquo
pur*?], we believe that those pigs are damaging those gardens,' Guillaume
exclaimed. Bernard looked out, saw them, and immediately hastened
downstairs to chase them away. At the main door of the Belots' he
bumped into Bernard Belot, and exchanged a few courtesies with him
before rushing on outside.
Once the rogue pigs had been driven away, Bernard wanted to
return to the Belots'. But then, he later claimed, he saw his brother
Pierre Clergue standing on the balcony which was above the main
door of his parents' home. The balcony opened from his first-floor
study, and he had presumably come to see what the commotion in the
garden was about. When he saw the rector, Bernard Clergue dared not
return to the Belots' in full view of him, because his brother mocked
him for being besotted with Raymonde Belot.
This, in essence, was Bernard Clergue's case to the Inquisition on
Friday 7 August 1310. He offered a two-pronged defence. First, the
reason why he repeatedly visited the Belots' house and Guillaume
Authié in it was because he was desperately in love with a daughter of
their house, and therefore with anything relating to it; in other words,
his contacts with a famous Perfect were caused by the madness of love.
Second, his seemingly casual reference to a disapproving elder brother
cleared the rector from any charge of collusion.
By offering a love-story in mitigation and cunningly fleshing it out

with authenticating narrative details such as rampaging pigs, Bernard Clergue shrouded the truth from the panel who interrogated him. Not that it was all that difficult, since the panel included the Clergues' powerful ally Jacques de Polignac. That the story of a romantic Bernard Clergue still enjoys currency is disconcerting, since there is *prima facie* evidence for a different view in the records themselves.

The bare facts are these. In July or August 1307 some time before Assumption Day, Bernard Clergue, who was then in his early thirties, became engaged to his neighbour Raymonde Belot. After a short engagement Bernard married his fiancée towards the middle of September 1307 (FR, f.173r). This date is not in doubt. The point needs stressing, because the date of Bernard Clergue's marriage in 1307 is crucial for a reading of Sybille Peyre's testimony and as regards Fabrisse Rives's assertion about Guillaume Authié's visit to the rector at Easter 1308.

There are two major reasons for being sceptical about the love-match scenario proposed by Bernard: the evidence of Sybille Peyre, and the fact that the Clergue–Belot match is the first of three Montalionian marriages which consolidated old alliances in the village against the backdrop, perhaps, of increasing pressure from the Inquisition. All three of these marriages involved Belots, and all of them joined Cathars. The fact that each of the couples would have been united in wedlock by Pierre Clergue does not inspire much Catholic trust either.

According to Sybille Peyre from Arques, Pierre Authié had claimed that Bernard Clergue married Raymonde Belot because the Belots were a soundly Cathar family; he could have secured a bigger dowry elsewhere. Pierre Authié's credibility is generally supported in the literature, and in his article on the Perfect, Duvernoy believes Sybille Peyre when she reports that Pierre Authié told her that he consoled the Count of Foix. After all, Duvernoy notes, true to his calling Pierre Authié never lied (Duvernoy 1970, 32). Was Sybille Peyre being equally honest?

If her evidence is truthful, then it demonstrates that the Authiés were back operating in Arques by late 1307, notwithstanding the fact that most of the Cathars of Arques had confessed themselves after the arrests of Jacques Authié and Prades Tavernier in 1305. Such renewed Cathar activity in Arques may explain why Sybille's husband Raymond Peyre ended up in prison after all, notwithstanding the indulgences granted him earlier. But there is also the possibility that she made it up; that she heard rumours about the Cathar inspiration behind the marriage of Bernard Clergue and Raymonde Belot, and was eager to impress the Inquisitor with such gobbets of gossip by attributing them to Pierre Authié.

Her reference to the Clergue–Belot match occurs at the very end of her statement, when she seemed eager to placate Fournier, who had already told her that her evidence up to then had left him sceptical. It is worth nothing that in the same few paragraphs she mistakenly called Roger-Bernard III 'Raymond-Roger', and she also claimed to have heard Pierre Authié say that Pierre Azéma was a Cathar loyalist, when in fact he was the opposite (FR, ff.66r, 206r). There *was* an Azéma who frequented her home village of Larnat, but this was the Montaillou *passeur* Raymond Azéma (d'AR, f.36v). As well as an Azéma and one '*r.beloti*' (i.e. Raymond Belot), the occasional presence of a Maury from Montaillou is reported at Larnat; on one occasion, and in broad daylight one Sunday, he arrived there with the Perfect Pierre-Raymond de Saint-Papoul (FR, ff.36v,39v).

Sybille Peyre's mistakes in her deposition years after the events may be little more than minor slips. My reason for highlighting them is that her evidence elswhere seems to be highly accurate, detailed and graphic. But even if the attribution to Pierre Authié of the motives behind Bernard Clergue's marriage were a fabrication, Sybille Peyre's testimony would still show that the Clergue–Belot union was rumoured to be a Cathar match as far afield as Arques.

The next wedding in Montaillou, probably still in the autumn of 1307, was that of Arnaud Belot, who was about thirty, to his neighbour opposite, the widowed Raymonde Lizier-Argelier.* Raymonde may have been somewhat older than Arnaud, because she was already the single mother of a son, Pierre Lizier, and had a teenage daughter. She was also considerably wealthier than her second husband, since Arnaud Belot's contribution was only a share of the Belots' fortune, and worth

---

* This union was promoted jointly by a family called Barbier from nearby Niort in the Aude, and by Bernard and Arnaud Marty of Montaillou. This may mean that the Barbiers and Martys were Raymonde Lizier's surviving 'family', with the right to give her away.

less than one third of her estate. Sixteen years later Fournier pressed her on why she would marry somebody who was so much poorer than herself, implying that Raymonde Lizier married Arnaud Belot for heretical reasons. By the time he interviewed Raymonde on 23 December 1323, Fournier was possessed of Sybille Peyre's deposition of 2 December 1322 and her claims about Bernard Clergue's marriage; he clearly suspected that this was another such union.*

It was probably in November or December 1307 that Alazaïs Guilabert married Arnaud Faure, who was in his forties and her senior by a generation. By marrying Arnaud Faure, Alazaïs Guilabert now became the twenty-five-year-old Pierre Maury's aunt, even though she may have been his junior by some six years. Her father Jean reneged on the promised dowry for his daughter, and this led to a deep rift between the two families. Jean Guilabert was a mean and cowardly character, and this was not the last time that he failed his family, as we shall see.

Like so many of the young women of Montaillou, including her sister Raymonde, the wife of Guillaume Authié (B) of Montaillou, Alazaïs had at some point been Pierre Clergue's mistress. Moreover, before marrying Arnaud Faure, she had a passionate affair with Arnaud Vital, and it was Vital whom she later blamed for instructing her in heresy. He may also have been the father of her child, and it is not impossible that she agreed to marry her middle-aged husband to have a father for her baby.†

*

* The underlying politics of the Lizier–Belot marriage would be consolidated in the years which followed when Raymonde's daughter married the rector's nephew Arnaud Clergue, the bastard son of Guillaume Clergue and Alazaïs Gonelle. Moreover, Raymonde's son Pierre later married Grazide Rives, whose mother Fabrisse was of course a Clergue; and the teenage Grazide in turn lost her virginity to her mother's cousin, the priest Pierre Clergue. But long before then Raymonde would again be widowed.

† The Guilabert–Faure link was further consolidated by the marriage of Raymonde Cléments of Gebets, the daughter of Alazaïs's sister Guillemette Cléments-Guilabert, to another Pierre Faure. This second Pierre Faure was probably of the generation of Pierre Maury. Even so he would have been older by up to twenty years than his bride Raymonde Cléments, who was probably born shortly after the turn of the century.

The third Belot marriage in this cycle took place in January 1308, when Bernard Belot took Guillemette Benet as his wife. We know that seven years earlier she and her sister Esclarmonde had been little girls of perhaps six or seven years of age so that in 1308 she would have been about fourteen or fifteen.

The man she married on that winter day in Montaillou was probably twice her age, and far from virginal. He had acted as a pander for Pierre Clergue and the former châtelaine, and for several years before his marriage he had been sexually involved with Vuissane Marty, as she then was. Some time before his marriage he seems to have asked Vuissane to leave the house. Although Vuissane was spurned, she apparently remained on good enough terms with Bernard's mother to visit there shortly after his marriage; but then Vuissane was poor, and could hardly take on, even if she were so inclined, a powerful clan like the Belots.

Worst of all, Bernard had tried to rape Raymonde Authié (B) (née Guilabert). For this serious offence Bernard Belot had been imprisoned and fined the large sum of twenty pounds, to be paid to the Count of Foix. This sum was the equivalent of half a house in Tarascon, or a rare illuminated Bible from Toulouse or Montpellier, or a herd of thirty-six sheep. No details of this sordid business have survived. It is certainly surprising that one of the powerful Belots was jailed at all, particularly since he was among the rector's factotums; and it is equally odd that the Authié (B) family lasted in Montaillou after pressing charges against Belot. It is possible that the châtelain was directly involved in prosecuting Belot. This brutal sexual predator was hardly an attractive prospect for a young bride.

At the time of Guillemette's marrying into the rich house of the Belots, her mother, Guillemette Benet, was probably in her late thirties. Three months earlier, in September 1307, she had been widowed. Her husband had been consoled by Prades Tavernier, who was then staying at the Rives'; his bones would later be dug up and burnt. Guillemette

---

That he was impotent, and that Raymonde desired to separate from him because of that, was widely known in the village. Not the least to get to hear of it was the priest of Montaillou, who made a play for Raymonde through her aunt Alazais. But this time he failed, and young Raymonde owed the preservation of her dignity to her courageous aunt.

Benet's absence from her daughter's winter wedding may have been due to the fact that she needed to stay at home to watch over the bride's two younger siblings, one of whom was only six in 1308 (assuming that she was alive); or perhaps she was still deeply in mourning. Bernard Benet, the bride's shepherd brother, was around, but again he did not attend the wedding, probably because transhumance had taken him into the lowlands far from Montaillou; nor did her sister Esclarmonde, who (later?) married one Guillaume Saint-Jean in Bélesta.

Young Guillemette Benet's family had tragically contracted in recent years and the Benets were now a spent force. But in the absence of Guillemette's relatives others made up the numbers, because through her cousin Gaillarde Authié-Benet young Guillemette's family included the most famous Perfects of Languedoc. Perhaps it was the expectation that the wedding would therefore be attended by the Belots' illustrious lodger, Guillaume Authié, which drew an exceptionally large crowd. Indeed, the size of the wedding party was such that the Belots' impoverished neighbour Alazais Azéma needed to lend Guillemette Belot a cooking pot for the occasion. Fourteen adults and one baby were present at the wedding festivities in the Belots' house. No record of the ceremony at Notre-Dame-de-Carnesses has survived, nor did Pierre Clergue visit the Belots' house that day. He probably could not afford to be seen in the same room as Guillaume Authié.

Apart from the bride and groom, the guests included Guillaume and Gaillarde Authié from Ax; Bernard Clergue and his new wife Raymonde; Guillemette Belot, the bridegroom's mother; Raymond Belot, the groom's eldest brother and now the figurehead of the house; Raymond Belot's brother Guillaume; Alazais den Torba-Belot, Raymond's sister, who had come with her husband Raymond and their baby daughter from Mijanès in the Donézan, along with Arnaude den Terras from the same place (she may have been a married Belot sister), Raymonde den Arsen, the recently rehired servant of the Belots, and Alissende Roussel, whose sister Gaillarde was married to Pierre Benet, the first-born Benet boy. A few years from now Alissende Roussel, her sister, and her husband were destined to be drawn into the tangled sexual web of the Clergues, before eventually collaborating with the Inquisition.

All the guests except for Guillaume Authié were gathered around the fire in the Belots' *foghana*, with Raymonde den Arsen sitting *behind* the central chimney as a servant. In her arms she was cradling Raymond Belot's niece, Alazais's daughter. The high point of this Cathar wedding was the entrance of the Perfect. Guillaume Belot went to get him from the locked loft, and Guillaume Authié descended the ladder, wearing a tunic and cloak or cape, which were of the same dark blue or dark green colour. When he stepped into the *foghana* everyone rose, with the exception of Raymonde den Arsen with the baby.

Nearly thirteen years later Gaillarde Authié was under the impression that Prades Tavernier had been her husband's companion on this night. But she was probably mistaken in this as in several other parts of her recollection, including the date of this marriage. Prades had no business being at the Belot–Benet wedding even if he did spend that evening in the Rives' barn just fifty yards away.

Guillaume Authié sat on a bench next to the three Belot brothers, Raymond, Bernard the groom, and Guillaume. No woman joined them there, but Guillaume Authié's wife sat close to him on a separate and, it seems, lower bench. He spoke to her in a hushed voice, as he did with the Belots and Arnaude den Terras, who was kneeling in front of him; she was, it seems, handing him money. Arnaude's supplicatory posture indicates that she was openly 'adoring' him in the *melhorier*. Moreover, Guillaume Authié and Arnaude seem to have briefly left the party together, because when Alazais Azéma went to retrieve her pot after the wedding ceremony she found Arnaude den Terras with the Perfect alone in a room off the *foghana*. She was being 'received' by him, just as Pierre Maury had been in similar circumstances in Arques in April 1304.

Guillaume Authié does not seem to have stayed long that night, and soon the three Belots accompanied him back upstairs into the mezzanine loft, which they locked from the outside. It must have been strange for Guillaume Authié to be sleeping alone in his comfortable bed with its silk cushion when, on this winter night after a wedding in Montaillou, the wife he loved was so near and yet now for ever beyond his reach.

From mid-January to early February 1308 Guillaume Authié generally stayed in the Belots' *solarium*, when he was not at Sybille

Baille's in Ax, where we know he spent Christmas of 1307. By now the loft was a well-appointed, self-contained flat with heating and cooking facilities, and probably complete sewing and shoe-mending kits. In the barn where the Belots kept their hay and straw were Raymonde den Arsen's quarters, including her bed; Vuissane had probably stayed there earlier. From here Raymonde saw smoke rising from the loft in the winter, a sure sign of habitation and also, in this case, of cooking. The house and barn were separate units with outside access, but the loft was an extension of the house. Its outside door was probably reached by a few steps from the courtyard. This external door, as well as Vuissane's dung-heap (see above, page 161), was in full view of the barn, and Raymonde den Arsen saw various people coming and visiting it.

Bernard Clergue and his wife left with Gaillarde Authié, and the entire party soon dispersed and retired to bed, leaving only Raymonde den Arsen and Guillaume Belot. Whatever she and Guillaume spoke of before she retired to her bed in the barn, it was almost certainly not, contrary to her subsequent claims, the identity of Guillaume Authié. She was fully aware of what was going on, and in May 1308, 'one day before Pierre de Luzenac came to Montaillou to search for and arrest the heretics', her sister-in-law Raymonde Vital met her at the (unidentified) spring of *cortal sec*. Raymonde den Arsen was carefully rinsing a flask because, as she explained to Arnaud Vital's wife, she intended to fill it with water for the Perfects who were staying in the Belots' loft. The Belots would never have taken her on if she had not had a Cathar pedigree.

It was towards Lent of 1308 (28 February to 14 April) that Gaillarde Authié of Ax was summoned to Carcassonne by the Inquisition. She was obviously singled out because of her husband, and she must have been dreading this call. As her travel companion, and to be safer, she took Arnaud Authié, Pierre Authié's son, with her.

Her first port of call was Montaillou, to seek advice from her husband. She and Arnaud checked in either at the Benets' or, if the Register's reading is correct, the Maurs' (rather than the Maurys'?). After dinner Gaillarde went to the Belots' to see her husband, who had been there for two days already.

She sat near the fire with her nephew Arnaud, along with Guillemette

Belot, Raymonde den Arsen, and three of the Belot brothers, Raymond, Bernard and his new wife, and Guillaume.*

Guillaume Authié came down from the loft and, standing, spoke to his wife and nephew for a long time. Eventually he accompanied them to the door. There he spoke to her again, and urged her not to betray them. She pointed out to him that she would have to tell the truth, and he replied that at least she should not reveal that she had seen them just then. He even seems to have stepped out of the house because he was so preoccupied with talking to her.

Her host, Raymond Belot, then walked her back the short distance to where she and Arnaud lodged, while Guillaume Authié returned to the loft with Guillaume Belot. Later that night the two of them departed from the house, presumably to a consolation.

The minutes of Gaillarde's interrogation in Carcassonne have not survived, but her deposition probably did not play a part in unleashing either the May or September raids on Montaillou. She would have done her utmost to protect her husband, and his allies the Clergues had probably taken steps to ensure that there would be no local fall-out from this. They had good reason to protect Gaillarde Authié, because it is probably from around this period that there survives the single eyewitness account which emphatically places Guillaume Authié and Pierre Clergue under one roof and even in the same room.

The information comes from the itinerant publican Fabrisse Rives-Clergue. Although she at first dated it to around Easter 1300, which is manifestly wrong, she also mentioned seeing Bernard Clergue '*and his wife Raymonde* [my emphasis]' a fortnight later in the same location, which therefore places these events after the autumn of 1307.† By a

* Arnaud was absent, presumably because after his wedding he moved with his wife into her big house next to the Clergues.
† She muddied the waters further when she claimed that at the time of her visit *Na* Roche was chatting with the Clergue and Belot matriarchs, when *Na* Roche had died three years earlier. Guillemette Belot and *Na* Roche may well have been '*commères*', and Mengarde Clergue was friendly with both of them. It may have been this that caused the confusion in Fabrisse's recollection. Would this also account for Vuissane Testanière's similar mistake, when she claims to have overheard Guillemette Belot and *Na* Roche discussing the recent marriage of Bernard Belot to Guillemette Benet? Both speakers would wrongly have us believe that *Na* Roche was alive in 1308.

process of elimination we may be reasonably confident that Fabrisse's visit to the Clergues' happened around Easter 1308, which fell on 14 April. It was between noon and 3 p.m. In her role as publican she was looking for a pewterware pint pitcher for dispensing wine, and the Clergues owned one such. She stopped by their house, and here, next to the ground-floor entrance, Mengarde Clergue and Guillemette Belot, who were now related, sat talking on a bench in the sun. It was a spot favoured by Pierre Clergue himself, and directly above it was his room.

Past the two women a staircase led up to the loft, which in the case of the Clergues' house consisted of a full first floor as well as, it seems, an attic. The priest's room boasted a balcony, which may have run the entire length of the first floor.

Fabrisse explained her reason for coming, and Mengarde directed her upstairs. When she reached the door and tried to get in, she found that it was guarded by Guillaume Belot. He demanded to know her business, and then instructed her to get her pitcher and hurry on out again. Fabrisse entered the hall of the loft, and here she met Pierre Clergue. He also asked her what she wanted, and then told her to be quick about it.

Fabrisse later maintained in evidence that she saw the pitcher on a table at the '*eastern*' end of the room, that is towards *a-la-cot* and the high mountains. As she crossed towards it, she noticed that on her right the door to the rector's room was ajar. In its window, which opened above the main entrance and 'looked towards *fontcanal*', stood Guillaume Authié (FR, f.63r).★ He was wearing a white tunic and blue overcoat, with a blue hood over his head. Fabrisse grabbed the pitcher and made her way to the door of the hall, while Pierre Clergue entered the room where Guillaume Authié was. She may have lingered for a moment, because Guillaume Belot again urged her to hurry up and leave.

★ Fabrisse's directionals, and particularly her pointed use of 'eastern', establish beyond a doubt that the front of the Clergue house and Pierre Clergue's room faced south to south-west into the junction of *capanal den belot*. This makes good sense, of course, since the side of the Clergue house facing the main track through Montaillou had a north-western aspect. The houses on the *bac* side of the road, on the other hand, could face the street and still enjoy optimum sunshine. For an imaginative reconstruction of fourteenth-century Montaillou Fabrisse Rives's evidence is of vital importance.

Guillaume Authié was still there, or perhaps back again, a fortnight later when she again called in at the loft. Although the Clergues were pitiless robber-barons, they were strangely forbearing of such unwelcome intrusions by an errant member of their family. On this occasion Fabrisse noticed the styling of Guillaume Authié's clothing, and the way his coarse-wool surcoat was split at the hood in front of his chest with buttons of a blue or red material; that is, he wore it like a cape. The white and blue colours of tunic, cloak, and hood were the same as before. This time it was Bernard Clergue who had to chase Fabrisse away.

From this it may appear that Guillaume Authié was now staying with the Clergues more often. There is a fitting irony about him lodging in the same loft where the Inquisition stayed whenever they stopped over in Montaillou on their way to Ax.

10. The Consolation of Guillaume Guilabert: May 1308

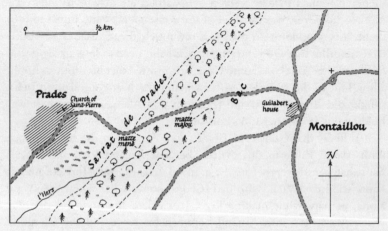

The Sarrat de Prades

In May 1308 a fifteen-year-old shepherd from Montaillou called Guillaume Guilabert started to spit blood. He probably suffered from some form of pulmonary consumption or tuberculosis. It quickly became clear that he was doomed.

He was the only son of Jean Guilabert and Alamande Fort. He had four sisters, three of whom (Alazais, Guillemette, Raymonde) were in their late teens or early twenties, while the youngest, Sybille, was only five at the time.

It was his father's flock that the young Guillaume used to tend on the pastures of Montaillou. He was a gregarious boy, and among his best friends had been two older boys and fellow shepherds: Guillaume Belot, the brother of the man who had assaulted his sister Raymonde Authié (B), and Raymond Benet, who had died three years earlier.*

* Raymond Benet was a kind of part-cousin on his mother Alamande's side, since her brother Guillaume Fort was married to a Sybille who was Guillemette Benet's sister.

202 *The Yellow Cross*

Guillaume Guilabert's sick-bed was set up in the *foghana* of the Guilabert house. Before noon on the day before he died, Guillaume Belot came to see him and, within his mother's hearing, addressed his dying friend: 'Friend,' he said, 'would you like me to go and fetch a doctor who can save both your soul and your body?' The young shepherd replied that he very much wished for that to happen. His mother, however, was terrified of the consequences and urged him to desist. 'My son, don't do that. It is too much already that I lose you. I have no other son. Do I into the bargain also need to lose all my goods for your sake?' But Guillaume Guilabert insisted that his mother should allow him to die consoled. After leaving the house Guillaume Belot sought out Arnaud Vital and told him that Alamande Guilabert was holding out against her son's consolation.

It is likely that Guillaume Belot asked Arnaud to use his influence with Alazais Faure in this matter, because Arnaud Vital and Alazais Faure had been lovers before she married Arnaud Faure. Indeed, Alazais Faure still loved Vital, who had tried to convert her when they were alone, perhaps while making love. It was late afternoon on that day when Alazais ran into Arnaud between his forge and the Clergues' house while heading to see her brother. He immediately urged her to prevail on her mother to let the consolation go ahead.

Alazais entered her father's house 'at the time of vespers' (6 p.m.), and spoke to her brother, eager to fulfil Arnaud Vital's bidding. The boy indicated that he wanted to be consoled, but only if his mother agreed. Alazais Faure found her mother pacing up and down in the house. She reasoned with her that consolation would secure her brother a place in paradise, and when her mother claimed to be very frightened, she said, using the polite form of address, 'You must not be afraid; from what Arnaud Vital says, Guillaume Benet and Raymond Maurs [he had died between September 1306 and May 1308] were "received" by the good Christians, and our rector, who is also a believer in the heretics, will not denounce us, any more than anybody else in the village.' She reassured her mother that the consolation would pass off in complete secrecy.

Alamande relented, and shortly afterwards Guillaume Belot revisited the house and conferred with Alazais and her mother, presumably about the practicalities of the consolation. Alazais then left with Guillaume to consult Arnaud Vital. The two men promised the utmost discretion, and added that far from being a threat the rector, Pierre Clergue, was in fact 'the guarantee of safety from the Inquisition'.

A decision must have been taken then that the safest time to console Guillaume Guilabert was the following night. Time was pressing, since Guillaume was very sick, but the cover of darkness was essential for the safe passage of the Perfect. It may have been during the course of that evening that Guillaume Guilabert's father Jean learnt of the plan to console his son.

Jean Guilabert complained to Guillemette Benet the following day that he could not under any circumstances witness the consolation. She advised him to resort to a subterfuge and retire to bed with his little daughter Sybille at the beginning of the night. This he did. Since his bedroom was off the *foghana* where the consolation took place, and since he closed the door, he did not see anything, nor did anyone see him. He thus escaped the clutches of the Inquisition. He must have heard every word that was uttered, but at no point did he join the group of mourners crowded into the main room of his house. His concern for his own safety outweighed his sense of duty and loyalty towards his son, whom he shamefully deserted at this all-important moment. Many years later Jean Guilabert's daughter Alazais discovered the truth about his stratagem that night, and expressed her contempt for her father.

The night that Guillaume Guilabert died, Guillaume Belot called on his neighbour young Bernard Benet in his garden. Judging from the distances involved in their night-time expedition, it was probably between 8 and 9 p.m., at the onset of darkness. He invited Bernard to accompany him on a mission to seek out either Guillaume Authié or Prades Tavernier in neighbouring Prades. Belot was the godson of Bernard's dead father, and he may have wanted to be accompanied on this journey by a Benet, because they were related to the Authiés. Young Bernard later claimed to have pleaded that he was a mere child and that he would not be able to keep up with Belot's marching pace. But Belot insisted, and the two of them duly headed west down the *bac* towards Prades.

The walk to Prades was not much more than a mile and a half. It led through a depression in the hump which hides the two villages from

each other's view. The dip was then known as *matte majou*, while the hump was called *sarrat de Prades* by the people of Montaillou (Pl. 19).*
The area down from the *sarrat* towards Prades was *matte menè*, and it was here that the two scouts forded the creek and advanced into the meadows beyond which Prades rises. Here, roughly in the area of the new cemetery, Guillaume Belot left Bernard Benet behind, while he entered Prades to look for the Perfects.

Belot's contact in Prades was Pierre Dejean, whose wife Gaillarde was the sister of Prades Tavernier and Alazais Rives. As a sound Cathar, Dejean regularly sheltered the Perfects, while his son Guillaume Dejean seems to have been another Perfects' mountain-guide. Dejean informed Belot that the Perfects had already left for the Sabartès by way of the Col de Marmare. Guillaume Belot rejoined young Benet, and they set off south-west into the valley and towards the *col*, a distance of about two and half miles.

At the apex of *pla del angle* Guillaume Belot called out into the dark, but received no reply. The two boys therefore climbed the escarpment to reach *superius del angle*, which means 'above the corner', and denotes the spot where today the D613 curves left in a wide sweep to start its climb into the Chioula (Pl. 20).

Guillaume Belot tried again, but to no avail. So he and Bernard penetrated up to the spring of the Coulobre, which has to be the crest where the Coulobre and Marmare converge and where the path towards Caussou starts its descent. Here Guillaume shouted into the night twice more. The second time a voice replied. They waited.

Two men emerged out of the dark and came towards them. One of them was Guillaume Dejean; the other one was tall, and although the boys could not make this out in the dark, he wore a brown cloak with a hood and a felt hat (FR, f.88r). This was Prades Tavernier. Guillaume and Bernard knelt in front of him and received his blessing in the manner of the *melhorier*. Then Guillaume Belot asked the Perfect to accompany them to Montaillou to console the dying Guillaume Guilabert. Prades Tavernier agreed, and so the foursome doubled back

---

* *Matte majou-mayou* (*LT*) is Occitan for the Latin text's '*matte maior*' (FR, f.80v). The spot is still known as 'la Matte', and is listed as such on the *PN* for Montaillou. So is '*Matéménigue*', which corresponds to the Latin '*matte minor*' or Occitan *matte menè* (or *menié, menic*: *LT*).

towards Prades, where the young Dejean split up from them to go home. It was about midnight (although Alazais and her mother later wrongly remembered it as dawn) when the three of them recrossed the Matte on their way to the Guilaberts' house.

In Montaillou, in the meantime, the same evening and night were tragically eventful. In the course of the day, the dying boy asked his sister to intercede with her husband Arnaud, to get him to come so that they could be reconciled. Since the withholding of Alazais's dowry the previous winter Arnaud Faure had not set foot in his wife's home, and the rift may have been compounded by young Guillaume Guilabert rallying to his father's support as the only other 'man' in the family.

When Arnaud returned from the wood that evening, his wife told him of her brother's mortal illness. Then she pleaded with him to make his peace with Guillaume. He agreed to follow her to the Guilaberts' after his dinner.

When he arrived there his wife and her mother were sitting next to the fire in the *foghana*, which was lit by candles. In another bed not far from Guillaume's lay his elder sister Guillemette Cléments, clutching a baby; she was sick and had come to her father's home to get better.

Guillaume Guilabert was sinking rapidly. His speech started to slur, but he was still conscious, and Arnaud and he made their peace and forgave each other everything. When Arnaud turned to go home, Alazais and Alamande told him to wait, because Guillaume Belot, they said, had gone to fetch 'a good Christian' who would save Guillaume's soul. So Arnaud stayed.

There were several others in the *foghana* awaiting the arrival of the Perfect. They included Guillaume Authié (B) from Montaillou, a brother-in-law of the dying boy. It was his wife Raymonde who had been assaulted by Bernard Belot, and he still felt at odds with the Belots. Also present were Guillaume Fort, young Guillaume's uncle, and his wife Sybille.

As Guillaume's speech was fading, his mother and sister Alazais became increasingly anxious in case he should die before the arrival of the Perfect. They urged Arnaud Faure and Guillaume Authié (B) to go to the hay-barn to see whether they could see the party with the Perfect in the *bac*, the slope of the hill which looks towards Prades. The two obliged, and from the barn, which must have overlooked the *bac*, they spotted them at once.* The three men entered through the barn, where they were greeted by the two look-outs who led them towards the *foghana*. At the 'second' door of the house Bernard Benet, according to Arnaud Faure, left without having entered the place of consolation. This was confirmed by his wife Alazais Faure's recollection, but Bernard himself later falsely claimed to have been present at the consolation (see below, page 370).

As the Perfect entered the *foghana* and bared his head, he noticed Guillaume Authié (B) in the light. Whether he did not recognize him, or whether he felt wary of someone who had litigated against the Cathar-friendly Belots, is not clear, but he exclaimed, 'Why is that one here? He should leave!' Alazais and Alamande reassured Prades that Authié (B) was a friend and that he had nothing to fear from him. Guillaume himself replied to the Perfect, 'But, sir, I also need my share of the Divine Good.'

Prades approached the bed of Guillaume Guilabert and called his name. But the boy could no longer speak; his breathing was spasmodic, and his mouth had filled with blood. Notwithstanding his friend Guillaume Belot's efforts to revive him, he failed to respond to Prades. He could not therefore voluntarily express his desire to be received into the Cathar faith, and Prades indicated that it was consequently too late for a consolation. But Guillaume Belot and Alazais begged him to proceed anyway, and protested that the boy had emphatically desired to be received into the Cathar faith while he was still lucid and of sound mind. At this Prades relented.

Guillaume Belot took his friend by the shoulders and sat him up in bed, while Prades put a small book on his head. Then, after several genuflections, he stood at the bottom of the bed and consoled Guillaume Guilabert.

* Later Alazais would confusedly remember that her husband and Guillaume left at the point of Prades's entry. Looking back nearly two decades later she wrongly attributed Guillaume Authié (B)'s momentary absence from the *foghana* to his unwillingness to share the same space with a Belot. Her belated attempt to insulate her husband from the consolation may have stemmed from a profound sense of guilt, because she had dragged him into heresy through her affair with Arnaud Vital, and later cheated on him with Pierre Clergue.

In the middle of these proceedings the young daughter of Guillaume and Sybille Fort, Esclarmonde, appeared in the doorway and called for her mother. She was asked to stay. Her father later called her an eight-year-old, while, according to Alazais Faure, she was thirteen. This is more likely to be correct, since the Forts belonged to Alamande's generation, and would have older children. In her testimony her aunt was careful to give the girl's age as under fourteen; had she been fourteen her presence on this night would have rendered her guilty of heresy. Esclarmonde would later marry Raymond Clergue, whose unflattering nickname was *morrut*, which means 'thick-lipped' or 'sullen'.

When the consolation was over, Prades sat down on a bench next to the fire. When Guillaume died, his friend Guillaume Belot turned to his distraught mother and told her that her son was saved. Then the party dissolved, leaving behind the grieving family and the Perfect.

Guillaume Guilabert's short journey on this earth was done. His face was splashed with water, and then covered with a cloth, as was the custom in the Pays d'Aillou. He was duly buried in the churchyard at Notre-Dame-de-Carnesses. His remains rested there until July 1322 when, on the orders of the Inquisition in Pamiers, his bones were exhumed and burnt as heretical. The afflictions of his loved ones and of those who stood by him in his hour of need were deferred until the spring of 1321.

Shortly after her son's death, Alamande Guilabert was talking to a neighbour in the doorway of her house, when Guillemette Benet called on her. Guillemette, who collected thanksgiving presents for the various consolations in Montaillou, told Alamande that she would do a great charity if she sent a gift to the 'good Christians', who were 'the friends of God'. A grateful Alamande gave Guillemette two fleeces of wool for the Perfects so that they would pray for the soul of her son. Guillemette took the fleeces, put them in the breast-pocket of her long mantle, and left.

The nature of Alamande's gift suggests that it was intended for Prades who, as a former weaver, would put the fleeces to good use. Prades was probably in the village on that day, along with Guillaume Authié, and that may have been why Guillemette collected an appropriate thanks-offering then from Alamande. Unlike Alamande, Guillemette Benet knew the Perfects' movements.

So, on this occasion, did the Carcassonne Inquisition. At some point in mid-morning of (probably) the day after the above conversation, a posse led by Pierre de Luzenac and the châtelain of Lordat raided Montaillou. The young de Luzenac probably lived in nearby Comus then, since in the winter of 1308 the chaplain of Comus carried an apologetic letter from him to the Inquisitor in Carcassonne. From Comus it would have been relatively easy to monitor the movements of Perfects in Montaillou, the more so since de Luzenac was an insider. It must have been the lure of Bernard Gui's monies that had turned this feckless gambler into a traitor, just as it had prompted Guillaume Peyre from Limoux to become a stool-pigeon.

What is intriguing about the raid is that de Luzenac struck without Pierre Clergue's prior knowledge. This suggests that the order was not given in Carcassonne, since the Clergues would then have been tipped off by the de Polignacs. The raid was probably triggered by the testimony given by Pierre Authié's nephew Géraud de Rodes to d'Ablis's deputies in Pamiers on 10 May 1308 (d'AR, ff.3v–4r). He let slip that Bernard Tavernier from Prades and the Belots of Montaillou had sheltered the Perfects Prades Tavernier and Jacques Authié. The instructions for the raid must have been issued shortly afterwards, although how de Luzenac came to lead it remains unknown.

It is not easy to approach Montaillou unnoticed, and in the Pays d'Aillou everyone knew everyone else or was related to them by marriage or sexual alliance. The strangers in the landscape were either spotted and at once identified as a raiding party, or else their approach from Prades, where they had rounded up suspects earlier that morning, had been betrayed.

But time was short when the bush-telegraph flashed a warning through to the Perfects in the Belot house. The chief *passeur* Arnaud Vital was alerted, and the two Perfects in the village donned ready-made disguises which clearly formed part of escape plans that were now activated.

It must have been about eleven in the morning on this day when the grandmother of the shepherd Jean Pélissier was collecting herbs in her garden for her cooking. It was then that she saw Arnaud Vital with Guillaume Authié and Prades Tavernier in tow. She had watched Arnaud collecting the Perfects at the Belots' house, but she failed to see that from the Belots' the Perfects were rushed to the house of Raymonde Belot-Lizier, probably because it sat directly above *a-la-cot* and was therefore strategically well placed for fleeing into the mountains. It is likely that the rector had a hand in this switching of hideouts, because he is reported at some point to have retrieved two Perfects from the Belots' house and assisted their flight down *a-la-cot*; that same night, it seems, the henchmen of the Inquisition burnt the house of Arnaud (?) Fort in the village (FR, f.152v).

The threesome hurried along the hedge of the Pélissiers' garden towards *comba del gazel*, while the Carcassonne Inquisition searched the houses of the Benets, Belots, and Rives. They knew where to look for the Cathar core of Montaillou, but they drew a blank. Nor did they find conclusive proof of organized, subversive activity, and the secret passage between the Rives and Benet houses remained undiscovered for another four months. Neither did the well-appointed loft of the Belots arouse undue suspicion.

Pierre de Luzenac and his party arrested the neighbours Pons Rives (wrongly called Bernard by Pélissier) and Guillemette Benet; Bernard Julia, whose wife (probably) Rixende Julia had sat on *Na* Roche's death-watch; Guillemette Maurs, the wife of Bernard Maurs; and Raymond Capelle. His family had traditionally been deeply Cathar, but it did not play any part in the latest Cathar revival. A remarkable feature of these arrests is that they included only two well-known Cathars, Guillemette Benet and Pons Rives. The reason why Guillemette Benet was among them was because Pierre de Luzenac knew, of course, that she was the aunt of Guillaume Authié's wife. But the small number of arrests suggests that de Luzenac was unaware of the scale of heretical penetration in Montaillou. Pierre Authié had not, it turns out, confided in him about who was and who was not Cathar at Montaillou. The Montalionians were added to the prisoners from Prades, who included Prades Tavernier's brother Bernard, and were locked up in the castle of Montaillou. From here they were subsequently moved to Lordat.

In the meantime Arnaud and the two Perfects progressed down past

la laviera and up into *comba del gazel* where the twenty-four-year-old
Jean Pélissier, ignorant of the events going on at that moment in the
village, was grazing his sheep. He was not alone. Here are his own
words from seventeen years later:

It was a year before, but I cannot in fact recall for certain whether it was the
same year, or the year before, the people of Montaillou were arrested on the
orders of the Lord Inquisitor of Carcassonne [Geoffroy d'Ablis] and gaoled in
the castle of Montaillou; nor can I be sure whether it was in summer after the
cutting of the grass, or in spring before the interdiction of the grass. It could
have been either spring or summer, when one morning I tended my sheep in
a place called *comba del gazel* which is within the territory of Montaillou. I was
in a meadow belonging to Guillaume Fort and his brothers. I was on the
left-hand side in this meadow close to the track which leads to the mountains
of Montaillou. Next to me, on my right-hand side, with the track between
us, Pierre Baille, the son of Raymond Baille of Montaillou, was grazing his
sheep in the meadows of Bernard Marty whose nickname was '*cabre*', and so
was Jean Marty in his meadow which was next to Raymond Marty's.

It was nearly noon. As Pierre Baille, Jean Marty and I were grazing our
sheep in those meadows there came away from Montaillou, on this same
track, the late Arnaud Vital, who was wearing a blue cloak and an axe around
his neck. With him walked two strangers who were not from Montaillou,
and I had neither seen them before nor did I know them. Over their other
clothes they each wore a large brown shepherd's cloak made from two pieces
of cloth so that the sides of their clothes were visible; their tunics or their
inner garments were of blue or green cloth, and each carried an axe on his
shoulder. These three men came towards me and the other two. When they
were next to the meadow of the Belots, they turned off the communal track
and crossed over a stone wall into the Belots' meadow. They walked through
the meadow and directly made their way to the meadow where Pierre Baille
was grazing his sheep. Arnaud Vital greeted him, and in return Pierre greeted
Arnaud. Then they reached Jean Marty whom they also greeted, as he did
them. After this I saw Arnaud Vital and the two strangers go cross-meadow
as far as the wood known as *comba fred*, which they entered. Immediately
afterwards Arnaud Vital came out from this wood bearing a huge faggot on
his shoulders which he balanced with his axe. He went up directly to Pierre
Baille and Jean Marty, while the two strangers stayed in the wood.

And when he joined Pierre and Jean he rebuked them, in my hearing, for allowing their sheep to stray into freshly sown fields. He did this because at the time Arnaud was the hayward of the village of Montaillou. But Jean jokingly said to Arnaud, 'And are those two woodcutters from Lavenalet? They look it,' to which Arnaud replied that, yes, they were from Lavelanet. I saw nothing else nor did I hear any more of the exchanges between Pierre and Jean. When Arnaud had gone, Jean and Pierre, while grazing their sheep on the meadows which intervened between them and *comba fred*, went straight up to it and its border. They then grazed their sheep in the meadows which verge on the wood, and sometimes, I saw it, they even entered it. I do not know whether Pierre and Jean entered this wood to confer with the two strangers, nor did they tell me this afterwards, as far as I recall. But when Jean and Pierre had passed a copse called *la peyra del fug*, they could enter and leave the wood at will. From where I stood I would not have seen them. Jean and Pierre grazed their sheep next to that wood until evening that day, and I saw no one else that day going to that wood. (FR, f.241v)

Jean Pélissier's directional uses of 'right' and 'left' here were from his perspective inside *comba del gazel*, looking towards Montaillou. He stood some way up from *la laviera*, and his reference to 'cross-meadow' signifies the meadows of *comba del gazel* as seen from his position on the edge of the path which led up into the mountains (Pl. 21).★

The reason why his fellow shepherds Pierre Baille and Jean Marty felt so at ease with the two strangers and their guide was perfectly clear to Jean Pélissier, even though later he at first tried to withhold this information from the Inquisition. Pélissier knew full well that Pierre Baille's brother Jacques was married to Sybille Rives, who was the niece of the Perfect Prades Tavernier. In other words, in *comba del gazel* Prades met his niece's brother-in-law, Pierre Baille. The Baille family

★ This path is still there and runs to the east of *GR*7B which today leads up to Jasse de Balaguès on the western flank of the Gazel. *Peyra del fug*, which Jean Pélissier called a *collis*, is the copse in front of the Bois de la Luzière. Today the part of *peyra del fug* which faces the village is grazing land and known as Fontanal. *Comba fred* has to be the spur which is directly north-east of the Gazel, the Bois de la Luzière. Since Pélissier stood in the south-western corner of *comba del gazel*, he could see only part of the wood of *comba fred*, but he could no longer see the shepherds' actions in *comba fred* once they moved behind the copse.

was deeply Cathar, and would pay a high price for this shortly. As for the cryptic exchange about 'woodcutters from Lavelanet', this may have been coded speak for Perfects, perhaps since Lavelanet sits so close to Montségur.

Jean Pélissier stayed in *comba del gazel* until evening, when he returned to Montaillou to hear news of the raid from his distressed and militantly Cathar grandmother.* Early the following morning Jean was up at *fontcanal* with his flock, and looking towards *la laviera* he spotted Arnaud Vital in *comba del gazel*. Arnaud was probably returning from feeding and briefing the Perfects, which suggests that they stayed in the woods all day and night waiting for news of the raid. Clearly it was essential that they should know who had been arrested, so that they could take appropriate evasive and defensive action.

By May 1308 the Catholic church's counter-campaign was in full swing. The first extant deposition in the Inquisitorial Register of Geoffroy d'Ablis is dated 10 May 1308, and a number of arrests and summonses undoubtedly predated May 1308. On 10 and 11 May 1308 the Carcassonne Inquisition briefly sat at Pamiers in the convent of the Dominicans, before settling at Carcassonne from 21 May 1308 to 27 September 1309. Only seventeen of the fifty-one depositions in the d'Ablis Register have survived, and among these none involves a Montalionian.

In order to appreciate the self-censorship in the seventeen extant depositions of the d'Ablis Register, we should remember that they were given *before* the arrest of the main Perfects and their followers. Repeatedly some of the accused are asked about the present where-abouts of various Perfects, in the knowledge that some of them may have been hiding within yards of the Inquisitor when he was in session in Ax. The reason why Raymond Authié kept Sybille Baille out of his evidence of 12 June 1308, for example, must be because at that stage she was probably on the run, and she may have been hiding in Ax itself. Unlike the Fournier statements of 1320–25, the d'Ablis ones are contemporary with the events; a number of them antedate the big

---

* She must have been his *maternal* grandmother, old 'Maura', whose Cathar days go back to the time of Montségur.

September 1308 raid on Montaillou, while others, including Pierre de Luzenac's, were taken shortly afterwards.

Up to this point Pierre Clergue had managed to stave off any in-depth investigation of his backyard. This was now becoming an untenable position, particularly since the May raid on Montaillou proved that the Church had intelligence about the village. Furthermore, if the Clergues suspected that Pierre de Luzenac had deliberately worked around them, because of local rumours about their Cathar sympathies, they would have known that urgent action was required to prove their good faith (in all senses of the word).

The Clergues now turned the necessity to survive into an opportunity for a major strike against their enemies. Their first act of retaliation may have been to clip de Luzenac's wings by ensuring that he in turn was summoned before d'Ablis to answer about *his* involvement with the Authiés. With the utmost cynicism they reinvented themselves in the months between May and 8 September 1308. These rural *padroni* must have reasoned that between them and the de Polignacs there was nothing the inhabitants of the village could do. To testify against the Clergues in the de Polignacs' gaol in Carcassonne was inconceivable. Moreover, the Clergues' friends would be protected, but from now on even the Belots and Rives would be beholden to them. Did Pierre Clergue at any point discuss this likely strategy with his friend Guillaume Authié, or was it only 'family' who were told?

11. The Martys of Junac: 1308–10

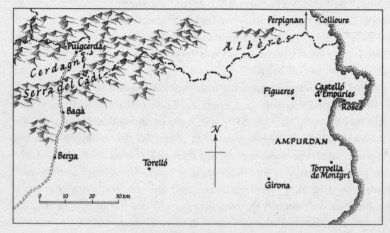

The road to freedom and exile

After a daring escape with Guillaume Bélibaste from Carcassonne in 1307 (see page 272), Philippe d'Aylarac returned to the Sabartès from the safety of Catalonia, and by October 1307 he was staying at the Martys of Junac. While there he was twice spotted by Arnaud Piquier in the square of Tarascon. Considering that the offices of Arnaud Sicre Senior gave on to the same square, d'Aylarac's exhibition of himself verges on the incomprehensible, even if Bayard and others had in some way guaranteed his safety. In January or February of 1308 he consoled Sybille, the sister of Philippe de Larnat, and from Lent to Easter, 14 April 1308, he stayed at the Issaurats' in Larnat.

By then the Inquisition was on the offensive, and the list of the d'Ablis depositions from May 1308 to September 1309 shows that the Rodes, Larnats, Issaurats and Piquiers were high on the Inquisitor's agenda. With their former comrades in the dock and naming fellow Cathars, it would be only a matter of time before the Martys were summoned (d'AR, f.56r), particularly after the de Junacs had been convoked.

In 1308 the family consisted of the father, Bernard de Junac (his wife Lombarde may already have died), four sons, Guillaume, Pierre, Gaillard and Jacques, and two daughters, Esclarmonde and Raymonde. Bernard de Junac was the first one to be ordered to Carcassonne, where he spent a week testifying. On his return he learnt that his sons had also been called. All of them except Jacques, who excused himself on the grounds of sickness but was in fact malingering, attended. The old châtelain was distraught by the prospect of his sons' departure and by his own experience of Carcassonne. On kissing him goodbye his son Guillaume assured him that he would stay in Carcassonne in his father's place. Old Bernard fell ill, but we know that he was still alive on the day after Whitsun, 3 June 1308.

It was around May 1308 that Arnaud Marty from Junac was finally ordained by Guillaume Authié, and the venue for the ceremony was probably again the Issaurats' house in Larnat. In late January or February 1308 he and Guillaume Authié had been seen together in Montaillou by Raymonde den Arsen (FR, f.74v); at that stage he was known to be an ardent follower of the Cathars.

Perhaps he had been in or near Montaillou during the raid, because one morning in May or early June, shortly after his ordination, he turned up panic-stricken outside Rixende Palharèse's house in Luzenac. She tried to calm him down, but failed. He had either chanced upon a hostile patrol or otherwise crossed the path of the Inquisition. Rixende offered him her usual hiding-place during daylight hours, a large chest. Then she locked the house and left. When she returned home, Arnaud Marty had escaped by breaking through the roof of her house. She did not see him for a long time after that. Arnaud's mission as a Perfect evidently got off to a terrifying start, and according to Rixende, she did not see him again for a year.

Shortly before Whitsun 1308 (2 June) both Guillaume and Arnaud Marty went on the run. Their brother-in-law Arnaud Piquier must have been summoned already, because by Thursday 13 June 1308 he was being interviewed in Carcassonne. To finance their flight they sold, among other things, twenty axes, a large quantity of coal from the forge's mills, and two oxen. They took a mule with them, and made their way to Sautel in what is now the Plantaurel, a rolling countryside of lush copses to the south of Pamiers and Mirepoix. Here, on the first or second day of their flight, around the weekend of 25–6 May, they stayed one night with friends who had formerly lived in Rabat. Then they took off for Mirepoix, and from there to Grenade in the Toulousain. Here they decided to split up to be less conspicuous, and they therefore sold their mule and the clothes and tools that they carried. Guillaume headed for Castelnaudary, while Arnaud returned into the Sabartès.

Not long after her brothers Blanche Marty also fled home, to escape her violent father after he had beaten her. When Bernard Marty returned to Junac from Rabat, where he continued to work for Guillaume-Arnaud de Castell, his contrite father asked him to go and find his sister and bring her back home. But if she refused, could Bernard give her three shillings from her father to help her fend for herself?

A few days later, on Whitsun, Bernard found his sister in the upper town at Castelnaudary, where she was staying with a Beguine, who would have been a pious, celibate woman, and one probably engaged in philanthropic work as much as prayer. Blanche flatly refused to return to Junac, and proudly declined the offer of her father's money, saying that she had enough cash on her. Then she instructed her brother on how to make his way back to Mirepoix.

On the southern outskirts of Castelnaudary Bernard ran into his brother Guillaume and told him that their sister was there. The two of them returned into the town, and met up again with Blanche who showed them an inn owned by one Raymond Marty, who may have been a relative. Here they took a room. That night Bernard and Guillaume shared a bed and spoke of their recent tribulations, and Guillaume urged Bernard, whose slate was officially clean as far as heresy was concerned, to return to Junac to run the forge, provided Bernard de Junac agreed to this.

Before Bernard set off for Junac his siblings told him that they would both be back there within the next eight days. Blanche had after all relented, it seems. After reporting back to his father and before Guillaume and Blanche reached Junac, Bernard made for Rabat intending to rejoin his flock there, which included twenty sheep and five lambs of his own. To his astonishment he discovered that his brother Arnaud had in his absence sold his entire livestock and had grossed a total of nineteen pounds from the sale: ten for the sheep (so one sheep cost ten shillings), six for the wool, and another three for the lambs.

Bernard furiously went in search of Arnaud. Towards dusk he found him sitting with his brother-in-law Arnaud Piquier outside the latter's house in Tarascon on a stone bench. He challenged Arnaud about the sale, and Arnaud pleaded an urgent need for cash, and promised to repay all of it as soon as he could. It seems likely from the large sum of money involved here that the cash was needed for buying favours from officials, and before long another Marty was forced to bribe his way out of trouble. For Arnaud Marty and Arnaud Piquier, as for d'Aylarac, to sit openly in Tarascon under the nose of the firm of Arnaud Sicre Senior beggars belief, since one of them had already been ordered to Carcassonne, and the other one was a Perfect on the run. It must be the case that Sicre was away at the time, perhaps in Carcassonne with the Inquisitors. For Marty capture meant certain death; for Piquier to have been seen so openly with a known Perfect, and after receiving his summons, spelt years in prison.

When Bernard returned home from this exchange with Arnaud, his sisters Raymonde and Blanche were sitting together in the *foghana* of their home. The fact that Raymonde stayed on in her father's house for the next eighteen months means that Piquier was convicted and imprisoned after his last recorded deposition of 23 October 1308; his house in Tarascon would therefore be declared forfeit, and this would have rendered Raymonde homeless.

Two days later Guillaume turned up, but there is no record of Arnaud doing so at any point. Rather, he now fled into Roussillon and from there crossed over into the county of Ampurdan (see below, page 222). But then, like several other Perfects, he returned to the Sabartès to continue with his ministry in the thick of the persecution. His mission was destined to be short-lived.

In the months which followed, and well into 1309, Bernard Marty worked mostly for one Raymond Goutas in Varilhes. He may even have seen the former châtelaine of Montaillou who lived there, and if he did not he probably knew about her presence here from his brother Arnaud.

While Bernard was at Varilhes, his father, Blanche, Raymonde, and

Guillaume were summoned to Carcassonne for preliminary hearings, probably in the course of the autumn of 1308 or early in 1309. One night Bernard's father visited him to brief him on his deposition, and around Easter, which in 1309 fell on 30 March, Guillaume turned up in Varilhes. He had spent seven weeks in remand custody in Carcassonne, and was under an injunction to return there after raising the funds required for settling a debt of fifteen pounds with the gaoler, who was de Polignac. To this end he intended to sell two pieces of land, which he could do only with his father's and brother's permission.* After the sale Guillaume took the money and fled. He was followed a few weeks later by his sister Blanche. It is likely that the siblings had hatched this contingency plan during the first week in June 1308, when they were both alone in Castelnaudary. The Inquisition never caught up with either of them, and Guillaume may have died in Catalonia in late 1323.

Both the Marty women were interviewed and released on licence. Blanche's session with Geoffroy d'Ablis is of particular interest. When she appeared before him she owned up to some minor heretical offences; she could hardly deny all knowledge of Catharism when her brother was a Perfect. But she artfully conveyed the impression that she was *orca*, that is lowly and a bit slow. The Inquisitor listened to her benevolently while she was confessing. She was prostrate before him and, with her arms wrapped around his legs, she pleaded for mercy. He repeatedly patted her gently on her shoulders, and told her not to be afraid, since he would not harm her. Then he let her go. 'I hadn't even confessed the half that I had done and knew of others,' she later remarked (FR, f.131r).

The intimacy of the scene, and particularly the physical proximity of judge and accused, is intriguing, as is d'Ablis's reassuring Blanche by physically touching her while she knelt before him in supplication. This episode also suggests that d'Ablis was a gentler and more gullible

---

* Since the fully audited average cost of a prisoner in Carcassonne in the early 1320s was twelve pounds a year or *per diem 8 d.* (*CR 1285–1314*, 8718–19), Guillaume Marty's debt was nearly eight times higher than it should have been. Did he make it up to cover his true intentions, as Pierre Authié had done earlier, or was the corrupt de Polignac trading prison privileges for money?

creature than Fournier. Blanche's role-playing deceived d'Ablis, but this did not lull her into a misplaced sense of security. As has already been mentioned, in the spring of 1309 Blanche fled the Sabartès. Her escape was funded by a 'wealthy man from the Sabartès', almost certainly a de Junac (FR, f.224r). There can be little doubt that it was also they who supported Raymonde in her later bid for freedom. It should be noted, however, that the same man who paid Blanche's expenses also gave her money so that she *should* flee, which might just lend some slight credibility to Bernard's story about his father's death.

Blanche's tale about d'Ablis became one of the exiled Cathars' favourite after-dinner stories in the years which followed. One late December night in 1320 she told it in Catalonia, and it provoked the usual merriment among a group of exiles which included a number of familiar characters from this story. Listening and laughing with them in their small circle sat, unbeknown to any of them, a mole of the Inquisition.

Before she left the Sabartès Blanche was anxious to ensure that some of her favourite possessions should be safe. Her best friend at Junac was Mersende, the wife of Pierre Ferrié, and formerly the lover of Arnaud Marty and then of Jacques de Junac. Blanche now entrusted her with a cape or hooded cloak, a blanket, and a pillow, on the understanding that if she failed to return these would go to her god-daughter Guillemette; if, on the other hand, she did come back, then she would retrieve these possessions.

After Blanche's and her brother's departure in April 1309, their father and Raymonde were alone at Junac. Both of them got off lightly in Carcassonne, since they were not even required to wear the yellow crosses. It must have been a bleak period for them, particularly since Raymonde's brother Arnaud was taken around this time and burnt at the stake. Then, in late December that year, or very early in January 1310, old Marty sickened. He recovered, but around Epiphany he suddenly died. Raymonde was not there when it happened, but it was she who found him, presumably in his house. According to her brother Bernard she thought that he had been strangled, and her reason for thinking this was because the veins in his neck bruised immediately after he died. Bernard claimed that she said, 'he had the artery or windpipe under his chin broken and squeezed; and I believe that he was strangled by those of the castle to stop him from revealing what he knew about their past heretical activities' (FR, f.279v).

Later Bernard claimed to share Raymonde's view of what had happened. But by early 1310 the persecutions were abating, since most of the last Perfects of the Sabartès were dead, and Pierre Authié himself had been captured. The 'murder' of old Marty was conceivably Bernard's invention, because by the time he appeared before Fournier in July 1324 he hated the de Junacs, and particularly Jacques and Gauserande de Junac. They had made it clear to Bernard earlier that he was no longer wanted around Junac, since he might endanger them all by staying. That an ill wind was blowing from Pamiers with the appointment of the new Bishop was clear to the de Junacs, and they must have known that it threatened to rekindle and fan the smouldering fires of the Inquisition. Bernard was to reply to this with a thinly veiled threat to take others down with him if he were summoned. Perhaps he projected his own imagined fate at the hands of the de Junacs on to his father's death, and maybe it was this which conjured up a murder scenario in his mind. That old Marty died of unnatural causes is not impossible, nor is it unimaginable that it was 'those of the castle'. But equally his death may have been caused by a spontaneous fight between the violent blacksmith and someone just as ill-tempered; or he may have had an apoplectic fit, or he may have died of convulsions from a stroke brought on by the illness from which he was supposedly recovering.

The most cogent reason for being sceptical about old Marty's 'murder' is that Raymonde Marty was, and remained, very close to her friends at the castle throughout her years in Catalonia, and they fully reciprocated her loyalty. This we know from the clinically objective evidence of the Inquisition's double agent Arnaud Sicre. It is a measure of the depth of the bond between the de Junacs and Raymonde that, eleven years after Raymonde Marty and Esclarmonde de Junac tearfully parted from each other, with Esclarmonde weeping bitterly on that occasion, they kept to an agreed strategy for communicating and thus scored a small but symbolic victory over a traitor (see below, pages 321–3).

All the signs are that the de Junacs loyally stuck by their friends even when they were 300 miles away across the Pyrenees. It is hard to imagine that the good-natured Raymonde would have displayed such warmth towards the murderers of her father.

Now that her father was gone and Bernard prepared to hire himself out as shepherd to the Catholic Issaurats of Larcat, who apparently taunted him with his brother's death at the stake, Raymonde decided to follow her sister and other brother and go underground. She may initially have shied away from the tough journey into exile because she suffered from a heart condition. But now, like her sister, she bequeathed a few precious items to friends who stayed behind. In Esclarmonde's and her brother Gaillard's safe-keeping she left a new cape made from a striped material, an ornate outer garment, and a veil or a silk shawl, as well as a ring and, it seems, a belt and a purse (FR, ff.128v, 274r). Such was the climate of suspicion that they agreed between them that the de Junacs would only ever release these items to a stranger on the production of a small knife owned by Raymonde. This *canivet* was probably similar, if not identical, to the small Parma knives owned by, among others, Pierre Clergue, Béatrice de Planisolles and Pierre de Luzenac, and given to them by Perfects.

Others of her prized things, such as her bedding, linen, pillows, and pillow-cases, and her tablecloths she left with her neighbour in Tarascon, a woman called *La Gasc*, who was probably Rixende de l'Aire, the wife of a Tarascon notary called Bérenger Gasc. He may have been the same Gasc who worked for Guillaume Bayard and who was uncharitably described by Bernard as small, fat and red-faced.

Having thus sorted her affairs, Raymonde vanished at some point in early 1310, never to return to Languedoc. She was spotted some time afterwards in Alairac, some eight miles south-west of Carcassonne, and in late 1313 or early 1314 Bernard Marty learnt from one Pierre Gasc of Junac, a relative (presumably) of the Tarascon Gascs and a friend of Raymonde's, that he had met Raymonde and Blanche in the Roussillon at Saint-Cyprien near Elne, south-east of Perpignan and ten miles up from Collioure, the now famous resort on the Côte Vermeille. The two Marty sisters told Gasc that they were aiming to cross over into Catalonia, but pledged him to secrecy.

The route they took was identical to the one chosen by their brother Guillaume Marty, Guillaume and Bernard Bélibaste, and Philippe d'Aylarac. It is likely that the Marty women were assisted in making their passage into Catalonia by Raymond Issaurat, whose various auditions before d'Ablis (the last recorded ones were on 21 and 22 March 1309) could have left him in little doubt about what lay in store for him. Even if the Inquisitor elicited only a fraction of Raymond's activities from his interviews with him, they were enough to put him away for ever, if not worse. It is fairly clear from Raymond Issaurat's recorded movements throughout Catalonia that he had become the Cathar church's chief *passeur* in the diaspora. His brother Pierre also fetched up in Catalonia.

They cut across the Albères mountains, and then proceeded to Ampurdan, the flatlands which lie between Figueres and the Costa Brava. Modern place-names such as 'Castelló d'Empúries' on the Figueres–Roses road and 'Empúria-brava' on the coast itself recall the medieval county which was wedged between Catalonia and Mallorca. Today the area forms part of the province of Girona.

They progressed as far as Torroella de Montgrí some twenty miles south-east of Figueres. This place was a kind of interim assembly point from where the Cathar exiles fanned out into different corners of Catalonia. At some time or other the two Bélibastes, Guillaume and Arnaud Marty, and Philippe d'Aylarac all stayed here, the latter two subsequently returning to Occitania and to self-immolation.

When we next encounter Raymonde and Blanche, they will be deep in Catalonia in the house of the Servels, the family of a blacksmith from Tarascon whom the Martys probably knew as members of the same guild. The year was 1312, and against the odds Raymonde had found happiness in a most unlikely quarter.

It was on the winter pastures of Catalonia that the persecuted Cathar church enjoyed a brief Indian summer, until its light was finally extinguished on a pyre in the Corbières and in the oubliettes of the Allemans fortress, which stood three miles east of Pamiers and is now called La Tour-du-Crieu (Pl. 22).

But before we join it in its twilight in Catalonia, it is necessary to return to Montaillou, because some of the most colourful characters in Catalonia got there as a direct consequence of the cataclysm that now engulfed the village.

12. The Day the Soldiers Came:
8 September 1308

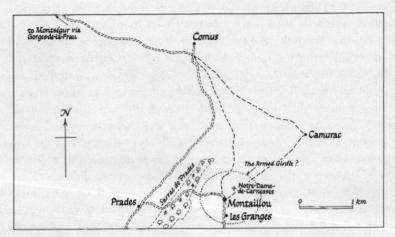

Montaillou under guard

Sunday 8 September 1308 was the feast of the Nativity of the Virgin Mary, the most important holiday of the year in the Montaillou calendar. The entire population would be expected to attend mass at the church of Sainte-Marie. It therefore afforded a perfect opportunity for a global arrest of the village.*

This time the raiding party took the village by surprise, and it can

---

* Pierre Maury stated that the Inquisition came to Montaillou 'around' (*circa*) the feast of the Nativity of the Virgin. Guillemette Arzelier, however, claimed that this happened on Assumption Day, Thursday 15 August, and unlike Pierre Maury she was in the village at the time (FR, f.242v). What may nevertheless tilt the balance in favour of 8 September is the absence of that month from the d'Ablis Register. Interviews took place from 10 May to 28 November 1308 (a session on 2 December was cancelled), *except* during September. By contrast there were six, if not seven, sessions in August 1308, including 12, 16, and 21 August, the dates surrounding Assumption Day. The blank for September may not be unconnected to the raid on Montaillou and the processing of information relating to it.

only have done so if the Clergues helped to orchestrate its arrival. The fact that no Perfects were apprehended further points in this direction. The men-at-arms from Carcassonne probably surrounded the village in the early hours of the morning, and set up posts at the points of exit of the different tracks to Ax, Prades, Gazel and Camurac. The girdle around the village must have been cast wide enough for its people and guardian animals to be caught completely off guard.

The hypothesis that the raid probably happened early in the morning may be supported by Guillemette Clergue (B)'s account of the spectacular escape of Pierre Maury's aunt Mersende 'in the morning'. *If* the people of Montaillou had been seized during the mid-morning service, this would not have been possible. Instead, the Inquisition probably ring-fenced Montaillou first, and then went from house to house gathering the inhabitants. But not everybody was caught in the first round. With a population in excess of 250 people, almost all of whom were strangers to the raiders, a watertight muster was a difficult task.

Perhaps Mersende Maury was out feeding or milking her animals when the soldiers came. We will never know. What is known, however, is that she put a loaf of bread and a sickle on her head, and calmly walked out of the village. At the checkpoint she convinced the soldiers that she was a migrant farm-labourer, who had come to help with the harvest. And so Mersende walked to freedom, leaving behind, though not for ever, her husband and one of her two children. It must have been hard for her on the road that eventually took her to Catalonia, but that morning of 8 September Mersende Maury inflicted a glorious personal defeat on the Inquisition.

She was not the only Montalionian to flee, and indeed several members of her family slipped through the net. Arnaud Belot also disappeared. After being arrested at his wife Raymonde's house, he was taken to the castle along with all the others, but then absconded without the soldiers noticing it at first. In the course of the day they reappeared at Raymonde's house to check whether Arnaud had returned there. His wife was upset to hear that he had fled, and she therefore sought out the commander of the raiders, Jacques de Polignac, who was probably staying at the Clergues', the next house up from Raymonde's. She and her son Pierre saw him, and with her own person and that of her son Raymonde stood security for her husband's turning himself in.

Later that day Arnaud turned up at the house, after hiding in a wood. By then the Inquisitors had departed.

What the case of Raymonde Belot-Lizier demonstrates is that not everybody was arrested. The orders were not, as Pierre Maury reports, to gather up everyone over fourteen, but to round up everyone over fourteen *who was suspected of heresy*. How did Carcassonne know who was who in the village, if not through a list provided by Pierre Clergue? Perhaps he and his brothers even accompanied the search parties. Thus in the Belot-Lizier house the arresting officers clearly knew that Arnaud Belot was Cathar and that his wife was not, and Raymonde's son was let off because he may have been under fourteen, or simply not Cathar like his mother; equally, Pierre Azéma was not fingered by Clergue, in spite of being an enemy, albeit perhaps so far an undeclared one.

According to Guillaume Maurs, de Polignac was assisted on this occasion by Arnaud Sicre Senior and Guillaume Peyre, who had been in protective custody at Carcassonne since 1305. He now conducted a search of his former hosts' home before declaring triumphantly, and in public, that he had discovered a secret passage between the Rives and Benet houses (FR, f.95v). He probably knew all along from his earlier visit that it was there.

In the course of this dramatic and traumatizing day, the people of Montaillou were herded together in the castle, where the Inquisitors seem to have conducted an impromptu roll-call, presumably assisted by the good offices of the Clergues. Some of the accused were apparently arraigned on the spot during these summary public hearings, which were probably very similar to the ones held at Saint-Paul-de-Fenouillet when Pierre Maury was interrogated (see below, page 273). De Polignac presided with, it seems, Sicre Senior at his side. The fact that Guillemette Benet uses *ibi* (FR, f.99r), meaning 'there at Montaillou', to describe where she had confessed to heresy, suggests that some confessions were extracted there and then, and witnessed by almost the whole village.

But time was short, and the accused were many. Most were probably issued dates on which to attend at Carcassonne, and that for the moment concluded the Inquisition's business. De Polignac seems to have departed for Ax, as was his wont, by the time Arnaud Belot turned up at his home later that day. This meant that towards 1 November he and his wife had to go all the way to Carcassonne for a preliminary hearing.

The business of coordinating the summonses was entrusted to 'those of the house of the rector of Montaillou and the rector himself' who carried out this task with some fervour (FR, f.75r). If the people of Montaillou were outraged by such duplicity, some may have reasoned that the Clergues' power-base inside the Inquisition's camp was their best bet in what was a desperate situation. No one could afford to call their bluff, since their tentacles reached deep into the prisons of Carcassonne, and nobody could know for certain whether or not de Polignac and Pierre Clergue were of one mind.

That night of 8 September the Clergues must have been quietly celebrating. They had snatched victory from the jaws of defeat. The powers of confiscation that were conferred on Bernard Clergue in his role of village *bayle* representing the Count of Foix allowed them to broaden their local economic base several times over, and they would take from friend and foe alike.

It was not long after the raid that Pierre Clergue visited his one-time lover Béatrice in her home in Varilhes. He was on his way to a synod in Pamiers, which may have been convened specially to discuss the latest developments in the Sabartès.

By the autumn of 1308 Béatrice was again widowed, and now she was seriously ill in her home. Had Clergue heard about this from a mutual acquaintance, or did he just happen to stop by because Varilhes lay on the road to Pamiers? In her room and in the presence of her eldest daughter, Béatrice, he sat on the frame of the bedstead on which she lay. Softly stroking her hand and arm, he asked her how she felt, and she replied that she was very sick. At this Clergue instructed her daughter to leave the room, saying that he needed to talk to her mother in private.

When young Béatrice was out of the room, Clergue asked his former lover how she felt in her heart. 'Weak and fearful,' she replied, because of their former conversations which she had never yet dared confess to a priest. Clergue urged her not to do so under any circumstances since God alone could and would absolve her. He assured her that she would soon be well again, and promised to call on her during his trips to Pamiers so that they could talk further about their earlier conversations.

He also filled her in about recent events at Montaillou, and boasted to her that he was using the Inquisition to keep the people of Montaillou under foot. She was shocked, and said, 'How can you now persecute the good Christians and their followers when previously you used to be so well disposed towards them?' Clergue replied that he continued to support them, but that he wanted to avenge himself on his enemies among the 'peasants' of Montaillou in whichever way he could. 'I'll make my peace with God later,' he concluded. Béatrice survived her illness and lived to love again, while Pierre Clergue proceeded to Pamiers before returning to his lair in Montaillou.

As it happens, the most tangible extant link between this medieval story and the present day dates from this period. On 2 and 3 August and 23 and 24 October 1308 Pierre de Gaillac appeared before d'Ablis, so that his first four appearances (there were a further three) straddle the raid of 8 September. He had been in custody at least since 25 July (d'AR, f.5r). A substantial part of his extant deposition, and all the material of Wednesday 23 October 1308, is in his own hand, and his is the *only* piece of autograph testimony in the Registers.★ All the others, including Pierre de Luzenac's first-person deposition in the d'Ablis Register, were taken down by clerks.

It was 690 years and six months later, and I sat at a desk in the Manuscripts section of the Richelieu in the Bibliothèque Nationale in Paris one April morning in 1999. MS 4269, better known as the Register of Geoffroy d'Ablis, was brought to me, and I was struck by its modest scale compared to the folio-sized Fournier Register. But the sheer immediacy of de Gaillac's wildly cursive long-hand renders this in some ways a more precious document. The paper that I now touched as I carefully turned the pages had once sat blank before this major player who, twelve years after writing on it, had dared to cross swords with the Clergues of Montaillou (see below, page 269). It was this identical writing that once filled the ledgers of Pierre Authié's son-in-law Arnaud Teisseyre in Lordat (Pl. 23). The same hand which had traced these scrawling lines had shaken the hands of the Authiés, of

---

★ Curiously, the following day de Gaillac read out his own deposition 'word for word and intelligibly in the common language', even though he wrote it in Latin (d'AR, f.57r). It is not clear why he should translate his own text into Occitan, since he and the Inquisitors were all fluent in Latin; indeed, Raymond Peyre witnessed de Gaillac talking to Jean de Beaune in Latin (FR, f.305v).

Pierre de Luzenac, and of many others. On the day in October 1308 when these pages of early-fourteenth-century Spanish paper were covered in ink, the three Authié Perfects, Pierre and Bernard Clergue, Béatrice de Planisolles, Guillaume Bélibaste, and Pierre Maury, were all alive. Moreover, on the same day that the statement was penned Pierre de Gaillac read it out to Geoffroy d'Ablis in person. At least de Gaillac was able to read his own handwriting, which is significantly harder to decipher than any of the other professional hands in this volume.

From the House of the Inquisition in Carcassonne on Wednesday 23 October 1308 to the Manuscripts Reading Room in the Richelieu on Monday 19 April 1999 seemed a very long trek, and I found myself musing about where de Gaillac's testimony, or any of our writings of today, might be in October 2689, when another 690 years and six months will have passed. How much would people living then know about the glorious library at the Richelieu, and how much of the world that we know, including London and Paris, would be extant? I felt oddly reassured by the thought that *comba del gazel* and the *haute montagne* above Montaillou would still look the same then as they do today. Later that evening, as I sat over a coffee in Les Deux Magots, not far from my hotel in Saint-Germain-des-Prés, I allowed myself the luxury of imagining de Gaillac on *his* night in Carcassonne after writing those pages. There would be no escaping prison after such a confession, and he was duly incarcerated. But that did not mean the end of Pierre de Gaillac, as we shall see.

Pierre Clergue's peculiar even-handedness in the aftermath of the raid is well illustrated by the summoning of Guillemette Benet early in 1309. Guillemette was at home when Arnaud Clergue, the illegitimate son of Guillaume Clergue and nephew of the rector, called on her. He had been sent by the rector to forewarn her of the arrival from Carcassonne of her summons, which was due to be served the following morning. Through his nephew Pierre Clergue advised Guillemette that if she did go to Carcassonne, she would certainly be gaoled. Could she therefore be in bed the following morning, when he would arrive with witnesses to serve the summons? She should say that she fell down a ladder and suffered multiple fractures; that way he could legitimately excuse her.

She followed his advice to the letter, and thus escaped gaol until, it seems, 1321. Clergue probably protected Guillemette to reward her for keeping his secret after her arrest earlier in May. At that time he had gone to see her in remand custody in Carcassonne and urged her not to implicate him or his family, but to own up to some of the things she had herself committed. If she did as instructed, he would do his best to free her.

In this he clearly succeeded, because Guillemette Benet was back in Montaillou by September 1308, and she had told d'Ablis nothing about the Clergues' heretical activities. At the same time that the rector was protecting Guillemette, however, his brother impounded fields or meadows belonging to her family, notably in an area known as *des molis*. Since *molis* means mills, these fields probably lay in what is still called the Coume du Moulin, an area east of Montaillou and on the way to Camurac. From now on the Benets were penurious as well as decimated, and the widowed Guillemette entered a long and sad twilight. Years later she was to tell Alazaïs Faure that she lost everything long before her eventual imprisonment near Pamiers.

It was after 8 September 1308 and *before* the death of Pons Clergue that open warfare erupted between Pierre Clergue and Guillaume Maurs. No family in Montaillou had suffered as much as the Maurs at the hands of Pierre Clergue, and three of them, Guillaume, and his brother and father who were both called Pierre, were interned at Carcassonne in the immediate aftermath of the September raid. Guillaume was the first to be released from remand custody, and although we cannot be sure of the timescale, his remand, like Guillaume Marty's, may have taken up to seven weeks.*

Guillaume was determined to free his brother and father. He enlisted the help of a couple of misfits from the Aude, a local hayward and a 'notary' (in reality a forger) from Limoux, who claimed that he could

---

* Since Guillaume was probably one of the younger sons, and since he was away for six years in the immediate period leading up to 1308, he may have struck the priest as less dangerous than his brother and father. Why his brothers Raymond and Arnaud and his two sisters were not summoned remains unclear. The fact that Guillaume's mother Mengarde is not mentioned may suggest that she was already dead, or else unable to testify because of the mutilation of her tongue.

free his father and his brother even if they were Perfects, so long as the fee was right. Guillaume paid for all three of them to go to the suburb of Carcassonne, where they stayed in a house next to the bridge, presumably to be as close as possible to the Inquisitor's palace and prisons. To raise the necessary funds, Guillaume Maurs sold thirty-six sheep, which would have grossed him around twenty pounds. He had been led to believe that such a sum would suffice to bribe the officials at Carcassonne as well as pay his two cronies. But however venal the de Polignacs' regime was, it lent a deaf ear to Guillaume Maurs's silver, almost certainly because the Clergues had briefed the de Polignacs about the Maurs. Many years later Bernard Clergue would trimphantly proclaim his enforcing powers in the prisons of Carcassonne.

Guillaume Maurs and his two hired hands now faked an Inquisitorial summons against Pierre Clergue, and they suborned two officers of the King of France to deliver it, at the same time as serving bogus summonses on two residents from Prades, Pierre Dejean and Prades Ayméric who had, allegedly, resisted an earlier summons by badly beating up the King's officers. Guillaume Maurs was naïvely hoping that, if Pierre Clergue were brought to Carcassonne, the Inquisitor would unmask him and thus break his stranglehold over Montaillou. His attempt to implicate Prades Ayméric was due to the fact that his son was married to Bernard Clergue's illegitimate daughter Mengarde, so that his appearance before the Inquisitor would further blacken the Clergue name.

When the two officers turned up in Montaillou with the fake summons, Pierre Clergue promptly had them arrested; the forgery was patently inept, since they had put the Inquisitorial seal in the wrong place on the summons.

Guillaume Maurs returned to Montaillou on the verge of bankruptcy in deepest winter, perhaps in January or February of 1309. He now learnt of the arrests of the two corrupt officials and that a warrant was out for his re-arrest. He therefore (probably) went into hiding or at least kept a very low profile at home with his brother Raymond and, perhaps, his sisters. Then, some time afterwards, he one day suddenly found himself face-to-face with Pierre Clergue and his father Pons.

This unplanned confrontation took place at *paret del colel* near the village square. Guillaume Maurs upbraided the priest for his vindictive behaviour towards his family, to which Clergue replied that he would cause all the Maurs to 'rot in gaol' in Carcassonne so that they would never cause trouble in Montaillou again. Guillaume retorted, 'I will leave this country, but first I will have my revenge on you. You had better watch out for me and my confederates. If I can, I will try and kill you. It will be either you or me.' On hearing this the rector's father Pons interjected, 'So you think that you can take on the Church and the King of France?' Guillaume Maurs replied that he did not desire to fight against either, but that he wanted revenge for the evil done to him (FR, f.152r).

On that note they parted. From now on Guillaume Maurs was on the run, knowing that after such an overt declaration of war Pierre Clergue would do everything in his power to destroy him. Guillaume, his brother Raymond, and one Jean Benet, who had also gone underground, went to Ax to Jean Benet's brother-in-law Julia, a relative almost certainly of Bernard Julia from Montaillou. Here, over bread and wine, they swore a ritual oath to kill Pierre Clergue and to support each other in everything in the carrying out of this task (FR, f.152).

For a spell of four or five weeks they stalked the rector of Montaillou, but no opportunity to kill him presented itself. At the end of this period Raymond Maurs was briefed in Ax by Guillaume Mathieu, who told him that the Clergues' sway with the Church and the Count of Foix would result in their arrests and destruction; they should make a move beyond the borders of France. Ironically it would be Guillaume Mathieu who would eventually help to arrest Guillaume Maurs after being 'turned' by Fournier.

Pierre Clergue lost no time in striking out at the Maurs by proscribing Guillaume as a heretic during mass (presumably) in Montaillou. Guillaume Maurs now left the Sabartès for Puigcerdà, but he continued to nurse his hatred of the priest until ten years later he planned another attempt on his life (see below, pages 308–9). Guillaume eventually reached the jurisdiction of the kingdom of Mallorca in the spring of 1309, and here, in the autumn, he encountered Pierre Maury, presumably as the latter was down from the summer pastures and getting ready for the transhumance south.

*

In the meantime the Clergues were experiencing their own share of life's vicissitudes. It was late in 1308 or early in 1309 that Pons Clergue, the rector's father, died. The records are silent about whether or not he was consoled, but the chances are that he was, since Guillaume Authié was still free, and may even have been sheltered by the Clergues.

Before Pons Clergue was shrouded, his face was splashed with water. Then he was laid out in the *foghana*, and a large number of people from the Pays d'Aillou came to pay their respects. Their obeisance anticipates the treatment accorded dead Mafia godfathers by their various *clientes*; even the funeral of 'Don Clergue' formed part of the rituals of power.

On the instructions of his widow Mengarde and in the presence of Pierre Clergue (Alazais Azéma later omitted this detail because she was covering for him: see below, page 365), Brune Pourcel and Alazais Azéma subsequently closed off the *foghana*, before taking hairs from the dead man's forehead and clippings from the nails of his hands and feet. This ritual was meant to ensure the continuing good fortune of the house of Pons Clergue. The hairs and nails were then given to the servant of the house, one Guillemette, while Brune was out of the room looking for string to sew the corpse into its shroud.

Mengarde Clergue did not survive her husband for long. She must, however, have felt fit enough in (probably) early 1309 to promise Alazais Rives to look after her daughter Guillemette and her many small children, when Alazais herself was summoned to Carcassonne. In the paternalistic culture of Montaillou, Mengarde's death did not attract the protection-paying masses that had flocked to pay their respects to her husband. But Pierre Clergue paid his mother a very special tribute by burying her next to the altar inside Notre-Dame-de-Carnesses. This was an act of hubris even by his standards, and it caused consternation in the village.

Alazais Azéma attended the funeral, along with Guillemette Belot, Alazais Rives, and others. As they walked back from the interment, they gossiped about the dead woman. When somebody suggested that she had produced a bad brood, the others praised her for her many kindnesses towards the Perfects. By the time Pierre Maury heard of the burial in Sainte-Marie-de-Carnesses several years later it had become a notorious local scandal, not least because Mengarde was almost certainly consoled in the teeth of the now unstoppable suppression of the Cathar church.

Through the centuries Notre-Dame-de-Carnesses has been remoulded, and the traces of this are discernible in the brickwork of this revered little church. Its height seems to have been raised, but most of its important features such as its narrow entrance door, the nave, and the apse are the same now as they were in the early fourteenth century (Pl. 24). There is no extant record to say that the priest's mother was ever exhumed as a heretic, and the odds are that she was not, because there would have been no witnesses to a consolation in the Clergue house other than the Clergues. Although Pierre Clergue's testimony, if there ever was one, has not survived, his brother's has, and it shows that Bernard Clergue was not asked about the consolation of either his mother or his father; and this in spite of the fact that his deposition comes *after* Alazais Azéma's, which first makes mention of Mengarde's funeral and therefore could be thought to throw up these questions. This suggests that at the time of writing Mengarde Clergue's remains may still be buried in the apse at Carnesses.

When in 1759 the grave of Fournier's papal predecessor in Avignon, Jean XXII (d. 1334), was opened, the diminutive eighty-five-year-old pontiff was found to be dressed in white silk with splashes of red tassels, white being the colour of Christ's innocence, red signifying his martyrdom. Four hundred and twenty-five years on he was still wearing a tiara and a ring. In her rock-hewn grave under the church in Montaillou Mengarde Clergue, a younger contemporary of Jean XXII, might be found to be similarly well preserved should she ever be disturbed. The thought that the remains of the mother of the infamous rector of Montaillou might be so close is an unsettling one to the modern visitor as he stands near the altar in Notre-Dame-de-Carnesses; and it was in this same apse, ten years before burying his mother here, that Pierre Clergue propositioned the châtelaine.

Pierre and Bernard Clergue were now the head and second-in-command of the Clergue 'family' respectively. At some point in that year 1309 Bernard Clergue went to Carcassonne to rescue his mother-in-law, who was ailing in the Inquisitor's gaol. He stood surety for her and brought her home on a mule.

The Clergues' star in Carcassonne was hardly waning, and although Bernard was implicated in heresy by several witnesses, he extricated himself by the well-rehearsed story of his deep love for Raymonde Belot. Clergue's rhetoric proved persuasive in a culture which in the preceding century had managed to foster the exquisite lyrics of troubadour love poetry while at the same time Simon de Montfort was wreaking the utmost devastation and bloodshed. But we may be sure that the Clergue monies spoke more eloquently in Bernard's defence than his weasel words.

No one can seriously doubt that Bernard Clergue's Cathar convictions were sincere, since he went all the way to Carcassonne to bring Guillemette Belot back to Montaillou to be consoled by Guillaume Authié (FR, ff.98v, 99r). He may have been almost the last Perfect to be free. When the rector from nearby Camurac, who was presumably standing in for the absent Pierre Clergue, entered the Belots' house to give the dying woman communion, she allegedly exclaimed, 'Holy Mary, Holy Mary, the devil is coming.'

In the evening of the day the matriarch died, her former servant and bearer of two of her illegitimate grandchildren, Vuissane Testanière-Marty, was coming up from *a-la-cot* of Montaillou. She had been working in the woods. At the junction of *capanal den belot*, she met, or caught up with, Guillemette, the wife of Pierre Azéma. By now Vuissane was hardly a friend of the Belots, and Guillemette Azéma had long been their enemy. But the Clergues' continuing, and indeed enhanced, hegemony in the village meant that hostilities needed to be contained where any member of their family was concerned; the fates of Mengarde Maurs and Arnaud Lizier had not been forgotten.

When Vuissane and Guillemette spotted Alazais Azéma and Guille-mette Benet whispering outside the door of Alazais's house, they at once realized that this must be about Guillemette Belot and therefore asked after her. Guillemette Benet's reply was tentative: she was weak, and she was getting better; however, she did not know if she was getting better because she was very weak.

When the two women passed the two Cathars on their way towards Pierre Azéma's house, they overheard them talking of Guillemette Belot's being put through the *endura* by Bernard Clergue. To goad them into a response, Guillemette Azéma said loudly, 'If she is so weak and close to death, how is it that we have not heard her daughters weeping for her?' It seems that Guillemette Benet walked straight into the trap when she whispered to Alazais Azéma, 'Those two are pretty silly. Why should one weep for Guillemette Belot who has had everything she needed, because her son-in-law made sure that she wanted nothing.' To this Guillemette Azéma responded by laughing out loud and saying to Vuissane that these 'bad people' had arranged for Guillemette to be consoled, hence the conference and exchange of words between the two women (FR, f.95v).

No sooner had the two women arrived at the house of Pierre Azéma than the death knell for Guillemette Belot started to toll. The body was immediately removed from the house and buried.

There was unmistakable venom between the foursome, which involved two Azéma sisters-in-law. The manifest desire on the part of Pierre Azéma's wife to give loud and public expression to the consolation of Guillemette Belot reflects perhaps the increasing frustration felt by orthodox Catholics in the village. Here they were within probably less than a year of the big raid, and the Cathars were still consoling.

13. Endgame, and a New Beginning: 1309–16

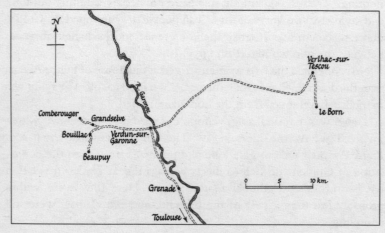

Pierre Authié's last hideout

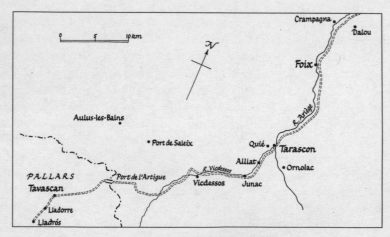

Béatrice's route into Pallars

Early in 1309 Jacques Authié was arrested, and by 3 March 1309 the prosecutor for the Count of Foix referred to his impending execution (Devic *et al.* 1872–1905, 10, cc. 484–9). Was the arrest of his nephew the reason why Guillaume Authié visited his brother Pierre in the Toulousain during the first week in Lent? Was he trying to shore up the movement in this time of supreme crisis?

Pierre Authié was then in his penultimate refuge in Verlhac-sur-Tescou, a mere twenty miles to the north-east of Toulouse, where, on Sunday 10 August 1309, Bernard Gui appealed to all the 'soldiers-in-Christ' of Languedoc to join him in capturing Pierre Authié, Pierre Sans and Sanche Mercadier, promising them 'eternal' wages *and* suitable temporal rewards.

The latter two were local men and had both been ordained by Pierre Authié. The middle-aged Pierre Sans from Verfeil had been the old Perfect's faithful runner from the days of exile in Lombardy and Toulouse at the turn of the century, and was ordained in the house of Raymond Durand of Beauvais-sur-Tescou around All Saints in 1306 (L,48,80,86). Sanche Mercadier from the nearby village of Le Born was young, good-looking and red-haired, a *juvenis pulcher ruphus* (L,102). His ordination in the house of Bertrand Salas in Verlhac-sur-Tescou was Pierre Authié's last one, and it happened only a short time before his arrest (L,80).

Some two weeks later, towards the end of August 1309, the old Perfect was arrested near the Garonne in the Toulousain. He was by now in his mid-seventies, hence the repeated references to him as *senex*. The day he was stopped he was wearing a blue coat, and he was accompanied by a woman.

His last refuge had been in a farm owned by two Burgundian brothers, Perrin and Arnaud Maurel, in the vicinity of the Cistercian abbey of Grandselve. This stood in a dip less than two miles north-east of Bouillac, where Pierre Authié's son-in-law Sartre *may* have had a house, if Latin *morabatur* is taken to mean 'he stayed there usually' (L,86). As the name of the abbey indicates, the entire area and the three localities of Bouillac, Beaupuy and their neighbour Comberouger once verged on a huge forest ('selve' = Latin *silva* = wood). Parts of the ancient wood remain, but of the medieval abbey nothing seems to be extant. Instead, this hollow in the midst of rolling acres of farmland is

occupied by a set of elegant, honey-coloured buildings whose front
porch exhibits, in a modest glass case, a reconstruction of the former
Notre-Dame de Grandselve. I drove past it several times before realizing
that this pastoral-looking farm with its poppies was in fact a long-distant
relative of the medieval abbey that I was searching for.

Pierre Authié was taken to his new hiding-place, the Maurels' farm
near Verdun-sur-Garonne, by his Verlhac hosts' twenty-year-old son
Pierre Salas.* The old Perfect hid here for some six weeks from 24 June
1309, and before leaving he gave three shillings to Arnaud Maurel for
his hospitality. At some point he sent Maurel back to Verlhac with a
mule to collect his belongings and his books; Maurel must have returned
for these before 25 July 1309, because that day the Inquisition raided
the Salas' house.

Pierre Authié was visited in his hideout by the freshly ordained Sanche
Mercadier, as well as Pierre Sans, and Sanche Mercadier's brother.
From here the old Perfect, Sanche Mercadier, and Pierre Sans were at
some point taken to Beaupuy for a few days by their hosts, probably
for a consolation; and Pierre Authié and Pierre Sans also visited the
village of Comberouger, which lies two miles north-west of Bouillac
and is today delicately restored.

To Pierre Authié during his last hours of freedom came a woman to
take him away to safety. This latter-day Antigone was either one of his
two daughters called Guillemette (the wives of Arnaud Teisseyre of
Lordat and of Guillaume Carramat of Tarascon), or she was Pierre
Maury's sister Guillemette. According to Perrin Maurel, 'a daughter of
Pierre Authié's whom I heard called "Guillemette" visited him there
and stayed there for a short time before leaving with him. The following
day Pierre Authié the heretic was arrested' (L, 102). Maurel ought to

* This latest location is put close to the hilltop hamlet of Beaupuy by both Vidal and
Duvernoy, but to do so may be to misread the text of Limborch. While it is true that
Pierre Authié's new hosts' father came from Beaupuy, and that they themselves had
'used' to live there in 1305–6, Pierre Authié's last hideout is in the text only ever
situated close to (*juxta*) Verdun-sur-Garonne by Arnaud Maurel and by Jeanne, the
wife of Perrin Maurel, and near (*prope*) Bouillac by Vidala Salas, the wife of Bertrand
Salas. In fact, Limborch clearly distinguishes between the Maurels living at Beaupuy
then (*modo*) and living now (*nunc*) near Verdun (L,123*bis*).

know, and one of Pierre Authié's daughters, Gaillarde, may even then have lived with her husband Sartre in Bouillac. But Pierre Maury states categorically that his sister Guillemette was arrested with the old Perfect, and that she was subsequently imprisoned in Toulouse before being transferred to Carcassonne (FR, f.256r). As for Guillemette Teisseyre-Authié, she was still living with her husband Arnaud at Lordat in the autumn of 1320, while no record survives about Guillemette Carramat (FR, f.159r).

It has always seemed more likely that the Guillemette with Pierre Authié was Pierre Maury's sister.★ We know that Guillemette's principal task after her march to freedom in June 1307 had been to keep house for Guillaume Bélibaste and his brother, and that they were pleased with her. If the Guillemette of Bouillac-Verdun was indeed Pierre Maury's sister, then one of her roles may have been to *pose* at times as the old Perfect's daughter, to deflect attention away from his ordained bachelor state; notwithstanding the fact that Guillemette Maury was little more than twenty years old at this time, and she may have found it hard to pass herself off as the old man's offspring. Raymonde Piquier-Marty would later similarly provide Bélibaste with a cover in Catalonia.

If Maurel is mistaken, we would have to conclude that he and his brother had not been fully received into the inner Authié circle to the point where Guillemette's true identity was revealed to them. The Perfects may well have proceeded on a strict 'need to know' basis.† Guillemette Maury probably came to the farm because the local Cathar intelligence network suspected that Pierre Authié's hiding-place was about to be discovered. Pierre de Luzenac was alleged by his contemporary Raymond Vaissière to have been involved in tracking the old Perfect to his final hiding-place, but this is not borne out by Limborch (FR, f.49v).

Pierre Authié was sentenced by Bernard Gui and Geoffroy d'Ablis

---

★ The use of *filia* in the quotation may stand in for the more inclusive *filiafamilias* (LS: *FILIA*, A), that is, a 'daughter' of the wider Authié clan, but not necessarily a physical child of the Perfect.

† But we should perhaps not entirely dismiss the Authié daughter from Lordat, not least because her husband Arnaud was close to the old Perfect and years later died an unrepentant Authié loyalist in Allemans (FR, ff.161v–162r); and in July 1312 Guillemette Teisseyre-Authié was in gaol in Carcassonne.

in the cathedral of Saint-Étienne in Toulouse, and on Thursday 9 April
1310, 'before Palm Sunday', as the Inquisition's Register points out
pedantically, he was burnt at the stake in front of Saint-Étienne (L, 93).
When he was on the point of being burnt, Pierre Authié apparently
remarked that, if he were allowed to speak and preach to the people,
he would convert all of them to his faith (FR, f.199r).

By the end of 1309 Guillaume Authié was finally arrested and, like
his brother, his nephew, and many of his friends and companions
including Arnaud Marty, Prades Tavernier, Philippe d'Aylarac, Amiel
de Perles,★ Sybille Baille and Pons Sicre, he perished in the flames of
the Inquisition. The records do not tell us where and when Guillaume
died, but it would have been at either Toulouse or Carcassonne, and
probably in 1310. Did his beloved Gaillarde share his last moments with
him, to give him strength as he faced the horror of the pyre? The
Cathar Good Men had taught that the material world and their own
flesh were the creation of the Evil God, and that they alone held the
keys to heaven. We may be sure that Guillaume Authié never doubted
that he was heading to meet the Maker of his soul, but it meant leaving
behind Gaillarde and his two children. If he and Gaillarde had jointly
plotted the contingency plans that would take their boys beyond the
reach of the Inquisition, the thought of this may have given him some
comfort when the powers of bigotry took his life. For Gaillarde the
years which followed must have been profoundly marked by the
knowledge that at least three members of her intimate circle had suffered
atrocious public deaths.

We know from the Inquisition's account books that on the pyre its
victims were forced to wear sacrifical liturgical garments. The cost of a
contemporary execution of four people was audited with eerie pedantry
by the same royal servant who, on another occasion, investigated the
de Polignacs' returns. The total expense of the materials, pyre, stakes,
pluvials, ropes, and communal grave came to 174 shillings and seven
pence ('*Summa: 8l.14s.7d.*', in *CR 1285–1314*: 8690), that is the equivalent of the value of around twenty sheep.

★ Amiel de Perles met Pierre Authié on at least one last occasion after both their
arrests. He openly acknowledged Pierre as his *Ancien*, and did him the *melhorier*. He
was sentenced on 23 October 1309 and surrendered to the secular arm for burning at
the stake (L, 37).

It seems that, mercifully, the condemned usually died of asphyxiation before the flames reached them. The spectacle was indeed a macabre one, as the fire stripped the condemned men and women of their clothes and hair before assaulting the flesh of their bodies. Although this grotesque nudity seems to have caused some concern at the time, the Inquisition remained resolutely gender-blind. At Casseneuil, the *Chanson de la Croisade Albigeoise* tells us, 'many beautiful heretical women' chose to be 'thrown into the fire' rather than convert, whereas at Minerve women ('mad female heretics') resisted as they were thrust on the pyre. The scorched corpses eventually collapsed around the stakes to which they were tied by rope (rather than chains), and after cooling down they were dumped into mass graves, 'so that the stench of that scum should not offend' the crusaders (*Chanson* 1931–61, 1.14.49).★

If these pseudo-judicial killings were intended to encourage the others, they signally failed. Few among the people believed that the Good Men were the devil's disciples, and these gruesome rituals rendered the Inquisitors' existence a more precarious one than their seemingly absolute sway might suggest. Neither people nor Church had forgotten the frenzied slaughter of Inquisitors at Avignonet.

Just as repugnant as live executions was the practice of posthumously burning the remains of the deceased. The exhumation of the dead by hand, as we saw in the case of Raymond Roche, was sometimes imposed on those who had buried them in the full knowledge that they had been consoled. The muddy piles of rotting flesh and bones were then spread on carts or hurdles, before being ceremoniously dragged through the streets of Toulouse or Carcassonne on their way to symbolic incineration on the scaffold.†

By 1310 the people of Languedoc were bereft of their spiritual guides, and the period from 8 September 1308 to 1310 was cataclysmic in Montaillou and throughout Occitania. Many Montalionians were

★ The Occitan text has '*Que no fesson pudor a nostra gent estranha/Aicelas malas res*'.
† The Inquisitors' sentence notes that the bones of the consoled are burnt after death to symbolize the ignominy of their offence: '*ut in signum perditionis ossa ipsorum si ab aliis Catholicorum ossibus possint discerni de sacris cimiteriis exhumentur & comburantur in detestationem criminis tam nephandi*' (L, 80).

shuttling between their village and Carcassonne, and many of them were interned, although not, it seems, for very long periods. Some of these journeys to Carcassonne were to attend summonses, others involved loved ones visiting their gaoled husbands, wives, mothers, and fathers, to take them money and food and, perhaps, to let them see their children. Whenever they returned from Carcassonne the visitors were anxiously debriefed by worried neighbours, for whom they might be carrying messages.

The case of Raymonde Belot-Lizier illustrates this well. During one of her two or three visits in 1310–12 to her husband Arnaud, who was in gaol at Carcassonne, she bumped into her brother-in-law, Raymond Belot, outside the prison gates. He told her to let Gauzia Clergue (B)-Longa know that she and her (dead) daughter had been denounced, but he would not say for what. He did not need to, since Raymonde knew that Gauzia's daughter had been consoled. Raymonde passed on this intelligence, which Gauzia received defiantly, saying that they should do their worst, as long as God saved her friends.

The fact that the Pays d'Aillou does not seem to have been littered with yellow crosses after the post-1308 sentences suggests that the Clergues delivered their part of the bargain as much as they could. If some of their friends and allies did not come back at all, or returned frail and dying like Guillemette Belot, it was because they were not strong enough to withstand, even for a relatively short time, the rigours of the prison regime, which were applied with varying degrees of severity as we shall see.

Pierre Maury's mother was summoned to Carcassonne in 1308 and then returned to Montaillou where she stayed 'for a long time', before she and members of her family were sentenced (FR, f.245v).

In the short term the Maurys lost everything, although their house in the square was still inhabited by Maurys several years later. This may suggest that the 'torching' of some heretical houses at Montaillou was primarily symbolic, even though Pierre Maury refers to the destruction of his parental home; perhaps the house had been made over to one of the younger Maury children in case of just such an eventuality. This was not an uncommon practice in Languedoc to safeguard the family's property against retaliatory destruction. Could this be why Pierre Maury ruefully remarked that he had forfeited his inheritance in Montaillou?

Pierre Maury's parents were gaoled in Carcassonne, and here Pierre's mother Alazais and his brother Guillaume died. Eventually, after serving only about a year or two, Pierre's father Raymond Maury was released in 1310–11. Wearing the yellow crosses, he returned to Montaillou where he seems to have died a broken man. According to Pierre Maury, his father's house had been ruined three times through heresy. Old Maury was saved from utter penury by a gift of sixty shillings from Pierre Maury, and probably more money from his other son Jean, who visited him regularly during the summers of the second decade of the fourteenth century.

Another occasional visitor to his house was Pierre Clergue, and together the old weaver and the priest may well have spoken of the not so old days. A kind of phoney peace prevailed at Montaillou now, with some of the wiser and chastened families henceforth wholly resigned to the Clergues' dual role.

Raymonde Belot-Lizier's husband Arnaud lasted less than two years in prison before dying at the age of around thirty-two some time after June 1312. His contemporary Arnaud Vital was similarly incarcerated at Carcassonne in 1310, and also died there. It is not possible to determine when this happened, but Arnaud was so deeply implicated in the Authiés' campaign that he was probably sentenced to a harsh prison regime. Raymonde Vital thus found herself widowed, and it may have been after this, or during Arnaud's stay in prison, that Pierre Clergue propositioned Raymonde, who then became his mistress before marrying one Bernard Guilhou from Vernaux.

Arnaud Vital was certainly dead by midsummer of 1312, because he is not mentioned in a set of accounts from the period which lists the prisoners of the Inquisition in Carcassonne and itemizes the cost of keeping them in custody (*CR 1314–1328*).

The document dates from Saturday 1 July 1312. We can determine its precise date because it refers to some fifteen inmates who were 'recently' (*noviter*) gaoled, while also noting that they had been incarcerated for forty days since sentence was passed on them on Monday 22 May 1312. The cost of keeping them was set at four pence per day, so that the global expenditure for each came to 160 pence or, as the entry records, 13 shillings and 4 pence. This expense was largely borne by the inmates, it seems, notwithstanding the contribution by the Crown to their upkeep. Furthermore, the preceding entry records the fact that the cost rose from three pence a day, during the first three weeks of 1312, to four pence thereafter to reflect the extra costs incurred by the shortage of bread due to the knock-on effect from the crop failures of 1310.

Among this group was one 'Philippe de Taylarac' (see similarly L, 76), who must be the Perfect of that same name from Coustaussau. If so, he remained at large longer than any of the others except Bélibaste. We know from Pierre Maury's reporting a conversation with Guillaume Bélibaste that d'Aylarac was arrested in a place called Roquefort in Fenouillèdes on a return mission into Roussillon, and that he was subsequently executed (FR, f.257r). His death therefore occurred after 1 July 1312.

The same minutes also list one *Alissendis de Martra, de Cameracho*. She may be the Algée (*sic*) de Martre who was a sister of Pierre Clergue's mother and the intended duenna of Béatrice if she eloped with her steward. At the very least Alissende was likely to be related to the Martres of Camurac, which would ally her to the Clergues of Montaillou.

In addition to these recent arrivals, the documents identify the names of a number of prisoners *De terra domini comitis Fuxi*, who had been there for at least the entire accounting period of 1 January 1312 to 1 July, and possibly longer. Although minute 15068 starts with *61 inmuratis, quorum nomina sunt a tergo*, only fifty-six are listed in the *a tergo* (i.e. 'on the back') minute 15069. The accounts moreover reveal that the figure of fifty-six, or something very near it, served as the basis for calculation, which comes out as '*163l.13s.8d*', that is just under £164. The missing five internees, including perhaps Arnaud Vital, may have died in the course of the six-month period, and the clerk may have realized this only after starting the ledger entry, if he was working from an established but out-of-date list which featured several familiar, or at least expected, names.

From Montaillou there are Arnaud Belot and his son Étienne, and Raymond Capelle and Bernard Maurs, whose wife had been arrested during the May 1308 round-up. He was the uncle of the Guillaume Maurs of the vendetta. For different reasons perhaps the Capelle and

Maurs families had attracted the attentions of the Inquisition as early as May 1308. But why were Arnaud Belot and his son lingering in prison as late as 1312? Had they fallen foul of the Clergues in some way, perhaps by daring to testify against them?*

With the exception of this quartet, the people of Montaillou who survived their spell in captivity were home again by the end of 1311. Others were less fortunate. The list includes no fewer than ten members of the extended Authié family. These were the dead Perfects' brother Raymond Authié and his wife Esclarmonde; Pierre Authié's elderly widow Alazais, and three of their children, Arnaud and his sisters Montane and Guillemette, the wife of Arnaud Teisseyre of Lordat; Blanche de Rodes (née Issaurat) and *G. de Redesio*, who was probably either her husband Guillaume de Rodes or her brother-in-law Géraud, both of them Pierre Authié's nephews, as well as one *Petrus de Rodesio*, who may be the character referred to in the Fournier Register as 'simple', and who was of the Authié–de Rodes family, perhaps a brother.

Before 26 July 1308 Blanche had been interned in Foix as (probably) a remand prisoner, but she was free by 1318, if not before, because by then she lived in the 'Bourg' of Carcassonne with her daughter and her son-in-law Pierre de Gaillac (L, 294). Her cousin Marguerite, sister of the fearless Issaurat brothers and wife of Amiel d'Ascou, was also in prison at Carcassonne.

The reference to *Galharda Bonetha* may be to Gaillarde Benet, the widow of the Perfect Guillaume Authié, although it would be unusual for her to be listed by her maiden name; her 'divorce' from Guillaume would not have been recognized by the Church. The fact that Raymond Authié and his wife as well as Gaillarde Authié and Lorda Bayard, the Carcassonne Inquisition's most high-ranking prisoner, were alive at all a decade later to face renewed pressures from Fournier supports the view that their prison regime at Carcassonne was a relatively light one, and that they had not been sentenced in perpetuity; and even perpetuity sometimes meant as little as five years.

In de Polignac's gaol the Authiés may even now have enjoyed the

---

* No heretical activity is ever attributed to Étienne Belot in the extant documents. He was eventually released with the crosses, and he was relieved of them in Pamiers by the Inquisitors Henry de Chamayou and Pierre Brun on 16 January 1329 (D 27, f.147v).

protection of Pierre Clergue, which might account for the fact that familiars of the Clergues got off comparatively lightly when contrasted with the Larnatians and Tarasconians.

In the same prison were Philippe de Larnat and three de Junac brothers, Guillaume, Pierre and Gaillard. In their absence Jacques took over the running of the castle, but Gaillard was back there by the time Arnaud Sicre passed through Junac for the first time in 1319. Others included Pierre 'Pauc' from Ax, whose wife Guillaume Authié would not console, and Bérengère Bourrel, the Cathar daughter of Pierre Maury's former employer. Like his mother-in-law, Pierre de Gaillac was also here, but his stay may have been a rather shorter one than hers.

While the rest of Montaillou was drowning, the Clergues were thriving, and the rector was having more sex than ever. By 1313 he was involved with Gaillarde, the wife of Pierre Benet of Montaillou.

That Gaillarde was his mistress was widely known in the village, and one day his cousin Fabrisse Rives gently berated him for it in front of her house, which Clergue had to pass on his way down to ring the church bells of Notre-Dame-de-Carnesses. The house she lived in now was almost certainly her former father-in-law's, because it had a separate barn just like the big Rives house. Fabrisse's teenage daughter Grazide was present during this banter. Fabrisse pointed out to the rector that Gaillarde was a married woman after all, to which Clergue replied cheerfully that one woman was as good as another, and that he believed he sinned as much with the one as with the other, because he did not sin with any of them. Before she could reply to this bit of sophistry Fabrisse's pot in the kitchen boiled over, and she rushed inside to see to it.

She may have come to rue this conversation with her cousin, because Clergue's physical needs verged on the pathological, and he now cast his eye on Fabrisse's teenage daughter. At this point the fourteen-year-old Grazide lived alone with her mother, while her father Pons may have languished in Carcassonne. One day in the high summer of 1313 she was on her own in the house when Pierre Clergue appeared. Her mother was out harvesting. He asked the young girl, who was his second cousin, for sex; indoctrinated as she was by his free-love cant, she agreed.

They went into the barn where a few years earlier Prades Tavernier used to sit reading in pools of sunshine. Here,

in the barn where the hay is kept, [Pierre Clergue] took my virginity, but he did it gently. After this he often had sex with me until the following January, and this always happened in my mother's house, with her knowledge and consent. (FR, f.56v)

In January 1314 Pierre Clergue gave Grazide Rives in marriage to Pierre Lizier. The idea of him joining these two in Christian wedlock in Notre-Dame-de-Carnesses, when all the parties concerned probably knew of the affair between bride and priest, is distinctly bizarre. Stranger still is the thought that the sexual relationship, which now became adulterous, continued, notwithstanding Grazide's claim to the contrary. Pierre Lizier had little choice but to connive with the continuing affair of his wife and the priest. He dared not put a stop to it, not least because his father had been murdered by the Clergues or their cronies. He rather feebly warned his wife against committing adultery with any man other than the priest, and Clergue had the doubtful delicacy not to possess Grazide in her house when her husband was in. Pierre Lizier died four years into the marriage in 1318, and it is not surprising that his mother Raymonde Belot-Lizier later sought to retaliate against the rector.

Grazide remained the mistress of Pierre Clergue throughout her teens until *c.*1320. As long as he and she enjoyed it, she later remarked, she saw nothing wrong with it. To Fournier's probing about her knowledge of the blood relationship between herself and the priest she replied evasively, and claimed to have been afraid of telling the truth, since the Clergues would have killed or ill-treated her. In any case, the priest fended off the charges of incest by stating that Fabrisse's mother had been his uncle's *filia*, that is she was a whore through whom anyone might have fathered Fabrisse.

But the insatiable priest needed more than one or two other men's wives, and around Easter 1315 he sent for Mengarde Buscailh from Prades. She had recently(?) been widowed and therefore, in the world according to Pierre Clergue, was footloose; there need be no complications, and he could have sex with her in her own house without having to worry about husbands.

He summoned her to Montaillou under the pretext that a senior law-officer of the Count of Foix desired to interview her in his house. When she arrived he was alone and told her that 'he had long loved me passionately (*adamaverat*) and desired to have sex with me'. She recoiled and tried to deny him, which Clergue countered with: 'How dare you cross me on this, when there isn't a single woman whom I couldn't have if I insisted as much with her as I have with you!' (FR, f.103r). She relented, because she had no choice. Clergue possessed her there and then in his house, and he did so again some time afterwards. Mostly, however, he visited her in her home in Prades at night. As she remarked ruefully, he always left after sex. Perhaps he enjoyed a brisk post-coital constitutional across the *sarrat de Prades*.

By the time Jean Maury reappeared in Montaillou in 1315 from the pastures of the Cerdagne and Catalonia, life in the village was settling into an uneasy truce. The twenty-five turbulent years since the arrival of Béatrice and Bérenger de Roquefort had seen the last generation of Occitan Perfects come and go, but the light they kindled in people's hearts was henceforth unquenchable. The price had been a heavy one for the village. By 1315 the Belots, Benets, Martys, Maurs, Maurys, and Rives were crushed, and many of the other families with very few exceptions had been affected as well. But the d'Ablis–Gui-led persecutions also drew many blanks, and it was left to the next investigator to uncover the 'real' story of Montaillou; and much though they hated him, many of the Cathars of Montaillou also applauded his bringing the Clergues to book at last.

Within nine months of Pierre Clergue's brutal pass at Mengarde Buscailh, his former lover Béatrice de Planisolles launched into a passionate love affair in Dalou. She was now about forty-two, and by her own account she had passed the menopause. Since her marriage to Othon she had lived mostly in her mansion on the south-western edge of the village square near the church of Dalou. Her two youngest daughters, the thirteen-year-old Ava and Philippa, who was about eleven, were still with her, but the other daughters had flown the nest, though not very far. Her new lover was a local priest called Barthélemy Amilhat, and he was considerably younger than her.

The rector of Dalou, Guillaume de Montaut, had repeatedly told

Barthélemy that Béatrice de Lagleize was a heretic and a whore whom anyone could have if they wanted to; which Barthélemy evidently did. This exchange suggests that Béatrice's affair with Pierre Clergue may have been widely known in the Dalou of 1315–16.

Before their involvement Barthélemy, perhaps at the behest of his rector, had once rebuked Béatrice for not attending church. From then on she did, probably because she liked the young priest and mass provided an opportunity to see him. Here are Barthélemy Amilhat's own words about how the affair started in January 1316:

During my last year in Dalou ... I conducted myself dishonestly with Béatrice, and we often had sex in her house near the church. It was she who propositioned me initially. One day when I was teaching pupils from Dalou and two of Béatrice's daughters, namely Philippa and Ava, in the church, Béatrice asked me to come and see her that evening. This I did. When I was in her house and there was nobody else there apart from her, I asked her what she wanted. Béatrice replied that she was passionately in love with me and wanted us to have sex. To this I consented, and we made love immediately in the hall of her home; and after this we had sex frequently. I did not, however, spend a night with her. Instead, she and I were always watching out for the moments when her daughters and her woman servant were out of the house during the day, and then we committed the sin of sex. (FR, f.45r)

Béatrice later claimed to have been 'bewitched' by Barthélemy. Like Shakespeare's Cleopatra she recalled wistfully that she was no longer in her salad days when she fell for the young priest: 'I loved him to distraction, and I desired to be with him, even though my periods had already stopped when I first met him' (FR, f.44v). That she was tenderly devoted to him is clear from her attempts to shield him to the last when giving evidence.

Barthélemy was from the Aragonian village of Lladrós in the rolling valley of the Cardós river in Pallars Sobirà. Lladrós lies about ten miles south-east of the Pyrenean border peaks of Estats and Montcalm, and in the Middle Ages, as today, several mountain tracks connected it with the Ariège and the Sabartès by way of Lladorre and Tavascan.

In the early fourteenth century a libertarian regime prevailed in the Pallars valley, and communes in which priests openly kept concubines were apparently widespread. Such women were 'married' to their lovers in civil ceremonies, and dowries were settled on them just as they were in proper church marriages. Vows of mutual support were exchanged, and the children of these unions were provided for by being named heirs to their parents' estates. This oddly Utopian world would seem to have been a cross between Plato's Republic and hippie culture, and for small bribes the local church turned a blind eye to its practices. Béatrice had heard about it from Barthélemy, and liked it. So they agreed to elope to Lladrós when, in the course of the first week in June 1316, rumours about their affair began to circulate in Dalou, and she feared that her brothers would harm her for her unseemly dalliance with Barthélemy.

It was probably to avoid further gossip, and perhaps to pre-empt a pursuit, that they decided to leave Dalou separately with a two-day interval between them. Carrying her clothes and thirty pounds, and accompanied by little Philippa, Béatrice set out for Vicdessos. The fact that Ava stayed behind suggests that she was left with one of her elder, married sisters, all of whom seem to have lived in the Varilhes–Dalou–Crampagna triangle south of Pamiers.

With Philippa in tow the trip from Dalou to Vicdessos would have taken her a solid two days. At Vicdessos mother and daughter waited for Barthélemy, and then together they made their way into the Pallars. The only direct route lies across the vertiginous Port de l'Artigue, which on the Catalan side is called Port de Lladorre. From Vicdessos it takes about six hours to reach the crest of l'Artigue by way of the valley of La Terre Rouge (Pl. 25), and from here Tavascan is two hours away. It would be the obvious crossing point were it not for the tantalizing cascade of massive boulders over the last half-mile up to the summit of l'Artigue. It is not easy to see how this could be negotiated by a party driving a mule, as they undoubtedly were. The Port de Saleix into the Couserans has therefore been proposed as an alternative route, the first part of a two-stage, and two-day, journey (Duvernoy 1978, 298n.1). The Saleix itself is a fairly gentle pass, but the passes from the Couserans into the Pallars are all of them situated close to l'Artigue and are equally inhospitable.

If the aspect of the lush and fertile Vall de Cardós may well have pleased the one-time châtelaine of Montaillou, it is harder to imagine what she made of Lladrós when she, her daughter, and her lover first laid eyes on it after turning a right-hand bend on the south-bound road from Lladorre. Almost 700 years on, this small, bleak village at the foot of a spur has no through road. Its grim, black-stone houses and its rocky tracks reach back into the Middle Ages. The churchyard and the path leading up to the church are overgrown and neglected, as if the village were resigned to oblivion (Pl. 26).

Of all the places that I visited in the slipstream of this medieval story, Lladrós was the most desolate, its melancholy feel set in relief by the luminous Pallars valley. Notwithstanding its derelict and archaic appearance, it was, perhaps, the least authentically medieval place that I encountered, because there can be little doubt that during the Middle Ages the valley was thriving. The area between Lladrós and the river is now a green expanse of meadows. Seven centuries ago every inch of it would have been farmed. The meagre revenues in the late twentieth century from the many discreetly hidden camp-sites in the valley can hardly compare to the buoyant economy here hundreds of years ago.

Béatrice at least had the comfort of feeling safe in her new lover's former home, and that summer he and she went through a civil ceremony of union before a notary. During it they promised to care for each other for better, for worse, and Béatrice offered her thirty pounds as dowry, while he pledged all his worldly belongings to her and Philippa, and to any children that might issue from their union; this latter must have been a formality, because Béatrice was of course past child-bearing. Their union was then sanctioned by a public 'spiritual' transaction overseen by the local priest, Pierre de Lubersu.

Barthélemy, Béatrice and Philippa lived in the same house in Lladrós for a year. It must have been odd for the little girl to witness at such close quarters this strange union of her mother and her priest-teacher. Béatrice and Barthélemy sometimes argued, and at such times he called her a malevolent old cowherdess and heretic, while also reproaching her with coming from a heretical region.

She repudiated his charges, but once in a moment of tenderness she opened up to him about her life in Montaillou. She mentioned the story of the fifteen-day *endura* of Guillemette Faure, and she told him how Stéphanie de Château-Verdun had repeatedly tried to coax her into visiting her. She recounted how in the end she consulted Pierre Clergue, her great friend and compadre, for guidance, and he told her that the Perfects were holy and righteous men who suffered persecution just as the early Christian martyrs had. In front of Fournier, Barthélemy later insisted that he had threatened Béatrice at this point with exposure, but she apparently only smiled at this and told him that much better priests than he were Cathars, meaning persumably Pierre Clergue and his ilk.

After a year in the Pallars, Béatrice and Barthélemy moved back to France, and for the next year, 1317–18, Barthélemy lived in the suburb* of Carcassonne, where he served at the church of Saint-Michel. It is not clear whether Béatrice moved there with him, or whether she and Philippa returned to Dalou, although the latter seems inherently more likely. It was one thing living openly as sexual partners in the emancipated environment of Lladrós, quite another to do so under the nose of the Inquisition in Carcassonne.

Béatrice probably returned to the Pamiers plain to see her children who lived locally, and perhaps in or near the little town of Rieux-de-Pelleport, because they refer to the rector from there as someone that all four of them, Condors, Esclarmonde, Philippa and Ava, knew well. This may explain why rather than settling in Dalou she took up residence again at Varilhes, probably in the same property where Pierre Clergue had visited her ten years earlier during her illness. It is to be doubted that up in Montaillou Clergue thought much of Béatrice this year, because he was now busy chasing Alazais Faure's niece Raymonde, whose husband Pierre Faure was impotent. In this pursuit, the middle-aged Clergue suffered his only recorded sexual defeat.

The following year, 1318–19, Barthélemy moved much closer to Varilhes by becoming priest at Sainte-Camelle, a hamlet eight miles south-east of Castelnaudary and almost equidistant from Avignonet; the small church of Sainte-Camelle is exquisitely preserved, with an interior that has changed little, if at all, since Barthélemy officiated in it. In 1319 he migrated again, this time only by a mile or so, to the nearby church of Mézerville which may have formed part of a priory. It is a strange fact that throughout this period Barthélemy committed a

---

* The Latin *burgus* means the suburb of an episcopal city.

string of petty thefts in the area, robbing (presumably) from his churches, but he was not held to account for these offences, perhaps because Fournier protected him. As for Béatrice's affair with Barthélemy, it was not over yet; not quite.

14. Jacques Fournier, Bishop of Pamiers: 1317

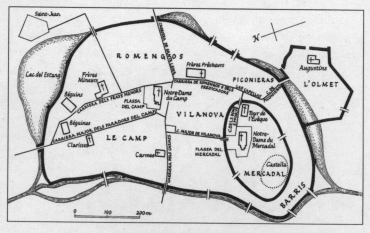

Pamiers in the fourteenth century

On Saturday 19 March 1317 the Cistercian Jacques Fournier became Bishop of Pamiers. Fournier had previously been Abbot of Fontfroide, where he had succeeded his maternal uncle Arnaud Novel in 1311. It was the murder on 14 January 1208 of a Cistercian from Fontfroide, the papal legate Pierre de Castelnau, which had caused Pope Innocent III to proclaim the first crusade of 1209. The Cistercians and the Inquisition had therefore been twinned even before the Dominicans entered the fray, and the latest Abbot of Fontfroide, and now Bishop of Pamiers, liked to think that his various callings were shaped by the hand of God; after all, this future Pope convinced everyone that he had never sought high office.

In his thirties Fournier may not have looked very different from the far from ascetic marble figure sculpted of him as Pope twenty-four years later during the last year of his life by Paolo da Siena. Although the sculpture appears to echo one of Boniface VIII by Arnolfo del Cambio, it is probably not generic, since da Siena is recorded as working on a monument for the Cardinal Matteo Orsini in Avignon in 1341 and would have known Benoît XII by sight. Moreover, the distinctive corpulence of the likeness of Fournier–Benoît XII is corroborated by other fourteenth-century testimonies.

This bust and a grateful inscription recording Benoît XII's repairs to the roof of the Basilica in Rome, which he sanctioned from his papal seat in Avignon, originally stood near the Altar of the Dead in the old Constantine Basilica, from where they were moved in due course to the new St Peter's. Today they occupy a discreet corner in one of the vaults of St Peter's not normally accessible to the public (Pl.27). In his late fifties his mandarin-like face was clean-shaven, plump, double-chinned, and coarse-featured with a thick and recessed nose, all of which made a leading writer on the sculpture call his profile '*mostruoso*' (Filippini 1908, 102). It is indeed the case that at Avignon Benoît XII was the butt of jokes because 'his natural obesity . . . stimulated caricature, and undeserved criticism' (*CE*, 431), and there is evidence in the Register that suggests that he was already corpulent when he arrived in Pamiers in 1317. A recent authority described him as 'tall, with a high colour, a deep voice, and sententious' (Amargier 1994, 206–8).

The new incumbent was a Paris-trained theologian, and his disputational skills were awesome. The hallmark of his forensic intelligence was his ability to elicit psychologically cohesive narratives from the people he interviewed during what became the Pamiers Inquisition.

Fournier has long enjoyed a reputation for zeal and integrity, not least because in July 1319 he judged the Minorite Bernard Délicieux on behalf of Pope Jean XXII and courageously refused to agree with his master (L, 273). But Fournier's incorruptibility was not primarily a matter of a monkish *contemptus mundi*. In fact, before his death as Pope Benoît XII at Avignon, he was accused of simony in a notorious contemporary pamphlet (Vingtain 1998, 91–2), a charge already levelled by Dante against three of Fournier's predecessors, including Boniface VIII (1294–1303). Money was indeed uppermost in Jacques Fournier's mind, but it was money collected primarily for the greater glory of God, His coffers and His buildings.

*

When Fournier arrived in Pamiers, the kidney-shaped bishopric on a bend in the Ariège probably counted between 5,000 and 6,000 inhabitants (Map 6). Economically it was thriving, notwithstanding years of excommunication and a fierce rivalry between the King of France and the Pope which was fought out on its territory.

Pamiers owed its affluence to its vineyards and the associated trades, from rich property-owning wine-merchants such as Bertrand de Taix to the coopers and casual labourers who serviced them. The number of taverns in Pamiers was another consequence of the city's flourishing wine trade; a tavern even perched above the church of the Mercadal towards the Castella. Such was the reputation of the vineyards of Pamiers that even the King of France drank its wines.

Apart from its wine trade the city boasted several mills, bakers, butchers, shoemakers, weavers, manufacturers of leather, and commodity shops. It was prosperous and charitable enough to sustain *two* leper colonies, the second one lying outside the city's northernmost points of Lestang, not far from the Minorites and down from the lake that used to fill the dip west of the cemetery.

Pamiers also harboured a number of Jews, who were thriving in the city until 1306, when the King of France initiated one of his periodic persecutions. In 1320 a German rabbi by the name of Baruch was engaged by Fournier in a fifty-nine-day-long theological debate in the course of which 'Baruch was roundly defeated' by the Bishop and had to convert to Christianity. In Toulouse Baruch had earlier escaped by the skin of his teeth from marauding gangs of militant Christian thugs, the infamous 'Pastoureaux', who had forcibly turned him into a Christian. By conducting his sham disputation with Baruch under the remit of the Inquisition Fournier did much the same thing, notwithstanding the pious pretence of a genuine debate. Two years earlier Fournier had similarly argued the finer points of theology with the Valdensian Raymond de la Côte, and later he was profoundly affected by watching Raymond and his wet-nurse Agnès burn at the stake for heresy, side by side.

No fewer than four religious orders had set up house in Pamiers by 1317. The most important at the time was the Dominicans, whose convent and church stood in the Romengos district in the north-eastern corner of the city. Here those who had been convicted of heresy were gathered by the Inquisition's officers before being taken for judgement in the cemetery of Saint-Jean (now Saint-Jean-Martyre). The Minorites had arrived in Pamiers at roughly the same time as the Dominicans and, towards the end of Fournier's tenure, they were joined in the district of Lestang by their sister order, the Clares or *Menoretas* (female Minorites); the contemporary street of Sainte-Claire recalls their presence here in the Middle Ages. The Carmelites settled in Pamiers six years before Fournier, in the *carriera dels Carmes*, which is still called after them today and from the west leads into the Place de la République, which ocupies the northern edge of the medieval *Vilanova* of Pamiers. Four years later the Augustinians arrived and took up residence in the suburb of Loumet (l'Olmet) south-east from Pamiers, across the Ariège.

But centuries earlier two monastic foundations had taken root to the south of Pamiers: the Mas-Saint-Antonin with its church and cloisters from where the capricious Bernard de Saisset had exercised his rule and, directly across the Ariège, the Mas-Vieux de Cailloup. Whereas by 1317 the Mas-Vieux was already reduced to little more than a hostelry with a skeletal staff, the influence wielded by the Mas-Saint-Antonin continued undiminished.

In addition to its various convents and the two monasteries, Pamiers boasted an episcopal residence or bishopric, which became Jacques Fournier's residence and the hub of the Pamiers Inquisition. This building was located inside the walls of the old city in the *carriera dels Bons Efforts* (now the rue du Collège), down east from the ancient centre of *Pamias*, which consisted of the Mercadal with its fortress of the Castella. Although the bulk of the former bishopric has long since been submerged in a Carmelite monastery, the Bishop's tower can still be glimpsed today. It was in various rooms in the bishopric and its tower that the people of the Register first appeared before Fournier.

In the fourteenth century a walnut tree grew near its entrance and an adjacent forge. Inside, a wide staircase rose to the upper floors. On the ground floor were the refectory and dormitory, as well as a great hall. This was one of at least two halls that Fournier used for interviewing a number of the accused and various witnesses. The other one was reached by a staircase, and was described as 'the upper chamber half-way up [literally in the middle of] the tower' (FR, f.307v). The Occitan words for *aula* and *camera* were used interchangeably by Raymond Peyre about the upstairs room in which he was interviewed.

In addition to these two large chambers, there was a loft at the top of the bishopric where some remand prisoners were kept, while others were sent to Allemans; in a few select cases such as that of the rector of Montaillou, they were interned under house-arrest in the Mas-Saint-Antonin. The bishopric rose close to the ramparts, and its prison-loft in the tower may have been almost flush with the rampart walk, which would help explain how, as we shall see, its inmates could be contacted fairly easily from outside.

When Boniface VIII established Pamiers as a bishopric in 1295, he contemporaneously granted the city a bull for a university. The university never materialized, but Pamiers became a hive of intellectual activity. By 1317 it seems to have been full of students of grammar, aged between sixteen and eighteen, who were taught in the various convents before going up to university in Toulouse. Since the cost of a university education at Toulouse was burdensome even for minor aristocracy like the de Luzenacs, many aspiring students were prepared to do menial tasks to fund their studies.

Someone who was well aware of their neediness was a lapsed Minorite from a noble and powerful Pamiers family, Arnaud de Verniolle, a friend incidentally of the Valdensian Raymond de la Côte. Arnaud's testimony reads like a picaresque journey through Jacques Fournier's Pamiers. It thereby affords an invaluable contemporary perspective on the fourteenth-century city from which Fournier launched his private crusade against the Cathars of the Sabartès. Above all, Arnaud's deposition was deeply damaging to the credibility of the local clergy, and this was why Fournier unscrupulously twisted the evidence until it fitted heresy. As such its contents could be dismissed as the product of the devil.

In 1323 Arnaud was about thirty-two years old and the father of two sons, one of whom was illegitimate, while the other one was old enough to have a fiancée. As a ten-year-old Arnaud had been seduced in a student dormitory by an older boy 'who already shaved', and who went on to become a priest. When Arnaud went up to Toulouse to train as a Minorite he in turn seduced a child whom he was teaching. For this paedophile offence he was jailed at the Minorites' convent in Mirepoix.

He somehow escaped, and at the age of twenty he left the order. It is an odd fact that he later moved freely through the streets of Pamiers and, indeed, in and out of the several convents of Pamiers including the Franciscans, without being challenged about leaving them. Perhaps his family's influence was locally strong enough to safeguard him.

Arnaud's inside view of the monastic life was that its acolytes were most adept at either sodomy or masturbation (FR, f.228v). He admitted that he himself could not exist for more than eight days to a fortnight without having sex with either a man or a woman. But a sexual encounter with a prostitute in Toulouse during his student days left him, temporarily, with a swollen face and the fear, unfounded, it turned out, of having contracted leprosy. It was for this reason, he claimed, that he turned to men exclusively. It was a combination of rampant sexuality and aborted calling that mapped out Arnaud's unhappy destiny.

By the time Arnaud became the gay bluebeard of Pamiers he seems to have been married, although no wife ever appears in his story. His widowed mother and a servant do, and of his two brothers only one, Guillaume, was alive. It was he who owned an island or bank in the river, called a *mediana*, while Arnaud lived next to the church of the Mercadal in a substantial house, which seems to have been the family home. Here he occupied the top floor, where he kept his study and his books. He also had the use of another house in the *Le Camp* district next to the Clares, on the way to Lestang.

After prison in Mirepoix Arnaud went to Rome, and then returned to Pamiers. From here he one day went up to the thermal waters at Ax, and on the way there popped into Notre-Dame-de-Sabart (also known as Sainte-Marie-de-Sabart) in Tarascon where, under a spurious pretext, he said mass. He carried it off successfully, but why would he want to do so? Was his former vocation still troubling him? Is that why he sought out, if he did, the Valdensian Raymond? We may never know, but the role of priest was one that Arnaud repeatedly, and plausibly, affected.

Not the least of the part's benefits, and perhaps for him the main one, was that it allowed him to hear confession. He later explained that he wanted to know whether others committed the same sins as he did.

The impersonation of a priest was already a serious offence, and it was compounded by the fact that Arnaud absolved people from sin. Because he had no consecrated power to do this he caused penitents to take communion in a state of mortal sin. His own sexual crimes of sodomy were so serious in the eyes of the Church that the sin could only be remitted by a Bishop in confession or by a priest with the Bishop's special dispensation.

Arnaud started to haunt the various churches and monasteries of Pamiers, as well as the school in front of the Carmelites, to pick up boys. He sometimes approached his victims while kneeling on the steps before the altar, as for instance the altar of Saint Barthélemy in the church of the Mercadal, or the chapel at the Dominicans' where theology was taught; and he had no qualms about discussing illicit sex after mass in the infamous Inquisitorial cemetery of Saint-Jean. Indeed, in this very place where people had been burnt in recent memory by the Church, Arnaud challenged the student Guillaume Boué on whether he thought masturbation or pederasty to be the worse offence.

Arnaud was a serial sex-offender, and no place was too sacred or too risky to prey on boys, not even a gallery 'between the dormitory and the lavatories of the Minorites in Pamiers' (FR, f.227r). If the testimony of the teenage Guillaume Rous can be believed, Arnaud may have forced himself on some of his young victims.

Arnaud met Guillaume at the Augustinians' convent in Loumet, and learnt that Guillaume's brother was not prepared to pay his fees at Toulouse. Arnaud led Guillaume into the convent's garden, and here he raised the possibility of Guillaume boarding free of charge with a canon of the church of Saint-Sernin in Toulouse. The price would be rubbing the canon's feet, procuring women for him, and compliance with his pederastic desires. This opening gambit allowed Arnaud to test the waters with the boy under the guise of helping out with accommodation. He then invited Guillaume home to show him his house and his books, the *Decretales*. Here he forced Guillaume to take off his underclothes, after which they had intercrural sex in the missionary position; Arnaud, the boy claimed, moved his penis between his thighs just as he would have done with a woman. After climaxing Arnaud invited the boy to do the same to him, and afterwards presented him with a book of ten leaves of parchment (Guillaume Rous) or, according to Arnaud, a copy of one of Ovid's books, which may have been the then popular *Ars amatoria* (Duvernoy 1978, 1068n.25).

On another occasion Arnaud committed buggery with Guillaume, who also accompanied Arnaud to his brother's island north of the city, in an area called *dels pomarols* or *al pomarol*, not far from the lepers' hospice at Lestang. The island had a cottage on it and lay next to a vineyard. Here Arnaud suggested that they undress because of the heat, and when the young man refused Arnaud chased him and allegedly raped him at knife-point.

There can be no doubt about the gist of the sexual allegations levelled against Arnaud by at least five young men; and by his own admission there were others. After such a confession it is astonishing that Arnaud denied ever masturbating, noting instead that one of his accusers, Guillaume Rous, was an accomplished master at it, presumably hoping thereby to discredit him. While one may reasonably surmise that his main judges such as the old Dominican Gaillard de Pomiès and Fournier himself had little or no experience of sodomy, there can be little doubt that they had all engaged in solipsistic sex.

According to Arnaud, Guillaume asked, 'Would you like me to demonstrate to you what one can do when one yearns to have sex with a man but has no opportunity to fulfil one's desire? I have often grabbed my member in my hand and rubbed it to sate my lust, and I can demonstrate to you how it is done' (FR, ff.231v, 232r). Guillaume Rous had apparently already had gay sex once before, and his relationship with Arnaud lasted over a period of several months.

The four students of grammar who accused Arnaud of sexual assault may have been rather more willing than they later let on. At least three of them, Guillaume Rous, Guillaume-Bernard Joc and Guillaume Pech, participated in a foursome orgy with Arnaud, in the course of which they all performed with one another for the erotic benefit of the others who looked on. That at least is what Arnaud told his cell-mate from Allemans, Brother Pierre Record. There is no real reason for doubting the veracity of this, even though Arnaud is the source of it. He was no Oscar Wilde, but he may nevertheless have supped with panthers.

When Arnaud was arrested he had recently returned from Toulouse, where he had gone with a young man with whom he had committed a homosexual act on the way. On remand Arnaud had rather sanguinely told Pierre Record that there were in excess of 3,000 gay men in Pamiers, and since this was more than Fournier would be able to handle, he would probably get off lightly (FR, f.229v). But on 9 August 1324 Arnaud was sentenced with exemplary harshness *as a heretic*; he would remain manacled in prison in perpetuity with only water and bread, and he was 'never to be extracted from there and freed'. Unlike his famous contemporary Dante, who never ceased revering his gay teacher Brunetto Latini (*Divina Commedia*, *Inferno* Canto XV), Fournier was not prepared to be indulgent of homosexual behaviour. Admittedly Arnaud's sexual misdemeanours were heinous and, since they included rape and paedophilia, would have attracted the severest penalties from the secular arm. But by charging Arnaud with heresy, which was the ballistic option for annihilating the opposition, Fournier brought him directly under the jurisdiction of the Church. This may have been to pre-empt any kind of mitigating intercession from Arnaud's wealthy and influential relatives. Fournier's adeptness at collapsing the spiritual and the secular spheres, as in this case of a former Minorite, would become the hallmark of his persecutions. It to some extent undermines the credibility of this churchman who has enjoyed a better press at the hands of posterity than he probably deserves.

Fournier's motives for relaunching the Inquisition in his own patch of Languedoc were substantially pragmatic. In the first instance it was his desire for raising new taxes that triggered the revolt among his truculent flock, who had won a similar round against his predecessor. The particular taxes that Fournier tried to exact related to *carnalagia*, that is livestock, and he intended to levy an eighth of all produce, consisting of a tithe (*decimalis*) of wheat crops and the firstlings (*primitiae*) of livestock.

Fournier needed the money to finance his ambitions for, among other things, an Inquisitorial Prison, perhaps because in Pamiers it was particularly important for the Church to be seen to be on an equal footing with the power of the state. Pamiers was expanding at the expense of Toulouse, and on his appointment to the see of Pamiers Fournier immediately negotiated a 15 per cent increase of revenues for his diocese from Jean XXII. To achieve it, he resorted to the excommunication of those who resisted his taxes.

But the people of Pamiers had spent the nine years from 1295 to 1304 under sentence of excommunication, and had stubbornly remained unimpressed, even when during this same period the original 'lesser' excommunication was upgraded to the 'greater' one. This banned them not only from all church sacraments, but all contracts and wills entered into by them became null and void by ecclesiastical decree, and they were not entitled to a Christian burial. The greater excommunication would normally be followed within a year by a charge of heresy, and the accused would then automatically face the Inquisition. It was this ultimate sanction that Fournier, unlike his predecessors, now chose to exercise.

That the people were perfectly aware of the Bishop's abuse of ecclesiastical authority is powerfully illustrated by the statements of two witnesses, who speak for all the poor and oppressed of fourteenth-century Languedoc.

Raymond de Laburat from Quié was a friend of the Clergues of Montaillou, an excommunicate, and the father of a priest. One Sunday morning the congregation was filing out from Notre-Dame-de-Sabart, which as an excommunicate he was prohibited from entering, when he started to upbraid them. The people, he railed, built and equipped the churches by their efforts and taxes only to see themselves excluded from them by the prelates. They were not, he protested, allowed to enjoy the fruits of their own labour. It would therefore be much better to pull down all the churches and say mass in an open field, because that way the priests could not hide the body of Christ from the people.

Raymond expressed a fervent desire to settle his differences with Fournier man-to-man on a lonely mountain top, scoffing, 'Then I would discover what he has in his big gut,' in other words, uncover the mettle of a coward. Raymond's use of the word *pansa* (*OED* relates Catalan *panxa* and Old French *panse* to English 'paunch') carries the additional implication of corpulence, so that Fournier is here called a fat coward whose authority was neither spiritual nor truly manly.

The Church described Raymond's harangue as 'vomit', but there is some retrospective satisfaction to be gleaned from the fact that Fournier had to listen to his bad faith being thus publicly exposed.

★

Raymond de Laburat's sentiments were echoed by many, including Bernard Clergue. But the anti-clerical case was put most forcefully by one of Clergue's enemies, Pierre den Hugol, who was also from Quié.*

One morning during the first year that Fournier had excommunicated the tax-refuseniks of the Sabartès, Pierre den Hugol was walking to hear mass at Notre-Dame-de-Sabart. Half-way between Quié and the mountain of Sabart he gave vent to his frustration at the Church's new taxes and enforcement strategies and excoriated them thus:

Since the Sabartès has come under the sway of the Church, I have not been able to make a profit, because the clerics in their hunger for power invented excommunication. God never Himself excommunicated anyone, neither did He order excommunication to be carried out, nor did He institute it. But the priests invented it to lord it over the people and thereby committed a great wickedness in excommunicating anyone. And why should we worry if we are excommunicated, since the people of Pamiers were so for seven [*sic*] years? This excommunication is not going to pierce our stomachs, and if we die thus excommunicated we will be saved just as surely as if we were not, and God will be merciful towards us. And what is the worth of that excommunication, since we are excommunicated for not paying tithes; since we never used to pay those, this excommunication is worthless. I wish that there were no clerics, neither on this side of the sea nor overseas, because if the priests did not exist we would be fine, because they cause us nothing but grief on a daily basis. There is no worse devil in the world than the Bishop: he has killed off our entire region on the pretexts of either heresy or witch-hunting, and because of the tithes he is constantly demanding and searching for, and for all the [other] bad things he is daily investigating. If by ill luck he should live long, he will destroy all the people of this region; then he can proceed against the rocks. It would be better for us to fall under the sway of bears and wolves than to be in the power of that devil; we could flee from wolf and bear, but him we can't escape at all. (FR, f.308v).

---

* Why he hated Bernard Clergue is not clear, though it may have been connected to his friendship with Guillaume Mathieu of Ax, whom Clergue later counted among his three mortal enemies.

17. Women carding, spinning, and weaving (from an illuminated fourteenth-century manuscript).

18. A judicial mutilation, in the thirteenth-century *Customary of Toulouse*.

19. Prades and the church of Saint-Pierre from *matte majou*.

20. *Superius del angle*, the Marmare, and the Coulobre.

21. *Comba del gazel*, through which a path led to the safety of the mountains.

22. The site of Allemans, now the square of La Tour-du-Crieu, with the church of Saint-Paul.

23. Pierre de Gaillac's long-hand deposition of 23 October 1308, in which he lists Cathars from Larnat, Montaillou (*de Alione*), and elsewhere, including Raymond Azéma and 'someone called Belot'.

24. Notre-Dame-de-Carnesses in Montaillou.

25. The valley of La Terre Rouge.

26. The church at Lladrós.

27. Paolo da Siena's bust of Jacques Fournier as Benoît XII.

28. The Perfects' fording point at Tournefort.

29. The grotesque (satyr?) drawing at the beginning of Jean Maury's testimony before Jacques Fournier. The framed writing spells 'Sperte', which abbreviates 'Esperte', the name of Jean Maury's mother-in-law.

30. The start of Pierre Maury's deposition before the Inquisition of Aragón.

31. Morella from the Sant Mateu road.

32. The Templars' fortress at Peñíscola, which was new when Pierre Maury sailed from here for Mallorca.

As this Brecht of the Sabartès demonstrates, the ordinary people of the Ariège readily appreciated the economic *Realpolitik* behind Fournier's persecutions, and they were accordingly irreverent about other rituals of a Church that exacted money in the name of the soul. Its practice, for example, of inserting a blessed candle into the mouth of a dying person elicited from Pierre Sabatier of Varilhes the comment that the candle would be just as usefully shoved up someone's anus. He similarly opined that the priests' chants and prayers during mass were merely a smoke-screen for extracting money from their parishioners; in this respect his view was remarkably similar to Pierre Clergue's.

Not only were Fournier's motives fairly transparent, but his mendacious example showed others the way, so that a number of ingratiating and plainly false· testimonies survive in the Register of the Pamiers Inquisition. One case which above all others illustrates the malign ripple effect of Fournier's policy concerned the deadly rivalry between Pierre de Gaillac and another lawyer. The issue was again money. Ironically, in this case Fournier tried his utmost to see justice done, and for once he was not too late. Almost like a Greek tragedy this particular story has a concluding chorus with which I propose to begin.

Within a stone's throw to the east of the Bishop's residence and virtually opposite the gates of the Mercadal there ran a street which survives almost intact today by the same name, the rue des Piconnières. In the early fourteenth century it led to the Piconieras bridge, beyond which lay the suburb of Loumet with its new Augustinian convent, hospital, tavern and lepers' hospice. A mile or so south-east from the bridge, wedged between what is now the Route de Foix and the rue Bernard Saisset, rose the Mas-Saint-Antonin.

Towards the bridge end of the Piconnières stood a tavern with stone benches for its customers. On Friday 10 August 1324, some time after 6 p.m., three men sat here, side by side, drinking wine. They were Pierre Peyre (on the Mercadal side), Pierre den Hugol (in the middle) and Jacques Tartier (on the bridge side); these last two must have made their peace since Tartier's attempt, in prison five years earlier, to report den Hugol.★

★ In 1318–19 Jacques Tartier, who served a long sentence in Carcassonne alongside the Peyre brothers Pierre and Raymond, had openly accused Pierre den Hugol and

They were discussing Bernard Clergue of Montaillou, who the day before had been found guilty of being an impenitent and relapsed heretic who should be surrendered to the secular arm to be burnt (D 28, f.48r). But Bernard Clergue's luck and influence held again when three days later he was leniently sentenced in the church of Notre-Dame-du-Camp, whereas the men who had prematurely gloated over his fate that summer evening in Pamiers were reported to the Bishop by the start of the following week which happened to be the feast of the Assumption.

Since their release from prison several years earlier, these three had stained their hands in the framing of a lawyer called Guillaume Tron, at the instigation of Pierre de Gaillac, who had himself died six months earlier. When Fournier started to inflict a vicious regime of cyclical betrayal on the Sabartès, Pierre de Gaillac saw his chance at last to destroy a hated rival. Rather than lying low after a spell in prison for past heresies, he decided to dice with the devil. The result was a murky, fourteenth-century version of the Dreyfus affair.

De Gaillac had once before, when he took on the powerful Simon Barre, exploited the opportunities afforded to mavericks by the lethal civil war between God's disciples. In 1308, on the eve of the collapse of the Cathars in the Sabartès, Pierre de Gaillac Senior found himself under sentence of death from Barre for a debt of twenty-two pounds, roughly the equivalent of a herd of forty-four sheep. How the debt arose is not known, but it is possible that the prosperous de Gaillacs' estate had become forfeit through heresy.

It was the younger Pierre de Gaillac who succeeded where others had failed. He secured a six-month reprieve for his father by bearding Barre on the main square of Tarascon. According to de Gaillac, Simon Barre agreed to postpone the execution since Pierre was a good Cathar. Barre allegedly relented with the words:

Certainly, for the love of God, and because I know and feel that you are of the good faith, that is the faith that Guillaume Authié preaches; I therefore will let you and your father go, for the moment, and will agree that the

---

Raymond de Laburat of heresy to de Polignac's face. The latter promptly informed Pierre Clergue, who alerted his friend Raymond de Laburat.

execution should not to take place just now. I will wait for your father a certain amount of time. (FR, f.56r)

It seems fairly clear that de Gaillac had blackmailed Barre with the threat of exposure, notwithstanding his own deep immersion in heresy and his multiple family links with the Authiés of Ax.

Both de Gaillac Junior and Barre ended up in prison in Carcassonne, but de Gaillac's Pyrrhic victory over Barre may have boosted his confidence when it came to tackling his next enemy, the lawyer Guillaume Tron. His first attempt at smearing Tron happened as early as Wednesday 21 May 1309. He claimed that on the way back to Tarascon from the assizes at Alet-les-Bains in the Aude earlier that year Tron had accused him of bad faith for confessing so quickly to heresy. Tron then, allegedly, claimed that as a student at Toulouse in about 1305 he had shared a room with another student of the natural sciences. This young man had repeatedly told him that he and nearly all the students of the natural sciences at Toulouse and Paris held the view that it was impossible, and even against nature, that bread and sacred words could transubstantiate into the body of Christ. De Gaillac's punchline was his last clause, 'and Guillaume Tron himself was nearly in agreement with this line of arguing'. If this attempt failed to destroy its intended victim, it was because no witnesses could be found to corroborate the charge of free-thinking levelled against Tron. There could not be any, since de Gaillac had made it up.

Nine years later, in the spring of 1318 and before a different Inquisitor, Jean de Beaune of Carcassonne, Pierre de Gaillac decided once more to play the heresy card against Guillaume Tron. By then he was out of prison and lived with his wife and mother-in-law in the rue des Faures in the suburb of Carcassonne. He had moved to Carcassonne from Tarascon for two reasons: first because of his inability to compete with Tron in the Sabartesian courts, and second because he desired to be close to the hub of the Inquisition, the winning side after 1308.

It was here that he confided in Raymond Peyre of Quié his intense hatred of Guillaume Tron and his wish to frame him, having already, it seems, similarly primed Peyre's brother Pierre. Peyre, a near neighbour and past fellow heretic, worked in the offices of the Carcassonne lawyer Frisco Ricomanni, and frequently visited de Gaillac in his first-floor apartment where he worked as a clerk.* This time, over the six-year period that the affair dragged on, from 1318 to 1324, de Gaillac co-opted several witnesses, including a fellow lawyer by the name of Guillaume Gautier.

Tron, de Gaillac argued, had treated all of them badly, and kept on referring to them as *iretialha*, that is 'heretical rubbish'. The Church forbade the taunting of convicted and penitent heretics, but Tron apparently flouted this injunction, and whenever they met in court he allegedly heaped abuse on de Gaillac. If Tron could be destroyed, de Gaillac advocated, then he in partnership with Gautier would plead all future cases in the Sabartès and thus they would earn large amounts of money.

What better revenge than to hoist Tron with his own Inquisitorial petard, by swearing in concert that Tron had met Guillaume Authié during a Cathar consolation at the house of Guillaume Delaire, a notorious former Cathar from Quié? If the Peyre brothers cooperated, de Gaillac undertook to plead all future cases for them free of charge, and to do the same for anyone they chose to name.

The case against Tron was put by de Gaillac to the Inquisitor Jean de Beaune, and Tron was duly summoned and arrested. He must have appealed to Fournier, because within a month Fournier and Gaillard de Pomiès had travelled to Carcassonne to satisfy themselves of his guilt. This probably happened early in 1319, because Gaillard de Pomiès did not team up with Fournier until 10 December 1318 (see below, page 306–7). The fact that Jacques de Polignac seemed to be convinced of Tron's guilt weighed with the men from Pamiers, and Guillaume Tron was gaoled. He may have spent some two years in de Polignac's prison at Carcassonne.

---

* Frisco Ricomanni was then the most famous lawyer of Languedoc, and as *patronus causarum regis*, that is royal advocate, he was paid a salary of ninety pounds in the 1302–3 tax year (Strayer 1970, 123–4,126), which is exactly what Carcassonne paid for the construction of the 'Chapelle Saint-Louis'. In 1320 he acquired forfeited property from a 'heretic' worth no less than 846 pounds, which he repaid to the Crown in instalments, starting with 100 pounds in 1320, 150 in 1321, and '80l.6s.7d' in 1322 (*CR 1285–1314*: 8462). His career affords clear proof of the scale of monies involved in the law in fourteenth-century Languedoc. Not only did de Gaillac live near him in Carcassonne and was trying to corrupt a clerk from his office, but three

This was not the end of it, even though in the short term de Gaillac achieved his ambition to dislodge his rival. The fact that around 1318– 19 de Gaillac and de Polignac rubbed along comfortably suggests that at this stage at least the Clergues and de Gaillac were not yet at odds. But de Gaillac may have overplayed his hand in trying to help the Inquisition, *if* he did, when its quarry became the rector of Montaillou.

In Ax, on Wednesday 23 September 1320, de Gaillac met Raymond Vaissière, who hailed him with, 'Come back, you of the law,' punning on de Gaillac's profession, while also meaning, as de Gaillac obligingly points out, 'you who are of *our* law [my emphasis]', that is, a fellow Cathar. They were clearly friendly, and Vaissière probably wanted to enlist de Gaillac's help against another Barre, Jean Barre, who was accusing Vaissière before Fournier of proselytizing for the faith of the Authiés.

Three weeks later, on Monday 13 October, Raymond Vaissière was being led to Pamiers as a prisoner of the Inquisition. At Tarascon he saw de Gaillac in his house and asked him for advice. De Gaillac claimed to have urged him to tell the entire truth. In response to this Vaissière blew in his hand in imitation of the fanning of flames, to show that if he did he would be burnt as a recidivist. He departed from de Gaillac without saying anything further. But thirteen days later Vaissière severely implicated Pierre Clergue, who was already in custody then, by reporting that Guillaume Authié had singled out the rector as a good friend.

It is possible that de Gaillac advised Vaissière that the time was right to reveal the truth about the Clergues. But if he did try to double-cross the rural seigneurs of Montaillou, his spoon was woefully short. In Lent 1321 Guillaume Tron was released from Carcassonne, probably because the Clergues desired it so now that they had identified Tron's detractor de Gaillac as one of their principal enemies.* Then, in July of 1321, de

---

of his earlier depositions, those of 23 and 24 October 1308 and of 18 April 1309, had been witnessed by Ricomanni (d'AR, f.58v).

* Pierre de Gaillac was undaunted and announced to his fellow conspirators that he shortly planned to visit Montaillou, and on the way there he proposed to pass through Ax to find more witnesses to testify against Tron. Bernard Clergue was by now sinking into paranoia as he was desperately trying to conceal his family's heretical past. But he probably guessed rightly that the removal of the crosses from Pierre de Gaillac's

Gaillac himself was arrested by the Carcassonne Inquisition, although he was released within six months. Pierre de Gaillac seems to have died on Tuesday 21 or Wednesday 22 February 1324 (FR, f.300v). The three Cathar carousers in the Piconnières probably held Bernard Clergue responsible, and this may be why they detested him so heartily and wanted him to pay for his many crimes. Eventually Guillaume Tron was reinstated and, indeed, went on thriving as a successful lawyer in the Sabartès.

If Jacques Fournier initially turned the Ariège into a Dantean hell for fiscal reasons, the Cathars in Catalonia unwittingly helped to transform his meretricious persecutions into a true crusade against heretics. We have seen already how several players from the story crossed the Pyrenees to safety. Among the last ones to do so was Pierre Maury.

---

wife at the 'Graces' of 8 March 1321 was evidence of complicity between Fournier and de Gaillac. In Bernard's mind, the release from the crosses was de Gaillac's reward from Fournier for getting Béatrice de Planisolles to incriminate Pierre Clergue. He was wrong about the specific connection to Béatrice, but repayment it very likely was; and so probably was the removal of the crosses on 4–5 July 1322 from Vaissière's wife Guillemette (L, 291–2).

15. From the Fenouillèdes into Catalonia: 1307–14

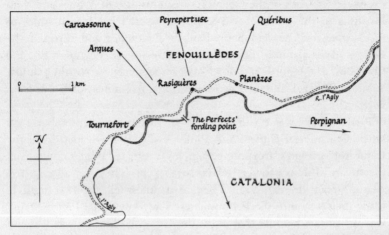

The ford on the Agly

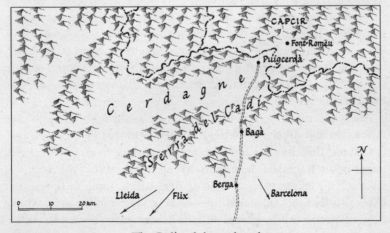

The Cadí and the road south

After Pierre Maury was dismissed by Barthélemy Bourrel at the end of June 1307, he hired himself out first to Pierre André, and then to Guillaume André, from Planèzes, a hamlet on the river Agly in deepest Fenouillèdes, situated half-way between Ax and Perpignan. Pierre Maury knew this hot region of valleys, scrubland, and rocky excrescences south of the Corbières from his days in Arques and from his visits to the Bélibastes in Cubières, which lies fifteen miles to the north-west, beyond Saint-Paul-de-Fenouillet and through the Gorges de Galamus. The ruined fortresses of Peyrepertuse and Quéribus, to the north and north-east respectively, lie within a similar radius of Planèzes, and Carcassonne is thirty-five miles north-east from here.

Pierre Maury was on the pastures of Planèzes in September 1307 when Guillaume Bélibaste and Philippe d'Aylarac escaped from the Inquisitor's gaol in Carcassonne, which was situated not far down from the square Bishop's tower (Poux 1931, 157). They hid all day in a nearby stream (L, 273, 297). Then, as darkness fell, the two fugitives made their way into the Fenouillèdes. They knew that Pierre Maury was at Planèzes because that night they searched him out, and he put them up. He fed and sheltered them, and it must have been Pierre Maury with his intimate knowledge of the region's geomorphology who showed them where best to cross the Agly. They forded the river 'between Rasiguères and Tournefort', which is about a mile west of Planèzes. Even today this marks a curve where the Agly narrows to a thin strip. Here, at about the midway point between Rasiguères and Tournefort, the Agly is crossed over a rough amalgam of boulders, while the flow of water is partly channelled through a central culvert (Pl. 28). This is almost certainly the ancient fording-point where the two Perfects crossed.

After crossing the Agly the two men pushed on through the Roussillon and Albères until they reached Torroella de Montgrí. But Guillaume Bélibaste did not stay put here, since in c.1310–11 he is found in the Berguedà, an area stretching from south of the Serra del Cadí and the hamlet of Guardiola de Berguedà to south of Berga. It is likely that Bélibaste inhabited the northern region of the area, which allowed him to visit Puigcerdà and the other regions bordering on the

County of Foix. It must have been here that he made contact with his brother Bernard.*

That a Perfect had stayed with Pierre Maury was known, or rumoured, within two days of the Agly fording, and Pierre was, it seems, briefly interned in Castelnou (in the Fenouillèdes near Thuir) at some point during the investigation into the Perfects' escape.† Eventually towards Easter (14 April) of 1308, Pierre appeared in the main square of the plains city of Saint-Paul-de-Fenouillet before his erstwhile fellow guest at the Bélibastes', Pierre Girard, the prosecutor of the Archbishop of Narbonne. He was charged with assisting Guillaume Bélibaste and Philippe d'Aylarac after their escape. But Pierre Maury repudiated the charge and insisted that he was without a flock at the time and had been in the vineyards of Guillaume André with the latter's sons and others. This was confirmed by a large number of people who were present, as well as by Othon de Corbolh, the lord of Saint-Paul who sat next to the prosecutor (on a dais presumably), and Arnaud de n'Ayglina, the town's *bayle*. They all bore false witness, but Girard could not overrule their solidarity, even if he had wanted to; and this former frequenter of a Perfect's family probably did not. Pierre Maury's popularity followed him, it seems, wherever he went.

Pierre was assigned another date to appear before Girard when he was duly absolved of complicity with the heretics. However, Girard ominously warned that the Sabartès and the Montaillou area were infested with heretics, 'but this year we're going to get them all and drag them out of there,' he threatened. Is it possible that Girard was trying to signal to one of the Perfects' chief *passeurs* that a purge was imminent? By May 1308 the machinery of persecution was in full swing, and the early raid on Montaillou meant that the village was clearly in the sight of the Inquisitors. Perhaps Pierre Maury ought to have relayed this back to base.

* Bernard Bélibaste had either fled Carcassonne gaol or he had been released (the Latin '*exiverat*' is ambiguous). He was accompanied by Pierre Issaurat at the time.
† Although during Inquisitorial hearings in 1307 and again in 1324 Pierre Maury consistently denied seeing the Perfect(s), there can be no doubt that Guillaume Maurs was telling the truth when he related that Pierre Maury had in fact confided in him about a visit by Guillaume Bélibaste.

Instead, in the early summer of 1308, he was accompanying a freight of salt from Planèzes destined for Bernard Tourte of Ax when, near the Bassin des Ladres, he ran into his brother Guillaume Maury and Guillaume Belot of Montaillou. They had dinner at Tourte's, and then they walked up to the *Vieille Ville*, where today the road rises past the church of Saint-Vincent. Here, it seems, they sat down, some distance away from the track to Prades and Montaillou, and Pierre Maury asked the two of them whether there were now many Cathars in his home town. They then offered a detailed census of a number of people from Montaillou who were of that faith.

Or so Pierre Maury claimed before Fournier in June 1324. While it is not impossible that some version of this conversation took place, it is hard to see the point of it. In 1308 all three of them were well aware of who the main Cathar families were, since they themselves belonged to two militant houses. And although Pierre Maury had spent the better part of the years from 1300 to 1308 away from the Pays de Sault, he had worked closely with a number of Perfects and undoubtedly knew the main Cathars in his home village, and indeed well beyond it.

The fact that the first name featured in Pierre Maury's testimony is that of Jean Guilabert makes one immediately suspect that old Guilabert, who was alive in 1321 when his daughter and wife lingered at Allemans, may no longer have been so in 1324. The list does not implicate Jean Pélissier, a belatedly eager Cathar who several years *after* the crackdown offered money to Pierre Maury's brother to pass on to the Catalonian Perfects. According to Pierre's 'memory' of events, there was no reference made by Guillaume Belot to the consolation of young Guilabert, even though he was present at it, and it would probably have happened only a month or so prior to this alleged conversation. Most striking of all, the Clergues are left out of Pierre Maury's account of the exchange entirely, in spite of the fact that by the summer of 1308 the Belot and Clergue houses were linked by marriage; and Pierre Maury elsewhere boasts of having first-hand knowledge of Pierre Clergue's Cathar sympathies. Moreover, by the time Pierre Maury testified, the power of the Clergues was broken, which he *knew*, and Bernard Clergue was dying.

Both Pierre Maury's interlocutors were dead by 1324, and therefore could not be cited to contradict him. Why would Pierre Maury provide such a list? Perhaps he was keen to give the impression of eagerly cooperating with Fournier, while at the same time not quite being able to bring himself to betray anyone directly?

Pierre Maury's roll-call has occasionally been cited in the literature as an insider's inventory of the village's heretics, but it adds nothing to our knowledge, or Fournier's, about Cathar contamination in Montaillou. It is, however, as we have already seen, invaluable for its topographical information. Although most of the layout of the village can be determined independently of Pierre Maury's survey, his account illuminates, corroborates, and consolidates various hypotheses; and is in turn borne out by them.

While Belot and his brother Guillaume returned to Montaillou, Pierre made his way back to Planèzes. In September 1308 he was up on the Quériu pass above Mérens when Bernard Tourte, who was delivering flour for the shepherds, brought him news of the raid on Montaillou. Pierre Maury's stoical reply, 'If they are taken now, they won't be for taking in the future,' angered Tourte, who pointedly asked, 'Aren't you afraid that all the guilty ones of the County of Foix will be caught now that they've started [the arrests]?' How Pierre Maury replied is not recorded.

Pierre stayed with Guillaume André until Easter 1309 (30 March) and then hired himself out to Pierre André en Constans of Rasiguères. He spent that summer in a pass above Mérens called *de la lose*, which *may* represent a mishearing of the Occitan version of '[Tute] de l'Ours', which is two miles above Mérens and three miles north of the Pédourrés and the Étang de Pédourrés, both of which were frequented by shepherds. Indeed, Pierre Maury was near this very pond with his flock one day when Raymond Clergue and Jacques Alsen, the lieutenant of the châtelain of Montaillou, suddenly turned up. They claimed to be looking for him and Jean Benet of Montaillou to arrest them as fugitives from the Inquisition. But they did not detain Pierre Maury. Instead they accepted provisions of food from him before carrying on with their search. In truth, they were not interested in Pierre Maury at all, but solely in Jean Benet, who with Guillaume Maurs had sworn to kill Pierre Clergue. The Clergues' counter-offensive, a part of their continuing vendetta against the Maurs, was well under way.

★

Pierre Maury remained in the passes above Mérens until *c*.29 September
1309 (St Michael's), when preparations for the winter transhumance
traditionally started. After leaving Pierre Constans he joined Raymond
Borser of Puigcerdà. Borser was either a major livestock-breeder in
Puigcerdà, or he was a steward acting for the Lady Brunissende of
Cervello. In any case, Pierre Maury, Guillaume Maurs, Jean Maury,
and young Guillaume Baille all worked for him and Brunissende at
some point or other during their Catalonian adventure.

In Puigcerdà, in September 1309, Pierre Maury met Guillaume
Maurs who was employed here from the end of September 1309 until
the end of June 1310. Maurs was relatively safe in Puigcerdà, since the
town lay outside the jurisdiction of the French Crown, but he can
hardly have been indifferent to reports of Pierre Maury's encounter
with the Clergues' posse up in the mountains.

Within a few months of arriving in Puigcerdà Pierre Maury was
joined by his baby brother Arnaud Maury and his other brother Jean
Maury, who was himself not much more than thirteen or fourteen
years old when the Maury parents were gaoled at Carcassonne. Bernard
Tourte's reply to Pierre Maury's jaunty remark on the Quériu was
coming true sooner than he could have anticipated. The Clergues'
willingness to turn over his own parents to the Inquisition, thereby
leaving his youngest brother effectively orphaned, must have come as
a shock.★ The fact that at Puigcerdà Arnaud was 'constantly' in the
company of his elder brother Pierre suggests that Pierre Maury took
his fostering task seriously (FR, f.153r).

In the meantime, and for the next two years, Jean Maury worked as
a shepherd for Jacques de Capcir in the Têt valley town of Villefranche-
de-Conflent, whose medieval houses, twelfth-century church and
Renaissance fortifications today attract a constant stream of tourists.
Also there at that time was a certain Arnaud Authié, who professed to
be a Cathar and with whom Jean Maury guarded sheep on *pass de canals*.

★ After collecting Arnaud in Montaillou Jean Maury had taken him to Quérigut in
Donézan, some twenty-five miles from Montaillou, where on the first day they were
put up by their uncle Guillaume Estèbe. Estèbe's wife, however, was unhappy about
their presence and particularly the fact that they openly discussed heresy among
themselves. Young Arnaud was then chaperoned by Jean Maury from Quérigut to
Puigcerdà, probably because Jean was too young himself to bring up his sibling.

Authié's nephew was a Pierre Cortil from Ascou with whom Jean Maury was to work two years from now when, in 1312, he arrived in Puigcerdà and joined the service of Pierre de Lilet. This Pierre Cortil was also Cathar and the grandson of one Raymond Authié of Vaychis near Ax, probably a cousin of the Perfect dynasty.*

Between the autumn of 1309 and the summer of 1310 Pierre Maury was ceaselessly on the move, and absented himself for extended spells from Puigcerdà. Moreover Pierre used to trek at night, an extraordinary feat on pitch-black mountain and woodland tracks. Pierre Maury's stated reason for these jaunts was the collection of a sum of twenty-five pounds that he had grossed from selling his sheep after leaving Planèzes.

The debt seems to have been real, and Guillaume Baille remarked that Pierre Maury was bitter about it not being settled. But it also provided an innocent pretext for operating a rearguard escape route for Cathars in the mountains above Mérens, Ax, and Arques. Was Pierre Maury on these night-time walks snooping around Montaillou and looking after Guillaume Authié, who was still free in the later stages of 1309? Did he liaise with the Clergues to try to negotiate his parents' return from Carcassonne? He gave his brother Bernard the considerable sum of sixty shillings to pass on to his father to save him from starving.

While Pierre Maury stayed put at Puigcerdà, perhaps to see matters through at Montaillou, in July 1310 Guillaume Maurs headed across the Cadí range south to Bagà, an important trading post on the southern slopes of the Serra del Cadí. Bagà lies some eighteen miles from Puigcerdà, and is today connected to the Cerdagne by the Túnel del Cadí. There were two major livestock-breeders in Bagà who employed Cerdagnian shepherds, Barthélemy Companho and Pierre Castell. After a spell with the former, Guillaume Maurs joined the latter, and that winter descended with his flock to the pastures of Tortosa.

---

* Raymond had notoriously died unconsoled, because on the short trek from Ax to Vaychis the Perfects had been caught in a tremendous storm which prevented them reaching him in time. The Cortils and the Maurys seem to have thought that theirs would be a sound alliance, because Pierre's mother Rixende met Jean Maury at their house in Ax in 1319 or 1320, apparently to discuss marriage plans between Jean Maury and Guillemette Cortil, Rixende's daughter. The truth, however, was almost certainly very different. As we shall see, Jean Maury had no intention of ever marrying, at least not in the conventional sense of the word.

It seems to have been during the summer of the following year
1311 that one day, near Notre-Dame de Puigcerdà, Pierre Maury was
suddenly grabbed from behind. His first thought was that he had been
arrested for heresy, but it was Bernard Bélibaste and Pierre Issaurat
who, as a prank, had crept up on him. Bernard told Pierre Maury that
his brother Guillaume Bélibaste was not far off: could Pierre join him
on the way to Berguedà, find Guillaume Bélibaste, and then together
make for the wine harvest at Cervera, a hilltop city half-way between
Cardona and Lleida? Pierre replied that he could not do so there and
then, but that he would look out for Guillaume Bélibaste during the
winter transhumance. Then they had dinner together.

A mere four days later, Pierre Maury reports, Bernard Bélibaste died
in the hospital at Puigcerdà and was interred in the cemetery of
Notre-Dame. No reason is given for Bernard Bélibaste's sudden death,
but it strangely anticipates the death from acute food poisoning of
Raymond Maurs a few years later. It is not impossible that Bernard
Bélibaste died of similar causes, since the time-span between meal and
death is almost identical to that of Raymond Maurs. He was certainly
not ill when he met Pierre Maury, since no sick man would be likely
to plan a summer of harvesting followed by an energetic search for a
brother and back-breaking work in vineyards.*

Pierre Maury joined Guillaume Maurs in Bagà in September 1311, and
young Arnaud Maury returned to Montaillou, where the situation was
perhaps bedding down to a semblance of normality. Arnaud was old
enough now to help his elder brother Bernard look after his father.
Pierre Maury hired himself out to Barthélemy Companho of Bagà for
two years, and alongside one Guillaume Gargalhet he grazed his sheep
near the port of Flix on the Ebre river (Map 7). These pastures were
favoured by the shepherds because they were free from wolves, which
meant that the herdsmen needed to be less vigilant and could go into
town for the odd night out.

The town of Flix is situated half-way between Lleida and the delta

* Bernard Bélibaste's death remains a minor mystery. Equally perplexing is the fact
that his Perfect brother Guillaume appeared at Puigcerdà at some stage after this death
to collect his sibling's clothes, but he and Pierre Maury did not then meet. It would
be another two and a half years before Pierre Maury encountered the Perfect in Flix.

town of Tortosa, which Pierre Maury knew from his stay in Catalonia years earlier. It had a large Saracen (i.e. Muslim and Arabic) population, some of whom became friends of Pierre Maury. As a port Flix was a melting-pot where the two main religious cultures of the Middle Ages, Muslim and Christian, coexisted peacefully. It was on the pastures of Flix in January 1313 that Pierre Maury heard from a local man that a relative of the Maurys wanted to see him. The following day, on the far bank of the Ebre at Flix, Pierre Maury for the first time met Raymond de Toulouse. Pierre warily circled around the stranger, who explained who he was. But it was not until Raymond de Toulouse knelt down by the river's bank and prayed like a Perfect that Pierre Maury felt reassured.

Raymond was about forty, tall, with a ruddy complexion and a sprinkling of white hairs on a closely cropped head (FR, f.215r). He spoke with a distinct Toulousain accent, but although he is always called 'de Toulouse' he was in fact from Castelnau d'Estrétefonds, above Toulouse and not far from Grenade. He had escaped from prison in Carcassonne, and he had been, it seems, one of the chief treasurers of the Cathar church. When the persecutions in Languedoc resumed (the faithful referred to this as '*scandalum*', which means outrage or struggle: FR, f.128v), he apparently entrusted a hoard of over 16,000 gold pieces to his nephew to smuggle to safety. This was a fabulous sum of money at the time. His nephew took the money to either of the two Cathar strongholds of Sicily or Lombardy, fully expecting his uncle to follow him there. Instead Raymond ended up in Catalonia where he was forever waiting to rendezvous with his nephew.

Raymond de Toulouse cuts a forlorn figure in the diaspora. His delicate constitution meant that he was ineffectual at earning a living, and he did not know a craft. When he tried his hand at being a trader, his shoulders became severely callused. From Raymond de Toulouse Pierre Maury learnt that Blanche and Raymonde Marty as well as Guillaume Bélibaste, who now called himself alternatively 'Pierre Bélibaste' and 'Pierre Pentiner' (i.e. 'Pierre-the-carder'), and Raymond Issaurat were at Sant Mateu. Pierre Maury invited the Perfect to join him for lunch at the home of his Saracen friend Moferret, who was a fellow shepherd. Moferret's mother duly prepared them a meal of dried figs and raisins, vegetables, bread and wine. Then they parted, with

Pierre Maury returning to his pastures while Raymond de Toulouse went back to Sant Mateu.

One morning in early March 1313, Pierre Maury was visited in his sheepfold on the pastures of Flix by Guillaume Bélibaste, Raymond de Toulouse, and Raymond Issaurat. This was the first time in five years that Pierre Maury and Guillaume Bélibaste had met, and much had happened since the fording of the Agly in September 1307.

When Pierre Maury as head-shepherd ordered Moferret to share with them some of their bread, Moferret was reluctant to oblige, presumably because he wanted the three strangers to earn their fare first. Pierre accordingly put them to work by getting them to erect enclosures for the sheep while he grazed his flock. Later that day his brother Jean Maury and, it seems, Pierre Cortil arrived at the sheepfold and were introduced to the newcomers. Then Pierre Maury, Guillaume Gargalhet, Jean Maury, Raymond de Toulouse, Moferret, and another Saracen called Cabitog all had dinner together, which consisted of a garlic dish, bread, and wine. The Cerdagnians were trusty friends, and the two Saracens were clearly part of the fold, not least because they too were enemies of the despised Catholic faith.

It was probably during this first visit to Pierre Maury that Guillaume Bélibaste broached the business of his remaining family in Cubières. He had a former wife, and a son and a daughter, whom he wanted to bring out of France. Bélibaste was particularly desirous to have his son with him in Catalonia to raise him as a *credens*, unaware of the fact that his wife and son had both died within the last two and a half years. It must have been heart-rending to learn this news now from Pierre, who had heard it from Guillaume's brother Bernard in Puigcerdà. Bélibaste also wanted his married sister, whose name was *de na Cavalha*, to come and join him. She was a Cathar who knew the Peyres of Arques, and she was alive and resident in Cubières, perhaps looking after Bélibaste's little girl.

The following morning the two Perfects and Raymond Issaurat departed for Lleida, some thirty-five miles north of Flix, to spend time with a family from Tarascon called Servel, and to work in the local vineyards. 'We already know them,' the Perfects remarked about the Servels.

★

It is indeed the case that the year before, in 1312, Raymond de Toulouse, Guillaume Bélibaste, Blanche and Raymonde had stopped off at the Servels' on their way to Morella, from where Bélibaste and the two sisters had proceeded to Sant Mateu. Raymond de Toulouse had stayed behind to help Bérenger Servel with the production of wrought iron in his forge. They had become friends, and Servel had paid Raymond de Toulouse well. In the meantime Bélibaste had moved his two women companions back up from Sant Mateu to Tortosa, because he was apprehensive lest he was recognized in a village which sat on a busy transit route to Valencia. His fears were to prove well founded. His sights were already set on Morella, but it would be another year and a half before he settled there for good.

The Servels were destined to connect in an important way with the Maurys of Montaillou, since Mathène Servel, Esperte's daughter, would become Pierre Maury's sister-in-law. Esperte Servel, née den Orta, may have been descended from the upwardly mobile bourgeoisie, while Bérenger Servel, like Pierre Marty of Junac, had been a prosperous blacksmith in Tarascon. The family's estate in the Sabartès had belonged to Esperte, but it had become forfeit when her husband was convicted of heresy, because he lived on it. Esperte herself had appeared at Carcassonne and got off lightly with a few *Pater Nosters*, *Ave Marias*, and a regime of penitential diets. Her husband had received the crosses, as had his friend Raymond Issaurat who met up with Esperte's husband in her house in Tarascon after their sentences.*

After being bankrupted in 1308–9 Esperte and her husband had decided to leave the Sabartès because they could not find the necessary work to survive. As they traversed the passes Bérenger divested himself of his crosses and hid them in a safe place, to put them on again if he returned into the jurisdiction of the Count of Foix. His friend Raymond

---

* Esperte's brother stood guarantor for her husband with the Inquisitor, and would later arrange for a formal death certificate to be issued by the priest at Tortosa in order to be released from his obligations.

Before 1308 the house of Esperte at Tarascon had been a haven for Perfects such as Jacques and Guillaume Authié, Raymond Faure and Amiel de Perles. At Tarascon she also knew by sight Sybille Baille's husband and the thirteen-year-old Arnaud Sicre. She could hardly have guessed that this teenager would years later metamorphose into the nemesis of the Cathar diaspora.

Issaurat did likewise, hanging his over a thornbush in the mountains.
The Servels had settled in Lleida, where they eventually set up home
in the 'street of Cugutz' near the bridge over the Segre, presumably
close to what is now the 'Pont Vell'.*

During that spring, or early summer, of 1313 Pierre Maury was making
his way up to the summer pastures in Bagà when he found himself at a
crossroads on the way out from La Palma d'Ebre, a small village eight
miles north-east of Flix and on the way to La Granadella. Here he
encountered Raymond de Toulouse with a woman from Tarascon
called Gaya, the widow of one Raymond Faure of Tarascon. She had
been brought out of the Sabartès by Raymond Issaurat who, true to
form, was operating a *filière* into Catalonia. Pierre Issaurat of Larnat was
also with them.

Raymond de Toulouse had been kneeling to pray behind a rock,
but spotted Pierre Maury when he rose. He was heading for La Granadella, but after learning in Flix the previous evening that Pierre Maury
had passed through earlier with his sheep, he came to look for him.
Why Raymond de Toulouse should be on the move is not clear, unless
he was still searching for his elusive nephew, or was on the way to a
consolation; although this practice was not nearly as extensive now and
here as it had been during the Authiés' reign in the Sabartès.

Pierre Maury instructed him to proceed to the head of the flock,
while he returned into La Palma d'Ebre to buy flour and wine so that
they could all eat together. After rejoining the flock, he and two
shepherds went on ahead with the flour and the herd's baggage, and
prepared a great loaf.

They had just started lunch when a posse of twelve men from
neighbouring La Bisbal de Falset swooped down on them to arrest Pierre

---

* Esperte later lost her two sons (to illness?) at Lleida in 1316, and the same year her
husband died in Tortosa, where he was buried in the cemetery of Sainte-Marie. She
claimed not to have been present at his death, and to have afterwards travelled to
Tortosa to arrange for masses to be said for his salvation. This may have been a ruse
to distract attention from the fact that he was consoled before dying; she also could
not remember where he was buried, a sure sign that she worried about a posthumous
heretical cremation. It is likely that Servel went specially to Tortosa to be consoled
by Guillaume Bélibaste; a death certificate was issued for him there.

Maury and the others for trespassing on the enclosures of the Bishop
of Lleida. But peace prevailed, and instead of arresting the Cerdagnian
shepherds, the Bishop's men joined the feast. After eating, Raymond de
Toulouse left for La Granadella with Gaya and Pierre Issaurat.

While Pierre Maury was up in Bagà for the summer, Guillaume
Bélibaste moved from Tortosa to Prades, a village near the Riu de
Siurana in the Muntanyes de Prades, some thirty miles north-east of
Flix and equidistantly south-east of Lleida. He lived here with Blanche
and Raymonde, who was meant to be his cover. As far as the outside
world was concerned, she and Guillaume Bélibaste were a couple,
whereas the Cathars pretended to think that theirs was a chaste relationship. They allegedly always slept in twin beds, and whenever they were
forced to share a single bed they kept their clothes on and did their
utmost not to touch each other, since Perfects were forbidden any form
of physical contact with women. The truth is that the diaspora Cathars
knew full well that Guillaume Bélibaste and Raymonde Marty-Piquier
were sexually involved.

Except Blanche Marty. It seems inconceivable that she should have
been unaware of the true nature of the relationship between Bélibaste
and her sister. Nevertheless this was the case, until one day Blanche
inadvertently walked into the room in which Bélibaste and Raymonde
usually slept. Guillaume was in a missionary position, but not the one
Blanche had in mind:

I saw Raymonde on the bed with her knees bent as if he were about to have
sex with her, or as if he had just had sex with her. After entering I exclaimed,
'O madam-the-misbegotten-bitch, you have compromised the entire cause
of our holy church.' (FR, f.265r)

Raymonde and Bélibaste jumped up from the bed, and a blazing row
erupted. Blanche made it clear that from now on she felt nothing
but contempt for Bélibaste. Her sister's subsequent reassurance that
Bélibaste had been re-ordained by Raymond de Toulouse to atone for
having had sex and to have his Perfect's female-free zone restored to
him did not impress Blanche. She was after all the sister of a martyred
Perfect, and a deeply devout Cathar. This *may* be the reason why she

did not marry, since the Cathars execrated all forms of sexual contact, including married intercourse.

The threesome had no option but to separate, and while Blanche stayed put at Prades, Raymonde and Bélibaste moved south-west to a place called Ortas or, today, Horta de Sant Joan, half-way between Flix and Morella, and forty-five miles south-west of Prades. It would be over seven years before Blanche again laid eyes on her sister and 'brother-in-law'.

Guillaume Bélibaste and Raymonde Marty probably met in Ampurdan, and Bélibaste may well have been living there since his daring escape from Carcassonne in September 1307. All the signs are that Raymonde and Bélibaste were a devoted and passionate couple, who moreover took the same size shoe (FR, f.266v)! When much later Bélibaste thought that he had lost her, he was heartbroken.

Even if Blanche had not surprised Bélibaste and her sister in the act, she would have discovered the truth when Raymonde became pregnant. Although she and Bélibaste must have been as conscientious about contraception as Pierre Clergue, on one occasion these pre-cautions failed. How they dealt with her pregnancy is not known, but the question is worth asking here because Raymonde's second pregnancy years later made Bélibaste dream up the most fantastical charade to disguise his paternity.

By the time Raymonde was rounding out, she and Guillaume Bélibaste had left Horta for Morella where, in the autumn of 1313, Bélibaste set up shop as a card-maker.* Raymond de Toulouse followed him and joined him as a business partner. It proved to be a very temporary arrangement. 'I could not work as hard as Guillaume,' de Toulouse complained afterwards, when his spending more than he earned led to a rift between them. Guillaume Bélibaste was notoriously

---

* Carding was used to prepare the wool for spinning. It came in from northern Italy and Catalonia in the twelfth and thirteenth centuries and gradually superseded the more traditional method of hand-combing the wool fibres because carding, unlike combing, left the short fibres intact. The card itself was a rectangular (not quite A4 size) wire brush with angled teeth on the inside, and the process of carding consisted of placing the wool on one card and then drawing the second card against it until the wool was fully transferred from the fixed card to the active one.

tight-fisted, and a craving for money, if not greed, was to contribute significantly to his undoing. His cupidity may have been accentuated by the fact that Raymonde was expecting a baby. Also business seems to have been slack, because before long Bélibaste was back in Tortosa with Raymonde, aiming to earn money from herding duties under Pierre Maury.

Although there were no permanent hard feelings between Raymond de Toulouse and Guillaume Bélibaste, by late December Raymond was on the road to Lleida and Urgell, where he expected to make a living as a trader. It was around Christmas 1313, and he was on his way from Morella, when he arrived at the hamlet of *les camposines*, which sat in the dip of a wide pasturing valley before Ascó and some four miles south of Flix. Today Camposines occupies the spot where the roads from Flix and Alcañiz intersect, and a handful of houses on the Gandesa-bound road testify to an enduring, if largely archaeological, presence here. A few yards east of the otherwise deserted junction stands a petrol station, as forlorn as Hopper's *MobilGas*.

It was Raymond de Toulouse's good fortune that he was spotted by Pierre Maury, who happened to be in a tavern here with two of his compadres, 'Raymond' and 'Pierre' Maurs, preparing eggs and meat on the tavern's stove. He stepped outside and spoke to him. Raymond explained about his clash with Guillaume Bélibaste and his plans, and inquired where he could find Pierre Maury if he found himself in this area again. 'At Raymond de Baias' in Tortosa,' Pierre countered.

Before they parted Pierre Maury kissed Raymond de Toulouse on the mouth, a customary ritual between *credens* and Perfect, and gave him five Barcelona shillings. Raymond de Toulouse asked Pierre Maury to accompany him into the Toulousain so that he could recover his books, which he had left at Castelsarrasin, and search further for his various nephews. Pierre's answer was: 'And how could I go into a country where Perfects and *credentes* are daily arrested?'

By Lent 1314 (20 February–7 April) the restless Guillaume Bélibaste in turn had left Morella and set up home in Tortosa. He was now renting a house at the end of the street 'de Moncade' where the streets of Moncade and Saint-Jean intersected. In this house he also had his workshop. When Pierre Maury visited him here he saw Pierre Issaurat,

whose whereabouts had two months earlier worried him, and a pregnant Raymonde Marty. He had never met Raymonde, and he could
hardly know that he had just then met the woman who six years later
would become his wife, albeit only for forty-eight hours.

Although Bélibaste now had a card-producing business, he hired
himself out for three months to Pierre Maury and his employer Pierre
Castell on the pastures of Tortosa in the plain of La Sénia. There was
better money to be made from herding.

He stayed with Pierre Maury and Guillaume and Pierre Maurs from
the end of February until the end of May 1314, when the shepherds
returned to the Pyrenees and Bélibaste to Tortosa. To the other
shepherds Pierre Maury introduced Bélibaste as a relative from Laroque
d'Olmes and commended him as an outstanding shepherd. It seems to
be only to the Maurs that Pierre Maury revealed the true identity of
the new recruit, and Guillaume Maurs's response was surprisingly
guarded. He observed that Bélibaste sometimes moved apart from them
to pray, raising his hands to heaven, and that he might thereby cause
them problems.

Bélibaste now started to urge Pierre Maury to sell up so that they
could gross enough money to take off to Lombardy or overseas with
Raymonde as housekeeper, somewhere far from persecutions. He and
Raymonde had clearly agreed to tie a knot of some sort. What line
Bélibaste spun Pierre Maury on the paternity of Raymonde's baby is
not known, but it convinced Pierre that Raymonde was not the
Perfect's concubine. Pierre Maury replied to Bélibaste's offer of a
business partnership that he was, and wanted to remain, for the rest of
his life a shepherd.

Before long awkward questions were being asked about Bélibaste,
who was, after all, not a regular herdsman. During this season of 1314
Guillaume Maurs and Pierre Maury were quartered at Raymond de
Baias's in Tortosa, and here they also probably kept some their provisions.
But the bulk of their stock was out on the pastures, and for a month
Guillaume Maurs slept there, presumably to guard their stuff. Their
nomadic existence must have been similar to that of desert caravans.

De Baias's place was evidently some kind of hostelry with special
storage facilities for shepherds on transhumance in Catalonia. Some
time not long before Easter (7 April) Guillaume Maurs had returned

from the pastures to de Baias's, when Bélibaste came to inquire after Pierre Maury. Raymond de Baias himself was present. In front of Bélibaste he asked Guillaume Maurs whether he knew him, and how Bélibaste was connected to Pierre Maury, and where Pierre Maury was from. Guillaume Maurs confirmed that Bélibaste was a relative of Pierre Maury's from Laroque d'Olmes.

But de Baias was suspicious and wanted to know why Bélibaste had come to Tortosa. 'To gain a living from making cards,' Bélibaste retorted, but then added that he was considering moving on, because one could not really make a good living from card-making in Tortosa: perhaps Morella or the mountains of Prades would be more propitious places. But Raymond insisted that Tortosa was one of the best places for that kind of cottage industry, and that perhaps Bélibaste had other reasons for wanting to move: 'I don't believe that you have the right religion,' he remarked.

Could de Baias's questions be attributed to anything more than just idle curiosity? Had there perhaps been an advance party of agents from the Fuxian Inquisition offering money for information? Whatever the answer may be, Bélibaste's cover was blown, and Guillaume Maurs immediately reported this to Pierre Maury on the pastures. But Pierre just smiled. There can be little doubt, however, that this was a signal to Bélibaste to make a move away from Tortosa. He and Raymonde duly seem to have made their way back to Horta de Sant Joan around Easter 1314 where he planned to work in the vineyards, and in their slipstream there shortly followed most of the Cathar exiled community.

In the meantime Pierre Maury was heading north from Tortosa to the summer pastures of *collado de pal*, a pass some fifteen miles east of the Cerdagne and not far from Prats-de-Mollo. On the way up he stopped off at Juncosa. Here he at last met up with his aunt, the bold, and probably widowed, Mersende Marty-Maury from Montaillou, her sister Guillemette Maury with her husband Bernard Marty, who was not Cathar, and their son Arnaud. It had been over seven years, and perhaps longer, since Pierre had last seen them in Montaillou. Since then his aunt Guillemette and Arnaud had been incarcerated at Carcassonne, but now they were free.

This Maury–Marty caucus had cast anchor in the unlikely village of

Juncosa in the hope of finding Perfects hiding in the area, and they had searched for them in vain in the mountains of Prades. They may have heard rumours about the presence here of Guillaume Authié's sons, but they were disappointed. The Maury sisters had lingered at Juncosa for five years since 1309, but now there was good news at last. They were delighted to learn from Pierre Maury that Guillaume Bélibaste was in Catalonia, and they eagerly took note of his whereabouts in Horta. They must also have been excited at the imminent prospect of further members of their families being spirited out of Languedoc. Indeed, Mersende's daughter Jeanne and her husband Befayt, her brother Pierre Maury of Gebets, and Guillemette Maury's other son, Jean Maury, were all on their way to Juncosa, and they were probably being chaperoned there by Raymond Issaurat.*

These additional Maurys arrived at Juncosa in the course of the summer of 1314, and from here the two reunited Maury families followed Guillaume Bélibaste and Raymonde to Horta. Pierre Maury of Gebets (*passim* Pierre Maury the Elder), however, pushed on to Sant Mateu probably to look for permanent quarters, while the others all converged on Horta and worked there during the wine harvest in October.

Two who did not work the vines in Horta were Bernard Marty and Raymonde Marty. Bernard had died early in the autumn that year, so that now both the Maury sisters were widows of the Marty brothers. At some point in the summer of 1314 Raymonde's daughter Guillemette was born, and Guillaume Bélibaste became a father for the third time. Raymonde could not, it seems, resist giving her daughter her lover's name. The birth of her daughter probably accounts for the fact that Raymonde was not listed among those who were out wine-harvesting.

It was in Horta in October 1314 that the little Cathar community and its resident luminary Guillaume Bélibaste experienced a rude awakening, literally so in Bélibaste's case. The recently arrived Jeanne Befayt-Marty, it turned out, detested the Cathar faith and was fearsomely

---

* Like her mother, Jeanne and Bernard Befayt had also given the Inquisition the slip, and Jean Maury later implied that Mersende Maury and her daughter and son-in-law had all fled together, because Mersende and Jeanne were jointly 'proclaimed' by the town crier at Carcassonne. Guillemette's brother Pierre Maury, who lived at Gebets, and his nephew Jean Maury, who also lived away from Montaillou, had similarly evaded capture in 1308.

shrewish. She must have been in her twenties, and she may have been rather large, because she was strong enough for her own mother to claim to fear for the lives of her nephews Arnaud and Jean when they offered to tackle her. By bringing Jeanne out from the Sabartès, the exiled church saddled itself with a tragi-comic Dickensian monster.

Guillaume Bélibaste's first, and only, experience of Jeanne as the Cathars' scourge was literally a morning call and another bedroom interruption. If Jeanne suspected that Bélibaste was the father of Raymonde's new-born daughter, this would have fuelled her antagonism.

It was before dawn, and Bélibaste was rising from his bed. He was not in the vineyard with the others because later that day he was due to press grapes, which meant that he would join several men in huge vats for the purpose. When Jeanne spotted him in bed, she turned on him with: 'If it isn't Mr Ugly-Mug! Are you still here? I promise you I shall yet make *roger* lick through your ribs' (FR, f.260r). Bélibaste was so shocked that he bolted in his nightshirt, without putting on shoes or collecting any clothes from his bed. He ran for 'two leagues' (anything between three and six miles), he later claimed, before stopping.

Although the scene of a shoeless Bélibaste in full flight from Jeanne is in itself comic, Jeanne's threat was not an idle one, and her use of what may in Occitan be an argotic phrase for fire struck a horrified chord in Bélibaste and his listeners. In Italian *rògo* (from Latin *rogus*) means pyre, and the phrase indeed features on the commemorative column to Giordano Bruno in the Campo dei Fiori in Rome where he was burnt on 17 February 1600.★

★

★ I happened to be working in the Vatican Library in Rome on the anniversary of Bruno's death. From the Via della Conciliazione, where I was staying to be near the library, I made my way every night across the Tiber to the Campo dei Fiori to pick up my dinner from a popular pizzeria next to the Carbonara hotel. On this particular night of 17 February the society of the *pensiero libero* had surrounded Giordano Bruno's statue with inscribed wreaths and lit candles. The wreaths execrated the death penalty and recorded the horrors of the Inquisition. It seemed a fitting time to be standing there just then after a day's work on Jacques Fournier's Register.

The contrast between the revered statue of Bruno in the Campo dei Fiori and the forlorn bust of Fournier as Pope Benoît XII in the vaults of St Peter's could hardly have been more striking. Although I had seen a life-size copy of the Fournier bust in

Bélibaste decided that he wanted to put a safe distance between Jeanne and himself, and to that end he and his family, as they now were, hit the road again, making for the place that they had always preferred to all the others, Morella.

In the fourteenth century the town was newly ring-fenced by massive ramparts which survive today, and at the apex of the dramatic wedding-cake mountain-top that is Morella sat a Saracen castle whose ruins still lord it over the surrounding countryside. Today the city and site are in the Comunidad Valenciana and form part of the Patrimonio Artístico Nacional. The south-eastern approach from the coast and Sant Mateu best conveys a sense of its magnificence. It remains as striking a vista in the age of the Internet as it was when Pierre Maury and Guillaume Bélibaste walked here (Pl. 31).

Guillaume Bélibaste moved his family into the 'houses of na Galiana, the widow of den Agremont', and this was to remain their home in Morella for the next five years. Galia himself lived next door and offered his services as soothsayer to Bélibaste. Although the whereabouts of his address in Morella cannot be discovered, we know that the location was inside the walls of Morella, and perhaps not far from the site of the Iglesia Arciprestal, where the medieval heart of Morella was and where tradesmen such as cobblers, weavers, card-makers, and others were to be found.

From my window in the Hotel Cardenal Ram I looked straight down into Morella's narrow and cobbled main street, the colonnaded calle Blasco de Alagón. Somewhere down there, and probably within my field of vision, the last Perfect of medieval Languedoc had resided

---

the Palais des Papes in Avignon, I was keen to view the original in order to photograph it for this book. After failing to find it in the rooms which were open to the public, I managed to prevail on a guard inside the cathedral to allow me to explore some of the closed vaults. He produced the largest key I had ever seen, and shortly afterwards I stood face-to-face with the effigy of the man who more than any other had hurt the people of the Registers. Since the likeness in the Vatican is almost certainly a true one from life (see above, pages 254–5), the odds were that I looked on the same features that their sculptor Paolo da Siena had gazed on; and twenty years earlier this bulky, tall prelate's face had balefully stared down at Béatrice de Planisolles and the short (but presumably not intimidated) Pierre Clergue. At least Pierre Maury, who was himself tall, would have stood level with Fournier.

with his 'family'. With hindsight it was impossible not to feel desperately sad at the thought of Guillaume Bélibaste, who had longed to see out his days in the clement climes of Catalonia, surrounded by his mistress and children. While I knew nothing about the lives of the busy people who started to move about down below from me now that the siesta had ended, I had learnt a great deal in a few short years about a character who resided on this identical rock of Morella centuries earlier. Sitting alone in the hotel's restaurant on my first night I was conscious of the fact that Bélibaste and his Raymonde had consumed their dinners within 100 yards or so from where I sat; and I knew what they had eaten on specific occasions, and that their guests had walked through the same Sant Mateu gate that every traveller and driver still needs to negotiate in the 1990s. And it was also here that Bélibaste and Raymonde conceived the son whom he subsequently tried to blame on his friend Pierre Maury, and it was again here that they raised little Guillemette. Medieval Morella seemed suddenly tangibly close; not just a state of mind.

At about the same time that Bélibaste set up home in Morella, Mersende and Jeanne and her husband moved to Beceite on the northern boundary of what is now the Reserva Nacional de Puertos de Beceite. Here, as a precautionary measure, Mersende assumed the name of Tarragona, and her sister similarly disguised hers when she moved to Sant Mateu. Beceite is twelve miles south-west of Horta, and some twenty-two miles from Morella. It is a curious place for this Maury group to have fetched up in, as by road it can now be reached only from Valderrobres to the north. From there a narrow road, wedged between the rock-face and the Río Matarraña, winds its way to the mouth of the canyon, before hitting the prospect of Beceite sitting across a ravine spanned by a Roman bridge. In the near distance beyond stretch the relatively gentle *puertos* of the Reserva Nacional.

In the Middle Ages there seems to have been another approach route across the mountains, and this was used by the shepherds descending from the Cerdagne to the pastures of Tortosa and Càlig. On his several visits Pierre Maury probably thus cut across the *puertos* from Morella.

Was it the relative seclusion of Beceite which recommended it to Mersende, since Jeanne had turned out to be a dangerous loose cannon?

At least here she was out of harm's way, since the most hazardous places for the Cathars in Catalonia were bustling trading towns such as Sant Mateu on the way to Valencia, buzzing inland ports like Flix, and estuary and coastal towns such as Tortosa and Tarragona. As we saw, it was this which motivated Bélibaste to settle in Morella; perhaps deep in his Cathar psyche Bélibaste also harboured a submerged recognition of the resemblance of Morella to Montségur, the famous Cathar shrine which he may have seen in the summer of 1307 when he stayed nearby at the time of Pierre Maury's sister's elopement.

When that winter Pierre Maury returned to Tortosa he went to their usual place (a miller's?) to collect their flour, and there received a message from his aunts that they had gone to Horta. He followed on and, arriving on a Saturday, he found Guillemette Maury and her two sons waiting for him. They spent Sunday together, and on the following Monday they proceeded to Tortosa, from where they pushed on to Sant Mateu to rejoin Pierre Maury the Elder from Gebets.

In January or February 1315 Guillemette Maury and her sons bought a house in Sant Mateu. It boasted a courtyard which doubled as a corral or sheepfold, and it must have been reasonably large, because up to fifteen people gathered there sometimes. Her brother is not mentioned as joint purchaser, perhaps because she wanted to ensure that the house would be handed down to her children after her death. She now called herself Mathena and pretended to be from Saverdun. Her house stood outside the ramparts not far from the south-facing Valencia gate, which rose on the site of today's Convento de las Monjas Agustinas in the calle Valencia. Their street was called the *carreria laboratorum*, or the street of the ploughmen, and their house was 'the house of the Cerdans'. The street where the Maurys lived is still so named, the *calle Llaurador* (cf. Castilian *labrador*), and among its handful of buildings is a small Red Cross station which may even sit on the site of the Maurys' family home. By the end of the winter of 1314–15, therefore, the Cathars in exile were settled: Guillaume Bélibaste, Raymonde, and their baby Guillemette in Morella; Mersende Marty, Jeanne and Bernard Befayt in Beceite; and the other Maurys, Guillemette and her sons Arnaud and Jean as well as her brother Pierre, in Sant Mateu. Blanche stayed on alone in Prades.

★

Shortly before Christmas 1314 Jean Maury, his friend Pierre Cortil, and other shepherds working for Pierre de Lilet of Puigcerdà huddled around a campfire on pastures between Flix and La Granadella. It was bitterly cold. Earlier Jean Maury had again met Raymond de Toulouse in La Granadella in the house of a Leridean called Guillaume Moliner. Now Raymond de Toulouse sought out Jean Maury because he was sick, and because he hoped for help from Pierre Maury's brother; and particularly, I suspect, because Jean Maury was an apprentice Perfect and Cortil the grandson of an Authié.

Jean Maury gave him an old brown coat and footwear of his to keep warm. That night Raymond de Toulouse preached at the encampment, while also complaining again about Bélibaste's meanness. The following day Raymond asked to stay with Jean Maury during his illness, but Jean Maury declined. He had other plans, it turned out, and so Raymond de Toulouse returned to La Granadella. Here he entered the house of one Dominique Ruig, and there he died, but not before, apparently, bequeathing his pedlar's stock and clothes to Bélibaste; months later these were taken to him by Jean Maury. Raymond de Toulouse was buried in the local cemetery, and Ruig paid the bill.

This, however, is at best a skeletal version of de Toulouse's death and related events, and two crucial details are almost certainly edited out: the presence of Bélibaste at de Toulouse's death-bed, and the true reasons why Jean Maury seemingly abandoned de Toulouse to go to see Blanche Marty in Prades at just this time.

According to the traitor Arnaud Sicre, Bélibaste confided in him that he had assisted a Catholic priest at Raymond's funeral, and had happily splashed a few drops of 'holy' water on members of the funeral party. It was, Bélibaste had suggested airily, no more harmful than a few drops of rain to a traveller on a journey. Throughout the priest's visit Guillaume Bélibaste had allegedly described himself punningly as 'a good Christian', meaning a heretic. Such equivocations were a popular defensive strategy with Perfects because they were not allowed to tell lies. In conversation with Arnaud Sicre, Pierre Maury independently corroborated Bélibaste's claim that he had been present at the Perfect's funeral, revealing in addition that Bélibaste had gone and *joined* Raymond de Toulouse as he approached death. Jean Maury makes no mention of any of this.

Why, if he was at the funeral, did the parsimonious Bélibaste not take with him the clothes de Toulouse left him, and why did Jean Maury visit Blanche in Prades just then? Rather than being vehemently at odds, as Pierre Maury reported them to be, was it not perhaps the case that Bélibaste and the younger Maury sometimes worked together as a consoling team, that Jean was Guillaume's *socius*, an apprentice Perfect? The only explicit reference to Jean Maury's *missionary* activities mentions Prades, and it was to Prades that Jean Maury now headed.

The source for the true version of events is again Arnaud Sicre, who was in Sant Mateu in the late autumn of 1320 and by chance witnessed the reporting of a shocking incident. One day one of the Maurys' donkeys, a she-ass, strayed into a field of wheat. In a fit of rage Jean Maury thrashed her severely and would have killed her, if Guillemette's son Jean had not intervened. This was especially serious since the Maurys depended on their two donkeys to operate their haulage business. Arnaud Sicre was present when Jean reported his cousin's action to his mother. According to Arnaud, Guillemette Maury furiously exclaimed, '*o del diable ia se fasia recebedor d'armas*,' which translates as 'O hell, and he was already turning himself into a receiver of souls,' that is, 'training to become a Cathar Perfect' so that the spilling of any blood was doubly heinous. When Arnaud Sicre asked whereabouts Jean Maury had received souls, Guillemette said at Prades, when Perfects were not to hand (FR, f.131r). In late December 1314 Bélibaste was busy attending the dying Raymond de Toulouse, and he may therefore have sent a 'deputy' to Prades; or perhaps he delegated the trip to Prades to Jean Maury because he and Blanche had not yet forgiven each other.

Guillemette apparently regretted this admission almost immediately. If Arnaud Sicre is reporting the conversation truthfully, then it is certain that Jean Maury was secretly training for the Cathar priesthood, without quite yet having become a *dominus*, that is a Perfect, by Christmas 1314. That this was also Fournier's view is evident from the theological probing of Jean Maury's testimony, and the clerk who copied Jean Maury's deposition expressed his contumely by drawing an obscene satyr-like figure at the start of his deposition at Pamiers; or perhaps he copied the figure from the original in front of him, in which case one of Fournier's own clerks, on this occasion Guillaume Nadin or Jean Strabaud, would have sketched it during Jean Maury's testimony (Pl.

29; see also Pl. 30). It would furthermore account for Pierre Maury's manifest gilding of the lily where his brother's anti-Cathar credentials are concerned, in the knowledge that Jean faced certain death if they could prove that he was a Perfect.

Jean Maury departed for Prades alone. The thirty-five miles on the road which separate La Granadella and Prades were a hard day's trek, rendered tougher by the stiff cold.

The beauty of the Serra de Montsant on a clear winter's day is breathtaking, and in the canyons down from Ulldemolins the light of Provence and the rich tones of Devon earth seem to blend together in a luminous harmony. In the extant records the Cerdagnian shepherds of the fourteenth century never express a lyrical response as such to the landscapes they inhabited and which sustained them. But we should not therefore assume that they were not stirred by the grandiose vistas that they encountered on an almost daily basis. A passionate love of outdoor nature must have fuelled their commitment to a way of life that seems in all of its aspects incredibly harsh to us today. At times they were every one of them a Wordsworth or a George Mallory. It was not just the camaraderie of the transhumance caravans and life in the mountains, but the intimate daily contact with the landscape that would have bonded them to the earth in no small measure.

Jean Maury had undoubtedly heard about Blanche from Guillaume Bélibaste and Pierre Maury. But they would hardly have commended the headstrong young woman, since even several years later Pierre Maury recalled that Bélibaste and Raymonde had told him how quarrelsome she was; and we may be sure that Bélibaste had not told anyone the truth about the cause of the rift with Blanche.

It was Tuesday 24 December 1314 when Jean Maury found Blanche, or Condors as she now called herself, in the house of a dyer or *parayre de draps*, who spoke the dialect of Toulouse and was from Fanjeaux, the very place from where St Dominic had launched his crusade against the Albigensians. Blanche was a servant in his household.

Jean Maury spent a couple of nights and Christmas Day 1314 at Prades talking, he later admitted, to Blanche about their faith. Not only did Blanche know that she was talking to a junior 'pre'-Perfect, but we may be fairly certain that she only received him because he was. What she made of her caller is not recorded, but it would be a long time before they met again. For the next six years Blanche lived a life cut off from all those whom she had known and loved.

Whom did Jean Maury console on this visit? We will never know. When Jean Maury returned to La Granadella, Ruig apparently asked him to reimburse him for Raymond's funeral, which Jean refused. Again, this sounds plausible, but like the bequeathed clothes it may have been intended to deflect attention from the fact that Bélibaste was with de Toulouse *and* Jean Maury all along. Conversely, given Bélibaste's niggardliness, it is not impossible that he tried to hive off the expenses of the funeral on the younger Maury.

16. Sant Mateu, Morella, Beceite, and Montaillou Again: 1315–18

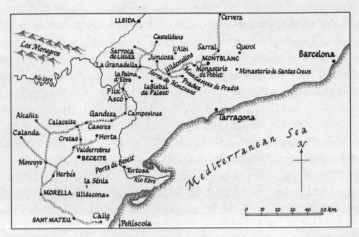

The Cathars' Catalonia

Around March 1315 Pierre Maury decided to go into business with his aunt Guillemette Maury in the plains of Càlig and Sant Mateu. In the early fourteenth century these lay at the gates of the kingdom of Valencia. The winter pastures here were superb. The entire area enjoys a clement micro-climate, the second warmest on the Iberian peninsula, and this is why the region was popular with Pyrenean shepherds. As well as boasting vast alluvial coastal plains between Tarragona and Valencia with lush olive groves and pastures, it has several low mountain ranges in which the shepherds could shelter with their flocks when in April the temperatures rose to 27° Celsius.

From being a shepherd Pierre Maury now hoped to become a livestock farmer, and to that end he opted for partnership, a herding practice that reaches back to the dawn of time.* The agreement was to

---

* The Latin of the Register reads '*posuit oves suas quas habebat in parsaria cum dicta guillelma*', that is, 'he put the sheep he owned in partnership with Guillemette' (FR, f.259r). It could be echoing the example given in LS from the *Digesta*, the classical

run for five years with profits and losses to be shared equally. The details of this were probably finalized between the two Pierre Maurys on the pastures of Tortosa.

But, as Pierre Maury was to discover to his cost, doing business with family can be a tricky affair, and in this case matters were not helped by Guillaume Bélibaste popping up again. He and Pierre had earlier purchased six sheep as a joint investment, but with Pierre Maury footing the initial bill. Since Pierre was doing all the tending work, Bélibaste had already done well. Even so he tried to take three of them with him to Morella, without settling his debt first. This time, however, Pierre Maury refused to yield, the more so since he had already given Bélibaste 'five shillings for the love of God'. But Bélibaste was tenacious, and if the sheep were not surrendered now, he knew where they were kept, and Morella was a good deal closer to Sant Mateu than the Pyrenean passes where Pierre Maury summered.

It was not long after, in late April or early May 1315, and it was hot. Pierre Maury was near La Sénia, which is part of the huge area of flatlands which stretch from Tortosa to Càlig and Castelló de la Plana. One day his brother Jean Maury, who was grazing his sheep at Castelldans, appeared carrying a parcel of clothes belonging to Raymond de Toulouse. He was apparently looking for Bélibaste, and Pierre directed him to Morella. The synchronized account by the two Maury brothers of Jean's searching out Bélibaste and then his aunt reads in all its details, including the freight of clothes, like a cover-up.

Jean claimed to have been well received at Bélibaste's, not least because he brought them Raymond de Toulouse's clothes and wares as well as a present of a blue or green tunic, either of which colours betokened a Perfect, and five shillings. The night of his arrival he dined with Guillaume Bélibaste and Raymonde. While Jean Maury and Raymonde sat up at a table eating fish, Bélibaste fetched bread from behind a reed curtain and ate it at the table after them. They did not, Jean Maury told Fournier, discuss their faith that night, but this flatly contradicts his Aragonian deposition of six months earlier (FR, ff.215r,213r).

---

treatises of jurisprudence, which under PARTIARIUS cites 'pecora partiaria pascenda suscipere' and glosses it 'so that their increase is shared between the owner and the herdsman'.

The following day Jean Maury left Morella and made for Beceite, where he called in on Mersende and Jeanne. He allegedly owed her compensation, because his sheep had earlier ruined a field of turnips belonging to her. He therefore paid her a sum of two-and-a-half shillings, and gave her a tunic worth twelve Barcelona pennies. He spent the night at Mersende's, and they discussed their faith. Jeanne Befayt does not seem to have been present.

Jean Maury rejoined his flock, and then made his way to Montaillou, where he arrived in July 1315 and stayed for six weeks. At least *four* separate references in the text agree on the date of this important visit, which appears to have been his first one since 1310 (FR, ff.212v,213bisv, 215v, 240r). In retrospect his stopovers at his brother's, Bélibaste's, and Mersende's look to have been an intelligence-gathering mission before his return to the Sabartès.

In Montaillou Jean Maury freely moved about in the village. Its people continued, it seems, a Cathar existence of a kind, although they were deprived now of the spiritual comforts provided by the Perfects. Jean Maury again stayed in his father's house in the square of Montaillou, where his sister Raymonde, the wife of Guillaume Marty, now lived. The Clergues were clearly aware of his presence, and Jean Maury was to solicit the help of Bernard Clergue towards the end of his stay.

A measure of freedom had returned to Montaillou, even though some in the village wore the yellow crosses. Officially the Cathar chapter was closed, and the priest's house had emerged richer, stronger, and more feared than ever from the repression. Nor had middle age dampened Pierre Clergue's ardour for women, and when Jean Maury reappeared on the scene Pierre Clergue was vigorously continuing his affair with the young Grazide Rives (now Madame Lizier) at the same time as having sex with Mengarde Buscailh. No one in Montaillou could have guessed that the worst was yet to come.

What rendered Jean Maury an object of considerable interest to most people in Montaillou was that he had come from Catalonia, where Good Men were known to live unmolested. Did anyone, the Clergues perhaps, know that he himself aspired to the Cathar priesthood?

Several Montalionians opened up to Jean Maury.* The most persistent among them was Jean Pélissier, who in 1315 was thought to be
dying. But he was well enough eight years later to testify, and he was
still alive in 1329 when he was gaoled. His grandmother, if he can be
believed, urged him to part with a gift of money for the Good Men in
Catalonia, and he persuaded Jean Maury's sister Raymonde to accept
five Barcelona shillings, saying that he and his grandmother wanted it
to go to the Perfects through Jean Maury. Raymonde suggested that
he should keep the money because he was ill and might need it, but
Pélissier insisted and pointed out that he might be dead soon. This must
be some of the money Jean Maury later gave to Guillaume Bélibaste in
the plain of La Sénia near Tortosa.

This simple exchange demonstrates that in their hearts the people of
the Sabartès remained unshakeably loyal to their dead Perfects. Towards
the end of his stay in Montaillou Jean Maury got into a fight in the
mountains with shepherds from Razès, and was injured in the face and
forehead. He complained about his injuries to Bernard Clergue as *bayle*,
and also to the châtelain of Montaillou, whose identity is not known.
Neither was prepared to pursue the matter.

The reasons behind this confrontation are unknown, but it was not
the only one, as we shall shortly see. The simmering tensions in the
Pyrenees over grazing rights and trespasses occasionally boiled over,
and raiding parties and posses could make life uncomfortable for the
shepherds. But in general transhumance was too important for all
concerned to allow any real degree of interference with it. It was only
when an all-out conflict broke out between two Catalonian warlords
that the shepherds needed to take note (see below, page 330).

From Montaillou Jean Maury returned with his flock into the Capcir,
and eventually, at Bagà in the Cadí, he found his brother Pierre
with Guillaume and Pierre Maurs tending the flock of Pierre Castell.
Freelancing for former employers was evidently one of Pierre Maury's
insurance policies while he was launching his business with his aunt in

---

* These included Brune Pourcel, Jean Maury's own brother Arnaud, Alazais, the
wife of Bernard Authié of Montaillou, one Raymond Malet from Prades d'Aillou
whose wife seems to have been the daughter of Raymond Peyre-Sabartès from
Arques, Raymonde, the wife of Guillaume Argelier, and 'Mondine', the former
Raymonde Lizier and now the widow of Arnaud Belot.

Sant Mateu. But now the time for dividends was approaching, and that winter Pierre Maury went to collect. When he arrived though at Sant Mateu, some time before Christmas 1315, he learnt that his aunt had invested the year's profits from wool in lambs, most of which had died in suspicious circumstances. Their balance sheet was therefore showing a deficit; moreover Guillaume Bélibaste had turned up and taken some of the wool with him to Morella.

Pierre Maury felt cheated, and in a pique he set off on the day-long, thirty-mile trek to Morella. That night they had dinner together, and Bélibaste enacted the full Cathar ritual. Then some neighbours visited and stayed late, and while they were present no mention was made of anything heretical. Later Pierre shared a bed with Bélibaste. In the end he let Bélibaste off lightly, pointing out to him, however, that he was generally thought to be too greedy, and that in future he and Bélibaste would go from groat to groat, that is count every penny.

The following morning Pierre Maury departed for Beceite. Here Mersende pleaded with him to get her brother in Sant Mateu to come and rescue her from her own daughter. Notwithstanding their guest, whom at that stage she did not know to be her cousin, Jeanne flew at her mother and called her an 'old heretic' who had made her leave Montaillou. It appears that Jeanne had been lured away from the Sabartès under some pretence or other, and that she intensely resented finding herself plunged deep into a fugitive Cathar cell in a far-away corner of Catalonia. 'You deserve to burn, and I'll see to it,' she threatened. Her mother defensively pointed out that Jeanne had herself once been a good Cathar, but this did not impress her daughter.

When Pierre Maury remonstrated with Jeanne for her abusive language to her mother, she called him a 'graduate in heresy'. As they were about to retire, Jeanne flew into another rage, because Pierre Maury was to share a bed with Jeanne's husband Bernard, while she had to sleep with her mother. She took the opportunity to bash Mersende about with a cushion or a pillow, at which point her husband intervened and in turn hit Jeanne, only to have her call *him* a heretic.

Did anyone sleep that night in this madhouse, and why did the resourceful Mersende allow herself to be maltreated by her daughter? The following morning Pierre Maury promised his aunt to arrange for her rescue, and then set out on the long haul to Sant Mateu. He reported there what he saw, but his uncle, Pierre Maury the Elder, was unmoved: 'My sister has the dough she kneaded,' he declared. He may have had a reputation for colourful expressions, because his nephew quotes his folksy sayings on at least two occasions. As the Elder's later comments indicate, he rather blamed his sisters for letting Jeanne come out of the Sabartès.

Pierre Maury was determined not to be intimidated by Jeanne, and a couple of months later, during Lent 1316 (25 February–11 April), he returned to Beceite in the company of his cousin Arnaud Maury. To his consternation Jeanne's behaviour towards her mother had, if anything, deteriorated. When Pierre Maury asked Mersende for eggs, Jeanne interjected, 'You'll have a good abscess before you're going to get any eggs.' He told her, 'Cousin, don't be so bad,' to which she replied, 'And how come that you are my cousin?' Pierre Maury explained that he was the son of Raymond Maury of Montaillou, which provoked from Jeanne the remark, 'And how did the old hag my mother hide that from me last time?' (FR, f.260r).

Pierre Maury gave her money for eggs and wine which she went out to get. But after drinking some wine, she became even more querulous. That evening when her husband came home Jeanne again cursed her mother, and Bernard Befayt and Mersende suggested that Pierre Maury and Arnaud should seek Belibaste's advice, because Jeanne might endanger all their work, not least because she had been to Sant Mateu and knew everything about them: 'My wife is a devil who has appeared to us,' her husband remarked, and they agreed that if she talked they would all be arrested.

Pierre Maury reported all this to Guillaume Bélibaste when, on their way back to Sant Mateu, he and Arnaud Maury stopped off at Morella. Bélibaste regaled him with his experience of Jeanne in Horta, and then, in a mini-sermon, he compared her inversely to St Paul: whereas on the road to Damascus the apostle converted from Saul to Paul, Jeanne had gone the other way, by turning from a well-brought-up Cathar girl into a lost soul. Either, Bélibaste suggested, they should take her to a remote village far from where they lived now, or she should be escorted back to Montaillou. On his return to Sant Mateu, Pierre Maury offered to take Jeanne as far as Ax at his own expense. According to Arnaud Sicre, Pierre Maury the Elder and his nephew Arnaud had considered taking Jeanne on a homebound journey, only to push her off an unbalustraded bridge high above a steep precipice. The bridge was fittingly called *mala mohler*, or 'Evil-Woman'. The reason for this drastic measure was that Jeanne had apparently threatened to go and see the Inquisitor at Carcassonne immediately on returning home. But no plan to contain Jeanne materialized.

On Friday 10 September 1316 Geoffroy d'Ablis, who had been active as Inquisitor until nearly the end, died and was buried in the Dominicans' convent in Lyon. The office of Inquisitor at Carcassonne now fell to Jean de Beaune. What d'Ablis's former victims in the diaspora made of this news is not recorded.

Not long afterwards a group of men was gathering in Puigcerdà. It consisted of a Bernard Laufre from Tignac, Raymond Maurs of the Montaillou Maurs brothers, and Baralher from Gebets. They (ostensibly?) set out from Puigcerdà to go to cut wood near Montblanc in the forests of the Monasterio de Poblet some twenty miles north-west from Tarragona and the coast. After they arrived in Cervera they lodged in a house near the north-facing gates. It was in a tavern at Cervera that they met Guillaume Bélibaste. Why he should be in Cervera, 110 miles north-east of Morella, in early October along with Raymonde and their toddler daughter is not clear, although we know that he was touting for work in the vines. Bélibaste was dedicated to hard graft, and seasonal work such as the wine harvest seems to have been particularly rewarding; perhaps autumn was a fallow period for carding. Otherwise it is hard to see how Bélibaste could absent himself from it for what was clearly some length of time, when later he protested that he could not afford even a few days away from Morella because he would thereby lose custom. But why would he venture as far afield as Cervera, when Horta, where he had earlier worked in the vineyards, was so much closer to Morella?

Laufre maintained to Fournier that he and his friends met Bélibaste by chance in a tavern. They noticed that he was buying sardines while everybody else was consuming meat. This, he claimed, alerted them to the fact that Bélibaste was a Perfect, the more so since he referred to their meat dish as *feresa*. Tragically *feresa* is exactly what Raymond

Maurs's black pudding turned out to be. Shortly after eating it he was taken violently sick. He was bled by the local barber, and after two days he felt well enough to set off for Montblanc. Their party got as far as Sarral, some sixteen miles south of Cervera. Here Raymond's condition worsened dramatically. After struggling to survive for three days and three nights, he died around noon on the fourth from what appears to have been a virulent case of food poisoning.

The people of Sarral organized a collection to pay for his funeral and to bury him in a local cemetery. Laufre was adamant that Raymond was not consoled before dying, but curiously could not recall whereabouts in the cemetery his grave was. The Inquisitors were naturally suspicious. Laufre's unlikely story was backed up by Pierre Maury, who claims to have heard from Guillaume Bélibaste that he and his family set out from Cervera with the others, but reached Sarral ahead of them because they were slowed down by a sick man. By the time Raymond Maurs died the Bélibaste group had gone. The true facts are probably rather different, namely that Raymond Maurs was consoled at Sarral and that the meeting with Bélibaste at Cervera was pre-arranged, perhaps because a Cathar *filière* ran through the town.

After the burial of Raymond the two parties met up in Montblanc, where they encountered what was perhaps the reason for Bélibaste's odd peregrinations. Here on the north-eastern fringe of the Muntanyes de Prades, six years after their father's death, they saw Arnaud and Pierre Authié, the sons of Guillaume and Gaillarde Authié. The two boys were accompanied by an unknown woman from Ax with three young daughters and a young man, a nephew of Jacques Rauzy of Ax. It is not likely that the woman was Gaillarde Authié, even though she was alive at this time and survived to give evidence to Fournier several years later, because Laufre would have recognized her. The survival in the diaspora of two male Authié children, the sons of Guillaume himself, must have seemed to local Cathars like a precious symbol of continuity with the famous Perfect dynasty; and Bélibaste, who had yearned to have his own son succeed him in his sacred office, may have felt the need to meet the young Authiés in the flesh. Did he, Raymonde, and their daughter stop off at nearby Prades on the way from Montblanc to Morella, to see Blanche? It seems not; and if they did attempt a reconciliation, it came to nothing.

After Bélibaste had returned from Montblanc, he was visited in Morella by Pierre Maury. From here, and with a loaf of bread blessed by Bélibaste for Mersende, Pierre Maury proceeded to Beceite, because Mersende was sick and Guillaume Bélibaste was anxious lest Jeanne might strangle her one of these days. By now Jeanne and her husband had moved into a different house from Mersende, but she was there when Pierre Maury arrived and told her mother that Bélibaste had sent her the loaf. Mersende said, '*Benedicite*,' and kissed it. Then she broke off a piece and gave it to Jeanne, noting that it was consecrated bread. 'Ouch, as if one didn't know you!' Jeanne exclaimed chortling, presumably meaning that Mersende was incorrigible, to which her mother replied, 'My daughter, you've forgotten everything.' However, on this occasion Jeanne did eat the bread with her mother, and that may have been why her mother invited her to dinner that evening, in honour of their guest Pierre Maury. This was a bad mistake.

When they were settling down for dinner, Jeanne started maltreating her mother, and again called her an old heretic whom she wanted to see burnt. She proceeded to beat Mersende so badly that the altercation drew a crowd of indignant neighbours. Then Jeanne's husband came up. He thrashed her fiercely and finally threw her down the stairs shouting, 'Let her go to the worst devil.' Then the three of them had dinner together, and Mersende shared some of Guillaume Bélibaste's bread with Bernard.

Bernard and his mother-in-law now put it to Pierre Maury that it would be best if Jeanne were dispatched, perhaps by pushing her into a ravine. Was this desperate thought inspired by the canyon-like trench which traces a semi-circle around the western approach to Beceite? This proposition had already been raised in Sant Mateu, and Pierre Maury replied tartly that Mersende should do as she wished, just as she had done when she got Jeanne out of Montaillou. Clearly the Catalonian Cathars increasingly held Mersende responsible for landing them with this psychotic cuckoo in their midst.

That Mersende may have attempted to poison her daughter by spiking her helpings of cabbage with hellebore is alleged by Arnaud Sicre. He furthermore claimed to have saved Jeanne's life by persuading his friend Bartholomeo den Amigo, the brother of the apothecary of Sant Mateu, not to part with medicinal red arsenic (*realgar*) to any customer, because Guillemette Maury had proposed dispatching Jeanne with that. When Pierre Maury the Elder therefore later turned up to purchase arsenic, ostensibly to treat his donkeys' sickness, Bartholomeo insisted that he bring the donkeys along for treatment rather than selling him the dangerous medication.*

Arnaud Sicre does not as a rule seem to make things up, and we may take it that this story is essentially true. Even Pierre Maury, who professed to abhor the idea of physical violence, apparently later proposed to Arnaud Sicre that they should kill Jeanne together by running her through with a spear and throwing her over a precipice. If hatching these murder plots hardly shows the Maurys at their best, it also underlines the depth of their fear of what Jeanne might inflict on them; and to their credit none of their schemes materialized.

After a spell on the pastures, Pierre Maury returned to Sant Mateu in February 1317 to see Guillaume Bélibaste, and that summer Jean Maury paid another short visit to Montaillou. He stayed there quite openly, but no one mentioned the *entendensa del be* this time. Since his visit in 1315 something had happened to silence the Cathars of Montaillou, and it can only have been the arrival in Pamiers some three months earlier of Jacques Fournier. What rendered the appointment of Fournier a matter of immediate concern for the villagers was the fact that a 'cousin' of his, Pierre Azéma, lived here. Up until now Azéma had been contained, because for twenty years the Inquisitorial winds blew from Carcassonne, and Carcassonne and the Clergues were one. Now all this was to change.

A year or so later, in May or June of 1318, Pierre Maury was up on the Puymorens pass when his younger brother Arnaud came to warn Pierre that he had already been proclaimed twice by the new Bishop of Pamiers. In fact there had probably been bounties on the heads of Pierre Maury and others like the Maurs brothers, the Issaurats, the Marty sisters, and of course Guillaume Bélibaste since the winter of 1317–18. In 1318, and to conform with the 1312 bull *Multorum querela* which

---

* If Arnaud did indeed prevent the poisoning of Jeanne, then we must conclude that she continued to behave outrageously until the winter of 1318 and beyond.

stipulated that Inquisitor and Bishop had to work as a team, Fournier asked Jean de Beaune to grant him the mandatory Inquisitor. He was allocated an elderly and feared Dominican from Pamiers, Brother Gaillard de Pomiès. By 10 December 1318 the Pamiers Inquisition was fully constituted.

Fournier's reputation was spreading fast. In Arnaud Maury's words, the Bishop 'was summoning the people of Montaillou and was proceeding bitterly against them, because many of them had not confessed to half of what they had committed by way of heresy'; the Bishop was said to be good at making '*exire las agnas*', however much it displeased the accused (FR, f.261v). The general meaning is that he was getting at the truth willy-nilly, but the precise idiom is a different matter.*

Pierre Maury left the Puymorens in late June 1318 and moved on to the passes of Château-Verdun, with his brother and other shepherds in tow. The Maurs and Guillaume Baille were not with them because, as we shall see shortly, they were otherwise engaged.

Pierre Maury was now on notice, and in spite of his cheerful fatalism he cannot have been impervious to worries about his safety. When they were in the mountains of Château-Verdun, Pierre and his companions usually seem to have pitched their camp at a place called Garsan to the north of Pic de Fontargenta. Here Pierre Maury as head shepherd made bread and cheeses.

It was at Garsan that Pierre Maury for the first time heard that Pierre Clergue was now nicknamed 'the little bishop' (*episcopus parvus*), almost certainly in imitation of the 'big' new bishop at Pamiers (FR, f.261v). Pierre Clergue was always a ruthless time-server when he was not a Cathar, and the people of the Sabartès knew that he had, not for the first time, opportunely reinvented himself as a Catholic zealot, modelling himself on Fournier. Although the phrase *parvus* is used here sarcastically, that is Clergue appears ridiculous while playing at being a powerful ecclesiastic, the parody was accentuated by the fact that Clergue was indeed short.

Nothing was more suggestive of Clergue's megalomania than the

---

* The phrase *agnas* may derive from Occitan *anha* (sloe: *LT*) rather than from Latin *agna* (blade, straw: LS), because the sharp and bitter taste of the sloe may connect with the idea of something resistant being drawn (*facit exire*) through the mouth, with sloes equating with the bitter truth.

fact that he buried his mother in Notre-Dame-de-Carnesses, and Pierre
Maury seems to have heard about this also for the first time at Garsan.
When Pierre Maury later told his aunt Mersende, she commented:

If the Bishop at Pamiers knew how worthy [that is, *un*worthy] Mengarde
Clergue was, he would order her to be dug up and thrown out of that church.
Pierre Clergue who is so powerful now and persecutes us is not himself so
Catholic that he should put the faithful to flight as he does (FR, f.261v).

While Pierre Maury and Jean Maury were at Garsan above Château-
Verdun, the Maurs stayed put on the Riucaut pass in the Capcir.★ It
was here that Guillaume Baille joined them from the pastures of the
Val d'Arques. The moment had at last come for the Maurs to strike at
Pierre Clergue, and the timing may not have been unconnected to the
new wave of oppression that, as a true quisling, he was spearheading.

Guillaume Baille had been on the Riucaut for a few days when
Guillaume Maurs arrived with two men. They were called Comi
and Pierre, and Guillaume Maurs had brought them with him from
Catalonia. They had been hired to murder Pierre Clergue, and Guillaume Baille was to take them to the fair at Ax on 14 September to
point Clergue out to them. One of them, Comi, was described as a
kind of 'light' shepherd, that is (probably) a shepherd who performed
ancillary tasks during transhumance rather than core herding duties
(FR, f.198*bis*r). The money that Guillaume Maurs had offered to Comi
and Pierre amounted to 500 shillings, or the equivalent of fifty sheep,
a true king's ransom. Guillaume Maurs told Guillaume Baille that he
wanted Comi to kill Pierre Clergue, but that he himself intended to
strike the first blow.

Shortly before the intended hit Guillaume Maurs returned to Montaillou one night to see his brother Pierre. His visit to Pierre's home
must have been intended as a briefing, to inform him that at last their
mother's suffering and their family's dishonour would be avenged. But
Pierre, who had come home to Montaillou from prison and was now

★ The Riucaut has sometimes been listed as a lost location, but in fact it extends from
the Cerdagne into the Capcir directly to the north-east of Font-Romeu. Among the
Riucaut pastures would have been the superb open areas stretching south of the dam
of La Bollosa and overlooked by the peaks of Puig Peric and El Petit Peric.

a trader in sheep's wool, pleaded with Guillaume not to assassinate the priest, because they would all then be lost. He must have found an accommodation of sorts with the Clergues since Carcassonne, otherwise he could not have survived in Montaillou. The fact that Guillaume Maurs himself often stayed openly in Ax, and usually slept at one of his two married sisters' homes, also suggests that from the Clergues' perspective the feud had abated.

It seems that his brother's representations may have weighed with Guillaume Maurs, but not enough for him to call off the operation quite yet. Having brought the two hitmen thus far, he made them at least get a good look at Clergue. In 1318 the fair in Ax was held on Thursday 14 September. Guillaume Baille, Comi, and Pierre stationed themselves in an area where the animals were corralled, and which later became the Place du Couloubret down left from the church of Saint-Vincent. In the fourteenth century it lay to the west of the *Vieille Ville*. Cattle markets were held here as late as the nineteenth and early twentieth centuries, and today the area is a spa town garden with casino and restaurants at the northern end, and a '*parking payant*' on its southern side.

As expected, Pierre Clergue turned up at the fair, and Guillaume Baille spotted him in the cattle enclosure. He pointed Clergue out to Comi, who at once remarked that Pierre Clergue was a 'little man' (FR, f.198*bisr*). The use of the word *parvus* confirms that Pierre Clergue was short as well as nasty. The charisma of the man must have been impressive, backed though it was by wealth and power. His fearsome reputation was such that Comi had clearly expected a tall man with an obviously imposing presence.

Eventually Guillaume Baille rejoined Guillaume Maurs, while Comi and, presumably, his companion Pierre returned to Puigcerdà. Perhaps Guillaume Maurs was swayed after all by his brother Pierre's reasoning. In retrospect Guillaume Maurs was literally fighting yesterday's battle, since in the meantime a much greater danger had crept up on them all in an unexpected shape and lay in wait for them in Catalonia.

Pierre Maury and his team rejoined the Maurs group on the Riucaut from Château-Verdun around St Matthew's (21 September), and that same night they were attacked by armed men from Andorra, who injured their companion Arnaud Moyshart. Guillaume Baille fled to Latour-de-Carol for help, and Guillaume Maurs went into Puigcerdà to report the incident to the law officers of the King of Mallorca. Many men responded by pouring out of those two towns to take on the Andorrans. The description of the assailants as 'Andorrans' and the enthusiastic response of the villagers suggest that this skirmish was a border incident provoked by territorial rivalries which had been inscripted into Andorra ever since 1278 when it it came under joint rule by the Counts of Foix and the Bishops of La Seu d'Urgell.

Towards St Michael's (29 September), the usual date for departure to the winter pastures, Pierre Maury paid 1,000 shillings (fifty pounds) for 100 sheep from Raymond Barri of Puigcerdà, another major live-stock farmer at Puigcerdà, to whom Pierre had previously hired himself out as a shepherd.* Arnaud Maurs or Jean Maury stood surety for him, and together Pierre Maury, Arnaud and Guillaume Maurs, Guillaume Baille, Jacques d'Odeillo, and Guillaume de Via descended on the pastures of Càlig, and from there pushed on to Sant Mateu. It seems that Guillaume Maurs and Pierre Maury were great buddies at this time, and Maurs is said to have almost hero-worshipped Pierre Maury and insisted that he be head shepherd.

On the pastures and sometimes at his aunt's in Sant Mateu Pierre Maury, who after all had known the greatest among the Perfects, found himself cast in the role of the one-eyed man among the blind. In the course of expounding various Cathar commonplaces, he was heard saying that transubstantiation was impossible because after eating the bread and drinking the wine the priests voided both in their excrement, which would hardly happen if God were in the wine and bread; He would surely not allow Himself to be eaten and rejected as waste.

During the winter of 1318–19 Jean Maury stayed in Castelldans in the diocese of Lleida, while Pierre Maury, it seems, sojourned in the plain of Sant Mateu with Guillaume Baille and Raymond Baralher, whose role was to keep the transhumance caravan fed by shuttling between the pastures and the provisions, which were kept at Càlig in

---

* Pierre Maury (probably) retrieved this vast sum while staying in the passes above Château-Verdun. It is not impossible that the source of these funds was a Cathar hoard kept in trust somewhere in the Ariège valley, perhaps even in Château-Verdun itself, which had traditionally been a Cathar stronghold.

the house of one Antoine le Cerdan. During the period leading up to Christmas 1318, Pierre Maury repeatedly absented himself from the flock with the excuse of going into Tortosa and Sant Mateu to buy juniper oil, which he claimed to need for himself, presumably as a diuretic. In reality, of course, he was visiting his relatives more frequently now, for a reason which will presently become apparent.

17. The Traitor, the Perfect, a Wedding and a Divorce: 1318–20

The Maurys' corner of a foreign field

It was in Sant Mateu, one day early in November 1318, that Guillemette Maury told Pierre Maury the exciting news of the arrival in Sant Mateu about a month earlier of Arnaud Sicre, the son of Sybille Baille of Ax and brother of a dead Perfect. Pierre Maury at once sent for Arnaud in his cobbler's workshop.

When Arnaud arrived inside the house Pierre Maury was sitting on a bench. He rose and greeted Arnaud with a big smile. Then they sat down, and Pierre Maury asked Arnaud whether he was indeed the son of Sybille Baille. When Arnaud confirmed this, Pierre Maury said, 'You are the son of an upright woman. I wish I were where your mother's soul is now, because she was the best and most dedicated of all the faithful' (FR, f.121r).

Arnaud was now in his early twenties. At the thought of Sybille Baille, whom he had last seen over ten years earlier, Pierre Maury mellowed and with Arnaud reminisced about seeing him at his mother's breast. He recalled that the six-year-old Arnaud had been sent away by his mother to prevent him inadvertently betraying the faithful by a childish indiscretion. Then Pierre Maury spoke about Guillaume Bélibaste, whom Arnaud Sicre had met three weeks earlier. Pierre sighed when he remarked to Arnaud that Bélibaste was a poor preacher compared to Pierre and Jacques Authié and that he lacked their education.

They drank some wine together, and then Pierre Maury got ready to return to the pastures. But when they were outside in the courtyard, he asked Arnaud Sicre why he had come to Sant Mateu. Arnaud explained that he had been ruined by the burning of his mother for heresy, and that he was in Catalonia searching for his rich aunt Alazaïs and his brother Bernard. He hoped that they could both start living with her. 'If you find them and bring them here so that we can live close to the *Be*, I should be very happy,' Pierre Maury replied; he would have remembered Bernard Baille, whom he had known in Ax.

Pierre Maury advised further that it was important to be near Perfects at the time of one's death in order to be consoled, since then forty-eight angels would appear and carry one's soul up to paradise. He compared the Good Men's dedication and dignity at the ritual of death with the mercenary opportunism of the Dominicans and the Minorites. These latter cultivated poverty but, Pierre Maury scoffed, punning on the Latin *minor* and *magnus*, they were often of substance, meaning that they were wealthy philistines. As for Arnaud Sicre's poverty, Pierre Maury told him how he himself had been bankrupted three times, and yet had always bounced back. Now he was richer than he had ever been, because he had the *entendensa del be* according to which one shared everything with one's needy brother. Pierre might have added that he was also blessed with the Midas touch as far as making money was concerned.

After this Pierre Maury returned to the pastures, promising to be back before long. Did he really not doubt Arnaud Sicre in these early stages, in spite of the fact that Arnaud had been brought up by his father, a man who was known to loathe the Cathars and had helped raid Montaillou? It beggars belief that Pierre Maury, who had only recently been apprised of the proclamation against him, made no causal or lateral connection between this and the appearance of a stranger in Sant Mateu, the first visitor from the Sabartès ever to have come to them under his own steam. No Issaurats were involved here as *passeurs*, only Sicre himself; that fact ought to have rendered them doubly wary of him.

Although the Catalonian Cathars repeatedly referred to their new recruit, as they saw him, as 'Arnaud Baille', I shall call him 'Arnaud Sicre' throughout, since 'Sicre' was Arnaud's father's name and the name by which he identified himself when he appeared before Fournier.

The records render the dating of Arnaud Sicre's first arrival in Sant Mateu an awkward, but not impossible, business. He states that he first started looking for Perfects in Catalonia some three and a half years before October 1321. This means that the consultation with his brother Pierre in La Seu d'Urgell which prompted the long trek to Catalonia happened in around May 1318. The minutes compiled by the clerks of the Inquisition clearly note that he first reported back to Fournier at Pamiers in October 1319. Careful scrutiny of the time scheme of the opening pages of his deposition establishes that he arrived in Sant Mateu during the first half of October 1318. By the time Guillaume Bélibaste told him to stall his search for his relatives in the Pallars because Christmas was near and the days were shortening, Arnaud Sicre had been in Sant Mateu for some seventy-three days (FR, f.124v). *If* Christmas closing in can be interpreted to mean that it was some ten days off, and if 'a few days' is taken to denote 'some three or four days' (since weeks and fortnights are usually specified in the Register), then Arnaud Sicre arrived in Sant Mateu around the beginning of October 1318, which is roughly Christmas 1318 minus eighty-three days. This date is consolidated by a close collation of Arnaud Sicre's deposition with those of Pierre Maury and particularly of Guillaume Maurs and Guillaume Baille.*

Arnaud's revenge, like Guillaume Maurs's, was a long time coming.

* Even so the evidence is repeatedly self-contradictory. Thus Pierre Maury correctly recalls the seasons of his first encounters with Arnaud Sicre, but he is a year early in his chronology. Guillaume Maurs offers a Lent and Easter date in 1318 (when he means 1319) for a meeting involving Arnaud Sicre, Pierre Maury, Guillaume Maurs, and, offstage as it were, Guillaume Bélibaste. In the same statement Maurs asserts that he first saw Arnaud Sicre in the company of Pierre Maury after Pierre had bought 100 sheep off Barri. This initially agrees with the correct date, but then Guillaume Maurs

Unlike Guillaume Maurs's, however, Arnaud Sicre's was a superbly executed, long-range sting which must rank as one of the more success-ful undercover operations in the annals of fourteenth-century counter-intelligence. That Arnaud Sicre kept his head during two and a half years, from October 1318 to Lent 1321, of living and sleeping with the enemy, of wining and dining them, and of receiving their hospitality in return, is an astonishing feat of persuasion, deviousness, and self-discipline. His cover was never blown, and this in turn proves how scrupulous and discreet Fournier was in dealing with this embittered and merciless agent, who blamed the Cathars for destroying his family and who had vowed to recover his inheritance, which his mother's support for the Authiès had lost them. Not even his father's sterling service to the Inquisition in 1308–9 could, it seems, return Sybille Baille's house in Ax to the Sicre boys, hence Arnaud's determination to cash in the bounties, and particularly the ones on the heads of the few remaining Perfects.*

As Arnaud Sicre's first encounter with Pierre Maury makes clear, he was keen to impress on Maury that he had a rich aunt and a lost brother. To this he added that his aunt lived somewhere in the Pallars, which, as we saw from Béatrice's elopement here, connects Catalonia to the borders of the County of Foix. The fictitious, and pointedly vague, location of his relative had two advantages. It allowed him to turn his specious search for her into an opportunity to report to the Bishop in the Sabartès without arousing suspicion, and it meant that, if he could lure Guillaume Bélibaste into this part of Aragón, he could have him arrested here because Fuxian jurisdiction extended to the Pallars.

Before long Arnaud Sicre was to refine and update his plan around another 'lost' member of his family, his younger sister Raymonde. She was to become the linchpin of Arnaud's fiction of a marriage between her and Arnaud Maury of Sant Mateu, Pierre Maury's cousin. Arnaud Sicre used these relatives of his perhaps because all of them, except his

---

adds that over that same Easter Pierre Maury and his aunt were arguing angrily over the revenue from wool that Pierre Maury felt was owing to him, when this row in fact happened several years earlier.

* Eventually Arnaud's career was to evolve from traitor and Cathar scalp-collector to his becoming a kind of civil servant, who is last heard of prospering some time after Fournier's departure from Pamiers.

brother Bernard, were dead. But *if* they were dead, he must have
gambled on no one in the Catalonian diaspora knowing about it. Since
Pierre Maury and Guillaume Maurs particularly had their ears very
close to the ground, Arnaud Sicre ran a serious risk of exposure. Not
only did the Catalonian exiles pick up news from itinerant pedlars and
Cerdagnian shepherds, but their own kith and kin regularly returned
to Ax, Tarascon, and other parts of the Ariège. Moreover, Arnaud Sicre
came from a family that, what with a burnt mother and a dead Perfect
brother, was legendary in Cathar lore, and infamous in the eyes of the
Catholic church. Would the fate of members of such a family not
be monitored and widely known? Nor were the Cathar intelligence
networks wholly extinct, notwithstanding the loss of all their major
leaders. Why did no one trouble to check out Arnaud Sicre, particularly
in Tarascon?

Arnaud Sicre's master plan was constantly adjusted, and he proved
to be a brilliant psychologist and flexible strategist. He understood that
the greed of others would be his most potent weapon, and after meeting
Guillaume Bélibaste and getting to hear about his tight-fistedness, he
knew how to play the fugitive Cathars. There is something daunting
about the scale of his enterprise, particularly in somebody so young.

It was Arnaud's brother Pierre who originally told him that bringing in
a Perfect to Pamiers would result in the restitution of their family's
fortune. And so Arnaud embarked on his personal crusade against his
mother's ghost in the kingdom of Aragón, where Cathars were known
to be hiding. Like Satan in the Book of Job (1:7) he walked to and fro
and up and down in Catalonia, but initially to no avail.

The vast spaces of Los Monegros and of the plain of the Ebre river
remain as deserted today as they were when Julius Caesar defeated
Pompey's legates here at Lleida (then 'Ilerda') in 49 BC. Nearly seven
centuries ago, during the summer of 1318, Arnaud Sicre doggedly
trekked through them, alone, in temperatures that regularly reached 38°
Celsius. In the end he arrived 'very wearily' in Sant Mateu. He decided
to stop over here for a few days and hired himself out to the cobbler
Jacques Vital, whose shop-premises stood on the corner of the main
street, probably the calle Morella, and the town square of Sant Mateu.

Arnaud was an able craftsman, and he excelled at shoemaking. Pierre

Maury maintained that Arnaud made him his best shoes ever from a single piece of Cordovan leather, and he more than once ordered shoes for Guillaume Bélibaste from him. Once Arnaud Sicre gently remonstrated with Pierre Maury for buying solid and expensive walking shoes for the sedentary Perfect in Morella, when more ordinary ones would do for him since, unlike Pierre Maury, he did not continually track through woodlands and pastures. Even Arnaud Sicre was impressed by generosity such as Pierre Maury's.

A few days after Arnaud's arrival in Sant Mateu a woman was heard shouting, 'Anyone having corn to grind?' in the street outside the cobbler's where Arnaud was working. It was Guillemette Maury advertising her freight business. A certain Garaut, who was in the shop with Arnaud, said to him, 'Arnaud, here is a farm-hand from your neck of the woods.' Arnaud Sicre stepped outside and went up to Guillemette to ask her where she was from. She answered, 'Saverdun,' but he pointed out to her that she spoke with the accent of Prades and Montaillou. 'Who are *you*?' she asked in return. When she heard that he was the son of Sybille Baille from Ax she relented and suggested that they should stay in touch on Sundays and on holidays.

Shortly afterwards it was market-day in Sant Mateu. Arnaud Sicre was in his workshop when Guillemette Maury and her son Jean entered, accompanied by Guillaume Bélibaste. They exchanged greetings, and Bélibaste looked intently at Arnaud Sicre. Then, without saying anything, he left, taking the others with him, but not before Guillemette had repeatedly said to Arnaud Sicre, 'Do, do, sir, in the name of God.' Arnaud Sicre had indeed told her earlier that he had the *entendensa del be*, but in fact this brief encounter made Guillaume Bélibaste suspect that he did not, because he failed to convey any knowledge of the *melhorier*, the ritual salutation of Perfects by the faithful.

But the shop was a public place, and some three weeks later Arnaud Sicre had another chance to prove that he had indeed, as he claimed, met the great Authié Perfects. Guillemette invited him to her home, and he reached Guillemette's door by executing an elaborate tour of the town's ramparts. It was a 'circuitous' route, as he called it, because it would have taken him a mere five minutes to cross to the Valencia gate from his master's workshop in the town's central square. But then his movements would have been observed, presumably because the

Maurys' house was visible from the gate where he would have needed to give his name. By doing a circuit, he left at one gate and re-entered at another. Arnaud was ever the master of indirections.

He entered the house and greeted Guillemette Maury, her brother and sons, and Guillaume Bélibaste who were standing near the fire. Guillaume Bélibaste was later to recall this encounter, and bitterly rued the fact that he had not followed his instinct then. When at Castellbó he and Arnaud were manacled together Bélibaste said, 'You Judas, when you first visited me I knew at once that you had lied when you told Guillemette that you had seen "*las bonas barbas*" ["the good beards"].* If you *had* seen them they would have taught you the *melhorier* that behoves someone who comes to see us.'

If Bélibaste entertained suspicions about Arnaud, this did not prevent him from accepting gifts of food and materials such as clothes and, probably, shoes, from this master craftsman. The same Arnaud Sicre who eventually sold him for a bounty also awaited the daily delivery of fresh sea-fish in the market at Sant Mateu before buying them as a special present for Guillaume Bélibaste in Morella. He positively plunged into a social round with the Maurys which involved frequent visits to their house carrying wine, bread, cheese, and fish. These extravagances were initially funded by his craftsmanship as a shoemaker, and only later did Fournier underwrite the mission. In retrospect one must wonder whether Arnaud Sicre's fortune could not have been made by plain, honest graft as a successful cobbler.

Although there would have been at most half a mile between their houses, Arnaud's blossoming friendship with the Maurys led to several overnight stays, probably because the gates of Sant Mateu closed late at night. The fact that the Maurys' house lay *extra muros* proved to be a blessing for Arnaud, as it provided him with a ready excuse for frequent overnight stays which allowed him to worm his way into their secrets more easily and to become intimate with them.

After dinner Guillaume Bélibaste usually preached. On one such occasion during the early days of Arnaud Sicre's staying with the Maurys he expounded the parable of the hired labourers in the vineyard, in

---

* They were so called because pre-crusadean Perfects used not to shave (Nelli 1969, 45).

which those who were hired at the eleventh hour get rewarded as generously as those who worked all day: 'So the last shall be first, and the first last' (Matthew 20:1–16). Turning to Arnaud, Guillaume Bélibaste said, 'Since you have the *entendensa del be* your reward will be as great and your hopes as high as mine who have for so long fasted and spent bad nights' (FR, f.122).

At this Guillemette Maury joyfully put her arms around Arnaud Sicre with, 'Arnaud, you should be happy because your reward will be as great as the lord's [Bélibaste] who has undergone so many penances.' In alluding to 'bad' nights, Guillaume Bélibaste referred to the fact that as a Perfect he needed to rise several times a night to pray, although Arnaud, who slept with him on several occasions, claimed that he did not fulfil this obligation to the letter.

That night Arnaud Sicre shared a bed with Guillaume Bélibaste, and he later recalled that Bélibaste did not remove his vest and underwear, which may suggest that Arnaud himself slept in a nightshirt. There is something chilling in this mundane domestic observation about a man whom he intended to deliver to the flames. While Guillaume Bélibaste and Arnaud Sicre were in bed, Pierre Maury was on his way over from the pastures. He arrived at the house in the early hours of the morning, and slept on a bench until daylight. He and Arnaud Sicre breakfasted that morning on a piece of bacon or ham which was suspended from the ceiling and which Pierre Maury cut using a ladder. The two of them drank wine that Arnaud Sicre provided.

Then Pierre Maury and Arnaud Sicre went into Sant Mateu to buy fish for Guillaume Bélibaste's lunch. They purchased two large fresh sea bass, for which they paid eleven pence in total, with Pierre Maury contributing nine; but when they returned with the fish to Bélibaste, Pierre Maury gave all the credit for them to Arnaud. Sea bass is a kind of perch also known as sea wolf, and Bélibaste joked that he wished that all the wolves of the mountains could be like those they had bought, that is dead and delicious to eat. He never imagined that it was the proverbial wolf in sheep's clothing of Pierre Cardenal's poem who was offering the sea bass to him.

Not long after this, and before Christmas 1318, Arnaud Sicre went up to see Bélibaste in Morella. He was on his way to Calanda, which was twenty-five miles north of Morella, to consult a Saracen divine about the whereabouts of his aunt and sister. At Morella he was instructed not to ask about Guillaume Bélibaste, but Raymonde gave him a piece of her clothing for the divine, to see whether he could advise on her heart ailment. Arnaud Sicre already carried a square of cloth from Guillemette Maury of Sant Mateu, because their herd, unlike others', had been decimated by illness, and she desired to know whether her house was jinxed. She seems to have lost as many as 150 animals. It is not impossible that the Maurys' losses ensued from sabotage rather than a random disease selecting their flock alone, particularly since three years earlier their herd had been similarly afflicted. If so, then there must have been smouldering tensions between the immigrant Cerdagnians and the local Catalans.

Arnaud Sicre went through with the charade at the Saracen's, because it would enhance his credibility with the Cathars. He must have felt a secret thrill in the presence of a soothsayer who never even suspected that his interlocutor was a traitor to the very people on whose behalf he was seeking guidance.

Around Easter 1319 Arnaud Sicre was introduced to Guillaume Maurs in Vital's shoemaker's shop. Shortly afterwards they met again at Guillemette Maury's, where Guillaume Maurs was staying for two days. It may have been Easter Sunday when they partook of a big fish lunch, because there were over a dozen other guests present, including Guillaume Bélibaste who ate in a separate room. When Guillaume Maurs protested that the meal was all fish which he did not like, Guillemette sent one of her sons out to buy a goat's liver, which Guillaume Maurs then shared with the others.

For some time now Pierre Maury had been keeping a woman on the pastures, and between Easter 1319 and his next visit to his relatives at the end of November 1319 the affair seems to have taken a rather more serious turn. As a result Pierre failed to make contact with either Guillaume Bélibaste or his family for an unusually long spell. When Bélibaste got to hear of Pierre's entanglement he decided to exploit it for a hare-brained scheme of his own.

That summer of 1319 Pierre Maury, presumably in the company of his mistress, was back on the passes of Château-Verdun, and he was working yet again for the Lady Brunissende. With Pierre Maury at Garsan was his brother Jean, who around Friday 14 September 1319, the feast of the Exaltation of the Holy Cross, returned to Montaillou and then went on to the fair at Ax. Among others at the fair Jean Maury also met up with Pierre Cortil and his mother, allegedly to discuss wedding plans; in reality, this may have been a crisis meeting to discuss events at Pamiers. Pierre Maury did not keep in close touch that summer with the Maurs or any of his usual associates. When in October 1319 therefore they and Guillaume Baille returned to Càlig, they had no news of him to pass on to his family.

In the meantime Pierre and Jean Maury wintered in the Tarragona plain with Brunissende's sheep. They were at Querol, which is on the edge of the plain and near the monastery of Santes Creus. They would have arrived here by the middle of October, but this time it was not until around St Andrew's (30 November) that Pierre Maury made his way to Beceite to see his aunt Mersende, so that he was more than a month later than usual in seeing them.

While Pierre Maury was taking time out from family and the *entendensa* for more mundane pursuits, Arnaud Sicre was heading towards the Pyrenees and Pamiers. It was late September or early October 1319. His professed intention was to search for his family in the Pallars, but in reality he was heading to Pamiers to offer Bélibaste to Jacques Fournier. On the outbound journey to Languedoc he stopped over at Bélibaste's in Morella, and before he departed Raymonde asked him to stop off at Tarascon and Junac to retrieve some of the cherished possessions that she had left in trust there before fleeing.

This Arnaud Sicre obligingly did. At Junac he went into the fish-monger's to buy salted fish. While the vendor was working out the price, Gaillard de Junac entered the shop. Arnaud Sicre recognized him, presumably from Raymonde's description, or from seeing him during his childhood in Tarascon. He beckoned Gaillard aside to have a confidential word with him. Then he passed on Raymonde Piquier's greetings. 'Where is she now?' Gaillard asked, and Arnaud Sicre replied that she was close by, and that she had sent him to collect her belongings from the de Junacs.

Gaillard invited Arnaud Sicre to accompany him up to the castle, and when they were there he called out to his sister Esclarmonde who joined them in the main hall from one of the rooms. Arnaud Sicre repeated his delegated request, and Esclarmonde told Arnaud to pass on her greetings to Raymonde, and that she was very eager to see her again. She and Gaillard agreed that they were looking after Raymonde Marty's possessions, and suggested that they would surrender them to him in Tarascon the following Tuesday. Then the three of them had a lunch of bread, wine, and cheese.

But that Tuesday in the main square of Tarascon Gaillard asked Arnaud whether he could escort Raymonde one night or towards dawn into a nearby place such as the church of Notre-Dame-de-Sabart or the castle of Junac: 'It is for her sake that we want to see her, and she is well aware of that.' The security arrangements between the de Junacs and the Martys had held fast.★

Arnaud Sicre did not forgive the de Junacs for daring to outwit him. Still smarting from this eighteen months later, he turned up at their castle in April 1321 to taunt them with *his* successful double-cross. He told them that he knew everything about the use of a knife (*canivet*) as a token of recognition, and he now demanded Raymonde's property on pain of exposing the de Junacs to his master Fournier. Gaillard de Junac must have known that the game was up, but he would not surrender without a fight. After all, he was aristocracy, and had powerful allies: 'Now we know that if we are betrayed it will only be by you,' he said, and added darkly, '*e bosom* [?], your master will not live for ever.' 'Are you threatening me?' Arnaud Sicre asked, to which Gaillard replied, 'No, but we've done you no harm, and we therefore expect you to do none to us' (FR, f.129r).

But this was a vain hope, the more so since Arnaud knew that, if he

---

★ Arnaud Sicre similarly drew a blank during his encounter with Raymonde's former neighbour *la Gasc*. He met her at a place that he describes as 'near the cross which stands below the city of Tarascon on the road to Ax', that is down by the Ariège on what is now the D23. Gasc's response was the same as the de Junacs', and Arnaud Sicre left empty-handed. The fact that Arnaud was prepared to take the Marty women's possessions back to Catalonia suggests that he was walking a mule on these long journeys, which he may have needed to do anyway in view of the sheer scope of these migrations.

did not get the de Junacs, they would dispose of him first. That he betrayed them is evident from his deposition, which itself implicates them. He undoubtedly reported them immediately after this interview, which may be why Jacques and Gauserande, and not Gaillard and Esclarmonde, were running the de Junacs' estate by the spring of 1323 when they urged Bernard Marty to leave the area for all their sakes (FR, f.281v; see above, page 220).

Arnaud Sicre arrived in Pamiers in October 1319. He reported finding Guillaume Bélibaste and other heretics, and offered to bring them in. Fournier agreed to his plan, and granted him a special dispensation to play the part of a Cathar and to participate in all their rituals. He also allowed him a considerable credit-line. Fournier's money now enabled Arnaud to give the Catalonian Cathars a taste of the comforts that his aunt's riches could bring them.

Arnaud Sicre returned to Catalonia with the good news that he had found his rich aunt. It is a mystery why it did not occur to anyone to check out the authenticity of his story until it was too late. Why, since Pierre Maury and others knew the Pallars, did they not make inquiries, the more so since they were uneasy about taking a journey north? In fact, the Catalonian Cathars had already instructed their chief scout, Raymond Issaurat, to explore the area around Murcia, in the hope of moving further south. Arnaud Sicre would have made sure, of course, that his fictitious aunt and sister were hard to trace, which would not have seemed unreasonable, since they were Cathars inhabiting an area under Fuxian jurisdiction.

When Pierre Maury finally visited Beceite in late November 1319, Mersende told him that she and Guillaume Bélibaste had feared that he might have been captured by Fournier. When he reported that Pierre Clergue was eager to lay his hands on both her and her sister Guillemette, she dismissed this defiantly as rhetorical posturing: 'Whatever he may say, he'll prefer me to be far rather than near,' implying that she could bring Clergue down with her. She then urged Pierre Maury no longer to return to the Sabartès, because it was too dangerous there now. Pierre laconically replied, 'I could not live in these parts, and nothing can take away my destiny.'

From his aunt and cousin Pierre Maury proceeded to Morella to see

Bélibaste, who was worried in case Pierre Maury had been turned into a spy for the Inquisition. Pierre Maury reassured him of his abiding loyalty, but Bélibaste insisted and also did not want him to return to the Sabartès. He pointed out to Pierre that if he were taken ill in the Sabartès, there might be no one there to console him, and his friends would not get to know about it. Pierre Maury replied, 'If I'm destined to be consoled in the end, I shall be so; if not, I shall follow in whatever tracks are allotted me.' Transhumance was his life, and he was determined to stay true to it. It was later that night that Bélibaste lampooned transubstantiation by comparing the body of Christ to 'a great mountain, like the mountain of Morella'.

Bélibaste's concern for Pierre Maury's safety was both genuine and self-serving. Pierre was after all a sound and tested friend, as well as, occasionally, a banker and provider of the Perfect's wardrobe. He had moreover risked much by helping Bélibaste escape from Fenouillèdes twelve years earlier, and he had never asked for anything in return.

Now Guillaume Bélibaste needed him again, but this time the cause was a delicate one. Raymonde was pregnant once more, and Guillaume Bélibaste wanted Pierre Maury to accept paternity of the new baby. He could not, however, openly ask him without losing face, and thus quite possibly forfeiting Pierre Maury's goodwill and esteem; his experience with Blanche Marty had taught him that lesson. So Guillaume Bélibaste and Raymonde agreed that she should 'marry' Pierre Maury, have sex with him, and then, soon after, separate from him.

Bélibaste's opening gambit came the night of Pierre's arrival in Morella, when he rebuked Pierre Maury for keeping a woman. He used the Occitan phrase *arloteiar*, which is a cognate of English 'harlotry', to describe Pierre Maury's relationship with this woman. Bélibaste suggested that since Pierre Maury could not do without women, he would try and find him one of the *entendensa*. In itself this was not unusual. The diaspora Cathars were keen to consolidate their position through the knitting of family units, hence their enthusiasm, not long after this, for two more prospective marriages of the *entendensa*. Moreover, Pierre Maury had already experienced just such a marriage proposal in Arques at the hands of the Peyres.

The following day Pierre and Guillaume took off for Sant Mateu, and for the first leg of the journey they were accompanied by two other travellers, one of whom was a mule-driver, who made Guillaume Bélibaste ride the first one and a half leagues on a donkey. The four of them stopped for lunch at *Na* Gargalha's, a '*beguda*' or tavern which they regularly frequented. Then Pierre and Bélibaste proceeded to Sant Mateu. It was at that point that Bélibaste again started pressing Pierre Maury to marry. When Pierre Maury asked whether he had anyone in mind for him, Bélibaste offered Raymonde. Pierre emphatically refused, and pointed out that her husband Piquier was still alive. But, without denying that Piquier was alive, Guillaume Bélibaste noted that he was hardly likely to come after Pierre.

Pierre Maury and Guillaume Bélibaste arrived at Sant Mateu late in the afternoon, and found Guillemette Maury dyeing wool with a woman whom Pierre Maury did not know. Guillemette served them a light supper, and then, when they were on their own, Bélibaste raised the issue of Raymonde again. He was, however, anxious that Pierre Maury should *not consult* his uncle Pierre Maury the Elder about this forthcoming event. While it is likely that in Pierre Maury's absence his family and friends had discussed the prospect of Pierre settling down, and particularly now that the *scandalum* was returning to the Sabartès, Bélibaste clearly doubted that they would approve of a match with Raymonde. Blood was thicker than water or even loyalty to a Perfect, and the wiser course would therefore be to present them with it *ex post facto*. In this he had judged right.

In the end Pierre Maury surrendered to Bélibaste's persuasiveness, and later that evening they had dinner with his uncle and aunt, the dyer, and a beggar whom Guillemette entertained 'for the love of God'. Over dinner Pierre Maury's uncle joined the chorus of voices warning him against a return to Languedoc with the perplexing statement, 'You are very keen to go into those bad lands, and one of these days you will there cover the cuckoo with feathers' (FR, f.262v). Did he mean that by his arrest Pierre Maury would be a 'feather' (or trophy) in the cap of the cuckoo Fournier? We have already encountered Pierre Maury the Elder's penchant for folksy diction. Perhaps his nephew quoted two of them because wisecracking folksiness was one of his uncle's most endearing, or infuriating, traits.

Now it was Guillemette's turn to raise the issue of marriage between men and women of the faith, and by doing so she unwittingly lent

Bélibaste a helping hand. Compatibility and the *entendensa* were particularly on her mind since her son Jean was very much in love with a
woman from Sant Mateu, who did not have the *entendensa*. Indeed,
the fact that he was absent on this night, the arrival of the *senher*
notwithstanding, indicates where his allegiances lay for the moment.
Guillaume Bélibaste seems to have felt that he only had stomach enough
for one fight about male–female affairs that day, and remarked that if
Jean loved this woman so much then they ought to let him have her;
but they need not bother inviting him to the wedding.

The following night Pierre Maury and Guillaume Bélibaste were
introduced to a renegade Gascon priest from Saint-Girons or Condom,
who was accompanied by a woman. The priest was about thirty, of
middling stature, and he was described as swarthy by Guillaume Maurs.
But Jean Maury claimed that he was of a rather pale complexion with
blue eyes, which may be another attempt by Jean Maury to throw the
Inquisitors off the scent through disinformation. The Gascon's first
name was Guillaume, but he did not volunteer his surname. His accent
was somewhere between Toulousain and Gascon, and he lived in a
house on the square of Sant Mateu near the Iglesia Arciprestal, which
still stands in the same place with its romanesque portico intact.

When Jean Maury discussed one of Guillaume Bélibaste's sermons
with him, the priest spoke in support of the Cathar faith, and revealed
that he was a Catholic priest only because he wanted to earn a living.
His father had apparently lost a vast fortune through heresy. The lapsed
priest also owned a heretics' Bible bound in red leather, and claimed
that there were more heretics in the Carcassonne, Toulouse, Agenais
and Quercy regions than in the Sabartès, confirming Raymond de
Toulouse's statements to this effect. Later when the Gascon learnt of
the arrest of Guillaume Bélibaste, he fled with the woman who seemed
to be his constant companion and mistress. The presence of the apostate
upset Guillaume Bélibaste, since he could not be sure whether he could
trust him. If only he had been similarly wary of Arnaud Sicre, who was
so much closer to home.

Two days later on the way back from Sant Mateu to Morella Pierre
Maury and Guillaume Bélibaste stopped off again at *Na* Gargalha's, and
after lunch Bélibaste once more belaboured Pierre, who then put it to

Bélibaste that he rather than Pierre should talk to Raymonde. Bélibaste took Raymonde aside and spoke to her. Then, as the four of them, including little Guillemette, sat next to the fire before dinner, Bélibaste talked Pierre Maury and Raymonde through the starkest ceremony of marriage, since marriage was regarded by the Perfects as a licence for the most sinful indulgence of the flesh. All that was required was for Raymonde and Pierre to state, before Guillaume Bélibaste, that they desired to be married. Pierre asked her and she accepted. Bélibaste was so delighted that he laughed. Now Pierre and Raymonde were man and wife, and indeed the Catalonian Cathars would henceforth refer to Raymonde as Pierre Maury's wife, even though some of them strongly protested at what Bélibaste had done to Pierre Maury.

After this short wedding ceremony in Morella in mid-December 1319, they had a dinner of conger, and Guillaume Bélibaste blessed the bread that they ate. That night Pierre and Raymonde had sex or, as he put it, 'we lay together carnally that night' (FR, f.263v). There can have been little privacy for sex in Bélibaste's home in Morella, and one wonders where little Guillemette slept that night. Moreover, whatever else was or was not going to happen, if Bélibaste's sleazy, face-saving plan was to work Raymonde needed to make Pierre emit. Pierre Maury may not have been a stud, but his recent sexual history seemed to suggest that he could be trusted to do the deed. And he did.

The morning following the night before, however, the previously game Bélibaste was sour and morose. He felt too depressed to get the food for the day, and therefore asked Pierre Maury to go and buy whatever he and Raymonde needed. This was a ruse to allow Bélibaste to confer with Raymonde alone. When Pierre returned with a pound of mutton his host was no more cheerful; nor could he explain to Pierre why he felt the way he did. Raymonde prepared lunch, putting the meat on the bottom stove and the conger on the top flame to ensure that no *feresa* should touch the Perfect's pot. After eating, Guillaume Bélibaste tried to work, but could not. He threw himself on the bed, and then started a penitential fast which lasted for three days and three nights. He refused to tell Pierre Maury what it was that had upset him so. What in all likelihood happened during Pierre's short absence was that Guillaume Bélibaste and Raymonde had sex, hence Guillaume Bélibaste's self-inflicted purificatory punishment.

During the three nights of Bélibaste's penance, Pierre and Raymonde probably slept together in one bed. Then, towards the end of Bélibaste's private Lent, Pierre at some point returned from outside and found Raymonde and Bélibaste quarrelling. She had, it seems, been impudent towards the Perfect, and had impertinently spoken back. 'You mustn't pay any attention to the caprices of women,' Pierre remarked, to which Bélibaste replied, 'Alas, it's for their whimsies that I've worked. I see that I cannot stay here any more.' One of the things that had wounded Guillaume Bélibaste particularly was that Raymonde had quoted his betrayed holiness back at him when she said, 'Don't you people claim that the mouth which has the power to bless must not curse?' (FR, f. 263v).

He started picking up his tools and gathered them in a holdall, as if to depart. Pierre Maury dissuaded him from doing so, and suggested that they lunch instead, as outside it was bitterly cold, and it was, probably, snowing. But neither Raymonde nor Bélibaste could eat anything, and so Pierre sat down for lunch with little Guillemette instead.

Pierre Maury was a simple man, but he was no fool. He knew that he had walked into a lovers' tiff. Why Bélibaste was so upset is not hard to guess. He adored Raymonde, and circumstances had forced him to surrender her to his friend, even if only for a few nights. Had she been too ardent during her encounters with Pierre Maury? It is as likely as not that it was something as basic, human, and poignant as jealousy which caused him such heartache.

The simmering atmosphere in Guillaume Bélibaste's rooms in Morella became too stifling for the roamer from Montaillou, and Pierre Maury therefore left the house and went for a stroll. For this epic walker there could be no question of staying in the town itself, and so he descended from the hill into the plain. But when he returned that evening, he seems to have run into a blizzard in the ascent to Morella. According to his aunt Mersende, who may have been exaggerating, it nearly cost him his life.

That evening they had dinner, and the three of them started to make up. The following morning Bélibaste and Pierre went for a walk beyond the city walls of the town, and Bélibaste proposed to Maury that he and Raymonde should get divorced, adding magnanimously, 'If you've made her pregnant, I shall send you the baby that Raymonde will have brought into the world, whether it be a boy or a girl.'

Pierre agreed to be separated from his 'wife' and Bélibaste arranged it, telling Pierre Maury that, like the hasty marriage, the perfunctory divorce four or five days later similarly had the sanction of the Almighty. Just to make sure, Bélibaste extracted a promise from Pierre Maury that he would no longer have sex with Raymonde. Pierre noticed that Raymonde had been similarly instructed, 'because she no longer behaved with me as a wife usually does with a husband' (FR, f.263v). When Pierre Maury specifies in his testimony that he and Raymonde ceased having sex between then (December 1319) and the arrest of Bélibaste in spring 1321, he appears to imply that he and Raymonde resumed a physical relationship after the disappearance of the Perfect. We will never know, because Pierre did not betray Raymonde Maury-Bélibaste-Piquier-Marty, and she, and her two children, and her sister got away.

Now that Raymonde and Bélibaste were reconciled after taking out, at some personal cost, an insurance policy against being discredited, they decided to square the circle at last by asking Pierre Maury to go and collect Blanche at Prades. Was it because Blanche might be needed to help her sister through the pregnancy and birth, or the rearing of a second baby? *De facto* the latter, since Blanche arrived in Morella some time after the birth. Bélibaste's son was due in about June or July, since Raymonde must have been pregnant by October or early November, hence the hurry to involve Pierre Maury. Pierre reminded his hosts that they had always described Blanche as a fractious woman, but they were adamant that they nevertheless wanted her to join them. Pierre Maury was to inquire after 'Condors' at the house of a notary by the name of Pierre Fontana. If she was not there, Fontana would know where she had gone.

From Morella Pierre Maury proceeded to Beceite and there stayed with Mersende, who took a distinctly dim view of Bélibaste's treatment of her nephew. She concluded that he lacked some of the sterling qualities that she recalled from the Perfects whom she had met at Montaillou, although she also disapproved of Raymonde's 'pride'. She recalled how two Cathar agents were consoled in her house and buried (presumably) in her garden. The Perfects who consoled the two had been able and gallant men, she said, and one of them had been Pons Baille. The young Perfect Baille was probably on Mersende's mind in those days, because his brother had resurfaced so unexpectedly in Catalonia. He and the other Perfect, another Pons, left for Condom before the last persecution, but Pons Baille did not in the end escape. We know that he was certainly dead by 2 April 1323, and probably long before then.

Mersende and her nephew that night spoke also about Montaillou and the wealth of the Clergues, and they did so without needing to worry about Jeanne, who was probably staying in her own house.

The following day Pierre Maury set off to Castelldans where he met his brother Jean. He informed Jean of his recent adventures at Morella, and later claimed that Jean was cross with Guillaume Bélibaste and mockingly referred to him as the *sent peire* (that is, the Pope) of Morella.

Pierre and Jean spent the rest of the winter of 1319–20 at Castelldans in the house of one Bérenger de Sagria. It was after this time that a turf war broke out between the lord of Castelldans and a neighbouring warlord, and so during the years 1320 and 1321, and perhaps beyond, the shepherds avoided Castelldans, but went to Sant Mateu instead with their flocks. During this same period of Christmas and New Year 1320 Jean Maury of Sant Mateu married his sweetheart Maria, and together the newlyweds planted a vineyard at Sant Mateu.

In the course of that winter or in early spring of 1320 Arnaud Sicre moved to Beceite for three months, where he again set up as a cobbler. He had learnt that Guillemette Maury's sister lived here, and he probably hoped to wheedle out further information from her before reporting back once more to his master in Pamiers. On his way north he also this time intended to take in the Cathar Servels in Lleida, whose pretty daughter Mathène his new friends were grooming as his wife.

Arnaud Sicre had been briefed about Jeanne before going to Beceite, and he instinctively recognized that the quickest way to gain Mersende's trust was through commiserating with her about her psychotic daughter. Mersende boasted to Arnaud Sicre that she had seen more than twenty Perfects in her time, including the Authiés. She also sang the praises of Jeanne's husband, Bernard Befayt. He was ill when Arnaud Sicre stayed in Beceite, but not, it seems, terminally, as he recovered enough to go back to working in the woods. Arnaud Sicre's account proves fairly conclusively that Befayt was still alive in the spring of 1320, notwithstanding the fact that Pierre Maury firmly put his death in 1319.*

After leaving Beceite, Arnaud Sicre returned to Sant Mateu for a three-day visit, and then set out for the Servels' at Lleida. He was instructed by the Maurys to identify himself with a kind of password. This consisted of recalling a terse exchange between Blanche Marty and Raymond de Toulouse regarding twenty shillings that he owed her. Arnaud passed the test, and now, just as Raymonde Marty had done the year before, Esperte asked Arnaud to bring back, if possible, some of her belongings that she had left in safe-keeping at Tarascon. On his way towards the Pyrenees in the late summer of 1320 Arnaud Sicre must have felt a sense of achievement, as he could reassure the Bishop that he now knew most, if not all, the secrets of the exiled Cathars.

Before leaving the winter pastures to head north, Pierre Maury honoured his promise to collect Blanche Marty, and in May 1320 he went to Prades. He found that Blanche had moved into the house of a woman whose name he later could not remember, but she was out when he called. He had obviously been given a description of her, probably by his brother Jean, and she may have looked like her sister, because when he saw her in the square of Prades he greeted her by her name. She asked him how he knew who she was, and he told her that the *senher* of Morella and her sister Raymonde sent greetings. On hearing this Blanche burst into tears of joy and hugged Pierre Maury. He told her that he had come to take her to them, and that they were sorry for saying to her the things they had.

---

* According to Pierre, it was over dinner with Mersende and Jeanne in late November 1319 that he learnt that Jeanne's husband had been killed in the woods of Benifassà, in what is now the Reserva Nacional de Puertos de Beceite south of Beceite. He was pulling away the stump of a tree, when roots and rocks above it came loose and fell on top of him. A rock crushed his stomach and killed him instantly. He was buried in Beceite. This version of events, but not the date specifically, was confirmed by Guillaume Maurs, and their versions and Arnaud Sicre's are not necessarily at odds, apart from being, surprisingly, one year out. There is no evidence that widowhood caused Jeanne to mellow.

Blanche agreed to accompany him, and Pierre Maury took her to Castelldans with him. There, that same night, she again met the same Jean Maury who five and a half years earlier had so mysteriously (to us) called on her in Prades. Pierre Maury promised to escort her from here to Morella on his way back from the mountains in early October. In the meantime she could hire herself out in Castelldans to help with the harvest. From Castelldans the two Maurys made their way north to the pass of Bacivier in, probably, the Isábena–Benasque mountains of Aragón.

At the same time as the Maurys were heading for Isábena, Pierre and Arnaud Maurs as well as Guillaume Baille were making their way towards the Riucaut from Càlig. Guillaume Maurs was not with them, but was making his way separately to Tortosa and was to rendezvous with his companions at the Ebre ferry in Flix. It is fairly clear that they drove their sheep across the Puertos de Beceite, and entered the village from its hinterland mountains. They were met by Mersende and Jeanne, who accompanied them out of the town and assisted the shepherds in keeping the sheep from trespassing on the same gardens and vineyards where earlier Jean Maury's sheep had damaged a field of turnips belonging to Mersende. Once they were safely beyond the town's lands, which probably means beyond the ravine and the bridge, they all ate a picnic together.

From the Riucaut Guillaume Baille and Pierre Maurs one day took themselves off to Montaillou, where they arrived around the feast of the Assumption, which in 1320 fell on Friday 15 August. Guillaume Baille stayed in his brother's house, presumably on the square of Montaillou. Guillaume had been too young in 1308 to be on the Inquisition's list, and therefore probably enjoyed some measure of immunity from persecution, as long as he had not offended in the meantime; which of course he had.

What neither he nor the Maurs could have anticipated was that they had walked into Montaillou at its most volatile since September 1308. At the very time that they arrived the châtelaine was giving her devastating evidence to the Bishop at Pamiers. Montalionians were being summoned again, and by Assumption Day it was known in the village that the unthinkable had happened: Pierre Clergue had been arrested in Pamiers. But this had not yet broken the Clergues' hold over the village, since Bernard Clergue remained its *bayle*, and was bound to use all means at his disposal to free his elder brother.

With news of this cataclysmic development Guillaume Baille headed for Puigcerdà and here, around 29 September 1320, he found Guillaume and Arnaud Maurs and two other shepherds who were getting ready to leave for Càlig. For some reason Guillaume Baille did not accompany them south, but instead returned to Montaillou; here he joined Pierre Maurs and Pierre Benet in making for Gascony.

18. The Sting

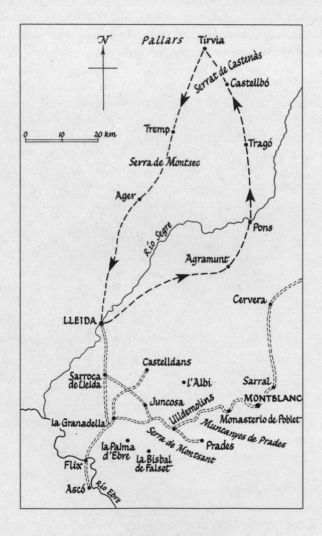

The Cathars' last trek

It was on the eve of All Saints in 1320 that Pierre Maury returned to Sant Mateu. He had not been able to collect Blanche in Castelldans on the way down, because he presumably dared not drive his flock through the plain there in case it was impounded by retainers from one or other of the warlords.

There was much news. He learnt that he was now the father of a boy, and he met his cousin Jean's new wife, Maria, who turned out to be a delightful girl, notwithstanding the fact that she was a Catholic and a Catalan. His family also told him that Arnaud Sicre had stayed there during the summer, and that they were expecting him back towards St Andrew's, that is around 30 November. Hadn't she done well, Guillemette Maury asked proudly, to have attracted good friends such as Arnaud Baille and the priest Guillaume?

The Sant Mateu Maurys were no more enthusiastic about Bélibaste's foisting Raymonde on their nephew than Mersende had been and his uncle told Pierre that Bélibaste and Raymonde were wary of putting him up at Morella in case he should try to have sex with Raymonde: 'If only they could have your goods, they wouldn't care to see you or put you up,' he remarked caustically.

The following morning Pierre Maury nevertheless set off for Morella to see Bélibaste, and to tell him that he would go and get Blanche, even though it would mean a round trip of at least a week. In Morella that night Guillaume Bélibaste and Pierre Maury slept together in the same bed. Pierre's loyalty to Bélibaste was that of a true friend and, above all perhaps, of a fellow Cathar who accepted Bélibaste's authority. Events would prove Pierre right, and *in extremis* Bélibaste became a true Perfect after all.

From Morella Pierre pushed on, as was his wont, to Beceite, where Mersende told him that Jeanne had recently nearly strangled her. So it was business as usual here, and Pierre explained to Mersende that he was on his way to collect Blanche and planned to bring her to Beceite on his way back. From Beceite to Castelldans, which must have been a tense place now, would have taken Pierre Maury two solid days. On arrival he discovered that Blanche had left for Lleida, to live with 'a woman and her daughter near the bridge'. Pierre Maury knew from this description that she had gone to join her old friends the Servels, and he followed on. From here Pierre and Blanche took off for Beceite.

They stayed at Mersende's for 'two nights and one day', and then departed on the morning of the third day. During the one full day they spent together Pierre Maury left the two women mostly alone, and Mersende seemed to take an instant liking to Blanche.

But on the second night Jeanne came for dinner, and after they had drunk rather a lot, Mersende ignited a row when she said that her daughter had reverted to being bad after a spell of being good. When she mentioned the strangulation, Jeanne scoffed, 'Ha, you old heretical cowherdess, you need a solid squeezing, since you're brimful of heresy!' Pierre Maury expostulated with her for carrying on like this, and Jeanne retaliated with, 'If it isn't our bachelor! You're about as full of heresy as her!' (FR, f.264v). The sarcastic address of Pierre Maury as 'bachelor', a phrase she had applied to him rather differently in a similar outburst some time earlier when she meant 'graduate', indicates that Mersende had filled Jeanne in on Guillaume Bélibaste's playing fast and loose with Pierre Maury (FR, f.260r). Jeanne continued with, 'There is another one of these villains left somewhere in this area, but I don't know where. At Ortas I did my utmost to have *roger* pass through his ribs, but he fled.'

Then Jeanne left. From Mersende's next remark, it is clear that Blanche had already confided in her why she had abandonded her sister and Guillaume Bélibaste. 'If,' Mersende said, 'you find it impossible to coexist peacefully with the *senher* and your sister Raymonde, then return here to me, and we will live together.' The prospect of returning '*du côté de chez Mersende–Jeanne*' was hardly an enticing one; a Perfect sleeping with her sister might have been preferable. When Pierre Maury told Blanche that her eyes must have played a trick on her, that she only *imagined* that she had seen them having sex, Blanche refused to accept this. The fact is that Pierre Maury knew full well what had happened, but he refused to admit it, as it showed him up for a fool.

The following day Pierre Maury set off with Blanche to Morella where they arrived later that day, in time to have dinner together. It must have been an emotional occasion for the two sisters. Since their parting seven years earlier, much had happened, and Raymonde now had a new baby as well as little Guillemette, whom her aunt Blanche had never seen. There can be no question that Blanche guessed who the father of the baby boy was; and if not, her sister may well have told her the following day when Pierre Maury and Guillaume Bélibaste hit the road to Sant Mateu.

Because he was in some haste Pierre missed the passing through Beceite of Guillaume Maurs at some point during the second week of November. When the people of Beceite saw the flock and said that it belonged to Cerdagnians, Mersende came out of her house to see who it was. She and Guillaume Maurs at once recognized each other from their days in Montaillou prior to 1308. Mersende asked after news from Montaillou, and Guillaume Maurs told her that Pierre Clergue had been arrested for heresy. In his own words, 'When she heard this, she raised her hands to heaven and said, "Thanks be to God, now it will all come out, because he was as much of a heretic as the rest of us whom he chased from the area"' (FR, ff.155v,156r).

Between 11 November and 30 November Guillaume Maurs was in the pastures of Peñíscola where he saw Jean Maury, Guillemette Maury, her sons Jean and Arnaud, her brother Pierre and Arnaud Sicre and then joined them in Sant Mateu. Pierre Maury and Guillaume Bélibaste had arrived there ahead of him, and had already left again for the pastures. Arnaud Sicre was due back shortly, and Jean Maury seems to have been working around Sant Mateu.

It was towards the middle of November, or perhaps slightly later in the month, when Jean Maury lost his temper and thrashed his aunt's donkey. We have already seen how his action provoked a rash indiscretion from Guillemette Maury. Did Guillemette know about Jean's consoling activities in Prades six years earlier because of something Blanche had let slip recently in Morella or Beceite?

Shortly after the donkey incident Jean Maury and Bélibaste allegedly clashed on the pastures of Sant Mateu. According to Pierre Maury, Jean first of all poked fun at Guillaume Bélibaste's blessing of the bread, and then, when Bélibaste asked to take a lamb with him to raise in Morella, Jean refused. It was a further sign of Jean's spiritual deterioration that he had, it seems, taken to calling the sheep *dels iregiasses* ('filthy heretics') whenever they annoyed him. Or so Pierre Maury alleged. None of this fooled Jacques Fournier, although there does indeed appear to have been tension between Jean Maury and Bélibaste.

★

Arnaud Sicre had returned from his second visit to Pamiers with a finely tuned strategy and funds to match. Fortune favours the brave, and the special bonus of Arnaud's return was his fortuitous discovery that Jean Maury was training to be a Perfect. In Sant Mateu he filled in the people he was set to betray on the state of affairs in the Sabartès, and he confirmed that Pierre Clergue had indeed been arrested. Pierre Maury interjected the curious fact that he and Pierre Clergue had once openly shared a meal with two Perfects, without Bernard Clergue ever knowing a thing about it. Arnaud Sicre now enthused about finding his aunt, who, he said, was as rich as Croesus and who was being well looked after by his sister in a village in the Pallars.

Since Christmas was approaching fast, Arnaud Sicre professed to be keen to treat Guillaume Bélibaste to a special Christmas with the gold angels (coins which were each worth up to ten shillings, or half a pound) that his 'aunt' had given him for his return journey. Arnaud and Pierre Maury agreed that Arnaud would this Christmas pay all his and Bélibaste's expenses, while Pierre Maury would fend for his 'wife' Raymonde and himself. Presumably the two children and Blanche were silently counted in.

On Christmas Eve Pierre Maury and Arnaud Sicre set off for Morella. On the way there Pierre Maury explained the ritual of the *melhorier* to Arnaud Sicre. By showing a certain amount of zeal Arnaud Sicre probably hoped to pre-empt any possible last-minute change of heart from Guillaume Bélibaste as far as visiting the Pallars was concerned.

That evening of 24 December 1320 Arnaud Sicre met Blanche Marty for the first time; what they made of each other is not recorded. Before dinner this impressive liar gave further details of his meeting with his 'aunt'. He told his hosts that his aunt was prevented by gout from travelling in person to Morella, and that his sister was her indispensable companion who could not leave her. His aunt was keen to see her niece married to a sound young man of the *entendensa*, and she offered to bestow a generous dowry on Arnaud Maury. She had once before, Arnaud Sicre explained, looked after the welfare of two Perfects for a while, and they were planning to return to her for Easter (19 April) 1321. In the meantime she had given Arnaud Sicre enough money to take Bélibaste to the Pallars on horseback, if necessary.

She had also expressed a keen desire to have her nephew Bernard with her, and she had urged Arnaud Sicre to find him. His aunt's longing to be reunited with Bernard Baille was of course an elaborate canard, and Arnaud Sicre must have had sound intelligence from Fournier to the effect that his brother had gone to Sicily. If he *had* found him, he would have been exposed as a traitor, but to be seen searching for him could only enhance his credibility in the eyes of the Cathar community.

Bernard had last been heard of in Valencia. The lengths to which Arnaud Sicre was prepared to go in pursuit of his goal are illustrated by his pushing on to Valencia a few weeks later, with Pierre Maury in tow, in the full knowledge that their quest was futile. His aunt's solicitous recommendation that they should delay their journey to the Pallars until Lent was similarly intended to lull Bélibaste into a false sense of security. The idea was that by travelling during Lent the Perfect's meat free diet was bound to be the same as everybody else's, and thus would not attract undue attention.

Arnaud Sicre was exceedingly plausible, and he was a double agent who was capable of switching to a different personality altogether when he needed to. Rather than playing a role, the role was him when he chose it. A part of Arnaud obviously felt at ease in these Cathar homes, and eagerly shared with them information and gossip about the Sabartès, and the malevolent actions of the new Bishop. When he told his Morella audience that Fournier was assisted by the Dominican Gaillard de Pomiès, Blanche exclaimed that she knew him, that he was already old; and then she added, '*O del dyable tant a viscut*,' meaning 'Why the devil has he lived so long!' (FR, f.130v). It would have depressed Blanche further to know that as late as Friday 13 January 1329 the old Dominican was still sitting on Inquisitorial panels (D 27, f.141v). Later that evening, and of course after dinner and at the fireside, Arnaud Sicre was treated to Blanche's tale of fooling d'Ablis.

That night of Christmas Eve 1320 the three men shared a bed, with Pierre Maury in the middle, since Guillaume Bélibaste needed to get up repeatedly from the side of the bed to pray. In Homeric epic the shepherds are said to cuddle up to their dogs and cattle for warmth. What was it like in these fourteenth-century bedrooms to share beds with two, and sometimes three, men? What went through Arnaud

Sicre's mind as he lay next to a man whom he was planning to betray to fire at the stake?

After Christmas lunch on Thursday 25 December 1320 the three men went for a constitutional, and Arnaud Sicre showed them a gold angel. He offered it, along with the seven which remained (he had already spent two), to the Perfect, saying that it was his aunt's express intention that Guillaume Bélibaste should have them. Bélibaste accepted the gift saying, 'Let it be for the love of God, and may God save our men and women friends.'

For Bélibaste the appearance of Arnaud Sicre's aunt as a wealthy patron must have seemed like the answer to his prayers. If before his ordination he had enjoyed a prosperous and moneyed lifestyle like the Authiés, he might have been less susceptible to the lure of Mammon and the comforts it could buy. But Guillaume Bélibaste was a hard-nosed shepherd-on-the-run from Cubières, and Arnaud Sicre dangled riches in front of his eyes, with the promise of more to come. It seems to have been during the course of this post-prandial Christmas stroll that Bélibaste proposed that he might be ready to go to the Pallars by the middle of Lent, that is at the end of March or early April. Arnaud Sicre more or less confirms this date by noting that they left from Sant Mateu for the Pallars some time after 15 March.

Pierre Maury and Arnaud Sicre stayed in Morella with Guillaume Bélibaste and his family until 29 December, and had to endure several of his sermons during this period. Then they departed for Valencia, sharing the cost on the way there, only to find that Bernard had long gone, of course. The two of them returned to Sant Mateu, where Pierre Maury sought out his flock and his brother, while Arnaud Sicre probably rejoined Vital's shoemaking business.

It was around 22 January 1321 that Guillaume Maurs went up to Sant Mateu to look for a shepherd to hire. He asked Pierre Maury to come and help him out, but Pierre could not because, apparently, he was ill; but he promised to follow on in a few days' time. In fact, it was his brother who was sick, and Pierre was looking after him out on the pastures. That was the last time Guillaume Maurs saw Pierre Maury, his brother, or any of the others from Sant Mateu.

It was early in February that Pierre Maury went to Morella, ostensibly to take some wool to Guillaume Bélibaste. He stayed only one night, and then hurried back. The true reason why he went to seek out Bélibaste was almost certainly because he thought Jean was dying, and he wanted the Perfect to come and console him. But Bélibaste declined, still perhaps smarting from Jean Maury's refusing him the lamb. Jean Maury was now so ill that they took him to their aunt's in Sant Mateu, where he would have a better chance of convalescing, or at least of dying in greater comfort. According to Pierre Maury, his brother Jean threatened to expose his own family to the Inquisition if they persisted in getting a Perfect, and Guillemette allegedly told Pierre that his brother, her nephew, was possessed by the devil and should be poisoned.

That there was a simmering antagonism between Jean Maury and his aunt over the beating of the donkey is quite possible, and Jean Maury may have been offended by his aunt's insistence for him to start the *endura*. What really happened during Jean Maury's near-fatal illness, however, is summed up succinctly by Arnaud Sicre:

In the same place [Sant Mateu] I heard Jean Maury tell me that, once when he was sick, he sent for Guillaume Bélibaste to be consoled by him, but Guillaume declined, pretending that he lacked the funds necessary for the journey. Jean denounced him for that, saying that he had acted badly and had not observed the proper practice of other Perfects; he should not have been found deficient in this matter, even if it meant crossing through fire. (FR, f.209r)

When Pierre Maury told what I believe to be an agreed version between the brothers to Fournier, he knew that his aunt and her sons were either dead or well beyond the reach of the Inquisition. He therefore seems to have done what the accused often did, pragmatically shift the blame full-scale on to the dead or disappeared, because they were beyond reprisal. Pierre Maury was obviously confident that Guillemette and her kin could not be hauled in, and only Arnaud Sicre's testimony stood against his and his brother's; and the two brothers had plenty of time after Guillaume Bélibaste's arrest during which to synchronize their stories, which was essential if Jean Maury was to escape the stake, as he did.

★

The time had come to visit Arnaud Sicre's fictitious aunt and organize the marriage of Raymonde Baille and Arnaud Maury. It would expand the Cathar constituency in Catalonia and promised to provide Bélibaste with the kind of pension that he craved.

The whole journey took nine days, and the episode is so significant that I propose to spell out the days separately.

DAY 1   Towards the middle of March an itinerary for this false errand had been agreed, and 'shortly afterwards' Pierre Maury the Elder, his cousin Arnaud, and Arnaud Sicre set off for Morella on the first leg of the journey to the Pallars. I would suggest that 'shortly afterwards' puts this around 20 March.* Guillaume Bélibaste had sum- moned Pierre Maury a few days earlier, but Pierre had been unable to go, and Bélibaste had similarly been unwilling to come to Sant Mateu instead. Something was on his mind, and when Pierre Maury met him in Morella, Bélibaste took Pierre aside and confided in him that his next-door neighbour's divination had augured badly for his trip to the Pallars; a prophetic shoe-test had forecast that he was destined not to come back. Pierre Maury told his friend not to be superstitious, but if he was indeed desperately worried he should just not go. But Bélibaste now declared solemnly that he would go at all costs, since he had promised it to Arnaud, and 'if God my Father calls me, the time will have come to go and join Him'.

The elixir of Fournier's money was now seriously clouding Béli- baste's judgement, and Arnaud made sure that it would continue to do so when he drafted a marriage contract at Morella that evening for Arnaud Maury and Raymonde Sicre-Baille. According to Arnaud Sicre, Raymonde's dowry was set at forty pounds in addition to a complete wardrobe and a mule to carry the clothes; though Pierre Maury remembered double the amount and two mules. This transaction was sealed by oath with Guillaume Bélibaste officiating.

* This is firmly supported by Mathène Servel, who dates her flight from Lleida *immediately* on hearing about Guillaume Bélibaste's arrest to 'eight days and some' before Palm Sunday, which in 1321 was on 12 April. Since the total time taken up by the expedition from Sant Mateu to the Pallars and its panic-stricken return adds up to eleven days, this means that they set out on 12 April minus 'eight days and some (*c.* three or four)' and minus eleven, which yields an approximate date of 20 March.

DAY 2   The following morning Pierre Maury's uncle returned to Sant Mateu, while Pierre Maury, Arnaud Sicre, Arnaud Maury and Guillaume Bélibaste proceeded to Beceite on the second leg of their journey. As they approached Beceite the two Maurys went on ahead to check whether Jeanne was staying at her mother's, since they did not want her to see the Perfect. When they saw that she was, they opted instead for the hotel of Pierre Prior in the square of Beceite, which was probably at the top of the village where the main square still is. Clearly Beceite was then substantial enough in size for Guillaume Bélibaste and the others to stay there without needing to fear that they would be spotted by Jeanne.

Before dinner the two Maury cousins went to see Mersende and alerted her to Bélibaste's presence in the town. They asked her to pretend to be ill and retire to bed to get Jeanne out of the house so that they could visit later. Then the quartet dined at the hotel and, when it was pitch-dark outside, Pierre Maury and Bélibaste adjourned to Mersende's. They had a second dinner with her, and after this they settled down to talk. Pierre Maury eventually turned in, but his aunt and Bélibaste chatted on into the early hours of the morning.

When Pierre woke up, Mersende started anxiously to press him to stop the trip, since so many Perfects had been betrayed. Given that Arnaud Sicre was as yet unproven, should not Pierre, or Arnaud, or Pierre Maury the Elder go to the Pallars first to make assurance doubly sure? There would still be time for Guillaume Bélibaste to follow on later. Pierre Maury quoted Guillaume Bélibaste's new-found fatalism to her, but later put the gist of Mersende's conversation to Arnaud Sicre and said, 'Arnaud, Arnaud, watch out that you do not betray us, since others in your family were wicked and traitors to the Church of God.'

DAY 3   That day the four went all the way to Ascó. In his testimony Pierre Maury recalled that Arnaud got drunk at Ascó, but from this he swiftly moved on to their next (literally) port of call, Flix. Arnaud Sicre's recollection of Ascó was rather more specific.

What happened was that Pierre Maury and Guillaume Bélibaste decided to put Arnaud to the test, in deference perhaps to Mersende's worries. They bought two wines, and Pierre stealthily mixed them to administer a particularly heady potion to Arnaud Sicre. But Arnaud was on to them at once, and decided to exploit this charade for his own ends. After drinking the spiked wine he pretended to be badly intoxicated, and fell down next to the table. Pierre Maury put him on the bed, from where Arnaud Sicre rose to urinate at the head of the bed. To stop him doing this, Pierre Maury dragged Arnaud into the street half-carrying him, and when they were alone whispered to him, 'Arnaud, why don't we take that heretic in there all the way to the Sabartès and collect fifty or a hundred pounds for him? From that we could live honourably, because that peasant in there talks nothing but bad rubbish.' Arnaud pretended to be outraged by the suggestion and protested that he would not stand by and see Pierre Maury betray Guillaume Bélibaste. Then, muttering, he returned into the house and threw himself on the bed, 'pretending to be stone-drunk'.

Pierre Maury removed his shoes, undressed him, and covered him up. While Arnaud Sicre pretended to sleep, Pierre told Bélibaste what had happened and that Arnaud Sicre was sound and would not betray them. Arnaud heard every word they spoke. The following morning Pierre asked him how he had slept and whether he could remember much from the night. Arnaud replied that he remembered drinking good wine, and that he had undressed and gone to bed by himself.

DAY 4　The following day they lunched at Flix at the house of Pons Ortola, a friend of Pierre Maury's, and then pushed on as far as Sarroca de Lleida, where they spent the night. The next morning they reached Esperte's in Lleida for lunch, and they stayed here for the rest of the day and that night. Since the living quarters of Esperte and Mathène seem to have been exiguous, the two women surrendered them to the quartet, while they slept at a neighbour's.

DAY 5　From Lleida they headed for Agramunt, some twenty-five miles to the north-east, and on the way there Bélibaste was urging Arnaud Sicre to marry Mathène because she was a good Cathar prospect.

DAY 6　From Agramunt their route took them to Pons, where they intended to lunch. Before they reached it, a magpie crossed the road three times in front of them, and each time it chattered. Bélibaste immediately took this to be a bad omen, and sat down on a stone, sad

and anxious. But between them Pierre Maury and Arnaud Sicre chiv-
vied him along, and they continued their journey, not before Bélibaste
had exhorted Arnaud Sicre to be sure to be taking him to a good place,
which Arnaud heartily confirmed. After lunch, they progressed to
Tragó, a small town on what is now the dam of Rialp. At some point
they had to ford a stream and, like St Christopher, the tall Pierre Maury
carried each of his companions across on his shoulders.

DAYS 7 AND 8   After one night in Tragó they made tracks as far as
Castellbó, and the following day they proceeded to Tírvia, which sits
high on a promontory to the right of the entrance to the Vall de Cardós.
A mere eight miles further up rises the village of Lladrós, where Béatrice
de Planisolles and Barthélemy Amilhat had lived five years earlier. It
was here at Tírvia that the intended bride of Arnaud Maury was
supposedly living. If so, why did they not make contact with this family
at once? Instead at Tírvia Pierre Maury noticed Arnaud Sicre talking
to the local *bayle* and heard him say the words 'It'll be all right.'

DAY 9   The next morning the *bayle*, accompanied by several other
men, arrived at the house where the quartet lodged and arrested the
entire party. They were taken to his house, and here Arnaud Sicre told
Pierre Maury and his cousin that they were free to go. 'I have no
quarrel with them,' he told the captors, adding that he did not desire
to harm them: 'I lost our family's assets because of the heretics, and I
want them back by arresting a Perfect,' he explained. In Pierre Maury's
hearing he told the *bayle* that the two Maurys were his associates, and
should therefore be set free. It seems that Arnaud Sicre could not quite
bring himself to hurt Pierre Maury; at least not yet. In conversation
later with his shepherd friends Pierre Maury dramatized his mundane
release into an abseiling escape (FR, f.199v).

Before he was taken away, Guillaume Bélibaste, who was already
under guard, gave Pierre Maury two Barcelona shillings, perhaps to
settle an old debt. The two friends would never meet again. Instead
Bélibaste now found himself sharing a leg-iron with the man who had
betrayed him for money. This manacling together of accused and
accuser may have been standard practice in certain circumstances to
pre-empt false accusations. Bélibaste now called Arnaud 'Judas', 'son of

a viper', and a bastard rather than the legitimate son of Sybille Baille. None of this moved Arnaud Sicre, who was determined to deliver a live Bélibaste to the Inquisition for burning. As soon as he was arrested, Bélibaste put himself into the *endura*, hoping to die before being dragged to the pyre. It is a measure of Arnaud Sicre's persuasive powers that even in these circumstances he tricked Bélibaste into believing that he repented of his deed and would help him escape, which Bélibaste could only do if he was fit. Bélibaste abandoned his fast.

Shortly after his arrest, and on the way to Ax, Guillaume Bélibaste and Arnaud Sicre found themselves on top of the main tower of the fortress of Castellbó, still shackled together. Bélibaste then said to Arnaud:

If you can rediscover your moral conscience and repent of what you've done to me, I will console you before we plunge down from this tower together. Both our souls will at once ascend to the Heavenly Father, where we will have crowns and thrones waiting for us; and forty-eight angels wearing golden coronets inset with precious stones will come and take us to the Father. (FR, f.128r)

He professed not to care about his body, because it belonged to the worms and was the creation of the god of the material world, the devil; God the Father was interested only in his soul, which the devil had long ago tricked into leaving heaven.

If Guillaume Bélibaste failed to impress Arnaud Sicre, he himself now experienced a spiritual renaissance. In this extremity the fallen Perfect from Cubières metamorphosed into an unlikely saint by refusing to save his life through recanting. Perhaps he wanted to prove his Maker right after all for choosing this unlikely vessel as an apostle of the true faith; perhaps he hoped his lover and his children would be proud of him.

While this was happening to Guillaume Bélibaste and Arnaud Sicre, the two distraught Maury cousins were on their return journey to Lleida. In the space of a mere two days they covered the distance from the Cardós valley to Beceite by way of Lleida, the equivalent of four ordinary days' march. After a strenuous forty-mile trek they reached

Ager to the south of the Serra de Montsec. From here they made for
Lleida the following morning, where they lunched with the Servels.
Esperte was devastated by the news, and she and her daughter left Lleida
almost immediately. According to Mathène they arrived at Juncosa
around 1 or 2 April. The reason they later gave for moving was the
wheat harvest which falls early in the Lleida plain.

As soon as Pierre Maury and Arnaud had fortified themselves, they
pushed on towards Beceite, another marathon of well over fifty miles.
Speed was of the essence, if the small Cathar community was to survive
in any form. It was night when they arrived in Beceite. In fact it was
probably in the early hours of the morning, and Mersende was astonished to see them. When Pierre Maury explained that Guillaume
Bélibaste had been arrested through the offices of Arnaud Sicre she
started to wail inconsolably.

Pierre Maury promised to return the following day to take Mersende
to safety, and then, after (perhaps) a very short rest, he and Arnaud set
off again, this time for Morella. Raymonde and Blanche broke into
prolonged lamentations at the news of the arrest and doom of their
lover and friend, newly found in Blanche's case. But there was no time
to grieve properly, because they needed to move urgently for their
safety. With Pierre Maury's assistance they immediately sold all Guillaume Bélibaste's assets in Morella, and then Pierre Maury walked the
two women as well as, presumably, Guillemette and her baby brother,
to Valderrobres. It must have been past midnight by the time they
reached their destination. In the course of this day Pierre Maury had
gone from Beceite to Morella, helped sell up his friend's estate, and
was now in Valderrobres. To do all this using a motor-car nowadays
would be a fair challenge; for a shepherd in 1321 it was an astonishing
feat.

While Pierre Maury was briefing Blanche and Raymonde, his cousin
Arnaud was making for Sant Mateu, packing the two days' journey
from Beceite to Morella and Sant Mateu into yet another single epic
day of marching. Pierre Maury's brother Jean was staying with his
aunt's family at the time. After the initial consternation at the news, the
Maurys sold or, it seems, leased, their house and newly acquired
vineyard. They all dispersed, although in the medium term they
returned to recover their property. Pierre Maury the Elder at once

made his way north to help his sister Mersende whom, with her daughter Jeanne, he took to Alcañiz.

He probably found them in Herbés, because that is where they fled in the immediate wake of Pierre Maury's visit. It was in this hamlet, half-way between Morella and Beceite, that Pierre Maury fetched up with them, and left them there, while he pushed on to Sant Mateu. Here he met his aunt Guillemette who was, allegedly, furious with Pierre Maury. 'It was you who sold the *senher*,' she told Pierre Maury, and added that she would have preferred the deaths of Pierre, Arnaud Sicre, and her own son Arnaud to the arrest of Bélibaste. Like several other blood-curdling statements that Pierre Maury attributed to his aunt, this sounds deeply implausible. One way or another she was evidently beyond Fournier's reach, and he therefore felt free to portray her as a fanatical Cathar and a homicidal maniac. By so doing he may have hoped to weaken the force of her evidence against his brother Jean as reported by Arnaud Sicre, because by far the most damaging statement against Jean Maury, that he was an aspiring Perfect, was attributed by Arnaud Sicre to the Maury brothers' aunt. Since there were no witnesses present when she said it, Arnaud Sicre's testimony on this was legally worthless, which mattered a great deal. Whatever else the Inquisition may have been guilty of, it did on the whole abide by its own laws. How did Pierre Maury know that she had let slip about Jean Maury that he stood in as Perfect in Prades? Because, I suspect, she owned up to it after the arrest of Guillaume Bélibaste.

The two Maury brothers spun the Inquisitor a well-rehearsed line, and in the absence of a corroborative testimony, which only Blanche Marty could have provided, Fournier was not prepared to send the younger Maury to the stake. By 7 July 1324 Guillemette Maury and her family were still at large, because on that day Raymonde Belot-Lizier referred to her as 'fugitive' while giving evidence in Pamiers.

Subsequently Pierre Maury sold his own sheep at Morella and grossed 700 Barcelona shillings. After helping his brother Jean to take his flock to Castelldans (from Sant Mateu presumably), he rejoined Mersende at Alcañiz and lent her a princely 500 shillings. Even the restless Pierre Maury can never have been as frantically active as he now had to be to save his family from the fall-out from the Bélibaste arrest. From Alcañiz he went down to Valderrobres to collect Blanche and Raymonde, but was directed towards Cretas where they had since gone. Were they hoping to return to Horta, since they knew the place well from having been there years earlier? Pierre Maury found them in Cretas, and told them to make the best of their chances, because he would probably go to Mallorca.

Since the party with Guillaume Bélibaste had left for the Pallars not much more than a fortnight had passed, but in that period the world of the Catalonian Cathar community had been turned inside out. It had seemed so solid only recently with the promise of new recruits and funds, and now it lay in ruins.

When shortly afterwards Guillaume Maurs drove his flock through Beceite on his way north to the Riucaut, he asked after Mersende and Jeanne. The neighbours told him that a cousin of theirs (Pierre Maury) had come and taken them away to Sant Mateu or Morella. What Maurs made of this is not recorded, but it must have struck him as odd, since he was almost certainly aware of the planned trip to Tírvia.

Pierre Maury returned to Sant Mateu, and from there went on to Peñíscola (Pl. 32). Its mighty Templar fortress would one day shelter the antipope Pedro de Luna; many centuries later the same dramatic silhouette served as the backdrop set for the Hollywood epic *El Cid*. Pierre Maury embarked for Mallorca, where he stayed for three weeks before deciding that he did not like it. Towards the end of April 1321, therefore, he touched base again at Tortosa, and he stayed here during the winters of 1321–2 and 1322–3 at Guillaume and Pierre Espa's. It was an area he knew well from earlier transhumances.

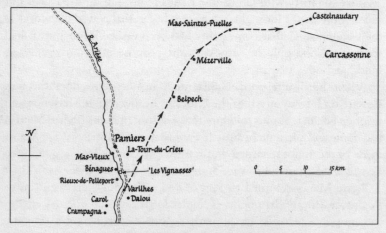

The route of Béatrice's flight from Fournier

A week or so before the Catalonian Cathars set out on their ill-fated journey for Tírvia, Béatrice de Planisolles and other penitents were gathered at the convent of the Dominicans in Pamiers. The time was before 9 a.m. on Sunday 8 March 1321. From here they were taken in a solemn procession to the cemetery of Saint-Jean-Martyr, there to be formally sentenced for heresy. They would have passed through the 'carriera dels Frays Menors' (the street of the Minorites), which is now called the rue Jacques Fournier, and then, beyond Notre-Dame-du-Camp, they would have turned right up past the Franciscans' convent and across the canal through the Porta dels Layros (gate of the thieves) towards the mount of the cemetery. Their itinerary can be retraced corner-by-corner. Later that day Béatrice and Barthélemy were both interned in Allemans. In its dungeons some prisoners were manacled hand and foot, and threatened with torture (FR, f.307v).

And yet in the early summer of 1320 Béatrice's life in Varilhes had entered a mellow phase. Her children were grown up, and she was now a grandmother several times over, with at least two boys among them. She must have derived pleasure from the fact that her daughters lived in the vicinity, since by her own account mother and daughters were close; and her youngest, Philippa, had become engaged to be married in 1320. Not that the daughters were always guided by their mother, as when Condors resisted Béatrice's suggestion that she should use the medicinal herb ive to cure her son's epilepsy. It is not easy to imagine what these young women made of a mother who in their lifetime had been twice married, and had lengthy sexual relationships with at least three other men who included the thug Pathau and two priests.

It is an opaque fact that Béatrice only once, and then not by name, mentions her sons by de Roquefort. They were after all her first-born. Had they died young, or had they severed their links with their mother and her family because of their Catharist leanings? By 1320 they would have been in their late twenties. It is not impossible that the de Roquefort family became the boys' guardians, and Béatrice's reference to settling up with her husband's 'heirs' (see above, page 53) may point in that direction.

For her children her love for Barthélemy may have been the most difficult to accept, as he was a priest, her junior by many years, and formerly her younger daughters' teacher. In the summer of 1320 Barthélemy lived at Mézerville, some eighteen miles north-east of Varilhes. After a spell in Carcassonne, he was back in the Pamiers plain, ready to resume, if it had ever stopped, his relationship with Béatrice. That there may have been some cooling off between them is suggested by her use of tense when describing her feelings for him. When Barthélemy asked her on 1 July 1320 whether she felt herself guilty of heresy, the Register records:

and she replied 'no', and that he ought to know that well, because if she had committed any offence of that nature she would have revealed it to him whom she had loved (*adamaverat*) very much. (FR, f.43v)

The use of the pluperfect here may imply that she no longer did so in the summer of 1320, although it may also just mark antecedence to the time of her actual testimony. But Barthélemy was not far away, and when Béatrice needed him, he came to her rescue.

It was on Thursday 19 June 1320 that at Pamiers one Guillaume Roussel of Dalou testified against Béatrice by quoting her views of ten years earlier on the absurdity of the belief that Christ could allow himself to be eaten by priests. He then provided a list of Béatrice's close friends who might be thought to know her secrets. These included Grazide, widow of Bernard Pujol from Dalou, Bernarde, wife of den Garsiot from Varilhes, Mabille, wife of Raymond Gouzy from l'Herm, Sybille, servant of Michel Dupont from Foix, Esperte, wife of Arnaud from Varilhes, and others. I am giving their names here principally to consolidate our sense of the former châtelaine as somebody with a circle of intimates, both male and female. The rector of Dalou's attempt to portray her to Barthélemy as a sexual pariah is belied by the fact that she was a popular woman friend.

Fournier almost certainly turned his fire on her now because he was preparing to move against the Clergues, and was using the former châtelaine to that end. The year before, a 'sorceress' had been arrested. She had spent one evening in Béatrice's house, and this was not disputed. That it should take almost a whole year for this affair to be wheeled out on the charge sheet now might provide a clue to how it fits into the wider frame. When it came to the Clergues, even Fournier needed to guard against the power of their friends in Carcassonne, the more so since the loyalty of Gaillard de Pomiès, Jean de Beaune's stand-in and mandatory presence at all major hearings, was to Carcassonne in the first instance.

I would submit that at some point in 1319–20 Fournier uncovered, or caught a tantalizing glimpse of, the scale of the Clergues' double-dealing. The most likely source must be Arnaud Sicre reporting back intelligence gathered from Pierre Maury, and other Maurys such as Pierre's aunt Mersende, and perhaps Guillaume Maurs. Clergue's belated enthusiasm for persecuting the faithful in the wake of Fournier's arrival in Pamiers generated immense loathing of him. In Montaillou itself the people were defenceless against the Clergues' reprisals, but abroad they were not so constrained. They consequently felt free to speak openly among themselves about them, unaware of the fact that the new Bishop's eyes and ears were literally present. It is not impossible that Arnaud Sicre remembered overheard conversations from his own childhood. Anyone with their ear close to the ground in the Sabartès in the 1290s would have had some idea about the Clergues' involvement, and particularly the son of Sybille Baille. Now that there was a Bishop in Pamiers who was not in the Clergues' pocket, the truth could out at last.

In little more than a week Béatrice realized that she had been reported and would probably be summoned. Pons Bole, a notary from Varilhes and a friend of the family, tipped her off. She reacted by sending a distress message to Barthélemy in Mézerville, who agreed that they should meet on Tuesday 1 July 1320, which was exactly a week after the Nativity of St John the Baptist.

Barthélemy arrived in Pamiers and dispatched a boy to Béatrice in Varilhes. According to Béatrice, what happened next was that Barthélemy met her near Varilhes, and 'we spoke'. He advised her to obey Fournier's summons, because the Bishop would not harm her if she was truly innocent. Then he left. This, however, is a sanitized version of what really took place, which seems to be as follows.

On his way from Pamiers to Varilhes Barthélemy's errand-boy met Béatrice's servant Alazais in Rieux-de-Pelleport, perhaps by prearrangement. Moreover, Béatrice's daughters may have lived in this locality. He instructed Alazais to return to her mistress in nearby Varilhes and to bring her to join Barthélemy at the ancient monastery of Mas-Vieux, which stood about half a mile directly to the south of Pamiers. Its romanesque church survives to this day in a peninsular spot formed by a west-curving loop of the Ariège. It is now called Cailloup and is currently undergoing extensive restoration. The Ariège divides here briefly into two, and flows close to the church.

While the wide and fertile valley must have invited habitation since the beginning of time, there is no mistaking the ease with which the flooding Ariège can wreak havoc here. It seems to be this which early on persuaded the monks to move across the river to the Mas-Saint-Antonin (Claeys 1981, 48), and by 1320 the Mas-Vieux seems to have been little more than a monastic outpost with a skeleton garrison. Indeed, if Barthélemy's deposition is taken literally, there may have been no more than a single resident monk who ran a modest hostelry.

Accompanied by her servant, Béatrice covered the five-mile distance from Varilhes to Mas-Vieux in time to have lunch with Barthélemy 'in the house of the monk of the church' (FR, f.46r). The monk may have been a friend of Barthélemy's, hence his choice of that particular venue. After lunch the threesome walked back together towards Varilhes on the western side of the river, which at the time was known as the 'upper road'. They passed the hamlet of Bénagues, and shortly afterwards Barthélemy and Béatrice entered a vineyard close to the road and had sex among the vines. Alazaïs waited in the road until they had finished. 'She had long known that I loved Béatrice very much,' Barthélemy explained later.

Such is the longevity of names in the Ariège that the place where this act of outdoor medieval intercourse happened can be fairly closely located 680 years later, since there is to this day an area directly south of Bénagues called 'Les Vignasses'. Vines grew here in living memory, although today the area consists of flat meadowlands. Were the two of them overcome by passion, or does this flush of enthusiasm suggest that they had been separated for a while?

They resumed their walk towards Rieux-de-Pelleport, and only now, it seems, did Béatrice tell her lover why she had called on him for help. Before they parted, Barthélemy gave her fifteen shillings and two to Alazaïs. It was not until Monday 28 July that he saw her again in Belpech.

On Wednesday 23 July 1320 the dreaded summons from the Inquisition was delivered by the rector of Varilhes; Béatrice was to appear before Fournier in Pamiers on Saturday 26 July.

When she appeared in the Inquisitor's Chamber that day she was intimidated by the presence in the chamber of a large archiepiscopal retinue, which she interpreted as a sign that she might be arrested there and then. She was accompanied by the Archdeacon of Mallorca and Pierre, the rector of Pelleport, who both interceded for her with Fournier.

Fournier did not yet question her under oath, but he received her harshly. He pressed her about her remark concerning the body of Christ and Margail. She denied ever saying it. He then asked whether in her house in Dalou she had ever welcomed and worshipped the Perfects Pierre, Jacques and Guillaume Authié, or other heretics, presumably thinking of Prades Tavernier, Arnaud Marty, Pons Sicre, and Philippe d'Aylarac. She owned up to seeing Pierre Authié when he acted as

solicitor in a sale by her husband, but she pointed out that at that stage
he was not yet reputed to be a heretic, and that she had not seen him
since. She admitted that she once let the 'sorceress' into her house.
Fournier warned her that he thought that she was lying, and he
pointedly reminded her of the fact that her father, Philippe, was a
former heretic who had been sentenced to the wearing of the crosses.
He rejected mitigatory intercessions on Béatrice's behalf by her two
friendly witnesses, stating that until she told the truth he would not
listen to anything in her favour. He then commanded her to reappear
before him the following Tuesday to testify under oath.

When later that day Béatrice returned home from Pamiers, her
daughters Condors, Esclarmonde, Ava and Philippa joined her and
wept loudly about her fate. They had been briefed by the rector of
Pelleport, who was probably their parish priest. He had told her daughters that Fournier was a nasty man who had flatly rejected his intercessions on their mother's behalf. He reported to them that he had told
Fournier that his persecutions for heresy were ruining the people of
the County of Foix, and that his actions deeply displeased the Countess
of Foix. Fournier dismissed this by noting that the Countess did not
like him, but that nothing would stop him doing his duty.

This information induced further desolation among Béatrice and her
daughters. What frightened Béatrice above all was the arrest again
of Lorda Bayard and her daughter (either Mathende or Ricarde),
notwithstanding the long arm of her husband's family. Her re-arrest
signalled that nobody was beyond Fournier's reach.

That same night Pons Bole, the Varilhes notary, advised Béatrice to
escape over the passes to put herself beyond Fournier's persecutions.
But Béatrice decided instead to flee to Limoux and there go into hiding
at her sister Gentille's. What she did not reveal was that a *filière* operated
from Limoux to Perpignan and hence into Catalonia (FR, f.159r). She
later claimed that no one except Barthélemy was aware of her decision
to give Fournier the slip. Unlike her lover she was eager not to implicate
anyone in her flight, not her daughters, nor the Pelleport rector, nor
the notary Pons Bole. She was well aware of the consequences of aiding
and abetting refugees from the Inquisition.

The next day, Sunday 27 July 1320, Béatrice prepared for her flight.
In addition to a whole array of clothes, she packed a number of items

that were later inventoried by the officers of the Inquisition. Then, early on the Monday, she told her daughter Condors that she was getting ready to go to Pamiers. After this she made straight for Belpech, some fifteen miles north-east of Varilhes and four miles south-west of Mézerville, where Barthélemy worked. She found lodgings there in a house near the castle, perhaps not far up the hill from where the post office now stands.

Next she sent a messenger to Mézerville. He was to tell Barthélemy that a friend of his wanted him to come and meet her at Belpech. Barthélemy asked the boy to describe this friend and realized that it was Béatrice. He at once set off for Belpech, where he found her. He arranged for her to leave her lodgings and took her to the home of Guillaume Mole, a parchment-maker of Belpech who may have been a friend of the book-owning Barthélemy. Here they could confer apart without witnesses.

He noticed the size of her luggage, and asked where she was heading. She explained that she was fleeing from Fournier, and then treated him to an account of her preliminary interrogation and the subsequent conference with her daughters and the Varilhes notary. When Barthélemy urged her nevertheless to present herself at Pamiers the following day, she protested that she would not do so under any circumstances. She tearfully implored him to join her on the way to Limoux. He agreed to help, but claimed that he could not get away from Mézerville until after the Invention of St Stephen (Sunday 3 August 1320), because it was the feast of the local altar at Mézerville. In the meantime, he suggested, he would accompany her to Mas-Saintes-Puelles, which was off the beaten track and safe from Fournier's searchers. Her hope was, she explained, that if the Inquisition could not find her they would eventually lose interest in her.

Béatrice and Barthélemy lunched together. When he realized that there was no stopping her, he offered her the sum of eight shillings for the journey. He also promised to raise additional money towards their journey to Limoux by pawning or selling a book, or by some other means. In Belpech that night they shared a 'single' bed and for this reason, according to Barthélemy, had sex.

The following day was Tuesday 29 July. Béatrice was scheduled to appear before Fournier on this day. Instead she was getting ready to flee to Mas-Saintes-Puelles. She and Barthélemy failed to find a mule or packhorse, but their host advised them that they would be sure to get one in Mas-Saintes-Puelles. Barthélemy therefore enlisted the services of a local man to carry Béatrice's luggage as far as Mas-Saintes-Puelles, and he paid him one shilling for his trouble. With another shilling he settled their bills in Belpech.

Half-way towards Mas-Saintes-Puelles, presumably at the junction where Barthélemy needed to turn off left to Mézerville, Béatrice started to cry again and entreated Barthélemy to accompany her all the way to Limoux. This he could not do, but he agreed to escort her to Mas-Saintes-Puelles.

Before he could return to his parish, he and she were both arrested by Fournier's henchmen. It had not taken them long to catch up with them after her failure to attend the Bishop's summons. The Inquisition's agents were well organized, swift, and on horseback, while the châtelaine and her young priest-lover were slow and, probably, conspicuous. Barthélemy was not called on to testify until Thursday 11 September, whereas Béatrice appeared briefly before Fournier on Lammastide, Friday 1 August. Fournier was anxious to press on with interviewing her, because he was after bigger prey that only she could deliver to him.

Her next appearance before him and Gaillard de Pomiès was on Thursday 7 August, and was much more substantial. It was towards the end of this testimony that she first implicated Pierre Clergue by relating his attempted seduction of her and his casuistic Cathar arguments to justify the deed. At this point her testimony stopped for the day. Did Fournier need time to assess the implications of this revelation?

The day after, on Friday 8 August, she seamlessly picked up the thread with Pierre Clergue. She now deeply implicated him in the spreading of heresy by relating, in this order, his views on incest, their sex during Holy Night, his scurrilous remarks about confession and the Pope, and his spiritual championing of the Good Men. She reported his Manichean doctrine of dualistic creation, his sharing the Cathars' belief in a nine-fold metempsychosis, and his denial of Christ's incarnation through the virgin birth.

In the course of her lengthy deposition on this day Béatrice shed all inhibitions about Clergue. We have already encountered a number of his views as reported by her. Here is what she now alleged Clergue said about confession:

He [Pierre Clergue] added that I must not confess to another priest the sin [of sex] that I was committing with him, because it was enough to confess to God. He knew our sin and could absolve it, which no man could do. And to induce me to believe that neither the supreme pontiff nor any bishop or priest who serve under him had the power to remit sins, Pierre Clergue alleged that St Peter was not Pope while he lived in this life, but only after his death; and that his bones were thrown into a pit where they stayed for many years. And when his bones were found, they were exalted and set on a throne in which the Roman pontiffs also sit. And because the bones of St Peter did not have the power of the remission of sins when they were enthroned and elevated to papal dignity, therefore neither Peter who thus became Pope, nor the Roman pontiffs who become Pope in that chair, can remit sins. The only ones who can do so are the good Christians who suffer persecution and death the way it was suffered by St Lawrence, St Stephen, and St Bartholomew. But the bishops and priests, who are the retainers of the Roman church and heretics and persecutors of the good Christians, do not have the power of absolution. God stripped them of this faculty and reserved it for Himself, and then handed it over to the good Christians foreknowing and prophesying their persecution . . . [Pierre Clergue] also told me that God created only the spirits and that which can be neither corrupted nor destroyed, because the works of God remain for ever, but all visible and tangible matter, namely the sky and the earth and everything that lives in them, with the sole exception of the spirits, were created by the devil, the ruler of the world; and because they are his creation all of them were corruptible because he could not create a firm and constant artefact. (FR, f.39v)

This was classic Cathar doctrine, and the man who listened to this evidence, a future Pope no less, can have harboured little doubt about the gravity of Pierre Clergue's offence. It does not seem to have occurred to Fournier that the châtelaine might be making any of this up to wreak revenge on her former lover. She appears to have been panic-stricken, and by now she was desperate to reveal everything, however scandalous or shocking it might be.

The following day, on Saturday 9 August, she started her testimony by recalling how Clergue visited her in the Pamiers plain after her marriage to Othon. Then she moved on to more general reminiscences of Montaillou at the height of the Cathar ferment there.

On Tuesday 12 August she testified again, and again the interrogation commenced with material relating to the Clergues, before becoming a question-and-answer session of a broader theological nature. These formed the substance also of her next appearance the day after, although she chose to apportion guilt to Clergue rather than to other heretics such as Raymond Roussel.

After 13 August she was given a respite until Friday 22 August, when she was summoned to reappear before Fournier and Gaillard de Pomiès. This time she was invited to enlarge on details of her sex life with the rector, and it was now that she revealed that he had used some form of contraception.

It is tempting to link this new track to the evidence provided on Tuesday 19 August by Grazide Lizier. She had arrived at Pamiers in the company of the now lame Alazais Azéma, and had testified against Pierre Clergue with whom she had been having sexual relations for six or seven years, since he had taken her virginity when she was fourteen. Did the young woman say more than is extant in the Register (which is incomplete)? Did she hint that Clergue had used contraception, which was itself sinful, and did Fournier want to elicit corroboration from the former châtelaine? Or was it because Clergue had consistently swayed her scruples about their affair with humbug about the illegitimacy of marriage and the pleasure principle?

The evidence against the rector was mounting, and Fournier issued a peremptory summons against him shortly after Béatrice's initial statements, probably on 8 or 9 August. Pierre Clergue must have been arrested by 12 or 13 August, because on 15 August his arrest was known in Montaillou. Bernard Clergue's reference on 2 November 1321 to his recently deceased brother's *fifteen* months in prison confirms a date in early August 1320 for his arrest.

Although Pierre Clergue was under guard now, this seems to have taken the form of a mild house-arrest, probably at the Mas-Saint-Antonin. It did not prevent him from wandering down into Pamiers and bearding witnesses, particularly if, like Béatrice perhaps, they were on remand in the loft of the bishopric.

Up to Friday 22 August Béatrice had not breathed a word about Barthélemy. She had tried not to implicate him, still hoping perhaps to be able to join her younger lover in due course. But after testifying on the Friday, she seems to have experienced a nervous collapse. By the time she appeared on Monday 25 August she was bedridden, and the Inquisition records that she was *very* likely to die. Fournier therefore admonished her to tell the truth on her soul. She responded by exonerating Pierre Clergue from the charges of Manicheism and from his denial of the virgin birth, and instead attributed those statements to Raymond Roussel, who was probably dead by now and beyond retribution; *and* he could no longer contradict her.

Why did she change her story, when the first version was probably true, and was bound to be corroborated by Barthélemy, in whom she had confided, and by others from Montaillou? It has been suggested that she may have been severely leant upon or even tortured, because her evidence so dramatically implicated in heresy a prominent collaborator of the Inquisition as Clergue had latterly become (Duvernoy 1978, 289n.59). But we know that torture was resorted to only once by Fournier during these proceedings, and it was not with regard to any of the characters from this story.* Also, at this stage Béatrice was in remand custody in the loft at the Archbishop's palace in Pamiers rather than in Allemans, which was the only place where she could have been tortured.

Moreover, Fournier refrained from torture in the case of the defiant Raymonde Guilhou, who had been married to Arnaud Vital of Montaillou. She also at first implicated the Clergues, but then retracted her

---

* In the one case where it was applied, the interrogation of the leper Guillaume Agasse from Pamiers, reference is made to it in a matter-of-fact manner in the minutes of the proceedings. Whatever was done to the unfortunate Agasse, the result was a string of rambling 'admissions' to a lepers' conspiracy to murder non-leprous Christians throughout the Toulousain. Agasse himself owned up to poisoning the Ariège and various wells of Pamiers. It is fairly evident that Fournier's clerks would not have tried to hide the use of torture, which had been legally enshrined in the Inquisition's juridical procedures since Pope Innocent IV's bull *Ad extirpanda* of 1252. But it is unimaginable that a man of Fournier's redoubtable intelligence should have believed a word of the frenzied testimony wrenched from Agasse. He wanted the truth, and he knew that a victim of torture would say whatever he wanted to hear.

deposition in favour of a manifest tissue of lies, after being visited by the Clergues during a temporary return home. Repeatedly, insistently, and over several sessions, Fournier urged her to revert to her original and circumstantially consolidated version, but she preferred to stay with her lie. It is a tribute to the Bishop that he exercised restraint and rejected her challenge to do his worst and burn her.

We may be reasonably confident that the châtelaine's illness, from which she clearly recovered well, was owing to natural causes that cannot now be determined. Why then did she suddenly retract? One obvious hypothesis must be that Pierre Clergue approached her in Pamiers over the weekend of 24 August 1320, just as eight months later, on 4 April 1321, he tried to tackle Alamande Guilabert from outside the Archbishop's loft. The ruined ramparts of Pamiers still closely skirt the top of the bishopric, and Clergue could easily have talked to her from the rampart walk. He may even have secured, through bribes, a full scale encounter with Béatrice inside the prison.

If so, was this first meeting between them since Varilhes in 1308 unexpectedly affectionate, and would that account for her implicating Amilhat at the same time as she attributed all Pierre Clergue's Cathar proselytizing statements to Raymond Roussel? But if the maturer Clergue momentarily may have seemed Hyperion to Barthélemy's satyr, it is also the case that sooner or later she would inevitably be made to confront her affair with Barthélemy, since they were arrested together.

Curiously, in view of his relentless pressing of Raymonde Guilhou, Fournier made no attempt to dissuade Béatrice from her partial retraction. All he needed was evidence of rampant sexual promiscuity, perhaps because the intelligence he had from Catalonia and elsewhere pointed to this as the most promising avenue.

20. The Last Trials of Montaillou

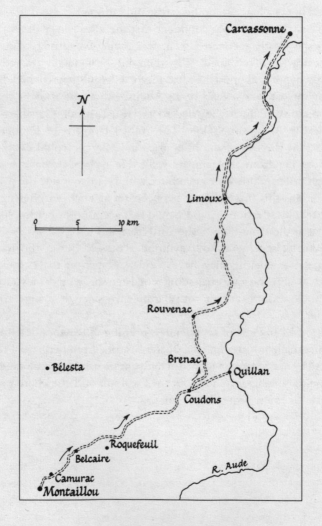

Clergue's and Benet's trek to Carcassonne

Fournier now turned on the men and women of Montaillou, and summonses were issued even as Béatrice was testifying. A number of women were ordered to attend Pamiers at short notice, and four among them, Grazide Lizier, Alazais Azéma, Alazais Faure and Esclarmonde Clergue-Fort, had been the rector's lovers. Also summoned were Gauzia Clergue (B), Alazais Faure's sister Guillemette Cléments, Fabrisse Rives, Guillemette Clergue (B), Raymonde den Arsen and Brune Pourcel, as well as Guillaume Authié (B) and Arnaud Faure.

A group from Montaillou including most, if not all, of the above set out together, but they did not arrive at the same time. Alazais Azéma 'could not walk well nor keep up with the others', presumably because she was arthritic, and the young Grazide Lizier lagged behind with her (FR, f.57v).

Béatrice had finished her fifth day (out of nine) of testifying when Gauzia Clergue (B), who was a first cousin of the rector, was detained in Allemans on Assumption Day, where she would remain until Christmas 1320. She had been summoned because on 9 August Béatrice had repeated her conversation of twenty years earlier with Pierre Maury's mother about the consolation of Guillemette Faure-Bar.

During her initial interview(s) in 1320 Gauzia gave little away, apart from mentioning that she had listened to heretical talk by Pierre Maury's aunt Mersende. Not that she had ever been sexually involved with the rector, but her daughter had been consoled, and she had herself been a loyal Cathar. That Gauzia did not incur a longer sentence for her exchange with Alazais Maury was perhaps because the only witness, apart from Béatrice, was the now dead Alazais. This suggests that the Inquisition's legal safeguards were being observed by Fournier, just as they had been by d'Ablis, that when there was no credible corroboration there could be no conviction. But there may be another reason, and one with far-reaching repercussions, and that was the emergence as a power in Montaillou of Pierre Azéma, the Catholic loyalist and relative of Jacques Fournier.

Gauzia later maintained that it was Pierre Azéma who in the autumn of 1320 dissuaded her from confessing to the consolation of her daughter, and Azéma apparently berated her for saying as much as she did about Pierre Maury's aunt's proselytizing. Because of that she would have to stay behind instead of joining him on the way home to

Montaillou, Azéma reputedly said. At the time Gauzia and Pierre
Azéma were both staying in the house of one Bernard Montanié, which
may have been an inn in Pamiers. Pierre Azéma claimed that he had
already secured permission from the Bishop to take Gauzia home with
him. He then told her that he could do her a lot of good, because 'as
long as this Lord Bishop lives I shall be of his house and will be able to
do many good things' (FR, f.295v). Not the least of his plans was to
marry his daughter to one of Gauzia's sons, but that, he indicated,
would be a viable proposition only so long as she did not lose everything
through heresy.

Pierre Azéma played for high stakes by trying to destroy the Clergues
through using Fournier. He must have fed the Bishop enough intelligence about the Clergues, the châtelaine, and others for his credit to
be good in Pamiers, but not to the point where it allowed him to distort
judicial procedure by swaying witnesses. When Azéma first made his
approach to the Bishop is not known, but like Arnaud Sicre he may
have done so after the initial proclamations of Pierre Maury and others
in the summer of 1318.

If so, he found himself now on the same zealous anti-Cathar side as
the Clergues. But unlike them this novice at playing the Inquisition
lacked the necessary funds to buy serious influence; and Fournier
professed to detest nepotism. As the case against the Clergues unfolded
from the middle of August 1320 to the summer and autumn of 1321,
Pierre Azéma's attempts to frame the already guilty became an increasing
liability and threatened the integrity of Fournier's entire investigation,
which after all required the approval of the Carcassonne Inquisitor Jean
de Beaune. Moreover, details of the proceedings at Pamiers were being
constantly leaked to the Clergues, and the source of these indiscretions
must have been their allies in the Carcassonne Inquisition.

From August 1320 until his own arrest by Carcassonne in July
1321 Pierre Azéma interfered with a number of witnesses, safe in the
knowledge, or so he hoped, that they would not dare reveal his part in
the business to his relative, the feared Bishop.

Four days after Gauzia, on Tuesday 19 August 1320, Grazide Lizier
testified. Nothing in Béatrice's evidence implicated her, because Grazide and Pierre Clergue became involved many years after the châtelaine's departure. Grazide's presence in Pamiers was very probably

owing to information received from Pierre Azéma, and Béatrice's wholly unrelated, and still ongoing, evidence at this point was merely a convenient pretext for summoning the witnesses from Montaillou without betraying the source.

Grazide Lizier's very first sentence, which was an answer to a question, at once implicated Pierre Clergue by telling how he seduced her as a virgin. Her subsequent remarks about Clergue's views on sex chimed remarkably with the châtelaine's. Grazide's forthright honesty saved her from severer punishment, and she walked free from prison, albeit with the crosses, on 4 July 1322. There is some tenuous evidence to suggest that she at least managed to rebuild her life by marrying a Guillaume Bonclergue from Montaillou, because on 16 January 1329, when her crosses were lifted, she was referred to as *uxor Guillelmi de Bene Clerici de Montealionis* (D 27, f.147v).

Her ingénue's candour about Pierre Clergue is the more remarkable because on the journey to Pamiers she was urged by that other lover of the priest, Alazais Azéma, not to implicate the rector in the course of her deposition. Alazais herself first testified on 20 August, and again on 23 August. She made no mention of Pierre Clergue, until towards the close of the second day's session Fournier asked her directly whether there had been a rumour in Montaillou about 'incest' between Clergue and Béatrice (FR, f.58v). She replied evasively that the châtelaine and Pathau Clergue, who was dead by 26 October 1320, were thought to be too close, and then refused to say anything more on the subject (FR, f.51r). But on 17 November she implicated Bernard Clergue, and on 4 January 1321 she came clean on Mengarde Clergue and also confessed that the rector had received a 'book called a calendar' from Guillaume Authié. Beyond that she did not implicate Clergue. Did she stay loyal because she saw him as the one remaining hope of the Cathar cause, or was it because she was impervious to her brother-in-law's pressures and blandishments?

Like Grazide, Alazais Faure confessed to an affair with Pierre Clergue, while others, like her husband Arnaud and her brother-in-law Guillaume Authié (B) of Montaillou, told it the way it had been at Montaillou while always carefully covering their own tracks. Although this batch of depositions has not survived, they may have intervened between Alazais Azéma's of 23 August and the next extant one, Fabrisse

Rives's of 26 September. They were obviously not available to the copyist of MS 4030 (the Fournier Register), nor was he aware of them, because the foliotation of MS 4030 does not show any gaps here.

These statements may additionally have included those of Guillemette Cléments and Esclarmonde Clergue-Fort, who were summoned to appear not long afterwards, specifically to testify against the rector. Somebody had told Fournier that Esclarmonde had been involved with her brother-in-law, which would mean that he and she both stood accused of incest. Was it Alazais Faure who told Fournier in the first place, and was it this which caused the hostility between the two women when they met back in Montaillou afterwards? If it was not, Alazais certainly made sure that Fournier had it confirmed from her when he interviewed her again, about a different matter this time, in April of the following year.

There was clearly method in Fournier's proceedings. After dealing with Clergue's lovers, Béatrice, Grazide, the two Alazaises, and probably Esclarmonde, and having thereby discredited the rector, he was ready to confront his full-blown heretical activities. We do not know what Arnaud Faure and Guillaume Authié (B) from Montaillou said about Pierre Clergue other than that their depositions accused the rector of being Cathar. So did three statements from the same period which *have* survived in MS 4030, those of Fabrisse Rives (26 September 1320) and of two Axians, Raymond Vaissière (26 October) and Guillaume Mathieu (31 December). Both men had given evidence to Geoffroy d'Ablis a decade earlier, and neither had then dared breathe a word against the Clergues.

Fabrisse Rives-Clergue was summoned particularly because she was reported as knowing 'many things' about Pierre Clergue. Her daughter Grazide *may* have been the source of this information, but once again the more likely finger points at Pierre Azéma. Fabrisse's evidence was devastating, particularly when she put the Perfect Guillaume Authié right into the rector's study. Equally damning was Raymond Vaissière's, because he confirmed Fabrisse's allegation that the rector and Guillaume Authié were friends and Cathar colleagues. Moreover, while adding more names from Ax to the list of Clergue's sexual conquests, he shrewdly attributed the clan's power to its exploitation of people's fear of the Inquisition.

Finally, on Wednesday 31 December 1320, Guillaume Mathieu provided further damning evidence against both Pierre and Bernard Clergue, pointing out that Pons Rives himself told him after the mass arrest in 1308 that the Clergue house was Cathar. Guillaume Mathieu was a turncoat who was now openly working for Fournier. Why he hated the Clergues is not clear, but years earlier he had assisted Guillaume Maurs in plotting against the rector's life. For Mathieu it was perfectly fitting that he and his fellow agent Arnaud Sicre should together arrest · his former comrade Guillaume Maurs in Puigcerdà in the autumn of 1321. It is little wonder that Azéma, Vaissière, and Mathieu were called his mortal enemies by Bernard Clergue, along with Pierre de Gaillac whose role in this, as in everything that he touched, was murky.

A formidable momentum was building up against the Clergues, and now Bernard Clergue and his brother, with whom he managed to communicate in spite of his sequestration, decided to strike back, unaware as yet, it seems, of the full extent to which Pierre Azéma was involved. This proves that Fournier's intelligence network was not only good but, unlike the *in camera* depositions, impenetrable even to the Clergues' various moles.

The Clergues' strategy was a high-risk and vengeful exercise in discrediting their opponents, and it could damagingly backfire. The plan was to expose the Guilabert consolation in Carcassonne by suborning Bernard Benet through bribes and intimidation. On that May night of 1308 he had after all accompanied Guillaume Belot in fetching Prades Tavernier, and as a child at the time would get off lightly, particularly if Bernard Clergue used his clout at Carcassonne.

It was an obvious, if desperate, plan, since several of the rector's accusers had been present. But there was a double snag. Thirteen years earlier a little girl, Esclarmonde Fort, had inadvertently stepped into the consolation of Guillaume Guilabert while looking for her mother. Now she was Madame Raymond Clergue, the rector's and Bernard's sister-in-law. She had been a child at the time and therefore enjoyed some immunity from prosecution, but there was her father's position to consider. If it should emerge that Guillaume Fort was present, it would be clear that in 1316 he had lied to the then Inquisitor.

★

It was around Ash Wednesday (4 March 1321) when Bernard Clergue called in to see Bernard Benet, who seems to have been living in the parental home opposite the Clergues. He was in his early twenties and was wearing the yellow crosses. Clergue invited him for a stroll beyond the Testanière house, which always meant important business. Here Clergue instructed Bernard to go to Carcassonne about the Guilabert consolation. He would underwrite the return journey and Bernard Benet was to testify to seeing at the consolation Guillaume Authié (B) of Montaillou, Arnaud Faure, Alazais Faure, and Guillemette Cléments-Guilabert. This left out the three Forts, as well as Alamande Guilabert and the by now dead Guillaume Belot. Clergue also specifically reminded Bernard Benet to leave out Jean Guilabert. Part of his reward, Bernard Clergue suggested, might be the removal of the crosses. Just to make sure, and to attend to other business, Bernard Clergue, his wife, and his nephew Pons Gary from Laroque d'Olmes would also head for Carcassonne that same day. Bernard Benet had little choice but to accept, and 12 March was set as the departure date for Carcassonne.

It is worth pausing briefly over the timing of this visit to Bernard Benet, since it very nearly coincides with Béatrice de Planisolles's next appearance before Fournier on Thursday 5 March 1321. On this occasion the Bishop was joined by the Carcassonne Inquisitor Jean de Beaune himself in the grand chamber of the archiepiscopal palace in Pamiers, and Béatrice was assigned Sunday 8 March 1321 for sentence in the cemetery of Saint-Jean. Present also were Brother Gaillard de Pomiès, who was usually de Beaune's substitute, and various other monks, priests, and the two notaries Guillaume Peyre-Barthe (for the Bishop) and Barthélemy Adalbert (for the Inquisition).

The presence in Pamiers on 5 March of both Jean de Beaune and his deputy may suggest that Fournier had alerted his superior to the highly charged information that was accumulating against the Clergues. Perhaps he wanted de Beaune to see the main prosecution witness, if only to establish his own good faith through her manifest guilelessness. Conversely, de Beaune may have insisted on seeing her for himself, thereby only doing what Fournier had himself done earlier when he feared that Tron was being framed in Carcassonne (see above, page 268).

I believe that there was a leak to the Clergues around Ash Wednesday; and if so, it would have been to the rector who may well have met Jean de Beaune at the Mas-Saint-Antonin or at the Dominican convent in Pamiers. It is hard to believe that there should not be a causal connection between these events in Pamiers and the Clergues' almost simultaneous decision over in Montaillou to take the fight to their enemies.

In the time which intervened between Ash Wednesday and 12 March 1321 Raymond Clergue called on Martin Guilabert from Montaillou, a relative of the Guilaberts of the consolation whose teenage wife Sybille was the baby sister and heir of Guillaume Guilabert; the wives of Raymond Clergue and Martin Guilabert were therefore cousins. Clergue told him that his brother was forcing Bernard Benet to testify to the consolation: could Martin give Bernard Benet some lambs or something else to stop him from going through with his testimony? Martin refused, saying that he felt himself wholly untainted, but that he would appear implicated if he tried to buy off Bernard Benet.

Raymond then asked Martin to talk to Arnaud Faure. Martin did so, but Arnaud Faure, who felt compromised, also refused to try to bribe his way out of the inevitable. Guillaume Authié (B), who was next briefed by Martin Guilabert passing on Raymond Clergue's remarks, similarly declined to pay Bernard Benet the thirty shillings that Guillaume Fort recommended they pay him to allow him to disappear. Instead Guillaume Authié (B)'s wife went to see Bernard and asked, 'Why do you want to divorce me?' because his revelations would ruin her marriage by landing her husband in prison.

But the Faures and Authié (B)s knew that the Guilabert consolation could no longer be kept a secret if the Clergues had decided to betray it. It was pointless to oppose it now. The most they could do was to pretend to take a principled stance against bribing their way out of it. They must have wondered whether Raymond Clergue was defying his brother by getting them to buy off Bernard Benet, because of his wife and father-in-law, or whether this was part of a concerted Clergue strategy. Certainly Raymond Clergue's treatment of Vuissane suggests that the Clergues' solidarity held fast (see below, pages 375–6), and that they may have been cynically trying to get their intended victims to pay Bernard Benet for their own demise, thus saving themselves the expense.

On Thursday 12 March, the morning of the departure for

Carcassonne, Bernard Benet could not be found, and the Clergue party left without their neighbour. Bernard Benet missed the apppointed hour, because as a convicted heretic he did not relish the prospect of facing the Inquisitor. Instead, he decided to let the Clergues take off and then waylay Alazaïs Faure.

He met her up on the castle plateau as she returned from a field; he had presumably gone up there because its commanding view would enable him easily to spot her. He asked her to give him enough livestock to enable him to disappear into the Narbonnais rather than go to Carcassonne. She firmly declined, telling him that he would only ask for more later.

Bernard Benet's last-ditch attempt to defy the Clergues had failed. It was time for him to join the party bound for Carcassonne. He caught up with them in time for lunch in a tavern at Brenac, which is fifteen miles from Montaillou. From here they proceeded in a straight line to Limoux by way of Rouvenac, although Benet momentarily changed his mind after lunch in Brenac and doubled back as far as Coudons. The next day they arrived in Carcassonne, and here Bernard Benet testified twice on two consecutive days to the Guilabert consolation; he included himself as a witness only after Bernard Clergue ordered him to, since otherwise his testimony would be worthless. When he confessed in Pamiers ten days later, Bernard Benet initially tried to suggest that his depositions in Carcassonne on 13 and 14 March were entirely bogus. But this did not fool Fournier, who rightly guessed that they were largely genuine.

While Bernard Benet testified in the House of the Inquisition, Bernard Clergue was trying to buy his imprisoned brother's freedom. He gave 300 pounds as a gift to the temporal ruler of Mirepoix, Gui de Lévis, who was heading for the Roman Curia in Avignon. He parted with a further 150 pounds as payment for the journey to his brother-in-law (probably Pons Gary), who accompanied de Lévis, and presented de Lévis's wife Constance, a daughter of Roger-Bernard III of Foix, with a mule as a gift so that she would intercede with the Bishop on behalf of his brother. It is a fact that as a result several cardinals and other powerful members of the Curia wrote a total of four intercessionary letters on Pierre Clergue's behalf to Fournier, but to no avail.

Bernard even paid money to various friends and familiars of Fournier, and to Arnaud Sicre Senior of Tarascon, which must have been a desperate move. But all of it proved futile. The more one begged (that is, attempted to bribe) the Bishop, Bernard concluded bitterly, the more he dug in. All in all, if Barthélemy Amilhat's evidence can be believed, Bernard spent a staggering 14,000 shillings (or 700 pounds) trying to free his brother Pierre.

Where was Pierre Azéma when the Clergues took off for Carcassonne, and why had he failed to stop the trip, or at least to intervene with Bernard Benet? Perhaps he was away in Pamiers in his new-found role as Fournier's relative. But he was back when Bernard returned home on his own. He had split from the Clergues in Limoux, probably on Sunday 15 March, and stopped off at his married sister's in Bélesta, which is some ten miles north-east of Montségur.

In Montaillou Pierre Azéma was waiting for him, and it may be the case that Alazais Faure went to see him after Bernard's eleventh-hour bid for extortion failed. He had learnt that land had been promised to Bernard Benet for perjuring himself, and so he confiscated all of Bernard's livestock in the name of the Count of Foix. If this was a legitimate claim, it may mean that Pierre Azéma was the new *bayle* of Montaillou, or that the office was temporarily suspended while the Clergues were under investigation.

But when Bernard Benet threatened to appeal to the *bayle* of Prades (rather than Bernard Clergue), Azéma asked him not to do so, promising that he would return Benet's livestock either the same day, or the following.

The new vicar of Montaillou, Raymond Trilh (perhaps the same family which gave the place name 'Trialh' to the village), was present during this exchange in the course of which Pierre Azéma sent his son Raymond to get Bernard Marty, the 'consul' of Montaillou, an office which did not play a role in Montaillou in the period leading up to 1308. Nor is it clear who Bernard Marty was, whether he came from one of the Cathar families of that name (and would therefore be well disposed to the Maurys, the Martys' invariable in-laws), or whether he was descended from the one non-Cathar Marty family, whose son had nevertheless married a Maury (see above, page 287).

In front of the consul and vicar Azéma demanded that Bernard Benet retract his Carcassonne deposition and that he be prepared to state under oath that he was neither present at, nor knew anything about, the consolation of Guillaume Guilabert. This was happening as they made their way up to the castle of Montaillou. Outside the castle Pierre Azéma suddenly ordered the lieutenant of the châtelain to arrest Bernard Benet and to put him in the dungeons of the castle's tower, for being a heretic and fugitive from the County of Foix (FR, f.82r).

Bernard stayed in the oubliettes for two days and two nights, with time to consider his options. Here he was beyond the reach of Bernard Clergue, who may not even have been aware of the fact that Bernard Benet was back in the village. Eventually Azéma collected him to take him to Lordat, on the first stage of his journey to Pamiers and Fournier. Since Bernard left Carcassonne on 15 March and testified in Pamiers on 25 March, we may date his stay in the dungeons of Montaillou to around the weekend of 22 March 1321.

On the track between Caussou and Lordat Pierre Azéma told Bernard Benet, who was probably manacled (FR, f.82r), that if he did not comply with his request to blame Bernard Clergue for the 'invented' consolation in front of Fournier, he would have him imprisoned in Lordat and hanged. Memories of the role played by the châtelain of Lordat in the first arrest of people from Montaillou in 1308 may still have been fresh in Bernard Benet's mind, since his mother had been among the prisoners that day. Bernard Benet realized that he had no choice, and on Wednesday 25 March he appeared before Fournier.

For the second time in the same month, now before the dreaded Bishop, Bernard Benet gave a false deposition, claiming that his testimony at Carcassonne was a fabrication by Bernard Clergue who intended to discredit those who had testified against the rector. Fournier disbelieved Benet's Azéma-inspired story, and even before Alazais Faure and the others arrived to give their version Fournier had extracted the truth from Bernard, including the manner in which Pierre Azéma had put him up to the false deposition. This demonstrates incidentally that Fournier and Pierre Azéma were not colluding in the framing of the Clergues, however much the Bishop may have valued Pierre Azéma's information on them. In this case Pierre Azéma manifestly tried to blacken Bernard Clergue without the Bishop knowing.

★

Once it was known in Montaillou that Bernard Benet had been taken to testify in Pamiers, Alamande Guilabert and her daughter, as well as Arnaud Faure and Guillaume Authié (B), decided to go before they were cited to confess themselves to Fournier. This is clear proof that they were not in cahoots with Pierre Azéma, who had urged Bernard Benet to deny the whole thing.

They had got as far as Les Cabannes when the Bishop's summons caught up with them so that at least they could demonstrate that they had gone to Pamiers of their own volition. Such details formed an important part of Inquisitorial judicial procedure. This group, who had not dared go to Carcassonne, now needed to trust the feared Bishop in Pamiers to protect them from the wrath of the Clergues, which might be worse than the fate decreed for them by the Inquisition.

Not in every case, though. Unlike his sister and niece, Guillaume Fort held back, not least because the Clergues had specifically exempted him from their private crusade. But on Monday 6 April 1321 a summons was issued for him, his sister-in-law Guillemette Benet, his daughter Esclarmonde Clergue-Fort, and Bernard Clergue and his wife Raymonde as well as Raymonde Testanière to appear the following Saturday 11 April before Fournier. It had taken less than a month for the Clergues' strategy to implode.

By then the two Faures, Alamande Guilabert and Guillaume Authié (B) had given their accounts of that tragic night in Montaillou thirteen years earlier. Throughout the period of their interviews, Alazais Faure, Alamande Guilabert, and later Guillemette Benet were on remand upstairs in the Archbishop's palace. Alamande Guilabert was here on either Friday 3 April or the day after when Pierre Clergue himself 'walked past the loft (*granerium*) of the bishopric in Pamiers where she was held' (FR, f.87r). He asked her whether she had confessed. When she said that she had, he walked away muttering that her daughter and son-in-law had killed him.

Guillaume Fort's account shortly afterwards of the Guilabert consolation merely corroborated the others', although he tried to play down his own role. Five years earlier he had got off lightly in Carcassonne when he was sentenced to the crosses by Geoffroy d'Ablis on 28 March 1316, some six months before d'Ablis himself died. He stood in no greater danger than any of the others until, inexplicably, he revealed during an interview on 21 April that he could not believe in the physical resurrection of the human body, because human bodies rot in the earth after death; and on 1 August that year, in front of a huge crowd of Church dignitaries, which included the Inquisitors from Carcassonne (Jean de Beaune) and from Toulouse (Bernard Gui), he confessed that he had returned to these heretical views and harboured them for the last three years. By doing so he wrote his own death sentence. The Church took the view of recidivism that 'As a dog returneth to his vomit, so a fool returneth to his folly' (Proverbs 26:11; L, 258).

Pierre Azéma by now hardly needed to bully witnesses any longer. Simply by telling the truth they were bound to implicate the Clergues ever more deeply. This was the case with Raymonde (Vuissane) Testan-ière, Raymonde Guilhou, and Guillemette Benet, the tragic matriarch from Montaillou. Vuissane's years as the Belots' servant and sex toy rendered her candid deposition about the goings-on in Guillaume Authié's headquarters in Montaillou a devastating indictment of the Clergues. Pierre Azéma did not urge her to say anything but the truth, but he asked her *not* to implicate herself, Gauzia Clergue (B), Raymonde Lizier, the Maurs brothers Raymond, Bernard and Pierre, and Vital Baille and his wife Esclarmonde. We have seen already that he was contemplating an alliance with Gauzia Clergue (B), and he would naturally make common cause with the Maurs, the Clergues' sworn enemies; but why the others?

After her last testimony on 30 April 1321 Vuissane returned to Montaillou where, rightly fearful of the consequences of her deposition, she withdrew into her house. It had a garden which commanded a view of the core of the village, and it is from here that three weeks later Vuissane saw two officers of the Count of Foix enforcing Bernard Clergue's house-arrest by one of them standing opposite the Clergues' house at the Benets' gate, and the other one down at the Liziers'.

Before this happened, however, Raymonde Clergue, formerly Belot, descended on her and launched into the following tirade:

You have gone and borne false witness against me, my husband, and monsignor Pierre Clergue, and yet you could not have said anything against me because I saw nothing with you nor you with me; nor have I wished to because I esteemed you too little [*parum*: LS]. You saw similarly too little [to provide evidence] with my husband, who felt no inclination to see anything with you because he did not consider you worthy enough. My husband and I have fully confessed ourselves if we did anything wrong, and now we have been to collect our letters of absolution in Carcassonne. We did not flee as some said, and no one can harm us with their testimony. Presently monsignor Pierre Clergue will be revenged on all those who testified against him, and they will answer before him about the allegations that they made against him. (FR, f.96v)

When Vuissane explained that all she had done was to report that Bernard Clergue and his brothers mingled with the Perfects at the Belots', Raymonde replied, 'You never saw any heretics in our house and therefore no one will believe your allegations; but for these reasons we will strip you of all your belongings.'

During the first two weeks or so of May 1321 Vuissane was repeatedly summoned to the Clergues' by messages from Bernard Clergue, but she was too frightened to see him at his home in case the Clergues harmed her there. Then, around 18 or 19 May, the soldiers of the Inquisition from Pamiers came and put Bernard under arrest for failing to attend Fournier's summons. Bernard would shortly need to accompany them to Pamiers, and with this in mind he now paid a visit in person to Vuissane in her brother's house and angrily threatened her with retaliation and exposure if she did not retract her statement and attribute it to the machinations of Pierre Azéma.

Bernard was taken away to Pamiers where he appeared on Friday 22 May for the first time. But the temporary removal of head and deputy did not emasculate the Clergues' power locally, and when Vuissane sickened she fled to Caussou (probably to her father's home), anxious to put some physical distance between herself and Montaillou.

It was here, on her sick-bed in Caussou in July, that she was visited by the new rector from Montaillou, Raymond Trilh, who had probably come to deliver her summons to the 'Graces' of 2 August to hear sentence. Her illness saved Vuissane from the horror of witnessing the execution of Guillaume Fort. She now 'confessed' to Trilh that she had wrongfully implicated the Clergues, and he duly reported this back to Raymond Clergue in Montaillou. The timing could hardly have been better, since one of the Clergues' most powerful allies, Hugues de Polignac, was poised to visit his friends in Montaillou; or he may already have been there.

He was ostensibly passing through Montaillou on his way to the baths at Ax, from where he was to progress to Pamiers to meet up with Jacques Fournier. The Clergues were now calling in favours that they were owed. The sick Vuissane was peremptorily summoned by Raymond Clergue, on pain of a huge fine, to appear before de Polignac formally to retract her charges against his brother. When the one-time Belot servant, who was ailing and frail, appeared before de Polignac in his usual quarters at Montaillou, Pierre Clergue's own upstairs rooms, her retraction was minuted by a French clerk who accompanied de Polignac. The Clergues' stooge de Polignac assured her that Fournier would take pity on her.

Vuissane survived the ordeal at the Clergues', and returned to her house in Montaillou. Here she was shortly afterwards visited by Pierre Azéma, who desired to know why she was 'not pleased with him' (FR, f.96v). She explained that she was keen to be in his good books and those of the Bishop, but that he must excuse her because she was very sick. Then, powerless and trapped in a pincer movement between the two cliques in Montaillou, she fled again as soon as she was well enough, this time further afield.

She was not alone in retracting her confession. Others such as Raymonde Lizier did likewise when they were summoned before de Polignac. It was probably he who had Pierre Azéma arrested during his stay at Montaillou, and taken to Carcassonne to be charged there. Azéma was certainly under arrest by 21 July, because by then Raymonde Gilhou in Allemans referred to his gaoling (FR, f.163v). It seems to be the case that de Polignac also scooped up Pierre de Gaillac in the same action.

21. Inside Allemans Prison in 1321

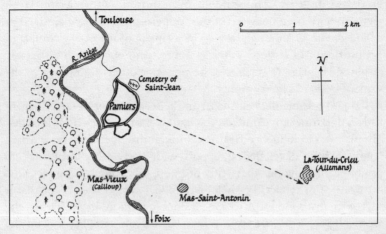

Pamiers with its monasteries and prison

Bernard Clergue arrived at Allemans on 25–6 May 1321, two weeks before Whitsun (7 June). Not the least of Fournier's reasons for exiling Bernard to the relative security of Allemans would have been the fact that his brother Pierre was contemporaneously under judicial supervision and partial house-arrest in Pamiers or at the Mas-Saint-Antonin. It was essential to keep the two Clergues apart.

By gaoling Bernard in Allemans, Fournier seemed to be locking the wolf into the sheepfold, since Bernard was bound to try to pressurize those who had testified against his brother, himself and their family. Here were Béatrice de Planisolles, Barthélemy Amilhat, Grazide Lizier, and others. Grazide's mother, Fabrisse Rives, followed later, as did the two Guilabert women, who started their sentences in Allemans after the 'Graces' of Sunday 2 August 1321, and thus came within his orbit.

True to the Clergues' energy and strategies, Bernard set to work inside. First he enlisted the goodwill of some of the key personnel such as the gaoler Garnot and his wife Honors by bribing them with a gift

of four fleeces of sheep's wool. After this bequest, a modest token by
Bernard's lavish standards, he was granted the free run of most of the
prison. When Garnot was absent, his wife even let Bernard have the
prison's keys so that he was completely at liberty to visit whomsoever
he wished; which he did, although as one of the witnesses remarked,
he did so stealthily. The warden of the prison, Maître Marc Rivel,
seems to have been unaware of this, or perhaps he tacitly connived or
colluded with it. Although he was the recipient of at least one complaint
against Bernard Clergue by Alazais Faure, who objected to his grossly
insulting language towards her, he does not otherwise feature in the
story of Bernard's imprisonment.

Bernard became the cell-mate, on the second floor of the Allemans
tower, of Barthélemy Amilhat, the last lover of Béatrice de Planisolles.
His plan was to influence Béatrice through this intermediary. Bernard
seems to have developed a rapport with Barthélemy Amilhat, and
promised him, among others, fifty florins (*c.* fifty pounds) if he prevailed
on Béatrice to retract. Barthélemy Amilhat would later claim that it
was twice that sum, eager to appear doubly virtuous in the eyes of the
ascetic Bishop (FR, f.175v). When Barthélemy Amilhat voiced the
legitimate fear that a retraction might lead Béatrice to the stake, Bernard
assured him that this would not ensue, because she would be blaming
it all on Pierre Azéma. His strategy was simple and effective: he would
get the witnesses to retract and then, to save themselves from the charge
of recidivism, they would have to implicate Pierre Azéma.

But the wily Bishop had laid a trap for Bernard Clergue, and if
Clergue had been less intoxicated with his own power he might have
smelled the rat when it started to share his cell. Barthélemy was a plant,
and Fournier had probably traded a lenient sentence in exchange
for good intelligence. By the time Bernard was alerted to Amilhat's
treachery, he no longer seemed to care (FR, f.176v). The scope of
Barthélemy's ingratiating testimony of 14 November 1321 regarding
Bernard Clergue's, and others', activities inside Allemans is impressive,
and he shamelessly records his various eavesdroppings.

About a fortnight after his committal, Bernard made his move. It
was during the first ten days of June. He descended to the ground floor
of the tower which connected, through a solid locked door, with a
large room which ran over the main or central hall of the fortress. This

room, to which Bernard did not have access, had a window (or several) which overlooked the castle moat. Here a number of women prisoners gathered, and their sleeping quarters or cells were probably off this room.

Although Béatrice sometimes moved between this chamber and the main hall underneath it, which was also at certain times frequented by the Guilabert women, Bernard did not manage in his five months' stay in prison to secure a face-to-face encounter with Béatrice, Grazide, Fabrisse, or anyone else from that group. Why this should have been so is not clear, since Bernard's cell-mate Barthélemy managed to communicate with Béatrice directly. Bernard had to suffer the indignity of soliciting a communication with Béatrice through third parties by kneeling down in front of the locked door and speaking through the crack of the door-sill. He knocked at the door and called for Grazide Lizier. Grazide, he must have known, shared a bed with Béatrice, and like Béatrice she had been his brother Pierre's concubine. He entreated Grazide either to get Béatrice to come and talk to him in person; or, if not, could she urge Béatrice to retract her confession? If Béatrice did, 'we will all be freed from this place,' he told her. 'A great evil has befallen us because of her,' he protested, and he pressed Grazide to find out whether Béatrice had been prompted by Pierre Azéma and Pierre de Gaillac to bear false witness against his family.

During the same subliminal negotiations Bernard also tried to get Grazide to retract. She had spent her teens under the spell and sexual yoke of Pierre Clergue, and even now she seemed momentarily prepared to retract and risk the stake for the Clergues. When she reminded Bernard that she had lost her possessions, he cynically retorted that she had plenty left since riches are bad things at best. She wavered, but she refused to implicate Azéma. It is true, she conceded, that he had occasionally asked her not to be afraid of speaking the truth because of Pierre Clergue, but he had never suggested framing the priest.

Grazide dutifully put Bernard's suggestion to Béatrice, whose response was contemptuously dismissive. She had not, she replied, seen Pierre Azéma in twenty years, and to the best of her knowledge she had never set eyes on Pierre de Gaillac. Grazide did not approach Béatrice again, even though she was afterwards bearded by Bernard on two or three occasions on the same matters.

In the summer Grazide's mother Fabrisse Rives was committed to Allemans, even though she had apparently been sentenced with the others on 8 March 1321. She now started to share the same prison-bed with her daughter and Béatrice. All three were linked intimately to the Clergues of Montaillou through sex and family ties. Two of them were from the same generation, and one of them was an aristocrat; and Fabrisse's brother was Pathau, who had raped the châtelaine twenty-four years earlier.

In bed one night Fabrisse and Béatrice spoke of Bernard Clergue's actions. Fabrisse told Béatrice how Bernard had insistently urged her to retract the confession for which she was wearing the crosses, and had promised that if she wished to comply he would arrange for two curates to hear her retraction. Béatrice advised against this by replying that for her own part she would not agree to this under any circumstances. Fabrisse then mentioned that Bernard had grievously threatened her because she had testified against him and other members of his family. To Béatrice's question whether she would retract, Fabrisse replied 'no', because she preferred it that Bernard should burn rather than herself.

Although Barthélemy Amilhat and Bernard were cell- and not soul-mates, a certain affinity seems to have developed between the turncoat Cathar Bernard and the now self-professedly reformed priest, even though Barthélemy refused to coax Béatrice into retracting. Bernard seems to have thought that he could exploit the services of the curate to more ends than one. Thus, if he refused to endanger his lover Béatrice, he could be relied on to act as a ready witness to a recantation, or just an unguarded statement that might come in useful at some point.

The two men passed their days sometimes sitting in the sun on the platform at the top of the Allemans tower, and at other times observing each other's idiosyncrasies. Bernard Clergue sneered at the priest for reciting his canonical hours (the seven offices of mattins, prime, terce, sext, none, vespers, compline), and invited him to stop this practice: 'You may well say your hours, because they have been of little or no use to you. Just look how your hours have helped you since you are now in this place. God is giving you a fat lot of thanks for your hours' (FR, f.176r).

Bernard also refused to fast except on the eve of All Saints (31 October), did not cross himself before going to sleep until prompted by Barthélemy Amilhat, and regularly failed to make the sign of the cross over his food. Bernard told Barthélemy Amilhat that the Cathars did not make the sign of the cross when entering a church, because they spurned it as a man would loathe the tree on which his father had been hanged. Instead they pretended to touch their noses, beards, and ears, saying to themselves, '*aysi es le front et aysi es la barba et aysi la una aurelha et aysi l'autra*' (FR, f.176v).*

Moreover, Bernard was openly hostile to the Bishop and supportive of the Valdensian Jean de Vienne, who was interned on the first floor of the tower under Bernard and Barthélemy Amilhat. The reason why the Bishop had moved against the people of the Sabartès, according to Bernard, as reported by Barthélemy Amilhat, was because they denied him his tithes on livestock. Bernard was no more a Marxist or intellectual than Pierre den Hugol (see above, pages 264–5), but he was rich enough to appreciate the specious spirituality of Fournier's agenda.

Bernard's experience of greasing the palms of the powerful from his mountain retreat had left him with the firm belief that everybody had their price; except, he discovered, Fournier, although Fournier's treatment of Bernard was to prove exceptionally genteel, as if the prelate were anxious to play by the book, to the point of instructing reluctant defence attorneys on Bernard's behalf. Was it because of the Clergues' questionable service to the state, or did the Bishop act in this way out of deference to the Inquisitor of Carcassonne, Jean de Beaune, who may have protected Bernard Clergue?

When Bernard heard the news of the arrests by de Polignac of Azéma and de Gaillac in July 1321, he responded ecstatically by kneeling down on the tower of Allemans and lifting his hands towards heaven:

Now I rejoice, because those two are arrested, because they are taken because of me, and it is because of me that my friends arrested them or had them arrested. And their arrest cost me dearly because those two traitors plotted for evil to befall our house and conspired against my brother the rector, and they made people come to the Lord Bishop. Now they are captured and will be put in a bad place. They will not emerge from it, however many or influential their friends are. I know that well, because Maître Jacques, the guardian of

---

* 'This is my forehead and this my beard, and this is one ear and this the other.'

the prison, is my friend to such an extent that it will go hard with those two prisoners in the Carcassonne prison; and if I could myself go there he would mete them out an even harsher treatment. There are two others whose arrest would render me happy, but one of them is already a prisoner here, notably Raymond Vaissière whom I will have burnt [as a recidivist], the other one is Guillaume Mathieu who is bad, false, and a traitor. And those two bore witness against my brother, and if I can get out of this place I shall do my utmost to ensure the arrest of that Guillaume Mathieu and to have him gaoled in the same place as Pierre Azéma and Pierre de Gaillac. (FR, f.176r)

Jacques de Polignac may have been as good as his word or Bernard's money, but Fournier's long-distance protection probably saved Pierre Azéma from the worst excesses of the Carcassonne prison. He survived there until 26 June of the following year, 1322, when he was taken from Carcassonne to Allemans to be brought face-to-face with Raymonde Guilhou; and he was alive in late July 1322 when he was confronted in turn with Vuissane Testanière, perhaps in late July or August 1322, because Vuissane was arrested on 22 July 1322 in Saurat (beyond Bédeilhac), and reincarcerated in Allemans. He was dead by 3 March 1323.

Pierre de Gaillac was allowed out of prison before long and relatively unscathed, since by Lent 1322, barely half a year after his arrest, he was back, seamlessly pursuing his feud with Tron who seems to have been released from Carcassonne in Lent 1321.* But de Gaillac died in February 1324, some four months before Pierre de Luzenac (FR, f.300v). Although he was himself ill, Bernard lived long enough to gloat over the death of one of his arch-foes.

The extent to which the Inquisition meant business was brought home to Bernard and everybody else in Allemans at the beginning of August. On Sunday 2 August 1321 the gentle Jean de Vienne was hauled from his first-floor cell and dragged to the cemetery of Saint-Jean at Pamiers. There he was burnt at the stake alongside his wife Huguette and Guillaume Fort of Montaillou.

---

* But there may be evidence which argues against this: see Duvernoy 1978, 1259n.1, which puts Guillaume Tron in a lawsuit in *1320*.

At the same infamous venue on the same day, Alazais Faure, Alamande Guilabert, and Guillemette Benet were sentenced to the 'strictest regime in prison, with bread, water, and in shackles'. If the reality of this daunting sentence turned out to be less dreadful than was intimated by the literal formula, Alazais and Alamande had to endure the grisly spectacle of seeing their uncle and brother Guillaume Fort burnt alive as a recidivist. Alazais's feelings of guilt would be mercilessly played on by Bernard Clergue, who was waiting for them in Allemans where the women arrived later that day.

They were imprisoned along with Guillemette Benet, Guillaume Fort's sister-in-law, and a woman called Alazais de Vernaux. Their cell was situated off the rampart gallery, next to the tower and to the left of the top of the staircase. Alazais de Vernaux had been sentenced on the same day as the other three women, though much more lightly, for meeting Guillaume Authié and another Perfect, a gross-looking man with a fat and round face, at a friend's house, and for sending them food. Her deposition is that of an innocent also-ran victim of the Inquisition. She appears to have been well liked by her local rector, who offered to accompany her to see the Bishop. In the end Alazais de Vernaux spent three years in Allemans, and was released on 12 August 1324 with crosses and pilgrimages.

Four years and four months later, after more than seven years in prison, Alazais Faure and her mother Alamande in turn walked out from Allemans to rejoin what was left of their family in Montaillou (D27, f.148r). Alazais's husband was freed on the same day from Carcassonne. The others who also left that day for Montaillou were Brune Pourcel, Guillaume Baille, Pierre Maury's sister Raymonde Marty, and Raymonde Castanière. The fearless Raymonde Guilhou and former Madame Vital was released the same day.

On Tuesday 4 or Wednesday 5 August 1321 Bernard met the two Guilabert women near their cell on the rampart gallery. Barthélemy Amilhat must have been aware of Bernard's movements, because he hid behind the door of the cell; perhaps Bernard had planted him there to act as a witness in case he managed to trap Alazais into a false testimony, since by his own admission Barthélemy Amilhat repeatedly spied on the women when Bernard was there.

On this first occasion the two Guilabert women seem to have been

delighted to encounter a familiar face from Montaillou, and told Bernard so. Bernard assured them that he had the run of the prison, and that he would do everything he could to make their lives more bearable.*
Then, inevitably, they spoke of the Sunday's 'Graces', and Alamande said, 'It would all have gone so well, if my brother had not died in these Graces.' Bernard agreed that the loss of Guillaume Fort was a bad blow, but, he said, 'all that is the fault of your daughter here, and not only did she do this bad thing, but she is responsible for many others, because she confessed that she was the whore of my brother the curate when, however, she was not. It would be a good thing if she retracted what she has alleged against my brother.' Then the three of them wept together and said that if this Bishop lived long then everything would perish, because he was the devil who had come to earth.

It was the following day that Alazais and Guillemette Benet found themselves alone in their cell, because Alazais's mother and Alazais de Vernaux had gone to a window on the rampart gallery. Alazais complained that they had both lost everything by being committed to prison. Guillemette replied that she had lost everything long before, but that Alazais had indeed suffered a heavy misfortune, since she and her husband were both now in prison, unlike Jean Guilabert, Alazais's father, who was holding on to his goods. It was then that Guillemette revealed to Alazais her father's calculated act of cowardice in May 1308. Guillemette, whose sister Sybille had died earlier in Carcassonne, was herself dead by late November 1321. She may have been ailing and eager therefore to clear her conscience of this well-kept secret.

How deeply Alazais was hurt by the revelation of her father's duplicity can be gauged from her unguarded expression of anguish shortly after this exchange. It was a few days later, on Monday 10 August 1321, when she climbed to the tower of the prison in the company of Bernard Clergue, and there they met Barthélemy Amilhat who was sunning himself. Clergue pointed towards the mountains of the Sabartès, which are clearly visible from La Tour-du-Crieu, and remarked that their '*pays*' and their lands lay over there. Alazais Faure answered that she and her mother had nothing left at all in those lands, to which Clergue

---

* He did not, however, have access to the area of the prison where Béatrice de Planisolles was kept.

replied that her father would purchase her freedom and restore their possessions to her. She retorted that her father had let them down: 'We have seen a bad father, because if he had wanted to we would not be here; he should have punished us, because at the time [May 1308] the entire region was already icy with fear and terror-stricken (*englassiada et empaurucada*). In spite of that my father put us in this misery' (FR, f.175v).

Would the affectionate Alazaïs have spoken thus, if she had known that she would probably never see her father again, because he seems to have died within two or three years of her incarceration? Bernard immediately nudged her with his elbow to signal that she should be silent, but it was too late. Alazaïs went very pale and still, and descended from the tower. The truth was out, and Barthélemy Amilhat now knew of Jean Guilabert's collusion with the Cathars.

Bernard had probably introduced Alazaïs to Amilhat in the hope of softening her up for an eventual retraction in front of this witness of the cloth. But he had not anticipated her gaffe about her father, with whom the Clergues had probably struck a deal. As long as the head of the family was 'uncontaminated' with the estate safe in his hands, he would be able, with the help of the Clergues and their Carcassonne cronies, to extract his family from Allemans, provided of course that they cooperated with the Clergues in other matters.

It is possible that Bernard Clergue had wanted to use his knowledge of old Guilabert's tacit complicity as his trump card to browbeat the two Guilabert women into cooperating, but Alazaïs's indiscretion let the cat out of the bag in front of Amilhat and *ipso facto* broke Bernard's hold over her.

Bernard and Barthélemy Amilhat stayed behind, and Barthélemy said, 'Bernard, those words spoken by your *commère* are bad and heretical,' to which Bernard replied, 'Certainly, yes, but let us look out that no evil befall either you or me.' With this veiled threat Bernard descended from the platform of the tower, and joined the Guilabert women in their cell. Up on the tower Barthélemy Amilhat tried to catch what was being said, but apart from Bernard's voice and Alamande's crying he could make out only one sentence spoken by Alazaïs's mother as she wept: 'Even now that one cannot keep quiet, even though she has already done so much harm.'

At around six o'clock that evening Barthélemy Amilhat left the tower, perhaps to attend some form of evening worship. When he passed the Guilaberts' cell, Alazais Faure emerged from it and went up to him with her arms crossed in supplication in front of her chest. She implored him not to let harm come to her because of the words she had spoken on the tower, and not to reveal them. Barthélemy Amilhat assured her of his discretion, provided Bernard kept *his* counsel. To this Alazais replied that she knew plenty to say against Bernard if he told on her, because it was in the Clergues' house that the Perfects stayed, ate and drank, and it was the Clergues who guided them through the village and the various houses.

Not long after, Bernard ascended the staircase towards the Guilabert women's cell. Leaning into the first window at the top left of the staircase, he addressed Alazais who was walking near her cell. Bernard had carefully stage-managed this occasion so that Barthélemy Amilhat was strategically positioned to overhear, and therefore be a witness to, the ensuing conversation; he was hiding in a room next to the tower from where he could hear everything.

Bernard told Alazais that the rector of Prades had been arrested by the Bishop because he conspired in secret with the rector of Montaillou (Trilh?). Bernard, congratulating himself, said, 'That traitor of a would-be priest is arrested, because he conspired with Pierre Azéma to destroy my brother the rector of Montaillou. Now the two who were the cause and organizers of my brother's arrest are prisoners.'

Presumably Bernard related this to Alazais to soften her up with a salutary tale of the likely fate of the Clergues' enemies, for he now asked her bluntly to retract her confession and to blame it all on Pierre Azéma's suborning her. Both for the sake of his hidden witness and more easily to sway Alazais, he pretended to believe that Azéma was indeed guilty of putting her up to a frame. He even seems to have suggested that she ought to state that he asked for sexual favours which she granted him. In short, he wanted to turn Azéma into the kind of villain that his brother was reputed to be according to a number of corroborative hostile depositions. If she complied, Bernard offered her in return the immediate release of her husband from Carcassonne. He had, Bernard assured her, plenty of money, and would pay Maître Jacques the necessary 'fee' to release Arnaud Faure.

But Alazais knew the dangers of retraction, and that she would most likely dig herself in ever more deeply. Weeping and perhaps stung by his cynicism, she turned on Bernard and, calling him a 'traitor', refused categorically to oblige him. 'You'll pay for this,' he threatened, and pointed out that some had already followed his advice to retract and implicate Azéma, including Raymonde Belot-Lizier, Gauzia Clergue (B), Vuissane Testanière, Fabrisse Rives, and Guillemette, the wife of Pierre Clergue (B) of Montaillou. He added triumphantly that Azéma and Pierre de Gaillac would never get out of the Carcassonne gaol. 'You said that you were my brother's whore to destroy him, when, however, you never were.' Alazais asserted that she had been, and that she was desperately sorry for it, and then, still crying, she walked away.

Bernard did not give up, and on three subsequent occasions pressed her on the same subject when they met on the rampart gallery. His insults to Alazais ranged from *na gossa* ('bitch') to *na canassa* ('nasty bitch'), and *canassa e truissa* ('nasty bitch and filthy sow'). Once, when he met her on the rampart gallery, he said to her with calculated cruelty:

You nasty bitch, you caused your uncle Guillaume Fort, your mother's brother, to be burnt. If you had not revealed before the Lord Bishop that he was present at the consolation of your brother, he would never have been denounced. Because of your confession that man was burnt. He was truly upright and decent, and a great family head of his home. Everything would have been all right if that worthy man had not been burnt. (FR, f.177v)

Often when Bernard met Alazais on her own he would repeat, 'You nasty bitch and sow, you caused your uncle to be burnt!'

One day she went downstairs into the great hall to complain to Maître Marc Rivel about Bernard's verbal abuses of her. When she had left the hall, Béatrice called out to her and asked, 'What is Bernard Clergue saying to you?' to which Alazais replied that he was trying to get her to retract her confession. Béatrice then told her that Bernard sent his messengers also to others in the same prison to get them to retract. She added, 'Take care not to do it.'

As late as 'the time of the wine harvest' he was urging Alamande to lean on her daughter to retract, which indicates that Pierre Clergue was still alive at the start of October 1321. Alamande explained to Bernard that she and Alazais were at odds, and that her daughter would not do anything on her prompting. Bernard then threatened her with '*velha malnada* [literally "bastard old woman"], if you don't do as I tell you, you have arrived in a bad place', meaning that he would make their lives in prison a hell.

One woman who *did* retract and who subsequently refused to retract her retraction in spite of the most urgent pressure from Fournier, was Raymonde Guilhou, who, like the guileless Alazais Vernaux, had latterly lived in the Pech. The extant record may suggest that Raymonde was either more frightened of the Clergues than of the Bishop, or that as the widow of Arnaud Vital and a Cathar at heart she in the end decided on the perilous course of defying the Inquisition; or did she still love Bernard Clergue with whom she had formerly been 'very intimate' (FR, f.95r)?

Her initial hearings were scheduled at Pamiers for 29 April and 2 May. After these were over she was allowed to return home to Vernaux, where her husband bitterly reproached her for misleading him about her former heretical sympathies. The Clergues were also waiting for her.

On Saturday 30 May she met Arnaud Clergue at Lordat. It is unlikely that Arnaud just happened to meet Raymonde in Lordat. His earlier career suggests that his uncles Pierre and Bernard used him to tip off their clients of imminent raids, or to present them with readily construed alibis. In this case we can be reasonably sure that Arnaud issued more than just a genteel reprimand. Arnaud told Raymonde, according to her second testimony, that she had caused his mother-in-law, Raymonde Belot-Lizier, to weep a great deal, because she had been implicated by Guilhou's declarations that Lizier was intimate with the Belots and had hidden Perfects on their behalf. Raymonde Guilhou claimed to have rejected this accusation, and indeed retracted it later. What she did not specifically retract were her charges against Pierre Clergue.

When Raymonde appeared again before the Bishop on Tuesday 21 July, she retracted her specific charges against Raymonde Belot-Lizier and against Mengarde Clergue. Moreover, she now implicated Pierre Azéma on exactly the lines suggested by Bernard Clergue to others in Allemans. It is impossible to know what brought about this change of heart, whether the Clergues offered to expose other members of her family, or whether they threatened to harm her children; or whatever else.

On Tuesday 21 July Raymonde was confined to Allemans for bearing false witness against Raymonde Belot-Lizier and Mengarde Clergue, as well as against herself, and also because Fournier suspected that her retraction in turn was false. It was between this date and Bernard Clergue's leaving Allemans on Sunday 2 November that an exchange between Bernard and Raymonde Guilhou was overheard by Barthélemy Amilhat.

Raymonde was interned above the stables on the second floor of the north side of the fortress, opposite the church of Saint-Paul. From a window on the rampart gallery Bernard often spoke with her. On one occasion she put her head through a hole in the castle's exterior wall facing the church and conferred with Clergue, who was in the upper window of the rampart gallery. She told him that she was terrified, but he urged her not to worry and just keep quiet.

She obliged at the risk of her own life and henceforth stood her ground with unshakeable conviction. The Inquisitors knew that she was lying about Azéma, and on Saturday 26 June 1322, eight months after Bernard's departure, she was summoned before Brothers Gaillard de Pomiès and Arnaud du Carla, as well as the warden Maître Marc Rivel and the notary Guillaume Peyre-Barthe, in session in the great hall in Allemans. She reiterated her retraction. Gaillard then confronted her with Azéma, who denied indoctrinating Raymonde. The most he had ever done, he insisted, was to urge her to tell the truth about her heretical activities, and if she did so the Bishop would have compassion on her. Raymonde refused to yield.

When she was threatened with further procedures, she stated that she would prefer burning to not telling the truth. She never deviated from this position, and was duly condemned as an 'obstinate and impenitent heretic'. Her sentence on 19 June 1323, however, was light under the circumstances: she was condemned to a regime of 'strict prison' and was set free with the bearing of the crosses on 17 January 1329. Did her resilience make her captors relent, or did they think that this was the one person whom Azéma had indeed succeeded in influencing? He did not, after all, deny instructing her to tell the truth, and the Inquisitors well knew that such 'instructions' could take many forms.

Were the Inquisitors soft on Raymonde Guilhou because she was at best a servant girl who had been manipulated by her Cathar employers, then her husband Arnaud Vital, and now the powerful Clergue clan? The Bishop was acutely aware of their long reach and their power to intimidate and hurt. He consequently refused to give out the names of his accusers to Bernard, even though Bernard of course guessed at some of them. Fournier's reason was that 'a great and evident danger would threaten many poor and weak people who have testified against Bernard, if their names were revealed to him' (FR, f.180v).

It was during Bernard's five-month stay in Allemans that his brother Pierre Clergue died. He would have been in his late forties. He was alive around 29 September, and probably at the start of October, when Bernard threatened Alamande Guilabert. But he was dead by Saturday 10 October 1321, when Guillaume Maurs referred to him as the 'deceased' Pierre Clergue (FR, ff.152r, 178r).

Bernard Clergue reacted to the news, which was delivered to him by Garnot, with a paroxysm of grief which was witnessed by Alazais Faure and most of Allemans. Weeping, he exclaimed again and again, 'Now my God is dead, and what shall I do about my God, because *le mieu capdel e le mieu dieu* ['the best head and the best God'] is dead, and I will never see him again' (FR, f.177v). Bernard would not stop until Esclarmonde, the wife of Maître Marc Rivel, told him not to utter such words, but to mourn his brother the way good people usually mourn their brothers.

Pierre Clergue's death probably occurred in the abbey precinct of the Mas-Saint-Antonin, even though his place of detention was called a 'prison' by the Inquisition on the one occasion when its charge-sheet against Bernard Clergue referred to Pierre Clergue's internment (FR, f.179r). Between August 1320 and his death in October 1321 he must have been interviewed repeatedly by Fournier, but no written record survives in MS 4030. Nor are there any cross-references to a testimony by Pierre Clergue in the same manuscript. That MS 4030 is incomplete can easily be demonstrated from internal evidence, as it lacks other depositions (see above, pages 365–6). In none of these cases does the copyist signal a lacuna, obviously because he was unaware of the existence of the minutes in question. We may be reasonably confident that the clerk similarly did not have access to papers or minutes relating to Pierre Clergue.

The absence of the testimony of Pierre Clergue cannot be attributed to an oversight. His would have been potentially the most subversive one, although his brother Bernard's claim that the rector gave nothing away during his interrogations might suggest otherwise. But then Pierre Clergue could hardly have invoked a right to silence in an Inquisitorial court in 1321, even though he may have tried to run rings around Fournier.

Why did his papers not reach the copyist? Were they retained in the abbey of the Mas-Saint-Antonin because the Carcassonne and Toulouse Inquisitions overruled Fournier and decided that the minutes of the priest's depositions were top-secret documents? That as such they could not even be preserved in a consolidated episcopal Register such as MS 4030 which Fournier may have been planning already then?

Of all the participants in this story Pierre Clergue remains the most enigmatic. We have multiple external accounts of him by his lovers, enemies, and brother, but the absence of his testimony remains a great loss. A minuted account of his verbal fencing with Fournier and of his rebuttals of accusations by the châtelaine and others about his nefarious reign in Montaillou would have provided invaluable insights into both the character and this story. Was he ever asked about burying his consoled mother in the church of Montaillou? The evidence from Fournier's other investigations suggests that he would have been, but since Mengarde's remains do not appear to have been disturbed Clergue probably won this round, notwithstanding the statements of witnesses. Most significant of all, perhaps, is the question whether Fournier ever confronted him directly with his involvement with the de Polignacs of Carcassonne. He undoubtedly harboured the strongest suspicion that the Clergues and Carcassonne were in cahoots, and if he did indeed pursue this highly charged line of inquiry and had it witnessed and minuted, as was standard procedure, then that might well account for the absence of this documentation from the extant records.

That Pierre Clergue enjoyed some freedom of movement between his arrest in August of 1320 and his encounter with Alamande Faure in

April 1321 is evident, but it is equally clear from Bernard Clergue's efforts inside Allemans that he was finding it impossible to convince Fournier of his brother's innocence. Moreover, the Bishop's lodging of Barthélemy Amilhat in Bernard Clergue's cell proves that between May and the rector's death in October 1321 Fournier continued to consolidate his case against the apostate priest.

Nothing is known about the circumstances surrounding Pierre Clergue's death. We have to assume that he fell ill and died of natural causes, even though the regime at the Mas-Saint-Antonin, if that was indeed where he stayed, would have been a comfortable one compared to the festering cells of Allemans. From the account of Bernard's reaction to news of his brother's demise it might appear that his death was unexpected, although we cannot be sure; Bernard would have been deeply affected by his brother's demise under any circumstances.

For Pierre Clergue the time of his captivity must have been a grim business. Over a period of twenty-five years he had enjoyed absolute power in his fee in the Pays de Sault, including '*droits de seigneur*' over women, and it was his former mistresses and victims who were now destroying him by testifying before the prelate from Saverdun. For the sexually insatiable Clergue life without women will have been a sharp reminder of his own mortality.

That he was in touch for part of the time with his brother at Allemans is a virtual certainty, since the timing of Bernard Clergue's targeting of various prisoners was very probably dictated by the course that the interviews between Fournier and the rector were taking. One can only guess at Pierre Clergue's frustrations as at last he found himself up against somebody who could not be bought, and who refused to yield to the entreaties of the cardinals who interceded for Clergue.

As the former rector of Montaillou lay dying he seems to have declined the spiritual comforts of the Catholic church, because seven years and three months later he was reported to have died an 'impenitent' (see below, page 400); like Pierre Authié's son-in-law Arnaud Teisseyre, who expired in a cell at Allemans on 29 May 1323 without abjuring Catharism, the rector of Montaillou may have haughtily rejected the sacraments of a church he despised. We can be fairly sure that his friendship with Guillaume Authié had resulted in the *convenenza*, and that this was the reason for his obduracy in the face of extinction.

He left no confession, it seems, and we shall never know what motivated his actions. Although the evidence in MS 4030 suggests that he made his peace with Béatrice de Planisolles, to the extent that she retracted her accusations against him, we cannot be sure. In the end he died within a mile and a half of the place where she and others among his many mistresses lingered in prison.

Where they buried him is not known, but the Mas-Saint-Antonin is as likely a place as any. With the death of Pierre Clergue, his family's stranglehold on local powers was broken, although the Clergues' genes ensured that they would continue to lord it over Montaillou for many more centuries.

It may have been the shock of Pierre Clergue's death that caused Bernard's health to fail. Certainly the panel who interviewed him on 2 November, consisting of Fournier, Gaillard de Pomiès, and others, noticed his pallor and were apparently moved to leniency (FR, f.175r). But they protested rather a lot in their report, and the clerk's comment that one of the mitigating circumstances of Bernard's situation was the length of his remand does not sound convincing, particularly when he also notes in parenthesis that Bernard had the run of the entire fortress, as if he were sceptical of what he needed to record. Bernard was released under judicial caution until St Lucy's day (13 December 1321), when he was ordered to reappear before the Bishop at Pamiers.

That same night of 2 November 1321 Bernard returned to Allemans a free man. He ascended to the inner rampart gallery, and there he jauntily bid farewell to his cell-mate Barthélemy Amilhat. Then, shouting into the well of the prison, he defiantly exhorted all the inmates to follow his and his brother's example and keep their mouths shut:

During my stay here I sent home for ten, or fifteen, or thirty shillings, and it was always sent to me at once, which would not have happened if the Count of Foix had confiscated my goods. If I had opened my mouth as widely as Arnaud Cocul or Arnaud de Savignan, who are in the dungeons, I would hardly have enjoyed such a good pension from my home, because the Count of Foix doesn't grant such a generous allowance to other prisoners. (FR, f.177v)

Between 2 November 1321 and his sentencing on 13 August 1324 the Bishop and the *padrone* from Montaillou engaged in a remarkable tug-of-war. Fournier's forbearance towards Bernard and his insistence on Clergue's enlisting counsel to prepare a defence, even if it meant Bernard freely travelling all the way to Toulouse, verge on the surreal. So does the coy reference to Bernard's having earlier spent vast sums of money to ensure that 'a certain person [Pierre Clergue] who was strongly suspected and accused of heresy should be freed from the prison where he was detained' (FR, f.179r). In the course of his various meetings with Bernard the otherwise intransigent prelate was determined to be seen to be emollient and scrupulously fair to the accused.

The testimonies of hostile witnesses, whose names were withheld, were copied out for him to prepare his defence, but he missed his appointment in Pamiers on 12 March 1323. His brother Raymond appeared in his stead to explain that Bernard was too sick at home in Montaillou to travel. Then, seventeen months later, on 7 August 1324, Bernard, forgoing a formal defence, submitted himself to the mercy of 'the Bishop and the Lord Inquisitor of Carcassonne'. On Thursday 9 August he was found guilty of impenitence, and it was recommended that he should be surrendered to the secular arm. The news of this spread through Pamiers, but the following Monday he was sentenced to prison in Carcassonne, his loyal friends' gaol. He must have been ailing, because he was dead by Friday 14 September 1324, when Gaillard de Pomiès O. P. referred to him as the 'late Bernard Clergue'.

It is doubtful that Bernard was ever imprisoned in Carcassonne in anything but name, the more so since we know that the de Polignacs had private quarters inside the prison where they probably lodged their old friend. By 8 October 1324 Arnaud Sicre Senior was also dead (FR, f.300r); latterly he had been collecting property forfeited by heresy on behalf of the Crown (*CR 1285–1314*: 8463, 8616–17 etc.). His son Arnaud, the nemesis of the Catalonian Cathars, was still alive and working for the Inquisition in 1329.

On 25 June 1324 Pierre Maury was interviewed by Fournier for the first time. Both he and his brother had been delivered into the Bishop's hands by Arnaud Sicre.

Together the Maury brothers, after Pierre's return from Mallorca, had spent the summer of 1321 in the pastures of Castanesa, the area of the Serrat de Castenàs which is wedged between Tírvia and Castellbó. It would seem to be the last place on earth for the Maurys to revisit so shortly after the arrest there of their friend and mentor Guillaume Bélibaste, since it was probably under the jurisdiction of Pinhana, the *bayle* of Tírvia.

Guillaume Bélibaste was already dead. He had been burnt at the stake by the Archbishop of Narbonne at Villerouge-Termenès, probably in the area between the castle and the church of Saint-Étienne; Jean Maury later pretended to think that this had happened at Carcassonne, as if to underline his distance from Bélibaste. Today, inside the fortress of Villerouge-Termenès, a three-dimensional 'Exposition Audiovisuelle' movingly pays tribute to the shepherd Perfect from nearby Cubières. The tour of 'Le Monde de Bélibaste, dernier Parfait Cathare' vividly recreates Bélibaste's journey from Morella and his subsequent (undocumented) confrontations with the Archbishop, Bernard de Farges, a nephew of Clément V.

While the Maurys were back in the Tírvia region, Guillaume and Arnaud Maurs were summering at Riucaut along with Vezian Tournier of Prades, Jacques d'Odeillo, and Bernard, the brother of Brune Pourcel, who was the daughter of the late Prades Tavernier. Guillaume Baille joined them there from Montaillou, which was then in a state of open civil war between the Clergues and Azéma.

Towards 2 September 1321, the feast of St Antonin, Arnaud Maurs went to the fair at Pamiers and there he was arrested while in the company of Raymond Bar from Montaillou, who must have been a cousin on his mother Mengarde Bar's side. His brother Guillaume Maurs was waiting at Puigcerdà and getting ready for the winter transhumance. Because of contradictory rumours about Arnaud's fate, Guillaume went up to Riucaut to search out Guillaume Baille and Jacques d'Odeillo. After conferring with them, he proposed going into Ax to find out. But Jacques d'Odeillo advised against it, because if Guillaume were himself to be arrested, then their flock would be forfeit.

Guillaume Maurs therefore asked Guillaume Baille to descend to Ax to visit his (Guillaume Maurs's) sister Guillemette, while he himself would return to Puigcerdà to sort out their provisions in readiness for Càlig. On the road between Ax and Mérens Baille bumped into Raymond Bar, who was taking his goats to Ax. Bar confirmed that Arnaud had been arrested in his presence, and he added that there was a well-attested rumour that all the shepherds from the Cerdagne would be rounded up by the Bishop of Pamiers.

Around 21 September Guillaume Maurs was arrested at Puigcerdà. At the time the shepherds of the Maurs–Baille–d'Odeillo team were either up at Campcardós (IGN 2249 OT), or on the pass of Guils above the village of Guils de Cerdanya near Puigcerdà. The sheep of Guillaume and Arnaud Maurs were impounded by the men of the King of Mallorca. Before they could be released, one Mathieu Pélissier from Puigcerdà had to stand surety for the sheep. Guillaume Baille and the other shepherds swore to Pélissier that they would deliver back the Maurs' sheep from Càlig and would not surrender them in the meantime to the Maurs.

Three months later, around Christmas, Pierre Maury visited Guillaume Baille and others at Càlig and learnt that the two Maurs were under arrest. At this news Pierre let fly angrily against Fournier, and claimed that an evil spirit had lighted on the bishopric of Pamiers in the form of Fournier; but, he vowed, Fournier would have less peace after death than anybody else, because he was 'a worse heretic than Guillaume Maurs or those who are called heretics'. Guillaume Baille later claimed to have believed Pierre Maury because he, Guillaume, was inspired by the Perfects' fortitude in facing death by fire for their faith (FR, f.199r).

Guillaume Baille was arrested by the Bishop's men around July or August 1322, and Guillaume Maurs was gaoled in Carcassonne on Monday 5 July 1322. In addition he was pilloried in both Pamiers and Carcassonne for forgery and extortion (L, 297). Maurs's gaoling in Carcassonne rather than Pamiers sounds a sinister note, for although the Clergues were on the wane, the de Polignacs' power was undented; and their friends' enemies were their enemies.

That summer of 1322 Pierre Maury seems to have stayed put in Catalonia. After calling on his brother Jean at Castelldans, he proceeded to Alcañiz to recover the money he had lent to his aunt and cousin, only to find that they had both died and were buried there. His money, some 500 shillings, had vanished with them.

Again, we have only Pierre Maury's word for this disappearance of loved ones, but it was one thing to spirit to oblivion Guillemette Maury and her family, quite another to do the same favour to a couple which included the Cathar-hating Jeanne, who might have stood to gain from the Inquisition. From a futile visit to Alcañiz Pierre Maury went on to seek out Blanche and Raymonde, and found them in Caseres not far from Cretas. In spite of suffering just then this staggering financial loss, he gave Raymonde twenty-five Barcelona shillings towards rearing 'his' son.

He spent the winter of 1322–3 in Tortosa. One evening around Whitsun (15 May) 1323 he bumped into Raymond Issaurat on that city's bridge across the Ebre. They bought bread, wine and cheese in Tortosa, and then left the town to sleep in the olive groves beyond the city boundaries. During this crepuscular meeting Pierre Maury shared with Issaurat the melancholy news that Guillaume Bélibaste was already dead. His compadre from the struggle was deeply affected and remarked, 'Until now I had hoped that I would still have good times and fun with him, and I wanted him to cross with me to Sicily, because it is a good land [for the faithful] and it is rich; I left Bernard Baille in Palermo, because he wanted to go and fight in Sardinia' (FR, f.267v).

That night the two of them compared notes on recent events and the difference between the two Sicre-Baille brothers, and Raymond asked where Blanche and her sister were. Pierre Maury explained that they were probably in the nearby Ulldecona region on the coast for the harvests, from where they would be likely to move on to the harvests in the mountains of Benifassà. Raymond told Pierre Maury that he wanted to see his brother Jean and that he intended to team up with the two Marty women 'to cheer myself up'.

The following morning they split. Pierre Maury made directly for Flix, and Raymond undertook to join him there after his various visits. At Flix, around 9 p.m., at dusk, Pierre Maury was apprehended by the local *bayle* acting on instructions from Arnaud Sicre. He was taken from Flix to Barcelona for a preliminary and perfunctory interview in Aragón. Then he was taken back all the way to Pamiers where, over thirteen months after his arrest, he finally came face-to-face with Jacques Fournier.

During the winter of 1321–2 Jean Maury was, apparently, instructed by the *bayle* of Castelldans that he would either have to marry a local girl, that is go native, or else remove his flock from the pastures of Castelldans. But it seems that no woman from there wanted him. The recurring claim in Jean Maury's testimony that the search for a marriage partner was the shaping force of his life sounds about as convincing as Bernard Clergue's protesting the most passionate love for his wife.

He left Castelldans for l'Albi, some twelve miles to the south-east, in search of a monk called Bérenger Moliner from the nearby monastery of Poblet, with whom he had, allegedly, pawned two rams. Was this monk a brother of the Guillaume Moliner from Lleida who had several years earlier provided accommodation in La Granadella to both Jean Maury and Raymond de Toulouse? If so, Moliner may well have been a part of a contingency strategy to save the younger Maury.

Moliner had conveniently left for Juncosa, and Jean Maury followed him. His real reason for going there was that his brother Pierre Maury had told him that Esperte Servel and her daughter Mathène had been staying there continuously since early April 1321. Jean Maury's claim later to have been unaware of the fact that his future wife Mathène was Cathar fooled no one, least of all Fournier. Mathène was Jean Maury's life insurance against the stake.

He and Mathène were engaged on Saturday 2 January 1322, and they married in church on Saturday 23 January; Mathène may have been eighteen years old, and Jean Maury was about twenty-six. Much is made in the Register of this public and orthodox ceremony, and the Inquisition elicited from young Mathène the curiously obvious fact that the written record of the marriage was deposed in the registers of Juncosa; and written into the marriage licence was the misleading statement that the bride's family hailed from Foix (rather than Tarascon), because Foix was a much less Cathar-contaminated area.

A wedding ceremony in church and written records were standard procedure. The reason why the Inquisition asked about them is because they suspected that this was a set-up to save Jean Maury. The newlyweds at once moved to Castelldans, taking Esperte with them. Together they enjoyed another year and a half of freedom, and no offspring, as befitted 'married' Perfects other than Bélibaste. They were still free around 15 May 1323, but were probably taken very shortly after Pierre Maury. Arnaud Sicre must have been eager to wind up his Catalonian assignments before transhumance took the Cerdagnian shepherds north to the passes, where they would be much harder to capture. It seems therefore likely that Jean Maury was arrested at Castelldans along with his wife and mother-in-law in mid- to late May 1323.

In Jean Maury the Inquisition at Pamiers arrested the last aspiring Perfect in Catalonia. It is evident from the scale of the two Maurys' interrogations that Fournier knew full well that they had been the most important Cathar players in the diaspora. But it was his Aragonian counterpart who elicited from Jean Maury the famous Cathar prayer, which the Register reproduces in the original Occitan. A literal translation reads as follows:

Holy Father, just God of the good spirits, who has no falsehood, nor lies, nor errs, nor hesitates for fear of death to sojourn in the world of the alien god, because we are not of the world nor the world of us, grant us to know that which You know and love that which You love. You treacherous pharisees who hover at the gates of the Kingdom and prevent those who desire to enter there from doing so, and you others who do not want to go there, this is why I pray to the Holy Father of the good spirits who has the power to save the souls, who for the good spirits causes seeding and flowering, and who, for the sake of the good ones, grants life to the bad ones, and will even cause them to go into the world of the good when in the lesser heavens of the seven kingdoms there are no more of mine who fell from paradise, out of which Lucifer pulled them under the cover of deceit saying that God promised them nothing but good. And because the devil was very false, he promised them bad and good, and undertook to give them women that they would love too much and grant them rule over one another; and there would among them be those who would be kings, and counts, and emperors, and they would have a bird with which to catch other birds, and one animal another; all the people would be the subjects of those who descended, and they would be gods and have the power to do evil and good just as God above, and they would never regret being gods with the power to do evil and good, when the one God above only ever gave them good; and thus they climbed on a glass heaven and as much as they climbed they fell and perished. And God descended from heaven with twelve apostles and shadowed Himself in St Mary. (FR, f.213v)

On Sunday 12 August 1324 Pierre and Jean Maury were both sentenced to the strict, but unshackled, prison regime of bread and water. Under the circumstances theirs ranged among the lighter sentences that were handed down by Fournier.

On 4 July 1322 Béatrice de Planisolles's prison sentence was commuted to the carrying of the double crosses, whereas Barthélemy Amilhat walked free from prison with minor penances; Fournier had kept his promise, it seems. Only Guillemette Clergue (B) got off just as lightly, for although she was sentenced to the double crosses on 2 August 1321, she may have served only about a year in Allemans. Also released on 4 July 1322 with the double crosses was Grazide Lizier. Her mother Fabrisse is not specifically mentioned, but she appeared with her daughter at the 'Graces' of Monday 16 January 1329 to have the crosses rescinded (L, 294; D 27, ff.147–8). The former châtelaine is not listed, but that may be because the *double* crosses were indeed, as her sentence stipulated, intended to last in perpetuity; or she may have been dead by then. Her brother Bernard from Caussou was sentenced to wearing the crosses for bearing false witness on that day (D 27, f.149r), but the main event of that Monday in 1329 was the posthumous condemnation of Pierre Clergue, the former rector of Montaillou.

On the Friday before (13 January), his case had been discussed in Pamiers, but a decision was deferred until the following day to allow the panel's legal expert further time (D 27, f.142v). Then, on Saturday 14 January it was agreed by all, *duobus exceptis* (with two exceptions), that Clergue's remains should be exhumed and posthumously burnt, as those of an impenitent proselytizer for heresy (D 27, f.145v). Were the two dissenting votes the de Polignacs', since we know that Jacques de Polignac had been present in Pamiers at an earlier Inquisitorial session on Saturday 17 December 1328 (D 27, f.140r)? The sentence was pronounced on 16 January 1329. It reads:

Infrascriptae personae defunctae obierunt impenitentes, et eorum ossa pronunciata fuerunt// exhumanda, et ignibus concremanda Petrus Clerici Rector olim Ecclesiae de Montealionis . . . (D 27, ff.148v–149r)★

★ 'The following deceased persons died as impenitents, and their bones were ordered to be exhumed and burnt in the fire: Pierre Clergue, the former rector of the church of Montaillou . . .'

The fact that the case of Pierre Clergue was being reopened now suggests that new evidence had come to light regarding his Cathar activities. Did Béatrice make a death-bed confession perhaps? We shall never know.

If Fournier had not been transferred to Mirepoix in 1326 and been created Cardinal in 1327, the records would be extant. Not only was he meticulous and kept copies of his Inquisitorial activities, but his later career took him and his books to Avignon, from where his library found its way to Rome. It is there today in the Biblioteca Apostolica Vaticana, and has thus escaped the ravages of the French Revolution.

Epilogue:
Benoît XII and the 'Citoyens'

Within ten years of these events Jacques Fournier was elected Pope at Avignon on 20 December 1334. He was crowned on 8 January 1335. In deference to his Cistercian origins he took the name of Benoît XII. The new Pope devoted seven years of his pontificate to erecting a palace to the Church in Avignon. Hundreds of thousands of people have since walked through the 'Vieux Palais' of Benoît XII, and his bedchamber, the room in which he died, is regularly invaded in the summer by scantily clad tourists.

Fournier's reputation for austerity is rather belied by the elaborate murals of his bedroom which, on a backdrop of a deep blue, exhibit a sumptuous mosaic of squirrels, birds, *trompe-l'œil* empty birdcages, vine-leaves, and ornate arabesques; and the intricate tapestry of tiles on the floor of his adjacent study survives intact from its laying in the mid-1330s. From his private apartments the apparently frugal Fournier, who had confined so many fifteen years earlier to the dank and festering cells and dungeons of Allemans, enjoyed fine views of his gardens and orchards which stretched east of the palace.

Like the Authiés, Fournier loved books, and particularly illuminated manuscripts. Between 27 April 1336 and 6 January 1338 his librarian, fellow Cistercian and private secretary, Jean Engilbert, spent 578 gold florins on the copying of books. It may be to Fournier's archival instincts that we owe the preservation of the otherwise undistinguished and austere MS 4030, which contains the bulk of our records for the Pamiers Inquisition. He was, we learn in Maurice Faucon's study of the pontifical library at Avignon, keen to preserve his own works (Faucon 1886, 47). It was not so much this particular vanity as allegations of simony, degeneracy and megalomania that incurred the wrath of several of his contemporaries, chief among whom was Petrarch.

Jacques Fournier died of gangrene on 25 April 1342. He was buried in Notre-Dame-des-Doms in Avignon, right next to the Papal Palace, in the middle of the fourth chapel towards the north transept. He rests across the aisle from Jean XXII, the construction of whose monument he had personally supervised. On 31 May 1342 the master mason Jean Lavenier from Paris was commissioned to execute Fournier's sepulchre. The mausoleum remained intact until 1689 when the upper parts, and particularly its pinnacles, were demolished, but not before a true likeness of the fourteenth-century structure was preserved in a drawing (Duhamel 1888, 32–3). But Benoît XII was not allowed to rest in peace, and like Jean XXII he suffered the indignity of being dug up even before the Revolution desecrated royal and ecclesiastical tombs across France.

On Monday 21 October 1765, six years after the opening of Jean XXII's grave and 423 years after being laid to rest, Jacques Fournier's remains were disturbed. The reason was that the Avignonese 'Guild of Master Tailors for men's and women's clothes' found the central position of the tomb and the uneven paving around it an irritation while worshipping in their designated chapel. They therefore requested permission to move the extant monument to the side of the chapel. This was granted. The irony of the fact that the craft of tailors is so closely connected to those of weavers and clothes-menders, the medieval Perfects' preferred two trades, may not have been apparent to the ecclesiastical officers who authorized the exhumation.

Three reliable accounts, including a scrupulously detailed 'Procès Verbal', survive regarding the opening of Fournier's tomb on this autumn afternoon in the mustiest and bleakest church of Provence. What was found were the pitiable and sparse remains of a badly rotten, ancient pine coffin which contained a few disintegrating bones of a strikingly tall man. Only small fragments of his head and jaw survived and, in the words of the eyewitness l'abbé Massilian, 'there were many bits of leather'. His slippers, which were made of cork, had retained their shape, but they crumbled on touching. Most of the bones had already disintegrated into ashes and dust. The cavity of Fournier's tomb, which measured six-and-a-half feet by just over one-and-a-half feet, and was not much more than three feet deep (so it was narrow and shallow), had for centuries been flooded by ground-water from the high-lying gardens which verge on the northern side of the church. It will hardly have exuded the legendary fragrance that in the Middle

Ages, when Fournier was active, was attributed to the corpses of the saints.

Three pieces of jewellery were found on the body. One was a substantial ring with an agate on which were carved, in relief, the heads of Christ and of the Virgin Mary, the whole being surrounded by twenty-one small garnets or rubies, nineteen of which still sat in their sockets. In addition, two small silver ornaments 'had been placed into the middle of the Pope's gloves' (Duhamel 1888, 22), that is, on his fingers. One of them showed the Virgin with *Ecce ancilla Domini* ('Behold the servant of the Lord'), and the other the archangel Gabriel with *Missus est Angelus* ('The Angel has been sent').

The jewellery was not returned with the remains into their new coffin but was retained by the Archbishop. If the Revolution did not lay its hands on them, then these three material links with the story of the last Cathars probably survive somewhere in either Avignon or Rome.

On Thursday 24 October 1765, around 3 p.m., the remains of Benoît XII were reinterred on the western side of the tailors' chapel so that they would face the altar. But the Revolution was waiting in the wings, and it desecrated the recently reconsecrated graves of the two medieval Popes Benoît XII and Jean XXII. Between 1765 and 1838 when they were finally laid to rest high up in the north wall of the same chapel, Fournier's remains underwent so many metamorphoses that one could be forgiven for thinking that a transmigratory Cathar curse was stalking them.

In the Middle Ages Fournier had caused the corpses of many to be dug up and to have their dignity further violated by burning them on pyres and thereby breaking their loved ones' hearts. The same Jacques Fournier had Guillaume Fort of Montaillou burnt at the stake for denying the physical resurrection of the human body, because it rotted in the earth. Did those who beheld the few mortal remains of Jacques Fournier really believe that these parts of him would one day be bound for heaven? During the cataclysmic revolt in 1789 against the tyranny of the Church – and this one, unlike the Cathars', unstoppable, totally secular, and still with us – his bones probably suffered a fate similar to Guillaume Guilabert's.

★

One night in February 1998 I sat with Alain Fayet, the current mayor of Montaillou, looking at video footage of 'his' village. As I left to head up to where medieval Montaillou had been, he urged me to watch my steps on the unlit parts of the site: '*Ne tombez pas là-haut,*' he said.

It was near the witching hour when I stood in the medieval square of Montaillou, in the same spot where once the Rives house rose. Opposite me had been Pierre Maury's home, and Guillemette Clergue (B)-Rives and her many children had lived right here. Behind me some sixty yards further up was the plateau of the castle and, although it was not really visible, I was aware of a luminous echo in the night sky from the searchlight on the ruin.

The moon was almost full, and the night was clement for the time of year. It was very still, and a smell of wood fires lingered in the air, as it does here throughout the winter. To my left, etched against the night, I could discern the silhouette of *matte majou*, the dip in the *sarrat de Prades* which Prades Tavernier crossed that night in May 1308 when he came to console Guillaume Guilabert. To my right, and high above *comba del gazel*, the Pic de Pénédis and the Col de Balaguès were covered with a dusting of snow which reflected the sheen of the moon. Lower down rose the copse of *peyra del fug*, where during that same month of May 1308 Guillaume Authié and Prades Tavernier had sheltered. Words from an English novel set in the moors of Yorkshire drifted into my mind then, '. . . how anyone could ever imagine unquiet slumbers for the sleepers in that quiet earth'. I thought of Agilo the Goth, who may have given his name to Montaillou, and I wondered again whether Mengarde Clergue still rested in the apse of Notre-Dame-de-Carnesses.

List of Abbreviations

acc.	accusative
CE	*The Catholic Encyclopaedia* (1907–18)
CR	Fawtier and Maillard, *Comptes royaux*
D	Doat, *La Collection Doat à la Bibliothèque Nationale* (1699)
d'AR	MS 4269, Bibliothèque Nationale, Paris (d'Ablis Register)
f.	folio
fem.	feminine
FR	MS 4030, Vatican Library (Fournier Register)
G	Gaffiot, *Dictionnaire Latin-Français* (1934)
IGN	Institut Géographique National
L	Limborch, *Historia Inquisitionis* (1692)
LS	Lewis and Short, *A Latin Dictionary* (1969)
LT	Mistral, *Lou Trésor dóu Félibrige* (1968)
N	Niermeyer, *Mediae Latinitatis Lexicon Minus* (1984)
OED	*The Oxford English Dictionary*
passim	throughout the text
PN	*Plan Napoléonien*

Bibliography

Allgemeines Lexikon der bildenden Künstler von der Antike bis zur Gegenwart, 26 vols. (H. Vollmer, Leipzig, 1907–).

Amargier, Paul, O. P., 'Benoît XII', in *Dictionnaire historique de la papauté*, sous la direction de Philippe Levillain (Fayard, Paris, 1994), pp.206–8.

Attwater, Donald, with John, Catherine Rachel, *The Penguin Dictionary of Saints*, 3rd edn (Penguin, Harmondsworth, 1995).

Baudrillart, A., *et al.*, *Dictionnaire d'histoire et de géographie ecclésiastiques* (Paris 1909–).

Belpech, André, 'Les Issaurat de Larnat', in *Heresis* no. 16 (Centre National d'Études Cathares, Villegly, 1991), pp.1–20.

Beugnot, Comte de (ed.), *Les Olim, ou registres des arrêts rendus par la Cour du Roi sous les règnes de Saint Louis, de Philippe le Hardi . . .* , 4 vols. (1839–48).

Bisson, Thomas N., *Medieval France and her Pyrenean Neighbours* (Hambledon Press, London, 1989).

Brenon, Anne, *Les femmes cathares* (Perrin, Paris, 1992).

Brundage, J. A., *Medieval Canon Law* (Longman, London, 1995).

Chalande, Jules M., *Histoire des rues de Toulouse* (1919; rpt. Laffitte Reprints, 1980).

La Chanson de la Croisade Albigeoise, éditée et traduite du provençal par E. Martin-Chabot, 3 vols. (Paris, 1931–61).

Cheney, C. R., *Handbook of Dates for Students of English History* (C.U.P., Cambridge, 1955).

Claeys, Louis, *et al.*, *Histoire de Pamiers* (Syndicat de Pamiers, Pamiers, 1981).

Cross, F. L. (ed.), *The Oxford Dictionary of the Christian Church* (O.U.P., Oxford, 1997).

Customary of Toulouse, 1286 (BN Lat.9187).

Dauzat, A., *Dictionnaire étymologique des noms de famille et prénoms de France* (Larousse, Paris, 1951).

Dauzat, A., and Rostaing, C., *Dictionnaire étymologique des noms de lieux en France* (Larousse, Paris, 1963).

Devic, Dom C., Vaissette, Dom J., and Molinier, Auguste, *Histoire générale de Languedoc*, 16 vols. (Toulouse, 1872–1905).

Doat, Jean de, *La Collection Doat à la Bibliothèque Nationale*, vols. 22, 23, 24, 27, 28, 34, 93 (1699).

Döllinger, I. von, *Beiträge zur Sektengeschichte des Mittelalters* (Munich, 1890).

Dondaine, Antoine, O. P., *Les hérésies et l'Inquisition, XIIe–XIIIe siècles. Documents et études*, édité par Yves Dossat (Variorum, Gower Publishing Company, Aldershot, 1990).

Douais, C., *Documents pour servir à l'histoire de l'inquisition dans le Languedoc* (Paris, 1900).

——, (ed.), *Practica inquisitionis heretice pravitatis, auctore Bernardo Guidonis O. F. P.* (Paris, 1886); édition partielle de G. Mollat, *Bernard Gui, Manuel de l'inquisition*, 2 vols. (Paris, 1926).

Dubin, Marc, *The Pyrenees* (Rough Guide, London, 1998).

DuCange (Charles du Fresne), *Glossarium ad Scriptores mediae et infimae latinitatis*, 7 vols. (Paris, 1840).

Duhamel, L., *Le tombeau de Jean XXII à Avignon* (Seguin, Avignon, 1887).

——, 'Le tombeau de Benoît XXII à la Métropole d'Avignon', *Bulletin Monumental* (1888), pp.3–23.

Dupré-Theseider, E., 'Le Catharisme languedocien et l'Italie', *Cahiers de Fanjeaux* no. 3 (Privat, Toulouse, 1968), pp. 299–316.

Duvernoy, Jean, *Le Registre d'Inquisition de Jacques Fournier, Évêque de Pamiers, 1318–1325 (MS Vat. Lat. 4030)*, 3 vols. (Privat, Toulouse, 1965).

——, *Le Registre d'Inquisition de Jacques Fournier, Évêque de Pamiers, 1318–1325*, 3 vols., traduit et annoté par Jean Duvernoy (Mouton, Paris, 1978).

——, 'Pierre Authié', *Cahiers d'études cathares* (1970), no. 47, pp.9–49.

——, *Le Dossier de Montségur*, 2 vols. (Pérégrinateur, Toulouse, 1998).

——, *La Religion des Cathares* (Privat, Toulouse, 1976).

Ehrle, Fr., *Historia Bibliothecae romanorum Pontificum tum Bonifatianae tum Avenionensis* (Imprimerie du Vatican, Rome, 1890).

Fabra, Pompeu, *Diccionari general de la llengua catalana* (15th edn, Edhasa, Barcelona, 1981).

Faucon, Maurice, *La Librairie des Papes d'Avignon, sa formation, sa composition, ses catalogues (1316–1420)* (Bibliothèque des Écoles françaises d'Athènes et de Rome, Paris, 1886).

Fawtier, Robert, and Maillard, François, *Comptes royaux, 1285–1314* (3 vols., Recueil des historiens de la France. Documents financiers vol. 3, Paris,

1953–6); *Comptes royaux, 1314–1328* (2 parts, Recueil des historiens de la France. Documents financiers vol. 4, Paris, 1961).

Fawtier Robert, *et al.*, *Les registres de Boniface VIII. Recueil des Bulles de ce Pape publiées ou analysées d'après les manuscrits originaux des Archives du Vatican* (Paris, 1884).

Fayet, Alain, *À la recherche de Montaillou* (pamphlet, mairie de Montaillou, 2000).

Filippini, Laura, 'Paolo da Siena', in *La Scultura nel Trecento in Roma* (S.T.E.N., Torino, 1908).

Gaffiot, F., *Dictionnaire Latin-Français* (Hachette, Paris, 1934).

Gilles, Henri, 'Les *Coutumes de Toulouse (1286)* et leur premier *Commentaire (1296)*', *Recueil de l'Académie de Législation* (1967–8).

Griffe, Élie, *Le Languedoc cathare et l'inquisition 1229–1329*, (Letouzey et Ané, Paris, 1980).

Guiraud, J., *Histoire de l'Inquisition au moyen âge*, 2 vols. (August Picard, Paris, 1935–8).

Le Roy Ladurie, Emmanuel, *Montaillou, village occitan de 1294 à 1324* (Gallimard, Paris, 1975; rev. edn 1982).

Levillain, Philippe (ed.), *Dictionnaire historique de la papauté* (Fayard, Paris, 1994).

Levy, E., *Provenzalisches Supplement-Wörterbuch*, 8 vols. (Leipzig, 1892–1924).

Lewis, Charlton, and Short, Charles, *A Latin Dictionary* (Clarendon Press, Oxford, 1879, 1969).

Limborch, Philip, *Historia Inquisitionis* (incl. *Liber Sententiarum Inquisitionis Tholosanae 1307–1323*), 1692.

Mistral, Frédéric, *Lou Trésor dóu Félibrige, ou Dictionnaire provençal-français embrassant les divers dialectes de la langue d'oc moderne . . .* Avec un supplément établi d'après les notes de Jules Ronjat, etc. (Troisième édition), 2 vols. (Is Edicioun Ramoun Berenguié, Aix-en-Provence, 1968).

Molinier, Ch., *L'Inquisition dans le Midi de la France au XIIIe et au XIVe siècle* (Toulouse, 1880).

Moulis, Adelin, *Ax-les-Thermes. Huis de l'Andorre* (C. Lacour, Nîmes, 1970, rpt 1996).

Nelli, René, *Les cathares du Languedoc au XIIIe siècle* (Hachette, Paris, 1969)

Nickson, A. E., 'Locke and the Inquisition of Toulouse', in *British Museum Quarterly*, vol. 36 (1972), pp.83–92.

Niermeyer, J. F., *Mediae Latinitatis Lexicon Minus* (Brill, Leiden, 1984).

Oldenbourg, Zoé, *Massacre at Montségur. A History of the Albigensian Crusade* (1959; English translation by Peter Green, Weidenfeld & Nicolson, London, 1961; Phoenix, London, 1998).

Ourgaud, J., *Notice historique sur la ville et le pays de Pamiers, ancien royaume de Frédelas* (Pamiers, 1865).

Pailhès, Claudine, *et al.*, *Histoire de Foix et de La Haute Ariège* (Privat, Toulouse, 1996).

Paladilhe, Dominique, *Les papes en Avignon ou l'exil de Babylone* (Perrin, Paris, 1974).

Pales-Gobilliard, Annette, *L'Inquisiteur Geoffroy d'Ablis et les Cathares du Comté de Foix (1308–1309)*, (*MS BN Latin 4269*), texte édité, traduit et annoté par Annette Pales-Gobilliard (CNRS, Paris, 1984).

—— 'Bernard Gui, inquisiteur', *Cahiers de Fanjeaux* no.16 (Privat, Toulouse, 1981), pp.253–64.

—— 'Passage de Languedoc en Italie à l'occasion du Jubilé de 1300', *Cahiers de Fanjeaux* no.15 (Privat, Toulouse, 1980), pp.245–55.

Paterson, Linda M., *The World of the Troubadours: Medieval Occitan Society, c. 1100-c.1300* (C.U.P., Cambridge, 1993).

Paul, Jacques, 'Jacques Fournier inquisiteur', *Cahiers de Fanjeaux*, no.26 (Privat, Toulouse, 1991), pp.39–67.

Peire Cardenal, *Poésies complètes du troubadour Peire Cardenal*, ed. R. Lavaud (Privat, Toulouse, 1957).

Poirion, Daniel, *Tacuinum Sanitatis*, ed. Daniel Poirion and Claude Thomasset as *L'art de vivre au moyen âge* (Félin, Paris, 1995).

Poux, Joseph, *La Cité de Carcassonne. Histoire et Description*, vol. 1. (Privat, Toulouse, 1931).

Ramet, Henri, *Histoire de Toulouse* (Impr. régionale, Toulouse, 1935).

Raynouard, F., *Lexique roman ou Dictionnaire de la Langue des Troubadours*, 6 vols. (Paris, 1838–44).

Runciman, Steven, *The Medieval Manichee. A Study of the Christian Dualist Heresy* (1947; C.U.P., Cambridge, 1969).

Sinclair, John D., *The Divine Comedy of Dante Alighieri*, with translation and comment, 3 vols. (O.U.P., Oxford, 1961).

Spufford, Peter, *Money and its Use in Medieval Europe* (C.U.P., Cambridge, 1988).

Strayer, Joseph R., *Les Gens de Justice du Languedoc sous Philippe le Bel* (Association Marc Bloch, Toulouse, 1970).

—— (editor in chief), *Dictionary of the Middle Ages*, 13 vols. (Charles Scribner's Sons, New York, 1982–9).

The Catholic Encyclopaedia, 17 vols. (Robert Appleton Co., New York, 1907–18).

The New Catholic Encyclopaedia, 15 vols. (McGraw-Hill Book Co., New York, 1967).

Vidal, J. M., *Le Tribunal d'Inquisition de Pamiers* (Privat, Toulouse, 1906).

—— 'Les derniers ministres de l'albigéisme en Languedoc, leur doctrine', *Revue des Questions historiques* (Paris, 1906b), pp.57–107.

Vingtain, Dominique, *Avignon: Le Palais des Papes* (*Le ciel et la pierre*, vol.2) (France, 1998).

Wakefield, Walter L., *Heresy, Crusade and Inquisition in Southern France 1100–1250* (George Allen & Unwin Ltd, London, 1974).

Wolff, P., 'Une ville pyrénéenne au XIIIe siècle, l'exemple de Foix', *Annales du Midi* (1965), pp.137–55.

Chronology

1208	Murder of the papal legate Pierre de Castelnau, which leads to the proclamation by Pope Innocent III of the first crusade against the Albigensians.
1209–11	Massacres of Béziers, Minerve, and Lavaur.
1233	Pope Gregory IX entrusts the purging of heresy to the Dominicans.
1244	Surrender of Montségur, the citadel of Occitan Catharism.
1255	Fall of Quéribus, the last Cathar stronghold.
1270s	Birth of Pierre Clergue in Montaillou.
c.1274	Béatrice de Planisolles born in (probably) Caussou.
c.1282	Birth of Pierre Maury in Montaillou.
c.1291	Béatrice de Planisolles marries Bérenger de Roquefort.
1294	*August*: attempted seduction by Raymond Roussel of Béatrice.
1295	*Summer*: birth of Béatrice's first daughter.
	July: Alazais Rives tries to get Béatrice to come and meet Prades Tavernier, while her daughter Guillemette Clergue (B) is in labour.
1296	*End of June*: Guillemette Clergue (B) goes to dance in Prades.
	October: Pierre and Guillaume Authié leave Languedoc for Lombardy to be ordained Perfects there. Prades Tavernier and Stéphanie de Château-Verdun depart for Catalonia.
	Autumn: return to Montaillou of Pierre Clergue as rector.
1297	*January, February?*: rape of Béatrice de Planisolles by Pathau Clergue.
1298	*February*: death of Bérenger de Roquefort; Béatrice moves out of the castle of Montaillou.
1299	*March*: Pierre Clergue propositions Béatrice behind the altar of Notre-Dame-de-Carnesses.
	Early July: surrender by Béatrice to Pierre Clergue and start of their relationship.
	Autumn: return of the Perfects to Toulouse; Pierre Authié is recognized by Pierre de Luzenac.
	All Saints 1299–spring 1300: the Perfects Guillaume Authié and

Pierre-Raymond de Saint-Papoul stay at the Martys' of Junac.

December: consolation of Guillemette Faure in Montaillou.

Christmas Eve: Béatrice and Pierre Clergue have sex on Holy Night.

1300   Béatrice moves to Prades, and Pierre Maury goes to Arques.

Late March—early April: return of the Authiés to their brother Raymond's house in Ax.

August: ordination in Larnat of Jacques Authié and Pons Sicre-Baille.

1301   *c.January*: end of Béatrice's affair with Pierre Clergue.

15 August: Béatrice leaves Prades to marry Guillaume-Othon de Lagleize and to set up home with him near Pamiers.

September: consolation of Gentille d'Ascou in the hospital in Ax.

October: Pierre Clergue visits Béatrice in her home in Dalou, and they have sex in the cellar there.

1303   Geoffroy d'Ablis becomes Inquisitor in Carcassonne.

1304   *c.April*: Pierre Maury is received into the Cathar faith in Arques by Pierre Authié.

August: consolation of Pierre de Gaillac's mother in Tarascon.

?: mutilation of Mengarde Maurs.

?: murder of Arnaud Lizier in Montaillou.

1305   *January*: death of *Na* Roche.

January—February: death of Alazais Benet of Montaillou, who was consoled by Guillaume Authié.

Spring ?: expulsion of Fabrisse Rives from her husband's home.

Easter: visit by Pierre Maury to Cubières, the home of Guillaume Bélibaste.

5 June: election of Clément V to Pope; he is crowned in Lyon on 14 November.

c.Whitsun: death of Raymond Benet.

?: visit by Béatrice to her sister in Limoux; she goes to mass in Notre-Dame-de-Marceille.

8 September: in Limoux Jacques Authié and Prades Tavernier walk into a trap, but they escape shortly afterwards.

Christmas: return of Pierre Maury to Montaillou.

1306   *Early*: Pierre Maury joins Barthélemy Bourrel in Ax and goes to Catalonia for the first time.

1307   *Early spring* ?: Geoffroy d'Ablis teams up with Bernard Gui,

Inquisitor in Toulouse.

June: Pierre Maury guides his sister Guillemette to freedom and leaves her with Bernard and Guillaume Bélibaste.

September: escape of the Perfects Guillaume Bélibaste and Philippe d'Aylarac from Carcassonne and across the Agly river.

c.15 September: marriage of Bernard Clergue and Raymonde Belot.

Autumn: wedding of Arnaud Belot and Raymonde Lizier.

December: Alazais Guilabert marries Arnaud Faure.

1308   *January*: marriage of Bernard Belot and Guillemette Benet.

Lent: Gaillarde Authié, the wife of the Perfect Guillaume Authié, is summoned to Carcassonne to testify.

c.14 April: sighting in Pierre Clergue's study of the Perfect Guillaume Authié.

May: death of Guillaume Guilabert, who was consoled by Prades Tavernier; shortly after 10 May (?) there follows the first raid on Montaillou led by Pierre de Luzenac.

8 September: major raid on Montaillou by the Inquisition.

Autumn: Pierre Clergue visits Béatrice, who is sick.

Late 1308–early 1309: death of Pons Clergue of Montaillou.

1309   *January, February*: arrest and sentence of Jacques Authié.

9 March: move of the papacy under Clément V from Rome to Avignon in Provence.

April: Blanche Marty flees Languedoc and heads for Catalonia.

?: death and burial of Mengarde Clergue.

End of August: arrest of Pierre Authié.

September: meeting of Pierre Maury and Guillaume Maurs in Puigcerdà.

End of the year: arrest of the Perfect Guillaume Authié.

1310   *9 April*: execution of Pierre Authié in Toulouse.

1311   *September*: departure of Pierre Maury for Bagà in Catalonia.

1312   Raymond de Toulouse, Guillaume Bélibaste, Blanche Marty, and Raymonde Piquier-Marty stay at the Servels' in Lleida.

1313   *January*: first meeting of Pierre Maury and Raymond de Toulouse in Flix in Catalonia.

April: Guillaume Bélibaste works with Pierre Maury until Easter.

Summer: Blanche Marty surprises Bélibaste and her sister in bed.

High summer: start of Pierre Clergue's affair in Montaillou with the teenage Grazide Rives.

Autumn: Bélibaste's first attempt at setting up a card-making business in Morella; Raymond de Toulouse joins him briefly as a business partner.

Christmas: meeting of Pierre Maury and Raymond de Toulouse at Camposines.

1314   *c.April*: Bélibaste is challenged about his religion in Tortosa and therefore moves to Horta de Sant Joan.

c.April–May: Pierre Maury meets members of his family in Juncosa.
Summer: birth of Bélibaste's and Raymonde's daughter Guillemette.
October: Jeanne Befayt threatens Bélibaste with exposure.
Winter?: Bélibaste, Raymonde, and Guillemette move to Morella.
c.Christmas: death of Raymond de Toulouse at La Granadella.
24 December: Jean Maury substitutes for Perfects in Prades in Catalonia, and here he meets Blanche Marty.

1314–15   Mersende Marty and Jeanne Befayt and her husband move to Beceite.

1315   *January, February?*: Pierre Maury's family settle in Sant Mateu.
c.Easter: Pierre Clergue propositions Mengarde Buscailh of Prades.
July: reappearance of Jean Maury in Montaillou.
December: first encounter of Pierre Maury and Jeanne Befayt.

1316   *January*: start of the affair between Béatrice and Barthélemy Amilhat.
June: departure of Béatrice, Barthélemy, and Philippa for Lladrós.
10 September: death of the Inquisitor Geoffroy d'Ablis, who is succeeded by Jean de Beaune.
c.October: sighting in Montblanc (Catalonia) of Guillaume Authié's two sons.

1317   *19 March*: Jacques Fournier becomes Bishop of Pamiers.
Summer: return to Languedoc of Béatrice and Barthélemy Amilhat; Jean Maury pays another visit to Montaillou.

1318   *May, June*: warning of Pierre Maury against Fournier's proclamations of him.
September: stalking of Pierre Clergue by two hired assassins.
Early October: arrival of Arnaud Sicre in Sant Mateu.
Early November: first meeting of Pierre Maury and Arnaud Sicre.
Before Christmas: visit by Arnaud Sicre to a Muslim soothsayer.

1319   *September–October*: Arnaud Sicre returns to Languedoc and visits

Jacques Fournier at Pamiers.

Middle of December: 'marriage' in Morella of Pierre Maury to the pregnant Raymonde, Bélibaste's companion; they 'divorce' a few days later.

1320 *May*: Pierre Maury meets Blanche Marty in Prades in Catalonia.

Late summer: second visit by Arnaud Sicre to Jacques Fournier in Pamiers.

26 July: first appearance of Béatrice before Jacques Fournier.

7 August: Béatrice implicates Pierre Clergue in her testimony.

c.10–11 August: arrest of Pierre Clergue of Montaillou.

24–9 December: Pierre Maury, Arnaud Sicre, Guillaume Bélibaste, Blanche, and Raymonde celebrate Christmas in Morella.

1321 *8 March*: sentencing of Béatrice at Pamiers.

End of March: arrest of Bélibaste at Tírvia.

3–4 April: Pierre Clergue approaches Alamande Guilabert in the Bishop's palace at Pamiers.

22 May: first appearance of Bernard Clergue before Fournier.

July: arrest of Pierre de Gaillac and Pierre Azéma.

2 August: burning at the stake of Guillaume Fort of Montaillou.

Early October: death of the rector Pierre Clergue.

2 November: release of Bernard Clergue from Allemans prison.

1322 *23 January*: marriage in Juncosa of Jean Maury to Mathène Servel.

4 July: release of Béatrice and Barthélemy Amilhat from Allemans prison.

1323 The affair Arnaud de Verniolles.

Middle of May: arrest by the Inquisition of Pierre Maury in Flix and of Jean Maury and the Servels shortly afterwards.

1324 *February*: death of Pierre de Gaillac.

Summer: death of Pierre de Luzenac.

25 June: first appearance of Pierre Maury before Fournier.

9 August: conviction of Bernard Clergue for heresy.

August–September: death of Bernard Clergue in Carcassonne.

1326 Transfer of Fournier to Mirepoix.

1327 Fournier is created Cardinal.

1329 *16 January*: sentencing of Pierre Clergue's remains to posthumous burning as those of an impenitent.

1334 *20 December*: election of Fournier to Pope at Avignon.

1342 *25 April*: Fournier dies and is buried in Notre-Dame-des-Doms.

Index

consolamentum (consolation) xxvi–xxvii, 90, 119–20, 127–31

consolation: of Guillaume Guilabert 206–7; by Jean Maury 294

consecrated bread *see* tinhol

Constantine Basilica 255

constitutional 80

consuls of Pamiers 123

contemptus mundi 73

contraception 58–9, 69, 284, 359

convenenza 90, 106, 131, 392

Convento de las Monjas Agustinas 292

Corbières xlvi, 222, 272

Corbolh, Othon 273

cordon sanitaire 83

corn mills in Ax 190

corruption in Carcassonne's Inquisitorial prisons 157, 218n., 226, 230, 382, 386–7

cortal 152

cortal sec 19, 197

Cortil family 277n.

Cortil, Guillemette 277n.

Cortil, Pierre 277, 277n., 280, 293, 321

Cortil, Rixende 277n.

Costa Brava 222

Coste of l'Assaladou 181–2

côte of Larnat-Bouan 90, 96

Côte Vermeille 221

Cotswolds 12

cottage industries of medieval Montaillou 15–16

Coudons 370

Coulobre 204

Coume d'Amont ('brook of Caussou') 9

Coume du Moulin 229

Count(s) of Foix xxviii, 12, 31, 65, 84, 89, 110, 118, 123, 125–6, 172, 191, 194, 226, 237, 248, 281, 310, 371, 374, 393

Countess of Foix 355

County of Foix 90, 103, 272, 275, 315, 355, 372

Couserans 250

Coustaussa 97, 97n., 132, 150–51, 156, 178–9, 244

craft of carding 284n., 287

Crampagna 67n., 68, 68n., 250

credens (*credentes*) xxvii, 75, 101, 110, 280, 285

cremation of bones 241n.

Cretas 349, 397

'crête de Gebets' xxxviii

cretinism 35n.

Crown 157, 244, 276

Cubières xlv–xlvi, 140, 150–52, 272, 280, 340, 346, 395

Cuneo 44n., 85

currency value li–lii

Dalou 67–70, 248–50, 252, 352, 354

Dante Alighieri 2, 9, 103, 114, 154, 255, 262, 270

dates li

dating the arrest of Guillaume Bélibaste 342

de la lose (mountain pass) 275

death: of Benoît XII 402; of Bernard Bélibaste 278; by fire 81, 138, 240–41; and lying in state of Pons Clergue 232; and suspected murder of Pierre Marty of Junac 219–20

death penalty 79

debt *see* money

decision of the Arques Cathars to confess to the Pope 154

Decretales 87, 87n., 260

defence of Bernard Clergue 381

defiance of the Cathar death ritual by a mother 146

Défilé d'Adouxes xxxviii

Dejean, Gaillarde (née Tavernier) 204

Dejean, Guillaume (*passeur* from Prades) 127, 204

Dejean, Guillaume (traitor) 114–16, 172, 179

Index

446   *Index*

Pont Vell 282

Pontilhs 155

Pope 155

population, crafts, and trades of Pamiers 256, 262

population grid of medieval Montaillou 26–40

Port d'Envalira xliii

Port de l'Artigue (port de Lladorre) xli, 250

Port de Querol xlv

Port de Saleix 250

Porta dels Layros 350

Portinari, Beatrice 9

portrait of Benoît XII in St Peter's 255

Post, Gentille den (née de Planisolles) 69–70, 128, 355

posthumous cremation of Pierre Clergue as heretic 400

Pourcel, Bernard 395

Pourcel, Brune (née Tavernier) 16, 39–40, 163–4, 164n., 165–7, 172–3, 232, 300n., 363, 383

Pourcel, Guillaume 39

Pourcel, Raymond 166

Poux, Joseph 272

Prade creek 20–21

Prades (Catalonia) 283–4, 288, 292–5, 304, 329, 331–2, 337, 348

Prades (Pays d'Aillou) xxxvi, xxxviii, xl, 2n., 8–9, 22, 22n., 26, 41, 43, 47–8, 50, 53–4, 62–3, 67, 67n., 68n., 78n., 168, 203–5, 208–9, 224, 230, 247–8, 274, 300n., 317, 395

Prades track: inner 22, 23, 38; outer 22, 33

prado lonc (Prat Loung) 98, 98n.

Pradon, Alissende 129

Prats-de-Mollo 287

pregnancy of Béatrice 41

presents: for the Perfects 207–8; between Perfects and *credentes* 165n.

primitiae 262

Prior, Pierre 343

proclamation of Pierre Authié by Bernard Gui 89

prophetic shoe-test 342

prostitute 259

protective custody of Guillaume Peyre 153

protest against Fournier's taxes and excommunication 263–5

Provence 2, 154n., 295, 403

Proverbs 374

psalmist 114

Psalms 114

Puig Peric 308n.

Puigcerdà 113, 126, 231, 272, 276–7, 278n., 280, 293, 303, 309–10, 333, 367, 395–6, 396

Pujol, Bernard and Grazide 352

pulcrum 91n.

Puymorens xxxv, xlii–xliv, 20n., 103, 113, 126, 306–7

Quercy 326

Quéribus xxix, 73n., 272

Quérigut 126, 276n.

Queriú pass 275–6

Querol 321

Quié 89, 93, 115–16, 124, 172, 263, 268

Quillan 126, 156

Rabassole 148–9, 151

Rabastens 184, 187

Rabat 90, 90n., 101, 216

railway viaduct 132

raising of new taxes 255, 262–5

Ramet, Henri 87n.

rampart wall of Pamiers 258

rape 125, 161, 261–2

Rasiguères xxxviii, 272, 275

Rauzy, Jacques 304

Rauzy, Pierre 10n.

Ravin du Correc 116